TENNYSON'S POETRY

AUTHORITATIVE TEXTS

JUVENILIA AND EARLY RESPONSES

CRITICISM

TENNYSON'S POETRY

AUTHORITATIVE TEXTS
JUVENILIA AND EARLY RESPONSES
CRITICISM

➤➤◄◄

Selected and Edited by

ROBERT W. HILL, JR.

MIDDLEBURY COLLEGE

W · W · NORTON & COMPANY

New York · London

W. W. Norton & Company, Inc., 500 Fifth Avenue, New York, N.Y. 10110

Copyright © 1971 by W. W. Norton & Company, Inc.

Library of Congress Catalog Card No. 68–12190

SBN 393-04331-2 {Cloth Edition}
SBN 393-09953-9 {Paper Edition}

PRINTED IN THE UNITED STATES OF AMERICA

2 3 4 5 6 7 8 9 0

Contents

79058

Songs from *The Princess* (1847, 1850), and Two
　　Poems Written before 1850

The Middle Period (1850–1872)

From *Idylls of the King*

The Late Period (1872–1892)

Juvenilia and Early Responses (1820—1835)

Juvenilia

From *Unpublished Early Poems* (1931) and *The Devil and the Lady* (1930)

From *Poems by Two Brothers* (1827)

Criticism

x · *Contents*

Preface

With a generous selection from Tennyson's earliest poetry and the inclusion of several poems from the middle and late periods not usually anthologized, I have tried to preserve most of what is generally taken to be the poet's finest work while retaining enough lesser pieces to make this book representative. One of the assumptions of this anthology is that to understand a poet well the reader must see his strengths and weaknesses juxtaposed, insofar as possible throughout the span of his productive life. Wordsworth writing on viaducts and railways or Tennyson seeking to rally the British against real or imagined invasion by the French are not at their best. But studying a poet's lesser works can often lead to a richer awareness of the conception of major poems.

Under the heading Juvenilia and Early Responses, following the texts of the poems, I have assembled a number of the earliest works —excerpts from *The Devil and the Lady*, selections from *Poems by Two Brothers* (1827), and selections from Sir Charles Tennyson's *Unpublished Early Poems* (1931). Any informed study of the poet's development depends upon a familiarity with the earliest work. Here his links with the past, particularly with Byron, Moore, and Scott, are most clearly evident. Students of Tennyson are, I believe, becoming increasingly aware of the value in locating the poet in that literary context as he emerges from his Romantic background; this anthology will provide them with material otherwise not available in a single collection. Similarly, the selections from reviews of the poems published in 1830, 1832, and 1842 are not easily come by and provide some continuity in a chronological representation of critical responses. Hopefully, they will lead the reader to a closer examination of those early poems where one is so often startled to find the germ of ideas developed much later. The hostile reviews of Wilson and Croker contributed to Tennyson's lifelong distrust of critics but at the same time forced him to a new self-appraisal that was responsible for the markedly superior poetry in the two 1842 volumes. The review by Hallam, Tennyson's closest friend, helped to encourage a dedication to his art during those difficult formative years, whereas J. S. Mill's perceptive and friendly review, published in 1835, was a welcome, balanced appraisal from a disinterested intelligence later to become a seminal mind of the Victorian age. Sterling and Spedding, both close friends of Tennyson, provide informative, contemporary evaluation of the 1842 volumes, while Knowles's "Reminiscence," one of several special obituary articles, contains valuable insights obtainable only from a source at first hand.

A word too is needed on the following critical selections. A tremendous amount of material on Tennyson exists. Rather than attempt to give a smattering of the various tastes and predilections, I have tried to represent major, often controversial voices in as much depth as space allowed. The reaction against Tennyson, especially virulent during the first three decades of this century, was severe —as indiscriminate in its waspishness as praise had been earlier. A. C. Bradley's defense and Douglas Bush's scholarly reappraisal indirectly reflect the nature and scope of the reaction, whereas the excerpt from Nicolson's biography, published in 1923, shows its indelible stamp. Arthur Carr's article, though easily accessible, is justifiably considered the high-water mark in the reappreciation. For interpretations of the major poems, I have simply taken large excerpts from the most perceptive commentary with which I am familiar. Eliot's and Baum's criticisms are both brilliant and controversial; Killham's essay on *Maud* is far and away the best shorter criticism of that poem; Priestley's evaluation of the *Idylls* properly considers it "one of Tennyson's most earnest and important efforts to deal with major problems of his time." Francis Golffing's discussion of the late poems gives them the emphasis long overdue. And finally, Georg Roppen's provocative study of Tennyson and the theory of evolution approaches that complicated and important subject with clarity and insight.

The poetry is arranged, as far as possible, roughly in the order of composition. The date after each selection is that of first publication. For poems not published fairly soon after they were written, conjectural or known dates of composition precede dates of publication. Dates in parentheses indicate substantial changes in subsequent publication.

Cross references to *In Memoriam* are made by section number, followed, where appropriate, by stanza number. Elsewhere, the practice has been to refer to poem and line numbers.

Page references are always given to the *Memoir* (the two-volume edition of 1897) because the index is so inadequate. Other notes by Tennyson himself either are identified by source or, where no explanation is given, are to be found in the Eversley edition of the poet's complete works. *Alfred Tennyson* refers to the biography by the poet's grandson.

In assembling the anthology and composing the notes and prefaces, my debts are numerous. I have made some use of nearly everything I could lay my hands on. The packets and notebooks in the Harvard collection are invaluable. William Clyde De Vane's notes in his *Selections from Tennyson* (1940) are still informative and provided useful suggestions. George Marshall's *A Tennyson Handbook* (1963) has, I hope, prevented mistakes in chronology which might otherwise have gone unnoticed. A. C. Bradley's recently republished *A Commentary on Tennyson's In Memoriam* (1901, 1966) is a necessary reference for any serious study of the poem. The text, with a few minor alterations, is that of the Cambridge Tennyson, edited with notes by W. J. Rolfe. Poems or excerpts not published there have been taken from *Tennyson's Unpublished Early Poems* (1931) and *The Devil and the Lady* (1930), both edited by Sir Charles Tennyson, and from the Eversley edition of the poet's works issued with notes by the poet's son. I have made extensive use of the *Memoir* (1897), also by Hallam Tennyson. As are all students of Tennyson, I am indebted to Sir Charles Tennyson's splendid biography of his grandfather. Middlebury College generously granted me a leave of absence to finish this work. To my friend William Noonan, whose wise counsel and patience in proofreading the manuscript cannot be measured, I wish to acknowledge publicly a private gratitude. Finally, what may be of value in this book I attribute to the guidance and friendship of two Tennysonians, my teachers Jerome Buckley and Douglas Bush. To them I dedicate it.

Middlebury, Vermont   ROBERT W. HILL, JR.

The Texts of
The Poems

The Early Period
(1830 — 1850)

FROM *POEMS, CHIEFLY LYRICAL* (1830)

Supposed Confessions[1]

OF A SECOND-RATE SENSITIVE MIND

O God! my God! have mercy now.
I faint, I fall.[2] Men say that Thou
Didst die for me, for such as *me*,
Patient of ill, and death, and scorn,
And that my sin was as a thorn   5
Among the thorns that girt Thy brow,
Wounding Thy soul.—That even now,
In this extremest misery
Of ignorance, I should require
A sign! and if a bolt of fire[3]   10
Would rive the slumbrous summer noon
While I do pray to Thee alone,
Think my belief would stronger grow!
Is not my human pride brought low?
The boastings of my spirit still?   15
The joy I had in my free-will
All cold, and dead, and corpse-like grown?
And what is left to me but Thou,
And faith in Thee? Men pass me by;
Christians with happy countenances—   20
And children all seem full of Thee!
And women smile with saint-like glances
Like Thine own mother's when she bow'd
Above Thee, on that happy morn

1. Reprinted in 1884 with the omission of 17 lines and a few minor changes, the poem was originally titled, "Supposed Confessions of a Second-rate Sensitive Mind not in Unity with Itself." Arthur Hallam praised the poem in his review of 1831 (excerpts of which are included in this book) for being "full of deep insight into human nature." He thought the title, however, "ill chosen" and "incorrect," for the mood portrayed to him "rather the clouded season of a strong mind than the habitual condition of one feeble and second-rate." It is possible that the title is deliberately ironic in an effort to create a dramatic voice and mask the personal, auto-biographical nature of the poem.
2. Compare Shelley's line, "I fall upon the thorns of life! I bleed!" in "Ode to the West Wind."
3. Perhaps a reference to Luther's experience with the bolt of lightning.

1

When angels spake to men aloud,   25
And Thou and peace to earth were born.
Good-will to me as well as all—
I one of them; my brothers they;
Brothers in Christ—a world of peace
And confidence, day after day;   30
And trust and hope till things should cease,
And then one Heaven receive us all.

How sweet to have a common faith!
To hold a common scorn of death!
And at a burial to hear   35
The creaking cords[4] which wound and eat
Into my human heart, whene'er
Earth goes to earth, with grief, not fear,
With hopeful grief, were passing sweet!
Thrice happy state[5] again to be   40
The trustful infant on the knee,
Who lets his rosy fingers play
About his mother's neck, and knows
Nothing beyond his mother's eyes!
They comfort him by night and day;   45
They light his little life alway;
He hath no thought of coming woes;
He hath no care of life or death;
Scarce outward signs of joy arise,
Because the Spirit of happiness   50
And perfect rest so inward is;
And loveth so his innocent heart,
Her temple and her place of birth,
Where she would ever wish to dwell,
Life of the fountain there, beneath   55
Its salient springs, and far apart,
Hating to wander out on earth,
Or breathe into the hollow air,
Whose chillness would make visible
Her subtil, warm, and golden breath,   60
Which mixing with the infant's blood,
Fulfils him with beatitude.
O, sure it is a special care
Of God, to fortify from doubt,
To arm in proof, and guard about   65
With triple-mailed trust, and clear
Delight, the infant's dawning year.

Would that my gloomed fancy were
As thine, my mother, when with brows
Propt on thy knees, my hands upheld   70

4. The straps which lower the casket into the grave.
5. Lines 40–67 seem clearly indebted to Wordsworth's "Ode: Intimations of Immortality."

In thine, I listen'd to thy vows,
For me outpour'd in holiest prayer—
For me unworthy!—and beheld
Thy mild deep eyes upraised, that knew
The beauty and repose of faith,   75
And the clear spirit shining thro'.
O, wherefore do we grow awry
From roots which strike so deep?[6] why dare
Paths in the desert? Could not I
Bow myself down, where thou hast knelt,   80
To the earth—until the ice would melt
Here, and I feel as thou hast felt?
What devil had the heart to scathe
Flowers thou hadst rear'd—to brush the dew
From thine own lily, when thy grave   85
Was deep, my mother, in the clay?[7]
Myself? Is it thus? Myself? Had I
So little love for thee? But why
Prevail'd not thy pure prayers? Why pray
To one who heeds not,[8] who can save   90
But will not? Great in faith, and strong
Against the grief of circumstance
Wert thou, and yet unheard. What if
Thou pleadest still, and seest me drive
Thro' utter dark a full-sail'd skiff,   95
Unpiloted i' the echoing dance
Of reboant whirlwinds,[9] stooping low

Unto the death, not sunk! I know
At matins and at evensong,
That thou, if thou wert yet alive,   100
In deep and daily prayers wouldst strive
To reconcile me with thy God.
Albeit, my hope is gray, and cold
At heart, thou wouldest murmur still—
"Bring this lamb back into Thy fold,   105
My Lord, if so it be Thy will."
Wouldst tell me I must brook the rod
And chastisement of human pride;
That pride, the sin of devils, stood

---

6. A question Wordsworth never really answered as he wondered why "Shades of the prison-house begin to close / Upon the growing Boy."
7. As in the poem's title, Tennyson here too may be attempting to conceal autobiographical material, for his mother was very much alive, living on until 1865.
8. Here the parallel to Wordsworth's poem ends. Wordsworth found comfort in recalling the thoughtless days of childhood, in the primal sympathy between God and child which once having been must ever be proof of our divine heritage.
9. For this image, Tennyson was probably thinking of Milton's *Samson Agonistes*, lines 197–200:

How could I once look up, or have the head,
Who like a foolish Pilot have shipwrack't
My vessel trusted to me from above,
Gloriously rigg'd; . . .

Compare *In Memoriam*, 4, 1.

Betwixt me and the light of God;   110
That hitherto I had defied
And had rejected God—that grace
Would drop from His o'er-brimming love,
As manna on my wilderness,
If I would pray—that God would move   115
And strike the hard, hard rock, and thence,
Sweet in their utmost bitterness,
Would issue tears of penitence
Which would keep green hope's life. Alas!
I think that pride hath now no place   120
Nor sojourn in me. I am void,
Dark, formless, utterly destroyed.

Why not believe then? Why not yet
Anchor thy frailty there, where man
Hath moor'd and rested? Ask the sea   125
At midnight, when the crisp slope waves
After a tempest rib and fret
The broad-imbased beach, why he
Slumbers not like a mountain tarn?
Wherefore his ridges are not curls   130
And ripples of an inland mere?[1]
Wherefore he moaneth thus, nor can
Draw down into his vexed pools
All that blue heaven which hues and paves
The other? I am too forlorn,   135
Too shaken: my own weakness fools
My judgment, and my spirit whirls,
Moved from beneath with doubt and fear.

"Yet," said I, in my morn of youth,
The unsunn'd freshness of my strength,   140
When I went forth in quest of truth,
"It is man's privilege to doubt,"[2]
If so be that from doubt at length
Truth may stand forth unmoved of change,
An image with profulgent[3] brows   145
And perfect limbs, as from the storm
Of running fires and fluid range
Of lawless airs, at last stood out
This excellence and solid form
Of constant beauty. For the ox[4]   150
Feeds in the herb, and sleeps, or fills
The horned valleys all about,

---

1. A small lake or pool, as distinguished from a "tarn," or mountain lake.
2. See *In Memoriam*, 96, 3.
3. Radiant.
4. This passage on the ox and lamb is indebted to Pope's *Essay on Man*, I, lines 81–84:

The lamb thy riot dooms to bleed today,
Had he thy Reason, would skip and play?
Pleased to the last, he crops the flowery food,
And licks the hand just raised to shed his blood.

And hollows of the fringed hills
In summer heats, with placid lows
Unfearing, till his own blood flows   155
About his hoof. And in the flocks
The lamb rejoiceth in the year,
And raceth freely with his fere,
And answers to his mother's calls
From the flower'd furrow. In a time   160
Of which he wots not, run short pains
Thro' his warm heart; and then, from whence
He knows not, on his light there falls
A shadow; and his native slope,
Where he was wont to leap and climb,   165
Floats from his sick and filmed eyes,
And something in the darkness draws
His forehead earthward, and he dies.
Shall man live thus, in joy and hope
As a young lamb, who cannot dream,   170
Living, but that he shall live on?
Shall we not look into the laws
Of life and death, and things that seem,
And things that be, and analyze
Our double nature, and compare   175
All creeds till we have found the one,
If one there be?" Ay me! I fear
All may not doubt, but everywhere
Some must clasp idols. Yet, my God,
Whom call I idol? Let Thy dove   180
Shadow me over, and my sins
Be unremember'd, and Thy love
Enlighten me. O, teach me yet
Somewhat before the heavy clod
Weighs on me, and the busy fret   185
Of that sharp-headed worm begins
In the gross blackness underneath.

O weary life! O weary death!
O spirit and heart made desolate!
O damned vacillating state![5]   190

1830

The Kraken[6]

Below the thunders of the upper deep,
Far, far beneath in the abysmal sea,
His ancient, dreamless, uninvaded sleep

5. The poem ends, it has zealously been stated, "with three lines of quintessential *Hamlet*." That irreducible play might, however, have been in the poet's thoughts.

6. A mythical Norwegian sea-beast from Scandinavian folklore, here identified with the beast of the Apocalypse. See *Revelation*, 13:1.

The Kraken sleepeth: faintest sunlights flee
About his shadowy sides; above him swell   5
Huge sponges of millennial growth and height;
And far away into the sickly light,
From many a wondrous grot and secret cell
Unnumber'd and enormous polypi[7]
Winnow with giant arms the slumbering green.   10
There hath he lain for ages, and will lie
Battening upon huge sea-worms in his sleep,[8]
Until the latter fire[9] shall heat the deep;
Then once by man and angels to be seen,
In roaring he shall rise and on the surface die. 15

1830

Mariana[1]

Mariana in the moated grange.
—*Measure for Measure*

With blackest moss the flower-plots
    Were thickly crusted, one and all;
The rusted nails fell from the knots
    That held the pear to the gable-wall.
The broken sheds look'd sad and strange: 5
    Unlifted was the clinking latch;
    Weeded and worn the ancient thatch
Upon the lonely moated grange.
        She only said, "My life is dreary,
            He cometh not," she said;   10
        She said, "I am aweary, aweary,
            I would that I were dead!"[2]

Her tears fell with the dews at even;
    Her tears fell ere the dews were dried;   15
She could not look on the sweet heaven,
    Either at morn or eventide.
After the flitting of the bats,
    When thickest dark did trance[3] the sky,

---

7. Sea-animals such as the hydra or octopus.
8. See Shelley's line, "the dull weed some sea-worm battens on," in *Prometheus Unbound*, IV, i, 542.
9. Fire which will consume the world at its end. See *Revelation*, 16:8–9.
1. In Shakespeare's play (III, i, 277) ". . . there, at the moated grange, resides this dejected Mariana," who waits for Angelo who has deserted her. The notion of desertion is the only parallel to the play; the theme of isolation is thoroughly Tennysonian. ("The Moated Grange," Tennyson said, "is an imaginary house in the fen." *Memoir*, I,

4–5.) "Mariana" was the poet's first really famous poem, receiving unqualified praise from even the most hostile reviewers. Later critics have noted that the poem in its emphasis upon mood and feeling anticipates the Pre-Raphaelites. As poetry of suggestion rather than direct statement, "Mariana," as one critic puts it, "is there to prove that the most sophisticated symbolist poetry could be written fifty years before the Symbolists."
2. Compare the last lines of "Supposed Confessions."
3. Entrance, line cited in O.E.D.

She drew her casement-curtain by,
And glanced athwart the glooming flats.
She only said, "The night is dreary,
He cometh not," she said;
She said, "I am aweary, aweary,
I would that I were dead!"

Upon the middle of the night,
Waking she heard the night-fowl crow;
The cock sung out an hour ere light;
From the dark fen the oxen's low
Came to her; without hope of change,
In sleep she seem'd to walk forlorn,
Till cold winds woke the gray-eyed morn
About the lonely moated grange.
She only said, "The day is dreary,
He cometh not," she said;
She said, "I am aweary, aweary,
I would that I were dead!"

About a stone-cast from the wall
A sluice with blacken'd waters slept,
And o'er it many, round and small,
The cluster'd marish-mosses[4] crept.
Hard by a poplar shook alway,
All silver-green with gnarled bark:
For leagues no other tree did mark
The level waste, the rounding gray.
She only said, "My life is dreary,
He cometh not," she said;
She said, "I am aweary, aweary,
I would that I were dead!"

And ever when the moon was low,
And the shrill winds were up and away,
In the white curtain, to and fro,
She saw the gusty shadow sway.
But when the moon was very low,
And wild winds bound within their cell,
The shadow of the poplar fell
Upon her bed, across her brow.
She only said, "The night is dreary,
He cometh not," she said;
She said, "I am aweary, aweary,
I would that I were dead!"

All day within the dreamy house,[5]
The doors upon their hinges creak'd;
The blue fly sung in the pane; the mouse
Behind the mouldering wainscot shriek'd,

4. Lumps of moss floating on the water.
5. Compare T. S. Eliot's "Gerontion" and the use of a decaying house to suggest the parallel decay of a soul.

Or from the crevice peer'd about. 65
  Old faces glimmer'd thro' the doors,
  Old footsteps trod the upper floors,
Old voices called her from without.
   She only said, "My life is dreary,
    He cometh not," she said; 70
   She said, "I am aweary, aweary,
    I would that I were dead!"

The sparrow's chirrup on the roof,
  The slow clock ticking, and the sound
Which to the wooing wind aloof 75
  The poplar made, did all confound
Her sense; but most she loathed the hour
  When the thick-moted sunbeam lay
  Athwart the chambers, and the day
Was sloping toward his western bower. 80
   Then said she, "I am very dreary,
    He will not come," she said;
   She wept, "I am aweary, aweary,
    O God, that I were dead!"

1830

The Poet[6]

The poet in a golden clime was born,
  With golden stars above;
Dower'd with the hate of hate, the scorn of scorn,
  The love of love.

He saw thro' life and death, thro' good and ill, 5
  He saw thro' his own soul.
The marvel of the everlasting will,
  An open scroll,

Before him lay; with echoing feet he threaded
  The secretest walks of fame: 10
The viewless arrows of his thoughts were headed
  And wing'd with flame,

Like Indian reeds blown from his silver tongue,
  And of so fierce a flight,
From Calpe[7] unto Caucasus they sung, 15
  Filling with light

6. Reflecting the Romantic poets' exalted notions of the poet as seer and prophet charged with high responsibilities, this piece seems directly indebted to Shelley's *Defence of Poetry* (written in 1821; published in 1840), which Tennyson may have seen in manuscript. Shelley's famous last sentence, "Poets are the unacknowledged legislators of the world," would have been a favorite concept of the Apostles, the Cambridge literary group Tennyson was for a while associated with and strongly influenced by.

7. From Gibraltar to the Caucasus Mountains, the western and eastern limits of the ancient world.

And vagrant melodies the winds which bore
    Them earthward till they lit;
Then, like the arrow-seeds of the field flower,[8]
    The fruitful wit   20

Cleaving took root, and springing forth anew
    Where'er they fell, behold,
Like to the mother plant in semblance, grew
    A flower all gold,

And bravely furnish'd all abroad to fling   25
    The winged shafts of truth,
To throng with stately blooms the breathing spring
    Of Hope and Youth.

So many minds did gird their orbs with beams,
    Tho' one did fling the fire;   30
Heaven flow'd upon the soul in many dreams
    Of high desire.

Thus truth was multiplied on truth, the world
    Like one great garden show'd,
And thro' the wreaths of floating dark upcurl'd,   35
    Rare sunrise flow'd.

And Freedom rear'd in that august sunrise
    Her beautiful bold brow,
When rites and forms before his burning eyes
    Melted like snow.[9]   40

There was no blood[1] upon her maiden robes
    Sunn'd by those orient skies;
But round about the circles of the globes
    Of her keen eyes

And in her raiment's hem was traced in flame   45
    WISDOM, a name to shake
All evil dreams of power—a sacred name.
    And when she spake,

Her words did gather thunder as they ran,
    And as the lightning to the thunder   50
Which follows it, riving[2] the spirit of man,
    Making earth wonder,

So was their meaning to her words. No sword
    Of wrath her right arm whirl'd,
But one poor poet's scroll, and with *his* word   55
    She shook the world.

1830

8. The dandelion.
9. This stanza, like the third, fourth, and last two, especially resembles in imagery and impulse Shelley's "Ode to the West Wind."

1. Freedom and wisdom are to be won in man's mind, not violent overthrown; perhaps an allusion to the French Revolution.
2. Splitting.

The Poet's Mind[3]

1

Vex not thou the poet's mind
　With thy shallow wit;
Vex not thou the poet's mind,
　For thou canst not fathom it.
Clear and bright it should be ever,　　　　5
Flowing like a crystal river,
Bright as light, and clear as wind.

2

Dark-brow'd sophist,[4] come not anear;
　All the place is holy ground;
　Hollow smile and frozen sneer　　　　10
　　　Come not here.
　　Holy water will I pour
　　Into every spicy flower
Of the laurel-shrubs that hedge it around.
The flowers would faint at your cruel cheer.　　　15
　In your eye there is death,
　There is frost in your breath
　Which would blight the plants.
　Where you stand you cannot hear
　　　From the groves within　　　　20
　　　The wild-bird's din.
In the heart of the garden the merry bird chants.
It would fall to the ground if you came in.
　In the middle leaps a fountain
　　　Like sheet lightning,　　　　25
　　　Ever brightening
　With a low melodious thunder;
All day and all night it is ever drawn
　From the brain of the purple mountain[5]
　Which stands in the distance yonder.　　　30
It springs on a level of bowery lawn,
And the mountain draws it from heaven above,
And it sings a song of undying love;
And yet, tho' its voice be so clear and full,
You never would hear it, your ears are so dull;　　35
So keep where you are; you are foul with sin;
It would shrink to the earth if you came in.

1830

---

3. A companion piece to "The Poet" and Wordsworthian in its notion of the poet's isolation; "The Palace of Art" becomes a partial corrective to this extreme posture of the retired aesthete.
4. Pure, rationalistic, scientific intelligence not in accord with the natural world. One thinks of Appollonius in Keats's "Lamia."
5. Suggests Parnassus. The eighteenth-century theory that rainwater is stored in hollow mountains may inform this image.

Sir Launcelot and Queen Guinevere[6]

A FRAGMENT

Like souls that balance joy and pain,
With tears and smiles from heaven again
The maiden Spring upon the plain
Came in a sunlit fall of rain.
    In crystal vapor everywhere   5
Blue isles of heaven laugh'd between,
And far, in forest-deeps unseen,
The topmost elm-tree gather'd green
    From draughts of balmy air.

Sometimes the linnet piped his song;   10
Sometimes the throstle whistled strong;
Sometimes the sparhawk,[7] wheel'd along,
Hush'd all the groves from fear of wrong;
    By grassy capes with fuller sound
In curves the yellowing river ran,   15
And drooping chestnut-buds began
To spread into the perfect fan,
    Above the teeming ground.

Then, in the boyhood of the year,
Sir Launcelot and Queen Guinevere   20
Rode thro' the coverts of the deer,
With blissful treble ringing clear.
    She seem'd a part of joyous Spring;
A gown of grass-green silk she wore,
Buckled with golden clasps before;   25
A light-green tuft of plumes she bore
    Closed in a golden ring.

Now on some twisted ivy-net,
Now by some tinkling rivulet,
In mosses mixt with violet   30
Her cream-white mule his pastern[8] set;
    And fleeter now she skimm'd the plains
Than she whose elfin prancer springs
By night to eery warblings,
When all the glimmering moorland rings   35
    With jingling bridle-reins.

6. According to Hallam Tennyson, the fragment was "partly if not wholly written in 1830" (*Memoir*, II, 122). FitzGerald recalled that some verses of it were handed about at Cambridge, and a fragment from FitzGerald's collection appears in the *Memoir*, I, 59. This poem marks the beginning of Tennyson's lifelong interest in the Arthurian legends for poetic purposes and anticipates in verse-form "The Lady of Shalott."
7. Sparrow-hawk.
8. Hoofprint.

As she fled fast thro' sun and shade,
The happy winds upon her play'd,
Blowing the ringlet from the braid.
She look'd so lovely, as she sway'd   40
      The rein with dainty finger-tips,
A man had given all other bliss,
And all his worldly worth for this,
To waste his whole heart in one kiss
      Upon her perfect lips.[9]   45

1830; 1842

FROM *POEMS* (1832, DATED 1833)

To Christopher North[1]

You did late review my lays,
    Crusty Christopher;
You did mingle blame and praise,
    Rusty Christopher.

When I learnt from whom it came,   5
I forgave you all the blame,
    Musty Christopher;
I could *not* forgive the praise,
    Fusty Christopher.

1832

My Life Is Full of Weary Days[2]

My life is full of weary days,
    But good things have not kept aloof,
Nor wander'd into other ways;
    I have not lack'd thy mild reproof,
Nor golden largess of thy praise.   5

9. Happily, the poem ends without a trace of authorial moral indignation, the stigma upon so much of the poetry in *Idylls of the King* treating of Guinevere's adultery.

1. The poem is addressed to John Wilson, who reviewed the 1830 volume in the May 1832 issue of *Blackwood's Edinburgh Magazine*. (Selections from the review are reprinted in the Early Responses section of this book.) Tennyson was acutely sensitive to Wilson's hostile criticism, for his pompous dismissal of much of his own work, and particularly for his offensive ridicule of Hallam's favorable review. Hallam vainly tried to get Tennyson to omit this squib from the 1832 edition and took a much more balanced view of the whole proceedings: "I suppose one ought to feel very savage at being attacked," he wrote to his friend, "but somehow I feel much more amused" (*Memoir*, I, 84).

2. In the 1832 volume printed with the heading, "To ———." ("All good things have not kept aloof.") In the *Quarterly* for April 1833 Croker savagely derided this piece for its indulgence in the pathetic fallacy. Among numerous revisions, Tennyson changed "sudden laughters of the jay" to "sudden scritches of the jay."

And now shake hands across the brink
  Of that deep grave to which I go,
Shake hands once more; I cannot sink
  So far—far down, but I shall know
  Thy voice, and answer from below.   10

When in the darkness over me
  The four-handed mole shall scrape,
Plant thou no dusky cypress-tree,
  Nor wreathe thy cap with doleful crape,
  But pledge me in the flowing grape.   15

And when the sappy field and wood
  Grow green beneath the showery gray,
And rugged barks begin to bud,
  And thro' damp holts new-flush'd with may,
  Ring sudden scritches of the jay,   20

Then let wise Nature work her will,
  And on my clay her darnel grow;
Come only, when the days are still,
  And at my headstone whisper low,
  And tell me if the woodbines blow.   25

1832 (1865, 1872)

The Lady of Shalott[3]

PART I

On either side the river lie
Long fields of barley and of rye,
That clothe the wold and meet the sky;
And thro' the field the road runs by
  To many-tower'd Camelot;[4]   5
And up and down the people go,
Gazing where the lilies blow[5]
Round an island there below,
  The island of Shalott.

Willows whiten,[6] aspens quiver,   10
Little breezes dusk and shiver
Thro' the wave that runs for ever

---

3. The 1842 version as printed here is significantly altered from the original, and comparison with the 1832 text reveals much about the poet's methods of revision. For the poem's source, Palgrave in his notes says it was suggested by "an Italian romance upon the Donna di Scalotta," confirming, as Tennyson said to his son, that he had not drawn upon Malory's *Morte d'Arthur*: "I do not think that I had ever heard of the latter [Malory's Elaine] when I wrote the former." Shalott from the Italian *Scalotta* is the same as Astolat; the Lady later becomes Elaine, "the lily maid of Astolat," in "Lancelot and Elaine" (1859).

4. The legendary city and site of Arthur's palace variously located in Winchester, Somersetshire and elsewhere. Unlike the kingdom of Celtic mythology, Camelot is placed by the sea in the Italian story.

5. Bloom.

6. The white underside of the leaves show in the wind.

By the island in the river
    Flowing down to Camelot.
Four gray walls, and four gray towers,   15
Overlook a space of flowers,
And the silent isle imbowers
    The Lady of Shalott.

By the margin, willow-veil'd,
Slide the heavy barges trail'd   20
By slow horses; and unhail'd
The shallop[7] flitteth silken-sail'd
    Skimming down to Camelot:
But who hath seen her wave her hand?
Or at the casement seen her stand?   25
Or is she known in all the land,
    The Lady of Shalott?

Only reapers, reaping early
In among the bearded barley,
Hear a song that echoes cheerly   30
From the river winding clearly,
    Down to tower'd Camelot;
And by the moon the reaper weary,
Piling sheaves in uplands airy,
Listening, whispers " 'T is the fairy   35
    Lady of Shalott."

PART II

There she weaves by night and day
A magic web with colors gay.
She has heard a whisper say,
A curse is on her if she stay   40
    To look down to Camelot.
She knows not what the curse may be,
And so she weaveth steadily,
And little other care hath she,
    The Lady of Shalott.   45

And moving thro' a mirror clear
That hangs before her all the year,
Shadows of the world appear.
There she sees the highway near
    Winding down to Camelot;   50
There the river eddy whirls,
And there the surly village-churls,
And the red cloaks of market girls,
    Pass onward from Shalott.

Sometimes a troop of damsels glad,   55
An abbot on an ambling pad,[8]

---

7. A light, open boat.   8. An easy-paced horse.

Sometimes a curly shepherd-lad,
Or long-hair'd page in crimson clad,
    Goes by to tower'd Camelot;
And sometimes thro' the mirror blue   60
The knights come riding two and two:
She hath no loyal knight and true,
    The Lady of Shalott.

But in her web she still delights
To weave the mirror's magic sights,   65
For often thro' the silent nights
A funeral, with plumes and lights
    And music, went to Camelot;
Or when the moon was overhead,
Came two young lovers lately wed: 70
"I am half sick of shadows,"[9] said
    The Lady of Shalott.

PART III

A bow-shot from her bower-eaves,
He rode between the barley-sheaves.
The sun came dazzling thro' the leaves,   75
And flamed upon the brazen greaves[1]
    Of bold Sir Lancelot.
A red-cross[2] knight for ever kneel'd
To a lady in his shield,
That sparkled on the yellow field,   80
    Beside remote Shalott.

The gemmy bridle glitter'd free,
Like to some branch of stars we see
Hung in the golden Galaxy.
The bridle bells rang merrily   85
    As he rode down to Camelot;

And from his blazon'd baldric[3] slung
A mighty silver bugle hung,
And as he rode his armor rung,
    Beside remote Shalott.   90

All in the blue unclouded weather
Thick-jewell'd shone the saddle-leather,
The helmet and the helmet-feather
Burn'd like one burning flame together,
    As he rode down to Camelot;   95

9. Tennyson commented: "The new-born love for something, for some one in the wide world from which she has been so long secluded, takes her out of the region of shadows into that of realities" (*Memoir*, I, 117). As an allegory of art and life, the poem offers no viable alternatives to a real artist.

1. Shin-guard armor.
2. Not one of Lancelot's usual emblems, though Malory once gives him such a shield. Perhaps Tennyson was thinking of Spenser's Red-Crosse Knight in Book I of the *Faerie Queene*.
3. A richly ornamented shoulder-belt.

As often thro' the purple night,
Below the starry clusters bright,
Some bearded meteor, trailing light,
    Moves over still Shalott.

His broad clear brow in sunlight glow'd;   100
On burnish'd hooves his war-horse trode;
From underneath his helmet flow'd
His coal-black curls as on he rode,
    As he rode down to Camelot.
From the bank and from the river   105
He flash'd into the crystal mirror,
"Tirra lirra," by the river
    Sang Sir Lancelot.

She left the web, she left the loom,
She made three paces thro' the room,   110
She saw the water-lily bloom,
She saw the helmet and the plume,
    She look'd down to Camelot.
Out flew the web and floated wide;
The mirror crack'd from side to side;   115
"The curse is come upon me," cried
    The Lady of Shalott.

PART IV

In the stormy east-wind straining,
The pale yellow woods were waning,
The broad stream in his banks complaining,   120
Heavily the low sky raining
    Over tower'd Camelot;
Down she came and found a boat
Beneath a willow left afloat,
And round about the prow she wrote   125
    The Lady of Shalott.

And down the river's dim expanse
Like some bold seër in a trance,
Seeing all his own mischance—
With a glassy countenance   130
    Did she look to Camelot.   ·
And at the closing of the day
She loosed the chain, and down she lay;
The broad stream bore her far away,
    The Lady of Shalott.   135

Lying, robed in snowy white
That loosely flew to left and right—
The leaves upon her falling light—
Thro' the noises of the night
    She floated down to Camelot;   140

And as the boat-head wound along
The willowy hills and fields among,
They heard her singing her last song,
    The Lady of Shalott.

Heard a carol, mournful, holy,   145
Chanted loudly, chanted lowly,
Till her blood was frozen slowly,
And her eyes were darken'd wholly,
    Turn'd to tower'd Camelot.
For ere she reach'd upon the tide   150
The first house by the water-side,
Singing in her song she died,
    The Lady of Shalott.

Under tower and balcony,
By garden-wall and gallery,   155
A gleaming shape she floated by,
Dead-pale between the houses high,
    Silent into Camelot.
Out upon the wharfs they came,
Knight and burgher, lord and dame,   160
And round the prow they read her name,
    The Lady of Shalott.[4]

Who is this? and what is here?
And in the lighted palace near
Died the sound of royal cheer;   165
And they cross'd themselves for fear,
    All the knights at Camelot:
But Lancelot mused a little space;
He said, "She has a lovely face;
God in his mercy lend her grace,   170
    The Lady of Shalott."[5]

1832 (1842)

Mariana in the South[6]

With one black shadow at its feet,
    The house thro' all the level shines,
Close-latticed to the brooding heat,
    And silent in its dusty vines;

4. Compare "Lancelot and Elaine," lines 1236–1274.
5. The 1832 text ended with the following stanza, which undercuts the sympathetic outside world by making it a bunch of Philistines:
> They crossed themselves, their stars they blest,
> Knight, minstrel, abbot, squire and guest.
> There lay a parchment on her breast, That puzzled more than all the rest,
>   The wellfed wits at Camelot;
> *"The web was woven curiously*
> *The charm is broken utterly,*
> *Draw near and fear not—this is I,*
>   *The Lady of Shalott."*

6. Much revised and improved from the 1832 text, this poem, as Arthur Hallam explains in a letter to W. B. Donne (1831), was obviously intended "as a kind of pendant to his former poem of

A faint-blue ridge upon the right,   5
  An empty river-bed before,
  And shallows on a distant shore,
In glaring sand and inlets bright.
    But "Ave Mary," made she moan,
      And "Ave Mary," night and morn,   10
    And "Ah," she sang, "to be all alone,
      To live forgotten, and love forlorn."

She, as her carol sadder grew,
  From brow and bosom slowly down
Thro' rosy taper fingers drew   15
  Her streaming curls of deepest brown
To left and right, and made appear
  Still-lighted in a secret shrine
  Her melancholy eyes divine,
The home of woe without a tear.   20
    And "Ave Mary," was her moan,
      "Madonna, sad is night and morn,"
    And "Ah," she sang, "to be all alone,
      To live forgotten, and love forlorn."

Till all the crimson changed, and past   25
  Into deep orange o'er the sea,
Low on her knees herself she cast,
  Before Our Lady murmur'd she;
Complaining, "Mother, give me grace
  To help me of my weary load."   30
And on the liquid mirror glow'd
  The clear perfection of her face.
    "Is this the form," she made her moan,
      "That won his praises night and morn?"
    And "Ah," she said, "but I wake alone,   35
      I sleep forgotten, I wake forlorn."

Nor bird would sing, nor lamb would bleat,
  Nor any cloud would cross the vault,
But day increased from heat to heat,
  On stony drought and steaming salt;   40
Till now at noon she slept again,
  And seem'd knee-deep in mountain grass,
  And heard her native breezes pass,
And runlets babbling down the glen.[7]

'Mariana,' the idea of both being the expression of desolate loneliness" (*Memoir*, I, 500). Conceived when "travelling between Narbonne and Perpignan" (*Memoir*, I, 117), the second "Mariana" draws heavily upon the scenery of Southern France (See notes to "Œnone") just as the earlier "Mariana" reflected the Lincolnshire countryside.

7. A comparison with the original 8 lines of this stanza readily indicates the quality of the poet's revisions:

> At noon she slumbered. All along
>   The silvery field, the large leaves talked
> With one another, as among
>   The spikèd maize in dreams she walked.
> The lizard leapt: the sunlight played:
>   She heard the callow nestling lisp,
>   And brimful meadow-runnels crisp,
> In the full-leavèd platan-shade.

She breathed in sleep a lower moan,   45
    And murmuring, as at night and morn,
She thought, "My spirit is here alone,
    Walks forgotten, and is forlorn."

Dreaming, she knew it was a dream;
    She felt he was and was not there.   50
She woke; the babble of the stream
    Fell, and, without, the steady glare
Shrank one sick willow sere and small.
    The river-bed was dusty-white;
    And all the furnace of the light   55
Struck up against the blinding wall.
    She whisper'd, with a stifled moan
        More inward than at night or morn,
    "Sweet Mother, let me not here alone
        Live forgotten and die forlorn."   60

And, rising, from her bosom drew
    Old letters, breathing of her worth,
For "Love," they said, "must needs be true,
    To what is loveliest upon earth."
An image seem'd to pass the door,   65
    To look at her with slight, and say
    "But now thy beauty flows away,
So be alone for evermore."
    "O cruel heart," she changed her tone,
        "And cruel love, whose end is scorn,   70
    Is this the end, to be left alone,
        To live forgotten, and die forlorn?"

But sometimes in the falling day
    An image seem'd to pass the door,
To look into her eyes and say,   75
    "But thou shalt be alone no more."
And flaming downward over all
    From heat to heat the day decreased,
    And slowly rounded to the east
The one black shadow from the wall.   80
    "The day to night," she made her moan,
        "The day to night, the night to morn,
    And day and night I am left alone
        To live forgotten, and love forlorn."

At eve a dry cicala[8] sung,   85
    There came a sound as of the sea;
Backward the lattice-blind she flung,
    And lean'd upon the balcony.
There all in spaces rosy-bright
    Large Hesper glitter'd on her tears,   90
    And deepening thro' the silent spheres

---

8. A cicada or locust.

Heaven over heaven rose the night.
And weeping then she made her moan,
   "The night comes on that knows not morn,
When I shall cease to be all alone,   95
   To live forgotten, and love forlorn."

1832 (1842)

Œnone[9]

There lies a vale in Ida, lovelier
Than all the valleys of Ionian[1] hills.
The swimming vapor slopes athwart the glen,
Puts forth an arm, and creeps from pine to pine,
And loiters, slowly drawn. On either hand   5
The lawns and meadow-ledges midway down
Hang rich in flowers, and far below them roars
The long brook falling thro' the cloven ravine
In cataract after cataract to the sea.
Behind the valley topmost Gargarus[2]   10
Stands up and takes the morning; but in front
The gorges, opening wide apart, reveal
Troas and Ilion's column'd citadel,
The crown of Troas.[3]
                 Hither came at noon
Mournful Œnone, wandering forlorn   15
Of Paris, once her playmate on the hills.
Her cheek had lost the rose, and round her neck
Floated her hair or seem'd to float in rest.
She, leaning on a fragment twined with vine,
Sang to the stillness, till the mountain shade   20
Sloped downward to her seat from the upper cliff.

9. Much altered from the 1832 version, "Œnone" is the first of the great classical idyls or little pictures in verse more or less indebted to Theocritus. Tennyson's primary sources for the story were probably Ovid's *Heroides* and James Beattie's *The Judgment of Paris*. Œnone, a nymph of Troas and the daughter of Mount Ida, was deserted by her husband Paris for Helen of Troy. Her abduction precipitated the Trojan War and the dire consequences darkly prophesied by the wild Cassandra at the end of the poem.

During the summer of 1830, from early July to the end of September, Tennyson and Arthur Hallam journeyed to the Pyrenees to aid a small band of insurgents led by Torrijos, a daring revolutionary whose abortive attempt to overthrow the Spanish government ended with his surrender and execution. On this dangerous and romantic excursion the two youths carried secret coded documents from an unknown source, perhaps from sympathizers within the British government, but the precise nature of their mission remains mysterious. See *Memoir*, I, 51–55.

Tennyson started work on "Œnone" in the valley of Cauteretz which provides the landscape infusing the poem. The scenery of the Pyrenees became a lasting source of natural imagery, but it took Tennyson 31 years to face up to a return trip to commemorate that first daring journey with Hallam. See "In the Valley of Cauteretz" (1864).
1. The west coast of Asia Minor on the Aegean Sea.
2. The highest peak in the Ida Mountains.
3. The district of Troy; Ilion, the city itself.

"O mother Ida, many-fountain'd Ida,
Dear mother Ida, harken ere I die.
For now the noonday quiet holds the hill;
The grasshopper is silent in the grass;   25
The lizard, with his shadow on the stone,
Rests like a shadow, and the winds are dead.
The purple flower droops, the golden bee
Is lily-cradled; I alone awake.
My eyes are full of tears, my heart of love,   30
My heart is breaking, and my eyes are dim,
And I am all aweary of my life.

"O mother Ida, many-fountain'd Ida,
Dear mother Ida, harken ere I die.
Hear me, O earth, hear me, O hills, O caves   35
That house the cold crown'd snake! O mountain brooks,
I am the daughter of a River-God,[4]
Hear me, for I will speak, and build up all
My sorrow with my song, as yonder walls
Rose slowly to a music[5] slowly breathed,   40
A cloud that gather'd shape; for it may be
That, while I speak of it, a little while
My heart may wander from its deeper woe.

"O mother Ida, many-fountain'd Ida,
Dear mother Ida, harken ere I die.   45
I waited underneath the dawning hills;
Aloft the mountain lawn was dewy-dark,
And dewy dark aloft the mountain pine.
Beautiful Paris, evil-hearted Paris,
Leading a jet-black goat white-horn'd, white-hooved,   50
Came up from reedy Simois all alone.

"O mother Ida, harken ere I die.
Far-off the torrent call'd me from the cleft;
Far up the solitary morning smote
The streaks of virgin snow. With downdropt eyes   55
I sat alone; white-breasted like a star
Fronting the dawn he moved; a leopard skin
Droop'd from his shoulder, but his sunny hair
Cluster'd about his temples like a God's;
And his cheeks brighten'd as the foam-bow brightens 60
When the wind blows the foam, and all my heart
Went forth to embrace him coming ere he came.

"Dear mother Ida, harken ere I die.
He smiled, and opening out his milk-white palm
Disclosed a fruit of pure Hesperian gold,[6]   65
That smelt ambrosially, and while I look'd

4. Simois.
5. Compare "Tiresias," line 96.
6. The golden apples of the Hesperides.

See notes to Tennyson's poem "The Hesperides" for part of the mythology.

And listen'd, the full-flowing river of speech
Came down upon my heart:
                   " 'My own Œnone,
Beautiful-brow'd Œnone, my own soul,
Behold this fruit, whose gleaming rind ingraven   70
"For the most fair," would seem to award it thine,
As lovelier than whatever Oread[7] haunt
The knolls of Ida, loveliest in all grace
Of movement, and the charm of married brows.'[8]

"Dear mother Ida, harken ere I die.   75
He prest the blossom of his lips to mine,
And added, 'This was cast upon the board,
When all the full-faced presence of the Gods
Ranged in the halls of Peleus;[9] whereupon
Rose feud, with question unto whom 't were due;   80
But light-foot Iris brought it yester-eve,
Delivering, that to me, by common voice
Elected umpire, Herè comes to-day,
Pallas and Aphrodite, claiming each
This meed of fairest. Thou, within the cave   85
Behind yon whispering tuft of oldest pine,
Mayst well behold them unbeheld, unheard
Hear all, and see thy Paris judge of Gods.'

"Dear mother Ida, harken ere I die.
It was the deep midnoon; one silvery cloud   90
Had lost his way between the piny sides
Of this long glen. Then to the bower they came,
Naked they came to that smooth-swarded bower,
And at their feet the crocus brake like fire,
Violet, amaracus, and asphodel,   95
Lotos and lilies; and a wind arose,
And overhead the wandering ivy and vine,
This way and that, in many a wild festoon
Ran riot, garlanding the gnarled boughs
With bunch and berry and flower thro' and thro'.   100

"O mother Ida, harken ere I die.
On the tree-tops a crested peacock lit,
And o'er him flow'd a golden cloud, and lean'd
Upon him, slowly dropping fragrant dew.
Then first I heard the voice of her to whom   105
Coming thro' heaven, like a light that grows
Larger and clearer, with one mind the Gods

---

7. A nymph.
8. In the classical age, eyebrows that met were considered a mark of beauty. Chaucer, in his description of Criseyde, wasn't so sure: "And save hire browes joyneden yfere, / Ther nas no lakke, in aught I kan espien."
9. The king of Thessaly who married Thetis; parents of Achilles. At their marriage Eris, the goddess of discord ("the abominable" of line 220), brought the golden apple marked "for the fairest." Hera (identified as Juno by the Romans), Athene, and Aphrodite all claimed it.

Rise up for reverence. She to Paris made
Proffer of royal power, ample rule
Unquestion'd, overflowing revenue   110
Wherewith to embellish state, 'from many a vale
And river-sunder'd champaign clothed with corn,
Or labor'd mine undrainable of ore.
Honor,' she said, 'and homage, tax and toll,
From many an inland town and haven large,   115
Mast-throng'd beneath her shadowing citadel
In glassy bays among her tallest towers.'

 "O mother Ida, harken ere I die.
Still she spake on and still she spake of power,
'Which in all action is the end of all;   120
Power fitted to the season; wisdom-bred
And throned of wisdom—from all neighbor crowns
Alliance and allegiance, till thy hand
Fail from the sceptre-staff. Such boon from me,
From me, heaven's queen, Paris,[1] to thee king-born,   125
A shepherd all thy life, but yet king-born.
Should come most welcome, seeing men, in power
Only, are likest Gods, who have attain'd
Rest in a happy place and quiet seats
Above the thunder, with undying bliss   130
In knowledge of their own supremacy.'

 "Dear mother Ida, harken ere I die.
She ceased, and Paris held the costly fruit
Out at arm's-length, so much the thought of power
Flatter'd his spirit; but Pallas where she stood   135
Somewhat apart, her clear and bared limbs
O'erthwarted with the brazen-headed spear
Upon her pearly shoulder leaning cold,
The while, above, her full and earnest eye
Over her snow-cold breast and angry cheek   140
Kept watch, waiting decision, made reply:

 " 'Self-reverence, self-knowledge, self-control,
These three alone lead life to sovereign power.
Yet not for power (power of herself
Would come uncall'd for) but to live by law,   145
Acting the law we live by without fear;
And, because right is right, to follow right
Were wisdom in the scorn of consequence.'

 "Dear mother Ida, harken ere I die.
Again she said: 'I woo thee not with gifts.   150
Sequel of guerdon could not alter me
To fairer. Judge thou me by what I am,

1. One of Priam's fifty sons, Paris as
a child was left to die on Mount Ida
because of a prophecy that he would
bring destruction on Troy; he was
saved and brought up by shepherds.

So shalt thou find me fairest.
      Yet, indeed,
If gazing on divinity disrobed
Thy mortal eyes are frail to judge of fair,   155
Unbias'd by self-profit, O, rest thee sure
That I shall love thee well and cleave to thee,
So that my vigor, wedded to thy blood,
Shall strike within thy pulses, like a God's,
To push thee forward thro' a life of shocks,   160
Dangers, and deeds, until endurance grow
Sinew'd with action, and the full-grown will,
Circled thro' all experiences, pure law,
Commeasure perfect freedom.'
       "Here she ceas'd,
And Paris ponder'd, and I cried, 'O Paris,   165
Give it to Pallas!' but he heard me not,
Or hearing would not hear me, woe is me!

 "O mother Ida, many-fountain'd Ida,
Dear mother Ida, harken ere I die.
Idalian Aphrodite beautiful,   170
Fresh as the foam, new-bathed in Paphian[2] wells,
With rosy slender fingers backward drew
From her warm brows and bosom her deep hair
Ambrosial, golden round her lucid throat
And shoulder; from the violets her light foot   175
Shone rosy-white, and o'er her rounded form
Between the shadows of the vine-bunches
Floated the glowing sunlights, as she moved.

 "Dear mother Ida, harken ere I die.
She with a subtle smile in her mild eyes,   180
The herald of her triumph, drawing nigh
Half-whisper'd in his ear, 'I promise thee
The fairest and most loving wife in Greece.'
She spoke and laugh'd; I shut my sight for fear;
But when I look'd, Paris had raised his arm,   185
And I beheld great Herè's angry eyes,
As she withdrew into the golden cloud,
And I was left alone within the bower;
And from that time to this I am alone,
And I shall be alone until I die.   190

 "Yet, mother Ida, harken ere I die.
Fairest—why fairest wife? am I not fair?
My love hath told me so a thousand times.
Methinks I must be fair, for yesterday,
When I past by, a wild and wanton pard,   195
Eyed like the evening star, with playful tail
Crouch'd fawning in the weed. Most loving is she?

---

2. Paphos, like Idalium, was a city in Cyprus sacred to Aphrodite.

Ah me, my mountain shepherd, that my arms
Were wound about thee, and my hot lips prest
Close, close to thine in that quick-falling dew   200
Of fruitful kisses, thick as autumn rains
Flash in the pools of whirling Simois!

"O mother, hear me yet before I die.
They came, they cut away my tallest pines,
My tall dark pines, that plumed the craggy ledge   205
High over the blue gorge, and all between
The snowy peak and snow-white cataract
Foster'd the callow eaglet—from beneath
Whose thick mysterious boughs in the dark morn
The panther's roar came muffled, while I sat   210
Low in the valley. Never, never more
Shall lone Œnone see the morning mist
Sweep thro' them; never see them overlaid
With narrow moonlit slips of silver cloud,
Between the loud stream and the trembling stars.   215

"O mother, hear me yet before I die.
I wish that somewhere in the ruin'd folds,
Among the fragments tumbled from the glens,
Or the dry thickets, I could meet with her
The Abominable, that uninvited came   220
Into the fair Peleïan banquet-hall,
And cast the golden fruit upon the board,
And bred this change; that I might speak my mind,
And tell her to her face how much I hate
Her presence, hated both of Gods and men.   225

"O mother, hear me yet before I die.
Hath he not sworn his love a thousand times,
In this green valley, under this green hill,
Even on this hand, and sitting on this stone?
Seal'd it with kisses? water'd it with tears?   230
O happy tears, and how unlike to these!
O happy heaven, how canst thou see my face?
O happy earth, how canst thou bear my weight?
O death, death, death, thou ever-floating cloud,
There are enough unhappy on this earth,   235
Pass by the happy souls, that love to live;
I pray thee, pass before my light of life,
And shadow all my soul, that I may die.
Thou weighest heavy on the heart within,
Weigh heavy on my eyelids; let me die.   240

"O mother, hear me yet before I die.
I will not die alone,[3] for fiery thoughts

3. Fatally wounded by Philoctetes' poisoned arrow, Paris finally sought help from Œnone, who alone had the gift to heal him. See lines 31–48 in "The Death of Œnone" for Tennyson's rendering of that part of the myth.

Do shape themselves within me, more and more,
Whereof I catch the issue, as I hear
Dead sounds at night come from the inmost hills,   245
Like footsteps upon wool. I dimly see
My far-off doubtful purpose, as a mother
Conjectures of the features of her child
Ere it is born. Her child!—a shudder comes
Across me: never child be born of me,   250
Unblest, to vex me with his father's eyes!

"O mother, hear me yet before I die.
Hear me, O earth. I will not die alone,
Lest their shrill happy laughter come to me
Walking the cold and starless road of death   255
Uncomforted, leaving my ancient love
With the Greek woman. I will rise and go
Down into Troy, and ere the stars come forth
Talk with the wild Cassandra,[4] for she says
A fire dances before her, and a sound   260
Rings ever in her ears of armed men.
What this may be I know not, but I know
That, wheresoe'er I am by night and day,
All earth and air seem only burning fire."

1832 (1842)

To ——

WITH THE FOLLOWING POEM[5]

I send you here a sort of allegory—
For you will understand it—of a soul,
A sinful soul possess'd of many gifts,
A spacious garden full of flowering weeds,
A glorious devil, large in heart and brain,   5
That did love beauty only—beauty seen
In all varieties of mould and mind—
And knowledge for its beauty; or if good,
Good only for its beauty, seeing not
That Beauty, Good, and Knowledge are three sisters   10
That doat upon each other, friends to man,
Living together under the same roof,
And never can be sunder'd without tears.
And he that shuts Love out, in turn shall be

4. One of Priam's daughters, she denied Apollo her love. He then rendered value-less his earlier gift of prophecy by causing her prophecies never to be believed.
5. Dedicated to Richard Trench, a member of the Cambridge Apostles. Trench, Tennyson noted late in his life, "said to me, when we were at Trinity together, 'Tennyson, we cannot live in art'" (*Memoir*, I, 118). See *In Memoriam*, 87, 6. The following allegory is a criticism of the doctrine of art for art's sake and may be contrasted to "The Poet's Mind" and "The Hesperides."

Shut out from Love, and on her threshold lie   15
Howling in outer darkness.[6] Not for this
Was common clay ta'en from the common earth
Moulded by God, and temper'd with the tears
Of angels to the perfect shape of man.

1832

The Palace of Art[7]

I built my soul a lordly pleasure-house,[8]
    Wherein at ease for aye to dwell.
I said, "O Soul, make merry and carouse,
        Dear soul, for all is well."

A huge crag-platform, smooth as burnish'd brass,   5
    I chose. The ranged ramparts bright
From level meadow-bases of deep grass
        Suddenly scaled the light.

Thereon I built it firm. Of ledge or shelf
    The rock rose clear, or winding stair.   10
My soul would live alone unto herself
        In her high palace there.

And "while the world runs round and round," I said,
    "Reign thou apart, a quiet king,
Still as, while Saturn whirls, his steadfast shade   15
        Sleeps on his luminous ring."[9]

To which my soul made answer readily:
    "Trust me, in bliss I shall abide
In this great mansion, that is built for me,
        So royal-rich and wide."   20

    ·   ·   ·   ·   ·   ·   ·   ·   ·

6. Compare *In Memoriam*, 54, 5: "an infant crying in the night . . . with no language but a cry," and *IM*, 124, 5–6. In 1890 Tennyson wrote: " 'The Palace of Art' is the embodiment of my own belief that the Godlike life is with man and for man" (*Memoir*, I, 118–119).

7. Circulating in manuscript by May 1832 the poem was extensively revised between 1832 and 1853. A number of stanzas were transposed, many were dropped, and several new ones were added. A couple of significant deletions are given in these notes; but a full comparison of the 1832 and 1842 texts is needed to reveal the extent of Tennyson's artistic development during the so-called ten years' silence.

    In a note to the 1832 version the poet acknowledged, "It is the most difficult of all things to *devise* a statue in verse." "When I first conceived the plan of the poem, I intended to have introduced both sculptures and paintings into it" (*Memoir*, I, 119). Many of the changes record the poet's often successful attempts at painting pictures in verse; for that, more than the moral, is the poem's achievement.

8. See note 2 to "Recollections of the Arabian Nights" for other evidence of Tennyson's debt to Coleridge's "Kubla Khan."

9. Saturn revolves every $10\frac{1}{2}$ hours, but the planet's shadow cast on the luminous ring appears stationary. Tennyson often, especially in *In Memoriam*, alludes to astronomical phenomena, a tendency which, for Yeats, contributed to what he called "that brooding over scientific opinion that so often extinguished the central flame in Tennyson."

Four courts I made, East, West and South and North,
    In each a squared lawn, wherefrom
The golden gorge of dragons spouted forth
    A flood of fountain-foam.

And round the cool green courts there ran a row   25
    Of cloisters, branch'd like mighty woods,
Echoing all night to that sonorous flow
    Of spouted fountain-floods;

And round the roofs a gilded gallery
    That lent broad verge to distant lands,   30
Far as the wild swan wings, to where the sky
    Dipt down to sea and sands.

From those four jets four currents in one swell
    Across the mountain stream'd below
In misty folds, that floating as they fell   35
    Lit up a torrent-bow.

And high on every peak a statue seem'd
    To hang on tiptoe, tossing up
A cloud of incense of all odor steam'd
    From out a golden cup.   40

So that she thought, "And who shall gaze upon
    My palace with unblinded eyes,
While this great bow will waver in the sun,
    And that sweet incense rise?"

For that sweet incense rose and never fail'd,   45
    And, while day sank or mounted higher,
The light aerial gallery, golden-rail'd,
    Burnt like a fringe of fire.

Likewise the deep-set windows, stain'd and traced,
    Would seem slow-flaming crimson fires   50
From shadow'd grots of arches interlaced,
    And tipt with frost-like spires.

  .   .   .   .

Full of long-sounding corridors it was,
    That over-vaulted grateful gloom,
Thro' which the livelong day my soul did pass,   55
    Well-pleased, from room to room.

Full of great rooms and small the palace stood,
    All various, each a perfect whole
From living Nature, fit for every mood
    And change of my still soul.   60

For some were hung with arras green and blue,
    Showing a gaudy summer-morn,
Where with puff'd cheek the belted hunter blew
    His wreathed bugle-horn.

One seem'd all dark and red—a tract of sand,   65
   And some one pacing there alone,
Who paced for ever in a glimmering land,
    Lit with a low large moon.

One show'd an iron coast and angry waves,
   You seem'd to hear them climb and fall
And roar rock-thwarted under bellowing caves,   70
    Beneath the windy wall.

And one, a full-fed river winding slow
   By herds upon an endless plain,
The ragged rims of thunder brooding low,   75
    With shadow-streaks of rain.

And one, the reapers at their sultry toil.
   In front they bound the sheaves. Behind
Were realms of upland, prodigal in oil,
    And hoary to the wind.[1]   80

And one a foreground black with stones and slags;
   Beyond, a line of heights; and higher
All barr'd with long white cloud the scornful crags;
    And highest, snow and fire.

And one, an English home—gray twilight pour'd   85
   On dewy pastures, dewy trees,
Softer than sleep—all things in order stored,
    A haunt of ancient Peace.

Nor these alone, but every landscape fair,
   As fit for every mood of mind,
Or gay, or grave, or sweet, or stern, was there,   90
    Not less than truth design'd.

  · · · · · · · · · · · ·

Or the maid-mother by a crucifix,
   In tracts of pasture sunny-warm,
Beneath branch-work of costly sardonyx[2]   95
    Sat smiling, babe in arm.

Or in a clear-wall'd city on the sea,
   Near gilded organ-pipes, her hair
Wound with white roses, slept Saint Cecily;[3]
    An angel look'd at her.   100

Or thronging all one porch of Paradise
   A group of Houris[4] bow'd to see
The dying Islamite, with hands and eyes
    That said, We wait for thee.

1. Probably an Italian landscape; the olive trees show their white undersides in the wind.
2. A kind of stone with orange-red layers.
3. St. Cecilia, the patron saint of music.
4. Nymphs of the Mohammedan paradise who would welcome the faithful.

Or mythic Uther's deeply-wounded son[5]   105
    In some fair space of sloping greens
Lay, dozing in the vale of Avalon,
    And watch'd by weeping queens.

Or hollowing one hand against his ear,
    To list a foot-fall, ere he saw   110
The wood-nymph, stay'd the Ausonian king[6] to hear
    Of wisdom and of law.

Or over hills with peaky tops and engrail'd,
    And many a tract of palm and rice,
The throne of Indian Cama[7] slowly sail'd   115
    A summer fann'd with spice.

Or sweet Europa's mantle blew unclasp'd,
    From off her shoulder backward borne;
From one hand droop'd a crocus; one hand grasp'd
    The mild bull's golden horn.[8]   120

Or else flush'd Ganymede,[9] his rosy thigh
    Half-buried in the eagle's down,
Sole as a flying star shot thro' the sky
    Above the pillar'd town.

Nor these alone; but every legend fair   125
    Which the supreme Caucasian mind
Carved out of Nature for itself was there,
    Not less than life design'd.

·   ·   ·   ·   ·   ·   ·   ·   ·   ·   ·   ·   ·   ·   ·

Then in the towers I placed great bells that swung,
    Moved of themselves, with silver sound;   130
And with choice paintings of wise men I hung
    The royal dais round.

For there was Milton like a seraph strong,
    Beside him Shakespeare bland and mild;
And there the world-worn Dante grasp'd his song,   135
    And somewhat grimly smiled.

And there the Ionian father[1] of the rest;
    A million wrinkles carved his skin;
A hundred winters snow'd upon his breast,
    From cheek and throat and chin.   140

Above, the fair hall-ceiling stately-set
    Many an arch high up did lift,

---

5. King Arthur. For Tennyson's rendering of this part of the myth, see "The Passing of Arthur," especially lines 361 to end.
6. Numa Pompilius, the second king of Rome.
7. Indian god of love.
8. Zeus loved Europa, the daughter of the king of Tyre, and in the form of a white bull he carried her off to Crete.
9. A mortal who, because of his extraordinary beauty, was carried off by the eagle of Zeus and made cupbearer to the gods.
1. Homer.

And angels rising and descending met
    With interchange of gift.

Below was all mosaic choicely plann'd   145
    With cycles of the human tale
Of this wide world, the times of every land
    So wrought they will not fail.

The people here, a beast of burden slow,
    Toil'd onward, prick'd with goads and stings;   150
Here play'd, a tiger, rolling to and fro
    The heads and crowns of kings;[2]

Here rose, an athlete, strong to break or bind
    All force in bonds that might endure,
And here once more like some sick man declined,   155
    And trusted any cure.

But over these she trod; and those great bells
    Began to chime. She took her throne;
She sat betwixt the shining oriels,
    To sing her songs alone.   160

And thro' the topmost oriels' colored flame
    Two godlike faces gazed below;
Plato the wise, and large-brow'd Verulam,[3]
    The first of those who know.

And all those names that in their motion were   165
    Full-welling fountain-heads of change,
Betwixt the slender shafts were blazon'd fair
    In diverse raiment strange;

Thro' which the lights, rose, amber, emerald, blue,
    Flush'd in her temples and her eyes,   170
And from her lips, as morn from Memnon,[4] drew
    Rivers of melodies.

No nightingale delighteth to prolong
    Her low preamble all alone,
More than my soul to hear her echo'd song   175
    Throb thro' the ribbed stone;

Singing and murmuring in her feastful mirth,
    Joying to feel herself alive,
Lord over Nature, lord of the visible earth,
    Lord of the senses five;   180

Communing with herself: "All these are mine,
    And let the world have peace or wars,

---

2. Perhaps a reference to the French Revolution of 1789, in which case the athlete and sick man in the following stanza may be democracy and anarchy respectively.
3. Francis Bacon.

4. King of the Ethiopians and immortalized by Zeus, his statue supposedly gave forth a musical sound when struck by the first rays of the morning sun.

'T is one to me." She—when young night divine
    Crown'd dying day with stars,

Making sweet close of his delicious toils—   185
    Lit light in wreaths and anadems,
And pure quintessences of precious oils
    In hollow'd moons of gems,

To mimic heaven; and clapt her hands and cried,
    "I marvel if my still delight   190
In this great house so royal-rich and wide
    Be flatter'd to the height.

"O all things fair to sate my various eyes!
    O shapes and hues that please me well!
O silent faces of the Great and Wise,   195
    My Gods, with whom I dwell![5]

"O Godlike isolation which art mine,
    I can but count thee perfect gain,
What time I watch the darkening droves of swine
    That range on yonder plain.   200

"In filthy sloughs they roll a prurient skin,
    They gaze and wallow, breed and sleep;
And oft some brainless devil enters in,
    And drives them to the deep."[6]

Then of the moral instinct would she prate   205
    And of the rising from the dead,
As hers by right of full-accomplish'd Fate;
    And at the last she said:

"I take possession of man's mind and deed.
    I care not what the sects may bawl.   210
I sit as God holding no form of creed,
    But contemplating all."

  .   .   .   .

Full oft the riddle of the painful earth
    Flash'd thro' her as she sat alone,
Yet not the less held she her solemn mirth,   215
    And intellectual throne.

5. After this stanza the following two verses appeared in the 1842 text:
  "From shape to shape at first within the womb
    The brain is moulded," she began,
  "And thro' all phases of all thought I come
    Unto the perfect man.

  All nature widens upward. Evermore
    The simpler essence lower lies,
  More complex is more perfect, owning more
    Discourse, more widely wise."

In the 1832 version the first of these stanzas began: "From change to change four times within the womb. . . ." These suppressed lines have been variously cited in arguments over the extent to which Tennyson anticipated the Theory of Evolution.
6. From two possessed men Christ cast out the devils who went into a herd of swine, "and behold the whole herd rushed down the steep bank into the sea, and perished in the waters" (*Matthew,* 8:28–34).

And so she throve and prosper'd; so three years
    She prosper'd; on the fourth she fell,
Like Herod,[7] when the shout was in his ears,
    Struck thro' with pangs of hell.   220

Lest she should fail and perish utterly,
    God, before whom ever lie bare
The abysmal deeps of personality,
    Plagued her with sore despair.

When she would think, where'er she turn'd her sight   225
    The airy hand confusion wrought,
Wrote, "Mene, mene,"[8] and divided quite
    The kingdom of her thought.

Deep dread and loathing of her solitude
    Fell on her, from which mood was born   230
Scorn of herself; again, from out that mood
    Laughter at her self-scorn.

"What! is not this my place of strength," she said,
    "My spacious mansion built for me,
Whereof the strong foundation-stones were laid   235
    Since my first memory?"

But in dark corners of her palace stood
    Uncertain shapes; and unawares
On white-eyed phantasms weeping tears of blood,
    And horrible nightmares,   240

And hollow shades enclosing hearts of flame,
    And, with dim fretted foreheads all,
On corpses three-months-old at noon she came,
    That stood against the wall.

A spot of dull stagnation, without light   245
    Or power of movement, seem'd my soul,
Mid onward-sloping motions infinite
    Making for one sure goal;

A still salt pool, lock'd in with bars of sand,
    Left on the shore, that hears all night   250
The plunging seas draw backward from the land
    Their moon-led waters white;

A star that with the choral starry dance
    Join'd not, but stood, and standing saw
The hollow orb of moving Circumstance   255
    Roll'd round by one fix'd law.

---

7. The people claimed Herod's voice was God's; "Immediately an angel of the Lord smote him, because he did not give God the glory; and he was eaten by worms, and died" (*Acts*, 12:18–23).

8. "This is the interpretation of the matter: mene, God has numbered the days of your kingdom and brought it to an end" (*Daniel*, 5:26).

Back on herself her serpent pride had curl'd.
   "No voice," she shriek'd in that lone hall,
"No voice breaks thro' the stillness of this world;
     One deep, deep silence all!"   260

She, mouldering with the dull earth's mouldering sod,
   Inwrapt tenfold in slothful shame,
Lay there exiled from eternal God,
     Lost to her place and name;

And death and life she hated equally,   265
   And nothing saw, for her despair,
But dreadful time, dreadful eternity,
     No comfort anywhere;

Remaining utterly confused with fears,
   And ever worse with growing time,   270
And ever unrelieved by dismal tears,
     And all alone in crime.

Shut up as in a crumbling tomb, girt round
   With blackness as a solid wall,
Far off she seem'd to hear the dully sound   275
     Of human footsteps fall:

As in strange lands a traveller walking slow,
   In doubt and great perplexity,
A little before moonrise hears the low
     Moan of an unknown sea;   280

And knows not if it be thunder, or a sound
   Of rocks thrown down, or one deep cry
Of great wild beasts; then thinketh, "I have found
     A new land, but I die."

She howl'd aloud, "I am on fire within.   285
   There comes no murmur of reply.
What is it that will take away my sin,
     And save me lest I die?"

So when four years were wholly finished,
   She threw her royal robes away.   290
"Make me a cottage in the vale," she said,
     "Where I may mourn and pray.

"Yet pull not down my palace towers, that are
   So lightly, beautifully built;
Perchance I may return with others[9] there   295
     When I have purged my guilt."

1832 (1842, 1853)

9. See *In Memoriam*, 58.

The Hesperides[1]

Hesperus and his daughters three,
That sing about the golden tree.
—*Comus* [MILTON]

The North-wind fall'n, in the new-starréd night
Zidonian Hanno,[2] voyaging beyond
The hoary promontory of Soloë
Past Thymiaterion,[3] in calméd bays,
Between the southern and the western Horn,   5
Heard neither warbling of the nightingale,
Nor melody of the Libyan lotus flute
Blown seaward from the shore; but from a slope
That ran bloom-bright into the Atlantic blue,
Beneath a highland leaning down a weight   10
Of cliffs, and zoned below with cedar shade,
Came voices, like the voices in a dream,
Continuous, till he reached the outer sea.

Song

1

The golden apple, the golden apple, the hallowed fruit,
Guard it well, guard it warily,   15
Singing airily,
Standing about the charméd root.
Round about all is mute,
As the snow-field on the mountain-peaks,
As the sand-field at the mountain-foot.   20
Crocodiles in briny creeks
Sleep and stir not: all is mute.
If ye sing not, if ye make false measure,
We shall lose eternal pleasure,
Worth eternal want of rest.   25

1. Never republished during the poet's lifetime. Tennyson expressed regret that he had done away with it from among his Juvenilia. See *Memoir*, I, 61. As a celebration of pure art, "The Hesperides" should be read along with "The Poet" and "The Poet's Mind" and contrasted with "A Palace of Art." As a recent critic has aptly said in arguing that the poem is more than mere picture painting, "The poem seems in fact to be an interpretation of the spiritual conditions under which the poetic experience comes to life."

In Greek mythology the Hesperides were the four daughters of the evening star Hesperus, and they lived near the Atlas Mountains on the north-west coast of Africa. With the dragon Ladon, they guarded the tree of the golden apples given by the Titan goddess of the Earth Gaea (or Gē) to Hera when she married Zeus. The eleventh labor of Heracles was to get the golden apples which he did, according to one version of the myth, by slaying Ladon. In another version he induced Atlas to fetch the apples while assuming his burden of holding up the world. The apples supposedly had the power of healing and were symbolic of happiness, love and wisdom. Tennyson's primary source was probably in Hesiod's rendering of the myth.

2. A Carthaginian commander who, around 500 B.C., navigated the west coast of Africa and recorded his experiences in the *Periplus*.

3. Like Soloë, a point on the African coast Hanno passed as he penetrated beyond the colony of Senegal on "the western Horn."

Laugh not loudly: watch the treasure
Of the wisdom of the West.[4]
In a corner wisdom whispers. Five[5] and three
(Let it not be preached abroad) make an awful mystery.
For the blossom unto threefold music bloweth;   30
Evermore it is born anew;
And the sap to threefold music floweth,
From the root
Drawn in the dark,
Up to the fruit,   35
Creeping under the fragrant bark,
Liquid gold, honeysweet, thro' and thro'.
Keen-eyed Sisters, singing airily,
Looking warily
Every way,   40
Guard the apple night and day,
Lest one[6] from the East come and take it away.

                                    2
Father Hesper, Father Hesper, watch, watch, ever and aye,
Looking under silver hair with a silver eye.
Father, twinkle not thy steadfast sight;   45
Kingdoms lapse, and climates change, and races die;
Honor comes with mystery;
Hoarded wisdom brings delight.
Number, tell them over and number
How many the mystic fruit-tree holds   50
Lest the red-combed dragon slumber
Rolled together in purple folds.
Look to him, father, lest he wink, and the golden apple be stol'n
          away,
For his ancient heart is drunk with overwatchings night and day,
Round about the hallowed fruit-tree curled—   55
Sing away, sing loud evermore in the wind, without stop,
Lest his scaléd eyelid drop,
For he is older than the world.
If he waken, we waken,
Rapidly levelling eager eyes.   60
If he sleep, we sleep,
Dropping the eyelid over the eyes.
If the golden apple be taken,
The world will be overwise.
Five links, a golden chain, are we,   65
Hesper, the dragon, and sisters three,
Bound about the golden tree.

---

4. In the symbolic geography here and in other early poems, the West stands for stability, twilight, rest, civilization whereas Tennyson connects the East with images of dawn, strength, vigor, strife.
5. The number five traditionally has mystic significance as the first number which contains the two primary odd and even numbers and is thus the original unification of opposites. The poet may also be thinking of the five senses.
6. Alludes to Heracles who came from Greece.

3

Father Hesper, Father Hesper, watch, watch, night and day,
Lest the old wound[7] of the world be healéd,
The glory unsealéd,   70
The golden apple stolén away,
And the ancient secret revealéd.
Look from west to east along:
Father, old Himala weakens, Caucasus[8] is bold and strong.
Wandering waters unto wandering waters call;   75
Let them clash together, foam and fall.
Out of watchings, out of wiles,
Comes the bliss of secret smiles.
All things are not told to all.
Half-round the mantling night is drawn,   80
Purple fringéd with even and dawn.
Hesper hateth Phosphor,[9] evening hateth morn.

4

Every flower and every fruit the redolent breath
Of this warm sea-wind ripeneth,
Arching the billow in his sleep;   85
But the land-wind wandereth,
Broken by the highland-steep,
Two streams upon the violet deep;
For the western sun and the western star,
And the low west-wind, breathing afar,   90
The end of day and beginning of night
Make the apple holy and bright;
Holy and bright, round and full, bright and blest,
Mellowed in a land of rest;
Watch it warily day and night;   95
All good things are in the west.
Till mid noon the cool east light
Is shut out by the round of the tall hillbrow.
But when the full-faced sunset yellowly
Stays on the flowering arch of the bough,   100
The lucious fruitage clustereth mellowly,
Golden-kernelled, golden-cored,
Sunset-ripened above on the tree.
The world is wasted with fire and sword,
But the apple of gold hangs over the sea   105
Five links, a golden chain are we,

7. A hint, as in line 27, where "wisdom of the West" suggests knowledge of good and evil, of the Fall from Eden. This line defies precise explication but is in keeping with the idea that mysteriousness somehow preserves vitality in art.
8. From the Himalayas to the Caucasian Mountains. Perhaps an allusion to the popular nineteenth-century notion that civilization was also moving northward. In many of the pieces in *Poems by Two Brothers* Tennyson conceives of the North and East as regions from which the barbarian hordes come to threaten the western civilizations. *Idylls of the King* essentially preserves this notion; see the end of the "Epilogue" for one of numerous allusions.
9. The morning star, specifically Venus. Classical astrologists believed the morning and evening star were two different stars.

Hesper, the dragon, and sisters three,
Daughters three,
Bound about
All round about   110
The gnarléd bole of the charméd tree.
The golden apple, the golden apple, the hallowed fruit,
Guard it well, guard it warily,
Watch it warily,
Singing airily,   115
Standing about the charméd root.

1832

A Dream of Fair Women[1]

I read, before my eyelids dropt their shade,
    "*The Legend of Good Women*," long ago
Sung by the morning star of song, who made
        His music heard below;

Dan[2] Chaucer, the first warbler, whose sweet breath   5
    Preluded those melodious bursts that fill
The spacious times of great Elizabeth
        With sounds that echo still.

And, for a while, the knowledge of his art
    Held me above the subject, as strong gales   10
Hold swollen clouds from raining, tho' my heart,
        Brimful of those wild tales,

Charged both mine eyes with tears. In every land
    I saw, wherever light illumineth,
Beauty and anguish walking hand in hand   15
        The downward slope to death.

Those far-renowned brides of ancient song
    Peopled the hollow dark, like burning stars,
And I heard sounds of insult, shame, and wrong,
        And trumpets blown for wars;   20

And clattering flints batter'd with clanging hoofs;
    And I saw crowds in column'd sanctuaries,
And forms that pass'd at windows and on roofs
        Of marble palaces;

1. A dream-vision in the medieval tra-
dition, the poem was suggested by
Chaucer's "Legend of Good Women"
though Chaucer praises women faithful
in love and from his list only Cleopatra
appears. Croker bludgeoned Tennyson's
poem (see excerpt from *Quarterly Re-
view* of 1833 in prose selections), and
it underwent considerable revision for
republication in 1842. Retouched in
1845, 1853, and 1884, these sketches
of uneven quality never materialized
into an organic whole.
2. From *dominus*, master. Spenser first
used the appellation: "Dan Chaucer,
well of English undefiled" (*The Faerie
Queen*, IV, ii, xxxii).

Corpses across the threshold, heroes tall   25
   Dislodging pinnacle and parapet
Upon the tortoise³ creeping to the wall,
    Lances in ambush set;

And high shrine-doors burst thro' with heated blasts
   That run before the fluttering tongues of fire;   30
White surf wind-scatter'd over sails and masts,
    And ever climbing higher;

Squadrons and squares of men in brazen plates,
Scaffolds, still sheets of water, divers woes,
Ranges of glimmering vaults with iron grates,   35
    And hush'd seraglios.⁴

So shape chased shape as swift as, when to land
   Bluster the winds and tides the selfsame way,
Crisp foam-flakes scud along the level sand,
    Torn from the fringe of spray.   40

I started once, or seem'd to start in pain,
   Resolved on noble things, and strove to speak,
As when a great thought strikes along the brain
    And flushes all the cheek.

And once my arm was lifted to hew down   45
   A cavalier from off his saddle-bow,
That bore a lady from a leaguer'd town;
    And then, I know not how,

All those sharp fancies, by down-lapsing thought
   Stream'd onward, lost their edges, and did creep   50
Roll'd on each other, rounded, smooth'd, and brought
    Into the gulfs of sleep.

At last methought that I had wander'd far
   In an old wood;⁵ fresh-wash'd in coolest dew
The maiden splendors of the morning star   55
    Shook in the steadfast blue.

Enormous elm-tree boles did stoop and lean
   Upon the dusky brushwood underneath
Their broad curved branches, fledged with clearest green,
    New from its silken sheath.   60

The dim red Morn had died, her journey done,
   And with dead lips smiled at the twilight plain,
Half-fallen across the threshold of the sun,
    Never to rise again.

There was no motion in the dumb dead air,   65
   Not any song of bird or sound of rill;
Gross darkness of the inner sepulchre
    Is not so deadly still

3. The "testudo," a close troop forma-   4. Harems.
tion made by soldiers overlapping their   5. I.e., into the past.
shields above their heads.

As that wide forest. Growths of jasmine turn'd
　　Their humid arms festooning tree to tree,　　　　　　70
And at the root thro' lush green grasses burn'd
　　　The red anemone.

I knew the flowers, I knew the leaves, I knew
　　The tearful glimmer of the languid dawn
On those long, rank, dark wood-walks drench'd in dew,　　75
　　　Leading from lawn to lawn.

The smell of violets, hidden in the green,
　　Pour'd back into my empty soul and frame
The times when I remember to have been
　　　Joyful and free from blame.　　　　　　　　　　80

And from within me a clear undertone
　　Thrill'd thro' mine ears in that unblissful clime,
"Pass freely thro'; the wood is all thine own
　　　Until the end of time."

At length I saw a lady[6] within call,　　　　　　　　　85
　　Stiller than chisell'd marble, standing there;
A daughter of the gods, divinely tall,
　　　And most divinely fair.

Her loveliness with shame and with surprise
　　Froze my swift speech; she turning on my face　　90
The star-like sorrows of immortal eyes,
　　　Spoke slowly in her place:

"I had great beauty; ask thou not my name:
　　No one can be more wise than destiny.
Many drew swords and died. Where'er I came　　　95
　　　I brought calamity."

"No marvel, sovereign lady: in fair field
　　Myself for such a face had boldly died,"
I answer'd free; and turning I appeal'd
　　　To one[7] that stood beside.　　　　　　　　　100

But she, with sick and scornful looks averse,
　　To her full height her stately stature draws;
"My youth," she said, "was blasted with a curse:
　　　This woman was the cause.

"I was cut off from hope in that sad place　　　　　105
　　Which men call'd Aulis in those iron years:
My father held his hand upon his face;
　　　I, blinded with my tears,

"Still strove to speak: my voice was thick with sighs
　　As in a dream. Dimly I could descry　　　　　110

6. Helen of Troy.
7. Iphigenia, Agamemnon's daughter, sacrificed to Artemis by her father so that the Greek fleet might have favorable winds in setting sail for Troy.

The stern black-bearded kings with wolfish eyes,
>Waiting to see me die.

"The high masts flicker'd as they lay afloat;
>The crowds, the temples, waver'd, and the shore;
The bright death quiver'd at the victim's throat—   115
>Touch'd—and I knew no more."

Whereto the other with a downward brow:
>"I would the white cold heavy-plunging foam,
Whirl'd by the wind, had roll'd me deep below,
>Then when I left my home."   120

Her slow full words sank thro' the silence drear,
>As thunder-drops fall on a sleeping sea:
Sudden I heard a voice that cried, "Come here,
>That I may look on thee."

I turning saw, throned on a flowery rise,   125
>One[8] sitting on a crimson scarf unroll'd;
A queen, with swarthy cheeks and bold black eyes,
>Brow-bound with burning gold.

She, flashing forth a haughty smile, began:
>"I govern'd men by change, and so I sway'd   130
All moods. 'T is long since I have seen a man.
>Once, like the moon, I made

"The ever-shifting currents of the blood
>According to my humor ebb and flow.
I have no men to govern in this wood: 135
>That makes my only woe.

"Nay—yet it chafes me that I could not bend
>One will; nor tame and tutor with mine eye
That dull cold-blooded Cæsar.[9] Prythee, friend,
>Where is Mark Antony?   140

"The man, my lover, with whom I rode sublime
>On Fortune's neck; we sat as God by God:
The Nilus would have risen before his time
>And flooded at our nod.

"We drank the Libyan Sun to sleep, and lit   145
>Lamps which out-burn'd Canopus.[1] O, my life
In Egypt! O, the dalliance and the wit,
>The flattery and the strife,

8. Cleopatra. Tennyson acknowledged he was thinking of Shakespeare's line, "Think on me / That am with Phoebus' amorous pinches black" (*Antony and Cleopatra*, I, v, 27–28).
9. Not Julius, whom she had loved, but Octavius, "the other" of line 155, whom Cleopatra failed to seduce. Consequently she took her own life rather than be led captive through the streets of Rome.
1. A first-magnitude star visible in the southern hemisphere.

"And the wild kiss, when fresh from war's alarms,
    My Hercules, my Roman Antony,   150
My mailed Bacchus leapt into my arms,
        Contented there to die!

"And there he died: and when I heard my name
    Sigh'd forth with life I would not brook my fear
Of the other; with a worm I balk'd his fame.   155
        What else was left? look here!"—

With that she tore her robe apart, and half
    The polish'd argent of her breast to sight
Laid bare. Thereto she pointed with a laugh,
        Showing the aspick's bite.—   160

"I died a Queen. The Roman soldier found
    Me lying dead, my crown about my brows,
A name for ever!—lying robed and crown'd,
        Worthy a Roman spouse."

Her warbling voice, a lyre of widest range   165
    Struck by all passion, did fall down and glance
From tone to tone, and glided thro' all change
        Of liveliest utterance.

When she made pause I knew not for delight;
    Because with sudden motion from the ground   170
She raised her piercing orbs, and fill'd with light
        The interval of sound.

Still with their fires Love tipt his keenest darts;
    As once they drew into two burning rings
All beams of love, melting the mighty hearts   175
        Of captains and of kings.

Slowly my sense undazzled. Then I heard
    A noise of some one[2] coming thro' the lawn,
And singing clearer than the crested bird
        That claps his wings at dawn: 180

"The torrent brooks of hallow'd Israel
    From craggy hollows pouring, late and soon,
Sound all night long, in falling thro' the dell,
        Far-heard beneath the moon.

"The balmy moon of blessed Israel   185
    Floods all the deep-blue gloom with beams divine;
All night the splinter'd crags that wall the dell
        With spires of silver shine."

As one that museth where broad sunshine laves
    The lawn by some cathedral, thro' the door   190

2. Jephthah's daughter (*Judges*, 11:30–40). Jephthah, "the warrior Gileadite," vowed he would sacrifice the first person to greet him on his return home were he victorious in the war against the children of Ammon.

Hearing the holy organ rolling waves
    Of sound on roof and floor

Within, and anthem sung, is charm'd and tied
    To where he stands,—so stood I, when that flow
Of music left the lips of her that died   195
    To save her father's vow;

The daughter of the warrior Gileadite,
    A maiden pure; as when she went along
From Mizpeh's[3] tower'd gate with welcome light,
    With timbrel and with song.   200

My words leapt forth: "Heaven heads the count of crimes
    With that wild oath." She render'd answer high:
"Not so, nor once alone; a thousand times
    I would be born and die.

"Single I grew, like some green plant, whose root   205
    Creeps to the garden water-pipes beneath,
Feeding the flower; but ere my flower to fruit
    Changed, I was ripe for death.

"My God, my land, my father—these did move
    Me from my bliss of life that Nature gave,   210
Lower'd softly with a threefold cord of love
    Down to a silent grave.

"And I went mourning, 'No fair Hebrew boy
    Shall smile away my maiden blame among
The Hebrew mothers'—emptied of all joy,   215
    Leaving the dance and song,

"Leaving the olive-gardens far below,
    Leaving the promise of my bridal bower,
The valleys of grape-loaded vines that glow
    Beneath the battled tower.   220

"The light white cloud swam over us. Anon
    We heard the lion roaring from his den;
We saw the large white stars rise one by one,
    Or, from the darken'd glen,

"Saw God divide the night with flying flame,   225
    And thunder on the everlasting hills.
I heard Him, for He spake, and grief became
    A solemn scorn of ills.

"When the next moon was roll'd into the sky,
    Strength came to me that equall'd my desire.   230
How beautiful a thing it was to die
    For God and for my sire!

3. A town in Gilead where Jephthah's house was.

"It comforts me in this one thought to dwell,
  That I subdued me to my father's will;
Because the kiss he gave me, ere I fell,   235
    Sweetens the spirit still.

"Moreover it is written that my race
  Hew'd Ammon, hip and thigh, from Aroer
On Arnon unto Minneth." Here her face
    Glow'd, as I look'd at her.   240

She lock'd her lips; she left me where I stood:
  "Glory to God," she sang, and past afar,
Thridding⁴ the sombre boskage of the wood,
    Toward the morning-star.

Losing her carol I stood pensively,   245
  As one that from a casement leans his head,
When midnight bells cease ringing suddenly,
    And the old year is dead.

"Alas! alas!" a low voice, full of care,
  Murmur'd beside me: "Turn and look on me;   250
I am that Rosamond,⁵ whom men call fair,
    If what I was I be.

"Would I had been some maiden coarse and poor!
  O me, that I should ever see the light!
Those dragon eyes of anger'd Eleanor   255
    Do hunt me, day and night."

She ceased in tears, fallen from hope and trust;
  To whom the Egyptian:⁶ "O, you tamely died!
You should have clung to Fulvia's waist, and thrust
    The dagger thro' her side."   260

With that sharp sound the white dawn's creeping beams,
  Stolen to my brain, dissolved the mystery
Of folded sleep. The captain⁷ of my dreams
    Ruled in the eastern sky.

Morn broaden'd on the borders of the dark   265
  Ere I saw her⁸ who clasp'd in her last trance
Her murder'd father's head, or Joan of Arc,
    A light of ancient France;

Or her⁹ who knew that Love can vanquish Death,
  Who kneeling, with one arm about her king,   270

4. Threading or making her way through the dark thicket.
5. Mistress of Henry II who was allegedly poisoned by his queen, Eleanor of Aquitaine.
6. Cleopatra. She substitutes Fulvia, Antony's wife, for Eleanor.
7. Venus, the morning star.
8. Margaret Roper, Sir Thomas More's daughter. She claimed her father's head, which, after his execution (1535), had been shown on London Bridge for two weeks. Allegedly, when her vault was opened in 1715, she was found clasping a leaden box containing the head.
9. Eleanor of Castile, wife of Edward I. When Edward was stabbed with a poisoned dagger, she sucked the poison from his wound.

Drew forth the poison with her balmy breath,
    Sweet as new buds in spring.

No memory labors longer from the deep
    Gold-mines of thought to lift the hidden ore
That glimpses, moving up, than I from sleep   275
    To gather and tell o'er

Each little sound and sight. With what dull pain
    Compass'd, how eagerly I sought to strike
Into that wondrous track of dreams again!
    But no two dreams are like.   280

As when a soul laments, which hath been blest,
    Desiring what is mingled with past years,
In yearnings that can never be exprest
    By signs or groans or tears;

Because all words, tho' cull'd with choicest art,   285
    Failing to give the bitter of the sweet,
Wither beneath the palate, and the heart
    Faints, faded by its heat.

1832 (1842)

To ———[1]

As when with downcast eyes we muse and brood,
And ebb into a former life, or seem
To lapse far back in some confused dream
To states of mystical similitude,
If one but speaks or hems or stirs his chair,   5
Ever the wonder waxeth more and more,
So that we say, "All this hath been before,
All this hath been, I know not when or where;"
So, friend, when first I look'd upon your face,
Our thought gave answer each to each, so true—   10
Opposed mirrors each reflecting each—
That, tho' I knew not in what time or place,
Methought that I had often met with you,
And either lived in either's heart and speech.

1832

To J. S.[2]

The wind that beats the mountain blows
More softly round the open wold,

1. The poem is probably addressed to Arthur Hallam.
2. James Spedding, a Cambridge Apostle and later famous as the biographer of Bacon. He was a close friend of Tennyson's from undergraduate days to Spedding's death in 1881. Selections from his favorable review of the 1842 volumes appear in the critical selections. This elegy is on the death of Spedding's younger brother, Edward.

And gently comes the world to those
    That are cast in gentle mould.

And me this knowledge bolder made,   5
    Or else I had not dared to flow
In these words toward you, and invade
    Even with a verse your holy woe.

'T is strange that those we lean on most,
    Those in whose laps our limbs are nursed,   10
Fall into shadow, soonest lost;
    Those we love first are taken first.

God gives us love. Something to love
    He lends us; but, when love is grown
To ripeness, that on which it throve   15
    Falls off, and love is left alone.

This is the curse of time. Alas!
    In grief I am not all unlearn'd;
Once thro' mine own doors Death did pass;
    One[3] went who never hath return'd.   20

He will not smile—not speak to me
    Once more. Two years his chair is seen
Empty before us. That was he
    Without whose life I had not been.

Your loss is rarer; for this star   25
    Rose with you thro' a little arc
Of heaven, nor having wander'd far
    Shot on the sudden into dark.

I knew your brother; his mute dust
    I honor and his living worth;
A man more pure and bold and just   30
    Was never born into the earth.

I have not look'd upon you nigh
    Since that dear soul hath fallen asleep.
Great Nature is more wise than I;   35
    I will not tell you not to weep.

And tho' mine own eyes fill with dew,
    Drawn from the spirit thro' the brain,
I will not even preach to you,
    "Weep, weeping dulls the inward pain."   40

Let Grief be her own mistress still.
    She loveth her own anguish deep
More than much pleasure. Let her will
    Be done—to weep or not to weep.

3. Tennyson's father, who had died on March 16, 1831. As the poet's grandson has observed, these lines show "how deep and sincere the son's feelings had been, in spite of all the father's weaknesses and the suffering which he had brought upon his family" (*Alfred Tennyson*, p. 134).

I will not say, "God's ordinance   45
    Of death is blown in every wind;"
For that is not a common chance
    That takes away a noble mind.

His memory long will live alone
    In all our hearts, as mournful light   50
That broods above the fallen sun,
    And dwells in heaven half the night.

Vain solace! Memory standing near
    Cast down her eyes, and in her throat
Her voice seem'd distant, and a tear   55
    Dropt on the letters as I wrote.

I wrote I know not what. In truth,
    How *should* I soothe you any way,
Who miss the brother of your youth?
    Yet something I did wish to say;   60

For he too was a friend to me.
    Both are my friends, and my true breast
Bleedeth for both; yet it may be
    That only silence suiteth best.

Words weaker than your grief would make   65
    Grief more. 'T were better I should cease
Although myself could almost take
    The place of him that sleeps in peace.

Sleep sweetly, tender heart, in peace;
    Sleep, holy spirit, blessed soul,   70
While the stars burn, the moons increase,
    And the great ages onward roll.[4]

Sleep till the end, true soul and sweet.
    Nothing comes to thee new or strange.
Sleep full of rest from head to feet;   75
    Lie still, dry dust, secure of change.[5]

1832

The Lotos-Eaters[6]

"Courage!" he[7] said, and pointed toward the land,
"This mounting wave will roll us shoreward soon."
In the afternoon they came unto a land

4. Compare the end of the "Epilogue" to *In Memoriam*.
5. The fear of change was characteristic of Tennyson and would, of course, become a major theme of *In Memoriam*.
6. Although the subject is based upon the episode in the *Odyssey* (IX, 82 ff) where Odysseus describes his weary mariners' brief stay with the Lotos-Eaters, only the opening stanzas and the sixth stanza of the choric song contain Homeric elements. The five introductory Spenserian stanzas were begun during the 1830 journey with Hallam through the Pyrenees (see notes to "Œnone") and reflect that scenery as

In which it seemed always afternoon.
All round the coast the languid air did swoon,   5
Breathing like one that hath a weary dream.
Full-faced above the valley stood the moon;
And, like a downward smoke, the slender stream
Along the cliff to fall and pause and fall did seem.

A land of streams! some, like a downward smoke,   10
Slow-dropping veils of thinnest lawn,[8] did go;
And some thro' wavering lights and shadows broke,
Rolling a slumbrous sheet of foam below.
They saw the gleaming river seaward flow
From the inner land; far off, three mountain-tops,   15
Three silent pinnacles of aged snow,
Stood sunset-flush'd; and, dew'd with showery drops,
Up-clomb the shadowy pine above the woven copse.

The charmed sunset linger'd low adown
In the red West; thro' mountain clefts the dale   20
Was seen far inland, and the yellow down
Border'd with palm, and many a winding vale
And meadow, set with slender galingale;[9]
A land where all things always seem'd the same!
And round about the keel with faces pale,   25
Dark faces pale against that rosy flame,
The mild-eyed melancholy Lotos-eaters came.

Branches they bore of that enchanted stem,
Laden with flower and fruit, whereof they gave
To each, but whoso did receive of them   30
And taste, to him the gushing of the wave
Far far away did seem to mourn and rave
On alien shores; and if his fellow spake,
His voice was thin, as voices from the grave;
And deep-asleep he seem'd, yet all awake,   35
And music in his ears his beating heart did make.

They sat them down upon the yellow sand,
Between the sun and moon upon the shore;
And sweet it was to dream of Fatherland,
Of child, and wife, and slave; but evermore   40
Most weary seem'd the sea, weary the oar,
Weary the wandering fields of barren foam.

---

well as drawing upon Spenser's descrip-
tions in *The Faerie Queene*, II, vi.
(Tennyson undoubtedly was also influ-
enced by Thomson's *Castle of Indo-
lence*.) Of numerous revisions for re-
publication in 1842, the additions of the
sixth and eighth stanzas of the choric
song were the most important.
7. Odysseus.
8. "When I printed this, a critic in-
formed me that 'lawn' was the material
used in theatres to imitate a waterfall,

and graciously added, 'Mr. T. should
not go to the boards of a theatre but
to nature herself for his suggestions.' "
Tennyson, who seldom erred in his
natural descriptions, could honestly say,
as he did, "And I *had* gone to Nature
herself"—to the Pyrenees in the Cirque
de Gavarnie where "lying among these
mountains before a waterfall that comes
down one thousand or twelve hundred
feet I sketched it . . . in these words"
(*Memoir*, I, 259).
9. An aromatic herb.

Then some one said, "We will return no more;"
And all at once they sang, "Our island home[1]
Is far beyond the wave; we will no longer roam."   45

CHORIC SONG[2]

1

There is sweet music here that softer falls
Than petals from blown roses on the grass,
Or night-dews on still waters between walls
Of shadowy granite, in a gleaming pass;
Music that gentlier on the spirit lies,   50
Than tired eyelids upon tired eyes;
Music that brings sweet sleep down from the blissful skies.
Here are cool mosses deep,
And thro' the moss the ivies creep,
And in the stream the long-leaved flowers weep,   55
And from the craggy ledge the poppy hangs in sleep.

2

Why are we weigh'd upon with heaviness,
And utterly consumed with sharp distress,
While all things else have rest from weariness?
All things have rest: why should we toil alone,   60
We only toil, who are the first of things,
And make perpetual moan,
Still from one sorrow to another thrown;
Nor ever fold our wings,
And cease from wanderings,   65
Nor steep our brows in slumber's holy balm;
Nor harken what the inner spirit sings,
"There is no joy but calm!"—
Why should we only toil, the roof and crown of things?

3

Lo! in the middle of the wood,   70
The folded leaf is woo'd from out the bud
With winds upon the branch, and there
Grows green and broad, and takes no care,
Sun-steep'd at noon, and in the moon
Nightly dew-fed; and turning yellow   75
Falls, and floats adown the air.
Lo! sweeten'd with the summer light,
The full-juiced apple, waxing over-mellow,
Drops in a silent autumn night.
All its allotted length of days   80
The flower ripens in its place,
Ripens and fades, and falls, and hath no toil,
Fast-rooted in the fruitful soil.

---

1. Ithaca. "But those who ate this honeyed plant, the Lotos, never cared to report, nor to return: they longed to stay forever, browsing on that native bloom, forgetful of their homeland" (*Odyssey,* Book IX, ll. 97–100).
2. Sung by the mariners.

4

Hateful is the dark-blue sky,
Vaulted o'er the dark-blue sea. 85
Death is the end of life; ah, why
Should life all labor be?
Let us alone. Time driveth onward fast,
And in a little while our lips are dumb.
Let us alone. What is it that will last? 90
All things are taken from us, and become
Portions and parcels of the dreadful past.
Let us alone. What pleasure can we have
To war with evil? Is there any peace
In ever climbing up the climbing wave?[3] 95
All things have rest, and ripen toward the grave
In silence—ripen, fall, and cease:
Give us long rest or death, dark death, or dreamful ease.

5

How sweet it were, hearing the downward stream,
With half-shut eyes ever to seem 100
Falling asleep in a half-dream!
To dream and dream, like yonder amber light,
Which will not leave the myrrh-bush on the height;
To hear each other's whisper'd speech;
Eating the Lotos day by day, 105
To watch the crisping ripples on the beach,
And tender curving lines of creamy spray;
To lend our hearts and spirits wholly
To the influence of mild-minded melancholy;
To muse and brood and live again in memory, 110
With those old faces of our infancy
Heap'd over with a mound of grass,
Two handfuls of white dust, shut in an urn of brass!

6

Dear is the memory of our wedded lives,
And dear the last embraces of our wives 115
And their warm tears; but all hath suffer'd change;
For surely now our household hearths are cold,
Our sons inherit us, our looks are strange,
And we should come like ghosts to trouble joy.
Or else the island princes[4] over-bold 120
Have eat our substance, and the minstrel sings
Before them of the ten years' war in Troy,
And our great deeds, as half-forgotten things.
Is there confusion in the little isle?
Let what is broken so remain. 125
The Gods are hard to reconcile;
'T is hard to settle order once again.

---

3. Compare "The Two Voices," lines
184–186.
4. Princes from the islands neighboring
Ithaca. The mariners cannot know, of
course, that they accurately describe the
activities of Penelope's suitors.

There *is* confusion worse than death,
Trouble on trouble, pain on pain,
Long labor unto aged breath,   130
Sore task to hearts worn out by many wars
And eyes grown dim with gazing on the pilot-stars.

7

But, propt on beds of amaranth and moly,[5]
How sweet—while warm airs lull us, blowing lowly—
With half-dropt eyelid still,   135
Beneath a heaven dark and holy,
To watch the long bright river drawing slowly
His waters from the purple hill—
To hear the dewy echoes calling
From cave to cave thro' the thick-twined vine—   140
To watch the emerald-color'd water falling
Thro' many a woven acanthus-wreath[6] divine!
Only to hear and see the far-off sparkling brine,
Only to hear were sweet, stretch'd out beneath the pine.

8

The Lotos blooms below the barren peak,   145
The Lotos blows by every winding creek;
All day the wind breathes low with mellower tone;
Thro' every hollow cave and alley lone
Round and round the spicy downs the yellow Lotos-dust is blown.
We have had enough of action, and of motion we,   150
Roll'd to starboard, roll'd to larboard, when the surge was seething
    free,
Where the wallowing monster spouted his foam-fountains in the sea.
Let us swear an oath, and keep it with an equal mind,
In the hollow Lotos-land to live and lie reclined
On the hills like Gods[7] together, careless of mankind.   155
For they lie beside their nectar, and the bolts[8] are hurl'd
Far below them in the valleys, and the clouds are lightly curl'd
Round their golden houses, girdled with the gleaming world;
Where they smile in secret, looking over wasted lands,
Blight and famine, plague and earthquake, roaring deeps and fiery
    sands,   160
Clanging fights, and flaming towns, and sinking ships, and praying
    hands.
But they smile, they find a music centred in a doleful song
Steaming up, a lamentation and an ancient tale of wrong,
Like a tale of little meaning tho' the words are strong;
Chanted from an ill-used race of men that cleave the soil,   165
Sow the seed, and reap the harvest with enduring toil,
Storing yearly little dues of wheat, and wine and oil;

5. Amaranth: the legendary flower which never faded; moly: a magical herb mentioned in Book X of the *Odyssey*, given by Hermes to Odysseus to protect him from Circe.
6. A prickly herbaceous plant the likeness of which often ornaments Corinthian columns.
7. This description of the indifferent gods derives from Lucretius' *De Rerum Natura*.
8. Thunderbolts.

Till they perish and they suffer—some, 't is whisper'd—down in hell
Suffer endless anguish, others in Elysian valleys dwell,
Resting weary limbs at last on beds of asphodel.[9]   170
Surely, surely, slumber is more sweet than toil, the shore
Than labor in the deep mid-ocean, wind and wave and oar;
O, rest ye, brother mariners, we will not wander more.

1832 (1842)

FROM *POEMS* (1842), INCLUDING
SEVERAL OTHER PIECES WRITTEN
BETWEEN 1833 AND 1846

Ulysses[1]

It little profits that an idle king,
By this still hearth, among these barren crags,
Match'd with an aged wife, I mete and dole
Unequal[2] laws unto a savage race,
That hoard, and sleep, and feed, and know not me.[3]   5
I cannot rest from travel; I will drink
Life to the lees. All times I have enjoy'd
Greatly, have suffer'd greatly, both with those
That loved me, and alone; on shore, and when
Thro' scudding drifts the rainy Hyades[4]   10
Vext the dim sea. I am become a name;
For always roaming with a hungry heart
Much have I seen and known,—cities of men

9. The yellow lilylike flower covering the Elysian Fields; the English daffodil and probably the narcissus to the early Greek poets.

1. "Ulysses," Tennyson said, "was written soon after Arthur Hallam's death, and gave my feeling about the need of going forward, and braving the struggle of life perhaps more simply than anything in *In Memoriam*" (*Memoir*, I, 196). Tennyson learned of Hallam's death (September 15, 1833) on October 1, and the earliest known draft of the poem in Harvard Notebook 16 suggests it was begun a few days later. Speaking of *In Memoriam*, Tennyson told James Knowles, "There is more about myself in 'Ulysses', which was written under the sense of loss and that all had gone by, but that still life must be fought out to the end" (from "A Personal Reminiscence," much of which is reprinted in the Early Responses section of this book).

Tennyson's source is first the *Odys-*

sey, XI, 100–137, where Ulysses learns from Tiresias' ghost that, after killing the suitors, he must undertake a final sea voyage. In Canto 26 of the *Inferno*, Dante has Ulysses give an account of that mysterious journey, and that episode forms the basis of Tennyson's poem.

2. I.e., fitting different situations. Ulysses' description of Ithaca bears little resemblance to Homer's, nor is Penelope aged when Ulysses returns. Perhaps Tennyson has Ulysses living in Ithaca for a long time before he departs, but there is no basis for that in the *Odyssey*.

3. Cf. *Hamlet*, IV, iv, 33 ff: "What is a man, / If his chief good and market of his time / Be but to sleep and feed? A beast, no more."

4. A *V*-shaped cluster of stars which, when they rose with the sun, were supposed to indicate the coming of the rainy season.

And manners, climates, councils, governments,
Myself not least, but honor'd of them all,—   15
And drunk delight of battle with my peers,
Far on the ringing plains of windy Troy.
I am a part of all that I have met;
Yet all experience is an arch wherethro'
Gleams that untravell'd world whose margin fades   20
For ever and for ever when I move.
How dull it is to pause, to make an end,
To rust unburnish'd, not to shine in use![5]
As tho' to breathe were life! Life piled on life
Were all too little, and of one to me   25
Little remains; but every hour is saved
From that eternal silence, something more,
A bringer of new things; and vile it were
For some three suns to store and hoard myself,
And this gray spirit yearning in desire   30
To follow knowledge like a sinking star,
Beyond the utmost bound of human thought.
    This is my son, mine own Telemachus,
To whom I leave the sceptre and the isle,—
Well-loved of me, discerning to fulfil   35
This labor, by slow prudence to make mild
A rugged people, and thro' soft degrees
Subdue them to the useful and the good.
Most blameless is he, centred in the sphere
Of common duties, decent not to fail   40
In offices of tenderness, and pay
Meet adoration to my household gods,
When I am gone. He works his work, I mine.[6]
    There lies the port; the vessel puffs her sail;
There gloom the dark, broad seas. My mariners,   45
Souls that have toil'd, and wrought, and thought with me,—
That ever with a frolic welcome took
The thunder and the sunshine, and opposed
Free hearts, free foreheads,—you and I are old;
Old age hath yet his honor and his toil.   50
Death closes all; but something ere the end,
Some work of noble note, may yet be done,
Not unbecoming men that strove with Gods.[7]
The lights begin to twinkle from the rocks;
The long day wanes; the slow moon climbs; the deep   55

5. Cf. Shakespeare's *Troilus and Cressida*, III, iii, 151 ff, where Ulysses speaks to Achilles: "To have done is to hang / Quite out of fashion, like a rusty mail / In monumental mock'ry."
6. The above passage about Telemachus has led a few critics to charge Ulysses with being irresponsible, the poem being, in the words of one commentator, "a dramatic portrayal of a type of human being who held a set of ideas which Tennyson regarded as destructive of the whole fabric of his society."
7. Cf. Ulysses' words to his mariners in the *Inferno*, XXVI, 119–121: "Consider your lineage; you were not made to live as brutes, but to follow virtue and knowledge."

Moans round with many voices. Come, my friends.
'T is not too late to seek a newer world.
Push off, and sitting well in order smite
The sounding furrows; for my purpose holds
To sail beyond the sunset, and the baths   60
Of all the western stars,[8] until I die.
It may be that the gulfs will wash us down;
It may be we shall touch the Happy Isles,
And see the great Achilles, whom we knew.[9]
Tho' much is taken, much abides; and tho'   65
We are not now that strength which in old days
Moved earth and heaven, that which we are, we are,—
One equal temper of heroic hearts,
Made weak by time and fate, but strong in will
To strive, to seek, to find, and not to yield.   70

1833; 1842

The Two Voices[1]

A still small voice spake unto me,
"Thou art so full of misery,
Were it not better not to be?"

Then to the still small voice I said:
"Let me not cast in endless shade   5
What is so wonderfully made."

To which the voice did urge reply:
"To-day I saw the dragon-fly
Come from the wells where he did lie.

"An inner impulse rent the veil   10
Of his old husk; from head to tail
Came out clear plates of sapphire mail.

"He dried his wings; like gauze they grew;
Thro' crofts and pastures wet with dew
A living flash of light he flew."[2]   15

---

8. The Homeric view of the ocean as a great river around the flat earth. In Dante, Ulysses sailed to these outer limits, glimpsed the Mount of Purgatory, and drowned in the "gulfs" for his presumption.
9. Carlyle said, "These lines do not make me weep, but there is in me what would fill whole Lachrymatories as I read" (*Memoir*, I, 214). The "Happy Isles," or Elysium, were supposed to be in the far west, the abode for the great heroes like Achilles whom Paris had slain in the Trojan War.
1. Begun in 1833, not long after Hallam's death, the poem in manuscript was called "Thoughts of a Suicide" and was written, as Hallam Tennyson says, "under the cloud of this overwhelming sorrow, which, as my father told me, for a while blotted out all joy from his life, and made him long for death" (*Memoir*, I, 109). In Tennyson's words, "When I wrote 'The Two Voices' I was so utterly miserable, a burden to myself and to my family, that I said, 'Is life worth anything?' " (*Memoir*, I, 193).

Many of the issues raised by the poem were anticipated in "Supposed Confessions" and would shortly be articulated more fully and thoughtfully as work on *In Memoriam* progressed. The struggle within the individual between faith and skepticism reminded Carlyle

I said: "When first the world began,
Young Nature thro' five cycles[3] ran,
And in the sixth she moulded man.

"She gave him mind, the lordliest
Proportion, and, above the rest,   20
Dominion in the head and breast."

Thereto the silent voice replied:
"Self-blinded are you by your pride;
Look up thro' night; the world is wide.

"This truth within thy mind rehearse,   25
That in a boundless universe
Is boundless better, boundless worse.

"Think you this mould of hopes and fears
Could find no statelier than his peers
In yonder hundred million spheres?"[4]   30

It spake, moreover, in my mind:
"Tho' thou wert scatter'd to the wind,
Yet is there plenty of the kind."

Then did my response clearer fall:
"No compound of this earthly ball   35
Is like another, all in all."

To which he answer'd scoffingly:
"Good soul! suppose I grant it thee,
Who'll weep for thy deficiency?

"Or will one beam be less intense,   40
When thy peculiar difference
Is cancell'd in the world of sense?"

I would have said, "Thou canst not know,"
But my full heart, that work'd below,
Rain'd thro' my sight its overflow.   45

Again the voice spake unto me:
"Thou art so steep'd in misery,
Surely 't were better not to be.

"Thine anguish will not let thee sleep,
Nor any train of reason keep;   50
Thou canst not think, but thou wilt weep."

"of passages in *Job*" (*Memoir*, I, 213).
And Tennyson clearly has *Hamlet* in
mind as he speculates on the nature of
human existence and the attractiveness
of suicide, which, in this poem at least,
the reader is convinced was real enough.
See Spedding's commentary in the
Early Responses section of this book.
2. The implication is that the dragon-
fly is as wonderfully made as man, the
beginning of the negative voice's long
argument to reduce man to the level of
beasts.
3. The Creation as described in *Genesis*.
4. Of numerous parallels in *In Memo-
riam*, see sections 3 and 61. Among the
late poems, the opening stanzas of
"Vastness" (1885) show the poet's last-
ing concern with man's significance in a
universe the proportions of which the
"new" science made increasingly in-
comprehensible.

I said: "The years with change advance;
If I make dark my countenance,
I shut my life from happier chance.

"Some turn this sickness yet might take,   55
Even yet." But he: "What drug can make
A wither'd palsy cease to shake?"

I wept: "Tho' I should die, I know
That all about the thorn will blow
In tufts of rosy-tinted snow;   60

"And men, thro' novel spheres of thought
Still moving after truth long sought,
Will learn new things when I am not."

"Yet," said the secret voice, "some time,
Sooner or later, will gray prime   65
Make thy grass hoar with early rime.

"Not less swift souls that yearn for light,
Rapt after heaven's starry flight,
Would sweep the tracts of day and night.

"Not less the bee would range her cells,   70
The furzy prickle fire the dells,
The foxglove cluster dappled bells."

I said that "all the years invent;
Each month is various to present
The world with some development.   75

"Were this not well, to bide mine hour,
Tho' watching from a ruin'd tower
How grows the day of human power?"

"The highest-mounted mind," he said,
"Still sees the sacred morning spread   80
The silent summit overhead.

"Will thirty seasons render plain
Those lonely lights that still remain,
Just breaking over land and main?

"Or make that morn, from his cold crown   85
And crystal silence creeping down,
Flood with full daylight glebe and town?

"Forerun thy peers, thy time, and let
Thy feet, millenniums hence, be set
In midst of knowledge, dream'd not yet.   90

"Thou hast not gain'd a real height,
Nor art thou nearer to the light,
Because the scale is infinite.

" 'T were better not to breathe or speak,
Than cry for strength, remaining weak,   95
And seem to find, but still to seek.[5]

"Moreover, but to seem to find
Asks what thou lackest, thought resign'd,
A healthy frame, a quiet mind."

I said: "When I am gone away,   100
'He dared not tarry,' men will say,
Doing dishonor to my clay."

"This is more vile," he made reply,
"To breathe and loathe, to live and sigh,
Than once from dread of pain to die.   105

"Sick art thou—a divided will
Still heaping on the fear of ill
The fear of men, a coward still.

"Do men love thee? Art thou so bound
To men that how thy name may sound   110
Will vex thee lying underground?

"The memory of the wither'd leaf
In endless time is scarce more brief
Than of the garner'd autumn-sheaf.

"Go, vexed spirit, sleep in trust;   115
The right ear that is fill'd with dust
Hears little of the false or just."

"Hard task, to pluck resolve," I cried,
"From emptiness and the waste wide
Of that abyss, or scornful pride!   120

"Nay—rather yet that I could raise
One hope that warm'd me in the days
While still I yearn'd for human praise.

"When, wide in soul and bold of tongue,
Among the tents I paused and sung,   125
The distant battle flash'd and rung.

"I sung the joyful Pæan clear,
And, sitting, burnish'd without fear
The brand, the buckler, and the spear—

"Waiting to strive a happy strife,   130
To war with falsehood to the knife,
And not to lose the good of life—

"Some hidden principle to move,
To put together, part and prove,
And mete the bounds of hate and love—   135

5. Contrast the conclusion of "Ulysses."

"As far as might be, to carve out
Free space for every human doubt,
That the whole mind might orb about—

"To search thro' all I felt or saw,
The springs of life, the depths of awe,   140
And reach the law within the law;[6]

"At least, not rotting like a weed,
But, having sown some generous seed,
Fruitful of further thought and deed,

"To pass, when Life her light withdraws,   145
Not void of righteous self-applause,
Nor in a merely selfish cause—

"In some good cause, not in mine own,
To perish, wept for, honor'd, known,
And like a warrior overthrown;   150

"Whose eyes are dim with glorious tears,
When, soil'd with noble dust, he hears
His country's war-song thrill his ears:

"Then dying of a mortal stroke,
What time the foeman's line is broke,   155
And all the war is roll'd in smoke."

"Yea!" said the voice, "thy dream was good,
While thou abodest in the bud.
It was the stirring of the blood.

"If Nature put not forth her power   160
About the opening of the flower,
Who is it that could live an hour?

"Then comes the check, the change, the fall,
Pain rises up, old pleasures pall.
There is one remedy for all.   165

"Yet hadst thou, thro' enduring pain,
Link'd month to month with such a chain
Of knitted purport, all were vain.

"Thou hadst not between death and birth
Dissolved the riddle of the earth.[7]   170
So were thy labor little worth.

"That men with knowledge merely play'd,
I told thee—hardly nigher made,
Tho' scaling slow from grade to grade;

"Much less this dreamer, deaf and blind,   175
Named man, may hope some truth to find,
That bears relation to the mind.

---

6. See "Supposed Confessions," lines 172 ff.
7. Cf. "The Palace of Art," line 213,
and Pallas' words in "Œnone," lines 142 ff.

"For every worm beneath the moon
Draws different threads, and late and soon
Spins, toiling out his own cocoon.   180

"Cry, faint not: either Truth is born
Beyond the polar gleam forlorn,
Or in the gateways of the morn.

"Cry, faint not, climb: the summits slope
Beyond the furthest flights of hope,   185
Wrapt in dense cloud from base to cope.[8]

"Sometimes a little corner shines,
As over rainy mist inclines
A gleaming crag with belts of pines.

"I will go forward, sayest thou,   190
I shall not fail to find her now.
Look up, the fold is on her brow.

"If straight thy track, or if oblique,
Thou know'st not. Shadows thou dost strike,
Embracing cloud, Ixion-like;[9]   195

"And owning but a little more
Than beasts,[1] abidest lame and poor,
Calling thyself a little lower

"Than angels. Cease to wail and brawl!
Why inch by inch to darkness crawl?   200
There is one remedy for all."

"O dull, one-sided voice," said I,
"Wilt thou make everything a lie,
To flatter me that I may die?

"I know that age to age succeeds,   205
Blowing a noise of tongues and deeds,
A dust of systems and of creeds.

"I cannot hide that some have striven,
Achieving calm, to whom was given
The joy that mixes man with Heaven;   210

"Who, rowing hard against the stream,
Saw distant gates of Eden gleam,
And did not dream it was a dream;

"But heard, by secret transport led,
Even in the charnels of the dead,   215
The murmur of the fountain-head—

8. Crown or top; ironically presented
here by the negative voice is the argu-
ment to which the Lotos-eaters suc-
cumbed (see particularly stanza 4).
9. When Ixion attempted to seduce
Hera, Zeus formed of the clouds a
phantom resembling her, and by it
Ixion became the father of the Cen-
taurs.
1. See *In Memoriam*, 27, 2, and 34, 4.

"Which did accomplish their desire,
Bore and forebore, and did not tire,
Like Stephen,[2] an unquenched fire.

"He needed not reviling tones,   220
Nor sold his heart to idle moans,
Tho' cursed and scorn'd, and bruised with stones;

"But looking upward, full of grace,
He pray'd, and from a happy place
God's glory smote him on the face."[3]   225

The sullen answer slid betwixt:
"Not that the grounds of hope were fix'd,
The elements were kindlier mix'd."

I said: "I toil beneath the curse,
But, knowing not the universe,   230
I fear to slide from bad to worse;

"And that, in seeking to undo
One riddle, and to find the true,
I knit a hundred others new;

"Or that this anguish fleeting hence,   235
Unmanacled from bonds of sense,
Be fix'd and frozen to permanence:

"For I go, weak from suffering here;
Naked I go, and void of cheer:
What is it that I may not fear?   240

"Consider well," the voice replied,
"His face, that two hours since hath died;
Wilt thou find passion, pain or pride?

"Will he obey when one commands?
Or answer should one press his hands?   245
He answers not, nor understands.

"His palms are folded on his breast;
There is no other thing express'd
But long disquiet merged in rest.

"His lips are very mild and meek;   250
Tho' one should smite him on the cheek,
And on the mouth, he will not speak.

"His little daughter, whose sweet face
He kiss'd, taking his last embrace,
Becomes dishonor to her race—   255

"His sons grow up that bear his name,
Some grow to honor, some to shame,—
But he is chill to praise or blame.

2. See *Acts*, 7:55-60.   3. Not one of Tennyson's happier lines.

"He will not hear the north-wind rave,
Nor, moaning, household shelter crave   260
From winter rains that beat his grave.

"High up the vapors fold and swim;
About him broods the twilight dim;
The place he knew forgetteth him."

"If all be dark, vague voice," I said,   265
"These things are wrapt in doubt and dread,
Nor canst thou show the dead are dead.

"The sap dries up: the plant declines.
A deeper tale my heart divines.
Know I not death? the outward signs?   270

"I found him⁴ when my years were few;
A shadow on the graves I knew,
And darkness in the village yew.

"From grave to grave the shadow crept;
In her still place the morning wept;   275
Touch'd by his feet the daisy slept.

"The simple senses crown'd his head:
'Omega! thou art Lord,' they said,
'We find no motion in the dead!'

"Why, if man rot in dreamless ease,   280
Should that plain fact, as taught by these,
Not make him sure that he shall cease?

"Who forged that other influence,
That heat of inward evidence,
By which he doubts against the sense?   285

"He owns the fatal gift of eyes,
That read his spirit blindly wise,
Not simple as a thing that dies.

"Here sits he shaping wings to fly;
His heart forebodes a mystery;   290
He names the name Eternity.

"That type of Perfect in his mind
In Nature can he nowhere find.⁵
He sows himself on every wind.

"He seems to hear a Heavenly Friend,   295
And thro' thick veils to apprehend
A labor working to an end.

"The end and the beginning vex
His reason: many things perplex,
With motions, checks, and counterchecks.   300

4. Death; possibly an allusion to his   5. See *In Memoriam,* 124, 2.
father's death in March, 1831.

"He knows a baseness in his blood[6]
At such strange war with something good,
He may not do the thing he would.

"Heaven opens inward, chasms yawn,
Vast images in glimmering dawn,   305
Half shown, are broken and withdrawn.

"Ah! sure within him and without,
Could his dark wisdom find it out,
There must be answer to his doubt,[7]

"But thou canst answer not again.   310
With thine own weapon art thou slain,
Or thou wilt answer but in vain.

"The doubt would rest, I dare not solve.
In the same circle we revolve.
Assurance only breeds resolve."   315

As when a billow, blown against,
Falls back, the voice with which I fenced
A little ceased, but recommenced:

"Where wert thou when thy father play'd
In his free field, and pastime made,   320
A merry boy in sun and shade?

"A merry boy they call'd him then,
He sat upon the knees of men
In days that never come again;

"Before the little ducts began   325
To feed thy bones with lime, and ran
Their course, till thou wert also man:

"Who took a wife, who rear'd his race,
Whose wrinkles gather'd on his face,
Whose troubles number with his days;   330

"A life of nothings, nothing worth,
From that first nothing ere his birth
To that last nothing under earth!"[8]

"These words," I said, "are like the rest;
No certain clearness, but at best   335
A vague suspicion of the breast:

"But if I grant, thou mightst defend
The thesis which thy words intend—
That to begin implies to end;

6. See *In Memoriam*, 51, 1.
7. An early MS in Harvard Papers 254
ends here as the poet struggled to bring
the poem to some satisfactory con-
clusion.
8. A somewhat later MS in Harvard
Notebook 21 ends here with the stanza,
  From when his baby pulses beat

To when his hands in their last heat
  Pick at the death-mote on the sheet,
suppressed as being perhaps too grue-
some in its accurate depiction of old
age facing death (*Memoir*, I, 109).
Conceivably Tennyson was still working
on a conclusion as late as 1837.

"Yet how should I for certain hold, 340
Because my memory is so cold,
That I first was in human mould?

"I cannot make this matter plain,
But I would shoot, howe'er in vain,
A random arrow from the brain. 345

"It may be that no life is found,
Which only to one engine bound
Falls off, but cycles always round.

"As old mythologies relate,
Some draught of Lethe might await 350
The slipping thro' from state to state;

"As here we find in trances, men
Forget the dream that happens then,
Until they fall in trance again;

"So might we, if our state were such 355
As one before, remember much,
For those two likes might meet and touch.

"But, if I lapsed from nobler place,
Some legend of a fallen race
Alone might hint of my disgrace; 360

"Some vague emotion of delight
In gazing up an Alpine height,
Some yearning toward the lamps of night;

"Or if thro' lower lives I came—
Tho' all experience past became 365
Consolidate in mind and frame—

"I might forget my weaker lot;
For is not our first year forgot?
The haunts of memory echo not.

"And men, whose reason long was blind, 370
From cells of madness unconfined,
Oft lose whole years of darker mind.

"Much more, if first I floated free,
As naked essence, must I be
Incompetent of memory; 375

"For memory dealing but with time,
And he with matter, could she climb
Beyond her own material prime?

"Moreover, something is or seems,
That touches me with mystic gleams, 380
Like glimpses of forgotten dreams—

"Of something felt, like something here;
Of something done, I know not where;
Such as no language may declare."

The still voice laugh'd. "I talk," said he,   385
"Not with thy dreams. Suffice it thee
Thy pain is a reality."

"But thou," said I, "hast missed thy mark,
Who sought'st to wreck my mortal ark,
By making all the horizon dark.   390

"Why not set forth, if I should do
This rashness, that which might ensue
With this old soul in organs new?

"Whatever crazy sorrow saith,
No life that breathes with human breath   395
Has ever truly long'd for death.

" 'T is life, whereof our nerves are scant,
O, life, not death, for which we pant;
More life, and fuller, that I want."

I ceased, and sat as one forlorn.   400
Then said the voice, in quiet scorn,
"Behold, it is the Sabbath morn."[9]

And I arose, and I released
The casement, and the light increased
With freshness in the dawning east.   405

Like soften'd airs that blowing steal,
When meres begin to uncongeal,
The sweet church bells began to peal.

On to God's house the people prest;
Passing the place where each must rest,   410
Each enter'd like a welcome guest.

One walk'd between his wife and child,
With measured footfall firm and mild,
And now and then he gravely smiled.

The prudent partner of his blood   415
Lean'd on him, faithful, gentle, good,
Wearing the rose of womanhood.

And in their double love secure,
The little maiden walk'd demure,
Pacing with downward eyelids pure.   420

These three made unity so sweet,
My frozen heart began to beat,
Remembering its ancient heat.

9. The ending, which produces no con-   ridiculed by several commentators.
clusion or solutions, has been roundly

I blest them, and they wander'd on;
I spoke, but answer came there none;   425
The dull and bitter voice was gone.

A second voice[1] was at mine ear,
A little whisper silver-clear,
A murmur, "Be of better cheer."

As from some blissful neighborhood,   430
A notice faintly understood,
"I see the end, and know the good."

A little hint to solace woe,
A hint, a whisper breathing low,
"I may not speak of what I know."   435

Like an Æolian harp that wakes
No certain air, but overtakes
Far thought with music that it makes;

Such seem'd the whisper at my side:
"What is it thou knowest, sweet voice?" I cried.   440
"A hidden hope," the voice replied;

So heavenly-toned, that in that hour
From out my sullen heart a power
Broke, like the rainbow from the shower,

To feel, altho' no tongue can prove,   445
That every cloud that spreads above
And veileth love, itself is love.

And forth into the fields I went,
And Nature's living motion lent
The pulse of hope to discontent.   450

I wonder'd at the bounteous hours,
The slow result of winter showers;
You scarce could see the grass for flowers.

I wonder'd, while I paced along;
The woods were fill'd so full with song,   455
There seem'd no room for sense of wrong;

And all so variously wrought,
I marvell'd how the mind was brought
To anchor by one gloomy thought;

And wherefore rather I made choice[2]   460
To commune with that barren voice,
Than him that said, "Rejoice! Rejoice!"

1833–34; 1842

1. Actually a third voice.   2. I.e., "Marvell'd" that he had ever made the choice.

Saint Simeon Stylites[3]

Altho' I be the basest of mankind,
From scalp to sole one slough and crust of sin,
Unfit for earth, unfit for heaven, scarce meet
For troops of devils, mad with blasphemy,
I will not cease to grasp the hope I hold   5
Of saintdom, and to clamor, mourn, and sob,
Battering the gates of heaven with storms of prayer,
Have mercy, Lord, and take away my sin!
    Let this avail, just, dreadful, mighty God,
This not be all in vain, that thrice ten years,   10
Thrice multiplied by superhuman pangs,
In hungers and in thirsts, fevers and cold,
In coughs, aches, stitches, ulcerous throes and cramps,[4]
A sign betwixt the meadow and the cloud
Patient on this tall pillar I have borne   15
Rain, wind, frost, heat, hail, damp, and sleet, and snow;
And I had hoped that ere this period closed
Thou wouldst have caught me up into thy rest,
Denying not these weather-beaten limbs
The meed of saints, the white robe and the palm.   20
    O, take the meaning, Lord! I do not breathe,
Not whisper, any murmur of complaint.
Pain heap'd ten-hundred-fold to this, were still
Less burthen, by ten-hundred-fold, to bear,
Than were those lead-like tons of sin that crush'd   25
My spirit flat before thee.
                                        O Lord, Lord,
Thou knowest I bore this better at the first,
For I was strong and hale of body then;
And tho' my teeth, which now are dropt away,
Would chatter with the cold, and all my beard   30
Was tagg'd with icy fringes in the moon,
I drown'd the whoopings of the owl with sound
Of pious hymns and psalms, and sometimes saw
An angel stand and watch me, as I sang.

---

3. Circulating by November 1833 among several of Tennyson's Cambridge friends, who called St. Simeon not "the watcher on the pillar to the end," but "to the *n*th" (*Memoir*, I, 130), the poem expresses satirically the poet's distrust of asceticism, with possibly a gibe at his Aunt Mary Bourne's brand of Calvinism (see note 2 to "Remorse").
   Simeon Stylites of Syria (c. 390–459) outdid all his contemporaries in the extremes to which he aspired to mortify the flesh. Tennyson's source was probably Edward Gibbon's derisive account in *The Decline and Fall of the Roman Empire:* "This voluntary martyrdom must have gradually destroyed the sensibility both of mind and body; nor can it be presumed that the fanatics, who torment themselves, are susceptible of any lively affection from the rest of mankind." Predictably, Robert Browning, the acknowledged master of the grotesque in his dramatic monologues, was fond of this poem.
4. "This is one of the poems A. T. would read with grotesque grimness, especially such passages as 'coughs, aches, stitches,' etc., laughing aloud at times" (FitzGerald's note, *Memoir*, I, 193).

Now am I feeble grown; my end draws nigh.   35
I hope my end draws nigh; half deaf I am,
So that I scarce can hear the people hum
About the column's base, and almost blind,
And scarce can recognize the fields I know;
And both my thighs are rotted with the dew;   40
Yet cease I not to clamor and to cry,
While my stiff spine can hold my weary head,
Till all my limbs drop piecemeal from the stone,
Have mercy, mercy! take away my sin!
   O Jesus, if thou wilt not save my soul,   45
Who may be saved? who is it may be saved?
Who may be made a saint if I fail here?
Show me the man hath suffer'd more than I.
For did not all thy martyrs die one death?
For either they were stoned, or crucified,   50
Or burn'd in fire, or boil'd in oil, or sawn
In twain beneath the ribs; but I die here
To-day, and whole years long, a life of death.
Bear witness, if I could have found a way—
And heedfully I sifted all my thought—   55
More slowly-painful to subdue this home
Of sin, my flesh, which I despise and hate,
I had not stinted practice, O my God!
   For not alone this pillar-punishment,
Not this alone I bore; but while I lived   60
In the white convent down the valley there,
For many weeks about my loins I wore
The rope that haled the buckets from the well,
Twisted as tight as I could knot the noose,
And spake not of it to a single soul,   65
Until the ulcer, eating thro' my skin,
Betray'd my secret penance, so that all
My brethren marvell'd greatly. More than this
I bore, whereof, O God, thou knowest all.
   Three winters, that my soul might grow to thee,   70
I lived up there on yonder mountain-side.
My right leg chain'd into the crag, I lay
Pent in a roofless close of ragged stones;
Inswathed sometimes in wandering mist, and twice
Black'd with thy branding thunder, and sometimes   75
Sucking the damps for drink, and eating not,
Except the spare chance-gift of those that came
To touch my body and be heal'd, and live.
And they say then that I work'd miracles,
Whereof my fame is loud amongst mankind,   80
Cured lameness, palsies, cancers. Thou, O God,
Knowest alone whether this was or no.
Have mercy, mercy! cover all my sin!

Then, that I might be more alone with thee,
Three years I lived upon a pillar, high   85
Six cubits, and three years on one of twelve;
And twice three years I crouch'd on one that rose
Twenty by measure; last of all, I grew
Twice ten long weary, weary years to this,
That numbers forty cubits from the soil.[5]   90
    I think that I have borne as much as this—
Or else I dream—and for so long a time,
If I may measure time by yon slow light,
And this high dial,[6] which my sorrow crowns—
So much—even so.

                       And yet I know not well,   95
For that the evil ones come here, and say,
'Fall down, O Simeon; thou hast suffer'd long
For ages and for ages!' then they prate
Of penances I cannot have gone thro',
Perplexing me with lies; and oft I fall,   100
Maybe for months, in such blind lethargies
That Heaven, and Earth, and Time are choked.

                                      But yet
Bethink thee, Lord, while thou and all the saints
Enjoy themselves in heaven, and men on earth
House in the shade of comfortable roofs,   105
Sit with their wives by fires, eat wholesome food,
And wear warm clothes, and even beasts have stalls,
I, 'tween the spring and downfall of the light,
Bow down one thousand and two hundred times,
To Christ, the Virgin Mother, and the saints;   110
Or in the night, after a little sleep,
I wake; the chill stars sparkle; I am wet
With drenching dews, or stiff with crackling frost.
I wear an undress'd goatskin on my back;
A grazing iron collar grinds my neck;   S11
And in my weak, lean arms I lift the cross,
And strive and wrestle with thee till I die.
O, mercy, mercy! wash away my sin!
    O Lord, thou knowest what a man I am;
A sinful man, conceived and born in sin.   120
'T is their own doing; this is none of mine;
Lay it not to me. Am I to blame for this,
That here come those that worship me? Ha! ha!
They think that I am somewhat. What am I?
The silly people take me for a saint,   125
And bring me offerings of fruit and flowers;

---

5. One cubit is approximately 18
inches, so the pillar is now about 60
feet high. Kemble, one of the Cam-
bridge friends mentioned above, wrote:
"Could you only have made the height
of the pillar a geometrical progression"
(*Memoir*, I, 130). There is clearly no
basis for the assumption, which a few
critics have held, that Tennyson's por-
trait is in any sense sympathetic.
6. I.e., a sundial.

And I, in truth—thou wilt bear witness here—
Have all in all endured as much, and more
Than many just and holy men, whose names
Are register'd and calendar'd for saints.   130
    Good people, you do ill to kneel to me.
What is it I can have done to merit this?
I am a sinner viler than you all.
It may be I have wrought some miracles,
And cured some halt and maim'd; but what of that?   135
It may be no one, even among the saints,
May match his pains with mine; but what of that?
Yet do not rise; for you may look on me,
And in your looking you may kneel to God.
Speak! is there any of you halt or maim'd?   140
I think you know I have some power with Heaven
From my long penance; let him speak his wish.
    Yes, I can heal him. Power goes forth from me.
They say that they are heal'd. Ah, hark! they shout
'Saint Simeon Stylites.' Why, if so,   145
God reaps a harvest in me. O my soul,
God reaps a harvest in thee! If this be,
Can I work miracles and not be saved?
This is not told of any. They were saints.
It cannot be but that I shall be saved,   150
Yea, crown'd a saint. They shout, 'Behold a saint!'
And lower voices saint me from above.
Courage, Saint Simeon! This dull chrysalis[7]
Cracks into shining wings, and hope ere death
Spreads more and more and more, that God hath now   155
Sponged and made blank of crimeful record all
My mortal archives.
                                    O my sons, my sons,
I, Simeon of the pillar, by surname
Stylites, among men; I, Simeon,
The watcher on the column till the end;   160
I, Simeon, whose brain the sunshine bakes;
I, whose bald brows in silent hours become
Unnaturally hoar with rime, do now
From my high nest of penance here proclaim
That Pontius and Iscariot by my side   165
Show'd like fair seraphs.[8] On the coals I lay,
A vessel full of sin; all hell beneath
Made me boil over. Devils pluck'd my sleeve,
Abaddon[9] and Asmodeus caught at me.
I smote them with the cross; they swarm'd again.   170

7. A cocoon; ironically the metaphor
reduces him to an insect in the midst of
his maniacal effort to purge himself of
the bestiality within.
8. Pontius Pilate and Judas Iscariot,
respectively Christ's judge and betrayer,
are angels compared with him.
9. A fallen angel in the abyss of Hell
whose name means destruction (see
Revelation, 9:11); Asmodeus, in
Jewish demonology, was an evil spirit,
demon of anger and lust.

In bed like monstrous apes they crush'd my chest;[1]
They flapp'd my light out as I read; I saw
Their faces grow between me and my book;
With coltlike whinny and with hoggish whine
They burst my prayer. Yet this way was left,   175
And by this way I 'scaped them. Mortify
Your flesh, like me, with scourges and with thorns;
Smite, shrink not, spare not. If it may be, fast
Whole Lents, and pray. I hardly, with slow steps,
With slow, faint steps, and much exceeding pain,   180
Have scrambled past those pits of fire, that still
Sing in mine ears. But yield not me the praise;
God only thro' his bounty hath thought fit,
Among the powers and princes of this world,
To make me an example to mankind,   185
Which few can reach to. Yet I do not say
But that a time may come—yea, even now,
Now, now, his footsteps smite the threshold stairs
Of life—I say, that time is at the doors
When you may worship me without reproach;   190
For I will leave my relics in your land,
And you may carve a shrine about my dust,
And burn a fragrant lamp before my bones,
When I am gather'd to the glorious saints.

  While I spake then, a sting of shrewdest pain   195
Ran shrivelling thro' me, and a cloudlike change,
In passing, with a grosser film made thick
These heavy, horny eyes. The end! the end!
Surely the end! What's here? a shape, a shade,
A flash of light. Is that the angel there   200
That holds a crown? Come, blessed brother, come!
I know thy glittering face. I waited long;
My brows are ready. What! deny it now?
Nay, draw, draw, draw nigh. So I clutch it. Christ!
'T is gone; 't is here again; the crown! the crown!   205
So now 't is fitted on and grows to me,
And from it melt the dews of Paradise,
Sweet! sweet! spikenard, and balm, and frankincense.
Ah! let me not be fool'd, sweet saints; I trust
That I am whole, and clean, and meet for Heaven.   210
  Speak, if there be a priest, a man of God,
Among you there, and let him presently
Approach, and lean a ladder on the shaft,
And climbing up into my airy home,
Deliver me the blessed sacrament;   215
For by the warning of the Holy Ghost,
I prophesy that I shall die to-night,

1. Ironic in that St. Simeon halluci-
nates fiends far more provocative than
anything external. See "Lucretius,"
lines 219 ff, for a similar phenomenon
arising from a different impulse.

A quarter before twelve.

But thou, O Lord,
Aid all this foolish people; let them take
Example, pattern; lead them to thy light.   220

1833; 1842

Tithonus[2]

The woods decay, the woods decay and fall,
The vapors weep their burthen to the ground,
Man comes and tills the field and lies beneath,
And after many a summer dies the swan.
Me only cruel immortality   5
Consumes; I wither slowly in thine arms,
Here at the quiet limit of the world,
A white-hair'd shadow roaming like a dream
The ever-silent spaces of the East,
Far-folded mists, and gleaming halls of morn.   10
   Alas! for this gray shadow, once a man—
So glorious in his beauty and thy choice,
Who madest him thy chosen, that he seem'd
To his great heart none other than a God!
I ask'd thee, "Give me immortality."   15
Then didst thou grant mine asking with a smile,
Like wealthy men who care not how they give.
But thy strong Hours indignant work'd their wills,
And beat me down and marr'd and wasted me,
And tho' they could not end me, left me maim'd   20
To dwell in presence of immortal youth,
Immortal age beside immortal youth,
And all I was in ashes. Can thy love,
Thy beauty, make amends, tho' even now,
Close over us, the silver star,[3] thy guide,   25
Shines in those tremulous eyes that fill with tears
To hear me? Let me go; take back thy gift.
Why should a man desire in any way
To vary from the kindly race of men,
Or pass beyond the goal of ordinance[4]   30
Where all should pause, as is most meet for all?

2. Started shortly after Hallam's death, "Tithonus" was, as Tennyson explained, "originally a pendent to the 'Ulysses' in my former volumes" and reflected his own desire to be released from the burdens of life. In 1860 he wrote that Thackeray had urged him to send a poem for publication in *Cornhill Magazine,* and he "found this 'Tithonus,' written upwards of a quarter of a century ago" (*Memoir,* I, 459; II, 9).

Eos or Aurora, the daughter of Hyperion and goddess of the dawn, begged Zeus to grant Tithonus eternal life but forgot to ask for eternal youth. In pity for his plight, the gods turned him into a grasshopper. (See Tennyson's earlier use of the myth in "The Grasshopper.")
3. Venus, the morning star.
4. The appointed span of life.

A soft air fans the cloud apart; there comes
A glimpse of that dark world where I was born.
Once more the old mysterious glimmer steals
From thy pure brows, and from thy shoulders pure,   35
And bosom beating with a heart renew'd.
Thy cheek begins to redden thro' the gloom,
Thy sweet eyes brighten slowly close to mine.
Ere yet they blind the stars, and the wild team[5]
Which love thee, yearning for thy yoke, arise,   40
And shake the darkness from their loosen'd manes,
And beat the twilight into flakes of fire.

    Lo! ever thus thou growest beautiful
In silence, then before thine answer given
Departest, and thy tears are on my cheek.   45

    Why wilt thou ever scare me with thy tears,
And make me tremble lest a saying learnt,
In days far-off, on that dark earth, be true?
"The Gods themselves cannot recall their gifts."

    Ay me! ay me! with what another heart   50
In days far-off, and with what other eyes
I used to watch—if I be he that watch'd—
The lucid outline forming round thee; saw
The dim curls kindle into sunny rings;
Changed with thy mystic change, and felt my blood   55
Glow with the glow that slowly crimson'd all
Thy presence and thy portals, while I lay,
Mouth, forehead, eyelids, growing dewy-warm
With kisses balmier than half-opening buds
Of April, and could hear the lips that kiss'd   60
Whispering I knew not what of wild and sweet,
Like that strange song I heard Apollo sing,
While Ilion like a mist rose into towers.[6]

    Yet hold me not for ever in thine East;
How can my nature longer mix with thine?   65
Coldly thy rosy shadows bathe me, cold
Are all thy lights, and cold my wrinkled feet
Upon thy glimmering thresholds, when the steam
Floats up from those fields about the homes
Of happy men that have the power to die,   70
And grassy barrows[7] of the happier dead.
Release me, and restore me to the ground.
Thou seest all things, thou wilt see my grave;
Thou wilt renew thy beauty morn by morn,
I earth in earth forget these empty courts,   75
And thee returning on thy silver wheels.

1833 ff.; 1860

5. Eos and her team of horses announce the sunrise.
6. Troy was built to the music of Apollo's lyre. Cf. "Œnone," lines 39–41, and "Tiresias," lines 95 ff.
7. Burial mounds.

Tiresias[8]

To E. FitzGerald

Old Fitz, who from your suburb grange,
   Where once I tarried for a while,
Glance at the wheeling orb of change,
   And greet it with a kindly smile;
Whom yet I see as there you sit   5
   Beneath your sheltering garden-tree,
And watch your doves about you flit,
   And plant on shoulder, hand, and knee,
Or on your head their rosy feet,
   As if they knew your diet spares   10
Whatever moved in that full sheet
   Let down to Peter at his prayers;[9]
Who live on milk and meal and grass;
   And once for ten long weeks I tried
Your table of Pythagoras,[1]   15
   And seem'd at first "a thing enskied,"[2]
As Shakespeare has it, airy-light
   To float above the ways of men,
Then fell from that half-spiritual height
   Chill'd, till I tasted flesh again   20
One night when earth was winter-black,
   And all the heavens flash'd in frost;
And on me, half-asleep, came back
   That wholesome heat the blood had lost,
And set me climbing icy capes   25
   And glaciers, over which there roll'd
To meet me long-arm'd vines with grapes
   Of Eshcol hugeness;[3] for the cold
Without, and warmth within me, wrought
   To mould the dream; but none can say   30
That Lenten fare makes Lenten thought
   Who reads your golden Eastern lay,[4]
Than which I know no version done
   In English more divinely well;

8. "The Prologue," Tennyson noted, "describes Edward FitzGerald, as we had seen him at Woodbridge in 1876" (*Memoir*, II, 316), and was composed shortly before FitzGerald's death on June 14, 1883. Much of the narrative poem, "dating many a year ago," was written at the time of "Ulysses"; the Epilogue was added for publication in 1885.

9. A reference to meat, fish, and fowl (see *Acts*, 10:11–12). FitzGerald was a vegetarian.

1. The sixth-century-B.C. Greek philosopher and vegetarian.

2. See *Measure for Measure*, I, iv, 34.

3. Of his vegetarian dream Tennyson said: "I had gone without meat for six weeks, living only on vegetables; and at the end of the time, when I came to eat a mutton-chop, I shall never forget the sensation. I never felt such joy in my blood. When I went to sleep, I dreamt that I saw the vines of the South, with huge Eshcol branches, trailing over the glaciers of the North." (*Memoir*, II, 317). For Eshcol, a fruitful valley, see *Numbers*, 13: 23.

4. FitzGerald's translation of the *Rubaiyat of Omar Khayyam*, published in 1859.

A planet equal to the sun   35
 Which cast it, that large infidel
Your Omar; and your Omar drew
 Full-handed plaudits from our best
In modern letters, and from two,
 Old friends outvaluing all the rest,   40
Two voices[5] heard on earth no more;
 But we old friends are still alive,
And I am nearing seventy-four,
 While you have touch'd at seventy-five,
And so I send a birthday line   45
 Of greeting; and my son, who dipt
In some forgotten book of mine
 With sallow scraps of manuscript,
And dating many a year ago,
 Has hit on this, which you will take,   50
My Fitz, and welcome, as I know,
 Less for its own than for the sake
Of one recalling gracious times,
 When, in our younger London days,
You found some merit in my rhymes,   55
 And I more pleasure in your praise.[6]

Tiresias[7]

I wish I were as in the years of old,
While yet the blessed daylight made itself
Ruddy thro' both the roofs of sight, and woke
These eyes, now dull, but then so keen to seek
The meanings ambush'd under all they saw,   5
The flight of birds, the flame of sacrifice,
What omens may foreshadow fate to man
And woman, and the secret of the Gods.
 My son,[8] the Gods, despite of human prayer,
Are slower to forgive than human kings.   10
The great God Arês burns in anger still
Against the guiltless heirs of him from Tyre,
Our Cadmus, out of whom thou art, who found
Beside the springs of Dircê, smote, and still'd

5. In the eighties, many of the closest of the old friends were dying. Here Tennyson is probably thinking of Thomas Carlyle and James Spedding, both of whom had died in 1881. See *Memoir*, II, 262–263.
6. FitzGerald had been an admirer of Tennyson's earlier poetry (through the 1842 volumes), but, as he said, "I am considered a great heretic, because like Carlyle, I gave up all hopes of him after 'The Princess'" (1847), for none of the songs had "the old champagne flavour" (*Memoir*, I, 253).

7. Tiresias, blinded by Athena when he surprised her while bathing, was granted the gift of prophecy but, like Cassandra, could not compel belief. In the poem he tries to persuade Menoeceus to sacrifice himself to save Thebes in its War of the Seven. Among many possible sources, Tennyson drew from the *Odyssey*, XI, 90–151.
8. Menoeceus, familiarly addressed. He was the son of Creon and descended from Cadmus, against whose offspring Ares (Mars) held his grudge.

Thro' all its folds the multitudinous beast,   15
The dragon, which our trembling fathers call'd
The God's own son.
               A tale, that told to me,
When but thine age, by age as winter-white
As mine is now, amazed, but made me yearn
For larger glimpses of that more than man   20
Which rolls the heavens, and lifts and lays the deep,
Yet loves and hates with mortal hates and loves,
And moves unseen among the ways of men.
    Then, in my wanderings all the lands that lie
Subjected to the Heliconian[9] ridge   25
Have heard this footstep fall, altho' my wont
Was more to scale the highest of the heights
With some strange hope to see the nearer God.
    One naked peak—the sister of the Sun
Would climb from out the dark, and linger there   30
To silver all the valleys with her shafts—
There once, but long ago, five-fold thy term[1]
Of years, I lay; the winds were dead for heat;
The noonday crag made the hand burn; and sick
For shadow—not one bush was near—I rose,   35
Following a torrent till its myriad falls
Found silence in the hollows underneath.
    There in a secret olive-glade I saw
Pallas Athene climbing from the bath
In anger; yet one glittering foot disturb'd   40
The lucid well; one snowy knee was prest
Against the margin flowers; a dreadful light
Came from her golden hair, her golden helm
And all her golden armor on the grass,
And from her virgin breast, and virgin eyes   45
Remaining fixt on mine, till mine grew dark
For ever, and I heard a voice that said,
"Henceforth be blind, for thou hast seen too much,
And speak the truth that no man may believe."
    Son, in the hidden world of sight that lives   50
Behind this darkness, I behold her still,
Beyond all work of those who carve the stone,
Beyond all dreams of Godlike womanhood,
Ineffable beauty, out of whom, at a glance,
And as it were, perforce, upon me flash'd   55
The power of prophesying—but to me
No power—so chain'd and coupled with the curse
Of blindness and their unbelief who heard
And heard not, when I spake of famine, plague,
Shrine-shattering earthquake, fire, flood, thunderbolt,   60

9. I.e., the lands that lie below the Helicon mountain range, regarded as sacred to the Muses.

1. In some legends, Tiresias was in his seventh year.

And angers of the Gods for evil done
And expiation lack'd—no power on Fate
Theirs, or mine own! for when the crowd would roar
For blood, for war, whose issue was their doom,
To cast wise words among the multitude   65
Was flinging fruit to lions; nor, in hours
Of civil outbreak, when I knew the twain
Would each waste each, and bring on both the yoke
Of stronger states, was mine the voice to curb
The madness of our cities and their kings.[2]   70
    Who ever turn'd upon his heel to hear
My warning that the tyranny of one
Was prelude to the tyranny of all?
My counsel that the tyranny of all
Led backward to the tyranny of one?   75
    This power hath work'd no good to aught that lives
And these blind hands were useless in their wars.
O, therefore, that the unfulfill'd desire,
The grief for ever born from griefs to be,
The boundless yearning of the prophet's heart—   80
Could *that* stand forth, and like a statue, rear'd
To some great citizen, win all praise from all
Who past it, saying, "That was he!"
                  In vain!
Virtue must shape itself in deed, and those   85
Whom weakness or necessity have cramp'd
Within themselves, immerging, each, his urn
In his own well, draws solace as he may.
    Menœceus, thou hast eyes, and I can hear
Too plainly what full tides of onset sap
Our seven high gates, and what a weight of war   90
Rides on those ringing axles! jingle of bits,
Shouts, arrows, tramp of the horn-footed horse
That grind the glebe to powder! Stony showers
Of that ear-stunning hail of Arês crash
Along the sounding walls. Above, below,   95
Shock after shock, the song-built towers[3] and gates
Reel, bruised and butted with the shuddering
War-thunder of iron rams; and from within
The city comes a murmur void of joy,
Lest she be taken captive—maidens, wives,   100
And mothers with their babblers of the dawn,
And oldest age in shadow from the night,

2. Passages like the above suggest the late Tennyson of "Locksley Hall Sixty Years After" and were perhaps altered from or added to the original. Here he identifies himself with the blind seer, feeling, like Tiresias, that his own prophecies and warnings fell on the deaf ears of his contemporaries. Since the Cambridge days, Tennyson had had a sometimes exaggerated notion that he was going blind, a fear which was particularly acute in the eighties. See *Memoir*, II, 311.

3. In legend, the walls of Thebes were built to the music of Amphion's harp. See note 6 to "Tithonus."

Falling about their shrines before their Gods,
And wailing, "Save us."
            And they wail to thee!
These eyeless eyes, that cannot see thine own,   105
See this, that only in thy virtue lies
The saving of our Thebes; for, yesternight,
To me, the great God Arês, whose one bliss
Is war and sacrifice—himself
Blood-red from battle, spear and helmet tipt   110
With stormy light as on a mast at sea,
Stood out before a darkness, crying, "Thebes,
Thy Thebes shall fall and perish, for I loathe
The seed of Cadmus—yet if one of these
By his own hand—if one of these—"
                      My son,   115
No sound is breathed so potent to coerce,
And to conciliate, as their names who dare
For that sweet mother land which gave them birth
Nobly to do, nobly to die. Their names,
Graven on memorial columns, are a song   120
Heard in the future; few, but more than wall
And rampart, their examples reach a hand
Far thro' all years, and everywhere they meet
And kindle generous purpose, and the strength
To mould it into action pure as theirs.   125
   Fairer thy fate than mine, if life's best end
Be to end well! and thou refusing this,
Unvenerable will thy memory be
While men shall move the lips; but if thou dare—
Thou, one of these, the race of Cadmus—then   130
No stone is fitted in yon marble girth
Whose echo shall not tongue thy glorious doom,
Nor in this pavement but shall ring thy name
To every hoof that clangs it, and the springs
Of Dircê laving yonder battle-plain,   135
Heard from the roofs by night, will murmur thee
To thine own Thebes, while Thebes thro' thee shall stand
Firm-based with all her Gods.
                  The Dragon's cave
Half hid, they tell me, now in flowing vines—
Where once he dwelt and whence he roll'd himself   140
At dead of night—thou knowest, and that smooth rock
Before it, altar-fashion'd, where of late
The woman-breasted Sphinx, with wings drawn back,
Folded her lion paws, and look'd to Thebes.
There blanch the bones of whom she slew, and these   145
Mixt with her own, because the fierce beast found
A wiser[4] than herself, and dash'd herself

---

4. Oedipus, who solved the riddle of the Sphinx.

Dead in her rage; but thou art wise enough,
Tho' young, to love thy wiser, blunt the curse
Of Pallas, bear, and tho' I speak the truth   150
Believe I speak it, let thine own hand strike
Thy youthful pulses into rest and quench
The red God's anger, fearing not to plunge
Thy torch of life in darkness, rather—thou
Rejoicing that the sun, the moon, the stars   155
Send no such light upon the ways of men
As one great deed.
           Thither, my son, and there
Thou, that hast never known the embrace of love,
Offer thy maiden life.
           This useless hand!
I felt one warm tear fall upon it. Gone!   160
He will achieve his greatness.
           But for me,
I would that I were gather'd to my rest,
And mingled with the famous kings of old,
On whom about their ocean-islets flash
The faces of the Gods—the wise man's word,   165
Here trampled by the populace underfoot,
There crown'd with worship—and these eyes will find
The men I knew, and watch the chariot whirl
About the goal again, and hunters race
The shadowy lion, and the warrior-kings,   170
In height and prowess more than human, strive
Again for glory, while the golden lyre
Is ever sounding in heroic ears
Heroic hymns, and every way the vales
Wind, clouded with the grateful incense-fume   175
Of those who mix all odor to the Gods
On one far height in one far-shining fire.[5]

"One height and one far-shining fire!"
    And while I fancied that my friend
For this brief idyll would require   180
    A less diffuse and opulent end,
And would defend his judgment well,
    If I should deem it over nice—
The tolling of his funeral bell
    Broke on my Pagan Paradise,   185
And mixt the dream of classic times,
    And all the phantoms of the dream,
With present grief, and made the rhymes,
    That miss'd his living welcome, seem

5. Tennyson liked to quote the above   verse" (*Memoir*, II, 318).
17 lines "as a sample of his blank

Like would-be guests an hour too late,   190
   Who down the highway moving on
With easy laughter find the gate
   Is bolted, and the master gone.
Gone into darkness, that full light
   Of friendship! past, in sleep, away   195
By night, into the deeper night![6]
   The deeper night? A clearer day
Than our poor twilight dawn on earth—
   If night, what barren toil to be!
What life, so maim'd by night, were worth   200
   Our living out? Not mine to me
Remembering all the golden hours
   Now silent, and so many dead,
And him the last; and laying flowers,
   This wreath, above his honor'd head,   205
And praying that, when I from hence
   Shall fade with him into the unknown,
My close of earth's experience
   May prove as peaceful as his own.

1833 ff.; 1885

Break, Break, Break[7]

Break, break, break,
   On thy cold gray stones, O Sea!
And I would that my tongue could utter
   The thoughts that arise in me.

O, well for the fisherman's boy,   5
   That he shouts with his sister at play!
O, well for the sailor lad,
   That he sings in his boat on the bay!

And the stately ships go on
   To their haven under the hill;   10
But O for the touch of a vanish'd hand,
   And the sound of a voice[8] that is still!

Break, break, break,
   At the foot of thy crags, O Sea!
But the tender grace of a day that is dead   15
   Will never come back to me.

1834?; 1842

---

6. In a letter to Fanny Kemble fondly describing Tennyson's short visit in 1876, FitzGerald concluded, "I suppose I may never see him again" (*Memoir,* II, 317).
7. Although the lyric is a seascape, Tennyson said it was "made in a Lincolnshire lane at 5 o'clock in the morning between blossoming hedges" (*Memoir,* I, 190).
8. Arthur Hallam's.

St. Agnes' Eve[9]

Deep on the convent-roof the snows
    Are sparkling to the moon;
My breath to heaven like vapor goes;
    May my soul follow soon!
The shadows of the convent-towers   5
    Slant down the snowy sward,
Still creeping with the creeping hours
    That lead me to my Lord.
Make Thou my spirit pure and clear
    As are the frosty skies,   10
Or this first snowdrop of the year
    That in my bosom lies.

As these white robes are soil'd and dark,
    To yonder shining ground;
As this pale taper's earthly spark,   15
    To yonder argent round;
So shows my soul before the Lamb,
    My spirit before Thee;
So in mine earthly house I am,
    To that I hope to be.   20
Break up the heavens, O Lord! and far,
    Thro' all yon starlight keen,
Draw me, thy bride, a glittering star,
    In raiment white and clean.

He lifts me to the golden doors;   25
    The flashes come and go;
All heaven bursts her starry floors,
    And strows her lights below,
And deepens on and up! the gates
    Roll back, and far within   30
For me the Heavenly Bridegroom[1] waits,
    To make me pure of sin.[2]
The Sabbaths of Eternity,
    One Sabbath deep and wide—
A light upon the shining sea—   35
    The Bridegroom with his bride!

1834; 1836, dated 1837

9. Titled "St. Agnes" until 1855, the poem, unlike Keats's famous secularized version, stresses the original religious elements of the legend. For her refusal to marry his son, the Roman prefect Sempronius condemned the young virgin of Christian parents to be violated by exposure in a brothel and martyred. A miracle preserved her virginity, but she was beheaded on January 21, 304. Subsequently she became the patron saint of young girls who, celebrating the eve of her death, were supposed to have a vision of their future husbands. See Keats's "The Eve of St. Agnes."
1. Christ.
2. Tennyson probably meant her asceticism to be taken as a corrective to the brand practiced by St. Simeon Stylites.

The Epic[3]

At Francis Allen's on the Christmas-eve,—
The game of forfeits done—the girls all kiss'd
Beneath the sacred bush[4] and past away—
The parson Holmes, the poet Everard Hall,[5]
The host, and I sat round the wassail-bowl,   5
Then half-way ebb'd; and there we held a talk,
How all the old honor had from Christmas gone,
Or gone or dwindled down to some odd games
In some odd nooks like this; till I, tired out
With cutting eights that day upon the pond,   10
Where, three times slipping from the outer edge,
I bump'd the ice into three several stars,
Fell in a doze; and half-awake I heard
The parson taking wide and wider sweeps,
Now harping on the church-commissioners,[6]   15
Now hawking at geology[7] and schism;
Until I woke, and found him settled down
Upon the general decay of faith
Right thro' the world: "at home was little left,
And none abroad; there was no anchor, none,   20
To hold by." Francis, laughing, clapt his hand
On Everard's shoulder, with "I hold by him."
"And I," quoth Everard, "by the wassail-bowl."
"Why yes," I said, "we knew your gift that way
At college; but another which you had—   25
I mean of verse (for so we held it then),
What came of that?" "You know," said Frank, "he burnt
His epic, his King Arthur, some twelve books"—
And then to me demanding why: "O, sir,
He thought that nothing new was said, or else   30
Something so said 't was nothing—that a truth
Looks freshest in the fashion of the day;
God knows; he has a mint of reasons; ask.
It pleased *me* well enough." "Nay, nay," said Hall,
"Why take the style of those heroic times?   35
For nature brings not back the mastodon,
Nor we those times; and why should any man

---

3. FitzGerald has said that when the "Morte d'Arthur" was read to him in 1835 from manuscript, it had no introduction or epilogue; "The Epic" was added later "to give a reason for telling an old-world tale" (*Memoir*, I, 194). Tennyson's early interest in the Arthurian legends as material for a grand epic had been abandoned or postponed by 1838, as the casual, almost flippant, tone of "The Epic" suggests. See *Alfred Tennyson*, p. 193.
4. Mistletoe.

5. May represent Tennyson himself with his friends at Cambridge.
6. Refers to the Ecclesiastical Commission, established in 1835 to administer the revenues of the Anglican Church.
7. Tennyson had been reading Lyell's *The Principles of Geology* (1830–33), one of the major contributions to the "new" science which challenged the Biblical interpretation of creation. Here and below, compare *In Memoriam*, 55 and 56.

Remodel models? these twelve books of mine
Were faint Homeric echoes, nothing-worth,
Mere chaff and draff, much better burnt." "But I,"   40
Said Francis, "pick'd the eleventh[8] from this hearth,
And have it; keep a thing, its use will come.
I hoard it as a sugar-plum for Holmes."
He laugh'd, and I, tho' sleepy, like a horse
That hears the corn-bin open, prick'd my ears;   45
For I remember'd Everard's college fame
When we were Freshmen. Then at my request
He brought it; and the poet, little urged,
But with some prelude of disparagement,
Read, mouthing out his hollow oes and aes,   50
Deep-chested music, and to this result.[9]

[Here follows "Morte d'Arthur," lines 170–440 of "The Passing of
Arthur," pp. 423–429, below. Then "The Epic" continues.]

Here ended Hall, and our last light, that long
Had wink'd and threaten'd darkness, flared and fell;
At which the parson, sent to sleep with sound,
And waked with silence, grunted "Good!" but we   55
Sat rapt: it was the tone with which he read—
Perhaps some modern touches here and there
Redeem'd it from the charge of nothingness—
Or else we loved the man, and prized his work;
I know not; but we sitting, as I said,   60
The cock crew loud, as at that time of year
The lusty bird takes every hour for dawn.
Then Francis, muttering, like a man ill-used,
"There now—that's nothing!" drew a little back,
And drove his heel into the smoulder'd log,   65
That sent a blast of sparkles up the flue.
And so to bed, where yet in sleep I seem'd
To sail with Arthur under looming shores,
Point after point; till on to dawn, when dreams
Begin to feel the truth and stir of day,   70
To me, methought, who waited with the crowd,
There came a bark that, blowing forward, bore
King Arthur, like a modern gentleman[1]
Of stateliest port; and all the people cried,
"Arthur is come again: he cannot die."   75
Then those that stood upon the hills behind
Repeated—"Come again, and thrice as fair;"
And, further inland, voices echoed—"Come

8. The "Morte d'Arthur," which in 1869 was incorporated into the *Idylls* but did not actually become the twelfth book until 1888.
9. "His voice, very deep and deep-chested, but rather murmuring than mouthing" was FitzGerald's comment on the poet's reading (*Memoir*, I, 194).

After line 51, there follows the "Morte d'Arthur," which, with a few changes and some expansion, becomes lines 170–440 of "The Passing of Arthur," pp. 423–429.
1. A phrase which in some ways anticipates the dedication of the *Idylls* in 1862 to Prince Albert.

With all good things, and war shall be no more."
At this a hundred bells began to peal,   80
That with the sound I woke, and heard indeed
The clear church-bells ring in the Christmas morn.

1838; 1842

"You Ask Me Why"[2]

You ask me, why, tho' ill at ease,
    Within this region I subsist,
    Whose spirits falter in the mist,
And languish for the purple seas.[3]

It is the land that freemen till,   5
    That sober-suited Freedom chose,
    The land, where girt with friends or foes
A man may speak the thing he will;

A land of settled government,
    A land of just and old renown,   10
    Where Freedom slowly broadens down
From precedent to precedent;

Where faction seldom gathers head,
    But, by degrees to fullness wrought,
    The strength of some diffusive thought   15
Hath time and space to work and spread.

Should banded unions[4] persecute
    Opinion, and induce a time
    When single thought is civil crime,
And individual freedom mute,   20

Tho' power should make from land to land
    The name of Britain trebly great—
    Tho' every channel of the State
Should fill and choke with golden sand—

Yet waft me from the harbor-mouth,   25
    Wild wind! I seek a warmer sky,
    And I will see before I die
The palms and temples of the South.

1833–34; 1842

2. Like the following two companion pieces, the poem was occasioned by the popular demonstrations arising from the House of Lords' rejection of the Reform Bill of 1832. See *Memoir,* I, 506. When it had been passed previously by the House of Commons, Tennyson had been jubilant: "This 'Firm Bill,' as the Lincolnshire people called it, had stirred all hearts; and my father and some of his brothers and sisters at once sallied out into the darkness, and began to ring the church bells madly" (*Memoir,* I, 93). But the political demonstrations, which helped to pressure the House of Lords into passing the bill (along with the threat that enough new Whig lords would be created to insure a majority vote), had moved Tennyson toward a conservative position.
3. Of the East. Cf. "Locksley Hall," lines 153 ff. The verse, as is that in "Of Old Sat Freedom on the Heights," is in the stanza form of *In Memoriam.*
4. Political factions or organizations.

"Of Old Sat Freedom on the Heights"[5]

Of old sat Freedom on the heights,
   The thunders breaking at her feet;
Above her shook the starry lights;
   She heard the torrents meet.

There in her place she did rejoice,   5
   Self-gather'd in her prophet-mind,
But fragments of her mighty voice
   Came rolling on the wind.

Then stept she down thro' town and field
   To mingle with the human race,   10
And part by part to men reveal'd
   The fullness of her face—

Grave mother of majestic works,
   From her isle-altar[6] gazing down,
Who, Godlike, grasps the triple forks,[7]   15
   And, king-like, wears the crown.

Her open eyes desire the truth.
   The wisdom of a thousand years
Is in them. May perpetual youth
   Keep dry their light from tears;   20

That her fair form may stand and shine,
   Make bright our days and light our dreams,
Turning to scorn with lips divine
   The falsehood of extremes!

1833–34; 1842

"Love Thou Thy Land"[8]

Love thou thy land, with love far-brought
   From out the storied past, and used
   Within the present, but transfused
Thro' future time by power of thought;

5. In 1842 Aubrey de Vere showed this and the preceding poem to Wordsworth, who, predisposed to dislike anything currently being published, said: "I must acknowledge that these two poems are very solid and noble in thought. Their diction also seems singularly stately" (*Memoir*, I, 209). Tennyson, in his own note, dryly commented: "They were the first poems of mine which he had read."
6. England.
7. According to his son, Tennyson meant "Zeus with his *triscula fulmina,* the thunderbolts," and not Britannia holding Neptune's trident.

8. Tennyson strongly denied the charge that either this poem or the preceding two had been versified from a speech by his friend Spedding at the Cambridge Union, and, accounting for similarities of thought, added: "Why not, for I thoroughly agreed with him about politics." See *Memoir*, I, 126–127 and 141. The poet's liberalism had almost certainly been tempered by his friends, particularly, one suspects, by Hallam, who from the start had "gloomily" viewed the proceedings surrounding passage of the Reform Bill. See *Memoir*, I, 93.

True love turn'd round on fixed poles,   5
    Love, that endures not sordid ends,
    For English natures, freemen, friends,
Thy brothers and immortal souls.

But pamper not a hasty time,
    Nor feed with crude imaginings   10
    The herd, wild hearts and feeble wings
That every sophister[9] can lime.

Deliver not the tasks of might
    To weakness, neither hide the ray
    From those, not blind, who wait for day,   15
Tho' sitting girt with doubtful light.

Make knowledge circle with the winds;
    But let her herald, Reverence, fly
    Before her to whatever sky
Bear seed of men and growth of minds.   20

Watch what main-currents draw the years;
    Cut Prejudice against the grain.
    But gentle words are always gain;
Regard the weakness of thy peers.

Nor toil for title, place, or touch   25
    Of pension, neither count on praise—
    It grows to guerdon[1] after-days.
Nor deal in watch-words overmuch;

Not clinging to some ancient saw,
    Not master'd by some modern term,   30
    Not swift nor slow to change, but firm;
And in its season bring the law,

That from Discussion's lip may fall
    With Life that, working strongly, binds—
    Set in all lights by many minds,   35
To close the interests of all.

For Nature also, cold and warm,
    And moist and dry, devising long,
    Thro' many agents making strong,
Matures the individual form.   40

Meet is it changes should control
    Our being, lest we rust in ease.
    We all are changed by still degrees,
All but the basis of the soul.

So let the change which comes be free   45
    To ingroove itself with that which flies,

9. Specifically a second- or third-year undergraduate at a British university, hence caught by sophomoric, specious reasoning. 1. Reward.

And work, a joint of state, that plies
Its office, moved with sympathy.

A saying hard to shape in act;
   For all the past of Time reveals   50
   A bridal dawn of thunder-peals,
Wherever Thought hath wedded Fact.

Even now we hear with inward strife
   A motion toiling in the gloom—
   The Spirit of the years to come   55
Yearning to mix himself with Life.

A slow-develop'd strength awaits
   Completion in a painful school;
   Phantoms of other forms of rule,[2]
New Majesties of mighty States—   60

The warders of the growing hour,
   But vague in vapor, hard to mark;
   And round them sea and air are dark
With great contrivances[3] of Power.

Of many changes, aptly join'd,   65
   Is bodied forth the second whole.
   Regard gradation, lest the soul
Of Discord race the rising wind;[4]

A wind to puff your idol-fires,
   And heap their ashes on the head;   70
   To shame the boast so often made,
That we are wiser than our sires.

O, yet, if Nature's evil star
   Drive men in manhood, as in youth,
   To follow flying steps of Truth   75
Across the brazen bridge of war—

If New and Old, disastrous feud,
   Must ever shock, like armed foes,
   And this be true, till Time shall close,
That Principles are rain'd in blood;   80

Not yet the wise of heart would cease
   To hold his hope thro' shame and guilt,
   But with his hand against the hilt,
Would pace the troubled land, like Peace;

Not less, tho' dogs of Faction bay,   85
   Would serve his kind in deed and word,
   Certain, if knowledge bring the sword,
That knowledge takes the sword away—

---

2. Democracy.
3. New inventions; see "Locksley

Hall," lines 120–124 and 182.
4. Of violent revolutionary change.

Would love the gleams of good that broke
    From either side, nor veil his eyes;   90
And if some dreadful need should rise
Would strike, and firmly, and one stroke.

To-morrow yet would reap to-day,
    As we bear blossom of the dead;
    Earn well the thrifty months, nor wed   95
Raw Haste, half-sister to Delay.

1833–34; 1842

"Move Eastward, Happy Earth"[5]

Move eastward, happy earth, and leave
    Yon orange sunset waning slow;
From fringes of the faded eve,
    O happy planet, eastward go,
Till over thy dark shoulder glow   5
    Thy silver sister-world,[6] and rise
    To glass herself in dewy eyes
That watch me from the glen below.

Ah, bear me with thee, smoothly borne,
    Dip forward under starry light,   10
And move me to my marriage-morn,
    And round again to happy night.

1836; 1842

The Progress of Spring[7]

1

The ground-flame of the crocus breaks the mould,
    Fair Spring slides hither o'er the Southern sea,
Wavers on her thin stem the snowdrop cold
    That trembles not to kisses of the bee.
Come, Spring, for now from all the dripping caves   5
    The spear of ice has wept itself away.
And hour by hour unfolding woodbine leaves
    O'er his uncertain shadow droops the day.

5. Chiefly of biographical interest, the poem suggests Tennyson's engagement to Emily Sellwood, whom he did not marry, however, until 1850. The poem was probably occasioned by the marriage in May 1836 of his brother Charles to Emily's sister Louisa. See "Love and Duty," p. 101.
6. The moon, or possibly Venus, as reflected in Emily's eyes.
7. Although Hallam Tennyson says the poem was "written in early youth," the precise time of composition cannot be fixed. When published in 1889, it was preceded by a dedication to Mary Boyle (see p. 488). As a happy catalogue of springtime phenomena, the poem is uncomplicated by the intellectual and scientific issues informing so much of the natural description in *In Memoriam*. Nevertheless, the poet's attitude toward nature is characteristic; the rendering of sights and sounds is accurate enough, but they all seem meditated upon and distilled through the poet's imagination. The ostensible subject is nature; the real subject is the sensibility which perceives it.

She comes! The loosen'd rivulets run;
 The frost-bead melts upon her golden hair;   10
Her mantle, slowly greening in the Sun,
  Now wraps her close, now arching leaves her bare
  To breaths of balmier air;

2

Up leaps the lark, gone wild to welcome her,
 About her glance the tits, and shriek the jays,   15
Before her skims the jubilant woodpecker,
  The linnet's bosom blushes at her gaze,
While round her brows a woodland culver flits,
 Watching her large light eyes and gracious looks,
And in her open palm a halcyon sits   20
 Patient—the secret splendor of the brooks.
Come, Spring! She comes on waste and wood,
 On farm and field; but enter also here,
Diffuse thyself at will thro' all my blood,
 And, tho' thy violet sicken into sere,   25
 Lodge with me all the year.

3

Once more a downy drift against the brakes,[8]
 Self-darken'd in the sky, descending slow!
But gladly see I thro' the wavering flakes
 Yon blanching apricot like snow in snow.   30
These will thine eyes not brook in forest-paths,
 On their perpetual pine, nor round the beech;
They fuse themselves to little spicy baths,
 Solved in the tender blushes of the peach;
They lose themselves and die   35
 On that new life that gems the hawthorn line;
Thy gay lent-lilies wave and put them by,
 And out once more in varnish'd glory shine
 Thy stars of celandine.

4

She floats across the hamlet. Heaven lours,[9]   40
 But in the tearful splendor of her smiles
I see the slowly-thickening chestnut towers
 Fill out the spaces by the barren tiles.
Now past her feet the swallow circling flies,
 A clamorous cuckoo stoops to meet her hand;   45
Her light makes rainbows in my closing eyes,
 I hear a charm of song thro' all the land.
Come, Spring! She comes, and Earth is glad
 To roll her North below thy deepening dome,
But ere thy maiden birk[1] be wholly clad,   50
 And these low bushes dip their twigs in foam,
 Make all true hearths thy home.

---

8. Thickets.   1. Birch.
9. Frowns.

5

Across my garden! and the thicket stirs,
 The fountain pulses high in summer jets,
The blackcap warbles, and the turtle purrs,   55
 The starling claps his tiny castanets.[2]
Still round her forehead wheels the woodland dove,
 And scatters on her throat the sparks of dew,
The kingcup fills her footprint, and above
 Broaden the glowing isles of vernal blue.   60
Hail, ample presence of a Queen,
 Bountiful, beautiful, apparell'd gay,
Whose mantle, every shade of glancing green,
 Flies back in fragrant breezes to display
 A tunic white as May!   65

6

She whispers, 'From the South I bring you balm,
 For on a tropic mountain was I born,
While some dark dweller by the coco-palm
 Watch'd my far meadow zoned with airy morn;
From under rose a muffled moan of floods;   70
 I sat beneath a solitude of snow;
There no one came, the turf was fresh, the woods
 Plunged gulf on gulf thro' all their vales below.
I saw beyond their silent tops
 The steaming marshes of the scarlet cranes,   75
The slant seas leaning on the mangrove copse.
 And summer basking in the sultry plains
 About a land of canes.

7

'Then from my vapor-girdle soaring forth
 I scaled the buoyant highway of the birds,   80
And drank the dews and drizzle of the North,
 That I might mix with men, and hear their words
On pathway'd plains; for—while my hand exults
 Within the bloodless heart of lowly flowers
To work old laws of Love to fresh results,   85
 Thro' manifold effect of simple powers—
I too would teach the man
 Beyond the darker hour to see the bright,
That his fresh life may close as it began,
 The still-fulfilling promise of a light   90
 Narrowing the bounds of night.'

8

So wed thee with my soul, that I may mark
 The coming year's great good and varied ills,
And new developments, whatever spark
 Be struck from out the clash of warring wills;   95

2. In 1889 Tennyson said, "This line
was written fifty-six years ago under
the elms on the sloping field at Som-
ersby."

Or whether, since our nature cannot rest,
    The smoke of war's volcano burst again
From hoary deeps that belt the changeful West,
    Old Empires, dwellings of the kings of men;
Or should those fail that hold the helm,   100
    While the long day of knowledge grows and warms,
And in the heart of this most ancient realm
    A hateful voice be utter'd, and alarms
    Sounding 'To arms! to arms!'

9

A simpler, saner lesson might he learn   105
    Who reads thy gradual process, Holy Spring.
Thy leaves possess the season in their turn,
    And in their time thy warblers rise on wing.
How surely glidest thou from March to May,
    And changest, breathing it, the sullen wind,   110
Thy scope of operation, day by day,
    Larger and fuller, like the human mind!
Thy warmths from bud to bud
    Accomplish that blind model in the seed,
And men have hopes, which race the restless blood,   115
    That after many changes may succeed
    Life which is Life indeed.

1833–38?; 1889

Dora[3]

With farmer Allan at the farm abode
William and Dora. William was his son,
And she his niece. He often look'd at them,
And often thought, 'I'll make them man and wife.'
Now Dora felt her uncle's will in all,   5
And yearn'd toward William; but the youth, because
He had been always with her in the house,
Thought not of Dora.
           Then there came a day
When Allan call'd his son, and said: 'My son,
I married late, but I would wish to see   10

3. Although plainer in style, "Dora" is representative of the group of poems which Tennyson assembled in the edition of 1884 and called "English Idyls." Domestic in theme and patterned after Theocritus, the "Idyls" helped to establish an English literary genre which Tennyson's contemporaries and followers practiced in with very irregular success.

For the story of "Dora," Tennyson partly drew upon Miss Mitford's pastoral tale "Dora Cresswell," which was, he noted, "cheerful in tone, whereas this is sad." There are also similarities to Crabbe and Wordsworth (compare "Michael"), who reportedly remarked: "I have been endeavouring all my life to write a pastoral like your 'Dora' and have not succeeded" (*Memoir*, I, 265). As "The Two Voices" had suggested passages in *Job* to Carlyle, "Your 'Dora,'" he said, "reminds me of the *Book of Ruth*" (*Memoir*, I, 213). Of the poem's composition, Tennyson said it "had to be told in the simplest possible poetical language, and therefore was one of the poems which gave most trouble" (*Memoir*, I, 196).

My grandchild on my knees before I die;
And I have set my heart upon a match.
Now therefore look to Dora; she is well
To look to; thrifty too beyond her age.
She is my brother's daughter; he and I   15
Had once hard words,[4] and parted, and he died
In foreign lands; but for his sake I bred
His daughter Dora. Take her for your wife;
For I have wish'd this marriage, night and day,
For many years.' But William answer'd short: 20
'I cannot marry Dora; by my life,
I will not marry Dora!' Then the old man
Was wroth, and doubled up his hands, and said:
'You will not, boy! you dare to answer thus!
But in my time a father's word was law,   25
And so it shall be now for me. Look to it;
Consider, William, take a month to think,
And let me have an answer to my wish,
Or, by the Lord that made me, you shall pack,
And never more darken my doors again.'   30
But William answer'd madly, bit his lips,
And broke away. The more he look'd at her
The less he liked her; and his ways were harsh;
But Dora bore them meekly. Then before
The month was out he left his father's house,   35
And hired himself to work within the fields;
And half in love, half spite, he woo'd and wed
A laborer's daughter, Mary Morrison.
     Then, when the bells were ringing, Allan call'd
His niece and said: 'My girl, I love you well;   40
But if you speak with him that was my son,
Or change a word with her he calls his wife,
My home is none of yours. My will is law.'
And Dora promised, being meek. She thought,
'It cannot be; my uncle's mind will change!'   45
     And days went on, and there was born a boy
To William; then distresses came on him,
And day by day he pass'd his father's gate,
Heart-broken, and his father helped him not.
But Dora stored what little she could save,   50
And sent it them by stealth, nor did they know
Who sent it; till at last a fever seized
On William, and in harvest time he died.
     Then Dora went to Mary. Mary sat
And look'd with tears upon her boy, and thought   55
Hard things of Dora. Dora came and said:
     'I have obey'd my uncle until now,
And I have sinn'd, for it was all thro' me

4. The quarrel is not in Miss Mitford's story.

This evil came on William at the first.
But, Mary, for the sake of him that 's gone,   60
And for your sake, the woman that he chose,
And for this orphan, I am come to you.
You know there has not been for these five years
So full a harvest. Let me take the boy,
And I will set him in my uncle's eye   65
Among the wheat; that when his heart is glad
Of the full harvest, he may see the boy,
And bless him for the sake of him that 's gone.'
   And Dora took the child, and went her way
Across the wheat, and sat upon a mound   70
That was unsown, where many poppies grew.
Far off the farmer came into the field[5]
And spied her not, for none of all his men
Dare tell him Dora waited with the child;
And Dora would have risen and gone to him,   75
But her heart fail'd her; and the reapers reap'd,
And the sun fell, and all the land was dark.
   But when the morrow came, she rose and took
The child once more, and sat upon the mound;
And made a little wreath of all the flowers   80
That grew about, and tied it round his hat
To make him pleasing in her uncle's eye.
Then when the farmer pass'd into the field
He spied her, and he left his men at work,
And came and said: 'Where were you yesterday?   85
Whose child is that? What are you doing here?'
So Dora cast her eyes upon the ground,
And answer'd softly, 'This is William's child!'
'And did I not,' said Allan, 'did I not
Forbid you, Dora?' Dora said again: 90
'Do with me as you will, but take the child,
And bless him for the sake of him that 's gone!'
And Allan said: 'I see it is a trick
Got up betwixt you and the woman there.
I must be taught my duty, and by you!   95
You knew my word was law, and yet you dared
To slight it. Well—for I will take the boy;
But go you hence, and never see me more.'
   So saying, he took the boy that cried aloud
And struggled hard. The wreath of flowers fell   100
At Dora's feet. She bow'd upon her hands,
And the boy's cry came to her from the field
More and more distant. She bow'd down her head,
Remembering the day when first she came,
And all the things that had been. She bow'd down   105

5. "From this line to the end of the   ford," Tennyson noted.
poem I have not followed Miss Mit-

And wept in secret; and the reapers reap'd,
And the sun fell, and all the land was dark.
   Then Dora went to Mary's house, and stood
Upon the threshold. Mary saw the boy
Was not with Dora. She broke out in praise   110
To God, that help'd her in her widowhood.
And Dora said: 'My uncle took the boy;
But, Mary, let me live and work with you:
He says that he will never see me more.'
Then answer'd Mary: 'This shall never be,   115
That thou shouldst take my trouble on thyself;
And, now I think, he shall not have the boy,
For he will teach him hardness, and to slight
His mother. Therefore thou and I will go,
And I will have my boy, and bring him home;   120
And I will beg of him to take thee back.
But if he will not take thee back again,
Then thou and I will live within one house,
And work for William's child, until he grows
Of age to help us.'
                 So the women kiss'd   125
Each other, and set out, and reach'd the farm.
The door was off the latch; they peep'd, and saw
The boy set up betwixt his grandsire's knees,
Who thrust him in the hollows of his arm,
And clapt him on the hands and on the cheeks,   130
Like one that loved him; and the lad stretch'd out
And babbled for the golden seal, that hung
From Allan's watch and sparkled by the fire.
Then they came in; but when the boy beheld
His mother, he cried out to come to her;   135
And Allan set him down, and Mary said:
   'O father!—if you let me call you so—
I never came a-begging for myself,
Or William, or this child; but now I come
For Dora; take her back, she loves you well.   140
O Sir, when William died, he died at peace
With all men; for I ask'd him, and he said,
He could not ever rue his marrying me—
I had been a patient wife; but, Sir, he said
That he was wrong to cross his father thus.   145
"God bless him!" he said, "and may he never know
The troubles I have gone thro'!" Then he turn'd
His face and pass'd—unhappy that I am!
But now, Sir, let me have my boy, for you
Will make him hard, and he will learn to slight   150
His father's memory; and take Dora back,
And let all this be as it was before.'
   So Mary said, and Dora hid her face

By Mary. There was silence in the room;
And all at once the old man burst in sobs: 155
    'I have been to blame—to blame. I have kill'd my son.
I have kill'd him—but I loved him—my dear son.
May God forgive me!—I have been to blame.
Kiss me, my children.'
                    Then they clung about
The old man's neck, and kiss'd him many times.   160
And all the man was broken with remorse;
And all his love came back a hundred-fold;
And for three hours he sobb'd o'er William's child
Thinking of William.
                    So those four abode
Within one house together, and as years   165
Went forward Mary took another mate;
But Dora lived unmarried till her death.

1834–35; 1842

A Farewell[6]

Flow down, cold rivulet, to the sea,
    Thy tribute wave deliver;
No more by thee my steps shall be,
    For ever and for ever.

Flow, softly flow, by lawn and lea,   5
    A rivulet, then a river;
Nowhere by thee my steps shall be,
    For ever and for ever.

But here will sigh thine alder-tree,
    And here thine aspen shiver;   10
And here by thee will hum the bee,
    For ever and for ever.

A thousand suns will stream on thee,
    A thousand moons will quiver;
But not by thee my steps shall be,   15
    For ever and for ever.

1837; 1842

Locksley Hall[7]

Comrades, leave me here a little, while as yet 't is early morn;
Leave me here, and when you want me, sound upon the bugle-horn.

6. The Tennyson family moved out of
the rectory at Somersby during the
spring of 1837. See *In Memoriam*, 103,
for the dream the poet had the night
before they left. The brook is also de-
scribed in "Ode to Memory," p. 532.

7. The poem is a dramatic monologue
which represents, according to Tenny-
son, "young life, its good side, its de-
ficiencies, and its yearnings" (*Memoir*,
I, 195). Speaker, place and incidents
are fictional. As the poet noted,

'T is the place, and all around it, as of old, the curlews call,
Dreary gleams[8] about the moorland flying over Locksley Hall;

Locksley Hall, that in the distance overlooks the sandy tracts,   5
And the hollow ocean-ridges roaring into cataracts.

Many a night from yonder ivied casement, ere I went to rest,
Did I look on great Orion sloping slowly to the west.

Many a night I saw the Pleiads,[9] rising thro' the mellow shade,
Glitter like a swarm of fireflies tangled in a silver braid.   10

Here about the beach I wander'd, nourishing a youth sublime
With the fairy tales of science, and the long result of time;

When the centuries behind me like a fruitful land reposed;
When I clung to all the present for the promise that it closed;

When I dipt into the future far as human eye could see,   15
Saw the vision of the world and all the wonder that would be.—

In the spring a fuller crimson comes upon the robin's breast;
In the spring the wanton lapwing gets himself another crest;

In the spring a livelier iris changes on the burnish'd dove;
In the spring a young man's fancy lightly turns to thoughts of love.   20

Then her cheek was pale and thinner than should be for one so young,
And her eyes on all my motions with a mute observance hung.

And I said, "My cousin Amy, speak, and speak the truth to me,
Trust me, cousin, all the current of my being sets to thee."

On her pallid cheek and forehead came a color and a light,   25
As I have seen the rosy red flushing in the northern night.

And she turn'd—her bosom shaken with a sudden storm of sighs—
All the spirit deeply dawning in the dark of hazel eyes—

Saying, "I have hid my feelings, fearing they should do me wrong,"
Saying, "Dost thou love me, cousin?" weeping, "I have loved thee long."   30

" 'Locksley Hall' is an imaginary place (tho' the coast is Lincolnshire) and the hero is imaginary" (*Memoir*, I, 195). Having been jilted by Amy, the speaker does, however, bear some resemblance to Tennyson's older brother Frederick, whose impetuous infatuation for his cousin Julia was thwarted by her parents. Similarly, Tennyson's more genuine relationship with Rosa Barring, to whom he had written several love poems between 1834 and 1836, was squelched by her parents. See *Alfred Tennyson*, pp. 162–163. Hallam recalls his father saying that Sir William Jones's prose translation of the *Moâllakât*, the seven Arabic poems hanging in the temple of Mecca, "gave him the idea of the poem," and the meter was reportedly suggested by Arthur Hallam's father, who thought "the English people liked verse in Trochaics" (*Memoir*, I, 195). 8. Tennyson said that the "gleams" do not refer to the curlews, as some commentators insist; he meant the line to read: "while dreary gleams of light are flying across a dreary moorland." 9. I. e., the Pleiades, a constellation which, like Orion, is especially brilliant in winter and early spring.

Love took up the glass of Time, and turn'd it in his glowing hands;
Every moment, lightly shaken, ran itself in golden sands.

Love took up the harp of Life, and smote on all the chords with
  might;
Smote the chord of Self, that, trembling, past in music out of sight.

Many a morning on the moorland did we hear the copses ring, 35
And her whisper throng'd my pulses with the fulness of the spring.

Many an evening by the waters did we watch the stately ships,
And our spirits rush'd together at the touching of the lips.

O my cousin, shallow-hearted! O my Amy, mine no more!
O the dreary, dreary moorland! O the barren, barren shore! 40

Falser than all fancy fathoms,[1] falser than all songs have sung,
Puppet to a father's threat, and servile to a shrewish tongue!

Is it well to wish thee happy?—having known me—to decline
On a range of lower feelings and a narrower heart than mine!

Yet it shall be; thou shalt lower to his level day by day, 45
What is fine within thee growing coarse to sympathize with clay.

As the husband is, the wife is; thou art mated with a clown,[2]
And the grossness of his nature will have weight to drag thee down.

He will hold thee, when his passion shall have spent its novel force,
Something better than his dog, a little dearer than his horse. 50

What is this? his eyes are heavy; think not they are glazed with wine.
Go to him, it is thy duty; kiss him, take his hand in thine.

It may be my lord is weary, that his brain is overwrought;
Soothe him with thy finer fancies, touch him with thy lighter
  thought.

He will answer to the purpose, easy things to understand— 55
Better thou wert dead before me, tho' I slew thee with my hand!

Better thou and I were lying, hidden from the heart's disgrace,
Roll'd in one another's arms, and silent in a last embrace.

Cursed be the social wants that sin against the strength of youth!
Cursed be the social lies that warp us from the living truth! 60

Cursed be the sickly forms that err from honest Nature's rule!
Cursed be the gold that gilds the straiten'd[3] forehead of the fool!

Well—'t is well that I should bluster!—Hadst thou less unworthy
  proved—
Would to God—for I had loved thee more than ever wife was loved.

Am I mad, that I should cherish that which bears but bitter fruit? 65
I will pluck it from my bosom, tho' my heart be at the root.

---

1. A verb, not a noun.   3. Narrowed, i. e., a "lowbrow."
2. A stupid, crude lout.

Never, tho' my mortal summers to such length of years should
    come
As the many-winter'd crow[4] that leads the clanging rookery home.

Where is comfort? in division of the records of the mind?
Can I part her from herself, and love her, as I knew her, kind?   70

I remember one that perish'd; sweetly did she speak and move;
Such a one do I remember, whom to look at was to love.

Can I think of her as dead, and love her for the love she bore?
No—she never loved me truly; love is love for evermore.

Comfort? comfort scorn'd of devils! this is truth the poet[5] sings,   75
That a sorrow's crown of sorrow is remembering happier things.

Drug thy memories, lest thou learn it, lest thy heart be put to proof,
In the dead unhappy night, and when the rain is on the roof.

Like a dog, he hunts in dreams, and thou art staring at the wall,
Where the dying night-lamp flickers, and the shadows rise and
    fall.   80

Then a hand shall pass before thee, pointing to his drunken sleep,
To thy widow'd[6] marriage-pillows, to the tears that thou wilt weep.

Thou shalt hear the "Never, never," whisper'd by the phantom
    years,
And a song from out the distance in the ringing of thine ears;

And an eye shall vex thee, looking ancient kindness on thy pain.   85
Turn thee, turn thee on thy pillow; get thee to thy rest again.

Nay, but Nature brings thee solace; for a tender voice will cry.
'T is a purer life than thine, a lip to drain thy trouble dry.

Baby lips will laugh me down; my latest rival brings thee rest.
Baby fingers, waxen touches, press me from the mother's breast.   90

O, the child too clothes the father with a dearness not his due.
Half is thine and half is his; it will be worthy of the two.

O, I see thee old and formal, fitted to thy petty part,
With a little hoard of maxims preaching down a daughter's heart.

"They were dangerous guides the feelings—she herself was not
    exempt—   95
Truly, she herself had suffer'd"—Perish in thy self-contempt!

Overlive it—lower yet—be happy! wherefore should I care?
I myself must mix with action, lest I wither by despair.

What is that which I should turn to, lighting upon days like these?
Every door is barr'd with gold, and opens but to golden keys.   100

Every gate is throng'd with suitors, all the markets overflow.
I have but an angry fancy; what is that which I should do?

4. The long-lived English rook.
5. Dante in the *Inferno*, V, 121–123.
6. His lack of attention has figuratively
widowed her. For a nocturnal visit
of the rejected lover, compare John
Donne's poem "The Apparition."

I had been content to perish, falling on the foeman's ground,
When the ranks are roll'd in vapor, and the winds are laid with
    sound.[7]

But the jingling of the guinea helps the hurt that Honor feels,   105
And the nations do but murmur, snarling at each other's heels.

Can I but relive in sadness? I will turn that earlier page.
Hide me from my deep emotion, O thou wondrous Mother-Age!

Make me feel the wild pulsation that I felt before the strife,
When I heard my days before me, and the tumult of my life;   110

Yearning for the large excitement that the coming years would
    yield,
Eager-hearted as a boy when first he leaves his father's field,

And at night along the dusky highway near and nearer drawn,
Sees in heaven the light of London flaring like a dreary dawn;[8]

And his spirit leaps within him to be gone before him then,   115
Underneath the light he looks at, in among the throngs of men;

Men, my brothers, men the workers, ever reaping something new;
That which they have done but earnest[9] of the things that they shall
    do.

For I dipt into the future, far as human eye could see,
Saw the Vision of the world, and all the wonder that would be;   120

Saw the heavens fill with commerce, argosies of magic sails,[1]
Pilots of the purple twilight, dropping down with costly bales;

Heard the heavens fill with shouting, and there rain'd a ghastly dew
From the nations' airy navies grappling in the central blue;

Far along the world-wide whisper of the south-wind rushing
    warm,   125
With the standards of the peoples plunging thro' the thunder-storm;

Till the war-drum throbb'd no longer, and the battle-flags were
    furl'd
In the Parliament of man, the Federation of the world.

There the common sense of most shall hold a fretful realm in awe,
And the kindly earth shall slumber, lapt in universal law.   130

So I triumph'd ere my passion sweeping thro' me left me dry,
Left me with the palsied heart, and left me with the jaundiced eye;

7. Cannon firing supposedly stilled the winds.
8. This couplet describes a night journey from High Beech, where the Tennysons moved after leaving Somersby, to London; the simile, Tennyson noted, was "from old times and the top of the mail-coach. They that go by train seldom see this."

9. A pledge, i. e., assurance of future achievements.
1. Much has been claimed for this line as making Tennyson a prophet of modern aviation. Manned balloon flights were a novelty in the England of the thirties, and he was probably thinking only of lighter-than-air craft.

Eye, to which all order festers, all things here are out of joint.
Science moves, but slowly, slowly, creeping on from point to point;

Slowly comes a hungry people, as a lion, creeping nigher,   135
Glares at one that nods and winks behind a slowly-dying fire.[2]

Yet I doubt not thro' the ages one increasing purpose runs,
And the thoughts of men are widen'd with the process of the suns.[3]

What is that to him that reaps not harvest of his youthful joys,
Tho' the deep heart of existence beat for ever like a boy's?   140

Knowledge comes, but wisdom lingers, and I linger on the shore,
And the individual withers, and the world is more and more.[4]

Knowledge comes, but wisdom lingers, and he bears a laden breast,
Full of sad experience, moving toward the stillness of his rest.

Hark, my merry comrades call me, sounding on the bugle-horn,   145
They to whom my foolish passion were a target for their scorn.

Shall it not be scorn to me to harp on such a moulder'd string?
I am shamed thro' all my nature to have loved so slight a thing.

Weakness to be wroth with weakness! woman's pleasure, woman's
  pain—
Nature made them blinder motions bounded in a shallower   150
  brain.

Woman is the lesser man, and all thy passions, match'd with mine,
Are as moonlight unto sunlight, and as water unto wine—

Here at least, where nature sickens, nothing. Ah, for some retreat
Deep in yonder shining Orient, where my life began to beat,

Where in wild Mahratta-battle[5] fell my father evil-starr'd;—   155
I was left a trampled orphan, and a selfish uncle's ward.

Or to burst all links of habit—there to wander far away,
On from island unto island at the gateways of the day.

Larger constellations burning, mellow moons and happy skies,
Breadths of tropic shade and palms in cluster, knots of Paradise.   160

Never comes the trader, never floats an European flag,
Slides the bird o'er lustrous woodland, swings the trailer[6] from the
  crag;

Droops the heavy-blossom'd bower, hangs the heavy-fruited tree—
Summer isles of Eden lying in dark-purple spheres of sea.

2. Suggests the gradual encroachment of democracy upon the dying aristocratic establishment. Contrast "Locksley Hall Sixty Years After," lines 247 ff, for a similarly expressed but completely unsympathetic point of view.
3. Compare Tennyson's dream on the night before leaving Somersby as recorded in *In Memoriam*, 103. Both the vision and the dream are involved with journeys, are conceivably variations of the single experience, and suggest that this part of "Locksley Hall" may have been composed concurrently with section 103 sometime in 1837.
4. A belief shared by a number of Tennyson's contemporaries, notably by John Stuart Mill in his "Essay on Civilization" (1836).
5. Alludes to wars in India violently fought in 1803 and 1817 by a Hindu tribe against the British.
6. A vine.

There methinks would be enjoyment more than in this march of
    mind,   165
In the steamship, in the railway, in the thoughts that shake man-
    kind.

There the passions cramp'd no longer shall have scope and breathing
    space;
I will take some savage woman, she shall rear my dusky race.

Iron-jointed, supple-sinew'd, they shall dive, and they shall run,
Catch the wild goat by the hair, and hurl their lances in the sun;   170

Whistle back the parrot's call and leap the rainbows of the brooks,
Not with blinded eyesight poring over miserable books—

Fool, again the dream, the fancy! but I *know* my words are wild,
But I count the gray barbarian lower than the Christian child.

I, to herd with narrow foreheads, vacant of our glorious gains,   175
Like a beast with lower pleasures, like a beast with lower pains![7]

Mated with a squalid savage—what to me were sun or clime?
I the heir of all the ages, in the foremost files of time—

I that rather held it better men should perish one by one,
Than that earth should stand at gaze like Joshua's moon in
    Ajalon![8]   180

Not in vain the distance beacons. Forward, forward let us range,
Let the great world spin for ever down the ringing grooves[9] of
    change.

Thro' the shadow of the globe we sweep into the younger day;
Better fifty years of Europe than a cycle of Cathay.[1]

Mother-Age,—for mine I knew not,—help me as when life
    begun;   185
Rift the hills, and roll the waters, flash the lightnings, weigh the
    sun.

O, I see the crescent promise of my spirit hath not set.
Ancient founts of inspiration well thro' all my fancy yet.

Howsoever these things be, a long farewell to Locksley Hall!
Now for me the woods may wither, now for me the roof-tree fall.   190

Comes a vapor from the margin, blackening over heath and holt,
Cramming all the blast before it, in its breast a thunderbolt.

Let it fall on Locksley Hall, with rain or hail, or fire or snow;
For the mighty wind arises, roaring seaward, and I go.

1835 ff.; 1842

7. Compare the opening of "Ulysses."
8. Joshua commanded that the sun and
moon stand still while the Israelites
continued the slaughter of their en-
emies in the valley of Ajalon. (See
Joshua, 10:12–13.)
9. "When I went by the first train from
Liverpool to Manchester (1830), I
thought that the wheels ran in a
groove" (*Memoir*, I, 195).
1. Ancient name for China; to the
progressive minds of the nineteenth
century a remote, static civilization.

Love and Duty[2]

Of love that never found his earthly close,
What sequel? Streaming eyes and breaking hearts?
Or all the same as if he had not been?
    Not so. Shall Error in the round of time
Still father Truth? O, shall the braggart shout   5
For some blind glimpse of freedom work itself
Thro' madness, hated by the wise, to law,
System, and empire? Sin itself be found
The cloudy porch oft opening on the sun?
And only he, this wonder, dead, become   10
Mere highway dust? or year by year alone
Sit brooding in the ruins of a life,
Nightmare of youth, the spectre of himself?
    If this were thus, if this, indeed, were all,
Better the narrow brain, the stony heart,   15
The staring eye glazed o'er with sapless days,
The long mechanic pacings to and fro,
The set gray life, and apathetic end.
But am I not the nobler thro' thy love?
O, three times less unworthy! likewise thou   20
Art more thro' Love, and greater than thy years,
The sun will run his orbit, and the moon
Her circle. Wait, and Love himself will bring
The drooping flower of knowledge changed to fruit
Of wisdom. Wait; my faith is large in Time,   25
And that which shapes it to some perfect end.
    Will some one say, Then why not ill for good?
Why took ye not your pastime? To that man
My work shall answer, since I knew the right
And did it; for a man is not as God,   30
But then most Godlike being most a man.—
So let me think 't is well for thee and me—
Ill-fated that I am, what lot is mine
Whose foresight preaches peace, my heart so slow
To feel it! For how hard it seem'd to me,   35
When eyes, love-languid thro' half tears would dwell
One earnest, earnest moment upon mine,
Then not to dare to see! when thy low voice,
Faltering, would break its syllables, to keep

---

2. Tennyson first met Emily Sellwood in 1830 when she and her family called at Somersby (*Memoir*, I, 148) and became engaged to her around the time of his brother Charles's wedding to Emily's sister in 1836 (see "Move Eastward, Happy Earth"). The engagement, not formally recognized by the Sellwoods until 1838, was broken off in 1840 when Emily's father forbade further correspondence between them. See *Memoir*, I, 167–176, and *Alfred Tennyson*, pp. 179–183. The poet's occupation, his lack of money, his bohemian manners and appearance—and perhaps particularly the dissolution of Charles and Louisa's marriage—were doubtless convincing arguments for the conservative Mr. Sellwood against losing another daughter to a Tennyson.

My own full-tuned,—hold passion in a leash,   40
And not leap forth and fall about thy neck,
And on thy bosom—deep desired relief!—
Rain out the heavy mist of tears, that weigh'd
Upon my brain, my senses, and my soul!
    For Love himself took part against himself   45
To warn us off, and Duty loved of Love—
O, this world's curse—beloved but hated—came
Like Death betwixt thy dear embrace and mine,
And crying, "Who is this? behold thy bride,"
She push'd me from thee.
                If the sense is hard   50
To alien ears, I did not speak to these—
No, not to thee, but to thyself in me.
Hard is my doom and thine; thou knowest it all.
    Could Love part thus? was it not well to speak,
To have spoken once? It could not but be well.   55
The slow sweet hours that bring us all things good,
The slow sad hours that bring us all things ill,
And all good things from evil, brought the night
In which we sat together and alone,
And to the want that hollow'd all the heart   60
Gave utterance by the yearning of an eye,
That burn'd upon its object thro' such tears
As flow but once a life.
               The trance gave way
To those caresses, when a hundred times
In that last kiss, which never was the last,   65
Farewell, like endless welcome, lived and died.
Then follow'd counsel, comfort, and the words
That make a man feel strong in speaking truth;
Till now the dark was worn, and overhead
The lights of sunset and of sunrise mix'd   70
In that brief night, the summer night, that paused
Among her stars to hear us, stars that hung
Love-charm'd to listen; all the wheels of Time
Spun round in station, but the end had come.
    O, then, like those who clench their nerves to rush   75
Upon their dissolution, we two rose,
There—closing like an individual life—
In one blind cry of passion and of pain,
Like bitter accusation even to death,
Caught up the whole of love and utter'd it,   80
And bade adieu for ever.
             Live—yet live—
Shall sharpest pathos blight us, knowing all
Life needs for life is possible to will?—
Live happy; tend thy flowers; be tended by
My blessing! Should my Shadow cross thy thoughts   85

Too sadly for their peace, remand it thou
For calmer hours to Memory's darkest hold,
If not to be forgotten—not at once—
Not all forgotten. Should it cross thy dreams,
O, might it come like one that looks content,   90
With quiet eyes unfaithful to the truth,
And point thee forward to a distant light,
Or seem to lift a burthen from thy heart
And leave thee freer, till thou wake refresh'd
Then when the first low matin-chirp hath grown   95
Full quire, and morning driven her plow of pearl
Far furrowing into light the mounded rack,
Beyond the fair green field and eastern sea.

1840?; 1842

Amphion[3]

My father left a park to me,
    But it is wild and barren,
A garden too with scarce a tree,
    And waster than a warren;
Yet say the neighbors when they call   5
    It is not bad but good land,
And in it is the germ of all
    That grows within the woodland.

O, had I lived when song was great
    In days of old Amphion,   10
And ta'en my fiddle to the gate,
    Nor cared for seed or scion!
And had I lived when song was great,
    And legs of trees were limber,
And ta'en my fiddle to the gate,   15
    And fiddled in the timber!

'T is said he had a tuneful tongue,
    Such happy intonation,
Wherever he sat down and sung
    He left a small plantation;   20
Wherever in a lonely grove
    He set up his forlorn pipes,
The gouty oak began to move,
    And flounder into hornpipes.

The mountain stirr'd its bushy crown,   25
    And, as tradition teaches,

3. In Greek mythology Amphion was a harper of such skill that the stones for the walls of Thebes were drawn into their places by his music. See "Tiresias," line 96. In Tennyson's allegory, Amphion is given similar powers over all nature. The poem expresses once more the notion of poetry's diminished state in the modern world. Compare "The Poet," p. 8.

Young ashes pirouetted down
   Coquetting with young beeches;
And briony-vine[4] and ivy-wreath
   Ran forward to his rhyming,   30
And from the valleys underneath
   Came little copses climbing.

The linden broke her ranks and rent
   The woodbine wreaths that bind her,
And down the middle, buzz! she went   35
   With all her bees behind her;
The poplars, in long order due,
   With cypress promenaded,
The shock-head willows two and two
   By rivers gallopaded.   40

Came wet-shod alder from the wave,
   Came yews, a dismal coterie;
Each pluck'd his one foot from the grave,
   Poussetting[5] with a sloe-tree;
Old elms came breaking from the vine,   45
   The vine stream'd out to follow,
And, sweating rosin, plump'd the pine
   From many a cloudy hollow.

And was n't it a sight to see,
   When, ere his song was ended,   50
Like some great landslip, tree by tree,
   The country-side descended;
And shepherds from the mountain-eaves
   Look'd down, half-pleased, half-frighten'd,
As dash'd about the drunken leaves   55
   The random sunshine lighten'd?

O, Nature first was fresh to men,
   And wanton without measure;
So youthful and so flexile then,
   You moved her at your pleasure.   60
Twang out, my fiddle! shake the twigs!
   And make her dance attendance;
Blow, flute, and stir the stiff-set sprigs,
   And scirrhous roots and tendons!

'T is vain! in such a brassy age   65
   I could not move a thistle;
The very sparrows in the hedge
   Scarce answer to my whistle;
Or at the most, when three-parts-sick
   With strumming and with scraping,   70
A jackass heehaws from the rick,
   The passive oxen gaping.

4. Vines with red or black fruit.
5. The poussette is a dance in which one or more couples join hands and move in a circle.

But what is that I hear? a sound
    Like sleepy counsel pleading;
O Lord!—'t is in my neighbor's ground,   75
    The modern Muses reading.
They read Botanic Treatises,
    And Works on Gardening thro' there,
And Methods of Transplanting Trees
    To look as if they grew there.   80

The wither'd Misses! how they prose
    O'er books of travell'd seamen,
And show you slips of all that grows
    From England to Van Diemen.[6]
They read in arbors clipt and cut,   85
    And alleys faded places,
By squares of tropic summer shut
    And warm'd in crystal cases.

But these, tho' fed with careful dirt,
    Are neither green nor sappy;   90
Half-conscious of the garden-squirt,
    The spindlings look unhappy.
Better to me the meanest weed
    That blows upon its mountain,
The vilest herb that runs to seed   95
    Beside its native fountain.

And I must work thro' months of toil,
    And years of cultivation,
Upon my proper patch of soil
    To grow my own plantation.   100
I'll take the showers as they fall,
    I will not vex my bosom;
Enough if at the end of all
    A little garden blossom.

1842

The Vision of Sin[7]

1

I had a vision when the night was late;
A youth came riding toward a palace-gate.

6. Tasmania.
7. This dream-allegory may be read as a companion poem to "The Palace of Art," and much of it may have been written in the thirties. The young aesthete can be the artist whose sin is the denial of the creative principle —the failure of the ideal poet to realize the true purposes of art. "This describes the soul of a youth," Tennyson noted, "who has given himself up to pleasure and Epicureanism. He at length is worn out and wrapt in the mists of satiety. Afterwards he grows into a cynical old man afflicted with the 'curse of nature,' and joining in the Feast of Death. Then we see the landscape which symbolizes God, Law and the future life."

He rode a horse[8] with wings, that would have flown,
But that his heavy rider kept him down.
And from the palace came a child of sin,⁵
And took him by the curls, and led him in,
Where sat a company with heated eyes,
Expecting when a fountain[9] should arise.
A sleepy light upon their brows and lips—
As when the sun, a crescent of eclipse,¹⁰
Dreams over lake and lawn, and isles and capes—
Suffused them, sitting, lying, languid shapes,
By heaps of gourds, and skins of wine, and piles of grapes.

2

Then methought I heard a mellow sound,
Gathering up from all the lower ground;¹⁵
Narrowing in to where they sat assembled,
Low voluptuous music winding trembled,
Woven in circles. They that heard it sigh'd,
Panted hand-in-hand with faces pale,
Swung themselves, and in low tones replied;²⁰
Till the fountain spouted, showering wide
Sleet of diamond-drift and pearly hail.
Then the music touch'd the gates and died,
Rose again from where it seem'd to fail,
Storm'd in orbs of song, a growing gale;²⁵
Till thronging in and in, to where they waited,
As 't were a hundred-throated nightingale,
The strong tempestuous treble throbb'd and palpitated;
Ran into its giddiest whirl of sound,
Caught the sparkles, and in circles,³⁰
Purple gauzes, golden hazes, liquid mazes,
Flung the torrent rainbow round.
Then they started from their places,
Moved with violence, changed in hue,
Caught each other with wild grimaces,³⁵
Half-invisible to the view,
Wheeling with precipitate paces
To the melody, till they flew,
Hair and eyes and limbs and faces,
Twisted hard in fierce embraces,⁴⁰
Like to Furies, like to Graces,[1]
Dash'd together in blinding dew;
Till, kill'd with some luxurious agony,
The nerve-dissolving melody
Flutter'd headlong from the sky.⁴⁵

---

8. Pegasus, the horse associated with the Muses, would have carried the poet aloft toward the realization of his poetic aspirations.
9. Here, as in section 2, description of the fountain and palace suggest possible debts to Coleridge's "Kubla Khan" and Keats's "Lamia."
1. Three goddesses who personified loveliness; the three Furies, winged women often represented with snakes about them, were the avengers of crime.

3

And then I look'd up toward a mountain-tract,
That girt the region with high cliff and lawn.
I saw that every morning, far withdrawn
Beyond the darkness and the cataract,
God made Himself an awful rose of dawn,   50
Unheeded; and detaching, fold by fold,
From those still heights, and, slowly drawing near,
A vapor heavy, hueless, formless, cold,
Came floating on for many a month and year,
Unheeded; and I thought I would have spoken,   55
And warn'd that madman ere it grew too late,
But, as in dreams, I could not. Mine was broken,
When that cold vapor touch'd the palace-gate,
And link'd again. I saw within my head
A gray and gap-tooth'd man as lean as death,   60
Who slowly rode across a wither'd heath,
And lighted at a ruin'd inn, and said:

4

   "Wrinkled ostler, grim and thin!
      Here is custom come your way;
   Take my brute, and lead him in,   65
      Stuff his ribs with mouldy hay.

   "Bitter barmaid, waning fast!
      See that sheets are on my bed.
   What! the flower of life is past;
      It is long before you wed.   70

   "Slip-shod waiter, lank and sour,
      At the Dragon[2] on the heath!
   Let us have a quiet hour,
      Let us hob-and-nob with Death.

   "I am old, but let me drink;   75
      Bring me spices, bring me wine;
   I remember, when I think,
      That my youth was half divine.

   "Wine is good for shrivell'd lips,
      When a blanket wraps the day,   80
   When the rotten woodland drips,
      And the leaf is stamp'd in clay.

   "Sit thee down, and have no shame,
      Cheek by jowl, and knee by knee;
   What care I for any name?   85
      What for order or degree?

   "Let me screw thee up a peg;
      Let me loose thy tongue with wine;

2. Name of the inn.

Callest thou that thing a leg?
    Which is thinnest? thine or mine?   90

"Thou shalt not be saved by works,
    Thou hast been a sinner too;
Ruin'd trunks on wither'd forks,
    Empty scarecrows, I and you!

"Fill the cup and fill the can,   95
    Have a rouse before the morn;
Every moment dies a man,
    Every moment one is born.

"We are men of ruin'd blood;
    Therefore comes it we are wise.   100
Fish are we that love the mud,
    Rising to no fancy-flies.

"Name and fame! to fly sublime
    Thro' the courts, the camps, the schools,
Is to be the ball of Time,   105
    Bandied by the hands of fools.

"Friendship!—to be two in one—
    Let the canting liar pack!
Well I know, when I am gone,
    How she mouths behind my back.   110

"Virtue!—to be good and just—
    Every heart, when sifted well,
Is a clot of warmer dust,
    Mix'd with cunning sparks of hell.

"O, we two as well can look   115
    Whited thought and cleanly life
As the priest, above his book
    Leering at his neighbor's wife.

"Fill the cup and fill the can,
    Have a rouse before the morn: 120
Every moment dies a man,
    Every moment one is born.

"Drink, and let the parties rave;
    They are fill'd with idle spleen,
Rising, falling, like a wave,   125
    For they know not what they mean.

"He that roars for liberty
    Faster binds a tyrant's power,
And the tyrant's cruel glee
    Forces on the freer hour.   130

"Fill the can and fill the cup;
    All the windy ways of men

Are but dust that rises up,
    And is lightly laid again.

"Greet her with applausive breath,   135
    Freedom, gaily doth she tread;
In her right a civic wreath,
    In her left a human head.[3]

"No, I love not what is new;
    She is of an ancient house,   140
And I think we know the hue
    Of that cap upon her brows.

"Let her go! her thirst she slakes
    Where the bloody conduit runs,
Then her sweetest meal she makes   145
    On the first-born of her sons.

"Drink to lofty hopes[4] that cool,—
    Visions of a perfect State;
Drink we, last, the public fool,
    Frantic love and frantic hate.   150

"Chant me now some wicked stave,
    Till thy drooping courage rise,
And the glow-worm of the grave
    Glimmer in thy rheumy[5] eyes.

"Fear not thou to loose thy tongue,   155
    Set thy hoary fancies free;
What is loathsome to the young
    Savors well to thee and me.

"Change, reverting to the years,
    When thy nerves could understand   160
What there is in loving tears,
    And the warmth of hand in hand.

"Tell me tales of thy first love—
    April hopes, the fools of chance—
Till the graves begin to move,   165
    And the dead begin to dance.

"Fill the can and fill the cup;
    All the windy ways of men
Are but dust that rises up,
    And is lightly laid again.   170

"Trooping from their mouldy dens
    The chap-fallen circle spreads—
Welcome, fellow-citizens,
    Hollow hearts and empty heads!

3. Probably an allusion to the French Revolution. Compare "The Palace of Art," lines 151–152.
4. Until the Reign of Terror, several of the first generation of Romantic poets, notably Coleridge and Wordsworth, had high hopes for the Revolution.
5. Diseased and watery.

"You are bones, and what of that?   175
    Every face, however full,
Padded round with flesh and fat,
    Is but modell'd on a skull.

"Death is king, and Vivat Rex!
    Tread a measure on the stones,   180
Madam—if I know your sex
    From the fashion of your bones.

"No, I cannot praise the fire
    In your eye—nor yet your lip;
All the more do I admire   185
    Joints of cunning workmanship.

"Lo! God's likeness—the ground-plan—
    Neither modell'd, glazed, nor framed;
Buss[6] me, thou rough sketch of man,
    Far too naked to be shamed!   190

"Drink to Fortune, drink to Chance,
    While we keep a little breath!
Drink to heavy Ignorance!
    Hob-and-nob with brother Death!

"Thou art mazed, the night is long,   195
    And the longer night is near—
What! I am not all as wrong
    As a bitter jest is dear.

"Youthful hopes, by scores, to all,
    When the locks are crisp and curl'd;   200
Unto me my maudlin gall
    And my mockeries of the world.

"Fill the cup and fill the can;
    Mingle madness, mingle scorn!
Dregs of life, and lees of man;   205
    Yet we will not die forlorn."

5

The voice grew faint; there came a further change;
Once more uprose the mystic mountain-range.
Below were men and horses pierced with worms,
And slowly quickening into lower forms;   210
By shards[7] and scurf of salt, and scum of dross,
Old plash of rains, and refuse patch'd with moss.
Then some one spake: "Behold! it was a crime
Of sense avenged by sense that wore with time."
Another said: "The crime of sense became   215
The crime of malice, and is equal blame."
And one: "He had not wholly quench'd his power;

---

6. Kiss.
7. Scales; "scurf," flakes. A devolution of life into the primeval state.

A little grain of conscience made him sour."
At last I heard a voice upon the slope
Cry to the summit, "Is there any hope?"   220
To which an answer peal'd from that high land,
But in a tongue no man could understand;
And on the glimmering limit far withdrawn
God made Himself an awful rose of dawn.[8]

1842

The New Timon and the Poets[9]

We know him, out of Shakespeare's art,
    And those fine curses which he spoke;
The old Timon, with his noble heart,
    That, strongly loathing, greatly broke.

So died the Old: here comes the New.   5
    Regard him: a familiar face:
I thought we knew him: What, it's you,
    The padded man—that wears the stays—

Who killed the girls and thrilled the boys
    With dandy pathos when you wrote!   10
A Lion, you, that made a noise,
    And shook a mane *en papillotes.*[1]

And once you tried the Muses too;
    You failed, Sir: therefore now you turn,
To fall on those who are to you   15
    As Captain is to Subaltern.[2]

But men of long-enduring hopes,
    And careless what this hour may bring,

8. When John Tyndall asked Tennyson to explain the line, he answered evasively: "the power of explaining such concentrated expressions of the imagination was very different from that of writing them" (*Memoir*, II, 475). More revealing is a passage from a letter to Emily Sellwood in 1839: "To me often the far-off world seems nearer than the present, for in the present is always something unreal and indistinct, but the other seems a good solid planet, rolling round its green hills and paradises to the harmony of more steadfast laws. There steam up from about me mists of weakness, or sin, or despondency, and roll between me and the far planet, but it is there still" (*Memoir*, I, 171–172).
9. In December 1845 Edward Bulwer-Lytton published the first part of his long satiric poem *The New Timon: A Romance of London;* on January 12, 1846, he followed up with a second issue in which he accused "*School-Miss Alfred*" of "outbabying Wordsworth and outglittering Keates [*sic*]." Tennyson sent his poem to his friend John Forster, who, without the poet's knowledge, sent it along to *Punch*, in which it appeared on February 28, signed "Alcibiades." See *Memoir*, I, 244–245, and *Alfred Tennyson*, pp. 208 ff. Tennyson would never authorize publication of his poem. "Let those wretched literary squabbles be forgotten," he said in 1872, "I hate spite: I am black-blooded like all the Tennysons. I remember all the malignant things said against me, but little of the praise" (*Memoir*, II, 120).
1. In curlpapers.
2. In the British army, a commissioned officer below the rank of captain, hence, a subordinate.

Can pardon little would-be Popes[3]
    And Brummels, when they try to sting.   20

An Artist, Sir, should rest in Art,
    And waive a little of his claim;
To have the deep Poetic heart
    Is more than all poetic fame.

But you, Sir, you are hard to please;   25
    You never look but half content;
Nor like a gentleman at ease,
    With moral breadth of temperament.

And what with spites and what with fears,
    You cannot let a body be: 30
It's always ringing in your ears,
    "They call this man as good as *me*."

What profits now to understand
    The merits of a spotless shirt—
A dapper boot—a little hand—   35
    If half the little soul is dirt?

You talk of tinsel! why, we see
    The old mark of rouge upon your cheeks.
You prate of Nature! you are he
    That spilt his life about the cliques.   40

A Timon you! Nay, nay, for shame:
    It looks too arrogant a jest—
The fierce old man—to take his name,
    You bandbox. Off, and let him rest.

1846

SONGS FROM *THE PRINCESS*[1] (1847, 1850), AND TWO POEMS WRITTEN BEFORE 1850

"Sweet and Low"

Sweet and low, sweet and low,
    Wind of the western sea,
Low, low, breathe and blow,
    Wind of the western sea!
Over the rolling waters go,   5
Come from the dying moon, and blow,
    Blow him again to me;
While my little one, while my pretty one sleeps.

3. The eighteenth-century satirist, Alexander Pope; Beau Brummel (1778–1840), the famous English dandy and wit.

1. "My book is out and I hate it, and so no doubt will you," Tennyson wrote FitzGerald (*Memoir*, I, 260). In this long didactic poem, Tennyson osten-

Sleep and rest, sleep and rest,
   Father will come to thee soon;   10
Rest, rest, on mother's breast,
   Father will come to thee soon;
Father will come to his babe in the nest,
Silver sails all out of the west
   Under the silver moon;   15
Sleep, my little one, sleep, my pretty one, sleep.

1850

"The Splendor Falls"[2]

The splendor falls on castle walls
   And snowy summits old in story;
The long light shakes across the lakes,
   And the wild cataract leaps in glory.
Blow, bugle, blow, set the wild echoes flying,   5
Blow, bugle; answer, echoes, dying, dying, dying.

O, hark, O, hear! how thin and clear,
   And thinner, clearer, farther going!
O, sweet and far from cliff and scar
   The horns of Elfland faintly blowing!   10
Blow, let us hear the purple glens replying,
Blow, bugle; answer, echoes, dying, dying, dying.

O love, they die in yon rich sky,
   They faint on hill or field or river;
Our echoes roll from soul to soul,   15
   And grow for ever and for ever.
Blow, bugle, blow, set the wild echoes flying,
And answer, echoes, answer, dying, dying, dying.

1850

sibly set out to argue for women's rights, specifically in higher education. After publication in 1847, the "medley" was much altered through numerous subsequent editions making it the most worked over of the longer poems. The constant tinkering showed the poet's continuing dissatisfaction with it. Although highly regarded through the sixties, the poem's declining popularity was marked by Gilbert and Sullivan's successful parody in the operetta *Princess Ida* (1884). Perhaps the confusion in point of view, largely the result of a half-serious, half-mocking tone—hence "medley" as the poet called it—contributes most to the poem's deserved obscurity. FitzGerald reportedly said that he "gave up all hope of Tennyson after 'The Princess'" (*Memoir*, I, 253). However, the splendid blank verse lyrics, which appeared in the first edition, and the so-called intercalary songs (in rhyme), which were added in 1850, are clearly among the finest in the language. The following selections are reproduced in the order they appear in the poem.

2. Inspired by the echoes of the boatsman's bugle over the lakes at Killarney, Ireland, which Tennyson visited in 1848. See *Memoir*, I, 291–292. "So you're the gentleman that brought the money to the place," a boatman told Tennyson on his last visit there—a measure of the lyric's popularity in terms of the tourist trade. Known as "The Bugle Song," it was the one song FitzGerald praised; none of the others, he felt, had "the old champagne flavour" (*Memoir*, I, 253).

"Tears, Idle Tears"[3]

Tears, idle tears, I know not what they mean,
Tears from the depth of some divine despair
Rise in the heart, and gather to the eyes,
In looking on the happy autumn-fields,
And thinking of the days that are no more.   5

Fresh as the first beam glittering on a sail,
That brings our friends up from the underworld,
Sad as the last which reddens over one
That sinks with all we love below the verge;
So sad, so fresh, the days that are no more.   10

Ah, sad and strange as in dark summer dawns
The earliest pipe of half-awaken'd birds
To dying ears, when unto dying eyes
The casement slowly grows a glimmering square;
So sad, so strange, the days that are no more.   15

Dear as remember'd kisses after death,
And sweet as those by hopeless fancy feign'd
On lips that are for others; deep as love,
Deep as first love, and wild with all regret;
O Death in Life, the days that are no more!   20

1847

"O Swallow, Swallow"[4]

O Swallow, Swallow, flying, flying south,
Fly to her, and fall upon her gilded eaves,
And tell her, tell her, what I tell to thee.

O, tell her, Swallow, thou that knowest each,
That bright and fierce and fickle is the South,   5
And dark and true and tender is the North.

O Swallow, Swallow, if I could follow, and light
Upon her lattice, I would pipe and trill,
And cheep and twitter twenty million loves.

O, were I thou that she might take me in,   10
And lay me on her bosom, and her heart
Would rock the snowy cradle till I died!

3. One of the most Virgilian of Tennyson's poems and perhaps his most famous lyric, it was written at Tintern Abbey, "full for me of its bygone memories." Wordsworth's "Tintern Abbey" had similarly expressed what Tennyson said his poem was about: "The passion of the past, the abiding in the transient" (*Memoir*, I, 253). One also thinks of Wordsworth's "thoughts that do often lie too deep for tears" in "Ode: Intimations of Immortality."
4. As with "Tears, Idle Tears," the fact that the poem is in blank verse is often missed.

Why lingereth she to clothe her heart with love,
Delaying as the tender ash delays
To clothe herself, when all the woods are green?   15

O, tell her, Swallow, that thy brood is flown;
Say to her, I do but wanton in the South,
But in the North long since my nest is made.

O, tell her, brief is life but love is long,
And brief the sun of summer in the North,   20
And brief the moon of beauty in the South.

O Swallow, flying from the golden woods,
Fly to her, and pipe and woo her, and make her mine,
And tell her, tell her, that I follow thee.

1847

"Ask Me No More"

Ask me no more: the moon may draw the sea;
   The cloud may stoop from heaven and take the shape,
   With fold to fold, of mountain or of cape;
But O too fond, when have I answer'd thee?
                    Ask me no more.   5

Ask me no more: what answer should I give?
   I love not hollow cheek or faded eye:
   Yet, O my friend, I will not have thee die!
Ask me no more, lest I should bid thee live;
                    Ask me no more.   10

Ask me no more: thy fate and mine are seal'd;
   I strove against the stream and all in vain;
   Let the great river take me to the main.
No more, dear love, for at a touch I yield;
                    Ask me no more.   15

1850

"Now Sleeps the Crimson Petal"

Now sleeps the crimson petal, now the white;
Nor waves the cypress in the palace walk;
Nor winks the gold fin in the porphyry font.
The fire-fly wakens; waken thou with me.

Now droops the milk-white peacock like a ghost,   5
And like a ghost she glimmers on to me.

Now lies the Earth all Danaë⁵ to the stars,
And all thy heart lies open unto me.

5. Warned by an oracle that his daughter's male offspring would kill him, Acrisius locked her up in a brass tower. Zeus managed to visit her in a shower of gold. Danaë's son was Perseus.

Now slides the silent meteor on, and leaves
A shining furrow, as thy thoughts in me.   10

Now folds the lily all her sweetness up,
And slips into the bosom of the lake.
So fold thyself, my dearest, thou, and slip
Into my bosom and be lost in me.

1847

"Come Down, O Maid"[6]

Come down, O maid, from yonder mountain height.
What pleasure lives in height (the shepherd sang),
In height and cold, the splendor of the hills?
But cease to move so near the heavens, and cease
To glide a sunbeam by the blasted pine,   5
To sit a star upon the sparkling spire;
And come, for Love is of the valley, come,
For Love is of the valley, come thou down
And find him; by the happy threshold, he,
Or hand in hand with Plenty in the maize,   10
Or red with spirted purple of the vats,
Or foxlike in the vine;[7] nor cares to walk
With Death and Morning on the Silver Horns,[8]
Nor wilt thou snare him in the white ravine,
Nor find him dropt upon the firths of ice,   15
That huddling slant in furrow-cloven falls
To roll the torrent out of dusky doors.[9]
But follow; let the torrent dance thee down
To find him in the valley; let the wild
Lean-headed eagles yelp alone, and leave   20
The monstrous ledges there to slope, and spill
Their thousand wreaths of dangling water-smoke,
That like a broken purpose waste in air.
So waste not thou, but come; for all the vales
Await thee; azure pillars[1] of the hearth   25
Arise to thee; the children call, and I
Thy shepherd pipe, and sweet is every sound,
Sweeter thy voice, but every sound is sweet;
Myriads of rivulets hurrying thro' the lawn,
The moan of doves in immemorial elms,   30
And murmuring of innumerable bees.

1847

---

6. "Written in Switzerland (chiefly at
Lauterbrunnen and Grindelwald, and
descriptive of the waste Alpine heights
and gorges" (*Memoir*, I, 252). Tenny-
son considered the poem to be among
his *"most successful work."* There is
some debt to Theocritus' *Idylls*, XI.

7. An image from the *Song of Solomon*,
2:15.
8. Mountain peaks.
9. Passageways cut by melting ice
through the mud and rocks at the foot
of a glacier.
1. Columns of chimney smoke.

To ———[2]

AFTER READING A LIFE AND LETTERS

> Cursed be he that moves my bones.
> —*Shakespeare's Epitaph*

You might have won the Poet's name,
    If such be worth the winning now,
    And gain'd a laurel for your brow
Of sounder leaf than I can claim;

But you have made the wiser choice,   5
    A life that moves to gracious ends
    Thro' troops of unrecording friends,
A deedful life, a silent voice.

And you have miss'd the irreverent doom
    Of those that wear the Poet's crown;   10
    Hereafter, neither knave nor clown
Shall hold their orgies at your tomb.

For now the Poet cannot die,
    Nor leave his music as of old,
    But round him ere he scarce be cold   15
Begins the scandal and the cry:

"Proclaim the faults he would not show;
    Break lock and seal, betray the trust;
    Keep nothing sacred, 't is but just
The many-headed beast should know."   20

Ah, shameless! for he did but sing
    A song that pleased us from its worth;
    No public life was his on earth,
No blazon'd statesman he, nor king.

He gave the people of his best;   25
    His worst he kept, his best he gave.
    My Shakespeare's curse on clown and knave
Who will not let his ashes rest!

Who make it seem more sweet to be
    The little life of bank and brier,   30
    The bird that pipes his lone desire
And dies unheard within his tree,

Than he that warbles long and loud
    And drops at Glory's temple-gates,

2. Probably addressed to the poet's brother Charles, who had exchanged the life of a poet for that of a country clergyman. The "Life and Letters" may be Richard Monckton Milnes's *Life, Letters and Literary Remains of John Keats* (1848). Tennyson "was indignant that Keats's wild love-letters should have been published," but he disclaimed any particular reference. He often expressed his own dread of trial by biographers, wanting his work to stand for his life. Compare "The Dead Prophet" (1885).

For whom the carrion vulture waits   35
To tear his heart before the crowd!

1849

The Eagle

FRAGMENT

He clasps the crag with crooked hands;
Close to the sun in lonely lands,
Ring'd with the azure world, he stands.

The wrinkled sea beneath him crawls;
He watches from his mountain walls,   5
And like a thunderbolt he falls.

1846?; 1851

In Memoriam A. H. H.   Arthur Henry Hallam died suddenly and un-
expectedly on September 15, 1833, while on a visit to Vienna with his
father. On February 1 he would have been 23 and was thus about 18
months Tennyson's junior. Some five years earlier Hallam had befriended
Tennyson at Cambridge, and the two remained inseparable. High points
in their relationship included the trip to the Pyrenees in 1830 (see note to
"Œnone") and a tour of the Rhineland in 1832. At Cambridge Hallam
was considered by all who knew him to be the most promising figure of
his generation, a statement substantiated by numerous reminiscences. As
titular leader of the Apostles, the Cambridge undergraduate literary group,
he introduced Tennyson to that society and its stimulating atmosphere.
Hallam's influence was profound. It was Hallam who helped Tennyson
through the difficult period following publication of *Poems, Chiefly Lyrical,*
in 1830 and who worked over the new volume for 1832. He was friend,
critic, and philosopher to a sometimes confused and lonely poet who des-
perately needed the guidance, warmth, and compassion Hallam freely
offered. Engaged to Tennyson's sister Emily, he was shortly to become a
member of the family. His loss was shattering.
    Tennyson learned of Hallam's death on October 1 and probably began
composing the lyrics which would eventually be assembled into his greatest
work sometime during early winter. See *Memoir,* I, 107. As he said much
later, "The sections were written at many different places, and as the
phases of our intercourse came to my memory and suggested them. I did
not write them with any view of weaving them into a whole, or for pub-
lication, until I found that I had written so many" (*Memoir,* I, 304).
Through internal evidence the composition of several sections can be dated
rather precisely. By far the majority of the lyrics were probably written

before 1842. And by 1849, with the composition of the "Prologue," the lyrics had been arranged for publication. One should not, therefore, expect a tightly knit structure. Rather, the poem is loosely organized around the three Christmas sections: 28, 78, and 104. What other unity is present largely results from recurrent theme and image. But "the way of the soul," as the poet subtitled his work, properly moves from doubt to tentative assertions of faith in an irregular fashion. Unlike Wordsworth in his *Prelude*, Tennyson was not out to program the growth of a poet's mind, and we should lay to rest once and for all the notion that the poem's lack of structure is somehow a measure of its inherent weakness.

Contrary to the practice imposed by anthologies, *In Memoriam* should be read as a whole, preferably at one sitting. Only then does the modern reader have a chance of grasping—possibly even feeling—the magnitude of the issues. In 1850 the "night of fear" had descended. Darwinism was in the air. Sir Charles Lyell's famous *Principles of Geology* (1830–33) had made it extremely difficult for any self-respecting intelligence to take the Biblical version of the Creation literally. At issue was the immortality of the soul, given special and immediate poignancy by the loss of Hallam. If that issue itself no longer moves us as it did Tennyson and his contemporaries, we nonetheless owe the poem a suspension of our disbelief. As in our reading of Dante's *Divine Comedy*, we believe in a belief—or, perhaps more accurately, in the expression of doubt.

IN MEMORIAM A. H. H.

OBIIT MDCCCXXXIII

Strong Son of God, immortal Love,[1]
  Whom we, that have not seen thy face,
  By faith, and faith alone, embrace,
Believing where we cannot prove;[2]

Thine are these orbs[3] of light and shade;   5
  Thou madest Life in man and brute;
  Thou madest Death; and lo, thy foot[4]
Is on the skull which thou hast made.

1. Probably influenced by George Herbert's poem "Love," which begins:
  Immortal Love, Author of this great frame,
    Sprung from that beauty which can never fade,
  How hath Man parcell'd out Thy glorious name,
And thrown it on the dust which Thou hast made · · ·
On the meter of the *In Memoriam* stanza, Tennyson commented: "I believed myself the originator of the metre, until after 'In Memoriam' came out, when some one told me that Ben Jonson and Sir Philip Sidney had used it" (*Memoir*, I, 306).
2. See *John*, 20:29, where Jesus speaks of His resurrection to the doubting Thomas: "Have you believed because you have seen me? Blessed are those who have not seen and yet believe."
3. The earth and other revolving planets; perhaps the sun and moon.
4. Possibly suggested by *Revelation*, 10:2, a chapter Tennyson particularly admired and often quoted. An angel appeared "and he set his right foot on the sea, and his left foot on the land."

Thou wilt not leave us in the dust:
    Thou madest man, he knows not why,   10
    He thinks he was not made to die;
And thou hast made him: thou art just.

Thou seemest human and divine,
    The highest, holiest manhood, thou.
    Our wills are ours, we know not how;   15
Our wills are ours, to make them thine.

Our little systems[5] have their day;
    They have their day and cease to be;
    They are but broken lights of thee,
And thou, O Lord, art more than they.   20

We have but faith: we cannot know,
    For knowledge is of things we see;
    And yet we trust it comes from thee,
A beam in darkness: let it grow.

Let knowledge grow from more to more,   25
    But more of reverence in us dwell;
    That mind and soul, according well,
May make one music as before,[6]

But vaster. We are fools and slight;
    We mock thee when we do not fear: 30
    But help thy foolish ones to bear;
Help thy vain worlds[7] to bear thy light.

Forgive what seem'd my sin in me,
    What seem'd my worth since I began;
    For merit lives from man to man,   35
And not from man, O Lord, to thee.

Forgive my grief for one removed,
    Thy creature, whom I found so fair.
    I trust he lives in thee, and there
I find him worthier to be loved.   40

Forgive these wild and wandering cries,
    Confusions of a wasted[8] youth;
    Forgive them where they fail in truth,
And in thy wisdom make me wise.

1849

---

5. Of philosophy and theology.
6. Before the split between faith and knowledge which the "new science" was rapidly widening. Compare Matthew Arnold's "Dover Beach" for a similar expression in a different metaphor: "The Sea of Faith / Was once, too, at the full. . . ."
7. Tennyson often implied that he believed in a number of inhabited planets.
8. Desolated. Bradley remarks, "surely, not 'squandered,'" but see line 2 in "Remorse," p. 522.

1

I held it truth, with him[9] who sings
　　To one clear harp in divers tones,
　　That men may rise on stepping-stones
Of their dead selves to higher things.

But who shall so forecast the years　　　　　　5
　　And find in loss a gain to match?
　　Or reach a hand thro' time to catch
The far-off interest[1] of tears?

Let Love clasp Grief lest both be drown'd,
　　Let darkness keep her raven gloss.　　　　　10
　　Ah, sweeter to be drunk with loss,
To dance with Death, to beat the ground,

Than that the victor Hours should scorn
　　The long result of love, and boast,
　　"Behold the man that loved and lost,　　　　15
But all he was is overworn."

2

Old yew,[2] which graspest at the stones
　　That name the underlying dead,
　　Thy fibres net the dreamless head,
Thy roots are wrapt about the bones.

The seasons bring the flower again,　　　　　　5
　　And bring the firstling to the flock;
　　And in the dusk of thee the clock[3]
Beats out the little lives of men.

O, not for thee the glow, the bloom,
　　Who changest not in any gale,　　　　　　　10
　　Nor branding summer suns avail
To touch thy thousand years of gloom;

And gazing on thee, sullen tree,
　　Sick for[4] thy stubborn hardihood,
　　I seem to fail from out my blood　　　　　　15
And grow incorporate into thee.

3

O Sorrow, cruel fellowship,
　　O Priestess in the vaults of Death,
　　O sweet and bitter in a breath,
What whispers from thy lying lip?

"The stars," she whispers, "blindly run;　　　　5
　　A web is woven across the sky;

9. Goethe, according to Tennyson (see *Memoir*, II, 391), but the reference never has been located.
1. Reward. The use of economic terms in religious context also suggests the influence of George Herbert.
2. Hallam was buried January 3, 1834, at Clevedon Church, Somersetshire, overlooking the Bristol Channel. The scene of this section is, however, prob-ably a composite picture in part suggested by the graveyard at Somersby where Tennyson's father was buried. See "The Two Voices," lines 271 ff, "darkness in the village yew." "I myself did not see Clevedon till years after the burial" (*Memoir*, I, 305).
3. In the church-tower behind the yew.
4. In envy of.

From out waste places comes a cry,
And murmurs from the dying sun;[5]

"And all the phantom, Nature, stands—
With all the music in her tone,   10
A hollow echo of my[6] own,—
A hollow form with empty hands."[7]

And shall I take a thing so blind,
Embrace her[8] as my natural good;
Or crush her, like a vice of blood,   15
Upon the threshold of the mind?

4

To Sleep I give my powers away;
My will is bondsman to the dark;
I sit within a helmless bark,
And with my heart I muse and say:

O heart, how fares it with thee now,   5
That thou shouldst fail[9] from thy desire,
Who scarcely darest to inquire,
"What is it makes me beat so low?"

Something it is which thou hast lost,
Some pleasure from thine early years.   10
Break thou deep vase of chilling tears,
That grief hath shaken into frost!

Such clouds of nameless trouble cross
All night below the darken'd eyes;
With morning wakes the will, and cries,   15
"Thou shalt not be the fool of loss."

5

I sometimes hold it half a sin
To put in words the grief I feel:
For words, like Nature, half reveal
And half conceal the Soul within.

But, for the unquiet heart and brain,   5
A use in measured language lies;
The sad mechanic exercise,
Like dull narcotics, numbing pain.

In words, like weeds,[1] I'll wrap me o'er,
Like coarsest clothes against the cold;   10

---

5. An allusion to the nebular hypothesis.
6. Sorrow's. The stanza would make better sense if the quotation marks closed "sun," and "my" referred to the poet.
7. Sorrow's words reflect Tennyson's growing concern with the mechanistic theory of the universe, which held that all life works out its predestined course according to natural laws over which neither God nor man has any control.
8. Sorrow.
9. Lose the capacity for desiring.
1. Garments. Contrast section 38. From his initial feeling that writing is merely an antidote for despair, the poet later moves toward a more positive conception of his art.

But that large grief which these enfold
Is given in outline and no more.

6

One writes, that "other friends remain,"
 That "loss is common to the race"—
 And common is the commonplace,
And vacant chaff well meant for grain.

That loss is common would not make   5
 My own less bitter, rather more.
 Too common! Never morning wore
To evening, but some heart did break.

O father, wheresoe'er thou be,
 Who pledgest now thy gallant son,   10
 A shot, ere half thy draught be done,
Hath still'd the life that beat from thee.

O mother, praying God will save
 Thy sailor,—while thy head is bow'd,
 His heavy-shotted hammock-shroud   15
Drops in his vast and wandering grave.

Ye know no more than I who wrought
 At that last hour to please him well;
 Who mused on all I had to tell,
And something written, something thought; 20

Expecting still his advent home;
 And ever met him on his way
 With wishes, thinking, "here to-day,"
Or "here to-morrow will he come."

O, somewhere, meek, unconscious dove,   25
 That sittest ranging[2] golden hair;
 And glad to find thyself so fair,
Poor child, that waitest for thy love!

For now her father's chimney glows
 In expectation of a guest;   30
 And thinking "this will please him best,"
She takes a riband or a rose,

For he will see them on to-night;
 And with the thought her color burns;
 And, having left the glass, she turns   35
Once more to set a ringlet right;

And, even when she turn'd, the curse
 Had fallen, and her future lord
 Was drown'd in passing thro' the ford,
Or kill'd in falling from his horse.   40

---

2. Arranging. This section was prob-
ably written sometime between sum-
mer 1840 and Christmas 1841. See
Memoir, I, 201–202.

O, what to her shall be the end?
  And what to me remains of good?
  To her perpetual maidenhood,
And unto me no second friend.

7

Dark house,[3] by which once more I stand
  Here in the long unlovely street,
  Doors, where my heart was used to beat
So quickly, waiting for a hand,

A hand that can be clasp'd no more—   5
  Behold me, for I cannot sleep,
  And like a guilty thing[4] I creep
At earliest morning to the door.

He is not here; but far away
  The noise of life begins again,   10
  And ghastly thro' the drizzling rain
On the bald street breaks the blank day.

8

A happy lover who has come
  To look on her that loves him well,
  Who 'lights and rings the gateway bell,
And learns her gone and far from home;

He saddens, all the magic light   5
  Dies off at once from bower and hall,
  And all the place is dark, and all
The chambers emptied of delight:

So find I every pleasant spot
  In which we two were wont to meet,   10
  The field, the chamber, and the street,
For all is dark where thou art not.

Yet as that other, wandering there
  In those deserted walks, may find
  A flower beat with rain and wind,   15
Which once she foster'd up with care;

So seems it in my deep regret,
  O my forsaken heart, with thee
  And this poor flower of poesy
Which, little cared for, fades not yet.   20

But since it pleased a vanish'd eye,
  I go to plant it on his tomb,
  That if it can it there may bloom,
Or, dying, there at least may die.[5]

---

3. Hallam's home at 67 Wimpole Street, London. See section 119.
4. Like a ghost. Tennyson was thinking of Horatio's description of Hamlet's father's ghost in *Hamlet*, I, i, 148:

"And then it started like a guilty thing."
5. Continuing the theme of section 5, the speaker takes some solace in recalling Hallam's appreciation of his poetry.

9

Fair ship,[6] that from the Italian shore
  Sailest the placid ocean-plains
  With my lost Arthur's loved remains,
Spread thy full wings, and waft him o'er.

So draw him home to those that mourn   5
  In vain; a favorable speed
  Ruffle thy mirror'd mast, and lead
Thro' prosperous floods his holy urn.

All night no ruder air perplex
  Thy sliding keel, till Phosphor,[7] bright   10
  As our pure love, thro' early light
Shall glimmer on the dewy decks.

Sphere all your lights around, above;
  Sleep, gentle heavens, before the prow;
  Sleep, gentle winds, as he sleeps now,   15
My friend, the brother of my love;

My Arthur, whom I shall not see
  Till all my widow'd[8] race be run;
  Dear as the mother to the son,
More than my brothers are to me.   20

10

I hear the noise about thy keel;
  I hear the bell struck in the night;
  I see the cabin-window bright;
I see the sailor at the wheel.

Thou bring'st the sailor to his wife,   5
  And travell'd men from foreign lands;
  And letters unto trembling hands;
And, thy dark freight, a vanish'd life.

So bring him; we have idle dreams;
  This look of quiet flatters thus   10
  Our home-bred fancies. O, to us,
The fools of habit, sweeter seems

To rest beneath the clover sod,
  That takes the sunshine and the rains,
  Or where the kneeling hamlet drains   15
The chalice of the grapes of God;[9]

6. Sections 9–17 form a group all concerned with the return of Hallam's body. They are probably among the first written of the elegies, mostly composed, one assumes, before the end of the year. On December 31, 1833, Tennyson received a letter from Hallam's father saying his son's body had arrived.
7. The morning star.
8. The speaker alternately thinks of himself as a widow or widower (see opening of section 13) and a careless reviewer of the first edition referred to the poem: "These touching lines evidently come from the full heart of the widow of a military man" (*Memoir*, I, 298).
9. The speaker imagines the possibility of burial inside the church where the villagers kneel to receive the sacrament. A good example of Tennysonian over-refinement.

Than if with thee the roaring wells
    Should gulf him fathom-deep in brine,
    And hands so often clasp'd in mine,
Should toss with tangle[1] and with shells.   20

11

Calm is the morn without a sound,
    Calm as to suit a calmer grief,
    And only thro' the faded leaf
The chestnut pattering to the ground;

Calm and deep peace on this high wold,[2]   5
    And on these dews that drench the furze,
    And all the silvery gossamers
That twinkle into green and gold;

Calm and still light on yon great plain
    That sweeps with all its autumn bowers,   10
    And crowded farms and lessening[3] towers,
To mingle with the bounding main;

Calm and deep peace in this wide air,
    These leaves that redden to the fall,
    And in my heart, if calm at all,   15
If any calm, a calm despair;

Calm on the seas, and silver sleep,
    And waves that sway themselves in rest,
    And dead calm in that noble breast
Which heaves but with the heaving deep.   20

12

Lo, as a dove when up she springs
    To bear thro' heaven a tale of woe,
    Some dolorous message knit below
The wild pulsation of her wings;

Like her I go, I cannot stay;   5
    I leave this mortal ark behind,
    A weight of nerves without a mind,
And leave the cliffs, and haste away

O'er ocean-mirrors rounded large,
    And reach the glow of southern skies,   10
    And see the sails at distance rise,
And linger weeping on the marge,

And saying, "Comes he thus, my friend?
    Is this the end of all my care?"
    And circle moaning in the air,   15
"Is this the end? Is this the end?"

---

1. Seaweed.
2. The scene reflects the Lincolnshire landscape near Somersby. The ship returning Hallam's body actually departed later in the year, and not in autumn, as the poet imagines.
3. As his vision reaches toward the sea in the distance, the church towers in the foreground appear to grow smaller.

And forward dart again, and play
   About the prow, and back return
   To where the body sits,[4] and learn
That I have been an hour away.   20

13

Tears of the widower, when he sees
   A late-lost form that sleep reveals,
   And moves his doubtful arms, and feels
Her place is empty, fall like these;

Which weep a loss for ever new,   5
   A void where heart on heart reposed;
   And, where warm hands have prest and closed,
Silence, till I be silent too;

Which weep the comrade of my choice,
   An awful thought, a life removed,   10
   The human-hearted man I loved,
A Spirit, not a breathing voice.

Come, Time, and teach me, many years,[5]
   I do not suffer in a dream;
   For now so strange do these things seem,   15
Mine eyes have leisure for their tears,

My fancies time[6] to rise on wing,
   And glance about the approaching sails,
   As tho' they brought but merchants' bales,
And not the burthen that they bring.   20

14

If one should bring me this report,
   That thou[7] hadst touch'd the land to-day,
   And I went down unto the quay,
And found thee lying in the port;

And standing, muffled round with woe,   5
   Should see thy passengers in rank
   Come stepping lightly down the plank
And beckoning unto those they know;

And if along with these should come
   The man I held as half-divine,   10
   Should strike a sudden hand in mine,
And ask a thousand things of home;

And I should tell him all my pain,
   And how my life had droop'd of late,
   And he should sorrow o'er my state   15
And marvel what possess'd my brain;

---

4. Not a happy choice of verb; the "body" is, of course, the poet's. He has imagined his soul departing to meet the ship bringing Hallam home.
5. Through many years.
6. The sense is: Since the passage of years has not yet come to teach him to accept the full meaning of his loss, his fancy has the time or leisure to imagine the ship brings only merchants' wares.
7. The ship.

And I perceived no touch of change,
    No hint of death in all his frame,
    But found him all in all the same,
I should not feel it to be strange.   20

15

To-night the winds begin to rise
    And roar from yonder dropping day;
    The last red leaf[8] is whirl'd away,
The rooks are blown about the skies;

The forest crack'd, the waters curl'd,   5
    The cattle huddled on the lea;
    And wildly dash'd on tower and tree
The sunbeam strikes along the world:

And but for fancies, which aver
    That all thy[9] motions gently pass   10
    Athwart a plane of molten glass,
I scarce could brook the strain and stir

That makes the barren branches loud;
    And but for fear it is not so,
    The wild unrest that lives in woe   15
Would dote and pore on yonder cloud

That rises upward always higher,
    And onward drags a laboring breast,
    And topples round the dreary west,
A looming bastion fringed with fire.   20

16

What words are these have fallen from me?
    Can calm despair and wild unrest[1]
    Be tenants of a single breast,
Or Sorrow such a changeling be?

Or doth she only seem to take   5
    The touch of change in calm or storm,
    But knows no more of transient form
In her deep self, than some dead lake

That holds the shadow of a lark
    Hung in the shadow of a heaven?   10
    Or has the shock, so harshly given,
Confused me like the unhappy bark

That strikes by night a craggy shelf,
    And staggers blindly ere she sink?
    And stunn'd me from my power to think   15
And all my knowledge of myself;

8. Tennyson may have been indebted to Coleridge's "Christabel" for this image, "The one red leaf, the last of its clan / That dances as often as dance it can" (lines 49–50).
9. The ship's.
1. The moods of sections 11 and 15.

And made me that delirious man
   Whose fancy fuses old and new,
   And flashes into false and true,
And mingles all without a plan?   20

17

Thou comest, much wept for; such a breeze
   Compell'd thy canvas, and my prayer
   Was as the whisper of an air
To breathe thee over lonely seas.

For I in spirit saw thee move   5
   Thro' circles of the bounding sky,
   Week after week; the days go by;
Come quick, thou bringest all I love.

Henceforth, wherever thou mayst roam,
   My blessing, like a line of light,   10
   Is on the waters day and night,
And like a beacon guards thee home.

So may whatever tempest mars
   Mid-ocean spare thee, sacred bark,
   And balmy drops in summer dark   15
Slide from the bosom of the stars;

So kind an office hath been done,
   Such precious relics brought by thee,
   The dust of him I shall not see
Till all my widow'd race be run.   20

18

'T is well; 't is something; we may stand
   Where he in English earth is laid,[2]
   And from his ashes may be made
The violet of his native land.

'T is little; but it looks in truth   5
   As if the quiet bones were blest
   Among familiar names to rest
And in the places of his youth.

Come then, pure hands, and bear the head
   That sleeps or wears the mask of sleep,   10
   And come, whatever loves to weep,
And hear the ritual of the dead.

Ah yet, even yet, if this might be,
   I, falling on his faithful heart,
   Would breathing thro' his lips impart   15
The life that almost dies in me;

2. Hallam was buried inside the church. Tennyson was not present at Hallam's interment. His first visit to Clevedon seems to have been on June 14, 1850, the day after his marriage to Emily Sellwood. At her wish, together "they saw Arthur Hallam's resting-place." " 'It seemed a kind of consecration to go there' " (*Memoir,* I, 332).

That dies not, but endures with pain,
    And slowly forms the firmer mind,
    Treasuring the look it cannot find,
The words that are not heard again.   20

19

The Danube to the Severn[3] gave
    The darken'd heart that beat no more;
    They laid him by the pleasant shore,
And in the hearing of the wave.

There twice a day the Severn fills;   5
    The salt sea-water passes by,
    And hushes half the babbling Wye,
And makes a silence in the hills.

The Wye is hush'd nor moved along,
    And hush'd my deepest grief of all,   10
    When fill'd with tears that cannot fall,
I brim with sorrow drowning song.

The tide flows down, the wave again
    Is vocal in its wooded walls;
    My deeper anguish also falls,   15
And I can speak a little then.

20

The lesser griefs that may be said,
    That breathe a thousand tender vows,
    Are but as servants in a house
Where lies the master newly dead;

Who speak their feeling as it is,   5
    And weep the fulness from the mind.
    "It will be hard," they say, "to find
Another service such as this."

My lighter moods are like to these,
    That out of words a comfort win;   10
    But there are other griefs within,
And tears that at their fountain freeze;

For by the hearth the children sit
    Cold in that atmosphere of death,
    And scarce endure to draw the breath,   15
Or like to noiseless phantoms flit;

But open converse is there none,
    So much the vital spirits sink
    To see the vacant chair, and think,
"How good! how kind! and he is gone."   20

3. Vienna, where Hallam died, is on the Danube. The tides flow up the Bristol Channel, which, further up, becomes the Severn, and eventually enter the Wye. Like "Tears, Idle Tears," this section was written at Tintern Abbey, on the Wye River.

21

I sing to him that rests below,
    And, since the grasses round me wave,
    I take the grasses of the grave,[4]
And make them pipes whereon to blow.

The traveller hears me now and then,
    And sometimes harshly will he speak:
    "This fellow would make weakness weak,
And melt the waxen hearts of men."

Another answers: "Let him be,
    He loves to make parade of pain,
    That with his piping he may gain
The praise that comes to constancy."

A third is wroth: "Is this an hour
    For private sorrow's barren song,
    When more and more the people throng
The chairs and thrones of civil power?[5]

"A time to sicken and to swoon,
    When Science[6] reaches forth her arms
    To feel from world to world, and charms
Her secret from the latest moon?"

Behold, ye speak an idle thing;
    Ye never knew the sacred dust.
    I do but sing because I must,
And pipe but as the linnets sing;

And one is glad; her note is gay,
    For now her little ones have ranged;
    And one is sad; her note is changed,
Because her brood is stolen away.

22

The path by which we twain did go,
    Which led by tracts that pleased us well,
    Thro' four sweet years arose and fell,
From flower to flower, from snow to snow;

And we with singing cheer'd the way,
    And, crown'd with all the season lent,
    From April on to April went,
And glad at heart from May to May.

---

4. See note on section 18. Sections 21–25 form an interlude. Working within the conventions of the classical pastoral elegy, the poet continues the theme begun in sections 5 and 8. His recourse to the pastoral convention allows him to think of his verses in terms of a larger, more durable context than that suggested by the previous comparison of his lines to a dying flower.
5. Possibly an allusion to the Chartist Movement of 1838–39.
6. Apparently the section was written late, since the poet probably is referring to the discovery of Neptune in September 1846. Neptune's single moon was discovered a month later. By "moon" Tennyson may mean either planet or satellite. Late in life he reportedly said, "at least one of the planets belonging to each sun should be inhabited" (*Memoir*, II, 336).

But where the path we walk'd began
    To slant the fifth autumnal slope,[7]   10
    As we descended following Hope,
There sat the Shadow[8] fear'd of man;

Who broke our fair companionship,
    And spread his mantle dark and cold,
    And wrapt thee formless in the fold,   15
And dull'd the murmur on thy lip,

And bore thee where I could not see
    Nor follow, tho' I walk in haste,
    And think that somewhere in the waste
The Shadow sits and waits for me.   20

23

Now, sometimes in my sorrow shut,
    Or breaking into song by fits,
    Alone, alone, to where he sits,
The Shadow cloak'd from head to foot,

Who keeps the keys[9] of all the creeds,   5
    I wander, often falling lame,
    And looking back to whence I came,
Or on to where the pathway leads;

And crying, How changed from where it ran
    Thro' lands where not a leaf was dumb,   10
    But all the lavish hills would hum
The murmur of a happy Pan;[1]

When each by turns was guide to each,
    And Fancy light from Fancy caught,
    And Thought leapt out to wed with Thought   15
Ere Thought could wed itself with Speech;

And all we met was fair and good,
    And all was good that Time could bring,
    And all the secret of the Spring
Moved in the chambers of the blood;   20

And many an old philosophy
    On Argive[2] heights divinely sang,
    And round us all the thicket rang
To many a flute of Arcady.[3]

24

And was the day of my delight
    As pure and perfect as I say?

---

7. Hallam died September 15, 1833, in
the fifth year of the friendship.
8. Death, which at this stage the poet
does not seem anxious to avoid. The
so-called "death-wish" should not, how-
ever, be overemphasized in the whole
poem.

9. Death answers all questions of mor-
tality.
1. God of all nature.
2. Greek; specifically, the city of Ar-
gos, known for its music.
3. Arcadia, the mountainous region in
central Greece celebrated as the home
of pastoral poetry.

The very source and fount of day
Is dash'd with wandering isles of night.[4]

If all was good and fair we met,   5
   This earth had been the Paradise
   It never look'd to human eyes
Since our first sun arose and set.

And is it that the haze of grief
   Makes former gladness loom so great?   10
   The lowness of the present state,
That sets the past in this relief?

Or that the past will always win
   A glory from its being far,
   And orb into the perfect star[5]   15
We saw not when we moved therein?

25

I know that this was Life,—the track
   Whereon with equal feet we fared;
   And then, as now, the day prepared
The daily burden for the back.

But this it was that made me move   5
   As light as carrier-birds in air;
   I loved the weight I had to bear,
Because it needed help of Love;

Nor could I weary, heart or limb,
   When mighty Love would cleave in twain   10
   The lading[6] of a single pain,
And part it, giving half to him.

26

Still onward winds the dreary way;
   I with it, for I long to prove
   No lapse of moons can canker Love,
Whatever fickle tongues may say.

And if that eye which watches guilt   5
   And goodness, and hath power to see
   Within the green the moulder'd tree,
And towers fallen as soon as built—

O, if indeed that eye foresee
   Or see—in Him is no before—   10
   In more of life true life no more
And Love the indifference to be,

Then might I find, ere yet the morn
   Breaks hither over Indian seas,

---

4. Sunspots.
5. From a distance the earth would appear a perfect disc, just as the rough edges of their past friendship appear to vanish with time.
6. A loading; burden.

That Shadow waiting with the keys,   15
To shroud me from my proper[7] scorn.

27

I envy not in any moods
    The captive void of noble rage,
    The linnet born within the cage,
That never knew the summer woods;

I envy not the beast that takes   5
    His license in the field of time,
    Unfetter'd by the sense of crime,
To whom a conscience never wakes;

Nor, what may count itself as blest,
    The heart that never plighted troth   10
    But stagnates in the weeds of sloth:
Nor any want-begotten rest.[8]

I hold it true, whate'er befall;
    I feel it, when I sorrow most;
    'T is better to have loved and lost   15
Than never to have loved at all.

28

The time draws near the birth of Christ.[9]
    The moon is hid, the night is still;
    The Christmas bells from hill to hill
Answer each other in the mist.

Four voices of four hamlets round,   5
    From far and near, on mead and moor,
    Swell out and fail, as if a door
Were shut between me and the sound;

Each voice four changes[1] on the wind,
    That now dilate, and now decrease,   10
    Peace and goodwill, goodwill and peace,
Peace and goodwill, to all mankind.

This year I slept and woke with pain,
    I almost wish'd no more to wake,
    And that my hold on life would break   15
Before I heard those bells again;

But they my troubled spirit rule,
    For they controll'd me when a boy;
    They bring me sorrow touch'd with joy,
The merry, merry bells of Yule.   20

7. Own; means scorn of himself. This stanza poses one of the larger questions asked in the poem: Does love live outside of time?
8. Ill-deserved rest resulting from "want" or deficiency.
9. The second part of the poem begins here, and the predominant concern is for Hallam's immortality. The time is the first Christmas after his friend's death (1833); the scene is the Tennyson family home at Somersby.
1. In different sequence, four churches each with four bells ring the four syllables in each of the four phrases of lines 11 and 12.

29

With such compelling cause to grieve
   As daily vexes household[2] peace,
   And chains regret to his decease,
How dare we keep our Christmas-eve,

Which brings no more a welcome guest   5
   To enrich the threshold of the night
   With shower'd largess of delight
In dance and song and game and jest?

Yet go, and while the holly boughs
   Entwine the cold baptismal font,   10
   Make one wreath more for Use and Wont,
That guard the portals of the house;

Old sisters[3] of a day gone by,
   Gray nurses, loving nothing new—
   Why should they miss their yearly due   15
Before their time? They too will die.

30

With trembling fingers did we weave
   The holly round the Christmas hearth;
   A rainy cloud possess'd the earth,
And sadly fell our Christmas-eve.

At our old pastimes in the hall   5
   We gamboll'd, making vain pretence
   Of gladness, with an awful sense
Of one mute Shadow[4] watching all.

We paused: the winds were in the beech;
   We heard them sweep the winter land;   10
   And in a circle hand-in-hand
Sat silent, looking each at each.

Then echo-like our voices rang;
   We sung, tho' every eye was dim,
   A merry song we sang with him   15
Last year; impetuously we sang.

We ceased; a gentler feeling crept
   Upon us: surely rest is meet.[5]
   "They rest," we said, "their sleep is sweet,"
And silence follow'd, and we wept.   20

Our voices took a higher range;
   Once more we sang: "They do not die
   Nor lose their mortal sympathy,
Nor change to us, although they change;

2. Our household, where thoughts of Hallam's death are daily present.
3. I.e., Use and Wont.
4. Not Death but the spirit of Hallam.

A draft of this section was probably made in 1833. See *Memoir,* I, 109.
5. Fitting or appropriate.

"Rapt from the fickle and the frail   25
    With gather'd power, yet the same,
    Pierces the keen seraphic flame
From orb to orb, from veil to veil."[6]

Rise, happy morn, rise, holy morn,
    Draw forth the cheerful day from night: 30
    O Father, touch the east, and light
The light that shone when Hope was born.

31

When Lazarus[7] left his charnel-cave,
    And home to Mary's house return'd,
    Was this demanded—if he yearn'd
To hear her weeping by his grave?

"Where wert thou, brother, those four days?"   5
    There lives no record of reply,
    Which telling what it is to die
Had surely added praise to praise.

From every house the neighbors met,
    The streets were fill'd with joyful sound,
    A solemn gladness even crown'd   10
The purple brows of Olivet.[8]

Behold a man raised up by Christ!
    The rest remaineth unreveal'd;
    He[9] told it not, or something seal'd   15
The lips of that Evangelist.[1]

32

Her[2] eyes are homes of silent prayer,
    Nor other thought, her mind admits
    But, he was dead, and there he sits,
And he that brought him back is there.

Then one deep love doth supersede   5
    All other, when her ardent gaze
    Roves from the living brother's face,
And rests upon the Life[3] indeed.

All subtle thought, all curious fears,
    Borne down by gladness so complete,
    She bows, she bathes the Saviour's feet   10
With costly spikenard[4] and with tears.

---

6. The soul, freed from the instabilities and frailties of the flesh though unchanged in essence, is now empowered to assume different embodiments passing from world to world.
7. Sections 31–36 are a group dealing directly with questions of love and individual immortality. For Christ's raising of Lazarus from the dead, see *John*, 11.
8. The Mount of Olives, a hill near Jerusalem.
9. Lazarus.
1. St. John, who alone records the story.
2. Mary, Lazarus' sister.
3. "Jesus said to her, 'I am the resurrection and the life; he who believes in me, though he die, yet shall he live'" (*John*, 11:25).
4. A fragrant ointment.

Thrice blest whose lives are faithful prayers,
　　Whose loves in higher love endure;
　　What souls possess themselves so pure,　　15
Or is there blessedness like theirs?

33

O thou[5] that after toil and storm
　　Mayst seem to have reach'd a purer air,
　　Whose faith has centre everywhere,
Nor cares to fix itself to form,

Leave thou thy sister when she prays　　5
　　Her early heaven, her happy views;
　　Nor thou with shadow'd hint confuse
A life that leads melodious days.

Her faith thro' form is pure as thine,
　　Her hands are quicker unto good.　　10
　　O, sacred be the flesh and blood
To which she links a truth divine!

See thou, that countest reason ripe
　　In holding by the law within,
　　Thou fail not in a world of sin,　　15
And even for want of such a type.

34

My own dim life should teach me this,
　　That life shall live for evermore,
　　Else earth is darkness at the core,
And dust and ashes all that is;

This round of green, this orb of flame,[6]　　5
　　Fantastic beauty; such as lurks
　　In some wild poet, when he works
Without a conscience or an aim.

What then were God to such as I?
　　'T were hardly worth my while to choose　　10
　　Of things all mortal, or to use
A little patience ere I die;

'T were best at once to sink to peace,
　　Like birds the charming serpent[7] draws,
　　To drop head-foremost in the jaws　　15
Of vacant darkness and to cease.

35

Yet if some voice that man could trust
　　Should murmur from the narrow house,
　　"The cheeks drop in, the body bows;
Man dies, nor is there hope in dust;"

5. Addressed to no one in particular.
Tennyson is supporting the less intel-
lectualized faith of simple believers like
the sister.

6. The earth and the sun.
7. Some snakes, like the cobra, are
supposed to be able to cast a spell over
their prey.

Might I not say? "Yet even here,   5
    But for one hour, O Love, I strive
    To keep so sweet a thing alive."
But I should turn mine ears and hear

The moanings of the homeless sea,
    The sound of streams that swift or slow   10
    Draw down Æonian[8] hills, and sow
The dust of continents to be,

And Love would answer with a sigh,
    "The sound of that forgetful shore[9]
    Will change my sweetness more and more,   15
Half-dead to know that I shall die."

O me, what profits it to put
    An idle case? If Death were seen
    At first as Death,[1] Love had not been,
Or been in narrowest working shut,   20

Mere fellowship of sluggish moods,
    Or in his coarsest Satyr-shape
    Had bruised the herb and crush'd the grape,
And bask'd and batten'd[2] in the woods.

36

Tho' truths in manhood darkly join,[3]
    Deep-seated in our mystic frame,
    We yield all blessing to the name
Of Him that made them current coin;

For Wisdom dealt with mortal powers,   5
    Where truth in closest words shall fail,
    When truth embodied in a tale[4]
Shall enter in at lowly doors.

And so the Word[5] had breath, and wrought
    With human hands the creed of creeds[6]   10
    In loveliness of perfect deeds,
More strong than all poetic thought;

Which he may read that binds the sheaf,
    Or builds the house, or digs the grave,

---

8. Hills that have lasted for aeons. This is one of several sections which seem clearly indebted to Tennyson's reading of Lyell's *Principles of Geology* (1830–33), in which, during some months of 1837, he was "deeply immersed" (*Memoir*, I, 162). Lyell familiarized English readers with Lamarck's concept of "uniformitism" as opposed to "catastrophism," expounding the theory that the whole surface of the earth changed not by sudden catastrophe but gradually, in obedience to natural laws.

9. The shore of Lethe, the river of forgetfulness.

1. I.e., only as extinction. The idea is: Love, to exist in more than a physical sense, must have perceived intimations of our immortality.

2. Fed on grossly. See "The Kraken."

3. Obscurely meet, hence dimly perceived. See "dim" in 34, 1.

4. The Gospels, not just the Parables.

5. Tennyson explained: " 'The Word' as used by St. John, the Revelation of the Eternal Thought of the Universe" (*Memoir*, I, 312).

6. Christ's life.

And those wild eyes[7] that watch the wave   15
In roarings round the coral reef.

37

Urania[8] speaks with darken'd brow:
   "Thou pratest here where thou art least;
   This faith has many a purer priest,
And many an abler voice than thou.

"Go down beside thy native rill,   5
   On thy Parnassus[9] set thy feet,
   And hear thy laurel whisper sweet
About the ledges of the hill."

And my Melpomene[1] replies,
   A touch of shame upon her cheek: 10
   "I am not worthy even to speak
Of thy prevailing mysteries;

"For I am but an earthly Muse,
   And owning but a little art
   To lull with song an aching heart,   15
And render human love his dues;

"But brooding on the dear one dead,
   And all he said of things divine,—
   And dear to me as sacred wine
To dying lips is all he said,—   20

"I murmur'd, as I came along,
   Of comfort clasp'd in truth reveal'd,
   And loiter'd in the master's field,
And darken'd sanctities with song."

38

With weary steps I loiter on,
   Tho' always under alter'd skies
   The purple from the distance dies,
My prospect and horizon gone.

No joy the blowing season gives,   5
   The herald melodies of spring,
   But in the songs I love to sing
A doubtful gleam of solace[2] lives.

If any care for what is here
   Survive in spirits render'd free,   10
   Then are these songs I sing of thee
Not all ungrateful to thine ear.

---

7. Savages on Pacific Islands currently being Christianized.

8. Originally, Muse of Astronomy. Tennyson is indebted to the invocation to Book VII, of Milton's *Paradise Lost*, where she is made Muse of Heavenly Poetry.

9. The mountain in Greece sacred to Apollo and the Muses. Laurel grows on its slopes, and poets are traditionally crowned with laurel-wreaths.

1. Muse of Tragedy, or, as here, of Elegy.

2. Contrast sections 5 and 8.

39

Old warder[3] of these buried bones,
    And answering now my random stroke
    With fruitful cloud and living smoke,[4]
Dark yew, that graspest at the stones

And dippest toward the dreamless head,   5
    To thee too comes the golden hour
    When flower is feeling after flower;[5]
But Sorrow,—fixt upon the dead,

And darkening the dark graves of men,—
    What whisper'd from her lying lips?   10
    Thy gloom is kindled at the tips,
And passes into gloom again.[6]

40[7]

Could we forget the widow'd hour
    And look on Spirits breathed away,
    As on a maiden in the day
When first she wears her orange-flower!

When crown'd with blessing she doth rise   5
    To take her latest leave of home,
    And hopes and light regrets that come
Make April of her tender eyes;

And doubtful joys the father move,
    And tears are on the mother's face,   10
    As parting with a long embrace
She enters other realms of love;

Her office there to rear, to teach,
    Becoming as is meet and fit
    A link among the days, to knit   15
The generations each with each;

And, doubtless, unto thee[8] is given
    A life that bears immortal fruit
    In those great offices that suit
The full-grown energies of heaven.   20

Ay me, the difference I discern!
    How often shall her old fireside

---

3. The yew-tree of section 2. Section 39 was written in 1868 and retained thereafter. See *Memoir*, II, 53.
4. When shaken ("random stroke") the male flowers of the yew give off a cloud of yellow pollen. Cf. "The Holy Grail," line 15.
5. Male and female flowers sometimes grow on the same tree. In contrast to section 2, the poet sees a renewal of life taking place in the ancient yew.
6. Sorrow's "lying lips" take us back to section 3. Sorrow lied before in sug-gesting the sun never touched the yew's "thousand years of gloom" (section 2). The speaker knows she also lies in lines 11 and 12 in disparaging the springtime phenomenon. In admitting her earlier distortion of nature, Sorrow confirms her untrustworthiness.
7. Sections 40–47 return to the theme of 31–36. The poet further speculates upon some eventual reunion with Hallam's spirit.
8. Hallam.

Be cheer'd with tidings of the bride,
    How often she herself return,

And tell them all they would have told,   25
    And bring her babe, and make her boast,
      Till even those that miss'd her most
Shall count new things as dear as old;

But thou and I have shaken hands,
    Till growing winters lay me low;   30
      My paths are in the fields I know,
And thine in undiscover'd lands.[9]

41

Thy spirit ere our fatal loss
    Did ever rise from high to higher,
    As mounts the heavenward altar-fire,
As flies the lighter thro' the gross.

But thou art turn'd to something strange,   5
    And I have lost the links that bound
      Thy changes; here upon the ground,
No more partaker of thy change.

Deep folly![1] yet that this could be—
    That I could wing my will with might   10
      To leap the grades of life and light,
And flash[2] at once, my friend, to thee!

For tho' my nature rarely yields
    To that vague fear implied in death,
      Nor shudders at the gulfs beneath,   15
The howlings from forgotten fields;[3]

Yet oft when sundown skirts the moor
    An inner trouble I behold,
      A spectral doubt which makes me cold,
That I shall be thy mate no more,   20

Tho' following with an upward mind
    The wonders that have come to thee,
      Thro' all the secular to-be,
But evermore a life behind.[4]

42

I vex my heart with fancies dim.
    He still outstript me in the race;

---

9. See *Hamlet*, III, i, 78–82:
    But that the dread of something after
        death—
    The undiscover'd country, from
        whose bourn
    No traveller returns—puzzles the will,
    And makes us rather bear those ills
        we have
    Than fly to others that we know not
        of?
1. Refers to the wish of lines 10–12.
2. See section 95, 9.

3. The horrors of the underworld imagined by Dante and perhaps Virgil. "Forgotten" seems to imply the general loss of belief in those visions.
4. The speaker has imagined Hallam in afterlife advancing through stages which he cannot follow or even comprehend while on earth himself (stanza 2). When he dies, even if he could follow in his friend's steps (which he doubts he would be able to), he would remain a step behind through all time.

It was but unity of place
That made me dream I rank'd with him.

And so may Place retain[5] us still,   5
　And he the much-beloved again,
　A lord of large experience, train
To riper growth the mind and will;

And what delights can equal those
　That stir the spirit's inner deeps,   10
　When one that loves, but knows not, reaps
A truth from one that loves and knows?

43

If Sleep and Death be truly one,
　And every spirit's folded bloom
　Thro' all its intervital[6] gloom
In some long trance should slumber on;

Unconscious of the sliding hour,   5
　Bare of the body, might it last,
　And silent traces of the past
Be all the color of the flower:

So then were nothing lost to man;
　So that still garden of the souls   10
　In many a figured leaf enrolls
The total world since life began;

And love will last as pure and whole
　As when he loved me here in Time,
　And at the spiritual prime   15
Rewaken with the dawning soul.

44

How fares it with the happy dead?
　For here the man is more and more;
　But he forgets the days before
God shut the doorways of his head.[7]

The days have vanish'd, tone and tint,   5
　And yet perhaps the hoarding sense
　Gives out at times—he knows not whence—
A little flash, a mystic hint;

And in the long harmonious years—
　If Death so taste Lethean springs—   10

---

5. Keep us together.
6. Between an individual's death and the general resurrection, "the spiritual prime."
7. Bradley offers several possible interpretations of this difficult section, the most plausible being: "The man" of line 2 and "he" of line 3 refer to living man, who, as he grows up, forgets the first two years of infancy before the closing of the sutures of the skull.

Stanza 2 continues with the Wordsworthian notion that we receive mystic impulses from those earliest years, but does not, I think, suggest flashings from a prenatal existence. Stanza 3 then shifts to the dead, who have forgotten their earthly life ("taste Lethean springs") but may have sudden glimpses of it parallel to our recollections from earliest childhood.

May some dim touch of earthly things
 Surprise thee ranging with thy peers.

If such a dreamy touch should fall,
 O, turn thee round, resolve the doubt;
 My guardian angel will speak out   15
In that high place, and tell thee all.

45

The baby new to earth and sky,
 What time his tender palm is prest
 Against the circle of the breast,
Has never thought that "this is I;"

But as he grows he gathers much,   5
 And learns the use of "I" and "me,"
 And finds "I am not what I see,
And other than the things I touch."

So rounds he to a separate mind
 From whence clear memory may begin, 10
 As thro' the frame that binds him in
His isolation[8] grows defined.

This use may lie in blood and breath,
 Which else were fruitless of their due,
 Had man to learn himself anew   15
Beyond the second birth of death.[9]

46

We ranging down this lower track,
 The path we came by, thorn and flower,
 Is shadow'd by the growing hour,
Lest life should fail in looking back.[1]

So be it: there[2] no shade can last   5
 In that deep dawn behind the tomb,
 But clear from marge to marge[3] shall bloom
The eternal landscape of the past;

A lifelong tract of time reveal'd,
 The fruitful hours of still increase;   10
 Days order'd in a wealthy peace,
And those five years its richest field.

O Love, thy province were not large,
 A bounded field, nor stretching far;

---

8. Compare Wordsworth, "Ode: Intimations of Immortality," V, 67–68: "Shades of the prison-house begin to close / Upon the growing Boy."
9. The speaker undercuts the proposition of section 44, arguing that if the dead did forget their earthly life, they would have to acquire an identity all over again.
1. Living man's concern with the present and future ("growing hour")
makes memory imperfect. But neither can man live in the past.
2. In the spiritual world these imperfections do not exist.
3. From birth to death. The word "shall" creates ambiguities. He cannot be thinking of his friend's present state, but looks to the indefinite future. Then perhaps he, his friend, or both of them together will look back on the five-year friendship.

Look also, Love, a brooding star,   15
A rosy warmth from marge to marge.

47

That each, who seems a separate whole,
    Should move his rounds, and fusing all
    The skirts of self again, should fall
Remerging in the general Soul,[4]

Is faith as vague as all unsweet.   5
    Eternal form shall still divide
    The eternal soul from all beside;
And I shall know him when we meet;

And we shall sit at endless feast,
    Enjoying each the other's good.   10
    What vaster dream can hit the mood
Of Love on earth? He seeks at least

Upon the last and sharpest height,
    Before the spirits fade away,
    Some landing-place, to clasp and say,   15
"Farewell! We lose ourselves in light."

48

If these brief lays, of Sorrow born,
    Were taken to be such as closed[5]
    Grave doubts and answers here proposed,
Then these were such as men might scorn.

Her[6] care is not to part and prove;   5
    She takes, when harsher moods remit,
    What slender shade of doubt may flit,
And makes it vassal unto love;

And hence, indeed, she sports with words,
    But better serves a wholesome law,   10
    And holds it sin and shame to draw
The deepest measure from the chords;

Nor dare she trust a larger lay,
    But rather loosens from the lip
    Short swallow-flights of song, that dip   15
Their wings in tears, and skim away.

49

From art, from nature, from the schools,[7]
    Let random influences glance,

---

4. A medieval theory known as Averroism denied individual immortality, claiming the spirit was merged back into the universal soul from whence it came. If this must be, and we cannot endlessly enjoy each other's company, let us at least share a moment of recognition before our souls are absorbed and "we lose ourselves in light." Apparently alluding to this section, Tennyson said: "If the absorption into the divine in the after-life be the creed of some, let them at all events allow us many existences of individuality before this absorption; since this short-lived individuality seems to be but too short a preparation for so mighty a union" (*Memoir*, I, 319).
5. Concluded.
6. Sorrow's.
7. Of theology and philosophy.

Like light in many a shiver'd lance
That breaks about the dappled pools.

The lightest wave of thought shall lisp,   5
    The fancy's tenderest eddy wreathe,
    The slightest air of song shall breathe
To make the sullen surface crisp.[8]

And look thy[9] look, and go thy way,
    But blame not thou the winds that make   10
    The seeming-wanton ripple break,
The tender-pencill'd shadow play.

Beneath all fancied hopes and fears
    Ay me, the sorrow deepens down,
    Whose muffled motions blindly drown   15
The bases of my life in tears.

50

Be near me when my light is low,
    When the blood creeps, and the nerves prick
    And tingle; and the heart is sick,
And all the wheels of being slow.

Be near me when the sensuous frame   5
    Is rack'd with pangs that conquer trust;
    And Time, a maniac scattering dust,
And Life, a Fury slinging flame.

Be near me when my faith is dry,
    And men the flies of latter spring,   10
    That lay their eggs, and sting and sing
And weave their petty cells and die.

Be near me when I fade away,
    To point the term[1] of human strife,
    And on the low dark verge of life   15
The twilight of eternal day.

51[2]

Do we indeed desire the dead
    Should still be near us at our side?
    Is there no baseness we would hide?
No inner vileness that we dread?

Shall he for whose applause I strove,   5
    I had such reverence for his blame,
    See with clear eye some hidden shame
And I be lessen'd in his love?

I wrong the grave with fears untrue.
    Shall love be blamed for want of faith?   10

8. A verb; curl or ripple.
9. Any observer such as the traveller
of section 21.
1. Reach the limit or end.
2. See note to section 6. Probably

composed in December 1841. At Christ-
mas time Tennyson showed it to Ed-
mund Lushington, who wrote for the
Memoir (I, 203) that Tennyson "liked
it better than most he had done lately."

There must be wisdom with great Death;
    The dead shall look me thro' and thro'.

Be near us when we climb or fall;
    Ye watch, like God, the rolling hours
    With larger other eyes than ours,   15
To make allowance for us all.

52

I cannot love thee as I ought,
    For love reflects the thing beloved;
    My words are only words, and moved
Upon the topmost froth of thought.

"Yet blame not thou thy plaintive song,"   5
    The Spirit of true love replied;
    "Thou canst not move me from thy side,
Nor human frailty do me wrong.

"What keeps a spirit wholly true
    To that ideal which he bears?
    What record? not the sinless years[3]   10
That breathed beneath the Syrian blue;

"So fret not, like an idle girl,
    That life is dash'd with flecks of sin.
    Abide; thy wealth is gather'd in,   15
When Time hath sunder'd shell from pearl."[4]

53

How many a father have I seen,
    A sober man, among his boys,
    Whose youth was full of foolish noise,
Who wears his manhood hale and green;

And dare we to this fancy give,[5]   5
    That had the wild oat not been sown,
    The soil, left barren, scarce had grown
The grain by which a man may live?

Or, if we held the doctrine sound[6]
    For life outliving heats of youth,
    Yet who would preach it as a truth   10
To those that eddy round and round?

Hold thou the good, define it well;
    For fear divine Philosophy
    Should push beyond her mark, and be   15
Procuress to the Lords of Hell.

54

O, yet we trust that somehow good
    Will be the final goal[7] of ill,

---

3. The record of Christ's sinless earthly life.
4. Not body from spirit, but what is worthless from what is valuable in him.
5. Yield.
6. Which Tennyson apparently doesn't.
7. A notion that makes little sense. How could evil ever have good as its

To pangs of nature, sins of will,
Defects of doubt, and taints of blood;

That nothing walks with aimless feet;   5
    That not one life shall be destroy'd,
    Or cast as rubbish to the void,
When God hath made the pile complete;

That not a worm is cloven in vain;
    That not a moth with vain desire   10
    Is shrivell'd in a fruitless fire,
Or but subserves another's gain.

Behold, we know not anything;
    I can but trust that good shall fall
    At last—far off[8]—at last, to all,   15
And every winter change to spring.

So runs my dreams; but what am I?
    An infant crying in the night;
    An infant crying for the light,
And with no language but a cry.[9]   20

55

The wish, that of the living whole
    No life may fail beyond the grave,
    Derives it not from what we have
The likest God within the soul?

Are God and Nature then at strife,   5
    That Nature lends such evil dreams?
    So careful of the type[1] she seems,
So careless of the single life,

That I, considering everywhere
    Her secret meaning in her deeds,   10
    And finding that of fifty seeds
She often brings but one to bear,

I falter where I firmly trod,
    And falling with my weight of cares
    Upon the great world's altar-stairs   15
That slope thro' darkness up to God,

---

goal—final or otherwise? Tennyson may have been thinking of Pope's conclusion to Part I of the *Essay on Man:*

    All Nature is but Art, unknown to thee;
    All Chance, Direction, which thou canst not see;
    All Discord, Harmony not understood;
    All partial Evil, universal Good.

8. See the poem's concluding lines.

9. See 124, 5.
1. Species. As in section 35, here and in section 56 Lyell's influence is apparent. "The lavish profusion too in the natural world appals me, from the growths of the tropical forest to the capacity of man to multiply, the torrent of babies. . . . If we look at Nature alone, full of perfection and imperfection, she tells us that God is disease, murder and rapine" (Tennyson in *Memoir*, I, 314).

I stretch lame hands of faith, and grope,
    And gather dust and chaff, and call
    To what I feel is Lord of all,
And faintly trust the larger hope.[2]   20

56[3]

"So careful of the type?" but no.
    From scarped[4] cliff and quarried stone
    She[5] cries, "A thousand types are gone;
I care for nothing, all shall go.

"Thou makest thine appeal to me.   5
    I bring to life, I bring to death;
    The spirit does but mean the breath:
I know no more." And he, shall he,

Man, her last work, who seem'd so fair,
    Such splendid purpose in his eyes,   10
    Who roll'd the psalm to wintry skies,
Who built him fanes of fruitless prayer,

Who trusted God was love indeed
    And love Creation's final law—
    Tho' Nature, red in tooth and claw   15
With ravine, shriek'd against his creed—

Who loved, who suffer'd countless ills,
    Who battled for the True, the Just,
    Be blown about the desert dust,
Or seal'd[6] within the iron hills?   20

No more? A monster then, a dream,
    A discord. Dragons of the prime,
    That tare each other in their slime,
Were mellow music match'd with him.[7]

O life as futile, then, as frail!   25
    O for thy[8] voice to soothe and bless!
    What hope of answer, or redress?
Behind the veil, behind the veil.

---

2. "He means," his son says, "that the whole human race would through, perhaps, ages of suffering, be at length purified and saved" (*Memoir*, I, 321–322). The "hope" is larger, I take it, than the wish in stanza one that no individual lose his immortality.

3. In 1844 Tennyson wrote his publisher to obtain a copy of Chambers's *Vestiges of Creation* (1844), a book which, Tennyson rightly noted from an advertisement, "seems to contain many speculations with which I have been familiar for years" (*Memoir*, I, 222–223). Probably written before 1844,

section 56 is important because it helps support the claim that Tennyson anticipated Darwin.

4. Cut vertically exposing the strata.

5. Nature. For the poet's response, see section 118.

6. As fossils.

7. Man. The thought that man may perish as did the lost species makes the human condition monstrous and more terrifying to contemplate than the fate of prehistoric beasts, which at least worked out their destinies in harmony with natural law.

8. Hallam's.

57

Peace; come away: the song of woe
  Is after all an earthly song.
  Peace; come away: we do him wrong
To sing so wildly: let us go.[9]

Come; let us go: your cheeks are pale;   5
  But half my life I leave behind.
  Methinks my friend is richly shrined;
But I shall pass, my work will fail.

Yet in these ears, till hearing dies,
  One set slow bell will seem to toll   10
  The passing of the sweetest soul
That ever look'd with human eyes.

I hear it now, and o'er and o'er,
  Eternal greetings to the dead;
  And "Ave, Ave, Ave,"[1] said,   15
"Adieu, adieu," for evermore.

58

In those sad words I took farewell.
  Like echoes in sepulchral halls,
  As drop by drop the water falls
In vaults and catacombs, they fell;

And, falling, idly broke the peace   5
  Of hearts that beat from day to day,
  Half-conscious of their dying clay,
And those cold crypts where they shall cease.

The high Muse[2] answer'd: "Wherefore grieve
  Thy brethren with a fruitless tear?   10
  Abide a little longer here,[3]
And thou shalt take a nobler leave."

59

O Sorrow,[4] wilt thou live with me
  No casual mistress, but a wife,
  My bosom-friend and half of life;
As I confess it needs must be?

O Sorrow, wilt thou rule my blood,   5
  Be sometimes lovely like a bride,
  And put thy harsher moods aside,
If thou wilt have me wise and good?

9. Perhaps addressed to Tennyson's sister Emily, who had been Hallam's fiancée. See *Memoir*, I, 306, for the unpublished section "The Grave," originally section 57.
1. Of Catullus' farewell to his brother Tennyson said that no "modern elegy, so long as men retain the least hope in the after-life of those whom they loved, [can] equal in pathos the desolation of that everlasting farewell, 'Atque in perpetuum frater ave atque vale'" (*Memoir*, II, 239).
2. Urania, as in the opening to section 37.
3. By the grave.
4. Contrast section 3. Section 59 was added in the fourth edition, 1851.

My centred passion cannot move,
 Nor will it lessen from to-day;   10
 But I'll have leave at times to play
As with the creature of my love;

And set thee forth, for thou art mine,
 With so much hope for years to come,
 That, howsoe'er I know thee, some   15
Could hardly tell what name were thine.

60[5]

He past, a soul of nobler tone;
 My spirit loved and loves him yet,
 Like some poor girl whose heart is set
On one whose rank exceeds her own.

He mixing with his proper sphere,   5
 She finds the baseness of her lot,
 Half jealous of she knows not what,
And envying all that meet him there.

The little village looks forlorn;
 She sighs amid her narrow days,
 Moving about the household ways,   10
In that dark house where she was born.

The foolish neighbors come and go,
 And tease her till the day draws by;
 At night she weeps, "How vain am I!   15
How should he love a thing so low?"

61

If, in thy second state sublime,
 Thy ransom'd reason[6] change replies
 With all the circle of the wise,
The perfect flower of human time;

And if thou cast thine eyes below,   5
 How dimly character'd and slight,
 How dwarf'd a growth of cold and night,
How blanch'd with darkness must I grow!

Yet turn thee to the doubtful shore,[7]
 Where thy first form was made a man;   10
 I loved thee, Spirit, and love, nor can
The soul of Shakespeare love thee more.

62

Tho' if an eye that's downward cast
 Could make thee somewhat blench[8] or fail,
 Then be my love an idle tale
And fading legend of the past;

5. Sections 60–65 form a group similar to group 40–47, but here the emphasis is on the speaker's desire that his friend think of him.
6. Compare "spirits render'd free" in 38, 3; "change" means exchange.
7. Earthly life, where man is in doubt and only dimly perceives.
8. Flinch.

And thou, as one that once declined,[9]   5
  When he was little more than boy,
  On some unworthy heart with joy,
But lives to wed an equal mind,

And breathes a novel world, the while
  His other passion wholly dies,   10
  Or in the light of deeper eyes
Is matter for a flying smile.

63

Yet pity for a horse o'er-driven,
  And love in which my hound has part
  Can hang no weight upon my heart
In its assumptions up to heaven;

And I am so much more than these,   5
  As thou, perchance, art more than I,
  And yet I spare them sympathy,
And I would set their pains at ease.

So mayst thou watch me where I weep,
  As, unto vaster motions bound,[1]   10
  The circuits of thine orbit round
A higher height, a deeper deep.

64

Dost thou look back on what hath been,
  As some divinely gifted man,
  Whose life in low estate began
And on a simple village green;

Who breaks his birth's invidious bar,   5
  And grasps the skirts of happy chance,
  And breasts the blows of circumstance,
And grapples with his evil star;

Who makes by force his merit known
  And lives to clutch the golden keys,   10
  To mould a mighty state's decrees,
And shape the whisper of the throne;

And moving up from high to higher,
  Becomes on Fortune's crowning slope
  The pillar of a people's hope,   15
The centre of a world's desire;

Yet feels, as in a pensive dream,
  When all his active powers are still,
  A distant dearness in the hill,
A secret sweetness in the stream,   20

The limit of his narrower fate,
  While yet beside its vocal springs

---

9. Stooped.
1. Hallam's spirit may be re-embodied on a planet with an orbit larger than earth's.

He play'd at counsellors and kings,
  With one that was his earliest mate;

Who ploughs with pain his native lea   25
  And reaps the labor of his hands,
  Or in the furrow musing stands:
"Does my old friend remember me?"

65

Sweet soul, do with me as thou wilt;
  I lull a fancy trouble-tost
  With "Love's too precious to be lost,
A little grain shall not be spilt."

And in that solace can I sing,   5
  Till out of painful phases wrought
  There flutters up a happy thought,
Self-balanced on a lightsome wing;

Since we deserved the name of friends,
  And thine effect so lives in me,   10
  A part of mine may live in thee
And move thee on to noble ends.

66

You[2] thought my heart too far diseased;
  You wonder when my fancies play
  To find me gay among the gay,
Like one with any trifle pleased.

The shade by which my life was crost,   5
  Which makes a desert in the mind,
  Has made me kindly with my kind,
And like to him whose sight is lost;

Whose feet are guided thro' the land,
  Whose jest among his friends is free,   10
  Who takes the children on his knee,
And winds their curls about his hand.

He plays with threads, he beats his chair
  For pastime, dreaming of the sky;
  His inner day can never die,   15
His night of loss is always there.

67

When on my bed the moonlight falls,
  I know that in thy place of rest[3]
  By that broad water of the west
There comes a glory on the walls:

Thy marble bright in dark appears,   5
  As slowly steals a silver flame

2. Addressed to some unidentified friend or perhaps to no one in particular. The section marks a transition between groups. Sections 67–71 are loosely connected by references to night, sleep, and dreams.
3. At Clevedon, by the Severn River.

Along the letters of thy name,
And o'er the number of thy years.

The mystic glory swims away,
　　From off my bed the moonlight dies;   10
　　And closing eaves of wearied eyes
I sleep till dusk is dipt in gray;

And then I know the mist is drawn
　　A lucid veil from coast to coast,
　　And in the dark church[4] like a ghost   15
Thy tablet glimmers to the dawn.

68

When in the down I sink my head,
　　Sleep, Death's twin-brother, times my breath;
　　Sleep, Death's twin-brother, knows not Death,
Nor can I dream of thee as dead.

I walk as ere I walk'd forlorn,   5
　　When all our path was fresh with dew,
　　And all the bugle breezes blew
Reveillée to the breaking morn.

But what is this? I turn about,
　　I find a trouble in thine eye,   10
　　Which makes me sad I know not why,
Nor can my dream resolve the doubt;

But ere the lark hath left the lea
　　I wake, and I discern the truth;
　　It is the trouble of my youth   15
That foolish sleep transfers to thee.

69

I dream'd there would be Spring no more,
　　That Nature's ancient power was lost;
　　The streets were black with smoke and frost,
They chatter'd trifles at the door;

I wander'd from the noisy town,   5
　　I found a wood with thorny boughs;
　　I took the thorns to bind my brows,
I wore them like a civic crown;

I met with scoffs, I met with scorns
　　From youth and babe and hoary hairs: 10
　　They call'd me in the public squares
The fool that wears a crown of thorns.

---

4. See notes to sections 2 and 18. "In later editions of 'In Memoriam' I altered the word 'chancel,' which was the word used by Mr. Hallam in his Memoir, to 'dark church'" (*Memoir*, I, 305). The tablet is "in the manor isle of the church"; the epitaph, written by Hallam's father, is reproduced in the *Memoir*, I, 296.

They call'd me fool, they call'd me child:
    I found an angel[5] of the night;
      The voice was low, the look was bright;   15
He look'd upon my crown and smiled.

He reach'd the glory of a hand,
    That seem'd to touch it into leaf:
      The voice was not the voice of grief,
The words were hard to understand.   20

70

I cannot see the features right,
    When on the gloom I strive to paint
      The face I know; the hues are faint
And mix with hollow[6] masks of night;

Cloud-towers by ghostly masons wrought,   5
    A gulf that ever shuts and gapes,
      A hand that points, and palled[7] shapes
In shadowy thoroughfares of thought;

And crowds that stream from yawning doors,
    And shoals of pucker'd faces drive;   10
      Dark bulks that tumble half alive,
And lazy lengths on boundless shores;

Till all at once beyond the will
    I hear a wizard music roll,
      And thro' a lattice on the soul   15
Looks thy fair face and makes it still.

71

Sleep, kinsman thou to death and trance
    And madness, thou hast forged at last
      A night-long present of the past
In which we went thro' summer France.[8]

Hadst thou such credit with the soul?   5
    Then bring an opiate trebly strong,
      Drug down the blindfold sense of wrong,
That so my pleasure may be whole;

While now we talk as once we talk'd
    Of men and minds, the dust of change,   10
      The days that grow to something strange,
In walking as of old we walk'd

Beside the river's wooded reach,
    The fortress, and the mountain ridge,
      The cataract flashing from the bridge,   15
The breaker breaking on the beach.

5. According to Bradley, Tennyson told Knowles the angel was "the divine Thing in the gloom." The stanza reminds one of similar visions in Blake.
6. Lacking substance.
7. Veiled, hence dimly seen.

8. In 1830, Tennyson and Hallam journeyed through the Pyrenees to see Torrijos, who was leading a revolt against the Spanish King. See notes to "Œnone," p. 20.

72

Risest thou thus, dim dawn,[9] again,
　And howlest, issuing out of night,
　With blasts that blow the poplar white,
And lash with storm the streaming pane?

Day, when my crown'd estate[1] begun　　　　　　　5
　To pine in that reverse of doom,
　Which sicken'd every living bloom,
And blurr'd the splendor of the sun;

Who usherest in the dolorous hour
　With thy quick tears that make the rose　　　10
　Pull sideways, and the daisy close
Her crimson fringes to the shower;

Who mightst have heaved a windless flame
　Up the deep East, or, whispering, play'd
　A chequer-work of beam and shade　　　　　　15
Along the hills, yet look'd the same,

As wan, as chill, as wild as now;
　Day, mark'd as with some hideous crime,
　When the dark hand struck down thro' time,
And cancell'd nature's best: but thou,　　　　　20

Lift as thou mayst thy burthen'd brows
　Thro' clouds that drench the morning star,
　And whirl the ungarner'd sheaf afar,
And sow the sky with flying boughs,

And up thy vault with roaring sound　　　　　　25
　Climb thy thick noon, disastrous day;
　Touch thy dull goal[2] of joyless gray,
And hide thy shame beneath the ground.

73

So many worlds, so much to do,
　So little done, such things to be,
　How know I what had need of thee,[3]
For thou wert strong as thou wert true?

The fame is quench'd that I foresaw,　　　　　　5
　The head hath miss'd an earthly wreath:
　I curse not Nature, no, nor Death;
For nothing is that errs from law.

We pass; the path that each man trod
　Is dim, or will be dim, with weeds.　　　　　　10

9. September 15, 1834, the first anni-
versary of Hallam's death. See *Mem-
oir*, I, 305. Contrast section 99.
1. As a poet. "Crown'd" recalls those
happy days recorded in section 22, 2.
2. The sun's zenith or noon; line 28
suggests the sunset. Perhaps both lines
refer to the sunset.
3. Hallam. Here and through section
77, Tennyson seems indebted to Mil-
ton's "Lycidas," particularly on the
subject of fame.

What fame is left for human deeds
In endless age? It rests with God.

O hollow wraith[4] of dying fame,
    Fade wholly, while the soul exults,
    And self-infolds the large results   15
Of force that would have forged a name.

74

As sometimes in a dead man's face,
    To those that watch it more and more,
    A likeness, hardly seen before,
Comes out—to some one of his race;

So, dearest, now thy brows are cold,   5
    I see thee what thou art, and know
    Thy likeness to the wise below,[5]
Thy kindred with the great of old.

But there is more than I can see,
    And what I see I leave unsaid,   10
    Nor speak it, knowing Death has made
His darkness beautiful with thee.

75

I leave thy praises unexpress'd
    In verse that brings myself relief,[6]
    And by the measure of my grief
I leave thy greatness to be guess'd.

What practice howsoe'er expert   5
    In fitting aptest words to things,
    Or voice the richest-toned that sings,
Hath power to give thee as thou wert?

I care not in these fading days
    To raise a cry that lasts not long,   10
    And round thee with the breeze of song
To stir a little dust of praise.

Thy leaf has perish'd in the green,
    And, while we breathe beneath the sun,
    The world which credits what is done
Is cold to all that might have been.   15

So here shall silence guard thy fame;
    But somewhere, out of human view,
    Whate'er thy hands are set to do
Is wrought with tumult of acclaim.   20

76

Take wings of fancy, and ascend,
    And in a moment set thy face

---

4. Apparition. See section 70, 1.
5. The famous dead; lines 7 and 8 are in apposition.

6. Contrast the "sad mechanic exercise" of 5, 2.

Where all the starry heavens of space
Are sharpen'd to a needle's end;

Take wings of foresight; lighten thro'   5
   The secular abyss to come,
   And lo, thy deepest lays are dumb
Before the mouldering of a yew;

And if the matin songs,[7] that woke
   The darkness of our planet, last,   10
   Thine own shall wither in the vast,
Ere half the lifetime of an oak.

Ere these[8] have clothed their branchy bowers
   With fifty Mays, thy songs are vain;
   And what are they when these remain   15
The ruin'd shells of hollow towers?

77

What hope is here for modern rhyme
   To him who turns a musing eye
   On songs, and deeds, and lives, that lie
Foreshorten'd in the tract of time?

These mortal lullabies of pain   5
   May bind a book, may line a box,
   May serve to curl a maiden's locks;
Or when a thousand moons shall wane

A man upon a stall may find,
   And, passing, turn the page that tells   10
   A grief, then changed to something else,
Sung by a long-forgotten mind.

But what of that? My darken'd ways
   Shall ring with music all the same;
   To breathe my loss is more than fame,   15
To utter love more sweet than praise.

78

Again at Christmas[9] did we weave
   The holly round the Christmas hearth;
   The silent snow possess'd the earth,
And calmly fell our Christmas-eve.

The yule-clog[1] sparkled keen with frost,   5
   No wing of wind the region swept,
   But over all things brooding slept
The quiet sense of something lost.

7. Of the great early poets.
8. The long-lived yew and oak.
9. The second Christmas (1834) after Hallam's death. The third part of the poem begins here. For Bradley, this section marks the "turning-point in the general feeling of *In Memoriam.* . . .

It seems true that in spite of gradual change, the tone of the poem so far is, on the whole, melancholy, while after LXXVIII. the predominant tone can scarcely be called even sad." But see my note to section 95.
1. Scottish dialect for yule-log.

As in the winters left behind,
  Again our ancient games had place,   10
  The mimic picture's[2] breathing grace,
And dance and song and hoodman-blind.[3]

Who show'd a token of distress?
  No single tear, no mark of pain—
  O sorrow, then can sorrow wane?   15
O grief, can grief be changed to less?

O last regret, regret can die!
  No—mixt with all this mystic frame,
  Her deep relations are the same,
But with long use her tears are dry.   20

79

"More than my brothers[4] are to me,"—
  Let this not vex thee, noble heart!
  I know thee of what force thou art
To hold the costliest love in fee.[5]

But thou and I are one in kind,   5
  As moulded like in Nature's mint;
  And hill and wood and field did print
The same sweet forms in either mind.

For us the same cold streamlet curl'd
  Thro' all his eddying coves, the same   10
  All winds that roam the twilight came
In whispers of the beauteous world.

At one dear knee we proffer'd vows,
  One lesson from one book we learn'd,
  Ere childhood's flaxen ringlet turn'd   15
To black and brown on kindred brows.

And so my wealth resembles thine,
  But he was rich where I was poor,
  And he supplied my want the more
As his unlikeness fitted mine.   20

80

If any vague desire should rise,
  That holy Death ere Arthur died
  Had moved me kindly from his side,
And dropt the dust on tearless eyes;

Then fancy shapes, as fancy can,   5
  The grief my loss in him had wrought,
  A grief as deep as life or thought,
But stay'd[6] in peace with God and man.

---

2. Tableaux vivants. A game like charades in which the participants assume poses of well-known figures in paintings or statues while the rest of the group guesses their identity.
3. Blind-man's buff.

4. Addressed to Tennyson's favorite brother, Charles Tennyson Turner. See the last line of section 9.
5. Full possession.
6. Propped.

I make a picture in the brain;
    I hear the sentence that he speaks;   10
    He bears the burthen of the weeks,
But turns his burthen into gain.

His credit[7] thus shall set me free;
    And, influence-rich to soothe and save,
    Unused example from the grave   15
Reach out dead hands to comfort me.

81

Could I have said while he was here,
    "My love shall now no further range;
    There cannot come a mellower change,
For now is love mature in ear"?[8]

Love, then,[9] had hope of richer store: 5
    What end is here to my complaint?
    This haunting whisper makes me faint,
"More years had made me love thee more."

But Death returns an answer sweet:
    "My sudden frost was sudden gain,   10
    And gave all ripeness to the grain[1]
It might have drawn from after-heat."

82

I wage not any feud with Death
    For changes wrought on form and face;
    No lower life that earth's embrace
May breed with him can fright my faith.

Eternal process moving on,   5
    From state to state the spirit walks;
    And these[2] are but the shatter'd stalks,
Or ruin'd chrysalis of one.

Nor blame I Death, because he bare
    The use of virtue out of earth;   10
    I know transplanted human worth
Will bloom to profit, otherwhere.

For this alone on Death I wreak
    The wrath that garners in my heart:
    He put our lives so far apart   15
We cannot hear each other speak.

---

7. The capacity to turn burden into gain which, in the poet's fancy, Hallam would have done had Tennyson died.
8. Ear of grain.
9. At that time. The meaning of these complicated five lines seems to be: if, when Hallam was alive, I could have said our love was complete, I could have anticipated then a fuller store of love were he to die than I could have by assuming our relationship to be incomplete.
1. His love for Hallam was ripened through sudden death, as some fruit is ripened by a sudden frost.
2. "Changes" of line 2.

83

Dip down upon the northern shore,
    O sweet new-year delaying long;
    Thou doest expectant Nature wrong;
Delaying long, delay no more.

What stays thee from the clouded noons,[3]   5
    Thy sweetness from its proper place?
    Can trouble live with April days,
Or sadness in the summer moons?[4]

Bring orchis, bring the foxglove spire,
    The little speedwell's darling blue,   10
    Deep tulips dash'd with fiery dew,
Laburnums, dropping-wells of fire.

O thou, new-year, delaying long,
    Delayest the sorrow in my blood,
    That longs to burst a frozen bud   15
And flood a fresher throat with song.

84

When I contemplate all alone
    The life that had been thine below,
    And fix my thoughts on all the glow
To which thy crescent would have grown,

I see thee sitting crown'd with good,   5
    A central warmth diffusing bliss
    In glance and smile, and clasp and kiss,
On all the branches of thy blood;

Thy blood, my friend, and partly mine;
    For now the day was drawing on,   10
    When thou shouldst link thy life with one[5]
Of mine own house, and boys of thine

Had babbled "Uncle" on my knee;
    But that remorseless iron hour
    Made cypress of her orange flower,[6]   15
Despair of hope, and earth of thee.

I seem to meet their least desire,
    To clap their cheeks, to call them mine.
    I see their unborn faces shine
Beside the never-lighted fire.   20

I see myself an honor'd guest,
    Thy partner in the flowery walk
    Of letters, genial table-talk,
Or deep dispute, and graceful jest;

3. The "new-year," or Spring, has not caught up with these April days whose cloudiness suggests an earlier season.
4. Contrast section 38.
5. Emily Tennyson, to whom Hallam was engaged.
6. See 40, 1. The orange-blossom is symbolic of weddings; the cypress, of death and mourning.

While now thy prosperous labor fills 25
  The lips of men with honest praise,
  And sun by sun the happy days
Descend below the golden hills

With promise of a morn as fair;
  And all the train of bounteous hours 30
  Conduct, by paths of growing powers,
To reverence and the silver hair;

Till slowly worn her earthly robe,
  Her lavish mission richly wrought,
  Leaving great legacies of thought, 35
Thy spirit should fail from off the globe;

What time mine own might also flee,
  As link'd with thine in love and fate,
  And, hovering o'er the dolorous strait
To the other shore, involved in thee, 40

Arrive at last the blessed goal,
  And He that died in Holy Land
  Would reach us out the shining hand,
And take us as a single soul.

What reed was that on which I leant? 45
  Ah, backward fancy, wherefore wake
  The old bitterness again, and break
The low beginnings of content?

85[7]

This truth came borne with bier and pall,
  I felt it, when I sorrow'd most,
  'T is better to have loved and lost,
Than never to have loved at all—[8]

O true in word, and tried in deed, 5
  Demanding, so to bring relief
  To this which is our common grief,
What kind of life is that I lead;

And whether trust in things above
  Be dimm'd of sorrow, or sustain'd; 10
  And whether love for him have drain'd
My capabilities of love;

Your words have virtue such as draws
  A faithful answer from the breast,
  Thro' light reproaches, half exprest, 15
And loyal unto kindly laws.

7. Addressed to Edmund Lushington, who married Tennyson's sister Cecilia on October 10, 1842. See the "Epilogue." A draft of this section was made in 1833 but clearly was much altered later.
8. See 27, 4.

My blood an even tenor kept,
    Till on mine ear this message falls,
    That in Vienna's fatal walls
God's finger touch'd him, and he slept.   20

The great Intelligences[9] fair
    That range above our mortal state,
    In circle round the blessed gate,
Received and gave him welcome there;

And led him thro' the blissful climes,   25
    And show'd him in the fountain fresh
    All knowledge that the sons of flesh
Shall gather in the cycled times.

But I remain'd, whose hopes were dim,
    Whose life, whose thoughts were little worth,   30
    To wander on a darken'd earth,
Where all things round me breathed of him.

O friendship, equal-poised control,
    O heart, with kindliest motion warm,
    O sacred essence, other form,   35
O solemn ghost, O crowned soul!

Yet none could better know than I,
    How much of act at human hands
    The sense of human will demands
By which we dare to live or die.   40

Whatever way my days decline,
    I felt and feel, tho' left alone,
    His being working in mine own,
The footsteps of his life in mine;

A life that all the Muses deck'd   45
    With gifts of grace, that might express
    All-comprehensive tenderness,
All-subtilizing intellect:

And so my passion hath not swerved
    To works of weakness, but I find   50
    An image comforting the mind,
And in my grief a strength reserved.

Likewise the imaginative woe,
    That loved to handle spiritual strife,
    Diffused the shock thro' all my life,   55
But in the present broke the blow.

My pulses therefore beat again
    For other friends that once I met;
    Nor can it suit me to forget
The mighty hopes[1] that make us men.   60

9. Angels.
1. Compare 55, 5, and see *Memoir*, I, 321: "We cannot give up the mighty hopes that make us men."

I woo your love: I count it crime
  To mourn for any overmuch;
  I, the divided half of such
A friendship as had[2] master'd Time;

Which masters Time indeed, and is   65
  Eternal, separate from fears.
  The all-assuming[3] months and years
Can take no part away from this;

But Summer on the steaming floods,
  And Spring that swells the narrow brooks,   70
  And Autumn, with a noise of rooks,
That gather in the waning woods,

And every pulse of wind and wave
  Recalls, in change of light or gloom,
  My old affection of the tomb,   75
And my prime passion in the grave.

My old affection of the tomb,
  A part of stillness, yearns to speak:
  "Arise, and get thee forth and seek
A friendship for the years to come.   80

"I watch thee from the quiet shore;
  Thy spirit up to mine can reach;
  But in dear words of human speech
We two communicate no more."

And I, "Can clouds of nature stain   85
  The starry clearness of the free?[4]
  How is it? Canst thou feel for me
Some painless sympathy with pain?"

And lightly does the whisper fall:
  " 'T is hard for thee to fathom this;   90
  I triumph in conclusive bliss,
And that serene result of all."

So hold I commerce with the dead;
  Or so methinks the dead would say;
  Or so shall grief with symbols play   95
And pining life be fancy-fed.

Now looking to some settled end,
  That these things pass, and I shall prove
  A meeting somewhere, love with love,
I crave your pardon, O my friend;   100

If not so fresh, with love as true,
  I, clasping brother-hands, aver
  I could not, if I would, transfer
The whole I felt for him to you.

2. Would have.   4. From the body, as in 38, 3.
3. All-devouring.

For which be they that hold apart 105
   The promise of the golden hours?
   First love, first friendship, equal powers,
That marry with the virgin heart.

Still mine, that cannot but deplore,
   That beats within a lonely place, 110
   That yet remembers his embrace,
But at his footstep leaps no more,

My heart, tho' widow'd, may not rest
   Quite in the love of what is gone,
   But seeks to beat in time with one 115
That warms another living breast.

Ah, take the imperfect gift I bring,
   Knowing the primrose yet is dear,
   The primrose of the later year,
As not unlike to that of Spring. 120

86[5]

Sweet after showers, ambrosial air,
   That rollest from the gorgeous gloom
   Of evening over brake and bloom
And meadow, slowly breathing bare

The round of space,[6] and rapt below 5
   Thro' all the dewy tassell'd wood,
   And shadowing down the horned[7] flood
In ripples, fan my brows and blow

The fever from my cheek, and sigh
   The full new life that feeds thy breath 10
   Throughout my frame, till Doubt and Death,
Ill brethren, let the fancy fly

From belt to belt of crimson seas
   On leagues of odor streaming far,
   To where in yonder orient star 15
A hundred spirits whisper "Peace."

87

I past beside the reverend walls[8]
   In which of old I wore the gown;
   I roved at random thro' the town,
And saw the tumult of the halls;

And heard once more in college fanes 5
   The storm their high-built organs make,
   And thunder-music, rolling, shake
The prophet blazon'd on the panes;

5. Answering section 83, this was written at Barmouth (see *Memoir*, I, 313), which Tennyson first visited in 1839 and described as "a flat sand shore, a sea with breakers, looking Mablethorpe-like, and sand hills, and close behind them huge crags and a long estuary with cloud-capt hills" (*Memoir*, I, 173–174).
6. The wind clears the sky of clouds.
7. Winding water, indented by land.
8. Of Trinity College, Cambridge.

And caught once more the distant shout,
 The measured pulse of racing oars   10
 Among the willows; paced the shores
And many a bridge, and all about

The same gray flats again, and felt
 The same, but not the same; and last
 Up that long walk of limes I past   15
To see the rooms in which he dwelt.

Another name was on the door.
 I linger'd; all within was noise
 Of songs, and clapping hands, and boys
That crash'd the glass and beat the floor;   20

Where once we held debate, a band[9]
 Of youthful friends, on mind and art,
 And labor, and the changing mart,
And all the framework of the land;

When one would aim an arrow fair,   25
 But send it slackly from the string;
 And one would pierce on outer ring,
And one an inner, here and there;

And last the master-bowman,[1] he,
 Would cleave the mark. A willing ear   30
 We lent him. Who but hung to hear
The rapt oration flowing free

From point to point, with power and grace
 And music in the bounds of law,
 To those conclusions when we saw   35
The God within him light his face,

And seem to lift the form, and glow
 In azure orbits heavenly-wise;
 And over those ethereal eyes
The bar of Michael Angelo?[2]   40

88

Wild bird,[3] whose warble, liquid sweet,
 Rings Eden thro' the budded quicks,[4]
 O, tell me where the senses mix,
O, tell me where the passions meet,

Whence radiate: fierce extremes employ   5
 Thy spirits in the darkening[5] leaf,
 And in the midmost heart of grief
Thy passion clasps a secret joy;

9. The Apostles.
1. Hallam.
2. "These lines I wrote from what Arthur Hallam said after reading of the prominent ridge of bone over the eyes of Michael Angelo: 'Alfred, look over my eyes; surely I have the bar of Michael Angelo' " (*Memoir*, I, 38).
3. The nightingale.
4. Hedgerows.
5. As night approaches.

And I—my harp would prelude woe—
    I cannot all command the strings;   10
    The glory of the sum of things
Will flash along the chords and go.

89

Witch-elms that counterchange[6] the floor
    Of this flat lawn with dusk and bright;
    And thou, with all thy breadth and height
Of foliage, towering sycamore;

How often, hither wandering down,   5
    My Arthur found your shadows fair,
    And shook to all the liberal air
The dust and din and steam of town!

He brought an eye for all he saw;
    He mixt in all our simple sports;   10
    They pleased him, fresh from brawling courts
And dusty purlieus of the law.[7]

O joy to him in this retreat,
    Immantled in ambrosial dark,
    To drink the cooler air, and mark   15
The landscape winking thro' the heat!

O sound to rout the brood of cares,
    The sweep of scythe in morning dew,
    The gust that round the garden flew,
And tumbled half the mellowing pears!   20

O bliss, when all in circle drawn
    About him, heart and ear were fed
    To hear him, as he lay and read
The Tuscan[8] poets on the lawn!

Or in the all-golden afternoon   25
    A guest, or happy sister, sung,
    Or here she brought the harp and flung
A ballad to the brightening moon.

Nor less it pleased in livelier moods,
    Beyond the bounding hill to stray,
    And break the livelong summer day   30
With banquet in the distant woods;

Whereat we glanced from theme to theme,
    Discuss'd the books to love or hate,
    Or touch'd the changes of the state,   35
Or threaded some Socratic dream;[9]

6. Checker. The section looks back to Hallam's visits to Somersby.
7. After leaving Cambridge, Hallam became a law student.
8. Dante and Petrarch.

9. "Arthur Hallam could take in the most abstruse ideas with the utmost rapidity and insight" (Tennyson in *Memoir*, I, 45).

But if I praised the busy town,
 He loved to rail against it still,
 For "ground in yonder social mill
We rub each other's angles down,   40

"And merge," he said, "in form and gloss
 The picturesque of man and man."
 We talk'd: the stream beneath us ran,
The wine-flask lying couch'd in moss,

Or cool'd within the glooming wave;   45
 And last, returning from afar,
 Before the crimson-circled star[1]
Had fallen into her father's[2] grave,

And brushing ankle-deep in flowers,
 We heard behind the woodbine veil   50
 The milk that bubbled in the pail,
And buzzings of the honeyed hours.

90[3]

He tasted love with half his mind,
 Nor ever drank the inviolate spring
 Where nighest heaven, who first could fling
This bitter seed[4] among mankind:

That could the dead, whose dying eyes   5
 Were closed with wail, resume their life,
 They would but find in child and wife
An iron welcome when they rise.

'T was well, indeed, when warm with wine,
 To pledge them with a kindly tear,   10
 To talk them o'er, to wish them here,
To count their memories half divine;

But if they came who past away,
 Behold their brides in other hands;
 The hard heir strides about their lands,   15
And will not yield them for a day.

Yea, tho' their sons were none of these,
 Not less the yet-loved sire would make
 Confusion worse than death, and shake
The pillars of domestic peace.   20

1. Venus, surrounded by the sunset, sinks after the sun.
2. Tennyson is thinking of the nebular hypothesis (see section 3, 2) which held that the planets were born from the gaseous matter thrown from the sun. In *The Princess*, (II, 101–104), Lady Psyche gives an account of the earth's beginnings:
 "This world was once a fluid haze of light,
 Til toward the centre set the starry tides,
 And eddied into suns, that wheeling cast
 The planets."
3. Sections 90–95 form a group concerned with communion between the living and dead.
4. The notion expressed in the following stanza.

Ah, dear, but come thou back to me!
  Whatever change the years have wrought,
  I find not yet one lonely thought
That cries against my wish for thee.

91

When rosy plumelets tuft the larch,
  And rarely[5] pipes the mounted thrush,
  Or underneath the barren bush
Flits by the sea-blue bird[6] of March;

Come, wear the form by which I know   5
  Thy spirit in time[7] among thy peers;
  The hope of unaccomplish'd years
Be large and lucid round thy brow.

When summer's hourly-mellowing change
  May breathe, with many roses sweet,   10
  Upon the thousand waves of wheat
That ripple round the lowly grange,

Come; not in watches of the night,
  But where the sunbeam broodeth warm,
  Come, beauteous in thine after form,[8]   15
And like a finer light in light.

92

If any vision should reveal
  Thy likeness, I might count in vain
  As but the canker of the brain;
Yea, tho' it spake and made appeal

To chances where our lots were cast   5
  Together in the days behind,
  I might but say, I hear a wind
Of memory[9] murmuring the past.

Yea, tho' it spake and bared to view
  A fact within the coming year;   10
  And tho' the months, revolving near,
Should prove the phantom-warning true,

They might not seem thy prophecies,
  But spiritual presentiments,[1]
  And such refraction of events   15
As often rises ere they rise.

93

I shall not see thee. Dare I say
  No spirit ever brake the band

---

5. Exquisitely.
6. The kingfisher.
7. In earthly life.
8. In whatever maturer form he is in
now.
9. My own memory.

1. Of my own, which can often arise
in the unconscious mind and not be
recognized until the event. The meta-
phor is of a mirage; refraction can
make an object below the horizon
visible.

That stays him from the native land
Where first he walk'd when claspt in clay?

No visual shade of some one lost,   5
 But he, the Spirit himself, may come
 Where all the nerve of sense is numb,
Spirit to Spirit, Ghost to Ghost.

O, therefore from thy sightless range[2]
 With gods in unconjectured bliss,   10
 O, from the distance of the abyss
Of tenfold-complicated change,

Descend, and touch, and enter; hear
 The wish too strong for words to name,
 That in this blindness of the frame   15
My Ghost may feel that thine is near.

94

How pure at heart and sound in head,
 With what divine affections bold
 Should be the man whose thought would hold
An hour's communion with the dead.

In vain shalt thou, or any, call   5
 The spirits from their golden day,
 Except, like them, thou too canst say,
My spirit is at peace with all.

They haunt the silence of the breast,
 Imaginations calm and fair,   10
 The memory like a cloudless air,
The conscience as a sea at rest;

But when the heart is full of din,
 And doubt beside the portal waits,
 They can but listen at the gates,   15
And hear the household jar within.

95[3]

By night we linger'd on the lawn,[4]
 For underfoot the herb was dry;
 And genial warmth; and o'er the sky
The silvery haze of summer drawn;

And calm that let the tapers burn   5
 Unwavering: not a cricket chirr'd;
 The brook alone far-off was heard,
And on the board the fluttering urn.[5]

2. The invisible height where his friend's spirit ranges.
3. Section 78 may mark the turning-point in the poem, but its climax comes here. Tennyson says in the *Memoir* (I, 320) that he had from boyhood the capacity to put himself into "a kind of waking trance" in which "out of the intensity of the consciousness of individuality, the individuality itself seemed to dissolve and fade away into boundless being." See note to "The Mystic," p. 535.
4. At Somersby, where a family gathering has taken place.
5. A teapot which is boiling.

And bats went round in fragrant skies,
    And wheel'd or lit the filmy shapes[6]   10
    That haunt the dusk, with ermine capes
And woolly breasts and beaded eyes;

While now we sang old songs that peal'd
    From knoll to knoll, where, couch'd at ease,
    The white kine[7] glimmer'd, and the trees   15
Laid their dark arms about the field.

But when those others, one by one,
    Withdrew themselves from me and night,
    And in the house light after light
Went out, and I was all alone,   20

A hunger seized my heart; I read
    Of that glad year[8] which once had been,
    In those fallen leaves which kept their green,
The noble letters of the dead.

And strangely on the silence broke   25
    The silent-speaking words, and strange
    Was love's dumb cry defying change
To test his worth; and strangely spoke

The faith, the vigor, bold to dwell
    On doubts that drive the coward back,   30
    And keen thro' wordy snares to track
Suggestion to her inmost cell.

So word by word, and line by line,
    The dead man touch'd me from the past,
    And all at once it seem'd at last   35
The living soul was flash'd on mine,

And mine in this[9] was wound, and whirl'd
    About empyreal heights of thought,
    And came on that which is, and caught
The deep pulsations of the world,   40

Æonian music[1] measuring out
    The steps of Time—the shocks of Chance—
    The blows of Death. At length my trance
Was cancell'd, stricken thro' with doubt.

Vague words! but ah, how hard to frame   45
    In matter-moulded forms of speech,

6. Night-moths, especially the ermine moth.
7. Cattle.
8. The five years of the friendship.
9. Originally "His living soul" and "mine in his." According to Bradley, Tennyson remarked to Knowles: "perchance the Deity. . . . My conscience is troubled by 'his.'" Bradley suggests the poet's conscience was troubled by "a doubt whether the soul that seemed to be flashed on his, and seemed to be Hallam's, *was* Hallam's."
1. The music of the spheres which has gone on for eons. For a moment he senses the harmony in an otherwise unintelligible universe.

Or even for intellect to reach
Thro' memory that which I became;

Till now the doubtful dusk reveal'd
    The knolls once more where, couch'd at ease,   50
    The white kine glimmer'd, and the trees
Laid their dark arms about the field;

And suck'd from out the distant gloom
    A breeze began to tremble o'er
    The large leaves of the sycamore,   55
And fluctuate all the still perfume,

And gathering freshlier overhead,
    Rock'd the full-foliaged elms, and swung
    The heavy-folded rose, and flung
The lilies to and fro, and said,   60

"The dawn, the dawn," and died away;
    And East and West, without a breath,
    Mixt their dim lights, like life and death,
To broaden into boundless day.

96

You say, but with no touch of scorn,
    Sweet-hearted, you,[2] whose light-blue eyes
    Are tender over drowning flies,
You tell me, doubt is Devil-born.

I know not: one[3] indeed I knew   5
    In many a subtle question versed,
    Who touch'd a jarring lyre at first,
But ever strove to make it true;

Perplext in faith, but pure in deeds,
    At last he beat his music out.   10
    There lives more faith in honest doubt,
Believe me, than in half the creeds.

He fought his doubts and gather'd strength,
    He would not make his judgment blind,
    He faced the spectres of the mind   15
And laid them; thus he came at length

To find a stronger faith his own;
    And Power was with him in the night,
    Which makes the darkness and the light,
And dwells not in the light alone,   20

But in the darkness and the cloud,
    As over Sinai's peaks of old,
    While Israel made their gods of gold,
Altho' the trumpet blew so loud.[4]

2. Some imaginary woman of simple beliefs. See 33.
3. Hallam, according to Tennyson.
4. The stanza refers to Moses receiving the Commandments on Mount Sinai while the Israelites lawlessly idolized a golden calf. See *Exodus,* 19:16–25, and 32:1–6.

97

My love[5] has talk'd with rocks and trees;
　　He finds on misty mountain-ground
　　His own vast shadow glory-crown'd;[6]
He sees himself in all he sees.

Two partners of a married life—　　　　　　　　5
　　I look'd on these and thought of thee[7]
　　In vastness and in mystery,
And of my spirit as of a wife.

These two—they dwelt with eye on eye,
　　Their hearts of old have beat in tune,　　　10
　　Their meetings made December June,
Their every parting was to die.

Their love has never past away;
　　The days she never can forget
　　Are earnest[8] that he loves her yet,　　　15
Whate'er the faithless people say.

Her life is lone, he sits apart;
　　He loves her yet, she will not weep,
　　Tho' rapt in matters dark and deep
He seems to slight her simple heart.　　　　20

He thrids[9] the labyrinth of the mind,
　　He reads the secret of the star,
　　He seems so near and yet so far,
He looks so cold: she thinks him kind.

She keeps the gift of years before,　　　　25
　　A wither'd violet is her bliss;
　　She knows not what his greatness is,
For that, for all, she loves him more.

For him she plays, to him she sings
　　Of early faith and plighted vows;　　　30
　　She knows but matters of the house,
And he, he knows a thousand things.

Her faith is fixt and cannot move,
　　She darkly feels him great and wise,
　　She dwells on him with faithful eyes,　　35
"I cannot understand; I love."

98

You[1] leave us: you will see the Rhine,
　　And those fair hills I sail'd below,

---

5. A personification of love, not Hallam. Compare 60.
6. With a halo.
7. Hallam.
8. A pledge.
9. Threads.
1. Tennyson's brother Charles, who was married in 1836 and here is about to set off on his honeymoon for the Rhine valley (where Tennyson travelled with Hallam in 1832) and Vienna (where Hallam died). See *Memoir*, I, 148.

When I was there with him; and go
By summer belts of wheat and vine

To where he breathed his latest breath,   5
That city. All her splendor seems
No livelier than the wisp that gleams
On Lethe in the eyes of Death.

Let her great Danube rolling fair
Enwind her isles, unmark'd of me;[2]   10
I have not seen, I will not see
Vienna; rather dream that there,

A treble darkness, Evil haunts
The birth, the bridal; friend from friend
Is oftener parted, fathers bend   15
Above more graves, a thousand wants

Gnarr at the heels of men, and prey
By each cold hearth, and sadness flings
Her shadow on the blaze of kings.
And yet myself have heard him say,   20

That not in any mother town[3]
With statelier progress to and fro
The double tides of chariots flow
By park and suburb under brown

Of lustier leaves; nor more content,   25
He told me, lives in any crowd,
When all is gay with lamps, and loud
With sport and song, in booth and tent,

Imperial halls, or open plain;
And wheels the circled dance, and breaks   30
The rocket molten into flakes
Of crimson or in emerald rain.

99

Risest thou thus, dim dawn, again,[4]
So loud with voices of the birds,
So thick with lowings of the herds,
Day, when I lost the flower of men;

Who tremblest thro' thy darkling red[5]   5
On yon swollen brook that bubbles fast
By meadows breathing of the past,
And woodlands holy to the dead;

Who murmurest in the foliage eaves
A song that slights the coming care,   10
And Autumn laying here and there
A fiery finger on the leaves;

2. Unseen by me; Tennyson never did go to Vienna.
3. Metropolis.
4. The second anniversary (September 15, 1835) of Hallam's death. See section 72.
5. The clouds in the sunset fading into darkness.

Who wakenest with thy balmy breath
  To myriads on the genial earth,
  Memories of bridal, or of birth,   15
And unto myriads more, of death.

O, wheresoever those[6] may be,
  Betwixt the slumber[7] of the poles,
  To-day they count as kindred souls;
They know me not, but mourn with me.   20

                100[8]

I climb the hill: from end to end
  Of all the landscape underneath,
  I find no place that does not breathe
Some gracious memory of my friend;

No gray old grange, or lonely fold,   5
  Or low morass and whispering reed,
  Or simple stile from mead to mead,
Or sheepwalk up the windy wold;

Nor hoary[9] knoll of ash and haw
  That hears the latest linnet trill,   10
  Nor quarry trench'd along the hill
And haunted by the wrangling daw;

Nor runlet tinkling from the rock;
  Nor pastoral rivulet that swerves
  To left and right thro' meadowy curves,   15
That feed the mothers of the flock;

But each has pleased a kindred eye,
  And each reflects a kindlier day;
  And, leaving these, to pass away,
I think once more he seems to die.   20

                101

Unwatch'd, the garden bough shall sway,
  The tender blossom flutter down,
  Unloved, that beech will gather brown,
This maple burn itself away;

Unloved, the sunflower, shining fair,   5
  Ray round with flames her disk of seed,
  And many a rose-carnation feed
With summer spice the humming air;

Unloved, by many a sandy bar,
  The brook shall babble down the plain,   10

6. The "myriads" who remember death.
7. At the poles, the earth seems not to
be rotating.
8. Sections 100–103 are concerned with
the Tennyson family's move from
Somersby to High Beech, north of
London. The group makes a transition
to the last part of the poem. Compare
"A Farewell," p. 94.
9. An autumnal scene. The move from
Somersby had been contemplated for
many months. As nearly as I can make
out, it actually took place in the spring
of 1837.

At noon or when the Lesser Wain[1]
Is twisting round the polar star;

Uncared for, gird the windy grove,
    And flood the haunts of hern[2] and crake,
    Or into silver arrows break   15
The sailing moon in creek and cove;

Till from the garden and the wild
    A fresh association blow,
    And year by year the landscape grow
Familiar to the stranger's child;   20

As year by year the laborer tills
    His wonted glebe, or lops the glades,
    And year by year our memory fades
From all the circle of the hills.

102

We leave the well-beloved place
    Where first we gazed upon the sky;
    The roofs that heard our earliest cry
Will shelter one of stranger race.

We go, but ere we go from home,   5
    As down the garden-walks I move,
    Two spirits[3] of a diverse love
Contend for loving masterdom.

One[4] whispers, "Here thy boyhood sung
    Long since its matin song,[5] and heard   10
    The low love-language of the bird
In native hazels tassel-hung."

The other answers, "Yea, but here
    Thy feet have stray'd in after hours
    With thy lost friend among the bowers,   15
And this hath made them trebly dear."

These two have striven half the day,
    And each prefers his separate claim,
    Poor rivals in a losing game,
That will not yield each other way.   20

I turn to go; my feet are set
    To leave the pleasant fields and farms;
    They mix in one another's arms
To one pure image of regret.

---

1. Ursa Minor, whose axis is the North Star.
2. The heron and corncrake, a kind of short-billed rail.
3. "Referring to the double loss of his father and of his friend" (*Memoir*, I, 72).
4. Not to be taken as either Hallam's or Tennyson's father's spirit. The poet glossed: "First, the love of the native place; second, this enhanced by the memory of A. H. H."
5. His earliest poetry.

103

On that last night[6] before we went
    From out the doors where I was bred,
    I dream'd a vision of the dead,
Which left my after-morn content.

Methought I dwelt within a hall,   5
    And maidens[7] with me; distant hills
    From hidden summits[8] fed with rills
A river sliding by the wall.

The hall with harp and carol rang.
    They sang of what is wise and good   10
    And graceful. In the centre stood
A statue[9] veil'd, to which they sang;

And which, tho' veil'd, was known to me,
    The shape of him I loved, and love
    For ever. Then flew in a dove   15
And brought a summons from the sea;

And when they learnt that I must go,
    They wept and wail'd, but led the way
    To where a little shallop lay
At anchor in the flood below;[1]   20

And on by many a level mead,
    And shadowing bluff that made the banks,
    We glided winding under ranks
Of iris and the golden reed;

And still as vaster grew the shore   25
    And roll'd the floods in grander space,
    The maidens gather'd strength and grace
And presence, lordlier than before;

And I myself, who sat apart
    And watch'd them, wax'd in every limb;   30
    I felt the thews of Anakim,[2]
The pulses of a Titan's heart;

As one would sing the death of war,
    And one would chant the history
    Of that great race which is to be,[3]   35
And one the shaping of a star;

6. This section recalls a dream Tennyson actually had on the night before leaving Somersby for the last time.
7. Tennyson said: "They are the Muses, poetry, arts—all that make life beautiful here, which we hope will pass with us beyond the grave." According to Knowles, he explained them as, "all the human powers and talents that do not pass with life but go along with it." Clearly the dream concerns the poet's own life, his poetry, and especially these lyrics which grow and depart with

him (Bradley).
8. "The high—the divine—the origin of Life"; the river is "Life"; the sea in line 16, "Eternity" (Tennyson to Knowles).
9. Of Hallam.
1. Compare the conclusion of "The Passing of Arthur."
2. Powerful giants, the sons of Anak. See *Numbers*, 13:33.
3. Compare "Locksley Hall," lines 119–130, and the "Epilogue," lines 136 ff.

Until the forward-creeping tides
   Began to foam, and we to draw
   From deep to deep, to where we saw
A great ship lift her shining sides.   40

The man we loved was there on deck,
   But thrice as large as man he bent
   To greet us. Up the side I went,
And fell in silence on his neck;

Whereat those maidens with one mind   45
   Bewail'd their lot; I did them wrong:
   "We served thee here," they said, "so long,
And wilt thou leave us now behind?"

So rapt I was, they could not win
   An answer from my lips, but he   50
   Replying, "Enter likewise ye
And go with us:" they enter'd in.

And while the wind began to sweep
   A music out of sheet and shroud,
   We steer'd her toward a crimson cloud   55
That landlike slept along the deep.

104[4]

The time draws near the birth of Christ;
   The moon is hid, the night is still;
   A single church[5] below the hill
Is pealing, folded in the mist.

A single peal of bells below,   5
   That wakens at this hour of rest
   A single murmur in the breast,
That these are not the bells I know.

Like strangers' voices here they sound,
   In lands where not a memory strays,   10
   Nor landmark breathes of other days,
But all is new unhallow'd ground.

105

To-night ungather'd let us leave
   This laurel, let this holly stand:
   We live within the stranger's land,
And strangely falls our Christmas-eve.

Our father's dust[6] is left alone   5
   And silent under other snows:
   There in due time the woodbine blows,
The violet comes, but we are gone.

---

4. The third Christmas (1835) after Hallam's death. The fourth part of the poem begins here. In the poem's chronology the time is 1835–36, in biographical time 1837–38, since the Tennyson family has moved to High Beech, the setting here.
5. Waltham Abbey.
6. Tennyson's father died in March 1831 and was buried at Somersby.

No more shall wayward grief abuse[7]
    The genial hour with mask and mime;   10
    For change of place, like growth of time,
Has broke the bond of dying use.

Let cares that petty shadows cast,
    By which our lives are chiefly proved,
    A little spare the night I loved,   15
And hold it solemn to the past.

But let no footstep beat the floor,
    Nor bowl of wassail mantle[8] warm;
    For who would keep an ancient form
Thro' which the spirit breathes no more?   20

Be neither song, nor game, nor feast;
    Nor harp be touch'd, nor flute be blown;
    No dance, no motion, save alone
What lightens in the lucid East

Of rising worlds[9] by yonder wood.   25
    Long sleeps the summer in the seed;
    Run out your measured arcs, and lead
The closing cycle rich in good.[1]

106

Ring out, wild bells, to the wild sky,
    The flying cloud, the frosty light:
    The year is dying in the night;
Ring out, wild bells, and let him[2] die.

Ring out the old, ring in the new,   5
    Ring, happy bells, across the snow:
    The year is going, let him go;
Ring out the false, ring in the true.

Ring out the grief that saps the mind,
    For those that here we see no more;   10
    Ring out the feud of rich and poor,
Ring in redress to all mankind.

Ring out a slowly dying cause,
    And ancient forms of party strife;
    Ring in the nobler modes of life,   15
With sweeter manners, purer laws.

Ring out the want, the care, the sin,
    The faithless coldness of the times;
    Ring out, ring out my mournful rhymes,
But ring the fuller minstrel in.   20

7. Wrong.
8. Become frothy.
9. Rising stars.
1. Let the old cycle fulfill its appointed revolution and the new cycle, which closes the old, begin. See 106, 7, and "Epilogue," lines 128 ff.
2. The old year; the time is New Year's Eve.

Ring out false pride in place and blood,
　　The civic slander and the spite;
　　Ring in the love of truth and right,
Ring in the common love of good.

Ring out old shapes of foul disease;　　　　　　25
　　Ring out the narrowing lust of gold;
　　Ring out the thousand wars of old,
Ring in the thousand years[3] of peace.

Ring in the valiant man and free,
　　The larger heart, the kindlier hand;　　　　30
　　Ring out the darkness of the land,
Ring in the Christ that is to be.[4]

107

It is the day when he was born,[5]
　　A bitter day that early sank
　　Behind a purple-frosty bank
Of vapor, leaving night forlorn.

The time admits not flowers or leaves　　　　　5
　　To deck the banquet. Fiercely flies
　　The blast of North and East, and ice
Makes daggers at the sharpen'd eaves,

And bristles all the brakes and thorns
　　To yon hard crescent, as she hangs　　　　10
　　Above the wood which grides[6] and clangs
Its leafless ribs and iron horns

Together, in the drifts[7] that pass
　　To darken on the rolling brine
　　That breaks the coast. But fetch the wine,　　15
Arrange the board and brim the glass;

Bring in great logs and let them lie,
　　To make a solid core of heat;
　　Be cheerful-minded, talk and treat
Of all things even as he were by;　　　　　　20

We keep the day. With festal cheer,
　　With books and music, surely we
　　Will drink to him, whate'er he be,
And sing the songs he loved to hear.

108

I will not shut me from my kind,
　　And, lest I stiffen into stone,

---

3. See *Revelation*, 20.
4. "My father expressed his conviction . . . that the forms of Christian religion would alter; but that the spirit of Christ would still grow from more to more 'in the roll of the ages' . . . when Christianity without bigotry will triumph, when the controversies of creeds shall have vanished" (*Memoir*, I, 325–326).
5. Hallam's birthday was February 1; he was born in 1811.
6. Grate; "iron" may either describe the frozen branches or the sound of their grinding together.
7. Snow-clouds; perhaps snow.

I will not eat my heart alone,
Nor feed with sighs a passing wind:

What profit lies in barren[8] faith,   5
    And vacant yearning, tho' with might
    To scale the heaven's highest height,
Or dive below the wells of death?

What find I in the highest place,
    But mine own phantom chanting hymns?   10
    And on the depths of death there swims
The reflex of a human face.[9]

I'll rather take what fruit may be
    Of sorrow under human skies:
    'T is held that sorrow makes us wise,   15
Whatever wisdom sleep with thee.[1]

109[2]

Heart-affluence in discursive talk
    From household fountains[3] never dry;
    The critic clearness of an eye
That saw thro' all the Muses' walk;

Seraphic intellect and force   5
    To seize and throw the doubts of man;
    Impassion'd logic, which outran
The hearer in its fiery course;

High nature amorous of the good,
    But touch'd with no ascetic gloom;   10
    And passion pure in snowy bloom
Thro' all the years of April blood;

A love of freedom rarely felt,
    Of freedom in her regal seat
    Of England; not the schoolboy heat,   15
The blind hysterics of the Celt;[4]

And manhood fused with female grace
    In such a sort, the child would twine
    A trustful hand, unask'd, in thine,
And find his comfort in thy face;   20

All these have been, and thee mine eyes
    Have look'd on: if they look'd in vain,
    My shame is greater who remain,
Nor let thy wisdom make me wise.

---

8. Faith without deeds.
9. His own.
1. Hallam.
2. Sections 109–114 form a group in which the poet forthrightly attempts to describe his friend's character, a task which he shied away from as late as section 65.
3. From within himself; original.
4. The French Revolution of 1789. See 127, 2.

110

Thy converse drew us with delight,
    The men of rathe[5] and riper years;
    The feeble soul, a haunt of fears,
Forgot his weakness in thy sight.

On thee the loyal-hearted hung,   5
    The proud was half disarm'd of pride,
    Nor cared the serpent at thy side
To flicker with his double[6] tongue.

The stern were mild when thou wert by,
    The flippant put himself to school   10
    And heard thee, and the brazen fool
Was soften'd, and he knew not why;

While I, thy nearest, sat apart,
    And felt thy triumph was as mine;
    And loved them more, that they were thine,   15
The graceful tact, the Christian art;

Nor mine the sweetness or the skill,
    But mine the love that will not tire,
    And, born of love, the vague desire
That spurs an imitative will.   20

111

The churl in spirit, up or down
    Along the scale of ranks, thro' all,
    To him who grasps a golden ball,[7]
By blood a king, at heart a clown,—

The churl in spirit, howe'er he veil   5
    His want in forms for fashion's sake,
    Will let his coltish nature break
At seasons thro' the gilded pale;

For who can always act?[8] but he,
    To whom a thousand memories call,   10
    Not being less but more than all
The gentleness he seem'd to be,

Best seem'd the thing he was, and join'd
    Each office of the social hour
    To noble manners, as the flower   15
And native growth of noble mind;

Nor ever narrowness or spite,
    Or villain[9] fancy fleeting by,
    Drew in the expression of an eye
Where God and Nature met in light;[1]   20

5. Early.
6. Hypocritical.
7. The king's scepter, topped by a golden ball.
8. Play a part.
9. Ignoble; the antithesis of gentle, as in "gentleman."
1. Compare 87, 9, and see 55, 2.

And thus he bore without abuse
    The grand old name of gentleman,
    Defamed by every charlatan,
And soil'd with all ignoble use.

112

High wisdom holds my wisdom less,
    That I, who gaze with temperate eyes
    On glorious insufficiencies,
Set light by narrower perfectness.[2]

But thou[3], that fillest all the room   5
    Of all my love, art reason why
    I seem to cast a careless eye
On souls, the lesser lords[4] of doom.

For what wert thou? some novel power
    Sprang up for ever at a touch,   10
    And hope could never hope too much,
In watching thee from hour to hour,

Large elements in order brought,
    And tracts of calm from tempest made,
    And world-wide fluctuation sway'd   15
In vassal tides that follow'd thought.

113

'T is held that sorrow makes us wise;[5]
    Yet how much wisdom sleeps with thee
    Which not alone had guided me,
But served the seasons that may rise;

For can I doubt, who knew thee keen   5
    In intellect, with force and skill
    To strive, to fashion, to fulfil—
I doubt not what thou wouldst have been:

A life in civic action warm,
    A soul on highest mission sent,   10
    A potent voice of Parliament,
A pillar steadfast in the storm,

Should licensed boldness gather force,
    Becoming, when the time has birth,
    A lever to uplift the earth   15
And roll it in another course,

With thousand shocks that come and go,
    With agonies, with energies,

2. This confusing stanza may be para-phrased thus: Some wise friend chas-tises me because, although I indulge men of uneven but glorious qualities, I make light of others who, within their limited capacities, have nonetheless de-veloped their lives to comparative per-fection.
3. Hallam.

4. The men of line 4, who, though they control their destinies, are lesser than those of "glorious insufficiencies." Tennyson said the latter referred to "unaccomplished greatness such as Arthur Hallam's," but the last two stanzas certainly suggest he had no "insufficiencies."
5. See 108, 4.

With overthrowings, and with cries,
And undulations to and fro.   20

114

Who loves not Knowledge? Who shall rail
   Against her beauty? May she mix
   With men and prosper! Who shall fix
Her pillars?[6] Let her work prevail.

But on her forehead sits a fire;   5
   She sets her forward countenance
   And leaps into the future chance,
Submitting all things to desire.

Half-grown as yet, a child, and vain—
   She cannot fight the fear of death.   10
   What is she, cut from love and faith,
But some wild Pallas[7] from the brain

Of demons? fiery-hot to burst
   All barriers in her onward race
   For power. Let her know her place;   15
She is the second, not the first.

A higher hand[8] must make her mild,
   If all be not in vain, and guide
   Her footsteps, moving side by side
With Wisdom, like the younger child;   20

For she is earthly[9] of the mind,
   But Wisdom heavenly of the soul.
   O friend, who camest to thy goal
So early, leaving me behind,

I would the great world grew like thee,   25
   Who grewest not alone in power
   And knowledge, but by year and hour
In reverence and in charity.

115

Now fades the last long streak of snow,
   Now burgeons every maze of quick[1]
   About the flowering squares,[2] and thick
By ashen roots[3] the violets blow.

Now rings the woodland loud and long,   5
   The distance takes a lovelier hue,
   And drown'd in yonder living blue
The lark becomes a sightless song.[4]

6. The Pillars of Hercules, which marked the known boundaries of the ancient world.
7. Athena, goddess of wisdom, who sprang fully armed from the brain of Zeus.
8. Wisdom's.
9. See "Prologue," 6, 7, and 8, espe-cially, "For knowledge is of things we see," and also "Locksley Hall," lines 141–144.
1. Hedgerows sprouting and budding.
2. Fields.
3. Roots of the ash trees.
4. Compare Shelley's "To a Skylark."

Now dance the lights on lawn and lea,
   The flocks are whiter down the vale,   10
   And milkier every milky sail
On winding stream or distant sea;

Where now the seamew pipes, or dives
   In yonder greening gleam,[5] and fly
   The happy birds, that change their sky   15
To build and brood, that live their lives

From land to land; and in my breast
   Spring wakens too, and my regret
   Becomes an April violet,
And buds and blossoms like the rest.   20

116

Is it, then, regret for buried time
   That keenlier in sweet April wakes,
   And meets the year,[6] and gives and takes
The colors of the crescent prime?

Not all: the songs, the stirring air,   5
   The life re-orient out of dust,
   Cry thro' the sense to hearten trust
In that which made the world so fair.

Not all regret: the face will shine
   Upon me, while I muse alone,   10
   And that dear voice, I once have known,
Still speak to me of me and mine.

Yet less of sorrow lives in me
   For days of happy commune dead,
   Less yearning for the friendship fled   15
Than some strong bond which is to be.

117

O days and hours, your work is this,
   To hold me from my proper place,
   A little while from his embrace,
For fuller gain of after bliss;

That out of distance might ensue   5
   Desire of nearness doubly sweet,
   And unto meeting, when we meet,
Delight a hundredfold accrue,

For every grain of sand that runs,
   And every span of shade that steals,
   And every kiss of toothed wheels,[7]   10
And all the courses of the suns.

---

5. The sea.
6. As in 83, 1, the year is thought of as beginning in spring.
7. Gears of a clock. The four lines of the stanza refer to different ways of measuring time: the hourglass, the sundial, the clock, and the movements of the stars, including our sun.

118[8]

Contemplate all this work of Time,
    The giant laboring in his youth;
    Nor dream of human love and truth,
As dying Nature's earth and lime;

But trust that those we call the dead   5
    Are breathers of an ampler[9] day
    For ever nobler ends. They[1] say,
The solid earth whereon we tread

In tracts of fluent heat began,
    And grew to seeming[2]-random forms,   10
    The seeming prey of cyclic storms,
Till at the last arose the man;

Who throve and branch'd from clime to clime,
    The herald of a higher race,
    And of himself in higher place,   15
If so he type[3] this work of time

Within himself, from more to more;
    Or, crown'd with attributes of woe
    Like glories, move his course, and show
That life is not as idle ore,   20

But iron dug from central gloom,
    And heated hot with burning fears,
    And dipt in baths of hissing tears,
And batter'd with the shocks of doom

To shape and use. Arise and fly   25
    The reeling Faun, the sensual feast;
    Move upward, working out the beast,
And let the ape and tiger die.

119

Doors,[4] where my heart was used to beat
    So quickly, not as one that weeps
    I come once more; the city sleeps;
I smell the meadow in the street;

I hear a chirp of birds; I see   5
    Betwixt the black fronts long-withdrawn
    A light-blue lane of early dawn,
And think of early days and thee,

And bless thee, for thy lips are bland,
    And bright the friendship of thine eye;   10
    And in my thoughts with scarce a sigh
I take the pressure of thine hand.

8. Compare sections 55, 56, and 123, and see 89, note 2.
9. Virgil's "largior aether" (*Aeneid*, VI, 640).
1. Geologists and astronomers, particularly Lyell and Laplace in his nebular hypothesis.
2. That is, apparently without a plan or order.
3. Prefigure.
4. Hallam's house; see section 7.

120

I trust I have not wasted breath:
    I think we are not wholly brain,
    Magnetic mockeries;[5] not in vain,
Like Paul with beasts, I fought with Death;[6]

Not only cunning casts in clay: 5
    Let Science prove we are, and then
    What matters Science unto men,
At least to me? I would not stay.

Let him, the wiser man[7] who springs
    Hereafter, up from childhood shape   10
    His action like the greater ape,
But I was *born*[8] to other things.

121

Sad Hesper[9] o'er the buried sun
    And ready, thou, to die with him,
    Thou watchest all things ever dim
And dimmer, and a glory done.

The team is loosen'd from the wain,[1]   5
    The boat is drawn upon the shore;
    Thou listenest to the closing door,
And life is darken'd in the brain.

Bright Phosphor, fresher for the night,
    By thee the world's great work is heard   10
    Beginning, and the wakeful bird;[2]
Behind thee comes the greater light.

The market boat is on the stream,
    And voices hail it from the brink;
    Thou hear'st the village hammer clink,   15
And see'st the moving of the team.

Sweet Hesper-Phosphor, double name[3]
    For what is one, the first, the last,
    Thou, like my present and my past,
Thy place is changed; thou art the same.   20

5. Automatons; machines turned on by electrical impulse.

6. "What do I gain if, humanly speaking, I fought with beasts at Ephesus? If the dead are not raised, 'Let us eat and drink, for tomorrow we die' " (Paul the Apostle in *I Corinthians*, 15:32).

7. According to Tennyson, "Spoken ironically against materialism, not against evolution."

8. Italicized sometime between 1875 and 1878. Tennyson had welcomed the publication of Darwin's *Origin of Species* (1859) but later grew increasingly hostile toward the theory as interpreted by those who sought to deny man's spiritual existence. To Tyndall he once said: "No evolutionist is able to explain the mind of Man or how any possible physiological change of tissue can produce conscious thought" (*Memoir*, I, 323)—a sentiment in keeping with the stress on *"born"* and a qualification of Tennyson's note to line 9. See "By an Evolutionist."

9. The evening star; Phosphor (line 9), the morning star. The ancients thought Venus to be two different stars.

1. A farmer's wagon.

2. The nightingale.

3. "The evening star is also the morning star, death and sorrow brighten into death and hope" (Tennyson's note).

122

O, wast thou with me, dearest,[4] then,
   While I rose up against my doom,[5]
   And yearn'd to burst the folded gloom,
To bare the eternal heavens again,[6]

To feel once more, in placid awe,   5
   The strong imagination roll
   A sphere of stars about my soul,
In all her motion one with law?

If thou wert with me, and the grave
   Divide us not, be with me now,   10
   And enter in at breast and brow,
Till all my blood, a fuller wave,

Be quicken'd with a livelier breath,
   And like an inconsiderate boy,
   As in the former flash of joy,   15
I slip[7] the thoughts of life and death;

And all the breeze of Fancy blows,
   And every dewdrop paints a bow,[8]
   The wizard lightnings[9] deeply glow,
And every thought breaks out a rose.   20

123[1]

There rolls the deep where grew the tree.
   O earth, what changes hast thou seen!
   There where the long street roars hath been
The stillness of the central sea.

The hills are shadows, and they flow   5
   From form to form, and nothing stands;
   They melt like mist, the solid lands,
Like clouds they shape themselves and go.

But in my spirit will I dwell,
   And dream my dream, and hold it true;   10
   For tho' my lips may breathe adieu,
I cannot think the thing farewell.

124

That which we dare invoke to bless;
   Our dearest faith; our ghastliest doubt;

---

4. "If anybody thinks I ever called even him 'dearest' in his life they are much mistaken, for I never called him 'dear'" (Tennyson to Knowles).
5. His grief at Hallam's death.
6. "Again" and "once more" (line 5) probably refer to the time Hallam was alive. "Then" in line 1 strongly suggests the experience of section 95. Another possibility is that "again" presupposes an experience prior to "then" or that of section 95—perhaps that of section 86. In this case, although the first part of the present section alludes to 95 in either interpretation, the last nine lines may recall 86.
7. Escape from.
8. Rainbow.
9. Probably not conventional lightning but the northern lights.
1. Another section in which the influence of Lyell's *Geology* appears obvious.

He, They, One, All; within, without;
The Power in darkness whom we guess,—

I found Him not in world or sun,   5
    Or eagle's wing, or insect's eye,
    Nor thro' the questions men may try,
The petty cobwebs we have spun.[2]

If e'er when faith had fallen asleep,
    I heard a voice, "believe no more,"   10
    And heard an ever-breaking shore
That tumbled in the Godless deep,

A warmth within the breast would melt
    The freezing reason's colder part,[3]
    And like a man in wrath the heart   15
Stood up and answer'd, "I have felt."

No, like a child in doubt and fear:
    But that blind clamor made me wise;
    Then was I as a child that cries,
But, crying, knows his father near;[4]   20

And what I am beheld again
    What is, and no man understands;
    And out of darkness came the hands
That reach thro' nature, moulding men.

125

Whatever I have said or sung,
    Some bitter notes my harp would give,
    Yea, tho' there often seem'd to live
A contradiction on the tongue,

Yet Hope had never lost her youth,   5
    She did but look through dimmer eyes;
    Or Love but play'd with gracious lies,
Because he felt so fix'd in truth;

And if the song were full of care,
    He breathed the spirit of the song;   10
    And if the words were sweet and strong
He set his royal signet there;

Abiding with me till I sail
    To seek thee on the mystic deeps,
    And this electric force, that keeps   15
A thousand pulses dancing, fail.

2. In this stanza Tennyson is not saying that God is not present in nature but that he can find no proof of His existence using the old eighteenth-century argument from design. In March 1833, when he and Hallam were looking through microscopes at "moths' wings, gnats' heads, and at all the lions and tigers which lie perdus in a drop of spring water," Tennyson said: "Strange that these wonders should draw some men to God and repel others. No more reason in one than in the other" (*Memoir*, I, 102). See "Love," p. 536.
3. Reason argues that the universe is in meaningless flux.
4. See section 54, 5.

126

Love is and was my lord and king,
   And in his presence I attend
   To hear the tidings of my friend,
Which every hour his couriers bring.

Love is and was my king and lord,   5
   And will be, tho' as yet I keep
   Within the court on earth, and sleep
Encompass'd by his faithful guard,

And hear at times a sentinel
   Who moves about from place to place,   10
   And whispers to the worlds of space,
In the deep night, that all is well.

127

And all is well, tho' faith and form[5]
   Be sunder'd in the night of fear;
   Well roars the storm to those that hear
A deeper voice across the storm,

Proclaiming social truth shall spread,   5
   And justice, even tho' thrice[6] again
   The red fool-fury of the Seine
Should pile her barricades with dead.[7]

But ill for him that wears a crown,
   And him, the lazar,[8] in his rags!   10
   They tremble, the sustaining crags;
The spires of ice are toppled down,

And molten up, and roar in flood;
   The fortress crashes from on high,
   The brute[9] earth lightens to the sky,   15
And the great Æon[1] sinks in blood,

And compass'd by the fires of hell,
   While thou, dear spirit, happy star,
   O'erlook'st the tumult from afar,
And smilest, knowing all is well.   20

128

The love that rose on stronger wings,
   Unpalsied when he met with Death,
   Is comrade of the lesser faith
That sees the course of human things.

No doubt vast eddies in the flood   5
   Of onward time shall yet be made,

---

5. Social order and religious dogma.
6. Does not refer to the three revolutions of 1789, 1830, and 1848 since the section was written, as Tennyson confirmed, before 1848.
7. The Revolution of 1830.
8. A diseased beggar.

9. Ponderous.
1. Not, obviously, the "closing cycle" of 105, 7, but the cataclysmic collapse of the Western world or, perhaps, of all civilization. Within qualifications, the concept of cycles within cycles anticipates Yeats.

And throned races may degrade;[2]
Yet, O ye mysteries of good,

Wild Hours that fly with Hope and Fear,
  If all your office had to do   10
  With old results that look like new[3]—
If this were all your mission here,

To draw, to sheathe a useless sword,
  To fool the crowd with glorious lies,
  To cleave a creed in sects and cries,   15
To change the bearing of a word,

To shift an arbitrary power,
  To cramp the student at his desk,
  To make old bareness picturesque
And tuft with grass a feudal tower,   20

Why, then my scorn might well descend
  On you and yours. I see in part
  That all, as in some piece of art,
Is toil coöperant to an end.[4]

129

Dear friend, far off, my lost desire,
  So far, so near in woe and weal,
  O loved the most, when most I feel
There is a lower and a higher;

Known and unknown, human, divine;   5
  Sweet human hand and lips and eye;
  Dear heavenly friend that canst not die,
Mine, mine, for ever, ever mine;

Strange friend, past, present, and to be;
  Loved deeplier, darklier understood;   10
  Behold, I dream a dream of good,
And mingle all the world with thee.

130

Thy voice is on the rolling air;
  I hear thee where the waters run;
  Thou standest in the rising sun,
And in the setting thou art fair.

What art thou then? I cannot guess;   5
  But tho' I seem in star and flower
  To feel thee some diffusive power,
I do not therefore love thee less.

2. Races now highest and even those to come may degenerate. See "Locksley Hall Sixty Years After," lines 235–236.
3. The idea is not that the past repeats itself in what seems new in the present, but that there really is progress through the cycles. Put awkwardly: what seems ("look like new"), then seems not, may be.
4. Compare "The Two Voices," lines 295–297.

My love involves the love before;
   My love is vaster passion now;   10
   Tho' mix'd with God and Nature thou,[5]
I seem to love thee more and more.

Far off thou art, but ever nigh;
   I have thee still, and I rejoice;
   I prosper, circled with thy voice;   15
I shall not lose thee tho' I die.

131

O living will[6] that shalt endure
   When all that seems shall suffer shock,
   Rise in the spiritual rock,[7]
Flow thro' our deeds and make them pure,

That we may lift from out of dust[8]   5
   A voice as unto him that hears,
   A cry above the conquer'd years[9]
To one that with us works, and trust,

With faith that comes of self-control,
   The truths that never can be proved   10
   Until we close with all we loved,
And all we flow from, soul in soul.

———

O true and tried, so well and long,
   Demand not thou a marriage lay;
   In that it is thy marriage day
Is music more than any song.[1]

Nor have I felt so much of bliss   5
   Since first he[2] told me that he loved
   A daughter of our house, nor proved
Since that dark day[3] a day like this;

Tho' I since then have number'd o'er
   Some thrice three years;[4] they went and came,   10
   Remade the blood and changed the frame,
And yet is love not less, but more;

---

5. This section hints at the idea, developed much later in "The Higher Pantheism," that the material universe may either be God himself or a projection of God.

6. Tennyson explained "as that which we know as Free-will, the higher and enduring part of man" (*Memoir*, I, 319). Compare "Prologue," stanza 4. "Free-will was undoubtedly, he said, the 'main miracle, apparently an act of self-limitation by the Infinite, and yet a revelation by Himself of Himself'" (*Memoir*, I, 316–317).

7. "And did all drink the same spiritual drink; for they drank of that spiritual Rock that followed them: and that Rock was Christ" (I *Corinthians*,

10:4).

8. Our perishable bodies.

9. "The victor Hours" of 1, 4.

1. The "Epilogue" is an epithalamion celebrating the marriage on October 10, 1842, of Edmund Lushington and Tennyson's youngest sister Cecilia. (See 85 and notes). To Knowles, Tennyson said of *In Memoriam*: It begins with a funeral and ends with a marriage—begins with death and ends in promise of a new life—a sort of Divine Comedy, cheerful at the close." See also *Memoir* I, 304.

2. Hallam, who was to marry Emily.

3. Of Hallam's death.

4. Confirms the composition date as 1842.

No longer caring to embalm
    In dying songs a dead regret,
    But like a statue solid-set,   15
And moulded in colossal calm.

Regret is dead, but love is more
    Than in the summers that are flown,
    For I myself with these have grown
To something greater than before;   20

Which makes appear the songs I made
    As echoes out of weaker times,
    As half but idle brawling rhymes,
The sport of random sun and shade.

But where is she, the bridal flower,   25
    That must be made a wife ere noon?
    She enters, glowing like the moon
Of Eden on its bridal bower.

On me she bends her blissful eyes
    And then on thee; they meet thy look   30
    And brighten like the star[5] that shook
Betwixt the palms of Paradise.

O, when her life was yet in bud,
    He too foretold the perfect rose.
    For thee she grew, for thee she grows   35
For ever, and as fair as good.

And thou art worthy, full of power;
    As gentle; liberal-minded, great,
    Consistent; wearing all that weight
Of learning[6] lightly like a flower.   40

But now set out: the noon is near,
    And I must give away the bride;
    She fears not, or with thee beside
And me behind her, will not fear.

For I that danced her on my knee,   45
    That watch'd her on her nurse's arm,
    That shielded all her life from harm,
At last must part with her to thee;

Now waiting to be made a wife,
    Her feet, my darling, on the dead;[7]   50
    Their pensive tablets round her head,
And the most living words[8] of life

---

5. The stars shook when Jupiter approved the marriage of Thetis and Peleus.

6. Lushington was professor of Greek at Glasgow.

7. The bride stands on the stones covering those buried in the church's chancel; the tablets on the walls above commemorate them.

8. Probably refers to the exchange of vows in the next stanza.

Breathed in her ear. The ring is on,
   The "Wilt thou?" answer'd, and again
   The "Wilt thou?" ask'd, till out of twain   55
Her sweet "I will" has made you one.

Now sign your names,[9] which shall be read,
   Mute symbols of a joyful morn,
   By village eyes as yet unborn.
The names are sign'd, and overhead   60

Begins the clash and clang that tells
   The joy to every wandering breeze;
   The blind wall rocks, and on the trees
The dead leaf trembles to the bells.

O happy hour, and happier hours   65
   Await them. Many a merry face
   Salutes them—maidens of the place,
That pelt us in the porch with flowers.

O happy hour, behold the bride
   With him to whom her hand I gave.   70
   They leave the porch, they pass the grave
That has to-day its sunny side.

To-day the grave is bright for me,
   For them the light of life increased,
   Who stay to share the morning feast,   75
Who rest to-night beside the sea.

Let all my genial spirits advance
   To meet and greet a whiter sun;[1]
   My drooping memory will not shun
The foaming grape of eastern France.   80

It circles round, and fancy plays.
   And hearts are warm'd and faces bloom,
   As drinking health to bride and groom
We wish them store of happy days.

Nor count me all to blame if I   85
   Conjecture of a stiller guest,[2]
   Perchance, perchance, among the rest,
And, tho' in silence, wishing joy.

But they must go, the time draws on,
   And those white-favor'd horses wait: 90
   They rise, but linger; it is late;
Farewell, we kiss, and they are gone.

A shade falls on us like the dark
   From little cloudlets on the grass,

9. In the parish register.   2. Hallam's spirit.
1. Brighter days.

But sweeps away as out we pass   95
To range the woods, to roam the park,

Discussing how their courtship grew,
    And talk of others that are wed,
    And how she look'd, and what he said,
And back we come at fall of dew.   100

Again the feast, the speech, the glee,
    The shade of passing thought, the wealth
    Of words and wit, the double health,
The crowning cup, the three-times-three,[3]

And last the dance;—till I retire.   105
    Dumb is that tower which spake so loud,
    And high in heaven the streaming cloud,
And on the downs a rising fire:

And rise, O moon, from yonder down,
    Till over down and over dale   110
    All night the shining vapor sail
And pass the silent-lighted town,

The white-faced halls, the glancing rills,
    And catch at every mountain head.
    And o'er the friths that branch and spread   115
Their sleeping silver thro' the hills;

And touch with shade the bridal doors,
    With tender gloom the roof, the wall;
    And breaking let the splendor fall
To spangle all the happy shores   120

By which they rest, and ocean sounds,
    And, star and system rolling past,
    A soul shall draw from out the vast
And strike his being into bounds,

And, moved thro' life of lower phase,[4]   125
    Result in man, be born and think,
    And act and love, a closer link
Betwixt us and the crowning race

Of those that, eye to eye, shall look
    On knowledge; under whose command   130
    Is Earth and Earth's, and in their hand
Is Nature like an open book;

No longer half-akin to brute,
    For all we thought and loved and did,
    And hoped, and suffer'd, is but seed   135
Of what in them is flower and fruit;

---

3. The cheer.
4. Stages in the development of the human fetus appear to resemble lower forms of animal life. See note to line 196 of "The Palace of Art."

Whereof the man that with me trod
  This planet was a noble type
  Appearing ere the times were ripe,
That friend of mine who lives in God,   140

That God, which ever lives and loves,
  One God, one law, one element,
  And one far-off divine event,
To which the whole creation moves.

1833–1849; 1850

The Middle Period
(1850 – 1870)

De Profundis[1]

The Two Greetings

1

Out of the deep,[2] my child, out of the deep,
Where all that was to be, in all that was,
Whirl'd for a million æons thro' the vast
Waste dawn of multitudinous-eddying light—
Out of the deep, my child, out of the deep,   5
Thro' all this changing world of changeless law,
And every phase of ever-heightening life,
And nine long months of antenatal gloom,
With this last moon, this crescent—her dark orb
Touch'd with earth's light—thou comest, darling boy;   10
Our own; a babe in lineament and limb
Perfect, and prophet of the perfect man;
Whose face and form are hers and mine in one,
Indissolubly married like our love.
Live, and be happy in thyself, and serve   15
This mortal race thy kin so well that men
May bless thee as we bless thee, O young life
Breaking with laughter from the dark; and may
The fated channel where thy motion lives
Be prosperously shaped, and sway thy course   20
Along the years of haste and random youth
Unshatter'd; then full-current thro' full man;
And last in kindly curves, with gentlest fall,
By quiet fields, a slowly-dying power,
To that last deep where we and thou are still.   25

2

I

Out of the deep, my child, out of the deep,
From that great deep, before our world begins,
Whereon the Spirit of God moves as he will—

---

1. Begun after the birth of the poet's first son Hallam on August 11, 1852, the poem was not completed until much later. Toward the end of his life, Tennyson interpreted the poem for Mr. Ward, who wrote of the first section: "Life is viewed as we see it in the world, and as we know it by physical science." In the second greeting, "we gaze into that other deep—the world of spirit, the world of realities." For two of Tennyson's many remarks on the reality of the spiritual world, see notes to *The Devil and the Lady* (Act 2), p. 504.
2. The title means "from the depths" or "out of the deep." Compare "The Passing of Arthur," lines 443–445, and *In Memoriam,* "Epilogue," lines 121 ff.

Out of the deep, my child, out of the deep,
From that true world[3] within the world we see,   30
Whereof our world is but the bounding shore—
Out of the deep, Spirit, out of the deep,
With this ninth moon, that sends the hidden sun
Down yon dark sea, thou comest, darling boy.

II

For in the world which is not ours They said,   35
"Let us make man," and that which should be man,
From that one light no man can look upon,
Drew to this shore lit by the suns and moons
And all the shadows. O dear Spirit, half-lost
In thine own shadow and this fleshly sign   40
That thou art thou—who wailest being born
And banish'd into mystery, and the pain
Of this divisible-indivisible world
Among the numerable-innumerable
Sun, sun, and sun, thro' finite-infinite space   45
In finite-infinite Time—our mortal veil
And shatter'd phantom of that infinite One,
Who made thee unconceivably Thyself
Out of His whole World-self and all in all—
Live thou! and of the grain and husk, the grape   50
And ivy-berry, choose; and still depart
From death to death thro' life and life, and find
Nearer and ever nearer Him, who wrought
Not matter, nor the finite-infinite,
But this main-miracle, that thou art thou,   55
With power on thine own act and on the world.

The Human Cry[4]

1

Hallowed be Thy name—Halleluiah!—
    Infinite Ideality!
    Immeasurable Reality!
    Infinite Personality!   60
Hallowed be Thy name—Halleluiah!

2

We feel we are nothing—for all is Thou and in Thee;
We feel we are something—*that* also has come from Thee;
We know we are nothing—but Thou wilt help us to be.
Hallowed be Thy name—Halleluiah!   65

1852 ff.; 1880

3. "At times I have possessed the power of making my individuality as it were dissolve and fade away into boundless being, and this not a confused state but the clearest of the clearest, the surest of the surest, utterly beyond words, where death was an almost laughable impossibility, and the loss of personality, if so it were, seem-ing no alteration but the only true life" (Tennyson's note to section 2). See *In Memoriam*, 95 and notes.
4. This prayer, really a second poem published under the title "De Profundis," was designed to show the futility in man's effort to comprehend fundamental religious truths.

Britons, Guard Your Own[5]

Rise, Britons, rise, if manhood be not dead;
The world's last tempest darkens overhead;
> The Pope has bless'd him;
> The Church caress'd him;
He triumphs; maybe we shall stand alone.   5
> Britons, guard your own.

His ruthless host is bought with plunder'd gold,
By lying priests the peasants' votes controll'd.
> All freedom vanish'd,
> The true men banish'd,   10
He triumphs; maybe we shall stand alone.
> Britons, guard your own.

Peace-lovers we—sweet Peace we all desire—
Peace-lovers we—but who can trust a liar?—
> Peace-lovers, haters   15
> Of shameless traitors,
We hate not France, but this man's heart of stone.
> Britons, guard your own.

We hate not France, but France has lost her voice.
This man is France, the man they call her choice.   20
> By tricks and spying,
> By craft and lying,
And murder was her freedom overthrown.
> Britons, guard your own.

'Vive l'Empereur' may follow by and by;[6]   25
'God save the Queen' is here a truer cry.
> God save the Nation,
> The toleration,
And the free speech that makes a Briton known.
> Britons, guard your own.   30

Rome's dearest daughter now is captive France,
The Jesuit laughs, and reckoning on his chance,
> Would, unrelenting,
> Kill all dissenting,
Till we were left to fight for truth alone.   35
> Britons, guard your own.

---

5. This and the following companion poem were published in January and February respectively. Louis Napoleon's *coup d'état* in December 1851 had been met with seeming indifference by The House of Lords, and a bill to mobilize the home militia had been rejected. Although published anonymously or under the pseudonym "Merlin," the poems show Tennyson in his new role as poet laureate, responding to what he considered dangerous apathy toward possible invasion. For such pieces as these, his detractors would later label him a jingoist. Although the poems have most of the faults of most occasional verse, they nonetheless reflect a side of Tennyson that should not be ignored— from his super-patriotism to his strong anti-Catholic prejudice. Contrast such earlier poems as "Love Thou Thy Land."
6. Later in the year Louis became Napoleon III.

Call home your ships across Biscayan[7] tides,
To blow the battle from their oaken sides.
    Why waste they yonder
    Their idle thunder?   40
Why stay they there to guard a foreign throne?
    Seamen, guard your own.

We were the best of marksmen long ago,
We won old battles with our strength, the bow.
    Now practise, yeomen,   45
    Like those bowmen,
Till your balls fly as their true shafts have flown.
    Yeomen, guard your own.

His soldier-ridden Highness might incline
To take Sardinia, Belgium, or the Rhine: 50
    Shall we stand idle,
    Nor seek to bridle
His rude aggressions, till we stand alone?
    Make their cause your own.

Should he land here, and for one hour prevail,   55
There must no man go back to bear the tale:
    No man to bear it—
    Swear it! we swear it!
Although we fight the banded world alone,
    We swear to guard our own.   60

1852

Hands All Round[8]

First pledge our Queen this solemn night,
    Then drink to England, every guest;
That man 's the best Cosmopolite
    Who loves his native country best.
May freedom's oak for ever live   5
    With stronger life from day to day;
That man 's the true Conservative
    Who lops the moulder'd branch away.
        Hands all round!
    God the traitor's hope confound!   10
To this great cause of Freedom drink, my friends,
    And the great name of England, round and round.

To all the loyal hearts who long
    To keep our English Empire whole!
To all our noble sons, the strong   15
    New England of the Southern Pole!

7. From the Spanish coast.
8. "I know I wrote these lines," Tennyson remarked, "with the Tears running down my Cheeks." (This version, as republished in 1882, is much condensed from the original.)

To England under Indian skies,
    To those dark millions of her realm!
To Canada whom we love and prize,
    Whatever statesman hold the helm.   20
        Hands all round!
    God the traitor's hope confound!
To this great name of England drink, my friends,
    And all her glorious empire, round and round.

To all our statesmen so they be   25
    True leaders of the land's desire!
To both our Houses, may they see
    Beyond the borough and the shire!
We sail'd wherever ship could sail,
    We founded many a mighty state;   30
Pray God our greatness may not fail
    Thro' craven fears of being great!
        Hands all round!
    God the traitor's hope confound!
To this great cause of Freedom drink, my friends,   35
    And the great name of England, round and round.

1852 (1882)

Ode on the Death of the Duke of Wellington[9]

1

Bury the Great Duke
    With an empire's lamentation;
Let us bury the Great Duke
    To the noise of the mourning of a mighty nation;
Mourning when their leaders fall,   5
Warriors carry the warrior's pall,
And sorrow darkens hamlet and hall.

2

Where shall we lay[1] the man whom we deplore?
Here, in streaming London's central roar.
Let the sound of those he wrought for,   10
And the feet of those he fought for,
Echo round his bones for evermore.

3

Lead out the pageant: sad and slow,
As fits an universal woe,
Let the long, long procession go,   15
And let the sorrowing crowd about it grow,

And let the mournful martial music blow;
The last great Englishman is low.

4

Mourn, for to us he seems the last,
Remembering all his greatness in the past.   20
No more in soldier fashion will he greet
With lifted hand the gazer in the street.
O friends, our chief state-oracle is mute!
Mourn for the man of long-enduring blood,
The statesman-warrior, moderate, resolute,   25
Whole in himself, a common good.
Mourn for the man of amplest influence,
Yet clearest of ambitious crime,
Our greatest yet with least pretence,
Great in council and great in war,   30
Foremost captain of his time,
Rich in saving common-sense,
And, as the greatest only are,
In his simplicity sublime.
O good gray head which all men knew,   35
O voice from which their omens all men drew,
O iron nerve to true occasion true,
O fallen at length that tower of strength
Which stood four-square to all the winds that blew!
Such was he whom we deplore.   40
The long self-sacrifice of life is o'er.
The great World-victor's victor² will be seen no more.

5

All is over and done.
Render thanks to the Giver,
England, for thy son.   45
Let the bell be toll'd.
Render thanks to the Giver,
And render him to the mould.
Under the cross of gold³
That shines over city and river,   50
There he shall rest for ever
Among the wise and the bold.
Let the bell be toll'd,
And a reverent people behold
The towering car, the sable steeds.   55
Bright let it be with its blazon'd deeds,⁴
Dark in its funeral fold.
Let the bell be toll'd,
And a deeper knell in the heart be knoll'd;
And the sound of the sorrowing anthem roll'd   60
Thro' the dome of the golden cross;

---

2. The conqueror of Napoleon.
3. On top of St. Paul's.

4. Wellington's victories were emblazoned in gold on his bier.

And the volleying cannon thunder his loss;
He knew their voices of old.
For many a time in many a clime
His captain's-ear has heard them boom   65
Bellowing victory, bellowing doom.
When he with those deep voices wrought,
Guarding realms and kings from shame,
With those deep voices our dead captain taught
The tyrant, and asserts his claim   70
In that dread sound to the great name
Which he has worn so pure of blame,
In praise and in dispraise the same,
A man of well-attemper'd frame.
O civic muse, to such a name,   75
To such a name for ages long,
To such a name,
Preserve a broad approach of fame,
And ever-echoing avenues of song!

6

"Who is he that cometh, like an honor'd guest,   80
With banner and with music, with soldier and with priest,
With a nation weeping, and breaking on my rest?"—
Mighty Seaman,[5] this is he
Was great by land as thou by sea.
Thine island loves thee well, thou famous man,   85
The greatest sailor since our world began.
Now, to the roll of muffled drums,
To thee the greatest soldier comes;
For this is he
Was great by land as thou by sea.   90
His foes were thine; he kept us free;
O, give him welcome, this is he
Worthy of our gorgeous rites,
And worthy to be laid by thee;
For this is England's greatest son,   95
He that gain'd a hundred fights,
Nor ever lost an English gun;
This is he that far away
Against the myriads of Assaye[6]
Clash'd with his fiery few and won;   100
And underneath another sun,
Warring on a later day,
Round affrighted Lisbon[7] drew

5. Lord Nelson, the speaker above, whose series of naval victories during the Napoleonic Wars culminated with his triumph and death at Trafalgar in 1805.
6. In India, where, in 1803, Wellington defeated a far superior force.
7. From 1808 to 1814, the Iron Duke waged his Peninsular Campaign against the French from Spain, first in a holding action and then in a series of increasingly successful offensive strikes. His decisive victory at Vitoria in northern Spain (June 21, 1813) exposed France to invasion through the Pyrenees, and Napoleon's abdication followed.

The treble works, the vast designs
Of his labor'd rampart-lines,   105
Where he greatly stood at bay,
Whence he issued forth anew,
And ever great and greater grew,
Beating from the wasted vines
Back to France her banded swarms,   110
Back to France with countless blows,
Till o'er the hills her eagles flew
Beyond the Pyrenean pines,
Follow'd up in valley and glen
With blare of bugle, clamor of men,   115
Roll of cannon and clash of arms,
And England pouring on her foes.
Such a war had such a close.
Again their ravening eagle rose[8]
In anger, wheel'd on Europe-shadowing wings,   120
And barking for the thrones of kings;
Till one that sought but Duty's iron crown
On that loud Sabbath[9] shook the spoiler down;
A day of onsets of despair!
Dash'd on every rocky square,   125
Their surging charges foam'd themselves away;
Last, the Prussian[1] trumpet blew;
Thro' the long-tormented air
Heaven flash'd a sudden jubilant ray,
And down we swept and charged and overthrew.   130
So great a soldier taught us there
What long-enduring hearts could do
In that world-earthquake, Waterloo!
Mighty Seaman, tender and true,
And pure as he from taint of craven guile,   135
O saviour of the silver-coasted isle,
O shaker of the Baltic and the Nile,[2]
If aught of things that here befall
Touch a spirit among things divine,
If love of country move thee there at all,   140
Be glad, because his bones are laid by thine
And thro' the centuries let a people's voice
In full acclaim,
A people's voice,
The proof and echo of all human fame,   145
A people's voice, when they rejoice

8. Napoleon, whose symbol was the eagle, returned from Elba in 1815 and reassembled much of his army.
9. The Battle of Waterloo was fought on Sunday, June 18, 1815.
1. The arrival of the Prussian army under Blücher decided the outcome.
2. In 1798, at the mouth of the Nile, Nelson destroyed major elements of the French fleet through an original and daring maneuver by which he simultaneously sent his ships, broadsides firing, down both sides of the French line. In 1801 in the Baltic he neutralized the Danish fleet.

At civic revel and pomp and game,
Attest their great commander's claim
With honor, honor, honor, honor to him,
Eternal honor to his name.   150

7

A people's voice! we are a people yet.
Tho' all men else their nobler dreams forget,
Confused by brainless mobs and lawless Powers,
Thank Him who isled us here, and roughly set
His Briton in blown seas and storming showers,   155
We have a voice with which to pay the debt
Of boundless love and reverence and regret
To those great men who fought, and kept it ours.
And keep it ours, O God, from brute control!
O Statesmen, guard us, guard the eye, the soul   160
Of Europe, keep our noble England whole,
And save the one true seed of freedom sown
Betwixt a people and their ancient throne,
That sober freedom out of which there springs
Our loyal passion for our temperate kings!   165
For, saving that, ye help to save mankind
Till public wrong be crumbled into dust,
And drill the raw world for the march of mind,
Till crowds at length be sane and crowns be just.
But wink no more in slothful overtrust.   170
Remember him who led your hosts;
He bade you guard the sacred coasts.
Your cannons moulder on the seaward wall;
His voice is silent in your council-hall
For ever; and whatever tempests lour   175
For ever silent; even if they broke
In thunder, silent; yet remember all
He spoke among you, and the Man who spoke;
Who never sold the truth to serve the hour,
Nor palter'd with Eternal God for power;   180
Who let the turbid streams of rumor flow
Thro' either babbling world of high and low;
Whose life was work, whose language rife
With rugged maxims hewn from life;
Who never spoke against a foe;   185
Whose eighty[3] winters freeze with one rebuke
All great self-seekers trampling on the right.
Truth-teller was our England's Alfred named;
Truth-lover was our English Duke;
Whatever record leap to light   190
He never shall be shamed.

8

Lo! the leader in these glorious wars
Now to glorious burial slowly borne,

3. The Duke was 83 when he died.

Follow'd by the brave of other lands,
He, on whom from both her open hands   195
Lavish Honor shower'd all her stars,
And affluent Fortune emptied all her horn
Yea, let all good things await
Him who cares not to be great
But as he saves or serves the state.   200
Not once or twice in our rough island-story
The path of duty was the way to glory.
He that walks it, only thirsting
For the right, and learns to deaden
Love of self, before his journey closes,   205
He shall find the stubborn thistle bursting
Into glossy purples, which outredden
All voluptuous garden-roses.
Not once or twice in our fair island-story
The path of duty was the way to glory.   210
He, that ever following her commands,
On with toil of heart and knees and hands,
Thro' the long gorge to the far light has won
His path upward, and prevail'd,
Shall find the toppling crags of Duty scaled   215
Are close upon the shining table-lands
To which our God Himself is moon and sun.
Such was he: his work is done.
But while the races of mankind endure
Let his great example stand   220
Colossal, seen of every land,
And keep the soldier firm, the statesman pure;
Till in all lands and thro' all human story
The path of duty be the way to glory.
And let the land whose hearths he saved from shame   225
For many and many an age proclaim
At civic revel and pomp and game,
And when the long-illumined cities flame,
Their ever-loyal iron leader's fame,
With honor, honor, honor, honor to him,   230
Eternal honor to his name.

9

Peace, his triumph will be sung
By some yet unmoulded tongue
Far on in summers that we shall not see.
Peace, it is a day of pain   235
For one about whose patriarchal knee
Late the little children clung.
O peace, it is a day of pain
For one upon whose hand and heart and brain
Once the weight and fate of Europe hung.   240
Ours the pain, be his the gain!
More than is of man's degree

Must be with us, watching here
At this, our great solemnity.
Whom we see not we revere;   245
We revere, and we refrain
From talk of battles loud and vain,
And brawling memories all too free
For such a wise humility
As befits a solemn fane: 250
We revere, and while we hear
The tides of Music's golden sea
Setting toward eternity,
Uplifted high in heart and hope are we,
Until we doubt not that for one so true   255
There must be other nobler work to do
Than when he fought at Waterloo,
And Victor he must ever be.
For tho' the Giant Ages heave the hill
And break the shore, and evermore   260
Make and break, and work their will,
Tho' world on world in myriad myriads roll
Round us, each with different powers,
And other forms of life than ours,
What know we greater than the soul?   265
On God and Godlike men we build our trust.
Hush, the Dead March[4] wails in the people's ears;
The dark crowd moves, and there are sobs and tears;
The black earth yawns; the mortal disappears;
Ashes to ashes, dust to dust;   270
He is gone who seem'd so great.—
Gone, but nothing can bereave him
Of the force he made his own
Being here, and we believe him
Something far advanced in State,   275
And that he wears a truer crown
Than any wreath that man can weave him.
Speak no more of his renown,
Lay your earthly fancies down,
And in the vast cathedral leave him,   280
God accept him, Christ receive him!

1852 (1855)

To E. L., on His Travels in Greece[5]

Illyrian[6] woodlands, echoing falls
    Of water, sheets of summer glass,

4. From Handel's *Saul*.
5. The poem is addressed to Edward Lear, best known for his nonsense books, who was a close friend of the Tennysons and had sent the poet a copy of his new travel book, *Journal of*
a Landscape Painter in Greece and Albania (1851), to which the poem alludes.
6. Illyria was the ancient name for an area roughly equivalent to Albania.

The long divine Peneïan pass,
The vast Akrokeraunian[7] walls,

Tomohrit, Athos,[8] all things fair,   5
   With such a pencil, such a pen,
   You shadow forth to distant men,
I read and felt that I was there.

And trust me while I turn'd the page,
   And track'd you still on classic ground,   10
   I grew in gladness till I found
My spirits in the golden age.

For me the torrent ever pour'd
   And glisten'd—here and there alone
   The broad-limb'd Gods at random thrown   15
By fountain-urns;—and Naiads[9] oar'd

A glimmering shoulder under gloom
   Of cavern pillars; on the swell
   The silver lily heaved and fell;
And many a slope was rich in bloom,   20

From him that on the mountain lea
   By dancing rivulets fed his flocks
   To him who sat upon the rocks
And fluted to the morning sea.

1853

The Daisy

WRITTEN AT EDINBURGH

O love,[1] what hours were thine and mine,
In lands of palm and southern pine;
   In lands of palm, or orange-blossom,
Of olive, aloe, and maize and vine!

What Roman strength Turbìa[2] show'd   5
In ruin, by the mountain road;
   How like a gem, beneath, the city
Of little Monaco, basking, glow'd!

How richly down the rocky dell
The torrent vineyard streaming fell   10

---

7. Refers to the ancient fortress of Chimaera on the southern coast of Albania.
8. A mountain in northern Greece on the Aegean Sea; Tomohrit is a mountain in southern Albania.
9. Water nymphs in Greek mythology.
1. The poem is addressed to Tennyson's wife, Emily, who had been left behind at Richmond on a tour of Yorkshire, and celebrates their belated wedding trip to Italy in the summer of 1851. The original meter, involving a feminine ending in the third line of each stanza and an extra syllable in the fourth, Tennyson called "a far-off echo of the Horatian Alcaic" (*Memoir*, I, 341).
2. A village in southeastern France.

To meet the sun and sunny waters,
That only heaved with a summer swell!

What slender campanili grew
By bays, the peacock's neck in hue;
   Where, here and there, on sandy beaches   15
A milky-bell'd amaryllis blew!

How young Columbus seem'd to rove,
Yet present in his natal grove,
   Now watching high on mountain cornice,
And steering, now, from a purple cove,   20

Now pacing mute by ocean's rim;
Till, in a narrow street and dim,
   I stay'd the wheels at Cogoletto,[3]
And drank, and loyally drank to him!

Nor knew we well what pleased us most;   25
Not the clipt palm of which they boast,
   But distant color, happy hamlet,
A moulder'd citadel on the coast,

Or tower, or high hill-convent, seen
A light amid its olives green;   30
   Or olive-hoary cape in ocean;
Or rosy blossom in hot ravine,

Where oleanders flush'd the bed
Of silent torrents, gravel-spread;
   And, crossing, oft we saw the glisten   35
Of ice, far up on a mountain head.

We loved that hall,[4] tho' white and cold,
Those niched shapes of noble mould,
   A princely people's awful princes,
The grave, severe Genovese of old.   40

At Florence too what golden hours,
In those long galleries, were ours;
   What drives about the fresh Cascinè,[5]
Or walks in Boboli's ducal bowers!

In bright vignettes, and each complete,   45
Of tower or duomo, sunny-sweet,
   Or palace, how the city glitter'd,
Thro' cypress avenues, at our feet!

But when we crost the Lombard plain
Remember what a plague of rain;   50

---

3. Assumed, perhaps wrongly, to be
Columbus' birthplace.
4. In the Ducal Palace in Genoa, or
possibly in the ancient Bank of St.
George.
5. The park of Florence on the bank of
the Arno; the Boboli Gardens are be-
hind the Pitti Palace.

Of rain at Reggio, rain at Parma,
At Lodi rain, Piacenza rain.[6]

And stern and sad—so rare the smiles
Of sunlight—look'd the Lombard piles;
　　Porch-pillars on the lion resting,　　　　　55
And sombre, old, colonnaded aisles.

O Milan, O the chanting quires,
The giant windows' blazon'd fires,
　　The height, the space, the gloom, the glory!
A mount of marble, a hundred spires![7]　　　60

I climb'd the roofs at break of day;
Sun-smitten Alps before me lay.
　　I stood among the silent statues,
And statued pinnacles, mute as they.

How faintly-flush'd, how phantom-fair,　　　65
Was Monte Rosa,[8] hanging there
　　A thousand shadowy-pencill'd valleys
And snowy dells in a golden air!

Remember how we came at last
To Como; shower and storm and blast　　　70
　　Had blown the lake beyond his limit,
And all was flooded; and how we past

From Como, when the light was gray,
And in my head, for half the day,
　　The rich Virgilian rustic measure　　　75
Of "Lari Maxume,"[9] all the way,

Like ballad-burthen music, kept,
As on the Lariano[1] crept
　　To that fair port[2] below the castle
Of Queen Theodolind, where we slept;　　　80

Or hardly slept, but watch'd awake
A cypress in the moonlight shake,
　　The moonlight touching o'er a terrace
One tall agavè above the lake.

What more? we took our last adieu,　　　85
And up the snowy Splügen[3] drew;
　　But ere we reach'd the highest summit
I pluck'd a daisy, I gave it you.

---

6. The stanza alludes to towns in and around the Lombardy district in north-central Italy.
7. The great Gothic cathedral of Milan.
8. A mountain on the Swiss-Italian border; the highest point (over 15,000 feet) in the Pennine Alps.
9. "Larius the Greatest," in the *Geor-*
gics Virgil's name for Lake Como, north of Milan.
1. A small boat.
2. Varenna. Theodolind was the wife of a late-sixth-century ruler of the Lombards.
3. A pass across the Alps.

It told of England then to me,
And now it tells of Italy.   90
   O love, we two shall go no longer
To lands of summer across the sea,

So dear a life[4] your arms enfold
Whose crying is a cry for gold;
   Yet here to-night in this dark city,   95
When ill and weary, alone and cold,

I found, tho' crush'd to hard and dry,
This nursling of another sky
   Still in the little book you lent me,
And where you tenderly laid it by;   100

And I forgot the clouded Forth,[5]
The gloom that saddens heaven and earth,
   The bitter east, the misty summer
And gray metropolis of the North.[6]

Perchance to lull the throbs of pain,   105
Perchance to charm a vacant brain,
   Perchance to dream you still beside me,
My fancy fled to the South again.

1853; 1855

To the Rev. F. D. Maurice

Come, when no graver cares employ,
Godfather,[7] come and see your boy;
   Your presence will be sun in winter,
Making the little one leap for joy.

For, being of that honest few   5
Who give the Fiend himself his due,
   Should eighty thousand college-councils
Thunder "Anathema," friend, at you,

Should all our churchmen foam in spite
At you, so careful of the right,   10

4. The poet's son Hallam, born August
11, 1852.
5. Edinburgh.
6. "A Scotch professor objected to this.
So I asked him to call London if he
liked the 'black metropolis of the
south'."
7. Maurice and Henry Hallam, Ar-
thur's father, were the godfathers of
Tennyson's first son, Hallam. At Cam-
bridge, though before Tennyson's time,
Maurice had been a founder of the
Apostles. He was the moving force be-
hind the Christian Socialist Movement
and for his unorthodoxy had been
ejected from his professorship at King's
College. "Anathema" in line 8 is liter-
ally "accursed thing." According to
Tennyson, Maurice had merely pointed
out that "eternal" in "eternal punish-
ment" referred to the quality and not
to the duration of punishment.

Yet one lay-hearth would give you welcome—
Take it and come—to the Isle of Wight;[8]

Where, far from noise and smoke of town,
I watch the twilight falling brown
    All round a careless-order'd garden   15
Close to the ridge of a noble down.

You 'll have no scandal while you dine,
But honest talk and wholesome wine,
    And only hear the magpie gossip
Garrulous under a roof of pine;   20

For groves of pine on either hand,
To break the blast of winter, stand,
    And further on, the hoary Channel
Tumbles a billow on chalk and sand;

Where, if below the milky steep   25
Some ship of battle slowly creep,
    And on thro' zones of light and shadow
Glimmer away to the lonely deep,

We might discuss the Northern sin
Which made a selfish war[9] begin,   30
    Dispute the claims, arrange the chances,—
Emperor, Ottoman, which shall win;

Or whether war's avenging rod
Shall lash all Europe into blood;
    Till you should turn to dearer matters,   35
Dear to the man that is dear to God,—

How best to help the slender store,
How mend the dwellings, of the poor,
    How gain in life, as life advances,
Valor and charity more and more.   40

Come, Maurice, come; the lawn as yet
Is hoar with rime or spongy-wet,
    But when the wreath of March has blossom'd,—
Crocus, anemone, violet,—

Or later, pay one visit here,   45
For those are few we hold as dear;
    Nor pay but one, but come for many,
Many and many a happy year.

1854; 1855

8. Tennyson leased Farringford on the Isle of Wight in 1853 and bought the house in 1856.
9. The Crimean War (1854–56) in which the English and French ostensibly sought to preserve the Ottoman Empire from Russian occupation. Nicholas I of Russia and not Napoleon III must be the "Emperor" of line 32.

The Charge of the Light Brigade[1]

1

Half a league, half a league,
Half a league onward,
All in the valley of Death
　Rode the six hundred.
"Forward the Light Brigade!   5
Charge for the guns!" he said.
Into the valley of Death
　Rode the six hundred.

2

"Forward, the Light Brigade!"
Was there a man dismay'd?   10
Not tho' the soldier knew
　Some one had blunder'd.
　Theirs not to make reply,
　Theirs not to reason why,
　Theirs but to do and die.   15
　Into the valley of Death
　　Rode the six hundred.

3

Cannon to right of them,
Cannon to left of them,
Cannon in front of them   20
　Volley'd and thunder'd;
Storm'd at with shot and shell,
Boldly they rode and well,
Into the jaws of Death,
Into the mouth of hell   25
　Rode the six hundred.

4

Flash'd all their sabres bare,
Flash'd as they turn'd in air
Sabring the gunners there,
Charging an army, while   30
　All the world wonder'd.
Plunged in the battery-smoke
Right thro' the line they broke;
Cossack and Russian
Reel'd from the sabre-stroke   35

1. Written on December 2, 1854, "in a few minutes, after reading the description in the *Times* in which occurred the phrase 'some one had blundered,' and this was the origin of the metre of his poem" (*Memoir*, I, 381). This disastrous engagement, probably the stupidest exploit in British military history, took place at Balaklava on October 25, during the initial phases of the Crimean War. Through a misinterpretation of orders, the light brigade charged headlong into entrenched Russian artillery. Of some 700 men, only 195 returned. Learning that the soldiers liked his poem, Tennyson had 1000 copies sent over for distribution among the troops. Cecil Woodham-Smith gives a splendid account of the engagement in her book *The Reason Why* (1953).

Shatter'd and sunder'd.
Then they rode back, but not,
　Not the six hundred.

5

Cannon to right of them,
Cannon to left of them,
Cannon behind them
　Volley'd and thunder'd;
Storm'd at with shot and shell,
While horse and hero fell,
They that had fought so well
Came thro' the jaws of Death,
Back from the mouth of hell,
All that was left of them,
　Left of six hundred.

6

When can their glory fade?
O the wild charge they made!
　All the world wonder'd.
Honor the charge they made!
Honor the Light Brigade,
　Noble six hundred!

1854

Maud　The so-called germ of *Maud* is the poem, "O that 'twere possible,"
(section IV of Part 2), which apparently was in existence prior to 1834.
See *Memoir*, I, 139. At the suggestion of his friend Sir John Simeon, who
thought the earlier poem could be made more intelligible with a predeces-
sor, Tennyson "wrote it; the second poem too required a predecessor; and
thus the whole work was written, as it were, *backwards*" (Aubrey de Vere
in *Memoir*, I, 379). The poem was composed at Farringford on the Isle of
Wight in about a year (it was finished in July 1855), but the divisions as
we have them did not appear until the eleventh edition (1865). Although
Maud was not favorably received by the critics, it was widely read and very
remunerative. Gladstone, as did many others, faulted it for its seeming
support of the Crimean War as panacea for disaffected youth; Browning,
predictably, was enthusiastic in praise. Of more modern commentators,
T. S. Eliot has appreciated the poem's "lyrical resourcefulness." (See his
and Killham's articles in the criticism section of this book.) During Tenny-
son's lifetime, it became well known that *Maud* was one of his favorites,
a poem he particularly liked to read aloud. It was certainly with mixed
emotions, however, that, when an old man, Tennyson forced himself to sit
through a recitation of the entire work memorized by an American who
had worked his way over to England on a cattle ship for that single
purpose.

As in "Locksley Hall," many readers have supposed Tennyson was
reflecting his own views through his speakers. It is true that he was some-

times morbidly concerned with hereditary insanity in his own family, more than once referring to the "black blood" of the Tennysons out of fear of his own susceptibility. It is likewise true that the poet's father was a disinherited eldest son always in financial hardships and had been, in effect, a suicide, though he settled for the lingering version through drink. But as the poet's grandson has observed, if some original in real life must be found, heroes "so idealistic, passionate and unstable, have more than a little reference to Frederick," the poet's older brother (*Alfred Tennyson*, p. 194). The hero of *Maud*, or more properly the Byronic antihero, is clearly unbalanced, perhaps paranoiac, and in some ways prefigures those other angry young men of a century later. His neuroses, his obsession with violence and merciless introspection, are shared by protagonists of the "Spasmodic School," a group headed by Alexander Smith and Sydney Dobell whose poetry was in vogue during the 1850's and 1860's.

Tennyson called his poem "a little *Hamlet*" and explained to his son that it was "the history of a morbid poetic soul, under the blighting influence of a recklessly speculative age. He is the heir of madness, an egotist with the makings of a cynic, raised to sanity by a pure and holy love which elevates his whole nature, passing from the height of triumph to the lowest depth of misery, driven into madness by the loss of her whom he has loved, and, when he has at length passed through the fiery furnace, and has recovered his reason, giving himself up to work for the good of mankind through the unselfishness born of his great passion. . . . 'The pecularity of this poem,' my father added, 'is that different phases of passion in one person take the place of different characters' " (*Memoir*, I, 396). In that last sentence surely lies the key to the proper reading of the poem. If we are perhaps reluctant to grant the poet complete dramatic distance from his speaker, and authorship of such pieces as "The Charge of the Light Brigade" contributes to our reluctance, we should likewise hesitate to assert that the poem is an exercise in support of the Crimean War. *Maud* should be read on its own terms, without undue stress on its autobiographical elements or historical context. Then it is what it appears to be: a splendidly executed psychological study.

MAUD; A MONODRAMA

Part 1

I

1

I hate the dreadful hollow behind the little wood;
Its lips in the field above are dabbled with blood-red heath,[1]
The red-ribb'd ledges drip with a silent horror of blood,
And Echo there, whatever is ask'd her, answers "Death."

1. "In calling heath 'blood'-red, the hero," according to Tennyson, "showed his extravagant fancy, which is already on the road to madness." "His sus- picion that all the world is against him is as true to his nature as the mood when he is 'fantastically merry' " (*Memoir*, I, 396).

2

For there in the ghastly pit long since a body was found,   5
His who had given me life—O father! O God! was it well?—
Mangled, and flatten'd, and crush'd, and dinted into the ground;
There yet lies the rock that fell with him when he fell.

3

Did he fling himself down? who knows? for a vast speculation[2] had
    fail'd,
And ever he mutter'd and madden'd, and ever wann'd with de-
    spair,   10
And out he walk'd when the wind like a broken worldling wail'd,
And the flying gold of the ruin'd woodlands drove thro' the air.

4

I remember the time, for the roots of my hair were stirr'd
By a shuffled step, by a dead weight trail'd, by a whisper'd fright.
And my pulses closed their gates with a shock on my heart as I
    heard   15
The shrill-edged shriek of a mother divide the shuddering night.

5

Villainy somewhere! whose? One says, we are villains all.
Not he! his honest fame should at least by me be maintained;
But that old man, now lord of the broad estate and the Hall,
Dropt off gorged from a scheme that had left us flaccid and
    drain'd.   20

6

Why do they prate of the blessings of peace? we have made them a
    curse,
Pickpockets, each hand lusting for all that is not its own;
And lust of gain, in the spirit of Cain, is it better or worse
Than the heart of the citizen hissing in war on his own hearthstone?

7

But these are the days of advance, the works of the men of mind,   25
When who but a fool would have faith in a tradesman's ware or his
    word?
Is it peace or war? Civil war, as I think, and that of a kind
The viler, as underhand, not openly bearing the sword.

8

Sooner or later I too may passively take the print
Of the golden age—why not? I have neither hope nor trust;   30
May make my heart as a millstone, set my face as a flint,
Cheat and be cheated, and die—who knows? we are ashes and dust.

9

Peace sitting under her olive, and slurring the days gone by,
When the poor are hovell'd and hustled together, each sex, like
    swine,
When only the ledger lives, and when only not all men lie;   35
Peace in her vineyard—yes!—but a company forges the wine.

---

2. A venture, never specified, which had enriched Maud's father, the "old man" of
line 19.

10

And the vitriol madness flushes up in the ruffian's head,
Till the filthy by-lane rings to the yell of the trampled wife,
And chalk and alum and plaster are sold to the poor for bread,
And the spirit of murder works in the very means of life, 40

11

And Sleep must lie down arm'd, for the villainous centre-bits[3]
Grind on the wakeful ear in the hush of the moonless nights,
While another is cheating the sick of a few last gasps, as he sits
To pestle a poison'd poison behind his crimson lights.

12

When a Mammonite mother kills her babe for a burial fee, 45
And Timour[4]-Mammon grins on a pile of children's bones,
Is it peace or war? better, war! loud war by land and by sea,
War with a thousand battles, and shaking a hundred thrones!

13

For I trust if an enemy's fleet came yonder round by the hill,
And the rushing battle-bolt sang from the three-decker out of the
    foam, 50
That the smooth-faced, snub-nosed rogue would leap from his
    counter and till,
And strike, if he could, were it but with his cheating yardwand,
    home.

14

What! am I raging alone as my father raged in his mood?
Must *I* too creep to the hollow and dash myself down and die
Rather than hold by the law that I made, nevermore to brood 55
On a horror of shatter'd limbs and a wretched swindler's lie?

15

Would there be sorrow for *me?* there was *love* in the passionate
    shriek,
Love for the silent thing that had made false haste to the grave—
Wrapt in a cloak, as I saw him, and thought he would rise and
    speak
And rave at the lie and the liar, ah God, as he used to rave. 60

16

I am sick of the Hall and the hill, I am sick of the moor and the
    main.
Why should I stay? can a sweeter chance ever come to me here?
O, having the nerves of motion as well as the nerves of pain,
Were it not wise if I fled from the place and the pit and the fear?

17

Workmen up at the Hall!—they are coming back from abroad; 65
The dark old place will be gilt by the touch of a millionaire
I have heard, I know not whence, of the singular beauty of Maud;
I play'd with the girl when a child; she promised then to be fair.

3. A tool for boring holes, here used
in burglary.
4. Tamerlane, the ruthless descendant
of Genghis Khan, who ravaged Asia
during the last part of the fourteenth
century. At Sivas, Turkey, in 1400, he
was supposed to have crushed a thou-
sand children under the hoofs of his
horses.

18

Maud, with her venturous climbings and tumbles and childish
 escapes,
Maud, the delight of the village, the ringing joy of the Hall,   70
Maud, with her sweet purse-mouth when my father dangled the
 grapes,
Maud, the beloved of my mother, the moon-faced darling of all,—

19

What is she now? My dreams are bad. She may bring me a curse.
No, there is fatter game on the moor; she will let me alone.
Thanks; for the fiend best knows whether woman or man be the
 worse.   75
I will bury myself in myself, and the Devil may pipe to his own.

II

Long have I sigh'd for a calm; God grant I may find it at last!
It will never be broken by Maud; she has neither savor nor salt,
But a cold and clear-cut face, as I found when her carriage past,
Perfectly beautiful; let it be granted her; where is the fault?   80
All that I saw—for her eyes were downcast, not to be seen—
Faultily faultless, icily regular, splendidly null,
Dead perfection, no more; nothing more, if it had not been
For a chance of travel, a paleness, an hour's defect of the rose,
Or an underlip, you may call it a little too ripe, too full,   85
Or the least little delicate aquiline curve in a sensitive nose,
From which I escaped heart-free, with the least little touch of
 spleen.

III

Cold and clear-cut face, why come you so cruelly meek,
Breaking a slumber in which all spleenful folly was drown'd?
Pale with the golden beam of an eyelash dead on the cheek,   90
Passionless, pale, cold face, star-sweet on a gloom profound;
Womanlike, taking revenge too deep for a transient wrong
Done but in thought to your beauty, and ever as pale as before
Growing and fading and growing upon me without a sound,
Luminous, gemlike, ghostlike, deathlike, half the night long   95
Growing and fading and growing, till I could bear it no more,
But arose, and all by myself in my own dark garden ground,
Listening now to the tide in its broad-flung shipwrecking roar,[5]
Now to the scream of a madden'd beach dragg'd down by the wave,
Walk'd in a wintry wind by a ghastly glimmer, and found   100
The shining daffodil dead, and Orion low in his grave.

---

5. Tennyson commented that on the
Isle of Wight "the roar can be heard
nine miles away from the beach"
(*Memoir*, I, 402).

IV

1

A million emeralds break from the ruby-budded lime
In the little grove where I sit—ah, wherefore cannot I be
Like things of the season gay, like the bountiful season bland,
When the far-off sail is blown by the breeze of a softer clime,   105
Half-lost in the liquid azure bloom of a crescent of sea,
The silent sapphire-spangled marriage ring of the land?

2

Below me, there, is the village, and looks how quiet and small!
And yet bubbles o'er like a city, with gossip, scandal, and spite;
And Jack on his ale-house bench has as many lies as a Czar;   110
And here on the landward side, by a red rock, glimmers the Hall;
And up in the high Hall-garden I see her pass like a light;
But sorrow seize me if ever that light be my leading star!

3

When have I bow'd to her father, the wrinkled head of the race?
I met her to-day with her brother, but not to her brother I bow'd;   115
I bow'd to his lady-sister as she rode by on the moor,
But the fire of a foolish pride flash'd over her beautiful face.
O child, you wrong your beauty, believe it, in being so proud;
Your father has wealth well-gotten, and I am nameless and poor.

4

I keep but a man and a maid, ever ready to slander and steal;   120
I know it, and smile a hard-set smile, like a stoic, or like
A wiser epicurean, and let the world have its way.
For nature[6] is one with rapine, a harm no preacher can heal;
The Mayfly is torn by the swallow, the sparrow spear'd by the shrike,
And the whole little wood where I sit is a world of plunder and
          prey.[7]   125

5

We are puppets, Man in his pride, and Beauty fair in her flower;
Do we move ourselves, or are moved by an unseen hand at a game
That pushes us off from the board, and others ever succeed?
Ah yet, we cannot be kind to each other here for an hour;
We whisper, and hint, and chuckle, and grin at a brother's   130
          shame;

6

A monstrous eft was of old the lord and master of earth,
For him did his high sun flame, and his river billowing ran,
And he felt himself in his force to be Nature's crowning race.
As nine months go to the shaping an infant ripe for his birth,   135
So many a million of ages have gone to the making of man:
He now is first, but is he the last? is he not too base?[8]

6. Human as well as external nature.
7. Compare *In Memoriam*, 56.
8. Like several sections of *In Memo-riam*, this stanza is often cited in support of the claim that Tennyson anticipated Darwinism. An "eft" is literally a newt, though Tennyson was thinking of "the great old lizards of geology." His note suggests he may have had Chambers' *Vestiges of Creation* (1844) in mind.

7

The man of science himself is fonder of glory, and vain,
An eye well-practised in nature, a spirit bounded and poor;
The passionate heart of the poet is whirl'd into folly and vice.   140
I would not marvel at either, but keep a temperate brain;
For not to desire or admire, if a man could learn it, were more
Than to walk all day like the sultan of old in a garden of spice.

8

For the drift of the Maker is dark, an Isis[9] hid by the veil.
Who knows the ways of the world, how God will bring them
     about?   145
Our planet is one, the suns are many, the world is wide.
Shall I weep if a Poland fall? shall I shriek if a Hungary[1] fail?
Or an infant civilization be ruled with rod or with knout?
I have not made the world,[2] and He that made it will guide.

9

Be mine a philosopher's life in the quiet woodland ways,   150
Where if I cannot be gay let a passionless peace be my lot,
Far-off from the clamor of liars belied in the hubbub of lies;
From the long-neck'd geese of the world that are ever hissing dis-
     praise
Because their natures are little, and, whether he heed it or not,
Where each man walks with his head in a cloud of poisonous
     flies.   155

10

And most of all would I flee from the cruel madness of love
The honey of poison-flowers and all the measureless ill.
Ah, Maud, you milk-white fawn, you are all unmeet for a wife.
Your mother is mute in her grave as her image in marble above;
Your father is ever in London, you wander about at your will;   160
You have but fed on the roses and lain in the lilies of life.

V

1

A voice by the cedar tree
In the meadow under the Hall!
She is singing an air that is known to me,
A passionate ballad gallant and gay,   165
A martial song like a trumpet's call!
Singing alone in the morning of life,
In the happy morning of life and of May,
Singing of men that in battle array,
Ready in heart and ready in hand,   170
March with banner and bugle and fife
To the death, for their native land.

9. The Egyptian goddess of fertility.
1. In 1849 the Hungarian uprising against Austria failed; In 1846 and again in 1848 Russia and Austria had partitioned and reduced Poland.

2. See Housman's *Last Poems*, XII:
   And how am I to face the odds
   Of man's bedevilment and God's?
   I, a stranger and afraid
   In a world I never made.

2

Maud with her exquisite face,
And wild voice pealing up to the sunny sky,
And feet like sunny gems on an English green,   175
Maud in the light of her youth and her grace,
Singing of Death, and of Honor that cannot die,
Till I well could weep for a time so sordid and mean,
And myself so languid and base.

3

Silence, beautiful voice!   180
Be still, for you only trouble the mind
With a joy in which I cannot rejoice,
A glory I shall not find.
Still! I will hear you no more,
For your sweetness hardly leaves me a choice   185
But to move to the meadow and fall before
Her feet on the meadow grass, and adore,
Not her, who is neither courtly nor kind,
Not her, not her, but a voice.

VI

1

Morning arises stormy and pale,   190
No sun, but a wannish glare
In fold upon fold of hueless cloud;
And the budded peaks of the wood, are bow'd,
Caught, and cuff'd by the gale:
I had fancied it would be fair.   195

2

Whom but Maud should I meet
Last night, when the sunset burn'd
On the blossom'd gable-ends
At the head of the village street,
Whom but Maud should I meet?   200
And she touch'd my hand with a smile so sweet,
She made me divine amends
For a courtesy not return'd.

3

And thus a delicate spark
Of glowing and growing light   205
Thro' the livelong hours of the dark
Kept itself warm in the heart of my dreams,
Ready to burst in a color'd flame;
Till at last, when the morning came
In a cloud, it faded, and seems   210
But an ashen-gray delight.

4

What if with her sunny hair,
And smile as sunny as cold,

She meant to weave me a snare
Of some coquettish deceit,   215
Cleopatra-like as of old
To entangle me when we met,
To have her lion roll in a silken net
And fawn at a victor's feet.

                                5

Ah, what shall I be at fifty   220
Should Nature keep me alive,
If I find the world so bitter
When I am but twenty-five?
Yet, if she were not a cheat,
If Maud were all that she seem'd,   225
And her smile were all that I dream'd,
Then the world were not so bitter
But a smile could make it sweet.

                                6

What if, tho' her eye seem'd full
Of a kind intent to me,   230
What if that dandy-despot, he,
That jewell'd mass of millinery,
That oil'd and curl'd Assyrian bull
Smelling of musk and of insolence,
Her brother, from whom I keep aloof,   235
Who wants the finer politic sense
To mask, tho' but in his own behoof,
With a glassy smile his brutal scorn—
What if he had told her yestermorn
How prettily for his own sweet sake   240
A face of tenderness might be feign'd,
And a moist mirage in desert eyes,
That so, when the rotten hustings[3] shake
In another month to his brazen lies,
A wretched vote may be gain'd?   245

                                7

For a raven ever croaks, at my side,
Keep watch and ward, keep watch and ward,
Or thou wilt prove their tool.
Yea, too, myself from myself I guard,
For often a man's own angry pride   250
Is cap and bells for a fool.

                                8

Perhaps the smile and tender tone
Came out of her pitying womanhood,
For am I not, am I not, here alone
So many a summer since she died,   255
My mother, who was so gentle and good?
Living alone in an empty house,

3. Platforms on which candidates for   tion, hence a place for making cam-
Parliament formerly stood for nomina-   paign speeches.

Here half-hid in the gleaming wood,
Where I hear the dead at midday moan,
And the shrieking rush of the wainscot mouse, 260
And my own sad name in corners cried,
When the shiver of dancing leaves is thrown
About its echoing chambers wide,
Till a morbid hate and horror have grown
Of a world in which I have hardly mixt, 265
And a morbid eating lichen fixt
On a heart half-turn'd to stone.

9

O heart of stone, are you flesh, and caught
By that you swore to withstand?
For what was it else within me wrought 270
But, I fear, the new strong wine of love,
That made my tongue so stammer and trip
When I saw the treasured splendor, her hand,
Come sliding out of her sacred glove,
And the sunlight broke from her lip? 275

10

I have play'd with her when a child;
She remembers it now we meet.
Ah, well, well, well, I *may* be beguiled
By some coquettish deceit.
Yet, if she were not a cheat, 280
If Maud were all that she seem'd,
And her smile had all that I dream'd,
Then the world were not so bitter
But a smile could make it sweet.

VII

1

Did I hear it half in a doze 285
　　Long since, I know not where?
Did I dream it an hour ago,
　　When asleep in this arm-chair?

2

Men were drinking together,
　　Drinking and talking of me: 290
"Well, if it prove a girl, the boy
　　Will have plenty; so let it be."

3

Is it an echo of something
　　Read with a boy's delight,
Viziers[4] nodding together 295
　　In some Arabian night?

4. High executive offices in Mohamme-
dan countries. The two fathers are talk-
ing just before the birth of Maud, and,
as Part 1, section XIX 4 later clarifies,
have arranged a marriage if the child
proves to be a girl. I assume Maud's
father speaks first; the second voice is,
obviously, the protagonist's father's.

4

Strange, that I hear two men,
Somewhere, talking of me:
"Well, if it prove a girl, my boy
Will have plenty; so let it be."   300

VIII

She came to the village church,
And sat by a pillar alone;
An angel watching an urn
Wept over her, carved in stone;
And once, but once, she lifted her eyes,   305
And suddenly, sweetly, strangely blush'd
To find they were met by my own;
And suddenly, sweetly, my heart beat stronger
And thicker, until I heard no longer
The snowy-banded, dilettante,   310
Delicate-handed priest intone;
And thought, is it pride? and mused and sigh'd,
"No surely, now it cannot be pride."

IX

I was walking a mile,
More than a mile from the shore,   315
The sun look'd out with a smile
Betwixt the cloud and the moor;
And riding at set of day
Over the dark moor land,
Rapidly riding far away,   320
She waved to me with her hand.
There were two[5] at her side,
Something flash'd in the sun,
Down by the hill I saw them ride,
In a moment they were gone;   325
Like a sudden spark
Struck vainly in the night,
Then returns the dark
With no more hope of light.

X

1

Sick, am I sick of a jealous dread?   330
Was not one of the two at her side
This new-made lord, whose splendor plucks
The slavish hat from the villager's head?

5. Maud's brother and her suitor, the "new-made lord" of line 332.

Whose old grandfather has lately died,
Gone to a blacker pit, for whom   335
Grimy nakedness dragging his trucks
And laying his trams in a poison'd gloom
Wrought, till he crept from a gutted mine
Master of half a servile shire,
And left his coal all turn'd into gold   340
To a grandson, first of his noble line,
Rich in the grace all women desire,
Strong in the power that all men adore,
And simper and set their voices lower,
And soften as if to a girl, and hold   345
Awe-stricken breaths at a work divine,
Seeing his gewgaw[6] castle shine,
New as his title, built last year,
There amid perky larches and pine,
And over the sullen-purple moor—   350
Look at it—pricking a cockney ear.

2

What, has he found my jewel out?
For one of the two that rode at her side
Bound for the Hall, I am sure was he;
Bound for the Hall, and I think for a bride.   355
Blithe would her brother's acceptance be
Maud could be gracious too, no doubt,
To a lord, a captain, a padded shape,
A bought commission, a waxen face,
A rabbit mouth that is ever agape—   360
Bought? what is it he cannot buy?
And therefore splenetic, personal, base,
A wounded thing with a rancorous cry,
At war with myself and a wretched race,
Sick, sick to the heart of life, am I.   365

3

Last week came one to the county town,
To preach our poor little army down,
And play the game of the despot kings,
Tho' the state has done it and thrice as well.
This broad-brimm'd hawker[7] of holy things, 370
Whose ear is cramm'd with his cotton, and rings
Even in dreams to the chink of his pence,
This huckster put down war! can he tell
Whether war be a cause or a consequence?
Put down the passions that make earth hell! 375
Down with ambition, avarice, pride,

---

6. Gaudy.
7. The Quakers were identifiable by their "broad-brimm'd" hats. The *Westminster Review* said the figure was John Bright, who had vigorously op- posed the Crimean War. Tennyson, only half-convincingly, denied the allega- tion, saying, "I did not know at the time that he was a Quaker" (*Memoir*, I, 403).

Jealousy, down! cut off from the mind
The bitter springs of anger and fear!
Down too, down at your own fireside,
With the evil tongue and the evil ear,   380
For each is at war with mankind!

4

I wish I could hear again
The chivalrous battle-song
That she warbled alone in her joy!
I might persuade myself then   385
She would not do herself this great wrong,
To take a wanton dissolute boy
For a man and leader of men.

5

Ah God, for a man with heart, head, hand,
Like some of the simple great ones gone   390
For ever and ever by,
One still strong man in a blatant land,
Whatever they call him—what care I?—
Aristocrat, democrat, autocrat—one
Who can rule and dare not lie!   395

6

And ah for a man to arise in me,
That the man I am may cease to be!

XI

1

O, let the solid ground
    Not fail beneath my feet
Before my life has found   400
    What some have found so sweet!
Then let come what come may,
What matter if I go mad,
I shall have had my day.

2

Let the sweet heavens endure,   405
    Not close and darken above me
Before I am quite quite sure
    That there is one to love me!
Then let come what come may
To a life that has been so sad,   410
I shall have had my day.

XII

1

Birds in the high Hall-garden
    When twilight was falling,

Maud, Maud, Maud, Maud,
   They were crying and calling. 415

2

Where was Maud? in our wood;
   And I—who else?—was with her,
Gathering woodland lilies,
   Myriads blow[8] together.

3

Birds in our wood sang 420
   Ringing thro' the valleys,
Maud is here, here, here
   In among the lilies.

4

I kiss'd her slender hand,
   She took the kiss sedately; 425
Maud is not seventeen,
   But she is tall and stately.

5

I to cry out on pride
   Who have won her favor!
O, Maud were sure of heaven 430
   If lowliness could save her!

6

I know the way she went
   Home with her maiden posy,
For her feet have touch'd the meadows
   And left the daisies rosy.[9] 435

7

Birds in the high Hall-garden
   Were crying and calling to her,
Where is Maud, Maud, Maud?
   One is come to woo her.

8

Look, a horse at the door, 440
   And little King Charley[1] snarling!
Go back, my lord, across the moor,
   You are not her darling.

XIII

1

Scorn'd, to be scorn'd by one that I scorn,
Is that a matter to make me fret? 445
That a calamity hard to be borne?
Well, he may live to hate me yet.
Fool that I am to be vext with his pride!
I past him, I was crossing his lands;

8. Bloom.
9. "If you tread on the daisy," Tenny-
son pointed out of the English variety,
"it turns up a rosy underside."
1. A dog.

He stood on the path a little aside; 450
His face, as I grant, in spite of spite,
Has a broad-blown comeliness, red and white,
And six feet two, as I think, he stands;
But his essences turn'd the live air sick,
And barbarous opulence jewel-thick 455
Sunn'd itself on his breast and his hands.

2

Who shall call me ungentle, unfair?
I long'd so heartily then and there
To give him the grasp of fellowship;
But while I past he was humming an air, 460
Stopt, and then with a riding-whip
Leisurely tapping a glossy boot,
And curving a contumelious lip,
Gorgonized[2] me from head to foot
With a stony British stare. 465

3

Why sits he here in his father's chair?
That old man never comes to his place;
Shall I believe him ashamed to be seen?
For only once, in the village street,
Last year, I caught a glimpse of his face, 470
A gray old wolf and a lean.
Scarcely, now, would I call him a cheat;
For then, perhaps, as a child of deceit,
She might by a true descent be untrue;
And Maud is as true as Maud is sweet, 475
Tho' I fancy her sweetness only due
To the sweeter blood by the other side;
Her mother has been a thing complete,
However she came to be so allied.
And fair without, faithful within, 480
Maud to him is nothing akin.
Some peculiar mystic grace
Made her only the child of her mother,
And heap'd the whole inherited sin
On that huge scapegoat of the race, 485
All, all upon the brother.

4

Peace, angry spirit, and let him be!
Has not his sister smiled on me?

XIV

1

Maud has a garden of roses
And lilies fair on a lawn; 490

2. Medusa, one of the three Gorgon sisters, had a face so hideous that it turned to stone anyone who gazed directly upon it.

There she walks in her state
And tends upon bed and bower,
And thither I climb'd at dawn
And stood by her garden-gate.
A lion ramps at the top,   495
He is claspt by a passion-flower.

2

Maud's own little oak-room—
Which Maud, like a precious stone
Set in the heart of the carven gloom,
Lights with herself, when alone   500
She sits by her music and books
And her brother lingers late
With a roystering company—looks
Upon Maud's own garden-gate;
And I thought as I stood, if a hand, as white   505
As ocean-foam in the moon, were laid
On the hasp of the window, and my Delight
Had a sudden desire, like a glorious ghost, to glide,
Like a beam of the seventh heaven, down to my side,
There were but a step to be made.   510

3

The fancy flatter'd my mind,
And again seem'd overbold;
Now I thought that she cared for me,
Now I thought she was kind
Only because she was cold.   515

4

I heard no sound where I stood
But the rivulet on from the lawn
Running down to my own dark wood,
Or the voice of the long sea-wave as it swell'd
Now and then in the dim-gray dawn;   520
But I look'd, and round, all round the house I beheld
The death-white curtain drawn,
Felt a horror over me creep,
Prickle my skin and catch my breath,
Knew that the death-white curtain meant but sleep,   525
Yet I shudder'd and thought like a fool of the sleep of death.

XV

So dark a mind within me dwells,
  And I make myself such evil cheer,
That if I be dear to some one else,
  Then some one else may have much to fear;   530
But if I be dear to some one else,
  Then I should be to myself more dear.
Shall I not take care of all that I think,

Yea, even of wretched meat and drink,
If I be dear, 535
If I be dear to some one else?

XVI

1

This lump of earth has left his estate
The lighter by the loss of his weight;
And so that he find what he went to seek,
And fulsome pleasure clog him, and drown 540
His heart in the gross mud-honey of town,
He may stay for a year who has gone for a week.
But this is the day when I must speak,
And I see my Oread[3] coming down,
O, this is the day! 545
O beautiful creature, what am I
That I dare to look her way?
Think I may hold dominion sweet,
Lord of the pulse that is lord of her breast,
And dream of her beauty with tender dread, 550
From the delicate Arab arch of her feet
To the grace that, bright and light as the crest
Of a peacock, sits on her shining head,
And she knows it not—O, if she knew it,
To know her beauty might half undo it! 555
I know it the one bright thing to save
My yet young life in the wilds of Time,
Perhaps from madness, perhaps from crime,
Perhaps from a selfish grave.

2

What, if she be fasten'd to this fool lord, 560
Dare I bid her abide by her word?
Should I love her so well if she
Had given her word to a thing so low?
Shall I love her as well if she
Can break her word were it even for me? 565
I trust that it is not so.

3

Catch not my breath, O clamorous heart,
Let not my tongue be a thrall to my eye,
For I must tell her before we part,
I must tell her, or die. 570

XVII

Go not, happy day,
From the shining fields,

3. A mountain-nymph.

Go not, happy day,
   Till the maiden yields.
Rosy is the West,   575
   Rosy is the South,
Roses are her cheeks,
   And a rose her mouth.
When the happy Yes
   Falters from her lips,   580
Pass and blush the news
   Over glowing ships;
Over blowing seas,
   Over seas at rest,
Pass the happy news,   585
   Blush it thro' the West;
Till the red man dance
   By his red cedar-tree,
And the red man's babe
   Leap, beyond the sea.   590
Blush from West to East,
   Blush from East to West,
Till the West is East,
   Blush it thro' the West.
Rosy is the West,   595
   Rosy is the South,
Roses are her cheeks,
   And a rose her mouth.

XVIII[4]

1

I have led her home, my love, my only friend.
There is none like her, none.   600
And never yet so warmly ran my blood
And sweetly, on and on
Calming itself to the long-wish'd-for end,
Full to the banks, close on the promised good.

2

None like her, none.   605
Just now the dry-tongued laurels' pattering talk
Seem'd her light foot along the garden walk,
And shook my heart to think she comes once more.
But even then I heard her close the door;
The gates of heaven are closed, and she is gone.   610

3

There is none like her, none,
Nor will be when our summers have deceased.
O, art thou[5] sighing for Lebanon

4. This whole section is an Epithala-   5. The cedar of Lebanon tree in
mion, perhaps the most successful effort   Maud's garden.
of the kind since Spenser.

In the long breeze that streams to thy delicious East,
Sighing for Lebanon,   615
Dark cedar, tho' thy limbs have here increased,
Upon a pastoral slope as fair,
And looking to the South and fed
With honey'd rain and delicate air,
And haunted by the starry head   620
Of her whose gentle will has changed my fate,
And made my life a perfumed altar-flame;
And over whom thy darkness must have spread
With such delight as theirs of old, thy great
Forefathers of the thornless garden, there   625
Shadowing the snow-limb'd Eve from whom she came?

4

Here will I lie, while these long branches sway,
And you fair stars that crown a happy day
Go in and out as if at merry play,
Who am no more so all forlorn   630
As when it seem'd far better to be born
To labor and the mattock-harden'd hand
Than nursed at ease and brought to understand
A sad astrology,[6] the boundless plan
That makes you tyrants in your iron skies,   635
Innumerable, pitiless, passionless eyes,
Cold fires, yet with power to burn and brand
His nothingness into man.

5

But now shine on, and what care I,
Who in this stormy gulf have found a pearl   640
The countercharm of space and hollow sky,
And do accept my madness, and would die
To save from some slight shame one simple girl?—

6

Would die, for sullen-seeming Death may give
More life to Love than is or ever was   645
In our low world, where yet 't is sweet to live.
Let no one ask me how it came to pass;
It seems that I am happy, that to me
A livelier emerald twinkles in the grass,
A purer sapphire melts into the sea.   650

7

Not die, but live a life of truest breath,[7]
And teach true life to fight with mortal wrongs.
O, why should Love, like men in drinking-songs,
Spice his fair banquet with the dust of death?
Make answer, Maud my bliss,   655
Maud made my Maud by that long loving kiss,

---

6. "The *sad astrology* is modern as-
tronomy, for of old astrology was
thought to sympathise with and rule
man's fate" (Tennyson's note).
7. Tennyson said, "This is the central
idea—the holy power of Love."

Life of my life, wilt thou not answer this?
"The dusky strand of Death inwoven here
With dear Love's tie, makes Love himself more dear."

8

Is that enchanted moan only the swell   660
Of the long waves that roll in yonder bay?
And hark the clock within, the silver knell
Of twelve sweet hours that past in bridal white,
And died to live, long as my pulses play;
But now by this my love has closed her sight   665
And given false death[8] her hand, and stolen away
To dreamful wastes where footless fancies dwell
Among the fragments of the golden day.
May nothing there her maiden grace affright!
Dear heart, I feel with thee the drowsy spell.   670
My bride to be, my evermore delight,
My own heart's heart, my ownest own, farewell;
It is but for a little space I go.
And ye[9] meanwhile far over moor and fell
Beat to the noiseless music of the night!   675
Has our whole earth gone nearer to the glow
Of your soft splendors that you look so bright?
I have climb'd nearer out of lonely hell.
Beat, happy stars, timing with things below,
Beat with my heart more blest than heart can tell,   680
Blest, but for some dark undercurrent woe
That seems to draw—but it shall not be so;
Let all be well, be well.

XIX

1

Her brother is coming back to-night,
Breaking up my dream of delight.   685

2

My dream? do I dream of bliss?
I have walk'd awake with Truth.
O, when did a morning shine
So rich in atonement as this
For my dark-dawning youth,   690
Darken'd watching a mother decline
And that dead man[1] at her heart and mine;
For who was left to watch her but I?
Yet so did I let my freshness die.

3

I trust that I did not talk   695
To gentle Maud in our walk—
For often in lonely wanderings

8. Sleep.   1. The speaker's father.
9. The stars.

I have cursed him even to lifeless things—
But I trust that I did not talk,
Not touch on her father's sin.   700
I am sure I did but speak
Of my mother's faded cheek
When it slowly grew so thin
That I felt she was slowly dying
Vext with lawyers and harrass'd with debt;   705
For how often I caught her with eyes all wet,
Shaking her head at her son and sighing
A world of trouble within!

4²

And Maud too, Maud was moved
To speak of the mother she loved   710
As one scarce less forlorn,
Dying abroad and it seems apart
From him who had ceased to share her heart,
And ever mourning over the feud,
The household Fury sprinkled with blood   715
By which our houses are torn.
How strange was what she said,
When only Maud and the brother
Hung over her dying bed—
That Maud's dark father and mine   720
Had bound us one to the other,
Betrothed us over their wine,
On the day when Maud was born;
Seal'd her mine from her first sweet breath!
Mine, mine by a right, from birth till death!   725
Mine, mine—our fathers have sworn!

5

But the true blood spilt had in it a heat
To dissolve the precious seal on a bond,
That, if left uncancell'd, had been so sweet;
And none of us thought of a something beyond,   730
A desire that awoke in the heart of the child,
As it were a duty done to the tomb,
To be friends for her sake, to be reconciled;
And I was cursing them and my doom,
And letting a dangerous thought run wild   735
While often abroad in the fragrant gloom
Of foreign churches—I see her there,
Bright English lily, breathing a prayer
To be friends, to be reconciled!

6

But then what a flint is he!   740
Abroad, at Florence, at Rome,

2. Section XIX did not appear in the
first edition of 1855. As noted earlier,
this subsection clarifies the pledge of
marriage, about which the poem's first
readers were justifiably confused.

I find whenever she touch'd on me
This brother had laugh'd her down,
And at last, when each came home,
He had darken'd into a frown,   745
Chid her, and forbid her to speak
To me, her friend of the years before;
And this was what had redden'd her cheek
When I bow'd to her on the moor.

7

Yet Maud, altho' not blind   750
To the faults of his heart and mind,
I see she cannot but love him,
And says he is rough but kind,
And wishes me to approve him,
And tells me, when she lay   755
Sick once, with a fear of worse,
That he left his wine and horses and play,
Sat with her, read to her, night and day,
And tended her like a nurse.

8

Kind? but the death-bed desire   760
Spurn'd by this heir of the liar—
Rough but kind? yet I know
He has plotted against me in this,
That he plots against me still.
Kind to Maud? that were not amiss.   765
Well, rough but kind; why, let it be so,
For shall not Maud have her will?

9

For, Maud, so tender and true,
As long as my life endures
I feel I shall owe you a debt   770
That I never can hope to pay;
And if ever I should forget
That I owe this debt to you
And for your sweet sake to yours,
O, then, what then shall I say?—   775
If ever I *should* forget,
May God make me more wretched
Than ever I have been yet!

10

So now I have sworn to bury
All this dead body of hate,   780
I feel so free and so clear
By the loss of that dead weight,
That I should grow light-hearted, I fear,
Fantastically merry,
But that her brother comes, like a blight   785
On my fresh hope, to the Hall to-night.

XX

1

Strange, that I felt so gay,
Strange, that I tried to-day
To beguile her melancholy;
The Sultan, as we name him—   790
She did not wish to blame him—
But he vext her and perplext her
With his worldly talk and folly.
Was it gentle to reprove her
For stealing out of view   795
From a little lazy lover
Who but claims her as his due?
Or for chilling his caresses
By the coldness of her manners,
Nay, the plainness of her dresses?   800
Now I know her but in two,
Nor can pronounce upon it
If one should ask me whether
The habit, hat, and feather,
Or the frock and gipsy bonnet   805
Be the neater and completer;
For nothing can be sweeter
Than maiden Maud in either.

2

But to-morrow, if we live,
Our ponderous squire will give   810
A grand political dinner
To half the squirelings near;
And Maud will wear her jewels,
And the bird of prey will hover,
And the titmouse hope to win her   815
With his chirrup at her ear.

3

A grand political dinner
To the men of many acres,
A gathering of the Tory,
A dinner and then a dance   820
For the maids and marriage-makers,
And every eye but mine will glance
At Maud in all her glory.

4

For I am not invited,
But, with the Sultan's pardon,   825
I am all as well delighted,
For I know her own rose-garden,
And mean to linger in it
Till the dancing will be over;
And then, O, then, come out to me   830

For a minute, but for a minute,
Come out to your own true lover,
That your true lover may see
Your glory also, and render
All homage to his own darling,   835
Queen Maud in all her splendor.

XXI

Rivulet crossing my ground,
And bringing me down from the Hall
This garden-rose that I found,
Forgetful of Maud and me,   840
And lost in trouble and moving round
Here at the head of a tinkling fall,
And trying to pass to the sea;
O rivulet, born at the Hall,
My Maud has sent it by thee—   845
If I read her sweet will right—
On a blushing mission to me,
Saying in odor and color, "Ah, be
Among the roses to-night."

XXII

1

Come into the garden, Maud,   850
  For the black bat, night, has flown,
Come into the garden, Maud,
  I am here at the gate alone;
And the woodbine spices are wafted abroad,
  And the musk of the rose is blown.   855

2

For a breeze of morning moves,
  And the planet of Love is on high,
Beginning to faint in the light that she loves
  On a bed of daffodil sky,
To faint in the light of the sun she loves,   860
  To faint in his light, and to die.

3

All night have the roses heard
  The flute, violin, bassoon;
All night has the casement jessamine stirr'd
  To the dancers dancing in tune;   865
Till a silence fell with the waking bird,
  And a hush with the setting moon.

4

I said to the lily, "There is but one,
  With whom she has heart to be gay.

When will the dancers leave her alone?   870
   She is weary of dance and play."
Now half to the setting moon are gone,
   And half to the rising day;
Low on the sand and loud on the stone
   The last wheel echoes away.   875

5
I said to the rose, "The brief night goes
   In babble and revel and wine.
O young lord-lover, what sighs are those,
   For one that will never be thine?
But mine, but mine," so I sware to the rose,   880
   "For ever and ever, mine."

6
And the soul of the rose went into my blood,
   As the music clash'd in the hall;
And long by the garden lake I stood,
   For I heard your rivulet fall   885
From the lake to the meadow and on to the wood,
   Our wood, that is dearer than all;

7
From the meadow your walks have left so sweet
   That whenever a March-wind sighs
He sets the jewel-print of your feet   890
   In violets blue as your eyes,
To the woody hollows in which we meet
   And the valleys of Paradise.

8
The slender acacia would not shake
   One long milk-bloom on the tree;   895
The white lake-blossom fell into the lake
   As the pimpernel dozed on the lea;
But the rose was awake all night for your sake,
   Knowing your promise to me;
The lilies and roses were all awake,   900
   They sigh'd for the dawn and thee.

9
Queen rose of the rosebud garden of girls,
   Come hither, the dances are done,
In gloss of satin and glimmer of pearls,
   Queen lily and rose in one;   905
Shine out, little head, sunning over with curls,
   To the flowers, and be their sun.

10
There has fallen a splendid tear
   From the passion-flower at the gate.
She is coming, my dove, my dear;   910
   She is coming, my life, my fate.
The red rose cries, "She is near, she is near;"

And the white rose weeps, "She is late;"
The larkspur listens, "I hear, I hear;"
And the lily whispers, "I wait."[3]   915

11

She is coming, my own, my sweet;
  Were it ever so airy a tread,
My heart would hear her and beat,
  Were it earth in an earthy bed;
My dust would hear her and beat,   920
  Had I lain for a century dead,
Would start and tremble under her feet,
  And blossom in purple and red.

Part 2

I

1

"The fault was mine, the fault was mine"—
Why am I sitting here[4] so stunn'd and still,
Plucking the harmless wild-flower on the hill?—
It is this guilty hand!—
And there rises ever a passionate cry   5
From underneath in the darkening land—
What is it, that has been done?
O dawn of Eden bright over earth and sky,
The fires of hell brake out of thy rising sun,
The fires of hell and of hate;   10
For she, sweet soul, had hardly spoken a word,
When her brother ran in his rage to the gate,
He came with the babe-faced lord,
Heap'd on her terms of disgrace;
And while she wept, and I strove to be cool,   15
He fiercely gave me the lie,
Till I with as fierce an anger spoke,
And he struck me, madman, over the face,
Struck me before the languid fool,
Who was gaping and grinning by;   20
Struck for himself an evil stroke,
Wrought for his house an irredeemable woe.
For front to front in an hour we stood,
And a million horrible bellowing echoes broke
From the red-ribb'd hollow behind the wood,   25

---

3. In his famous chapter, "Of the Pathetic Fallacy" (*Modern Painters,* Part IV, ch. 12) Ruskin quotes this stanza as an "exquisite" example of how the "fallacy" can be properly, i.e., consciously, used.
4. The precise time and place are not clear. The landscape and Tennyson's note to the section, "The Phantom (after the duel with Maud's brother)," suggest that the speaker is still in England and that only a short time has elapsed since the duel. In Part 2, section II, lines 49 ff, he has crossed the Channel into Brittany.

And thunder'd up into heaven the Christless code[5]
That must have life for a blow.
Ever and ever afresh they seem'd to grow.
Was it he lay there with a fading eye?
"The fault was mine," he whisper'd, "fly!"   30
Then glided out of the joyous wood
The ghastly Wraith[6] of one that I know,
And there rang on a sudden a passionate cry,
A cry for a brother's blood;
It will ring in my heart and my ears, till I die, till I die.   35

2

Is it gone? my pulses beat—
What was it? a lying trick of the brain?
Yet I thought I saw her stand,
A shadow there at my feet,
High over the shadowy land.   40
It is gone; and the heavens fall in a gentle rain,
When they should burst and drown with deluging storms
The feeble vassals of wine and anger and lust,
The little hearts that know not how to forgive.
Arise, my God, and strike, for we hold Thee just,   45
Strike dead the whole weak race of venomous worms,
That sting each other here in the dust;
We are not worthy to live.

II

1

See what a lovely shell,[7]
Small and pure as a pearl,   50
Lying close to my foot,
Frail, but a work divine,
Made so fairly well
With delicate spire and whorl,
How exquisitely minute,   55
A miracle of design!

2

What is it? a learned man
Could give it a clumsy name.
Let him name it who can,
The beauty would be the same.   60

5. The code of honor. Although there were strict laws against it, dueling was primarily engaged in by the aristocracy. By mid-century, however, it had become an anachronism.
6. Maud. A "wraith" is an apparation in a person's exact likeness which portends his imminent death—a definition which fits my assumption in note 4 about the time. Maud soon dies, off-stage. We must remember that throughout Part 2 we are receiving the dis-torted impressions of a speaker who is at first unbalanced, then quite literally mad. Sequence in time and unity of place are appropriately blurred. The technique resembles Faulkner's in Benjy's narration opening *The Sound and the Fury*.
7. According to Tennyson, "The shell undestroyed amid the storm perhaps symbolizes to him his own first and highest nature preserved amid the storms of passion."

3

The tiny cell is forlorn,
Void of the little living will
That made it stir on the shore.
Did he stand at the diamond door
Of his house in a rainbow frill?
65
Did he push, when he was uncurl'd,
A golden foot or a fairy horn
Thro' his dim water-world?

4

Slight, to be crush'd with a tap
Of my finger-nail on the sand,
Small, but a work divine,
70
Frail, but of force to withstand,
Year upon year, the shock
Of cataract seas that snap
The three-decker's oaken spine
Athwart the ledges of rock,
75
Here on the Breton strand!

5

Breton, not Briton; here
Like a shipwreck'd man on a coast
Of ancient fable and fear—
Plagued with a flitting to and fro,
80
A disease, a hard mechanic ghost
That never came from on high
Nor ever arose from below,
But only moves with the moving eye,
Flying along the land and the main—
85
Why should it look like Maud?
Am I to be overawed
By what I cannot but know
Is a juggle born of the brain?
90

6

Back from the Breton coast,
Sick of a nameless fear,
Back to the dark sea-line
Looking, thinking of all I have lost;
An old song vexes my ear,
95
But that of Lamech[8] is mine.

7

For years, a measureless ill,
For years, for ever, to part—
But she, she would love me still;
And as long, O God, as she
100
Have a grain of love for me,

8. See *Genesis*, 4:23. Lamech had killed a young man and lamented his deed.

So long, no doubt, no doubt,
Shall I nurse in my dark heart,
However weary, a spark of will
Not to be trampled out.   105

8

Strange, that the mind, when fraught
With a passion so intense
One would think that it well
Might drown all life in the eye,—
That it should, by being so overwrought,   110
Suddenly strike on a sharper sense
For a shell, or a flower, little things
Which else would have been past by!
And now I remember, I,
When he lay dying there,   115
I noticed one of his many rings—
For he had many, poor worm—and thought,
It is his mother's hair.[9]

9

Who knows if he be dead?
Whether I need have fled?   120
Am I guilty of blood?
However this may be,
Comfort her, comfort her, all things good,
While I am over the sea!
Let me and my passionate love go by,   125
But speak to her all things holy and high,
Whatever happen to me!
Me and my harmful love go by;
But come to her waking, find her asleep,
Powers of the height, Powers of the deep,   130
And comfort her tho' I die!

III

Courage, poor heart of stone!
I will not ask thee why
Thou canst not understand
That thou art left for ever alone;   135
Courage, poor stupid heart of stone!—
Or if I ask thee why,
Care not thou to reply:
She is but dead, and the time is at hand
When thou shalt more than die.[1]   140

9. Set in the ring under glass.
1. These nine lines were added for the edition of 1856 and tell us what we otherwise could only assume—that he has learned of Maud's death.

IV

1

O that 't were possible
After long grief and pain
To find the arms of my true love
Round me once again!

2

When I was wont to meet her   145
In the silent woody places
By the home that gave me birth,
We stood tranced in long embraces
Mixt with kisses sweeter, sweeter
Than anything on earth.   150

3

A shadow flits before me,
Not thou, but like to thee.
Ah, Christ, that it were possible
For one short hour to see
The souls we loved, that they might tell us   155
What and where they be!

4

It leads me forth at evening,
It lightly winds and steals
In a cold white robe before me,
When all my spirit reels   160
At the shouts, the leagues of lights,
And the roaring of the wheels.

5

Half the night I waste in sighs,
Half in dreams I sorrow after
The delight of early skies;
In a wakeful doze I sorrow   165
For the hand, the lips, the eyes,
For the meeting of the morrow,
The delight of happy laughter,
The delight of low replies.   170

6

'T is a morning pure and sweet,
And a dewy splendor falls
On the little flower that clings
To the turrets and the walls;
'T is a morning pure and sweet,
And the light and shadow fleet.   175
She is walking in the meadow,
And the woodland echo rings;
In a moment we shall meet.
She is singing in the meadow,
And the rivulet at her feet   180

Ripples on in light and shadow
To the ballad that she sings.

7

Do I hear her sing as of old,
My bird with the shining head,   185
My own dove with the tender eye?
But there rings on a sudden a passionate cry,
There is some one dying or dead,
And a sullen thunder is roll'd;
For a tumult shakes the city,   190
And I wake, my dream is fled.
In the shuddering dawn, behold,
Without knowledge, without pity,
By the curtains of my bed
That abiding phantom cold!   195

8

Get thee hence, nor come again,
Mix not memory with doubt,
Pass, thou deathlike type of pain,
Pass and cease to move about!
'T is the blot upon the brain   200
That *will* show itself without.

9

Then I rise, the eave-drops fall,
And the yellow vapors choke
The great city sounding wide;
The day comes, a dull red ball   205
Wrapt in drifts of lurid smoke
On the misty river-tide.

10

Thro' the hubbub of the market
I steal, a wasted frame;
It crosses here, it crosses there,   210
Thro' all that crowd confused and loud,
The shadow still the same;
And on my heavy eyelids
My anguish hangs like shame.

11

Alas for her that met me,   215
That heard me softly call,
Came glimmering thro' the laurels
At the quiet evenfall,
In the garden by the turrets
Of the old manorial hall!   220

12

Would the happy spirit descend
From the realms of light and song,
In the chamber or the street,
As she looks among the blest,

Should I fear to greet my friend   225
Or to say "Forgive the wrong,"
Or to ask her, "Take me, sweet,
To the regions of thy rest"?

13

But the broad light glares and beats,
And the shadow flits and fleets
And will not let me be;   230
And I loathe the squares and streets,
And the faces that one meets,
Hearts with no love for me.
Always I long to creep
Into some still cavern deep,   235
There to weep, and weep, and weep
My whole soul out to thee.

V²

1

Dead, long dead,
Long dead!
And my heart is a handful of dust,   240
And the wheels go over my head,³
And my bones are shaken with pain,
For into a shallow grave they are thrust,
Only a yard beneath the street,
And the hoofs of the horses beat, beat,   245
The hoofs of the horses beat,
Beat into my scalp and my brain,
With never an end to the stream of passing feet,
Driving, hurrying, marrying, burying,
Clamor and rumble, and ringing and clatter;   250
And here beneath it is all as bad,
For I thought the dead had peace, but it is not so.
To have no peace in the grave, is that not sad?
But up and down and to and fro,
Ever about me the dead men go;   255
And then to hear a dead man chatter
Is enough to drive one mad.

2

Wretchedest age, since Time began,
They cannot even bury a man;
And tho' we paid our tithes in the days that are gone,   260
Not a bell was rung, not a prayer was read.
It is that which makes us loud in the world of the dead;

2. In section V the speaker has been consigned to an insane asylum and records in fragments some of his experience there.

3. Compare Part 1, section XXII, 11, where, in a rather different context, he also imagined he was buried.

There is none that does his work, not one.
A touch of their office might have sufficed,   265
But the churchmen fain would kill their church,
As the churches have kill'd their Christ.

                           3

See, there is one of us[4] sobbing,
No limit to his distress;
And another, a lord of all things, praying   270
To his own great self, as I guess;
And another, a statesman there, betraying
His party-secret, fool, to the press;
And yonder a vile physician, blabbing
The case of his patient—all for what?   275
To tickle the maggot born in an empty head,
And wheedle a world that loves him not,
For it is but a world of the dead.

                           4

Nothing but idiot gabble!
For the prophecy given of old[5]   280
And then not understood,
Has come to pass as foretold;
Not let any man think for the public good,
But babble, merely for babble.
For I never whisper'd a private affair   285
Within the hearing of cat or mouse,
No, not to myself in the closet alone,
But I heard it shouted at once from the top of the house;
Everything came to be known.
Who told *him*[6] we were there?   290

                           5

Not that gray old wolf,[7] for he came not back
From the wilderness, full of wolves, where he used to lie;
He has gather'd the bones for his o'ergrown whelp to crack—
Crack them now for yourself, and howl, and die.

                           6

Prophet, curse me the blabbing lip,   295
And curse me the British vermin, the rat;
I know not whether he came in the Hanover[8] ship,
But I know that he lies and listens mute
In an ancient mansion's crannies and holes.
Arsenic, arsenic, sure, would do it,   300
Except that now we poison our babes, poor souls!
It is all used up for that.

---

4. Other corpses, that is, inmates of the madhouse.
5. "Whatever you have said in the dark shall be heard in the light, and what you have whispered in private rooms shall be proclaimed upon the housetops" (*Luke*, 12:3).

6. Maud's brother.
7. Maud's father.
8. In 1714 the House of Hanover succeeded to the British throne, and the Jacobites claimed they brought with them the so-called Norwegian rat.

7

Tell him now: she is standing here at my head;
Not beautiful now, not even kind;
He may take her now; for she never speaks her mind,   305
But is ever the one thing silent here.
She is not *of* us, as I divine;
She comes from another stiller world of the dead,
Stiller, not fairer than mine.

8

But I know where a garden grows,   310
Fairer than aught in the world beside,
All made up of the lily and rose
That blow by night, when the season is good,
To the sound of dancing music and flutes:
It is only flowers, they had no fruits,   315
And I almost fear they are not roses, but blood;
For the keeper[9] was one, so full of pride,
He linkt a dead man there to a spectral bride;
For he, if he had not been a Sultan of brutes,
Would he have that hole in his side?   320

9

But what will the old man say?
He laid a cruel snare in a pit
To catch a friend of mine one stormy day;
Yet now I could even weep to think of it;
For what will the old man say   325
When he comes to the second corpse[1] in the pit?

10

Friend, to be struck by the public foe,
Then to strike him and lay him low,
That were a public merit, far,
Whatever the Quaker holds, from sin;   330
But the red life spilt for a private blow—
I swear to you, lawful and lawless war
Are scarcely even akin.

11

O me, why have they not buried me deep enough?
Is it kind to have made me a grave so rough,   335
Me, that was never a quiet sleeper?
Maybe still I am but half-dead;
Then I cannot be wholly dumb.
I will cry to the steps above my head
And somebody, surely, some kind heart will come   340
To bury me, bury me
Deeper, ever so little deeper.

9. Maud's brother; the "dead man" in the next line is the speaker himself.
1. Maud's brother. The first corpse would be the speaker's father, whom he now assumes Maud's father murdered.

Part 3

1

My life has crept so long[2] on a broken wing
Thro' cells of madness, haunts of horror and fear,
That I come to be grateful at last for a little thing.
My mood is changed, for it fell at a time of year
When the face of night is fair on the dewy downs,　　　　5
And the shining daffodil dies,[3] and the Charioteer
And starry Gemini hang like glorious crowns
Over Orion's grave low down in the west,
That like a silent lightning under the stars
She seem'd to divide in a dream from a band of the blest,　10
And spoke of a hope for the world in the coming wars—
"And in that hope, dear soul, let trouble have rest,
Knowing I tarry for thee," and pointed to Mars
As he glow'd like a ruddy shield on the Lion's[4] breast.

2

And it was but a dream, yet it yielded a dear delight　　15
To have look'd tho' but in a dream, upon eyes so fair,
That had been in a weary world my one thing bright;
And it was but a dream, yet it lighten'd my despair
When I thought that a war would arise in defence of the right,
That an iron tyranny[5] now should bend or cease,　　　20
The glory of manhood stand on his ancient height,
Nor Britain's one sole God be the millionaire.
No more shall commerce be all in all, and Peace
Pipe on her pastoral hillock a languid note,
And watch her harvest ripen, her herd increase,　　　　25
Nor the cannon-bullet rust on a slothful shore,
And the cobweb woven across the cannon's throat
Shall shake its threaded tears in the wind no more.

3

And as months ran on and rumor of battle grew,
"It is time, it is time, O passionate heart," said I,—　　30
For I cleaved to a cause that I felt to be pure and true,—
"It is time, O passionate heart and morbid eye,
That old hysterical mock-disease should die."
And I stood on a giant deck[6] and mixt my breath
With a loyal people shouting a battlecry,　　　　　　35
Till I saw the dreary phantom[7] arise and fly
Far into the North, and battle, and seas of death.

2. The period of insanity having passed, the speaker is left "sane but shattered." Tennyson added that this part of the poem was "written when the cannon was heard booming from the battle-ships in the Solent before the Crimean War" (*Memoir*, I, 405).
3. Late spring. "The Charioteer" is the constellation Auriga midway between the North Star and the constellation of Orion; "Gemini" are the twin stars, Castor and Pollux.
4. Mars (the god of war) is now in the constellation of the Lion (the symbol of Britain).
5. That of Czar Nicholas I of Russia.
6. Sailing off to the Crimea.
7. Throughout Part 2 he has been haunted by Maud's phantom, and now he finds the spirit exorcised as he seeks to lose himself in a cause larger than himself.

4

Let it go or stay, so I wake to the higher aims
Of a land that has lost for a little her lust of gold,
And love of a peace that was full of wrongs and shames,   40
Horrible, hateful, monstrous, not to be told;
And hail once more to the banner of battle unroll'd!
Tho' many a light shall darken, and many shall weep
For those that are crush'd in the clash of jarring claims
Yet God's just wrath shall be wreak'd on a giant liar,[8]   45
And many a darkness into the light shall leap,
And shine in the sudden making of splendid names,
And noble thought be freer under the sun,
And the heart of a people beat with one desire;
For the peace, that I deem'd no peace, is over and done,   50
And now by the side of the Black[9] and the Baltic deep,
And deathful-grinning mouths of the fortress, flames
The blood-red blossom of war with a heart of fire.

5

Let it flame or fade, and the war roll down like a wind,
We have proved we have hearts in a cause, we are noble still,   55
And myself have awaked, as it seems, to the better mind.
It is better to fight for the good than to rail at the ill;
I have felt with my native land, I am one with my kind,
I embrace the purpose of God, and the doom assign'd.[1]

1855 (1856)

Riflemen, Form[1]

There is a sound of thunder afar,
   Storm in the South that darkens the day!
Storm of battle and thunder of war!
   Well if it do not roll our way.
     Form! form! Riflemen, form!   5
     Ready, be ready to meet the storm!
     Riflemen, Riflemen, Riflemen, form!

Be not deaf to the sound that warns!
   Be not gull'd by a despot's plea!
Are figs of thistles, or grapes of thorns?   10

8. Nicholas I.
9. The Black Sea.
1. Nineteenth-century critics generally failed to distinguish between poet and speaker, and hence Part 3 was all too easily interpreted to show that Tennyson was a jingoist. Lucid, but nonetheless "shattered," the speaker is hardly one through whom Tennyson would elect to express his own views. Whatever similarities of thought may exist become irrelevant.
1. Originally titled "The War" and republished in 1892 with the title "Rifle-men, Form," this poem first appeared in *The Times* for May 9, 1859, "after the outbreak of war between France, Piedmont, and Austria; when more than one power seemed to be prepared to take the offensive against England; and it rang like a trumpet-call through the length and breadth of the Empire" (*Memoir*, I, 436). The piece was indeed influential, and "by the end of the year one hundred eighty thousand men had been enrolled" in the Volunteer Force (*Alfred Tennyson*, p. 317). Compare "Britons, Guard Your Own."

How should a despot set men Free?
　Form! form! Riflemen, form!
　Ready, be ready to meet the storm!
　Riflemen, Riflemen, Riflemen, form!

Let your reforms for a moment go!　　　　　　　　　15
　Look to your butts, and take good aims!
Better a rotten borough or so
　Than a rotten fleet or a city in flames!
　　Form! form! Riflemen, form!
　　Ready, be ready to meet the storm!　　　　　　20
　　Riflemen, Riflemen, Riflemen, form!

Form, be ready to do or die!
　Form in Freedom's name and the Queen's!
True that we have a faithful ally,[2]
　But only the devil can tell what he means.　　　25
　　Form! form! Riflemen, form!
　　Ready, be ready to meet the storm!
　　Riflemen, Riflemen, Riflemen, form!

1859

In the Valley of Cauteretz[3]

All along the valley, stream that flashest white,
Deepening thy voice with the deepening of the night,
All along the valley, where thy waters flow,
I walk'd with one I loved two and thirty years ago.
All along the valley, while I walk'd to-day,　　　　5
The two and thirty[4] years were a mist that rolls away;
For all along the valley, down thy rocky bed,
Thy living voice to me was as the voice of the dead,
And all along the valley, by rock and cave and tree,
The voice of the dead was a living voice to me.　　10

1861; 1864

Helen's Tower

[WRITTEN AT THE REQUEST OF MY FRIEND, LORD DUFFERIN.]

Helen's Tower,[5] here I stand,
Dominant over sea and land.
Son's love built me, and I hold

---

2. France, with whom England had
shared an uneasy truce since the ill-
conceived Crimean debacle.
3. Tennyson revisited the Pyrenees in
the summer of 1861, and his poem re-
calls his first visit there with Hallam in
1830. See the notes to "Œnone."
4. Actually one and thirty.
5. Lord Dufferin built this tower in
Belfast on the Irish coast and named it
after his mother.

Mother's love in letter'd gold.[6]
Love is in and out of time,   5
I am mortal stone and lime.
Would my granite girth were strong
As either love, to last as long!
I should wear my crown entire
To and thro' the Doomsday fire,   10
And be found of angel eyes
In earth's recurring Paradise.[7]

1861; 1884

Milton

(ALCAICS)[8]

O mighty-mouth'd inventor of harmonies,
O skill'd to sing of Time or Eternity,
  God-gifted organ-voice of England,
    Milton, a name to resound for ages;
Whose Titan angels, Gabriel, Abdiel,[9]   5
Starr'd from Jehovah's gorgeous armories,
  Tower, as the deep-domed empyrean
    Rings to the roar of an angel onset!
Me rather all that bowery loneliness,
The brooks of Eden mazily murmuring,   10
  And bloom profuse and cedar arches
    Charm, as a wanderer out in ocean,
Where some refulgent sunset of India
Streams o'er a rich ambrosial ocean isle,
  And crimson-hued the stately palm-woods   15
    Whisper in odorous heights of even.

1863

Enoch Arden[1]

Long lines of cliff breaking have left a chasm;
And in the chasm are foam and yellow sands;

6. "In it I have placed on a golden tablet the birthday verses which my mother wrote to me on the day I came of age" (Lord Dufferin's letter to Tennyson of September 24, 1861, requesting a poem, *Memoir*, I, 478).
7. "The fancy of some poets and theologians that Paradise is to be the renovated earth" (Tennyson's annotation when he sent his poem).
8. The Alcaic stanza, named for its reputed inventor, the Greek poet Alcaeus (c. 600 B.C.), is composed of two eleven-syllable lines followed by one of nine and one of ten syllables. As distinguished from English qualitative verse, in which the accent falls on stressed syllables, the classical quantitative verse places the accent on long vowels and short vowels when followed by two consonantal sounds. In commenting on this "experiment," Tennyson took care to distinguish between the Horatian Alcaic and the Greek Alcaic he imitates, which "had a much freer and lighter movement" (*Memoir*, II, 11).
9. Archangels of *Paradise Lost*, respectively the guardian of Paradise and the one angel among Satan's rebels who remained constant to God.
1. " 'Enoch Arden' (like 'Aylmer's Field') is founded on a theme given me by the sculptor Woolner. I believe that

Beyond, red roofs about a narrow wharf
In cluster; then a moulder'd church; and higher
A long street climbs to one tall-tower'd mill;   5
And high in heaven behind it a gray down
With Danish barrows;[2] and a hazel-wood,
By autumn nutters haunted, flourishes
Green in a cuplike hollow of the down.
Here on this beach a hundred years ago,   10
Three children of three houses, Annie Lee,
The prettiest little damsel in the port,
And Philip Ray, the miller's only son,
And Enoch Arden, a rough sailor's lad
Made orphan by a winter shipwreck, play'd   15
Among the waste and lumber of the shore,
Hard coils of cordage, swarthy fishing-nets,
Anchors of rusty fluke, and boats updrawn;
And built their castles of dissolving sand
To watch them overflow'd, or following up   20
And flying the white breaker, daily left
The little footprint daily wash'd away.

A narrow cave ran in beneath the cliff;
In this the children play'd at keeping house.
Enoch was host one day, Philip the next,   25
While Annie still was mistress; but at times
Enoch would hold possession for a week:
"This is my house and this my little wife."
"Mine too," said Philip; "turn and turn about;"
When, if they quarrell'd, Enoch stronger-made   30
Was master. Then would Philip, his blue eyes
All flooded with the helpless wrath of tears,
Shriek out, "I hate you, Enoch," and at this
The little wife would weep for company,

---

this particular story came out of Suf-
folk, but something like the same story
is told in Brittany" (Tennyson's note
in *Memoir*, II, 7). "Enoch Arden" was
immensely popular, was soon translated
into most European languages, and es-
tablished Tennyson as "The Poet of
the People." For twentieth-century
readers, however, its sentimentality and
prefabricated "realism" have reduced it
to the potted period piece it always
was, and no amount of reappreciation
for the Victorian sensibility is likely to
redeem the poem's two concluding lines.
Apart from the many who heaped praise
upon the poem just after its publica-
tion, Walter Bagehot was almost alone
in discerning its central failings: "So
much has not often been made of selling
fish. The essence of ornate art is in
this manner to accumulate round the
typical object, everything which can be
said about it, every associated thought
that can be connected with it." And he
added, "A dirty sailor who did *not* go
home to his wife is not an agreeable
being: a varnish must be put on him
to make him shine." One has only to
think of *Maud*, which was thoroughly
unappreciated, to be impressed again
by the truisms about the ephemerality
of a poet's most popular poem. A re-
viewer of the volume for *Harper's
Magazine* (October 1864) unknowingly
makes the point: "As his poems are the
most striking illustration of the fond-
ness of the literary spirit of the age
for the most gorgeous verbiage, so they
are the most noble examples of a lux-
uriant tendency constantly restrained
and tempered by the truest taste."
2. Burial mounds, many of which pre-
date the Danish invasions of the ninth
century.

And pray them not to quarrel for her sake,   35
And say she would be little wife to both.

But when the dawn of rosy childhood past,
And the new warmth of life's ascending sun
Was felt by either, either fixt his heart
On that one girl; and Enoch spoke his love,   40
But Philip loved in silence; and the girl
Seem'd kinder unto Philip than to him;
But she loved Enoch, tho' she knew it not,
And would if ask'd deny it. Enoch set
A purpose evermore before his eyes,   45
To hoard all savings to the uttermost,
To purchase his own boat, and make a home
For Annie; and so prosper'd that at last
A luckier or a bolder fisherman,
A carefuller in peril, did not breathe   50
For leagues along that breaker-beaten coast
Than Enoch. Likewise had he served a year
On board a merchantman, and made himself
Full sailor; and he thrice had pluck'd a life
From the dread sweep of the down-streaming seas,   55
And all men look'd upon him favorably.
And ere he touch'd his one-and-twentieth May
He purchased his own boat, and made a home
For Annie, neat and nestlike, halfway up
The narrow street that clamber'd toward the mill.   60

Then, on a golden autumn eventide,
The younger people making holiday,
With bag and sack and basket, great and small,
Went nutting to the hazels. Philip stay'd—
His father lying sick and needing him—   65
An hour behind; but as he climb'd the hill,
Just where the prone edge of the wood began
To feather toward the hollow, saw the pair,
Enoch and Annie, sitting hand-in-hand,
His large gray eyes and weather-beaten face   70
All-kindled by a still and sacred fire,
That burn'd as on an altar. Philip look'd,
And in their eyes and faces read his doom;
Then, as their faces drew together, groan'd,
And slipt aside, and like a wounded life   75
Crept down into the hollows of the wood;
There, while the rest were loud in merrymaking,
Had his dark hour unseen, and rose and past
Bearing a lifelong hunger in his heart.

So these were wed, and merrily rang the bells,   80
And merrily ran the years, seven happy years,
Seven happy years of health and competence,

And mutual love and honorable toil,
With children, first a daughter. In him woke,
With his first babe's first cry, the noble wish   85
To save all earnings to the uttermost,
And give his child a better bringing-up
Than his had been, or hers; a wish renew'd,
When two years after came a boy to be
The rosy idol of her solitudes,   90
While Enoch was abroad on wrathful seas,
Or often journeying landward; for in truth
Enoch's white horse, and Enoch's ocean-spoil
In ocean-smelling osier, and his face,
Rough-redden'd with a thousand winter gales,   95
Not only to the market-cross were known,
But in the leafy lanes behind the down,
Far as the portal-warding lion-whelp
And peacock yew-tree of the lonely Hall,
Whose Friday fare was Enoch's ministering.[3]   100

  Then came a change, as all things human change.
Ten miles to northward of the narrow port
Open'd a larger haven. Thither used
Enoch at times to go by land or sea;
And once when there, and clambering on a mast   105
In harbor, by mischance he slipt and fell.
A limb was broken when they lifted him;
And while he lay recovering there, his wife
Bore him another son, a sickly one.
Another hand crept too across his trade   110
Taking her bread and theirs; and on him fell,
Altho' a grave and staid God-fearing man,
Yet lying thus inactive, doubt and gloom.
He seem'd, as in a nightmare of the night,
To see his children leading evermore   115
Low miserable lives of hand-to-mouth,
And her he loved a beggar. Then he pray'd,
"Save them from this, whatever comes to me."
And while he pray'd, the master of that ship
Enoch had served in, hearing his mischance,   120
Came, for he knew the man and valued him,
Reporting of his vessel China-bound,
And wanting yet a boatswain. Would he go?
There yet were many weeks before she sail'd,
Sail'd from this port. Would Enoch have the place?   125
And Enoch all at once assented to it,
Rejoicing at that answer to his prayer.

---

3. Bagehot, citing lines 91–100, observed: "Everyone knows that in himself Enoch could not have been charming. People who sell fish about the country (and that is what he did, though Mr. Tennyson won't speak out, and wraps it up) never are beautiful."

So now that shadow of mischance appear'd
No graver than as when some little cloud
Cuts off the fiery highway of the sun,   130
And isles a light in the offing. Yet the wife—
When he was gone—the children—what to do?
Then Enoch lay long-pondering on his plans:
To sell the boat—and yet he loved her well—
How many a rough sea had he weather'd in her!   135
He knew her, as a horseman knows his horse—
And yet to sell her—then with what she brought
Buy goods and stores—set Annie forth in trade
With all that seamen needed or their wives—
So might she keep the house while he was gone.   140
Should he not trade himself out yonder? go
This voyage more than once? yea, twice or thrice—
As oft as needed—last, returning rich,
Become the master of a larger craft,
With fuller profits lead an easier life,   145
Have all his pretty young ones educated,
And pass his days in peace among his own.

Thus Enoch in his heart determined all;
Then moving homeward came on Annie pale,
Nursing the sickly babe, her latest-born.   150
Forward she started, with a happy cry,
And laid the feeble infant in his arms;
Whom Enoch took, and handled all his limbs,
Appraised his weight and fondled fatherlike,
But had no heart to break his purposes   155
To Annie, till the morrow, when he spoke.

Then first since Enoch's golden ring had girt
Her finger, Annie fought against his will;
Yet not with brawling opposition she,
But manifold entreaties, many a tear,   160
Many a sad kiss by day, by night, renew'd—
Sure that all evil would come out of it—
Besought him, supplicating, if he cared
For her or his dear children, not to go.
He not for his own self caring, but her,   165
Her and her children, let her plead in vain;
So grieving held his will, and bore it thro'.

For Enoch parted with his old sea-friend,
Bought Annie goods and stores, and set his hand
To fit their little streetward sitting-room   170
With shelf and corner for the goods and stores.
So all day long till Enoch's last at home,
Shaking their pretty cabin, hammer and axe,
Auger and saw, while Annie seem'd to hear
Her own death-scaffold raising, shrill'd and rang,   175

Till this was ended, and his careful hand,—
The space was narrow,—having order'd all
Almost as neat and close as Nature packs
Her blossom or her seedling, paused; and he,
Who needs would work for Annie to the last,   180
Ascending tired, heavily slept till morn.

And Enoch faced this morning of farewell
Brightly and boldly. All his Annie's fears,
Save as his Annie's, were a laughter to him.
Yet Enoch as a brave God-fearing man   185
Bow'd himself down, and in that mystery
Where God-in-man is one with man-in-God,
Pray'd for a blessing on his wife and babes,
Whatever came to him; and then he said:
"Annie, this voyage by the grace of God   190
Will bring fair weather yet to all of us.
Keep a clean hearth and a clear fire for me,
For I'll be back, my girl, before you know it;"
Then lightly rocking baby's cradle, "and he,
This pretty, puny, weakly little one,—   195
Nay—for I love him all the better for it—
God bless him, he shall sit upon my knees
And I will tell him tales of foreign parts,
And make him merry, when I come home again.
Come, Annie, come, cheer up before I go."   200

Him running on thus hopefully she heard,
And almost hoped herself; but when he turn'd
The current of his talk to graver things
In sailor fashion roughly sermonizing
On providence and trust in heaven, she heard,   205
Heard and not heard him; as the village girl,
Who sets her pitcher underneath the spring,
Musing on him that used to fill it for her,
Hears and not hears, and lets it overflow.

At length she spoke: "O Enoch, you are wise;   210
And yet for all your wisdom well know I
That I shall look upon your face no more."

"Well, then," said Enoch, "I shall look on yours.
Annie, the ship I sail in passes here"—
He named the day;—"get you a seaman's glass,   215
Spy out my face, and laugh at all your fears."

But when the last of those last moments came:
"Annie, my girl, cheer up, be comforted,
Look to the babes, and till I come again
Keep everything shipshape, for I must go.   220
And fear no more for me; or if you fear,
Cast all your cares on God; that anchor holds.

Is He not yonder in those uttermost
Parts of the morning? if I flee to these,
Can I go from Him? and the sea is His,   225
The sea is His; He made it."

                      Enoch rose,
Cast his strong arms about his drooping wife,
And kiss'd his wonder-stricken little ones;
But for the third, the sickly one, who slept
After a night of feverous wakefulness,   230
When Annie would have raised him Enoch said,
"Wake him not, let him sleep; how should the child
Remember this?" and kiss'd him in his cot.
But Annie from her baby's forehead clipt
A tiny curl, and gave it; this he kept   235
Thro' all his future, but now hastily caught
His bundle, waved his hand, and went his way.

    She, when the day that Enoch mention'd came,
Borrow'd a glass, but all in vain. Perhaps
She could not fix the glass to suit her eye;   240
Perhaps her eye was dim, hand tremulous;
She saw him not, and while he stood on deck
Waving, the moment and the vessel past.

    Even to the last dip of the vanishing sail
She watch'd it, and departed weeping for him;   245
Then, tho' she mourn'd his absence as his grave,
Set her sad will no less to chime with his,
But throve not in her trade, not being bred
To barter, nor compensating the want
By shrewdness, neither capable of lies,   250
Nor asking overmuch and taking less,
And still foreboding "what would Enoch say?"
For more than once, in days of difficulty
And pressure, had she sold her wares for less
Than what she gave in buying what she sold.   255
She fail'd and sadden'd knowing it; and thus,
Expectant of that news which never came,
Gain'd for her own a scanty sustenance,
And lived a life of silent melancholy.

    Now the third child was sickly-born and grew   260
Yet sicklier, tho' the mother cared for it
With all a mother's care; nevertheless,
Whether her business often call'd her from it,
Or thro' the want of what it needed most,
Or means to pay the voice who best could tell   265
What most it needed—howsoe'er it was,
After a lingering,—ere she was aware,—
Like a caged bird escaping suddenly,
The little innocent soul flitted away.

In that same week when Annie buried it,   270
Philip's true heart, which hunger'd for her peace,—
Since Enoch left he had not look'd upon her,—
Smote him, as having kept aloof so long.
"Surely," said Philip, "I may see her now,
May be some little comfort;" therefore went,   275
Past thro' the solitary room in front,
Paused for a moment at an inner door,
Then struck it thrice, and, no one opening,
Enter'd, but Annie, seated with her grief,
Fresh from the burial of her little one,   280
Cared not to look on any human face,
But turn'd her own toward the wall and wept.
Then Philip standing up said falteringly,
"Annie, I came to ask a favor of you."

He spoke; the passion in her moan'd reply,   285
"Favor from one so sad and so forlorn
As I am!" half abash'd him; yet unask'd,
His bashfulness and tenderness at war,
He set himself beside her, saying to her:

"I came to speak to you of what he wish'd,   290
Enoch, your husband. I have ever said
You chose the best among us—a strong man;
For where he fixt his heart he set his hand
To do the thing he will'd, and bore it thro'.
And wherefore did he go this weary way,   295
And leave you lonely? not to see the world—
For pleasure?—nay, but for the wherewithal
To give his babes a better bringing up
Than his had been, or yours; that was his wish.
And if he come again, vext will he be   300
To find the precious morning hours were lost.
And it would vex him even in his grave,
If he could know his babes were running wild
Like colts about the waste. So, Annie, now—
Have we not known each other all our lives?   305
I do beseech you by the love you bear
Him and his children not to say me nay—
For, if you will, when Enoch comes again
Why then he shall repay me—if you will,
Annie—for I am rich and well-to-do.   310
Now let me put the boy and girl to school;
This is the favor that I came to ask."

Then Annie with her brows against the wall
Answer'd, "I cannot look you in the face;
I seem so foolish and so broken down.   315
When you came in my sorrow broke me down;
And now I think your kindness breaks me down.

But Enoch lives; that is borne in on me;
He will repay you. Money can be repaid,
Not kindness such as yours."

                                And Philip ask'd,   320
"Then you will let me, Annie?"

                                     There she turn'd,
She rose, and fixt her swimming eyes upon him,
And dwelt a moment on his kindly face,
Then calling down a blessing on his head
Caught at his hand, and wrung it passionately,   325
And past into the little garth[4] beyond.
So lifted up in spirit he moved away.

    Then Philip put the boy and girl to school,
And bought them needful books, and every way,
Like one who does his duty by his own,
Made himself theirs; and tho' for Annie's sake,   330
Fearing the lazy gossip of the port,
He oft denied his heart his dearest wish,
And seldom crost her threshold, yet he sent
Gifts by the children, garden-herbs and fruit,
The late and early roses from his wall,   335
Or conies from the down, and now and then,
With some pretext of fineness in the meal
To save the offence of charitable, flour
From his tall mill that whistled on the waste.   340

    But Philip did not fathom Annie's mind;
Scarce could the woman, when he came upon her,
Out of full heart and boundless gratitude
Light on a broken word to thank him with.
But Philip was her children's all-in-all;   345
From distant corners of the street they ran
To greet his hearty welcome heartily;
Lords of his house and of his mill were they,
Worried his passive ear with petty wrongs
Or pleasures, hung upon him, play'd with him   350
And call'd him Father Philip. Philip gain'd
As Enoch lost, for Enoch seem'd to them
Uncertain as a vision or a dream,
Faint as a figure seen in early dawn
Down at the far end of an avenue,   355
Going we know not where; and so ten years,
Since Enoch left his hearth and native land,
Fled forward, and no news of Enoch came.

    It chanced one evening Annie's children long'd
To go with others nutting to the wood,   360
And Annie would go with them; then they begg'd

4. Garden.

For Father Philip, as they call'd him, too.
Him, like the working bee in blossom-dust,
Blanch'd with his mill, they found; and saying to him,
"Come with us, Father Philip," he denied;   365
But when the children pluck'd at him to go,
He laugh'd, and yielded readily to their wish,
For was not Annie with them? and they went.

But after scaling half the weary down,
Just where the prone edge of the wood began   370
To feather toward the hollow, all her force
Fail'd her; and sighing, "Let me rest," she said.
So Philip rested with her well-content;
While all the younger ones with jubilant cries
Broke from their elders, and tumultuously   375
Down thro' the whitening hazels made a plunge
To the bottom, and dispersed, and bent or broke
The lithe reluctant boughs to tear away
Their tawny clusters, crying to each other
And calling, here and there, about the wood.   380

But Philip sitting at her side forgot
Her presence, and remember'd one dark hour
Here in this wood, when like a wounded life
He crept into the shadow. At last he said,
Lifting his honest forehead, "Listen, Annie,   385
How merry they are down yonder in the wood.
Tired, Annie?" for she did not speak a word.
"Tired?" but her face had fallen upon her hands;
At which, as with a kind of anger in him,
"The ship was lost," he said, "the ship was lost!   390
No more of that! why should you kill yourself
And make them orphans quite?" And Annie said,
"I thought not of it; but—I know not why—
Their voices make me feel so solitary."

Then Philip coming somewhat closer spoke: 395
"Annie, there is a thing upon my mind,
And it has been upon my mind so long
That, tho' I know not when it first came there,
I know that it will out at last. O Annie,
It is beyond all hope, against all chance,   400
That he who left you ten long years ago
Should still be living; well, then—let me speak.
I grieve to see you poor and wanting help;
I cannot help you as I wish to do
Unless—they say that women are so quick—   405
Perhaps you know what I would have you know—
I wish you for my wife. I fain would prove
A father to your children; I do think
They love me as a father; I am sure

That I love them as if they were mine own; 410
And I believe, if you were fast my wife,
That after all these sad uncertain years
We might be still as happy as God grants
To any of his creatures. Think upon it;
For I am well-to-do—no kin, no care, 415
No burthen, save my care for you and yours,
And we have known each other all our lives,
And I have loved you longer than you know."

Then answer'd Annie—tenderly she spoke:
"You have been as God's good angel in our house. 420
God bless you for it, God reward you for it,
Philip, with something happier than myself.
Can one love twice? can you be ever loved
As Enoch was? what is it that you ask?"
"I am content," he answer'd, "to be loved 425
A little after Enoch." "O," she cried,
Scared as it were, "dear Philip, wait a while.
If Enoch comes—but Enoch will not come—
Yet wait a year, a year is not so long.
Surely I shall be wiser in a year. 430
O, wait a little!" Philip sadly said,
"Annie, as I have waited all my life
I well may wait a little." "Nay," she cried,
"I am bound: you have my promise—in a year.
Will you not bide your year as I bide mine?" 435
And Philip answer'd, "I will bide my year."

Here both were mute, till Philip glancing up
Beheld the dead flame of the fallen day
Pass from the Danish barrow overhead;
Then, fearing night and chill for Annie, rose 440
And sent his voice beneath him thro' the wood.
Up came the children laden with their spoil;
Then all descended to the port, and there
At Annie's door he paused and gave his hand,
Saying gently, "Annie, when I spoke to you, 445
That was your hour of weakness. I was wrong,
I am always bound to you, but you are free."
Then Annie weeping answer'd, "I am bound."

She spoke; and in one moment as it were,
While yet she went about her household ways, 450
Even as she dwelt upon his latest words,
That he had loved her longer than she knew,
That autumn into autumn flash'd again,
And there he stood once more before her face,
Claiming her promise. "Is it a year?" she ask'd. 455
"Yes, if the nuts," he said, "be ripe again;
Come out and see." But she—she put him off—

So much to look to—such a change—a month—
Give her a month—she knew that she was bound—
A month—no more. Then Philip with his eyes   460
Full of that lifelong hunger, and his voice
Shaking a little like a drunkard's hand,
"Take your own time, Annie, take your own time."
And Annie could have wept for pity of him;
And yet she held him on delayingly   465
With many a scarce-believable excuse,
Trying his truth and his long-sufferance,
Till half another year had slipt away.

　By this the lazy gossips of the port,
Abhorrent of a calculation crost,   470
Began to chafe as at a personal wrong.
Some thought that Philip did but trifle with her;
Some that she but held off to draw him on;
And others laugh'd at her and Philip too,
As simple folk that knew not their own minds;   475
And one, in whom all evil fancies clung
Like serpent eggs together, laughingly
Would hint at worse in either. Her own son
Was silent, tho' he often look'd his wish;
But evermore the daughter prest upon her   480
To wed the man so dear to all them
And lift the household out of poverty;
And Philip's rosy face contracting grew
Careworn and wan; and all these things fell on her
Sharp as reproach.

　　　　　　At last one night it chanced   485
That Annie could not sleep, but earnestly
Pray'd for a sign, "My Enoch, is he gone?"
Then compass'd round by the blind wall of night
Brook'd not the expectant terror of her heart,
Started from bed, and struck herself a light,   490
Then desperately seized the holy Book,
Suddenly set it wide to find a sign,
Suddenly put her finger on the text,
"Under the palm-tree."[5] That was nothing to her,
No meaning there; she closed the Book and slept.   495
When lo! her Enoch sitting on a height,
Under a palm-tree, over him the sun.
"He is gone," she thought, "he is happy, he is singing
Hosanna in the highest; yonder shines
The Sun of Righteousness, and these be palms   500
Whereof the happy people strowing cried

5. See *Judges*, 4:5. A method of divina-
tion in which the Bible is opened at
random and the first passage touched
by the finger portends something of
the future or reveals the unknown. The
practice is known as *Sortes Virgilianae*,
derived from similarly consulting the
Aeneid.

'Hosanna in the highest!' " Here she woke,
Resolved, sent for him and said wildly to him,
"There is no reason why we should not wed."
"Then for God's sake," he answer'd, "both our sakes,   505
So you will wed me, let it be at once."

So these were wed, and merrily rang the bells,
Merrily rang the bells, and they were wed.
But never merrily beat Annie's heart.
A footstep seem'd to fall beside her path,   510
She knew not whence; a whisper on her ear,
She knew not what; nor loved she to be left
Alone at home, nor ventured out alone.
What ail'd her then that, ere she enter'd, often
Her hand dwelt lingeringly on the latch,   515
Fearing to enter? Philip thought he knew:
Such doubts and fears were common to her state,
Being with child; but when her child was born,
Then her new child was as herself renew'd,
Then the new mother came about her heart,   520
Then her good Philip was her all-in-all,
And that mysterious instinct wholly died.

And where was Enoch? Prosperously sail'd
The ship "Good Fortune," tho' at setting forth
The Biscay, roughly ridging eastward, shook   525
And almost overwhelm'd her, yet unvext
She slipt across the summer of the world,
Then after a long tumble about the Cape
And frequent interchange of foul and fair,
She passing thro' the summer world again,   530
The breath of heaven came continually
And sent her sweetly by the golden isles,
Till silent in her oriental haven.

There Enoch traded for himself, and bought
Quaint monsters for the market of those times,   535
A gilded dragon also for the babes.

Less lucky her home-voyage: at first indeed
Thro' many a fair sea-circle, day by day,
Scarce-rocking, her full-busted figure-head
Stared o'er the ripple feathering from her bows: 540
Then follow'd calms, and then winds variable,
Then baffling, a long course of them; and last
Storm, such as drove her under moonless heavens
Till hard upon the cry of "breakers" came
The crash of ruin, and the loss of all   545
But Enoch and two others. Half the night,
Buoy'd upon floating tackle and broken spars,
These drifted, stranding on an isle at morn
Rich, but the loneliest in a lonely sea.

No want was there of human sustenance, 550
Soft fruitage, mighty nuts, and nourishing roots;
Nor save for pity was it hard to take
The helpless life so wild that it was tame.
There in a seaward-gazing mountain-gorge
They built, and thatch'd with leaves of palm, a hut, 555
Half hut, half native cavern. So the three,
Set in this Eden of all plenteousness,
Dwelt with eternal summer, ill-content.
For one, the youngest, hardly more than boy,
Hurt in that night of sudden ruin and wreck, 560
Lay lingering out a five-years' death-in-life.
They could not leave him. After he was gone,
The two remaining found a fallen stem;
And Enoch's comrade, careless of himself,
Fire-hollowing this in Indian fashion, fell 565
Sun-stricken, and that other lived alone.
In those two deaths he read God's warning "wait."

The mountain wooded to the peak, the lawns
And winding glades high up like ways to heaven,
The slender coco's drooping crown of plumes, 570
The lightning flash of insect and of bird,
The lustre of the long convolvuluses
That coil'd around the stately stems, and ran
Even to the limit of the land, the glows
And glories of the broad belt of the world,— 575
All these he saw; but what he fain had seen
He could not see, the kindly human face,
Nor ever hear a kindly voice, but heard
The myriad shriek of wheeling ocean-fowl,
The league-long roller thundering on the reef, 580
The moving whisper of huge trees that branch'd
And blossom'd in the zenith, or the sweep
Of some precipitous rivulet to the wave,
As down the shore he ranged, or all day long
Sat often in the seaward-gazing gorge, 585
A shipwreck'd sailor, waiting for a sail.
No sail from day to day, but every day
The sunrise broken into scarlet shafts
Among the palms and ferns and precipices;
The blaze upon the waters to the east; 590
The blaze upon his island overhead;
The blaze upon the waters to the west;
Then the great stars that globed themselves in heaven,
The hollower-bellowing ocean, and again
The scarlet shafts of sunrise—but no sail. 595

There often as he watch'd or seem'd to watch,
So still the golden lizard on him paused,

A phantom made of many phantoms moved
Before him haunting him, or he himself
Moved haunting people, things, and places, known   600
Far in a darker isle beyond the line;
The babes, their babble, Annie, the small house,
The climbing street, the mill, the leafy lanes,
The peacock yew-tree and the lonely Hall,
The horse he drove, the boat he sold, the chill   605
November dawns and dewy-glooming downs,
The gentle shower, the smell of dying leaves,
And the low moan of leaden-color'd seas.

     Once likewise, in the ringing of his ears,
Tho' faintly, merrily—far and far away—   610
He heard the pealing of his parish bells;
Then, tho' he knew not wherefore, started up
Shuddering, and when the beauteous hateful isle
Return'd upon him, had not his poor heart
Spoken with That which being everywhere   615
Lets none who speaks with Him seem all alone,
Surely the man had died of solitude.

     Thus over Enoch's early-silvering head
The sunny and rainy seasons came and went
Year after year. His hopes to see his own,   620
And pace the sacred old familiar fields,
Not yet had perish'd, when his lonely doom
Came suddenly to an end. Another ship—
She wanted water—blown by baffling winds,
Like the "Good Fortune," from her destined course,   625
Stay'd by this isle, not knowing where she lay;
For since the mate had seen at early dawn
Across a break on the mist-wreathen isle
The silent water slipping from the hills,
They sent a crew that landing burst away   630
In search of stream or fount, and fill'd the shores
With clamor. Downward from his mountain gorge
Stept the long-hair'd, long-bearded solitary,
Brown, looking hardly human, strangely clad,
Muttering and mumbling, idiot-like it seem'd,   635
With inarticulate rage, and making signs
They knew not what; and yet he led the way
To where the rivulets of sweet water ran,
And ever as he mingled with the crew,
And heard them talking, his long-bounden tongue   640
Was loosen'd, till he made them understand;
Whom, when their casks were fill'd, they took aboard.
And there the tale he utter'd brokenly,
Scarce-credited at first but more and more,
Amazed and melted all who listen'd to it;   645

And clothes they gave him and free passage home,
But oft he work'd among the rest and shook
His isolation from him. None of these
Came from his country, or could answer him,
If question'd, aught of what he cared to know.   650
And dull the voyage was with long delays,
The vessel scarce sea-worthy; but evermore
His fancy fled before the lazy wind
Returning, till beneath a clouded moon
He like a lover down thro' all his blood   655
Drew in the dewy meadowy morning-breath
Of England, blown across her ghostly wall.[6]
And that same morning officers and men
Levied a kindly tax upon themselves,
Pitying the lonely man, and gave him it;   660
Then moving up the coast they landed him,
Even in that harbor whence he sail'd before.

   There Enoch spoke no word to any one,
But homeward—home—what home? had he a home?—
His home, he walk'd. Bright was that afternoon,   665
Sunny but chill; till drawn thro' either chasm,
Where either haven open'd on the deeps,
Roll'd a sea-haze and whelm'd the world in gray,
Cut off the length of highway on before,
And left but narrow breadth to left and right   670
Of wither'd holt or tilth or pasturage.
On the nigh-naked tree the robin piped
Disconsolate, and thro' the dripping haze
The dead weight of the dead leaf bore it down.
Thicker the drizzle grew, deeper the gloom;   675
Last, as it seem'd, a great mist-blotted light
Flared on him, and he came upon the place.

   Then down the long street having slowly stolen,
His heart foreshadowing all calamity,
His eyes upon the stones, he reach'd the home   680
Where Annie lived and loved him, and his babes
In those far-off seven happy years were born;
But finding neither light nor murmur there—
   A bill of sale gleam'd thro' the drizzle—crept
Still downward thinking, "dead or dead to me!"   685

   Down to the pool and narrow wharf he went,
Seeking a tavern which of old he knew,
A front of timber-crost antiquity,
So propt, worm-eaten, ruinously old,
He thought it must have gone; but he was gone   690
Who kept it, and his widow Miriam Lane,
With daily-dwindling profits held the house;

6. The chalk cliffs on the southern coast.

A haunt of brawling seamen once, but now
Stiller, with yet a bed for wandering men.
There Enoch rested silent many days. 695

But Miriam Lane was good and garrulous,
Nor let him be, but often breaking in,
Told him, with other annals of the port,
Not knowing—Enoch was so brown, so bow'd,
So broken—all the story of his house: 700
His baby's death, her growing poverty,
How Philip put her little ones to school,
And kept them in it, his long wooing her,
Her slow consent and marriage, and the birth
Of Philip's child; and o'er his countenance 705
No shadow past, nor motion. Any one,
Regarding, well had deem'd he felt the tale
Less than the teller; only when she closed,
"Enoch, poor man, was cast away and lost,"
He, shaking his gray head pathetically, 710
Repeated muttering, "cast away and lost;"
Again in deeper inward whispers, "lost!"

But Enoch yearn'd to see her face again:
"If I might look on her sweet face again,
And know that she is happy." So the thought 715
Haunted and harass'd him, and drove him forth,
At evening when the dull November day
Was growing duller twilight, to the hill.
There he sat down gazing on all below;
There did a thousand memories roll upon him, 720
Unspeakable for sadness. By and by
The ruddy square of comfortable light,
Far-blazing from the rear of Philip's house,
Allured him, as the beacon-blaze allures
The bird of passage, till he madly strikes 725
Against it and beats out his weary life.

For Philip's dwelling fronted on the street,
The latest house to landward; but behind,
With one small gate that open'd on the waste,
Flourish'd a little garden square and wall'd, 730
And in it throve an ancient evergreen,
A yew-tree, and all round it ran a walk
Of shingle, and a walk divided it.
But Enoch shunn'd the middle walk and stole
Up by the wall, behind the yew; and thence 735
That which he better might have shunn'd, if griefs
Like his have worse or better, Enoch saw.

For cups and silver on the burnish'd board
Sparkled and shone; so genial was the hearth;

And on the right hand of the hearth he saw   740
Philip, the slighted suitor of old times,
Stout, rosy, with his babe across his knees;
And o'er her second father stoopt a girl,
A later but a loftier Annie Lee,
Fair-hair'd and tall, and from her lifted hand   745
Dangled a length of ribbon and a ring
To tempt the babe, who rear'd his creasy arms,
Caught at and ever miss'd it, and they laugh'd;
And on the left hand of the hearth he saw
The mother glancing often toward her babe,   750
But turning now and then to speak with him,
Her son, who stood beside her tall and strong,
And saying that which pleased him, for he smiled.

   Now when the dead man come to life beheld
His wife his wife no more, and saw the babe   755
Hers, yet not his, upon the father's knee,
And all the warmth, the peace, the happiness,
And his own children tall and beautiful,
And him, that other, reigning in his place,
Lord of his rights and of his children's love—   760
Then he, tho' Miriam Lane had told him all,
Because things seen are mightier than things heard,
Stagger'd and shook, holding the branch, and fear'd
To send abroad a shrill and terrible cry,
Which in one moment, like the blast of doom,   765
Would shatter all the happiness of the hearth.

   He therefore turning softly like a thief,
Lest the harsh shingle should grate underfoot,
And feeling all along the garden-wall,
Lest he should swoon and tumble and be found,   770
Crept to the gate, and open'd it and closed,
As lightly as a sick man's chamber-door,
Behind him, and came out upon the waste.

   And there he would have knelt, but that his knees
Were feeble, so that falling prone he dug   775
His fingers into the wet earth, and pray'd:

   "Too hard to bear! why did they take me thence?
O God Almighty, blessed Saviour, Thou
That didst uphold me on my lonely isle,
Uphold me, Father, in my loneliness   780
A little longer! aid me, give me strength
Not to tell her, never to let her know.
Help me not to break in upon her peace.
My children too! must I not speak to these?
They know me not. I should betray myself.   785
Never! no father's kiss for me—the girl
So like her mother, and the boy, my son."

There speech and thought and nature fail'd a little,
And he lay tranced; but when he rose and paced
Back toward his solitary home again,   790
All down the long and narrow street he went
Beating it in upon his weary brain,
As tho' it were the burthen of a song,
"Not to tell her, never to let her know."

He was not all unhappy. His resolve   795
Upbore him, and firm faith, and evermore
Prayer from a living source within the will,
And beating up thro' all the bitter world,
Like fountains of sweet water in the sea,
Kept him a living soul. "This miller's wife,"   800
He said to Miriam, "that you spoke about,
Has she no fear that her first husband lives?"
"Ay, ay, poor soul," said Miriam, "fear enow!
If you could tell her you had seen him dead,
Why, that would be her comfort;" and he thought,   805
"After the Lord has call'd me she shall know,
I wait His time;" and Enoch set himself,
Scorning an alms, to work whereby to live.
Almost to all things could he turn his hand.
Cooper he was and carpenter, and wrought   810
To make the boatmen fishing-nets, or help'd
At lading and unlading the tall barks
That brought the stinted commerce of those days,
Thus earn'd a scanty living for himself.
Yet since he did but labor for himself,   815
Work without hope, there was not life in it
Whereby the man could live; and as the year
Roll'd itself round again to meet the day
When Enoch had return'd, a languor came
Upon him, gentle sickness, gradually   820
Weakening the man, till he could do no more,
But kept the house, his chair, and last his bed.
And Enoch bore his weakness cheerfully.
For sure no gladlier does the stranded wreck
See thro' the gray skirts of a lifting squall   825
The boat that bears the hope of life approach
To save the life despair'd of, than he saw
Death dawning on him, and the close of all.

For thro' that dawning gleam'd a kindlier hope
On Enoch thinking, "after I am gone,   830
Then may she learn I loved her to the last."
He call'd aloud for Miriam Lane and said:
"Woman, I have a secret—only swear,
Before I tell you—swear upon the book
Not to reveal it, till you see me dead."   835

"Dead," clamor'd the good woman, "hear him talk!
I warrant, man, that we shall bring you round."
"Swear," added Enoch sternly, "on the book;"
And on the book, half-frighted, Miriam swore.
Then Enoch rolling his gray eyes upon her,   840
"Did you know Enoch Arden of this town?"
"Know him?" she said, "I knew him far away.
Ay, ay, I mind him coming down the street;
Held his head high, and cared for no man, he."
Slowly and sadly Enoch answer'd her: 845
"His head is low, and no man cares for him.
I think I have not three days more to live;
I am the man." At which the woman gave
A half-incredulous, half-hysterical cry:
"You Arden, you! nay,—sure he was a foot   850
Higher than you be." Enoch said again:
"My God has bow'd me down to what I am;
My grief and solitude have broken me;
Nevertheless, know you that I am he
Who married—but that name has twice been changed—   855
I married her who married Philip Ray.
Sit, listen." Then he told her of his voyage,
His wreck, his lonely life, his coming back,
His gazing in on Annie, his resolve,
And how he kept it. As the woman heard,   860
Fast flow'd the current of her easy tears,
While in her heart she yearn'd incessantly
To rush abroad all round the little haven,
Proclaiming Enoch Arden and his woes;   •
But awed and promise-bounden she forbore,   865
Saying only, "See your bairns[7] before you go!
Eh, let me fetch 'em, Arden," and arose
Eager to bring them down, for Enoch hung
A moment on her words, but then replied:

"Woman, disturb me not now at the last,   870
But let me hold my purpose till I die.
Sit down again; mark me and understand,
While I have power to speak. I charge you now,
When you shall see her, tell her that I died
Blessing her, praying for her, loving her;   875
Save for the bar between us, loving her
As when she laid her head beside my own.
And tell my daughter Annie, whom I saw
So like her mother, that my latest breath
Was spent in blessing her and praying for her.   880
And tell my son that I died blessing him.
And say to Philip that I blest him too;
He never meant us anything but good.

7. Children, in dialects of northern England and Scotland.

But if my children care to see me dead,
Who hardly knew me living, let them come, 885
I am their father; but she must not come,
For my dead face would vex her after-life.
And now there is but one of all my blood
Who will embrace me in the world-to-be.
This hair is his, she cut it off and gave it, 890
And I have borne it with me all these years,
And thought to bear it with me to my grave;
But now my mind is changed, for I shall see him,
My babe in bliss. Wherefore when I am gone,
Take, give her this, for it may comfort her; 895
It will moreover be a token to her
That I am he."

       He ceased; and Miriam Lane
Made such a voluble answer promising all,
That once again he roll'd his eyes upon her
Repeating all he wish'd, and once again 900
She promised.

       Then the third night after this,
While Enoch slumber'd motionless and pale,
And Miriam watch'd and dozed at intervals,
There came so loud a calling of the sea
That all the houses in the haven rang. 905
He woke, he rose, he spread his arms abroad,
Crying with a loud voice, "A sail! a sail!
I am saved;" and so fell back and spoke no more.

So past the strong heroic soul away.
And when they buried him the little port 910
Had seldom seen a costlier funeral.[8]

1862; 1864

Requiescat

Fair is her cottage in its place,
    Where yon broad water sweetly, slowly glides.
It sees itself from thatch to base
    Dream in the sliding tides.

And fairer she, but ah, how soon to die! 5
    Her quiet dream of life this hour may cease.
Her peaceful being slowly passes by
    To some more perfect peace.

1864

8. Tennyson's note doesn't help: "The costly funeral is all that poor Annie could do for him after he was gone. This is entirely introduced for her sake, and, in my opinion, quite necessary to the perfection of the Poem and the simplicity of the narrative."

Northern Farmer[9]

1

Wheer 'asta beän saw long and meä liggin' 'ere aloän?[1]
Noorse?[2] thoort nowt o' a noorse; whoy, Doctor's abeän an' agoän;
Says that I moänt 'a[3] naw moor aäle, but I beänt a fool;
Git ma my aäle, fur I beänt a-gawin' to breäk my rule.

2

Doctors, they knaws nowt, fur a[4] says what 's nawways true;   5
Naw soort o' koind o' use to saäy the things that a do.
I 've 'ed my point o' aäle ivry noight sin' I beän 'ere.
An' I 've 'ed my quart ivry market-noight for foorty year.

3

Parson's a beän loikewoise, an' a sittin' ere o' my bed.
"The Amoighty 's a taäkin o' you to 'issén,[5] my friend," a said,   10
An' a towd ma my sins, an' 's toithe were due,[6] an' I gied it in hond;
I done moy duty boy 'um, as I 'a done boy the lond.

4

Larn'd a ma' beä.[7] I reckons I 'annot sa mooch to larn.
But a cast oop, thot a did, 'bout Bessy Marris's barne.[8]
Thaw a knaws I hallus voäted wi' Squoire an' choorch an' staäte,   15
An' i' the woost o' toimes I wur niver agin the raäte.[9]

5

An' I hallus coom'd to 's choorch afoor moy Sally wur deäd,
An' 'eärd 'um a bummin' awaäy loike a buzzard-clock[1] ower my 'eäd,
An' I niver knaw'd whot a meän'd but I thowt a 'ad summut to saäy,
An' I thowt a said whot a owt to 'a said, an' I coom'd awaäy.   20

---

9. Of this and the following poem Tennyson said: "The first is founded on the dying words of a farm-bailiff, as reported to me by a great uncle of mine when verging upon 80,—'God A'mighty little knows what He's about, a-taking me. An' Squire will be so mad an' all.' I conjectured the man from that one saying. . . . [The second poem] is likewise founded on a single sentence, 'When I canters my 'erse along the ramper (highway) I 'ears proputty, proputty, proputty.' I had been told that a rich farmer in our neighbourhood was in the habit of saying this. I never saw the man and know no more of him" (*Memoir*, II, 9). Bagehot (see note 1 to "Enoch Arden"), in praise of the "Northern Farmer," complains: 'He could, if he only would, have given us the ideal sailor in like manner." Both these dramatic monologues in Lincolnshire dialect, more earthy than anything Browning ever did, give us a welcome but all too infrequent glimpse into Tennyson's sense of humor.

1. Where hast thou been so long and me lying here alone?
2. Nurse.
3. Must not have.
4. He.
5. Himself. "You" is pronounced with the *ou* as in *hour*.
6. And he told me my sins, and his tithe was due.
7. Learned he may be.
8. But he brought up, that he did, about Bessy Marris' child.
9. Rate, i.e., poor-tax.
1. Cockchafer, a large destructive beetle. A story Tennyson liked to tell was about "a Lincolnshire farmer coming home on Sunday after a sermon about the endless fires of hell and talking to his wife—'Noä, Sally, it woän't do, noä constitootion cud stan' it.' " Another "was of a Lincolnshire minister praying for rain: 'O God, send us rain, and especially on John Stubbs' field in the middle marsh, and if Thou doest not know it, it has a big thorn-tree in the middle of it' " (*Memoir*, II, 10).

6

Bessy Marris's barne! tha knaws she laäid it to meä.
Mowt a beän, mayhap, for she wur a bad un, sheä.
'Siver,[2] I kep 'um, I kep 'um, my lass, tha mun understond;
I done moy duty boy 'um, as I 'a done boy the lond.

7

But Parson a cooms an' a goäs, an' a says it eäsy an' freeä: 25
"The Amoighty 's taäkin o' to you to 'issén, my friend," say 'eä.
I weänt saäy men be loiars, thaw summun[3] said it in 'aäste;
But 'e reäds wonn sarmin a weeäk, an' I' a stubb'd[4] Thurnaby
    waäste.

8

D' ya moind the waäste, my lass? naw, naw, tha was not born then;
Theer wur a boggle[5] in it, I often 'eärd 'um mysén;   30
Moäst loike a butter-bump,[6] fur I 'eärd 'um about an' about,
But I stubb'd 'um oop wi' the lot, an' raäved an' rembled[7] 'um out.

9

Keäper's it wur; fo' they fun 'um theer a-laäid of 'is faäce[8]
Down i' the woild 'enemies[9] afor I com'd to the plaäce.
Noäks or Thimbleby—toäner[1] 'ed shot 'um as deäd as a naäil.   35
Noäks wur 'ang'd for it oop at 'soize[2]—but git ma my aäle.

10

Dubbut[3] looök at the waäste; theer warn't not feeäd for a cow;
Nowt at all but bracken an' fuzz, an' looök at it now—
Warn't worth nowt a haäcre, an' now theer 's lots o' feeäd,
Fourscoor[4] yows[5] upon it, an' some on it down i' seeäd.[6]   40

11

Nobbut a bit[7] on it 's left, an' I meän'd to 'a stubb'd it at fall,
Done it ta-year[8] I meän'd, an' runn'd plow thruff it an' all,
If Godamoighty an' parson 'ud nobbut let ma aloän,—
Meä, wi' haäte hoonderd haäcre o' Squoire's, an' lond o' my oän.

12

Do Godamoighty knaw what a 's doing a-taäkin' o' meä?   45
I beänt wonn as saws[9] 'ere a beän an' yonder a peä;
An' Squoire 'ull be sa mad an' all—a' dear, a' dear!
And I 'a managed for Squoire coom Michaelmas thutty year.

13

A mowt 'a taäen owd Joänes, as 'ant not a 'aäpoth o' sense,[1]
Or a mowt 'a taäen young Robins—a niver mended a fence;   50

2. Howsoever.
3. Someone, i.e., David: "I said in my haste, All men *are* liars" (*Psalms,* 116:11).
4. Cleared, perhaps ploughed.
5. Bogy or ghost.
6. A bittern or kind of heron, which makes loud booming noises during the mating season.
7. Tore up and threw away.
8. It was the gamekeeper's (ghost), for they found him there lying on his face.

9. Anemones.
1. One or the other.
2. Assizes or court trial.
3. Do but.
4. *ou* as in *hour.*
5. Ewes.
6. Clover.
7. Nought but a little.
8. This year.
9. I be not one that sows.
1. He might have taken old Jones, that hasn't a halfpenny-worth of sense.

But Godamoighty a moost taäke meä an' taäke ma now,
Wi' aäf the cows to cauve[2] an' Thurnaby hoälms[3] to plow!

14

Looök 'ow quoloty[4] smoiles when they seeäs ma a passin' boy,
Says to thessén,[5] naw doubt, "What a man a beä sewer-loy!"[6]
Fur they knaws what I beän to Squoire sin' fust a coom'd to the
    'All;   55
I done moy duty by Squoire an' I done moy duty boy hall.

15

Squoire 's i' Lunnon, an' summun I reckons 'ull 'a to wroite,
For whoä 's to howd[7] the lond ater meä, thot muddles ma quoit;[8]
Sartin-sewer[9] I beä thot a weänt niver give it to Joänes,
Naw, nor a moänt to Robins—a niver rembles the stoäns.[1]   60

16

But summon 'ull come ater meä mayhap wi' 'is kittle o' steäm[2]
Huzzin' an' maäzin'[3] the blessed feälds wi' the divil's oän teäm.
Sin' I mun doy I mun doy, thaw loife they says is sweet,
But sin' I mun doy I mun doy, for I couldn abeär to see it.

17

What atta stannin' theer fur, an' doesn bring ma the aäle?   65
Doctor 's a 'toättler,[4] lass, an a 's hallus i' the owd taäle;[5]
I weänt breäk rules fur Doctor, a knaws naw moor nor a floy;[6]
Git ma my aäle, I tell tha, an' if I mun doy I mun doy.

1861; 1864

Northern Farmer

1

Dosn't thou 'ear my 'erse's[7] legs, as they canters awaäy?
Proputty,[8] proputty, proputty—that 's what I 'ears 'em saäy.
Proputty, proputty, proputty—Sam, thou 's an ass for thy païns;
Theer 's moor sense i' one o' 'is legs, nor in all thy braïns.

2

Woä—theer 's a craw to pluck[9] wi' tha, Sam: yon 's parson's
    'ouse—   5
Dosn't thou knaw that man mun be eäther a man or a mouse?
Time to think on it then; for thou 'll be twenty to weeäk.[1]
Proputty, proputty—woä then, woä—let ma 'ear mysén[2] speäk.

2. Calve.
3. Low lands.
4. Quality or gentry.
5. Themselves.
6. Surely.
7. Hold.
8. Quite.
9. Certain sure.
1. No, nor he must not (give the land) to Robbins—he never removes the stones.

2. The newfangled steam thresher.
3. Worrying and confusing.
4. Teetotaler.
5. And he's always in (telling) the same old tale.
6. Fly.
7. Horse's.
8. Property.
9. A crow to pluck, a dispute to settle.
1. This week.
2. Myself.

3
Me an' thy muther, Sammy, 'as beän a-talkin' o' thee;
Thou 's beän talkin' to muther, an' she beä a-tellin' it me.   10
Thou 'll not marry for munny—thou's sweet upo' parson's lass—
Noä—thou 'll marry for luvv—an' we boäth on us thinks tha an ass.

4
Seeä'd her to-daäy goä by—Saäint's-daäy—they was ringing the
    bells.
She 's a beauty, thou thinks—an' soä is scoors o' gells,[3]
Them as 'as munny an' all—wot 's a beauty?—the flower as blaws. 15
But proputty, proputty sticks, an' proputty, proputty graws.

5
Do'ant be stunt;[4] taäke time. I knaws what maäkes tha sa mad.
Warn't I craäzed fur the lasses mysén when I wur a lad?
But I knaw'd a Quaäker feller as often 'as towd[5] ma this:
"Doänt thou marry for munny, but goä wheer munny is!"   20

6
An' I went wheer munny war;[6] an' thy muther coom to 'and,
Wi' lots o' munny laaïd by, an' a nicetish bit o' land.
Maäybe she warn't a beauty—I niver giv it a thowt—
But warn't she as good to cuddle an' kiss as a lass as 'ant nowt?[7]

7
Parson's las 'ant nowt, an' she weänt 'a nowt when 'e 's deäd,   25
Mun be a guvness, lad, or summut, and addle[8] her breäd.
Why? fur 'e 's nobbut[9] a curate, an' weänt niver get hissén clear,
An' 'e maäde the bed as 'e ligs[1] on afoor 'e coom'd to the shere.[2]

8
An' thin 'e coom'd to the parish wi' lots o' Varsity debt,
Stook to his taail they did, an' 'e 'ant got shut on[3] 'em yet.   30
An' 'e ligs on 'is back i' the grip,[4] wi' noän to lend 'im a shove,
Woorse nor a far-welter'd yowe;[5] fur, Sammy, 'e married fur luvv.

9
Luvv? what 's luvv? thou can luvv thy lass an' 'er munny too,
Maäkin' 'em goä togither, as they 've good right to do.
Couldn I luvv thy muther b' y cause o' 'er munny laaïd by?   35
Naäy—fur I luvv'd 'er a vast sight moor fur it; reäson why.

10
Ay, an' thy muther says thou wants to marry the lass,
Cooms of a gentleman burn;[6] an' we boäth on us thinks tha an ass.
Woä then, proputty, wiltha?[7]—an ass as near as mays nowt[8]
Woä then, wiltha? dangtha!—the bees is as fell as owt.[9]   40

3. Scores of girls.
4. Stubborn.
5. Told.
6. "It was also reported of the wife of
this worthy that, when she entered the
salle à manger of a sea bathing-place,
she slapt her pockets and said, 'When I
married I brought him £5000 on each
shoulder' " (*Memoir*, II, 9).
7. Has nothing.
8. Earn.

9. Nothing but.
1. Lies.
2. Shire.
3. Clear of.
4. Ditch.
5. Ewe lying on her back.
6. Born.
7. Wilt thou.
8. Makes nothing.
9. The flies are as fierce as anything.

11

Breäk me a bit o' the esh for his 'eäd,[1] lad, out o' the fence!
Gentleman burn! what 's gentleman burn? is it shillins an' pence?
Proputty, proputty 's ivrything 'ere, an', Sammy, I 'm blest
If it is n't the saäme oop yonder, fur them as 'as it 's the best.

12

Tis 'n them as 'as munny as breäks into 'ouses an' steäls,   45
Them as 'as coäts to their backs an' taäkes their regular meäls.
Noä, but it 's them as niver knaws wheer a meäl 's to be 'ad.
Taäke my word for it, Sammy, the poor in a loomp is bad.

13

Them or thir feythers, tha sees, mun 'a beän a laäzy lot,
Fur work mun 'a gone to the gittin' whiniver munny was got.   50
Feyther 'ad ammost nowt; leästways 's munny was 'id.
But 'e tued an' moil'd issén deäd,[2] an' 'e died a good un, 'e did.

14

Looök thou theer wheer Wrigglesby beck[3] cooms out by the 'll!
Feyther run oop to the farm, an' I runs oop to the mill;
An' I 'll run oop to the brig,[4] an' that thou 'll live to see;   55
And if thou marries a good un I 'll leäve the land to thee.

15

Thim 's my noätions, Sammy, wheerby I meäns to stick;
But if thou marries a bad un, I 'll leäve the land to Dick.—
Com oop, proputty, proputty—that 's what I 'ears 'im saäy—
Proputty, proputty, proputty—canter an' canter awaäy.   60

1866; 1869

Lucretius[5]

Lucilia, wedded to Lucretius, found
Her master cold; for when the morning flush

1. An ash branch to keep the flies off the horse's head.
2. But he toiled and drudged himself to death.
3. Brook.
4. Bridge.
5. At the center of Victorian thought, particularly after mid-century, was the problem to which Tennyson addresses his poem: the materialists, buttressed by the rapid advances being made in the sciences, presented increasingly impressive evidence that the universe was governed by natural laws and not by a supreme being. The general resurgence of interest in Lucretius (c. 99–55 B.C.) was understandable. In his famous poem *De Rerum Natura* ("On the Nature of Things"), he had argued for the Epicurean philosophy, which denied the immortality of the soul and held the pursuit of pleasure to be the legitimate end of existence. (Epicureanism, it should be observed, was originally an ascetic doctrine; although it claimed the world was knowable through the senses, it sought to realize the higher virtues of the mind, such as honor, duty, and justice.) Tennyson based his poem on the probably apocryphal version of Lucretius' death as supplied by St. Jerome (c. 340–420), who in his *Chronicle* was out to discredit Roman philosophy.

When it was published, "Lucretius" was alternately praised and damned. Tennyson was charged with imitating Swinburne's libertinism (*Poems and Ballads* appeared in 1866) or attempting to outdo Browning in his speciality, the dramatic monologue. "What a mess little Swinburne would have made of this," Tennyson reportedly once said in the midst of a reading (*Alfred Tennyson*, p. 375). But as a condensation of the *De Rerum Natura*, Tennyson's poem happily strikes that seldom-realized balance which he never quite achieved in *Idylls of the King*—he looked to the past for a means of focusing on contemporary issues.

Of passion and the first embrace had died
Between them, tho' he loved her none the less,
Yet often when the woman heard his foot   5
Return from pacings in the field, and ran
To greet him with a kiss, the master took
Small notice, or austerely, for—his mind
Half buried in some weightier argument,
Or fancy-borne perhaps upon the rise   10
And long roll of the hexameter—he past
To turn and ponder those three hundred scrolls
Left by the Teacher,[6] whom he held divine.
She brook'd it not, but wrathful, petulant,
Dreaming some rival, sought and found a witch   15
Who brew'd the philtre which had power, they said,
To lead an errant passion home again.
And this, at times, she mingled with his drink,
And this destroy'd him; for the wicked broth
Confused the chemic labor of the blood,   20
And tickling the brute brain within the man's
Made havoc among those tender cells, and check'd
His power to shape. He loathed himself, and once
After a tempest woke upon a morn
That mock'd him with returning calm, and cried: 25

    "Storm in the night! for thrice I heard the rain
Rushing; and once the flash of a thunderbolt—
Methought I never saw so fierce a fork—
Struck out the streaming mountain-side, and show'd
A riotous confluence of watercourses   30
Blanching and billowing in a hollow of it,
Where all but yester-eve was dusty-dry.

    "Storm, and what dreams, ye holy Gods, what dreams!
For thrice I waken'd after dreams. Perchance
We do but recollect the dreams that come   35
Just ere the waking. Terrible: for it seem'd
A void was made in Nature; all her bonds
Crack'd; and I saw the flaring atom-streams
And torrents of her myriad universe,
Ruining along the illimitable inane,   40
Fly on to clash together again, and make
Another and another frame of things
For ever. That was mine, my dream, I knew it—
Of and belonging to me, as the dog
With inward yelp and restless forefoot plies   45
His function of the woodland; but the next!

6. Epicurus (c. 342–270 B.C.)

I thought that all the blood by Sylla[7] shed
Came driving rainlike down again on earth,
And where it dash'd the reddening meadow, sprang
No dragon warriors from Cadmean teeth,[8]   50
For these I thought my dream would show to me,
But girls, Hetairai,[9] curious in their art,
Hired animalisms, vile as those that made
The mulberry-faced Dictator's orgies worse
Than aught they fable of the quiet Gods.   55
And hands they mixt, and yell'd and round me drove
In narrowing circles till I yell'd again
Half-suffocated, and sprang up, and saw—
Was it the first beam of my latest day?

   "Then, then, from utter gloom stood out the breasts,   60
The breasts of Helen, and hoveringly a sword
Now over and now under, now direct,
Pointed itself to pierce, but sank down shamed
At all that beauty; and as I stared, a fire,
The fire that left a roofless Ilion,   65
Shot out of them, and scorch'd me that I woke.

   "Is this thy vengeance,[1] holy Venus, thine,
Because I would not one of thine own doves,
Not even a rose, were offer'd to thee? thine,
Forgetful how my rich proœmion[2] makes   70
Thy glory fly along the Italian field,
In lays that will outlast thy deity?

   "Deity? nay, thy worshippers. My tongue
Trips, or I speak profanely. Which of these
Angers thee most, or angers thee at all?   75
Not if thou be'st of those who, far aloof
From envy, hate and pity, and spite and scorn,
Live the great life which all our greatest fain
Would follow, centred in eternal calm.

   "Nay, if thou canst, O Goddess, like ourselves   80
Touch, and be touch'd, then would I cry to thee
To kiss thy Mavors,[3] roll thy tender arms
Round him, and keep him from the lust of blood
That makes a steaming slaughter-house of Rome.

---

7. Sulla, self-appointed dictator (line 54) of Rome from 82 to 79 B.C. He was known for his ruthlessness and dissolute life recorded in Plutarch's *Lives*.
8. Cadmus, the founder of Thebes, killed a dragon from whose teeth, which Athena had instructed him to sow, sprang up armed warriors.
9. Courtesans.
1. That is, for sending such lustful visions.
2. In his introduction to the *De Rerum Natura*, Lucretius invoked Venus as the symbol of nature's generative forces.
3. Mars.

"Ay, but I meant not thee; I meant not her   85
Whom all the pines of Ida shook to see
Slide from that quiet heaven of hers, and tempt
The Trojan,[4] while his neatherds were abroad;
Nor her that o'er her wounded hunter[5] wept
Her deity false in human-amorous tears;   90
Nor whom her beardless apple-arbiter[6]
Decided fairest. Rather, O ye Gods,
Poet-like, as the great Sicilian[7] called
Calliope to grace his golden verse—
Ay, and this Kypris[8] also—did I take   95
That popular name of thine to shadow forth
The all-generating powers and genial heat
Of Nature, when she strikes thro' the thick blood
Of cattle, and light is large, and lambs are glad
Nosing the mother's udder, and the bird   100
Makes his heart voice amid the blaze of flowers;
Which things appear the work of mighty Gods.

"The Gods! and if I go *my* work is left
Unfinish'd—*if* I go. The Gods, who haunt
The lucid interspace of world and world,   105
Where never creeps a cloud, or moves a wind,
Nor ever falls the least white star of snow,
Nor ever lowest roll of thunder moans,
Nor sound of human sorrow mounts to mar
Their sacred everlasting calm! and such,   110
Not all so fine, nor so divine a calm,
Not such, nor all unlike it, man may gain
Letting his own life go. The Gods, the Gods!
If all be atoms, how then should the Gods
Being atomic not be dissoluble,   115
Not follow the great law? My master[9] held
That Gods there are, for all men so believe.
I prest my footsteps into his, and meant
Surely to lead my Memmius[1] in a train
Of flowery clauses onward to the proof   120
That Gods there are, and deathless. Meant? I meant?
I have forgotten what I meant; my mind
Stumbles, and all my faculties are lamed.

"Look where another of our Gods, the Sun,
Apollo, Delius, or of older use   125

---

4. Anchises, whom Venus seduced; their son was Aeneas.
5. Adonis, also loved by Venus, was killed by a boar while hunting.
6. Paris judged Venus fairest, and she received the golden apples. See "Œnone" for the myth.
7. Empedocles, who invoked Calliope, the muse of epic poetry.
8. Cyprus, where Venus was worshiped.
9. Epicurus.
1. Caius Memmius Gemellus, Sulla's son-in-law, to whom the *De Rerum Natura* was dedicated.

All-seeing Hyperion—what you will—
Has mounted yonder; since he never sware,
Except his wrath were wreak'd on wretched man,
That he would only shine among the dead
Hereafter—tales! for never yet on earth   130
Could dead flesh creep, or bits of roasting ox
Moan round the spit—nor knows he what he sees;
King of the East altho' he seem, and girt
With song and flame and fragrance, slowly lifts
His golden feet on those empurpled stairs   135
That climb into the windy halls of heaven
And here he glances on an eye new-born,
And gets for greeting but a wail of pain;
And here he stays upon a freezing orb
That fain would gaze upon him to the last;   140
And here upon a yellow eyelid fallen
And closed by those who mourn a friend in vain,
Not thankful that his troubles are no more.
And me, altho' his fire is on my face
Blinding, he sees not, nor at all can tell   145
Whether I mean this day to end myself.
Or lend an ear to Plato where he says,
That men like soldiers may not quit the post
Allotted by the Gods.[2] But he that holds
The Gods are careless, wherefore need he care   150
Greatly for them, nor rather plunge at once,
Being troubled, wholly out of sight, and sink
Past earthquake—ay, and gout and stone, that break
Body toward death, and palsy, death-in-life,
And wretched age—and worst disease of all,   155
These prodigies of myriad nakednesses,
And twisted shapes of lust, unspeakable,
Abominable, strangers at my hearth
Not welcome, harpies miring every dish,
The phantom husks of something foully done,   160
And fleeting thro' the boundless universe,
And blasting the long quiet of my breast
With animal heat and dire insanity?

"How should the mind, except it loved them, clasp
These idols to herself? or do they fly   165
Now thinner, and now thicker, like the flakes
In a fall of snow, and so press in, perforce
Of multitude, as crowds that in an hour
Of civic tumult jam the doors, and bear
The keepers down, and throng, their rags and they   170

2. "We men are as it were on guard, from it, nor to run away." See *Phaedo*,
and a man ought not to free himself vi.

The basest, far into that council-hall
Where sit the best and stateliest of the land?

"Can I not fling this horror off me again,
Seeing with how great ease Nature can smile,
Balmier and nobler from her bath of storm,   175
At random ravage? and how easily
The mountain there has cast his cloudy slough,
Now towering o'er him in serenest air,
A mountain o'er a mountain,—ay, and within
All hollow as the hopes and fears of men?   180

"But who was he[3] that in the garden snared
Picus and Faunus, rustic Gods? a tale
To laugh at—more to laugh at in myself—
For look! what is it? there? yon arbutus
Totters; a noiseless riot underneath   185
Strikes through the wood, sets all the tops quivering—
The mountain quickens into Nymph and Faun,
And here an Oread[4]—how the sun delights
To glance and shift about her slippery sides,
And rosy knees and supple roundedness,   190
And budded bosom-peaks—who this way runs
Before the rest!—a satyr, a satyr, see,
Follows; but him I proved impossible;
Twy-natured is no nature. Yet he draws
Nearer and nearer, and I scan him now   195
Beastlier than any phantom of his kind
That ever butted his rough brother-brute
For lust or lusty blood or provender.
I hate, abhor, spit, sicken at him; and she
Loathes him as well; such a precipitate heel,   200
Fledged as it were with Mercury's ankle-wing,
Whirls her to me—but will she fling herself
Shameless upon me? Catch her, goatfoot! nay,
Hide, hide them, million-myrtled wilderness,
And cavern-shadowing laurels, hide! do I wish—   205
What?—that the bush were leafless? or to whelm
All of them in one massacre? O ye Gods,
I know you careless, yet, behold, to you
From childly wont and ancient use I call—
I thought I lived securely as yourselves—   210
No lewdness, narrowing envy, monkey-spite,
No madness of ambition, avarice, none;

3. Numa, who in legend was Romulus' successor as king of Rome. The goddess Egeria counseled him to ensnare Picus and his son Faunus, divinities who could reveal the secrets of the gods. See Ovid's *Fasti*, III, 291 ff.

4. A mountain nymph. The visions which follow are brought on by the love potion. In the *De Rerum Natura* Lucretius had claimed that nature could not produce such things as satyrs.

No larger feast than under plane or pine
With neighbors laid along the grass, to take
Only such cups as left us friendly-warm,   215
Affirming each his own philosophy—
Nothing to mar the sober majesties
Of settled, sweet, Epicurean life.
But now it seems some unseen monster lays
His vast and filthy hands upon my will,   220
Wrenching it backward into his, and spoils
My bliss in being; and it was not great,
For save when shutting reasons up in rhythm,
Or Heliconian[5] honey in living words,
To make a truth less harsh, I often grew   225
Tired of so much within our little life,
Or of so little in our little life—
Poor little life that toddles half an hour
Crown'd with a flower or two, and there an end—
And since the nobler pleasure seems to fade,   230
Why should I, beastlike as I find myself,
Not manlike end myself?—our privilege—
What beast has heart to do it? And what man,
What Roman would be dragg'd in triumph thus?
Not I; not he, who bears one name with her[6]   235
Whose death-blow struck the dateless doom of kings,
When, brooking not the Tarquin in her veins,
She made her blood in sight of Collatine
And all his peers, flushing the guiltless air,
Spout from the maiden fountain in her heart.   240
And from it sprang the Commonwealth, which breaks
As I am breaking now!

       "And therefore now
Let her, that is the womb and tomb of all,
Great Nature, take, and forcing far apart
Those blind beginnings that have made me man,   245
Dash them anew together at her will
Thro' all her cycles—into man once more,
Or beast or bird or fish, or opulent flower.
But till this cosmic order everywhere
Shatter'd into one earthquake in one day   250
Cracks all to pieces,—and that hour perhaps
Is not so far when momentary man
Shall seem no more a something to himself,

5. In Greece, Helicon was a mountain sacred to the muses.
6. Lucretia, who was raped by Tarquin (Collatine), committed suicide. According to legend, the incident brought about an insurrection in which the Tarquins were expelled from Rome, which led to the establishment of the Roman Republic.

But he, his hopes and hates, his homes and fanes,
And even his bones long laid within the grave, 255
The very sides of the grave itself shall pass,
Vanishing, atom and void, atom and void,
Into the unseen for ever,—till that hour,
My golden work in which I told a truth
That stays the rolling Ixionian wheel, 260
And numbs the Fury's ringlet-snake, and plucks
The mortal soul from out immortal hell,
Shall stand. Ay, surely; then it fails at last
And perishes as I must; for O Thou,
Passionless bride, divine Tranquillity, 265
Yearn'd after by the wisest of the wise,
Who fail to find thee, being as thou art
Without one pleasure and without one pain,
Howbeit I know thou surely must be mine
Or soon or late, yet out of season, thus 270
I woo thee roughly, for thou carest not
How roughly men may woo thee so they win—
Thus—thus—the soul flies out and dies in the air."

    With that he drove the knife into his side.
She[7] heard him raging, heard him fall, ran in, 275
Beat breast, tore hair, cried out upon herself
As having fail'd in duty to him, shriek'd
That she but meant to win him back, fell on him,
Clasp'd, kiss'd him, wail'd. He answer'd, "Care not thou!
Thy duty? What is duty? Fare thee well!" 280

1865; 1868

"Flower in the Crannied Wall"

Flower in the crannied wall,
I pluck you out of the crannies,
I hold you here, root and all, in my hand,
Little flower—but *if* I could understand
What you are, root and all, and all in all, 5
I should know what God and man is.

1869

The Higher Pantheism[8]

The sun, the moon, the stars, the seas, the hills and the plains,—
Are not these, O Soul, the Vision of Him who reigns?

---

7. Lucilia.
8. The "lower," or old, pantheism pro-
poses that God is identified with nature
and has no existence outside the natural

Is not the Vision He, tho' He be not that which He seems?
Dreams are true while they last, and do we not live in dreams?

Earth, these solid stars, this weight of body and limb,   5
Are they not sign and symbol of thy division from Him?

Dark is the world to thee; thyself art the reason why,
For is He not all but thou, that hast power to feel "I am I"?

Glory about thee, without thee; and thou fulfillest thy doom,
Making Him broken gleams and a stifled splendor and gloom.   10

Speak to Him, thou, for He hears, and Spirit with Spirit can meet—
Closer is He than breathing, and nearer than hands and feet.

God is law, say the wise; O Soul, and let us rejoice,
For if He thunder by law the thunder is yet His voice.

Law is God, say some; no God at all, says the fool,   15
For all we have power to see is a straight staff bent in a pool;

And the ear of man cannot hear, and the eye of man cannot see;
But if we could see and hear, this Vision—were it not He?

1867; 1869

In the Garden at Swainston[9]

Nightingales warbled without,
   Within was weeping for thee;
Shadows of three dead men
   Walk'd in the walks with me,
     Shadows of three dead men, and thou wast one of the three.   5

---

world. Tennyson's version insists that the spirit is the only reality there is. From his earliest poetry through *In Memoriam*, he had been working toward an articulation of this philosophy. (See *The Devil and the Lady*, Act 1, Scene 1, 41–58, and note p. 503; also *In Memoriam*, 130.) Swinburne's savage but funny parody begins: "One, who is not, we see: but one, whom we see not, is;/ Surely this is not that: but that is assuredly this." It ends with the devastating couplet: "God, whom we see not, is: and God, who is not, we see;/ Fiddle, we know, is diddle: and diddle, we take it, is dee."

9. Swainston was Sir John Simeon's home on the Isle of Wight, near Tennyson's Farringford. Sir John (see note 1 to *Maud*) had been one of the poet's closest friends; he died suddenly and

unexpectedly in Switzerland. The moving account of the poem's composition deserves repeating in full: "He [Tennyson] arrived sometime before the procession was due to leave the house, and asked his old friend's eldest son if he could give him a pipe of his father's and one of his cloaks and hats. 'Come for me yourself,' he added, 'when it is time to start, and do not send a servant.' When the moment arrived young Simeon went to fetch the poet. He found him, stretched at full length on the ground, wearing the hat and cloak and smoking the pipe. The tears were streaming down his face, and in his hand was a scrap of paper on which he had roughly jotted down the beautiful lines 'In the Garden at Swainston.' " (*Alfred Tennyson*, p. 389).

Nightingales sang in his woods,
  The Master was far away;
Nightingales warbled and sang
    Of a passion that lasts but a day;
    Still in the house in his coffin the Prince of courtesy lay.   10

Two dead men have I known
  In courtesy like to thee;
Two dead men[1] have I loved
    With a love that ever will be;
    Three dead men have I loved, and thou art last of the three.   15

1870; 1874

1. Arthur Hallam and Henry Lushington.

Idylls of the King Few poems, if any, have been so widely acclaimed
and then so thoroughly maligned as Tennyson's *Idylls of the King*, his most
ambitious but never fully realized work. When Tennyson's star was at its
height, the praises heaped upon his poem obscured the poet's very real
defects; when appreciation of him reached its lowest, during the first third
of the twentieth century, the sometimes niggling, often ill-informed criti-
cism of the *Idylls* made a general appraisal of the poet's achievements im-
possible. Writing in 1872, Swinburne, who disparagingly called the poem
"The Morte d'Albert, or Idylls of the Prince Consort," was perhaps the
first clearly to perceive that Tennyson's greatest enemies were "those of his
own household," the close circle of friends who indiscriminately took every
utterance as prophecy from the Bard. But in the reaction against Tennyson
and those who had inflated his reputation, even Swinburne would have
been surprised to discover how right he had been.

    With varying degrees of intensity, Tennyson worked on his *Idylls* for
some fifty-five years, and therein lies an obvious cause of the poem's weak-
ness. In 1859 he published four *Idylls*: "Enid" (later divided into two
parts), "Vivien," "Elaine," and "Guinevere." His purpose here was simply
to contrast true and false love, and any thematic relationship to the first-
written of the idylls, the "Morte d'Arthur" (1833), was negligible. In
1869 he published "The Coming of Arthur," "Pelleas and Ettarre," "The
Holy Grail," and "The Passing of Arthur," which was based on the earlier
"Morte d'Arthur." The motivating impulse behind these poems, and what
later would be the central concern in the whole work, was to show the rise
and fall of a society and to suggest symbolically and allegorically a perti-
nence to the age in which he lived. The attempt was laudable and by no
means a complete failure, although one suspects that the Arthurian
legends, chiefly derived from Malory, never could fully lend themselves to
such an ambitious design. But a more immediate obstacle lay ahead—how
to bring together two essentially irreconcilable sets of poems. He wrote

"The Last Tournament" in 1871 and "Gareth and Lynette" in 1872; he published "Balin and Balan" in 1885 and divided "Enid" in 1888. (See chronology for more complete information on composition and publication dates.) But only extensive rewriting and rigorous cutting could have produced the coherence and structure necessary to the strict demands of the "Epic" he initially wished his poem to be. And even then, as I have just said, there is reason to believe that the source material could not sustain the larger purpose, or what Tennyson preferred to call the "parabolic drift in the poem" (*Memoir*, II, 127). What we have, to put it most simply, is a long poem in which the sum of the twelve parts is considerably more than the whole.

Criticism on the *Idylls* is all but endless, while criticism on the criticism has inevitably led to the neglect of the poem. Of the first four *Idylls*, Carlyle was one of the few who spoke derogatively; he saw an "inward perfection of vacancy" and sarcastically observed, "The lollipops were so Superlative." Matthew Arnold elaborated: "The real truth is that Tennyson, with all his temperament and artistic skill, is deficient in intellectual power." Of all the charges brought against the poem and the poet, this is the most serious and most frequently encountered in subsequent criticism. Before one too readily agrees, however, he could do worse than ponder the complexities of the problem to which Tennyson addressed his poem. In his *Science and the Modern World* (1925), Alfred North Whitehead wrote: "The history of thought in the eighteenth and nineteenth centuries is governed by the fact that the world had got hold of a general idea which it could neither live with nor live without." The idea is the mechanistic theory of nature or the theory of scientific materialism. The failure of the *Idylls* is not, as is so frequently maintained, that Tennyson avoided facing the consequences of materialistic thought because he lacked the intellectual equipment, but that the poem offers no working alternative to it. To support his belief in the spiritual, Tennyson could not get beyond his statement in the Prologue to *In Memoriam*, "By faith and faith alone, embrace, / Believing where we cannot prove." It would be up to later thinkers like William James and Whitehead to attempt to articulate a substitute for materialistic philosophies. But "even though mechanistic doctrines of the nineteenth century came to be repudiated," Professor Bush has written, "the new and more fluid conceptions were not much more reassuring, and the staggering fact of immensity or infinity has remained a part of the modern consciousness." The achievement of *Idylls of the King* is simply that it offered a repudiation. Those who look to *In Memoriam*, particularly to the notion expressed there "That mind and soul, according well, / May make one music as before," and from that point of departure conclude that Tennyson looked to the past for the harmony the modern world so conspicuously lacked, must also acknowledge that *Idylls* does diagnose the plights of modern life. King Arthur, in the dominant metaphor of the poem, sees that all his realm "Reels back into the beast and is no more." Our sophistication is not such that we can ignore, except at our peril, the implications of "The darkness of that battle in the west / Where all of high and holy dies away."

Idylls of the King: A Chronology

ORDER OF POEMS

"Dedication"

1. "The Coming of Arthur"

2. "Gareth and Lynette"

3. "The Marriage of Geraint"

4. "Geraint and Enid"

5. "Balin and Balan"

6. "Merlin and Vivien"

7. "Lancelot and Elaine"

8. "The Holy Grail"

9. "Pelleas and Ettarre"

10. "The Last Tournament"

11. "Guinevere"

12. "The Passing of Arthur"

To the Queen

ORDER OF FIRST PUBLICATION

"Merlin and Vivien" ("Nimuë"),* 1857, in trial copies privately printed.

"Geraint and Enid" ("Enid"), 1857.

"Guinevere," 1859.

"Elaine," 1859.

"Dedication," 1862.

"The Holy Grail," 1869 (dated 1870).

"The Coming of Arthur," 1869 (dated 1870).

"Pelleas and Ettarre," 1869 (dated 1870).

"The Passing of Arthur," 1869 (dated 1870). ("Morte d'Arthur" published 1842.)

"The Last Tournament," 1871.

"Gareth and Lynette," 1872.

"To the Queen," 1873.

"Balin and Balan," 1885.

"Geraint and Enid": "Enid" divided in 1888 into two idylls— "The Marriage of Geraint" and "Geraint and Enid" (see 3 and 4 in first column).

* The original titles of the poems are given in parentheses.

ORDER OF COMPOSITION

"Morte d'Arthur" composed 1833–35 (published 1842).

"Merlin and Vivien" ("Nimuë") started end of 1855; rough draft January 1856; completed March 1856.

"Geraint and Enid" ("Enid") started April 1856; worked on intensively September 1856; completed October 1856.

"Guinevere" started July 1857; completed January 1858; finishing touches added March 1858.

"Lancelot and Elaine" ("Elaine") conceived March 1858; mostly written winter 1858–59; completed end of February 1859.

"Dedication" (Prince Albert died December 18, 1861) set in type by January 9, 1862.

"The Holy Grail" started March 1868; re-started September 1868; completed November 1868.

"The Coming of Arthur" worked on winter 1868–69; completed end of February 1869.

"Pelleas and Ettarre" well under way May 1869; completed September 1869.

"The Passing of Arthur" ("Morte d'Arthur"): introduction and conclusion added to "Morte d'Arthur" September 1869.

"The Last Tournament" started April 1871; completed May 1871.

"Gareth and Lynette" started October 1869; worked on for a year; picked up again November 1871; completed summer 1872.

"To the Queen" composed toward end of 1872.

"Balin and Balan" composed during later part of 1872 and early 1873; completed 1874 (140 lines added to opening of "Merlin and Vivien" 1874).

FROM *IDYLLS OF THE KING*

Dedication[1]

These to His Memory—since he held them dear,
Perchance as finding there unconsciously
Some image of himself—I dedicate,
I dedicate, I consecrate with tears—
These Idylls.[2]

    And indeed he seems to me   5
Scarce other than my king's ideal knight,
'Who reverenced his conscience as his king;
Whose glory was, redressing human wrong;
Who spake no slander, no, nor listen'd to it;
Who loved one only and who clave to her—'[3]   10
Her—over all whose realms to their last isle,
Commingled with the gloom of imminent war,[4]
The shadow of his loss drew like eclipse,
Darkening the world. We have lost him; he is gone.
We know him now; all narrow jealousies   15
Are silent, and we see him as he moved,
How modest, kindly, all-accomplish'd, wise,
With what sublime repression of himself,
And in what limits, and how tenderly;
Not swaying to this faction or to that;   20
Not making his high place the lawless perch
Of wing'd ambitions, nor a vantage-ground
For pleasure; but thro' all this tract of years
Wearing the white flower of a blameless life,
Before a thousand peering littlenesses,   25
In that fierce light which beats upon a throne
And blackens every blot; for where is he
Who dares foreshadow for an only son
A lovelier life, a more unstain'd, than his?
Or how should England dreaming of *his* sons   30
Hope more for these than some inheritance
Of such a life, a heart, a mind as thine,
Thou noble Father of her Kings to be,
Laborious for her people and her poor—
Voice in the rich dawn of an ampler day—   35

1. To Prince Albert, husband of Queen Victoria, who died in December 1861. He had particularly liked the four *Idylls* published in 1859, and at his request Tennyson had sent him an autographed copy.
2. Tennyson used two *l*'s to distinguish them from his "English Idyls" concerning rural domestic life.
3. Paraphrased from "Guinevere," lines 465–472, where King Arthur summarizes the ideals of the Round Table.
4. Alludes to the *Trent* affair, in which two Confederate commissioners were taken off the British ship *Trent* by a Federal man-of-war. "The Queen and the Prince Consort," according to Tennyson's note, "were said to have averted war by their modification of a dispatch."

Far-sighted summoner of War and Waste
To fruitful strifes and rivalries of peace—[5]
Sweet nature gilded by the gracious gleam
Of letters, dear to Science, dear to Art,
Dear to thy land[6] and ours, a Prince indeed,   40
Beyond all titles, and a household name,
Hereafter, thro' all times, Albert the Good.

   Break not, O woman's-heart, but still endure;
Break not, for thou art royal, but endure,
Remembering all the beauty of that star   45
Which shone so close beside thee that ye made
One light together, but has past and leaves
The Crown a lonely splendor.

                 May all love,
His love, unseen but felt, o'ershadow thee,
The love of all thy sons encompass thee,   50
The love of all thy daughters cherish thee,
The love of all thy people comfort thee,
Till God's love set thee at his side again!

1862

         Flos Regum Arthurus.
       —JOSEPH OF EXETER[7]

The Coming of Arthur

Leodogran, the king of Cameliard,[8]
Had one fair daughter, and none other child;
And she was fairest of all flesh on earth,
Guinevere, and in her his one delight.

   For many a petty king ere Arthur came   5
Ruled in this isle and, ever-waging war
Each upon other, wasted all the land;
And still from time to time the heathen host
Swarm'd over-seas, and harried what was left.
And so there grew great tracts of wilderness,   10
Wherein the beast was ever more and more,
But man was less and less, till Arthur came.
For first Aurelius lived and fought and died,
And after him King Uther[9] fought and died,
But either fail'd to make the kingdom one.   15
And after these King Arthur for a space,

---

5. These lines refer to Prince Albert's efforts in planning the International Exhibitions of 1851 and 1862.
6. Albert's native land was Saxe-Coburg, in Germany.
7. "Arthur, the flower of kings." Joseph of Exeter was a medieval English poet who wrote epic verse in emulation of Virgil.
8. Sometimes located as far north as Scotland or, as probable here, in south Wales.
9. Aurelius' brother and, by some accounts, Arthur's father.

And thro' the puissance of his Table Round,
Drew all their petty princedoms under him,
Their king and head, and made a realm and reign'd.

And thus the land of Cameliard was waste, 20
Thick with wet woods, and many a beast therein,
And none or few to scare or chase the beast;
So that wild dog and wolf and boar and bear
Came night and day, and rooted in the fields,
And wallow'd in the gardens of the King. 25
And ever and anon the wolf would steal
The children and devour, but now and then,
Her own brood lost or dead, lent her fierce teat
To human sucklings; and the children, housed
In her foul den, there at their meat would growl, 30
And mock their foster-mother on four feet,
Till, straighten'd, they grew up to wolf-like men,
Worse than the wolves. And King Leodogran
Groan'd for the Roman legions here again
And Cæsar's eagle. Then his brother king, 35
Urien,[1] assail'd him; last a heathen horde,
Reddening the sun with smoke and earth with blood,
And on the spike that split the mother's heart
Spitting the child, brake on him, till, amazed,
He knew not whither he should turn for aid. 40

But—for he heard of Arthur newly crown'd,
Tho' not without an uproar made by those
Who cried, "He is not Uther's son"—the King
Sent to him, saying, "Arise, and help us thou!
For here between the man and beast we die." 45

And Arthur yet had done no deed of arms,
But heard the call and came; and Guinevere
Stood by the castle walls to watch him pass;
But since he neither wore on helm or shield
The golden symbol[2] of his kinglihood, 50
But rode a simple knight among his knights,
And many of these in richer arms than he,
She saw him not, or mark'd not, if she saw,
One among many, tho' his face was bare.
But Arthur, looking downward as he past, 55
Felt the light of her eyes into his life
Smite on the sudden, yet rode on, and pitch'd
His tents beside the forest. Then he drave
The heathen; after, slew the beast, and fell'd
The forest, letting in the sun, and made 60
Broad pathways for the hunter and the knight,
And so return'd.

---

1. King of North Wales.   2. A dragon.

For while he linger'd there,
A doubt that ever smoulder'd in the hearts
Of those great lords and barons of his realm
Flash'd forth and into war; for most of these, 65
Colleaguing with a score of petty kings,
Made head against him, crying: "Who is he
That he should rule us? who hath proven him
King Uther's son? for lo! we look at him,
And find nor face nor bearing, limbs nor voice, 70
Are like to those of Uther whom we knew.
This is the son of Gorloïs, not the King;
This is the son of Anton, not the King."

And Arthur, passing thence to battle, felt
Travail, and throes and agonies of the life, 75
Desiring to be join'd with Guinevere,
And thinking as he rode: "Her father said
That there between the man and beast they die.
Shall I not lift her from this land of beasts
Up to my throne and side by side with me? 80
What happiness to reign a lonely king,
Vext—O ye stars that shudder over me,
O earth that soundest hollow under me,
Vext with waste dreams? for saving I be join'd
To her that is the fairest under heaven, 85
I seem as nothing in the mighty world,
And cannot will my will nor work my work
Wholly, nor make myself in mine own realm
Victor and lord. But were I join'd with her,
Then might we live together as one life, 90
And reigning with one will in everything
Have power on this dark land to lighten it,
And power on this dead world to make it live."[3]

Thereafter—as he speaks who tells the tale—
When Arthur reach'd a field of battle bright 95
With pitch'd pavilions of his foe, the world
Was all so clear about him that he saw
The smallest rock far on the faintest hill,
And even in high day the morning star.[4]
So when the King had set his banner broad, 100
At once from either side, with trumpet-blast,
And shouts, and clarions shrilling unto blood,
The long-lanced battle let their horses run.

3. On the simplest allegorical level, Arthur represents the spirit and Guinevere the flesh. But, as I indicated in my introduction, the poem's scope is much wider. "The whole," Tennyson said, "is the dream of man coming into practical life and ruined by one sin. Birth is a mystery and death is a mystery, and in the midst lies the tableland of life, and its struggles and performances. It is not the history of one man or of one generation but of a whole cycle of generations" (*Memoir,* II, 127).
4. Compare "Armageddon," lines 171 ff., for an interesting early parallel to this mode of vision.

And now the barons and the kings prevail'd,
And now the King, as here and there that war 105
Went swaying; but the Powers who walk the world
Made lightnings and great thunders over him,
And dazed all eyes, till Arthur by main might,
And mightier of his hands with every blow,
And leading all his knighthood threw the kings, 110
Carádos, Urien, Cradlemont of Wales,
Claudius, and Clariance of Northumberland,
The King Brandagoras of Latangor,
With Anguisant of Erin, Morganore,
And Lot of Orkney.[5] Then, before a voice 115
As dreadful as the shout of one who sees
To one who sins, and deems himself alone
And all the world asleep, they swerved and brake
Flying, and Arthur[6] call'd to stay the brands
That hack'd among the flyers, "Ho! they yield!" 120
So like a painted battle the war stood
Silenced, the living quiet as the dead,
And in the heart of Arthur joy was lord.
He laugh'd upon his warrior[7] whom he loved
And honor'd most. "Thou dost not doubt me King, 125
So well thine arm hath wrought for me today."
"Sir and my liege," he cried, "the fire of God
Descends upon thee in the battle-field.
I know thee for my King!" Whereat the two,
For each had warded either in the fight, 130
Sware on the field of death a deathless love.
And Arthur said, "Man's word is God in man;[8]
Let chance what will, I trust thee to the death."

Then quickly from the foughten field he sent
Ulfius, and Brastias, and Bedivere, 135
His new-made knights, to King Leodogran,
Saying, "If I in aught have served thee well,
Give me thy daughter Guinevere to wife."

Whom when he heard, Leodogran in heart
Debating—"How should I that am a king, 140
However much he holp me at my need,
Give my one daughter saving to a king,
And a king's son?"—lifted his voice, and call'd
A hoary man, his chamberlain, to whom
He trusted all things, and of him required 145
His counsel: "Knowest thou aught of Arthur's birth?"

---

5. This list of conquered kings is from Malory, whom Tennyson follows quite closely in this idyll.
6. Contrast "The Last Tournament," lines 466–476, in which Arthur's commands go unheeded. One of the themes throughout the *Idylls* is the growing failure of communication, and its consequences.
7. Lancelot.
8. A central precept upon which the order of knights is founded and, in the poem's design, any social organization.

Then spake the hoary chamberlain and said:
"Sir King, there be but two old men that know;
And each is twice as old as I; and one
Is Merlin, the wise man that ever served   150
King Uther thro' his magic art, and one
Is Merlin's master—so they call him—Bleys,
Who taught him magic; but the scholar ran
Before the master, and so far that Bleys
Laid magic by, and sat him down, and wrote   155
All things and whatsoever Merlin did
In one great annal-book, where after-years
Will learn the secret of our Arthur's birth."

To whom the King Leodogran replied:
"O friend, had I been holpen half as well   160
By this King Arthur as by thee to-day,
Then beast and man had had their share of me;
But summon here before us yet once more
Ulfius, and Brastias, and Bedivere."

Then, when they came before him, the king said: 165
"I have seen the cuckoo chased by lesser fowl,
And reason in the chase; but wherefore now
Do these your lords stir up the heat of war,
Some calling Arthur born of Gorloïs,
Others of Anton? Tell me, ye yourselves,   170
Hold ye this Arthur for King Uther's son?"

And Ulfius and Brastias answer'd, "Ay."
Then Bedivere, the first of all his knights
Knighted by Arthur at his crowning, spake—
For bold in heart and act and word was he,   175
Whenever slander breathed against the King—

"Sir, there be many rumors on this head;
For there be those who hate him in their hearts,
Call him baseborn, and since his ways are sweet,
And theirs are bestial, hold him less than man;   180
And there be those who deem him more than man,
And dream he dropt from heaven. But my belief
In all this matter—so ye care to learn—
Sir, for ye know that in King Uther's time
The prince and warrior Gorloïs, he that held   185
Tintagil castle by the Cornish sea,
Was wedded with a winsome wife, Ygerne.
And daughters had she borne him,—one whereof,
Lot's wife, the Queen of Orkney,[9] Bellicent,
Hath ever like a loyal sister cleaved   190
To Arthur,—but a son she had not borne.
And Uther cast upon her eyes of love;

9. A kingdom in northeast Scotland.

But she, a stainless wife to Gorloïs,
So loathed the bright dishonor of his love
That Gorloïs and King Uther went to war,   195
And overthrown was Gorloïs and slain.
Then Uther in his wrath and heat beseiged
Ygerne within Tintagil, where her men,
Seeing the mighty swarm about their walls,
Left her and fled, and Uther enter'd in,   200
And there was none to call to but himself.
So, compass'd by the power of the king,
Enforced she was to wed him in her tears,
And with a shameful swiftness; afterward
Not many moons, King Uther died himself,   205
Moaning and wailing for an heir to rule
After him, lest the realm should go to wrack.
And that same night, the night of the new year,
By reason of the bitterness and grief
That vext his mother, all before his time   210
Was Arthur born, and all as soon as born
Deliver'd at a secret postern-gate
To Merlin, to be holden far apart
Until his hour should come, because the lords
Of that fierce day were as the lords of this,   215
Wild beasts, and surely would have torn the child
Piecemeal among them, had they known; for each
But sought to rule for his own self and hand,
And many hated Uther for the sake
Of Gorloïs. Wherefore Merlin took the child,   220
And gave him to Sir Anton, an old knight
And ancient friend of Uther; and his wife
Nursed the young prince, and rear'd him with her own;
And no man knew. And ever since the lords
Have foughten like wild beasts among themselves,   225
So that the realm has gone to wrack; but now,
This year, when Merlin—for his hour had come—
Brought Arthur forth, and set him in the hall,
Proclaiming, 'Here is Uther's heir, your king,'
A hundred voices cried: 'Away with him!   230
No king of ours! a son of Gorloïs he,
Or else the child of Anton, and no king,
Or else baseborn.' Yet Merlin thro' his craft,
And while the people clamor'd for a king,
Had Arthur crown'd; but after, the great lords   235
Banded, and so brake out in open war.''

Then while the king debated with himself
If Arthur were the child of shamefulness,
Or born the son of Gorloïs after death,
Or Uther's son and born before his time.   240
Or whether there were truth in anything

Said by these three, there came to Cameliard,
With Gawain and young Modred, her two sons,
Lot's wife, the Queen of Orkney, Bellicent;
Whom as he could, not as he would, the king   245
Made feast for, saying, as they sat at meat:
"A doubtful throne is ice on summer seas.
Ye come from Arthur's court. Victor his men
Report him! Yea, but ye—think ye this king—
So many those that hate him, and so strong,   250
So few his knights, however brave they be—
Hath body enow to hold his foemen down?"

     "O King," she cried, "and I will tell thee: few,
Few, but all brave, all of one mind with him;
For I was near him when the savage yells   255
Of Uther's peerage died, and Arthur sat
Crowned on the daïs, and his warriors cried,
'Be thou the king, and we will work thy will
Who love thee.' Then the King in low deep tones,
And simple words of great authority,   260
Bound them by so strait vows to his own self
That when they rose, knighted from kneeling, some
Were pale as at the passing of a ghost,
Some flush'd, and others dazed, as one who wakes
Half-blinded at the coming of a light.   265

     "But when he spake, and cheer'd his Table Round
With large, divine, and comfortable words,
Beyond my tongue to tell thee—I beheld
From eye to eye thro' all their Order flash
A momentary likeness of the King;   270
And ere it left their faces, thro' the cross
And those around it and the Crucified,
Down from the casement over Arthur smote
Flame-color, vert, and azure, in three rays,
One falling upon each of three fair queens[1]   275
Who stood in silence near his throne, the friends
Of Arthur, gazing on him, tall, with bright
Sweet faces, who will help him at his need.

     "And there I saw mage Merlin, whose vast wit
And hundred winters are but as the hands   280
Of loyal vassals toiling for their liege.

     "And near him stood the Lady of the Lake,[2]
Who knows a subtler magic than his own—
Clothed in white samite, mystic, wonderful.

1. They may represent Faith, Hope, and Charity. To those who offered that interpretation Tennyson responded: "They are right, and they are not right. They mean that and they do not. They are three of the noblest of women. They are also those three Graces, but they are much more. I hate to be tied down to say, '*This* means *that*' " (*Memoir*, II, 127). They reappear in "The Passing of Arthur," line 366.
2. She represents the Church.

She gave the King his huge cross-hilted sword,   285
Whereby to drive the heathen out. A mist
Of incense curl'd about her, and her face
Wellnigh was hidden in the minster gloom;
But there was heard among the holy hymns
A voice as of the waters, for she dwells   290
Down in a deep—calm, whatsoever storms
May shake the world—and when the surface rolls,
Hath power to walk the waters like our Lord.

"There likewise I beheld Excalibur
Before him at his crowning borne, the sword   295
That rose from out the bosom of the lake,
And Arthur row'd across and took it—rich
With jewels, elfin Urim,[3] on the hilt,
Bewildering heart and eye—the blade so bright
That men are blinded by it—on one side,   300
Graven in the oldest tongue of all this world,
'Take me,' but turn the blade and ye shall see,
And written in the speech ye speak yourself,
'Cast me away!' And sad was Arthur's face
Taking it, but old Merlin counsell'd him,   305
'Take thou and strike! the time to cast away
Is yet far-off.' So this great brand the king
Took, and by this will beat his foemen down."

Thereat Leodogran rejoiced, but thought
To sift his doubtings to the last, and ask'd,   310
Fixing full eyes of question on her face,
"The swallow and the swift are near akin,
But thou art closer to this noble prince,
Being his own dear sister;" and she said,
"Daughter of Gorloïs and Ygerne am I;"   315
"And therefore Arthur's sister?" ask'd the king.
She answer'd, "These be secret things," and sign'd
To those two sons to pass, and let them be.
And Gawain went, and breaking into song
Sprang out, and follow'd by his flying hair   320
Ran like a colt, and leapt at all he saw;
But Modred laid his ear beside the doors,
And there half-heard—the same that afterward
Struck for the throne, and striking found his doom.

And then the Queen made answer: "What know I?   325
For dark my mother was in eyes and hair,
And dark in hair and eyes am I; and dark
Was Gorloïs; yea, and dark was Uther too,
Wellnigh to blackness; but this king is fair
Beyond the race of Britons and of men.   330

3. Refers to precious stones, which the   of revelation. See *Exodus,* 28:30.
Jewish high priests took to be symbols

Moreover, always in my mind I hear
A cry from out the dawning of my life,
A mother weeping, and I hear her say,
'O that ye had some brother, pretty one,
To guard thee on the rough ways of the world.' "   335

"Ay," said the king, "and hear ye such a cry?
But when did Arthur chance upon thee first?"

"O King!" she cried, "and I will tell thee true.
He found me first when yet a little maid.
Beaten I had been for a little fault   340
Whereof I was not guilty; and out I ran
And flung myself down on a bank of heath,
And hated this fair world and all therein,
And wept, and wish'd that I were dead; and he—
I know not whether of himself he came,   345
Or brought by Merlin, who, they say, can walk
Unseen at pleasure—he was at my side,
And spake sweet words, and comforted my heart,
And dried my tears, being a child with me.
And many a time he came, and evermore   350
As I grew greater grew with me; and sad
At times he seem'd, and sad with him was I,
Stern too at times, and then I loved him not,
But sweet again, and then I loved him well.
And now of late I see him less and less,   355
But those first days had golden hours for me,
For then I surely thought he would be king.

"But let me tell thee now another tale:
For Bleys, our Merlin's master, as they say,
Died but of late, and sent his cry to me,   360
To hear him speak before he left his life.
Shrunk like a fairy changeling⁴ lay the mage;
And when I enter'd told me that himself
And Merlin ever served about the king,
Uther, before he died; and on the night   365
When Uther in Tintagil past away
Moaning and wailing for an heir, the two
Left the still king, and passing forth to breathe,
Then from the castle gateway by the chasm
Descending thro' the dismal night—a night   370
In which the bounds of heaven and earth were lost—
Beheld, so high upon the dreary deeps
It seem'd in heaven, a ship, the shape thereof
A dragon wing'd, and all from stem to stern
Bright with a shining people on the decks,   375

4. The elves the fairies substituted for the human children they stole could supposedly be recognized by their shriv- elled appearance. "Mage" is an archaic form of *Magus*, "a magician."

And gone as soon as seen. And then the two
Dropt to the cove, and watch'd the great sea fall,
Wave after wave, each mightier than the last,
Till last, a ninth one,[5] gathering half the deep
And full of voices, slowly rose and plunged   380
Roaring, and all the wave was in a flame;
And down the wave and in the flame was borne
A naked babe, and rode to Merlin's feet,
Who stoopt and caught the babe, and cried, 'The King!
Here is an heir for Uther!' And the fringe   385
Of that great breaker, sweeping up the strand,
Lash'd at the wizard as he spake the word,
And all at once all round him rose in fire,
So that the child and he were clothed in fire.
And presently thereafter follow'd calm,   390
Free sky and stars. 'And this same child,' he said,
'Is he who reigns; nor could I part in peace
Till this were told.' And saying this the seer
Went thro' the strait and dreadful pass of death,
Not ever to be question'd any more   395
Save on the further side; but when I met
Merlin, and ask'd him if these things were truth—
The shining dragon and the naked child
Descending in the glory of the seas—
He laugh'd as is his wont, and answer'd me   400
In riddling triplets of old time, and said:—

    " 'Rain, rain, and sun! a rainbow in the sky!
A young man will be wiser by and by;
An old man's wit may wander ere he die.

    " 'Rain, rain, and sun! a rainbow on the lea![6]   405
And truth is this to me, and that to thee;
And truth or clothed or naked let it be.

    " 'Rain, sun, and rain! and the free blossom blows;
Sun, rain, and sun! and where is he who knows?
From the great deep to the great deep he goes.'   410

    "So Merlin riddling anger'd me; but thou
Fear not to give this King thine only child,
Guinevere; so great bards of him will sing
Hereafter, and dark sayings from of old
Ranging and ringing thro' the minds of men,   415
And echo'd by old folk beside their fires
For comfort after their wage-work is done,
Speak of the King; and Merlin in our time
Hath spoken also, not in jest, and sworn
Tho' men may wound him that he will not die,   420

5. In Welsh folklore the ninth wave is thought to be larger than its predecessors.

6. The two rainbows may respectively be taken to reveal spiritual and earthly truth.

But pass, again to come, and then or now
Utterly smite the heathen underfoot,
Till these and all men hail him for their king."

She spake and King Leodogran rejoiced,
But musing "Shall I answer yea or nay?"   425
Doubted, and drowsed, nodded and slept, and saw,
Dreaming, a slope of land that ever grew,
Field after field, up to a height, the peak
Haze-hidden, and thereon a phantom king,
Now looming, and now lost; and on the slope   430
The sword rose, the hind fell, the herd was driven,
Fire glimpsed; and all the land from roof and rick,
In drifts of smoke before a rolling wind,
Stream'd to the peak, and mingled with the haze
And made it thicker; while the phantom king   435
Sent out at times a voice; and here or there
Stood one who pointed toward the voice, the rest
Slew on and burnt, crying, "No king of ours,
No son of Uther, and no king of ours;"
Till with a wink his dream was changed, the haze   440
Descended, and the solid earth became
As nothing, but the King stood out in heaven,
Crown'd. And Leodogran awoke, and sent
Ulfius, and Brastias, and Bedivere,
Back to the court of Arthur answering yea.   445

Then Arthur charged his warrior whom he loved
And honor'd most, Sir Lancelot, to ride forth
And bring the Queen, and watch'd him from the gates;
And Lancelot past away among the flowers—
For then was latter April—and return'd   450
Among the flowers, in May, with Guinevere.
To whom arrived, by Dubric the high saint,
Chief of the church in Britain, and before
The stateliest of her altar-shrines, the King
That morn was married, while in stainless white,   455
The fair beginners of a nobler time,[7]
And glorying in their vows and him, his knights
Stood round him, and rejoicing in his joy.
Far shone the fields of May thro' open door,
The sacred altar blossom'd white with May,   460
The sun of May descended on their King,
They gazed on all earth's beauty in their Queen,
Roll'd incense, and there past along the hymns

7. Throughout the *Idylls* Tennyson does attempt to preserve a consistency of color symbolism and seasonal motif. As he noted, "The Coming of Arthur is on the night of the New Year [i.e., spring]; when he is wedded 'the world is white with May'; on a summer night the vision of the Holy Grail appears; and the 'Last Tournament' is in the 'yellowing autumntide.' Guinevere flees thro' the mists of autumn, and Arthur's death takes place at midnight in mid-winter" (*Memoir*, II, 133).

A voice as of the waters, while the two
Sware at the shrine of Christ a deathless love.   465
And Arthur said, "Behold, thy doom is mine.
Let chance what will, I love thee to the death!"
To whom the Queen replied with drooping eyes,
"King and my lord, I love thee to the death!"
And holy Dubric spread his hands and spake: 470
"Reign ye, and live and love, and make the world
Other, and may thy Queen be one with thee,
And all this Order of thy Table Round
Fulfil the boundless purpose of their King!"[8]

So Dubric said; but when they left the shrine   475
Great lords from Rome before the portal stood,
In scornful stillness gazing as they past;
Then while they paced a city all on fire
With sun and cloth of gold, the trumpets blew,
And Arthur's knighthood sang before the King:—   480

"Blow trumpet, for the world is white with May!
Blow trumpet, the long night hath roll'd away!
Blow thro' the living world—'Let the King reign!'

"Shall Rome or Heathen rule in Arthur's realm?
Flash brand and lance, fall battle-axe upon helm,   485
Fall battle-axe, and flash brand! Let the King reign!

"Strike for the King and live! his knights have heard
That God hath told the King a secret word.
Fall battle-axe, and flash brand! Let the King reign!

"Blow trumpet! he will lift us from the dust.   490
Blow trumpet! live the strength, and die the lust!
Clang battle-axe, and clash brand! Let the King reign!

"Strike for the King and die! and if thou diest,
The King is king, and ever wills the highest.
Clang battle-axe, and clash brand! Let the King reign!   495

"Blow, for our Sun is mighty in his May!
Blow, for our Sun is mightier day by day!
Clang battle-axe, and clash brand! Let the King reign!

"The King will follow Christ, and we the King,
In whom high God hath breathed a secret thing.   500
Fall battle-axe, and clash brand! Let the King reign!"

So sang the knighthood, moving to their hall.
There at the banquet those great lords from Rome,

---

8. The question of the King's reality, as that of any ideal, is met with increasing skepticism in the later idylls as the dissolution of the Order approaches. Leodogran's acknowledgment of the King, in what amounts to the acceptance of divine revelation, signifies the health of the society in its early stages. Tennyson said he meant the King to be "mystic and no mere British Prince" (quoted in Buckley's *Tennyson*, p. 176). But one of the faults often found with the *Idylls* is that Tennyson stressed "ideal manhood" at the expense of developing the King's human qualities.

The slowly-fading mistress of the world,
Strode in and claim'd their tribute as of yore.   505
But Arthur spake: "Behold, for these have sworn
To wage my wars, and worship me their King;
The old order changeth, yielding place to new,
And we that fight for our fair father Christ,
Seeing that ye be grown too weak and old   510
To drive the heathen from your Roman wall,
No tribute will we pay." So those great lords
Drew back in wrath, and Arthur strove with Rome.

    And Arthur and his knighthood for a space
Were all one will, and thro' that strength the King   515
Drew in the petty princedoms under him,
Fought, and in twelve great battles overcame
The heathen hordes, and made a realm and reign'd.

1869

Following "The Coming of Arthur" are three idylls, "Gareth and Lynette," "The Marriage of Geraint," and "Geraint and Enid," in which the poet's purpose is to show how hardships and obstacles may be overcome while the founding principles of the Order are fresh and believable. In the first, Gareth, the youngest son of Bellicent, is eager to set forth for Camelot to seek his fame and fortune. To prove his knighthood, Arthur assigns him a quest. Into a land green with promise, he sets out with Lynette as guide to free her sister imprisoned in the Castle Perilous. Lynette, bitter at having the task entrusted to an untried youth, is more difficult to win than the several battles, but knight and lady are finally united. In the second and third idylls, roles are reversed. Geraint, through a series of adventures in which the obstacles are far more formidable than those Gareth encountered, first wins Enid and then, in the next idyll, tests his blameless wife's fidelity in every conceivable manner. Like Spenser's Red Cross Knight, Geraint is besieged with self-doubts, and the wastelands he must traverse are as much a psychological condition within himself. Many readers, with some justification, have found the two Geraint idylls tediously drawn out, but they do manage to stress the viability of the Order while it strives to maintain its ideals.

"Geraint and Enid" is the last idyll to end happily, and it concludes what can be conveniently thought of as a tripartite division of the poem into sets of four idylls. In the middle group, seeds of discontent have been sown; rumors of Guinevere's adulterous relationship with Lancelot are generally bruited about. The sequence begins with "Balin and Balan." The idyll opens on a note of discord, and the leisurely pace of the Geraint idylls gives way to a relentless rush of events which bring two brother knights to their deaths. Their identities hidden, the two brothers slay each other in an argument over the Queen's faithfulness, "brainless bulls/Dead for one heifer," as Vivien cynically puts it. "Merlin and Vivien" follows and carries the process of disintegration closer to the center of Arthur's court. In the allegorical scheme, intellect, wisdom, and age prove unable to resist the sensuality personified by Vivien. [Editor's note.]

Merlin and Vivien

A storm was coming, but the winds were still,
And in the wild woods of Broceliande,[9]
Before an oak, so hollow, huge, and old
It look'd a tower of ivied masonwork,
At Merlin's feet the wily Vivien lay.   5

    For he that always bare in bitter grudge[1]
The slights of Arthur and his Table, Mark
The Cornish King, had heard a wandering voice,
A minstrel of Caerleon[2] by strong storm
Blown into shelter at Tintagil, say   10
That out of naked knight-like purity
Sir Lancelot worshipt no unmarried girl,
But the great Queen herself, fought in her name,
Sware by her—vows like theirs that high in heaven
Love most, but neither marry nor are given   15
In marriage, angels of our Lord's report.

    He ceased, and then—for Vivien sweetly said—
She sat beside the banquet nearest Mark,—
"And is the fair example follow'd, sir,
In Arthur's household?"—answer'd innocently: 20

    "Ay, by some few—ay, truly—youths that hold
It more beseems the perfect virgin knight
To worship woman as true wife beyond
All hopes of gaining, than as maiden girl.
They place their pride in Lancelot and the Queen.   25
So passionate for an utter purity
Beyond the limit of their bond are these,
For Arthur bound them not to singleness.
Brave hearts and clean! and yet—God guide them!—young."

    Then Mark was half in heart to hurl his cup   30
Straight at the speaker, but forbore. He rose
To leave the hall, and, Vivien following him,
Turn'd to her: "Here are snakes within the grass;
And you methinks, O Vivien, save ye fear
The monkish manhood, and the mask of pure   35
Worn by this court, can stir them till they sting."

---

9. A forest in Brittany.
1. Lines 6–147 were added in 1874.

2. In Monmouthshire, in Wales, where Arthur frequently held court.

And Vivien answer'd, smiling scornfully:
"Why fear? because that foster'd at *thy* court
I savor of thy—virtues? fear them? no,
As love, if love be perfect, casts out fear,   40
So hate, if hate be perfect, casts out fear.
My father died in battle against the King,
My mother on his corpse in open field;
She bore me there, for born from death was I
Among the dead and sown upon the wind—   45
And then on thee! and shown the truth betimes,
That old true filth, and bottom of the well,
Where Truth is hidden. Gracious lessons thine,
And maxims of the mud! 'This Arthur pure!
Great Nature thro' the flesh herself hath made   50
Gives him the lie! There is no being pure,
My Cherub; saith not Holy Writ[3] the same?'—
If I were Arthur, I would have thy blood.
Thy blessing, stainless King! I bring thee back,
When I have ferreted out their burrowings,   55
The hearts of all this Order in mine hand—
Ay—so that fate and craft and folly close,
Perchance, one curl of Arthur's golden beard.
To me this narrow grizzled fork of thine
Is cleaner-fashion'd—Well, I loved thee first;   60
That warps the wit."

        Loud laugh'd the graceless Mark.
But Vivien, into Camelot stealing, lodged
Low in the city, and on a festal day
When Guinevere was crossing the great hall
Cast herself down, knelt to the Queen, and wail'd.   65

    "Why kneel ye there? What evil have ye wrought?
Rise!" and the damsel bidden rise arose
And stood with folded hands and downward eyes
Of glancing corner and all meekly said:
"None wrought, but suffer'd much, an orphan maid!   70
My father died in battle for thy King,
My mother on his corpse—in open field,
The sad sea-sounding wastes of Lyonnesse—
Poor wretch—no friend!—and now by Mark the king,
For that small charm of feature mine, pursued—   75
If any such be mine—I fly to thee.
Save, save me thou! Woman of women—thine
The wreath of beauty, thine the crown of power,
Be thine the balm of pity, O heaven's own white
Earth-angel, stainless bride of stainless King—   80
Help, for he follows! take me to thyself!
O yield me shelter for mine innocency
Among thy maidens!"

3. "How then can man be righteous   of woman be clean?" (*Job*, 25:4).
before God? How can he who is born

Here her slow sweet eyes
Fear-tremulous, but humbly hopeful, rose
Fixt on her hearer's, while the Queen who stood   85
All glittering like May sunshine on May leaves
In green and gold, and plumed with green replied:
"Peace, child! of over-praise and over-blame
We choose the last. Our noble Arthur, him
Ye scarce can overpraise, will hear and know.   90
Nay—we believe all evil of thy Mark—
Well, we shall test thee farther; but this hour
We ride a-hawking with Sir Lancelot.
He hath given us a fair falcon which he train'd;
We go to prove it. Bide ye here the while."   95

    She past; and Vivien murmur'd after, "Go!
I bide the while." Then thro' the portal-arch
Peering askance, and muttering brokenwise,
As one that labors with an evil dream,
Beheld the Queen and Lancelot get to horse.   100

    "Is that the Lancelot? goodly—ay, but gaunt;
Courteous—amends for gauntness—takes her hand—
That glance of theirs, but for the street, had been
A clinging kiss—how hand lingers in hand!
Let go at last!—they ride away—to hawk   105
For waterfowl. Royaller game is mine.
For such a supersensual sensual bond
As that gray cricket[4] chirpt of at our hearth—
Touch flax with flame—a glance will serve—the liars!
Ah little rat that borest in the dyke   110
Thy hole by night to let the boundless deep
Down upon far-off cities while they dance—
Or dream—of thee they dream'd not—nor of me
These—ay, but each of either; ride, and dream
The mortal dream that never yet was mine—   115
Ride, ride and dream until ye wake—to me!
Then, narrow court and lubber King, farewell!
For Lancelot will be gracious to the rat,
And our wise Queen, if knowing that I know,
Will hate, loathe, fear—but honor me the more."   120

    Yet while they rode together down the plain,
Their talk was all of training, terms of art,
Diet and seeling,[5] jesses, leash and lure.
"She is too noble," he said, "to check at pies,[6]
Nor will she rake:[7] there is no baseness in her."   125
Here when the Queen demanded as by chance,

4. The "minstrel of Caerleon," line 9.
5. Part of the taming process of a
young hawk, in which its eyelids are
partly stitched together; "jesses" are

straps of leather attached to the legs.
6. Fly at magpies instead of pursuing
the game bird.
7. Fly off at other unintended game.

"Know ye the stranger woman?" "Let her be,"
Said Lancelot, and unhooded casting off
The goodly falcon free; she tower'd;[8] her bells,
Tone under tone, shrill'd; and they lifted up 130
Their eager faces, wondering at the strength,
Boldness, and royal knighthood of the bird,
Who pounced her quarry and slew it. Many a time
As once—of old—among the flowers—they rode.

But Vivien half-forgotten of the Queen 135
Among her damsels broidering sat, heard, watch'd,
And whisper'd. Thro' the peaceful court she crept
And whisper'd; then, as Arthur in the highest
Leaven'd the world, so Vivien in the lowest,
Arriving at a time of golden rest, 140
And sowing one ill hint from ear to ear,
While all the heathen lay at Arthur's feet,
And no quest came, but all was joust and play,
Leaven'd his hall. They heard and let her be.

Thereafter, as an enemy that has left 145
Death in the living waters[9] and withdrawn,
The wily Vivien stole from Arthur's court.

She hated all the knights, and heard in thought
Their lavish comment when her name was named.
For once, when Arthur walking all alone, 150
Vext at a rumor issued from herself
Of some corruption crept among his knights,
Had met her, Vivien, being greeted fair,
Would fain have wrought upon his cloudy mood
With reverent eyes mock-loyal, shaken voice, 155
And flutter'd adoration, and at last
With dark sweet hints of some who prized him more
Than who should prize him most; at which the King
Had gazed upon her blankly and gone by.
But one had watch'd, and had not held his peace; 160
It made the laughter of an afternoon
That Vivien should attempt the blameless King.
And after that, she set herself to gain
Him, the most famous man of all those times,
Merlin, who knew the range of all their arts, 165
Had built the King his havens, ships, and halls,
Was also bard, and knew the starry heavens;
The people call'd him wizard; whom at first
She play'd about with slight and sprightly talk,
And vivid smiles, and faintly-venom'd points 170
Of slander, glancing here and grazing there;
And yielding to his kindlier moods, the seer
Would watch her at her petulance and play,

8. Soared.   9. I.e., poisoned wells or springs.

Even when they seem'd unlovable, and laugh
As those that watch a kitten. Thus he grew   175
Tolerant of what he half disdain'd, and she,
Perceiving that she was but half disdain'd,
Began to break her sports with graver fits,
Turn red or pale, would often when they met
Sigh fully, or all-silent gaze upon him   180
With such a fixt devotion that the old man,
Tho' doubtful, felt the flattery, and at times
Would flatter his own wish in age for love,
And half believe her true; for thus at times
He waver'd, but that other clung to him,   185
Fixt in her will, and so the seasons went.

  Then fell on Merlin a great melancholy;
He walk'd with dreams and darkness, and he found
A doom that ever poised itself to fall,
An ever-moaning battle in the mist,   190
World-war of dying flesh against the life,
Death in all life and lying in all love,
The meanest having power upon the highest,
And the high purpose broken by the worm.[1]

  So leaving Arthur's court he gain'd the beach,   195
There found a little boat and stept into it;
And Vivien follow'd, but he mark'd her not.
She took the helm and he the sail; the boat
Drave with a sudden wind across the deeps,
And, touching Breton sands, they disembark'd.   200
And then she follow'd Merlin all the way,
Even to the wild woods of Broceliande.
For Merlin once had told her of a charm,
The which if any wrought on any one
With woven paces and with waving arms,   205
The man so wrought on ever seem'd to lie
Closed in the four walls of a hollow tower,
From which was no escape for evermore;
And none could find that man for evermore,
Nor could he see but him who wrought the charm   210
Coming and going, and he lay as dead
And lost to life and use and name and fame.
And Vivien ever sought to work the charm
Upon the great enchanter of the time,

---

1. Lines 188–198 were added in 1873. A premonition of the last great battle in the west, they are an obvious attempt at making a link between idylls. Here, and often in the later idylls, Tennyson's notion of the final catastrophe, along with his cyclical view of history, remind us of Yeats. "The meanest having power upon the highest," a condition dramatized fully in the ironic ceremony of innocence in "The Last Tournament," finds a parallel expression in Yeats's "The Second Coming": "Everywhere/ The ceremony of innocence is drowned; / The best lack all conviction, while the worst/ Are full of passionate intensity."

As fancying that her glory would be great   215
According to his greatness whom she quench'd.

    There lay she all her length and kiss'd his feet,
As if in deepest reverence and in love.
A twist of gold was round her hair; a robe
Of samite without price, that more exprest   220
Than hid her, clung about her lissome limbs,
In color like the satin-shining palm
On sallows in the windy gleams of March.
And while she kiss'd them, crying, "Trample me,
Dear feet, that I have follow'd thro' the world,   225
And I will pay you worship; tread me down
And I will kiss you for it;" he was mute.
So dark a forethought roll'd about his brain,
As on a dull day in an ocean cave
The blind wave feeling round his long sea-hall   23c
In silence; wherefore, when she lifted up
A face of sad appeal, and spake and said,
"O Merlin, do ye love me?" and again,
"O Merlin, do ye love me?" and once more,
"Great Master, do ye love me?" he was mute.   235
And lissome Vivien, holding by his heel,
Writhed toward him, slided up his knee and sat,
Behind his ankle twined her hollow feet
Together, curved an arm about his neck,
Clung like a snake;[2] and letting her left hand   240
Droop from his mighty shoulder, as a leaf,
Made with her right a comb of pearl to part
The lists of such a beard as youth gone out
Had left in ashes. Then he spoke and said,
Not looking at her, "Who are wise in love   245
Love most, say least," and Vivien answer'd quick:
"I saw the little elf-god eyeless once
In Arthur's arras hall at Camelot;
But neither eyes nor tongue—O stupid child!
Yet you are wise who say it; let me think   250
Silence is wisdom. I am silent then,
And ask no kiss;" then adding all at once,
"And lo, I clothe myself with wisdom," drew
The vast and shaggy mantle of his beard
Across her neck and bosom to her knee,   255
And call'd herself a gilded summer fly
Caught in a great old tyrant spider's web,

2. It was such passages as this which prompted Swinburne of all people to say the theme of the *Idylls* was "rather a case for the divorce-court than for poetry." He particularly objected to this idyll: "The Vivien of Mr. Tennyson's idyl seems to me, to speak frankly, about the most base and repulsive person ever set forth in serious literature. . . . It is the utterly ignoble quality of Vivien which makes her so unspeakably repulsive and unfit for artistic treatment."

Who meant to eat her up in that wild wood
Without one word. So Vivien call'd herself,
But rather seem'd a lovely baleful star   260
Veil'd in gray vapor; till he sadly smiled:
"To what request for what strange boon," he said,
"Are these your pretty tricks and fooleries,
O Vivien, the preamble? yet my thanks,
For these have broken up my melancholy."   265

    And Vivien answer'd smiling saucily:
"What, O my Master, have ye found your voice?
I bid the stranger welcome. Thanks at last!
But yesterday you never open'd lip,
Except indeed to drink. No cup had we;   270
In mine own lady palms I cull'd the spring
That gather'd trickling dropwise from the cleft,
And made a pretty cup of both my hands
And offer'd you it kneeling. Then you drank
And knew no more, nor gave me one poor word;   275
O, no more thanks than might a goat have given
With no more sign of reverence than a beard.
And when we halted at that other well,
And I was faint to swooning, and you lay
Foot-gilt with all the blossom-dust of those   280
Deep meadows we had traversed, did you know
That Vivien bathed your feet before her own?
And yet no thanks; and all thro' this wild wood
And all this morning when I fondled you.
Boon, ay, there was a boon, one not so strange—   285
How had I wrong'd you? surely ye are wise,
But such a silence is more wise than kind."

    And Merlin lock'd his hand in hers and said:
"O, did ye never lie upon the shore,
And watch the curl'd white of the coming wave   290
Glass'd in the slippery sand before it breaks?
Even such a wave, but not so pleasurable,
Dark in the glass of some presageful mood,
Had I for three days seen, ready to fall.
And then I rose and fled from Arthur's court   295
To break the mood. You follow'd me unask'd;
And when I look'd, and saw you following still,
My mind involved yourself the nearest thing
In that mind-mist—for shall I tell you truth?
You seem'd that wave about to break upon me   300
And sweep me from my hold upon the world,
My use and name and fame. Your pardon, child.
Your pretty sports have brighten'd all again.
And ask your boon, for boon I owe you thrice,
Once for wrong done you by confusion, next   305

For thanks it seems till now neglected, last
For these your dainty gambols; wherefore ask,
And take this boon so strange and not so strange."

    And Vivien answer'd smiling mournfully:
"O, not so strange as my long asking it,   310
Not yet so strange as you yourself are strange,
Nor half so strange as that dark mood of yours.
I ever fear'd ye were not wholly mine;
And see, yourself have own'd ye did me wrong.
The people call you prophet; let it be;   315
But not of those that can expound themselves.
Take Vivien for expounder; she will call
That three-days-long presageful gloom of yours
No presage, but the same mistrustful mood
That makes you seem less noble than yourself,   320
Whenever I have ask'd this very boon,
Now ask'd again; for see you not, dear love,
That such a mood as that which lately gloom'd
Your fancy when ye saw me following you
Must make me fear still more you are not mine,   325
Must make me yearn still more to prove you mine,
And make me wish still more to learn this charm
Of woven paces and of waving hands,
As proof of trust. O Merlin, teach it me!
The charm so taught will charm us both to rest.   330
For, grant me some slight power upon your fate,
I, feeling that you felt me worthy trust,
Should rest and let you rest, knowing you mine.
And therefore be as great as ye are named,
Not muffled round with selfish reticence.   335
How hard you look and how denyingly!
O, if you think this wickedness in me,
That I should prove it on you unawares,
That makes me passing wrathful; then our bond
Had best be loosed for ever; but think or not, 340
By Heaven that hears, I tell you the clean truth,
As clean as blood of babes, as white as milk!
O Merlin, may this earth, if ever I,
If these unwitty wandering wits of mine,
Even in the jumbled rubbish of a dream,   345
Have tript on such conjectural treachery—
May this hard earth cleave to the nadir hell
Down, down, and close again and nip me flat,
If I be such a traitress! Yield my boon,
Till which I scarce can yield you all I am;   350
And grant my re-reiterated wish,
The great proof of your love; because I think,
However wise, ye hardly know me yet."

And Merlin loosed his hand from hers and said:
"I never was less wise, however wise,   355
Too curious Vivien, tho' you talk of trust,
Than when I told you first of such a charm.
Yea, if ye talk of trust I tell you this,
Too much I trusted when I told you that,
And stirr'd this vice in you which ruin'd man   360
Thro' woman the first hour; for howsoe'er
In children a great curiousness be well,
Who have to learn themselves and all the world,
In you, that are no child, for still I find
Your face is practised when I spell the lines,   365
I call it,—well, I will not call it vice;
But since you name yourself the summer fly,
I well could wish a cobweb for the gnat
That settles beaten back, and beaten back
Settles, till one could yield for weariness.   370
But since I will not yield to give you power
Upon my life and use and name and fame,
Why will ye never ask some other boon?
Yea, by God's rood, I trusted you too much!"

And Vivien, like the tenderest-hearted maid   375
That ever bided tryst at village stile,
Made answer, either eyelid wet with tears:
"Nay, Master, be not wrathful with your maid;
Caress her, let her feel herself forgiven
Who feels no heart to ask another boon.   380
I think ye hardly know the tender rhyme
Of 'trust me not at all or all in all.'
I heard the great Sir Lancelot sing it once,
And it shall answer for me. Listen to it.

     " 'In love, if love be love, if love be ours,   385
    Faith and unfaith can ne'er be equal powers:
    Unfaith in aught is want of faith in all.

     " 'It is the little rift within the lute,
    That by and by will make the music mute,
    And ever widening slowly silence all.   390

     " 'The little rift within the lover's lute,
    Or little pitted speck in garner'd fruit,
    That rotting inward slowly moulders all.

     " 'It is not worth the keeping; let it go:
    But shall it? answer, darling, answer, no.   395
    And trust me not at all or all in all.'

"O master, do ye love my tender rhyme?"

And Merlin look'd and half believed her true,
So tender was her voice, so fair her face,
So sweetly gleam'd her eyes behind her tears   400

Like sunlight on the plain behind a shower;
And yet he answer'd half indignantly:

"Far other was the song[3] that once I heard
By this huge oak, sung nearly where we sit;
For here we met, some ten or twelve of us,   405
To chase a creature that was current then
In these wild woods, the hart with golden horns.
It was the time when first the question rose
About the founding of a Table Round,
That was to be, for love of God and men   410
And noble deeds, the flower of all the world;
And each incited each to noble deeds.
And while we waited, one, the youngest of us,
We could not keep him silent, out he flash'd,
And into such a song, such fire for fame,   415
Such trumpet-blowings in it, coming down
To such a stern and iron-clashing close,
That when he stopt we long'd to hurl together,
And should have done it, but the beauteous beast
Scared by the noise upstarted at our feet,   420
And like a silver shadow slipt away
Thro' the dim land. And all day long we rode
Thro' the dim land against a rushing wind,
That glorious roundel echoing in our ears,
And chased the flashes of his golden horns   425
Until they vanish'd by the fairy well
That laughs at iron—as our warriors did—
Where children cast their pins and nails, and cry,
'Laugh, little well!' but touch it with a sword,
It buzzes fiercely round the point; and there   430
We lost him—such a noble song was that.
But, Vivien, when you sang me that sweet rhyme,
I felt as tho' you knew this cursed charm,
Were proving it on me, and that I lay
And felt them slowly ebbing, name and fame."   435

And Vivien answer'd smiling mournfully:
"O, mine have ebb'd away for evermore,
And all thro' following you to this wild wood,
Because I saw you sad, to comfort you.
Lo now, what hearts have men! they never mount   440
As high as woman in her selfless mood.
And touching fame, howe'er ye scorn my song,
Take one verse more—the lady speaks it—this:

" 'My name, once mine, now thine, is closelier mine,
For fame, could fame be mine, that fame were thine,   445
And shame, could shame be thine, that shame were mine.
So trust me not at all or all in all.'

3. The "Blow trumpet" song in "The Coming of Arthur," lines 481 ff.

"Says she not well? and there is more—this rhyme
Is like the fair pearl-necklace of the Queen,
That burst in dancing and the pearls were spilt;   450
Some lost, some stolen, some as relics kept;
But nevermore the same two sister pearls
Ran down the silken thread to kiss each other
On her white neck—so is it with this rhyme.
It lives dispersedly in many hands,   455
And every minstrel sings it differently;
Yet is there one true line, the pearl of pearls:
'Man dreams of fame while woman wakes to love.'
Yea! love, tho' love were of the grossest, carves
A portion from the solid present, eats   460
And uses, careless of the rest; but fame,
The fame that follows death is nothing to us;
And what is fame in life but half-disfame
And counterchanged with darkness? ye yourself
Know well that envy calls you devil's son,   465
And since ye seem the master of all art,
They fain would make you master of all vice."

    And Merlin lock'd his hand in hers and said:
"I once was looking for a magic weed,
And found a fair young squire who sat alone,   470
Had carved himself a knightly shield of wood,
And then was painting on it fancied arms,
Azure, an eagle rising or, the sun
In dexter chief;[4] the scroll, 'I follow fame.'
And speaking not, but leaning over him,   475
I took his brush and blotted out the bird,
And made a gardener putting in a graff,
With this for motto, 'Rather use than fame.'
You should have seen him blush; but afterwards
He made a stalwart knight. O Vivien,   480
For you, methinks you think you love me well;
For me, I love you somewhat. Rest; and Love
Should have some rest and pleasure in himself,
Not ever be too curious for a boon,
Too prurient for a proof against the grain   485
Of him ye say ye love. But Fame with men,
Being but ampler means to serve mankind,
Should have small rest or pleasure in herself,
But work as vassal to the larger love
That dwarfs the petty love of one to one.   490
Use gave me fame at first, and fame again
Increasing gave me use. Lo, there my boon!
What other? for men sought to prove me vile,

4. A representation of a coat of arms on the upper part of the shield to the
bearer's right.

Because I fain had given them greater wits;
And then did envy call me devil's son. 495
The sick weak beast, seeking to help herself
By striking at her better, miss'd, and brought
Her own claw back, and wounded her own heart.
Sweet were the days when I was all unknown,
But when my name was lifted up the storm 500
Brake on the mountain and I cared not for it.
Right well know I that fame is half-disfame,
Yet needs must work my work. That other fame,
To one at least who hath not children vague,
The cackle of the unborn about the grave, 505
I cared not for it. A single misty star,[5]
Which is the second in a line of stars
That seem a sword beneath a belt of three,
I never gazed upon it but I dreamt
Of some vast charm concluded in that star 510
To make fame nothing. Wherefore, if I fear,
Giving you power upon me thro' this charm,
That you might play me falsely, having power,
However well ye think ye love me now—
As sons of kings loving in pupilage 515
Have turn'd to tyrants when they came to power—
I rather dread the loss of use than fame;
If you—and not so much from wickedness,
As some wild turn of anger, or a mood
Of overstrain'd affection, it may be, 520
To keep me all to your own self,—or else
A sudden spurt of woman's jealousy,—
Should try this charm on whom ye say ye love."

And Vivien answer'd smiling as in wrath:
"Have I not sworn? I am not trusted. Good! 525
Well, hide it, hide it; I shall find it out,
And being found take heed of Vivien.
A woman and not trusted, doubtless I
Might feel some sudden turn of anger born
Of your misfaith; and your fine epithet 530
Is accurate too, for this full love of mine
Without the full heart back may merit well
Your term of overstrain'd. So used as I,
My daily wonder is, I love at all.
And as to woman's jealousy, O, why not? 535
O, to what end, except a jealous one,
And one to make me jealous if I love,
Was this fair charm invented by yourself?

5. "When this was written," Tennyson noted, "some astronomers fancied that this nebula in Orion was the vastest object in the universe—a firmament of suns too far away to be resolved into stars by the telescope, and yet so huge as to be seen by the naked eye."

I well believe that all about this world
Ye cage a buxom captive here and there,   540
Closed in the four walls of a hollow tower
From which is no escape for evermore."

    Then the great master merrily answer'd her:
"Full many a love in loving youth was mine;
I needed then no charm to keep them mine   545
But youth and love; and that full heart of yours
Whereof ye prattle, may now assure you mine;
So live uncharm'd. For those who wrought it first,
The wrist is parted from the hand that waved,
The feet unmortised from their anklebones   550
Who paced it, ages back—but will ye hear
The legend as in guerdon for your rhyme?

    "There lived a king in the most eastern East,
Less old than I, yet older, for my blood
Hath earnest in it of far springs to be.   555
A tawny pirate anchor'd in his port,
Whose bark had plunder'd twenty nameless isles;
And passing one, at the high peep of dawn,
He saw two cities in a thousand boats
All fighting for a woman on the sea.   560
And pushing his black craft among them all,
He lightly scatter'd theirs and brought her off,
With loss of half his people arrow-slain;
A maid so smooth, so white, so wonderful,
They said a light came from her when she moved.   565
And since the pirate would not yield her up,
The king impaled him for his piracy,
Then made her queen. But those isle-nurtured eyes
Waged such unwilling tho' successful war
On all the youth, they sicken'd; councils thinn'd,   570
And armies waned, for magnet-like she drew
The rustiest iron of old fighters' hearts;
And beasts themselves would worship, camels knelt
Unbidden, and the brutes of mountain back
That carry kings in castles bow'd black knees   575
Of homage, ringing with their serpent hands,
To make her smile, her golden ankle-bells.
What wonder, being jealous, that he sent
His horns of proclamation out thro' all
The hundred under-kingdoms that he sway'd   580
To find a wizard who might teach the king
Some charm which, being wought upon the queen,
Might keep her all his own. To such a one
He promised more than ever king has given,
A league of mountain full of golden mines,   585
A province with a hundred miles of coast,

A palace and a princess, all for him;
But on all those who tried and fail'd the king
Pronounced a dismal sentence, meaning by it
To keep the list low and pretenders back, 590
Or, like a king, not to be trifled with—
Their heads should moulder on the city gates.
And many tried and fail'd, because the charm
Of nature in her overbore their own;
And many a wizard brow bleach'd on the walls, 595
And many weeks a troop of carrion crows
Hung like a cloud above the gateway towers."

And Vivien breaking in upon him, said:
"I sit and gather honey; yet, methinks,
Thy tongue has tript a little; ask thyself. 600
The lady never made *unwilling* war
With those fine eyes; she had her pleasure in it,
And made her good man jealous with good cause.
And lived there neither dame nor damsel then
Wroth at a lover's loss? were all as tame, 605
I mean, as noble, as their queen was fair?
Not one to flirt a venom at her eyes,
Or pinch a murderous dust into her drink,
Or make her paler with a poison'd rose?
Well, those were not our days—but did they find 610
A wizard? Tell me, was he like to thee?"

She ceased, and made her lithe arm round his neck
Tighten, and then drew back, and let her eyes
Speak for her, glowing on him, like a bride's
On her new lord, her own, the first of men. 615

He answer'd laughing: "Nay, not like to me.
At last they found—his foragers for charms—
A little glassy-headed hairless man,
Who lived alone in a great wild on grass,
Read but one book, and ever reading grew 620
So grated down and filed away with thought,
So lean his eyes were monstrous; while the skin
Clung but to crate and basket, ribs and spine.
And since he kept his mind on one sole aim,
Nor ever touch'd fierce wine, nor tasted flesh, 625
Nor own'd a sensual wish, to him the wall
That sunders ghosts and shadow-casting men
Became a crystal, and he saw them thro' it,
And heard their voices talk behind the wall,
And learnt their elemental secrets, powers 630
And forces; often o'er the sun's bright eye
Drew the vast eyelid of an inky cloud,
And lash'd it at the base with slanting storm;
Or in the noon of mist and driving rain,

When the lake whiten'd and the pinewood roar'd,   635
And the cairn'd mountain was a shadow, sunn'd
The world to peace again. Here was the man;
And so by force they dragg'd him to the king.
And then he taught the king to charm the queen
In such-wise that no man could see her more,   640
Nor saw she save the king, who wrought the charm,
Coming and going, and she lay as dead,
And lost all use of life. But when the king
Made proffer of the league of golden mines,
The province with a hundred miles of coast,   645
The palace and the princess, that old man
Went back to his old wild, and lived on grass,
And vanish'd and his book came down to me."

    And Vivien answer'd smiling saucily:
"Ye have the book; the charm is written in it.   650
Good! take my counsel, let me know it at once;
For keep it like a puzzle chest in chest,
With each chest lock'd and padlock'd thirty-fold,
And whelm all this beneath as vast a mound
As after furious battle turfs the slain   655
On some wild down above the windy deep,
I yet should strike upon a sudden means
To dig, pick, open, find and read the charm;
Then, if I tried it, who should blame me then?"

    And smiling as a master smiles at one   660
That is not of his school, nor any school
But that where blind and naked Ignorance
Delivers brawling judgments, unashamed,
On all things all day long, he answer'd her:

    "Thou read the book, my pretty Vivien!   665
O, ay, it is but twenty pages long,
But every page having an ample marge,
And every marge enclosing in the midst
A square of text that looks a little blot,
The text no larger than the limbs of fleas;   670
And every square of text an awful charm,
Writ in a language that has long gone by,
So long that mountains have arisen since
With cities on their flanks—thou read the book!
And every margin scribbled, crost, and cramm'd   675
With comment, densest condensation, hard
To mind and eye; but the long sleepless nights
Of my long life have made it easy to me.
And none can read the text, not even I;
And none can read the comment but myself;   680
And in the comment did I find the charm.
O, the results are simple; a mere child

Might use it to the harm of any one,
And never could undo it. Ask no more;
For tho' you should not prove it upon me,   685
But keep that oath ye sware, ye might, perchance,
Assay it on some one of the Table Round,
And all because ye dream they babble of you."

And Vivien, frowning in true anger, said:
"What dare the full-fed liars say of me?   690
They ride abroad redressing human wrongs!
They sit with knife in meat and wine in horn.
They bound to holy vows of chastity!
Were I not woman, I could tell a tale.
But you are man, you well can understand   695
The shame that cannot be explain'd for shame.
Not one of all the drove should touch me—swine!"

Then answer'd Merlin careless of her words:
"You breathe but accusation vast and vague,
Spleen-born, I think, and proofless. If ye know,   700
Set up the charge ye know, to stand or fall!"

And Vivien answer'd frowning wrathfully:
"O, ay, what say ye to Sir Valence, him
Whose kinsman left him watcher o'er his wife
And two fair babes, and went to distant lands,   705
Was one year gone, and on returning found
Not two but three? there lay the reckling,[6] one
But one hour old! What said the happy sire?
A seven-months' babe had been a truer gift.
Those twelve sweet moons confused his fatherhood."   710

Then answer'd Merlin: "Nay, I know the tale.
Sir Valence wedded with an outland dame;
Some cause had kept him sunder'd from his wife.
One child they had; it lived with her; she died.
His kinsman travelling on his own affair   715
Was charged by Valence to bring home the child.
He brought, not found it therefore; take the truth."

"O, ay," said Vivien, "over-true a tale!
What say ye then to sweet Sir Sagramore,
That ardent man? 'To pluck the flower in season,'   720
So says the song, 'I trow it is no treason.'
O Master, shall we call him over-quick
To crop his own sweet rose before the hour?"

And Merlin answer'd: "Over-quick art thou
To catch a loathly plume fallen from the wing   725
Of that foul bird of rapine whose whole prey
Is man's good name. He never wrong'd his bride.

---

6. The runt in a litter of puppies, hence a weakling infant.

I know the tale. An angry gust of wind
Puff'd out his torch among the myriad-room'd
And many-corridor'd complexities   730
Of Arthur's palace. Then he found a door,
And darkling felt the sculptured ornament
That wreathen round it made it seem his own,
And wearied out made for the couch and slept,
A stainless man beside a stainless maid;   735
And either slept, nor knew of other there,
Till the high dawn piercing the royal rose
In Arthur's casement glimmer'd chastely down,
Blushing upon them blushing, and at once
He rose without a word and parted from her.   740
But when the thing was blazed about the court,
The brute world howling forced them into bonds,
And as it chanced they are happy, being pure."

   "O, ay," said Vivien, "that were likely too!
What say ye then to fair Sir Percivale   745
And of the horrid foulness that he wrought,
The saintly youth, the spotless lamb of Christ,
Or some black wether of Saint Satan's fold?
What, in the precincts of the chapel-yard,
Among the knightly brasses of the graves,   750
And by the cold Hic Jacets[7] of the dead!"

   And Merlin answer'd careless of her charge:
"A sober man is Percivale and pure,
But once in life was fluster'd with new wine,
Then paced for coolness in the chapel-yard,   755
Where one of Satan's shepherdesses caught
And meant to stamp him with her master's mark.
And that he sinn'd is not believable;
For, look upon his face!—but if he sinn'd,
The sin that practice burns into the blood,   760
And not the one dark hour which brings remorse,
Will brand us, after, of whose fold we be;
Or else were he, the holy king[8] whose hymns
Are chanted in the minster, worse than all.
But is your spleen froth'd out, or have ye more?"   765

   And Vivien answer'd frowning yet in wrath:
"O, ay; what say ye to Sir Lancelot, friend,
Traitor or true? that commerce with the Queen,
I ask you, is it clamor'd by the child,
Or whisper'd in the corner? do ye know it?"   770

   To which he answer'd sadly: "Yea, I know it.
Sir Lancelot went ambassador, at first,
To fetch her, and she watch'd him from her walls.

7. The "here lies" beginning the epi-   8. David.
taphs on tomb stones.

A rumor runs, she took him for the king,
So fixt her fancy on him; let them be.   775
But have ye no one word of loyal praise
For Arthur, blameless king and stainless man?"

　　She answer'd with a low and chuckling laugh:
"Man! is he man at all, who knows and winks?
Sees what his fair bride is and does, and winks?   780
By which the good King means to blind himself,
And blinds himself and all the Table Round
To all the foulness that they work. Myself
Could call him—were it not for womanhood—
The pretty, popular name such manhood earns,   785
Could call him the main cause of all their crime,
Yea, were he not crown'd king, coward and fool."

　　Then Merlin to his own heart, loathing, said:
"O true and tender! O my liege and King!
O selfless man and stainless gentleman,   790
Who wouldst against thine own eye-witness fain
Have all men true and leal, all women pure!
How, in the mouths of base interpreters,
From over-fineness not intelligible
To things with every sense as false and foul   795
As the poach'd filth that floods the middle street.
Is thy white blamelessness accounted blame!"

　　But Vivien, deeming Merlin overborne
By instance, recommenced, and let her tongue
Rage like a fire among the noblest names,   800
Polluting, and imputing her whole self,
Defaming and defacing, till she left
Not even Lancelot brave nor Galahad clean.

　　Her words had issue other than she will'd.
He dragg'd his eyebrow bushes down, and made   805
A snowy pent-house for his hollow eyes,
And mutter'd in himself: "Tell *her* the charm!
So, if she had it, would she rail on me
To snare the next, and if she have it not
So will she rail. What did the wanton say?   810
'Not mount as high!' we scarce can sink as low;
For men at most differ as heaven and earth,
But women, worst and best, as heaven and hell.
I know the Table Round, my friends of old;
All brave, and many generous, and some chaste.   815
She cloaks the scar of some repulse with lies.
I well believe she tempted them and fail'd,
Being so bitter; for fine plots may fail,
Tho' harlots paint their talk as well as face
With colors of the heart that are not theirs.   820

I will not let her know; nine tithes of times
Face-flatterer and backbiter are the same.
And they, sweet soul, that most impute a crime
Are pronest to it, and impute themselves,
Wanting the mental range, or low desire   825
Not to feel lowest makes them level all;
Yea, they would pare the mountain to the plain,
To leave an equal baseness; and in this
Are harlots like the crowd that if they find
Some stain or blemish in a name of note,   830
Not grieving that their greatest are so small,
Inflate themselves with some insane delight,
And judge all nature from her feet of clay,
Without the will to lift their eyes, and see
Her godlike head crown'd with spiritual fire,   835
And touching other worlds. I am weary of her."

  He spoke in words part heard, in whispers part,
Half-suffocated in the hoary fell
And many-winter'd fleece of throat and chin.
But Vivien, gathering somewhat of his mood,   840
And hearing "harlot" mutter'd twice or thrice,
Leapt from her session[9] on his lap, and stood
Stiff as a viper frozen; loathsome sight,
How from the rosy lips of life and love
Flash'd the bare-grinning skeleton of death!   845
White was her cheek; sharp breaths of anger puff'd
Her fairy nostril out; her hand half-clench'd
Went faltering sideways downward to her belt,
And feeling. Had she found a dagger there—
For in a wink the false love turns to hate—   850
She would have stabb'd him; but she found it not.
His eye was calm, and suddenly she took
To bitter weeping, like a beaten child,
A long, long weeping, not consolable.
Then her false voice made way, broken with sobs: 855

  "O crueller than was ever told in tale
Or sung in song! O vainly lavish'd love!
O cruel, there was nothing wild or strange,
Or seeming shameful—for what shame in love,
So love be true, and not as yours is?—nothing   860
Poor Vivien had not done to win his trust
Who call'd her what he call'd her—all her crime,
All—all—the wish to prove him wholly hers."

  She mused a little, and then clapt her hands
Together with a wailing shriek, and said: 865
"Stabb'd through the heart's affections to the heart!

---

9. In the archaic sense, the act of sitting or posture of being seated.

Seethed like the kid in its own mother's milk![1]
Kill'd with a word worse than a life of blows!
I thought that he was gentle, being great;
O God, that I had loved a smaller man!   870
I should have found in him a greater heart.
O, I, that flattering my true passion, saw
The knights, the court, the King, dark in your light,
Who loved to make men darker than they are,
Because of that high pleasure which I had   875
To seat you sole upon my pedestal
Of worship—I am answer'd, and henceforth
The course of life that seem'd so flowery to me
With you for guide and master, only you,
Becomes the sea-cliff pathway broken short,   880
And ending in a ruin—nothing left
But into some low cave to crawl, and there,
If the wolf spare me, weep my life away,
Kill'd with unutterable unkindliness."

    She paused, she turn'd away, she hung her head,   885
The snake of gold slid from her hair, the braid
Slipt and uncoil'd itself, she wept afresh,
And the dark wood grew darker toward the storm
In silence, while his anger slowly died
Within him, till he let his wisdom go   890
For ease of heart, and half believed her true;
Call'd her to shelter in the hollow oak,
"Come from the storm," and having no reply,
Gazed at the heaving shoulder and the face
Hand-hidden, as for utmost grief or shame;   895
Then thrice essay'd, by tenderest-touching terms,
To sleek her ruffled peace of mind, in vain.
At last she let herself be conquer'd by him,
And as the cageling newly flown returns,
The seeming-injured simple-hearted thing   900
Came to her old perch back, and settled there.
There while she sat, half-falling from his knees,
Half-nestled at his heart, and since he saw
The slow tear creep from her closed eyelid yet,
About her, more in kindness than in love,   905
The gentle wizard cast a shielding arm.
But she dislink'd herself at once and rose,
Her arms upon her breast across, and stood,
A virtuous gentlewoman deeply wrong'd,
Upright and flush'd before him; then she said: 910

    "There must be now no passages of love
Betwixt us twain henceforward evermore;
Since, if I be what I am grossly call'd,

---

1. See *Exodus*, 34:26.

What should be granted which your own gross heart
Would reckon worth the taking? I will go. 915
In truth, but one thing now—better have died
Thrice than have ask'd it once—could make me stay—
That proof of trust—so often ask'd in vain!
How justly, after that vile term of yours,
I find with grief! I might believe you then, 920
Who knows? once more. Lo! what was once to me
Mere matter of the fancy, now hath grown
The vast necessity of heart and life.
Farewell; think gently of me, for I fear
My fate or folly, passing gayer youth 925
For one so old, must be to love thee still.
But ere I leave thee let me swear once more
That if I schemed against thy peace in this,
May yon just heaven, that darkens o'er me, send
One flash that, missing all things else, may make 930
My scheming brain a cinder, if I lie."

  Scarce had she ceased, when out of heaven a bolt—
For now the storm was close above them—struck,
Furrowing a giant oak, and javelining
With darted spikes and splinters of the wood 935
The dark earth round. He raised his eyes and saw
The tree that shone white-listed[2] thro' the gloom.
But Vivien, fearing heaven had heard her oath,
And dazzled by the livid-flickering fork,
And deafen'd with the stammering cracks and claps 940
That follow'd, flying back and crying out,
"O Merlin, tho' you do not love me, save,
Yet save me!" clung to him and hugg'd him close;
And call'd him dear protector in her fright,
Nor yet forgot her practice in her fright, 945
But wrought upon his mood and hugg'd him close.
The pale blood of the wizard at her touch
Took gayer colors, like an opal warm'd.
She blamed herself for telling hearsay tales;
She shook from fear, and for her fault she wept 950
Of petulancy; she call'd him lord and liege,
Her seer, her bard, her silver star of eve,
Her God, her Merlin, the one passionate love
Of her whole life; and ever overhead
Bellow'd the tempest, and the rotten branch 955
Snapt in the rushing of the river-rain
Above them; and in change of glare and gloom
Her eyes and neck glittering went and came;
Till now the storm, its burst of passion spent,
Moaning and calling out of other lands, 960

---

2. White-striped.

Had left the ravaged woodland yet once more
To peace; and what should not have been had been,
For Merlin, overtalk'd and overworn,
Had yielded, told her all the charm, and slept.

Then, in one moment, she put forth the charm   965
Of woven paces and of waving hands,
And in the hollow oak he lay as dead,
And lost to life and use and name and fame.

Then crying, "I have made his glory mine,"
And shrieking out, "O fool!" the harlot leapt   970
Adown the forest, and the thicket closed
Behind her, and the forest echo'd "fool."

1855–56; 1859

Lancelot and Elaine[3]

Elaine the fair, Elaine the lovable,
Elaine, the lily maid of Astolat,[4]
High in her chamber up a tower to the east
Guarded the sacred shield of Lancelot;
Which first she placed where morning's earliest ray   5
Might strike it, and awake her with the gleam;
Then fearing rust or soilure fashion'd for it
A case of silk, and braided thereupon
All the devices blazon'd on the shield
In their own tinct, and added, of her wit,   10
A border fantasy of branch and flower,
And yellow-throated nestling in the nest.
Nor rested thus content, but day by day,
Leaving her household and good father, climb'd
That eastern tower, and entering barr'd her door,   15
Stript off the case, and read the naked shield,
Now guess'd a hidden meaning in his arms,
Now made a pretty history to herself
Of every dint a sword had beaten in it,
And every scratch a lance had made upon it,   20
Conjecturing when and where: this cut is fresh,
That ten years back; this dealt him at Caerlyle,[5]
That at Caerleon—this at Camelot[6]—

3. Although the primary source is Malory, the legend or versions of it had been in Tennyson's mind for many years. Compare "The Lady of Shalott," and see note on p. 13, in which Tennyson claims he did not know of Malory's Elaine in 1832. One cannot be certain just when he became familiar with Malory's account. He does say, "The vision of Arthur as I have drawn him had come upon me when, little more than a boy, I first lighted upon Malory" (*Memoir* II, 128), implying, perhaps, only partial familiarity.
4. The town of Guilford, in Surrey, according to Malory.
5. Carlisle, in Cumberland.
6. Arthur's capital has been variously located in Somersetshire, Winchester, and Wales; Caerleon (see line 9 in "Merlin and Vivien") was in Wales.

And ah, God's mercy, what a stroke was there!
And here a thrust that might have kill'd, but God   25
Broke the strong lance, and roll'd his enemy down,
And saved him: so she lived in fantasy.

How came the lily maid by that good shield
Of Lancelot, she that knew not even his name?
He left it with her, when he rode to tilt   30
For the great diamond in the diamond jousts,
Which Arthur had ordain'd, and by that name
Had named them, since a diamond was the prize.

For Arthur, long before they crown'd him king,
Roving the trackless realms of Lyonnesse,[7]   35
Had found a glen, gray boulder and black tarn.
A horror lived about the tarn, and clave
Like its own mists to all the mountain side;
For here two brothers, one a king, had met
And fought together, but their names were lost;   40
And each had slain his brother at a blow;
And down they fell and made the glen abhorr'd.
And there they lay till all their bones were bleach'd,
And lichen'd into color with the crags.
And he that once was king had on a crown   45
Of diamonds, one in front and four aside.
And Arthur came, and laboring up the pass,
All in a misty moonshine, unawares
Had trodden that crown'd skeleton, and the skull
Brake from the nape, and from the skull the crown   50
Roll'd into light, and turning on its rims
Fled like a glittering rivulet to the tarn.
And down the shingly scaur he plunged, and caught,
And set it on his head, and in his heart
Heard murmurs, 'Lo, thou likewise shalt be king.'   55

Thereafter, when a king, he had the gems
Pluck'd from the crown, and show'd them to his knights
Saying: 'These jewels, whereupon I chanced
Divinely, are the kingdom's, not the King's—
For public use. Henceforward let there be   60
Once every year, a joust for one of these;
For so by nine years' proof we needs must learn
Which is our mightiest, and ourselves shall grow
In use of arms and manhood, till we drive
The heathen,[8] who, some say, shall rule the land   65
Hereafter, which God hinder!' Thus he spoke.
And eight years past, eight jousts had been, and still
Had Lancelot won the diamond of the year,

7. According to legend, a land which lay between Land's End and Scilly, perhaps containing part of Cornwall. It supposedly sank into the sea.
8. Angles, Saxons, and Jutes. (See "The Coming of Arthur," line 59.)

With purpose to present them to the Queen
When all were won; but, meaning all at once   70
To snare her royal fancy with a boon
Worth half her realm, had never spoken word.

    Now for the central diamond and the last
And largest, Arthur, holding then his court
Hard on the river nigh the place which now   75
Is this world's hugest,[9] let proclaim a joust
At Camelot, and when the time drew nigh
Spake—for she had been sick—to Guinevere:
'Are you so sick, my Queen, you cannot move
To these fair jousts?' 'Yea, lord,' she said, 'ye know it.'   80
'Then will ye miss,' he answer'd, 'the great deeds
Of Lancelot, and his prowess in the lists,
A sight ye love to look on.' And the Queen
Lifted her eyes, and they dwelt languidly
On Lancelot, where he stood beside the King.   85
He, thinking that he read her meaning there,
'Stay with me, I am sick; my love is more
Than many diamonds,' yielded; and a heart
Love-loyal to the least wish of the Queen—
However much he yearn'd to make complete   90
The tale of diamonds for his destined boon—
Urged him to speak against the truth, and say,
'Sir King, mine ancient wound is hardly whole,
And lets me from the saddle;' and the King
Glanced first at him, then her, and went his way.   95
No sooner gone than suddenly she began:

    'To blame, my lord Sir Lancelot, much to blame!
Why go ye not to these fair jousts? the knights
Are half of them our enemies, and the crowd
Will murmur, "Lo the shameless ones, who take   100
Their pastime now the trustful King is gone!"'
Then Lancelot, vext at having lied in vain:
'Are ye so wise? ye were not once so wise,
My Queen, that summer when ye loved me first.
Then of the crowd ye took no more account   105
Than of the myriad cricket of the mead,
When its own voice clings to each blade of grass,
And every voice is nothing. As to knights,
Them surely can I silence with all ease.
But now my loyal worship is allow'd   110
Of all men; many a bard, without offence,
Has link'd our names together in his lay,
Lancelot, the flower of bravery, Guinevere,
The pearl of beauty; and our knights at feast
Have pledged us in this union, while the King   115

9. London.

Would listen smiling. How then? is there more?
Has Arthur spoken aught? or would yourself,
Now weary of my service and devoir,[1]
Henceforth be truer to your faultless lord?'

She broke into a little scornful laugh: 120
'Arthur, my lord, Arthur, the faultless King,
That passionate perfection, my good lord—
But who can gaze upon the sun in heaven?
He never spake word of reproach to me,
He never had a glimpse of mine untruth,   125
He cares not for me. Only here to-day
There gleamed a vague suspicion in his eyes;
Some meddling rogue has tampered with him—else
Rapt in this fancy of his Table Round,
And swearing men to vows impossible.   130
To make them like himself; but, friend, to me
He is all fault who hath no fault at all.
For who loves me must have a touch of earth;
The low sun makes the color. I am yours,
Not Arthur's, as ye know, save by the bond.   135
And therefore hear my words: go to the jousts;
The tiny-trumpeting gnat can break our dream
When sweetest; and the vermin voices here
May buzz so loud—we scorn them, but they sting.'

Then answer'd Lancelot, the chief of knights: 140
'And with what face, after my pretext made,
Shall I appear, O Queen, at Camelot, I
Before a king who honors his own word
As if it were his God's?'

            'Yea,' said the Queen,
'A moral child without the craft to rule,   145
Else had he not lost me; but listen to me,
If I must find you wit. We hear it said
That men go down before your spear at a touch,
But knowing you are Lancelot; your great name,
This conquers. Hide it therefore; go unknown.   150
Win! by this kiss you will; and our true King
Will then allow your pretext, O my knight,
As all for glory; for to speak him true,
Ye know right well, how meek soe'er he seem,
No keener hunter after glory breathes.   155
He loves it in his knights more than himself;
They prove to him his work. Win and return.'

Then got Sir Lancelot suddenly to horse,
Wroth at himself. Not willing to be known,
He left the barren-beaten thoroughfare,   160

1. Duty.

Chose the green path that show'd the rarer foot,
And there among the solitary downs,
Full often lost in fancy, lost his way;
Till as he traced a faintly-shadow'd track,
That all in loops and links among the dales   165
Ran to the Castle of Astolat, he saw
Fired from the west, far on a hill, the towers.
Thither he made, and blew the gateway horn.
Then came an old, dumb, myriad-wrinkled man,
Who let him into lodging and disarm'd.   170
And Lancelot marvell'd at the wordless man;
And issuing found the Lord of Astolat
With two strong sons, Sir Torre and Sir Lavaine,
Moving to meet him in the castle court;
And close behind them stept the lily maid   175
Elaine, his daughter; mother of the house
There was not. Some light jest among them rose
With laughter dying down as the great knight
Approach'd them; then the Lord of Astolat:
'Whence comest thou, my guest, and by what name   180
Livest between the lips? for by thy state
And presence I might guess thee chief of those,
After the King, who eat in Arthur's halls.
Him have I seen; the rest, his Table Round,
Known as they are, to me they are unknown.'   185

    Then answer'd Lancelot, the chief of knights:
'Known am I, and of Arthur's hall, and known,
What I by mere mischance have brought, my shield.
But since I go to joust as one unknown
At Camelot for the diamond, ask me not;   190
Hereafter ye shall know me—and the shield—
I pray you lend me one, if such you have,
Blank, or at least with some device not mine.'

    Then said the Lord of Astolat: 'Here is Torre's:
Hurt in his first tilt was my son, Sir Torre,   195
And so, God wot, his shield is blank enough.
His ye can have.' Then added plain Sir Torre,
'Yea, since I cannot use it, ye may have it.'
Here laugh'd the father saying: 'Fie, Sir Churl,
Is that an answer for a noble knight?   200
Allow him! but Lavaine, my younger here,
He is so full of lustihood, he will ride,
Joust for it, and win, and bring it in an hour,
And set it in this damsel's golden hair,
To make her thrice as wilful as before.'   205

    'Nay, father, nay, good father, shame me not
Before this noble knight,' said young Lavaine,
'For nothing. Surely I but play'd on Torre,

He seem'd so sullen, vext he could not go;
A jest, no more! for, knight, the maiden dreamt   210
That some one put this diamond in her hand,
And that it was too slippery to be held,
And slipt and fell into some pool or stream,
The castle-well, belike; and then I said
That *if* I went and *if* I fought and won it—   215
But all was jest and joke among ourselves—
Then must she keep it safelier. All was jest.
But, father, give me leave, an if he will,
To ride to Camelot with this noble knight.
Win shall I not, but do my best to win;   220
Young as I am, yet would I do my best.'

    'So ye will grace me,' answer'd Lancelot,
Smiling a moment, 'with your fellowship
O'er these waste downs whereon I lost myself,
Then were I glad of you as guide and friend;   225
And you shall win this diamond,—as I hear,
It is a fair large diamond,—if ye may,
And yield it to this maiden, if ye will.'
'A fair large diamond,' added plain Sir Torre,
'Such be for queens, and not for simple maids.'   230
Then she, who held her eyes upon the ground,
Elaine, and heard her name so tost about,
Flush'd slightly at the slight disparagement
Before the stranger knight, who, looking at her,
Full courtly, yet not falsely, thus return'd: 235
'If what is fair be but for what is fair,
And only queens are to be counted so,
Rash were my judgment then, who deem this maid
Might wear as fair a jewel as is on earth,
Not violating the bond of like to like.'   240

    He spoke and ceased; the lily maid Elaine,
Won by the mellow voice before she look'd,
Lifted her eyes and read his lineaments.
The great and guilty love he bare the Queen,
In battle with the love he bare his lord,   245
Had marr'd his face, and mark'd it ere his time.
Another sinning on such heights with one,
The flower of all the west and all the world,
Had been the sleeker for it; but in him
His mood was often like a fiend, and rose   250
And drove him into wastes and solitudes
For agony, who was yet a living soul.
Marr'd as he was, he seem'd the goodliest man
That ever among ladies ate in hall,
And noblest, when she lifted up her eyes.   255
However marr'd, of more than twice her years,

Seam'd with an ancient sword-cut on the cheek,
And bruised and bronzed, she lifted up her eyes
And loved him, with that love which was her doom.

Then the great knight, the darling of the court, 260
Loved of the loveliest, into that rude hall
Stept with all grace, and not with half disdain
Hid under grace, as in a smaller time,
But kindly man moving among his kind;
Whom they with meats and vintage of their best 265
And talk and minstrel melody entertain'd,
And much they ask'd of court and Table Round,
And ever well and readily answer'd he;
But Lancelot, when they glanced at Guinevere,
Suddenly speaking of the wordless man, 270
Heard from the baron that, ten years before,
The heathen caught and reft him of his tongue.
'He learnt and warn'd me of their fierce design
Against my house, and him they caught and maim'd;
But I, my sons, and little daughter fled 275
From bonds or death, and dwelt among the woods
By the great river in a boatman's hut.
Dull days were those, till our good Arthur broke
The Pagan yet once more on Badon hill.'[2]

'O, there, great lord, doubtless,' Lavaine said, rapt 280
By all the sweet and sudden passion of youth
Toward greatness in its elder, 'you have fought.
O, tell us—for we live apart—you know
Of Arthur's glorious wars.' And Lancelot spoke
And answer'd him at full, as having been 285
With Arthur in the fight which all day long
Rang by the white mouth of the violent Glem;
And in the four loud battles by the shore
Of Duglas; that on Bassa; then the war
That thunder'd in and out the gloomy skirts 290

---

2. The last of the twelve battles against the Angles and Saxons. Tennyson took the list which follows from Bohn's translation of Nennius' *Historia Britonum* (c. 796): "Thus it was that the magnanimous Arthur, with all the kings and military force of Britain, fought against the Saxons. And though there were many more noble than himself, yet he was twelve times chosen their commander, and was as often conqueror. The first battle in which he was engaged was at the mouth of the river Glem. The second, third, fourth, and fifth were on another river, by the Britons called Duglas, in the region Linuis. The sixth on the river Bassas. The seventh in the wood Celidon, which the Britons call Cat Coit Celidon. The eighth was near Gurnion Castle, where Arthur bore the image of the Holy Virgin, mother of God, upon his shoulders, and through the power of our Lord Jesus Christ, and the holy Mary, put the Saxons to flight, and pursued them the whole day with great slaughter. The ninth was at the City of Legion, which is called Caerleon. The tenth was on the banks of the river Trat Treuroit. The eleventh was on the mountain Breguoin, which we call Cat Bregion. The twelfth was a most severe contest, when Arthur penetrated to the hill of Badon. In this engagement, nine hundred and forty fell by his hand alone, no one but the Lord affording him assistance. In all these engagements the Britons were successful. For no strength can avail against the will of the Almighty."

Of Celidon the forest; and again
By Castle Gurnion, where the glorious King
Had on his cuirass³ worn our Lady's Head,
Carved of one emerald centred in a sun
Of silver rays, that lighten'd as he breathed;   295
And at Caerleon had he help'd his lord,
When the strong neighings of the wild White Horse⁴
Set every gilded parapet shuddering;
And up in Agned-Cathregonion too,
And down the waste sand-shores of Trath Treroit,   300
Where many a heathen fell; 'and on the mount
Of Badon I myself beheld the King
Charge at the head of all his Table Round,
And all his legions crying Christ and him,
And break them; and I saw him, after, stand   305
High on a heap of slain, from spur to plume
Red as the rising sun with heathen blood,
And seeing me, with a great voice he cried,
"They are broken, they are broken!" for the King,
However mild he seems at home, nor cares   310
For triumph in our mimic wars, the jousts—
For if his own knight casts him down, he laughs,
Saying his knights are better men than he—
Yet in this heathen war the fire of God
Fills him. I never saw his like; there lives   315
No greater leader.'

          While he utter'd this,
Low to her own heart said the lily maid,
'Save your great self, fair lord;' and when he fell
From talk of war to traits of pleasantry—
Being mirthful he, but in a stately kind—   320
She still took note that when the living smile
Died from his lips, across him came a cloud
Of melancholy severe, from which again,
Whenever in her hovering to and fro
The lily maid had striven to make him cheer,   325
There brake a sudden-beaming tenderness
Of manners and of nature; and she thought
That all was nature, all, perchance, for her.
And all night long his face before her lived,
As when a painter, poring on a face,   330
Divinely thro' all hindrance finds the man
Behind it, and so paints him that his face,
The shape and color of a mind and life,
Lives for his children, ever at its best
And fullest; so the face before her lived,   335
Dark-splendid, speaking in the silence, full

3. Breastplate.
4. The emblem of the English or Sax-
ons; the dragon was the emblem of the
Britons.

Of noble things, and held her from her sleep,
Till rathe⁵ she rose, half-cheated in the thought
She needs must bid farewell to sweet Lavaine.
First as in fear, step after step, she stole   340
Down the long tower-stairs, hesitating.
Anon, she heard Sir Lancelot cry in the court,
'This shield, my friend, where is it?' and Lavaine
Past inward, as she came from out the tower.
There to his proud horse Lancelot turn'd, and smooth'd   345
The glossy shoulder, humming to himself.
Half-envious of the flattering hand, she drew
Nearer and stood. He look'd, and, more amazed
Than if seven men had set upon him, saw
The maiden standing in the dewy light.   350
He had not dream'd she was so beautiful.
Then came on him a sort of sacred fear,
For silent, tho' he greeted her, she stood
Rapt on his face as if it were a god's.
Suddenly flash'd on her a wild desire   355
That he should wear her favor at the tilt.
She braved a riotous heart in asking for it.
'Fair lord, whose name I know not—noble it is,
I well believe, the noblest—will you wear
My favor at this tourney?' 'Nay,' said he,   360
'Fair lady, since I never yet have worn
Favor of any lady in the lists.
Such is my wont, as those who know me know.'
'Yea, so,' she answer'd; 'then in wearing mine
Needs must be lesser likelihood, noble lord,   365
That those who know should know you.' And he turn'd
Her counsel up and down within his mind,
And found it true, and answer'd: 'True, my child.
Well, I will wear it; fetch it out to me.
What is it?' and she told him, 'A red sleeve   370
Broider'd with pearls,' and brought it. Then he bound
Her token on his helmet, with a smile
Saying, 'I never yet have done so much
For any maiden living,' and the blood
Sprang to her face and fill'd her with delight;   375
But left her all the paler when Lavaine
Returning brought the yet-unblazon'd shield,
His brother's, which he gave to Lancelot,
Who parted with his own to fair Elaine:
'Do me this grace, my child, to have my shield   380
In keeping till I come.' ' A grace to me,'
She answer'd, 'twice to-day. I am your squire!'
Whereat Lavaine said laughing: 'Lily maid,
For fear our people call you lily maid

5. Early.

In earnest, let me bring your color back; 385
Once, twice, and thrice. Now get you hence to bed;'
So kiss'd her, and Sir Lancelot his own hand,
And thus they moved away. She staid a minute,
Then made a sudden step to the gate, and there—
Her bright hair blown about the serious face 390
Yet rosy-kindled with her brother's kiss—
Paused by the gateway, standing near the shield
In silence, while she watch'd their arms far-off
Sparkle, until they dipt below the downs.
Then to her tower she climb'd, and took the shield, 395
There kept it, and so lived in fantasy.

Meanwhile the new companions past away
Far o'er the long backs of the bushless downs,
To where Sir Lancelot knew there lived a knight
Not far from Camelot, now for forty years 400
A hermit, who had pray'd, labor'd and pray'd,
And ever laboring had scoop'd himself
In the white rock a chapel and a hall
On massive columns, like a shore-cliff cave,
And cells and chambers. All were fair and dry; 405
The green light from the meadows underneath
Struck up and lived along the milky roofs;
And in the meadows tremulous aspen-trees
And poplars made a noise of falling showers.
And thither wending there that night they bode. 410

But when the next day broke from underground,
And shot red fire and shadows thro' the cave,
They rose, heard mass, broke fast, and rode away.
Then Lancelot saying, 'Hear, but hold my name
Hidden, you ride with Lancelot of the Lake,' 415
Abash'd Lavaine, whose instant reverence,
Dearer to true young hearts than their own praise,
But left him leave to stammer, 'Is it indeed?'
And after muttering, 'The great Lancelot,'
At last he got his breath and answer'd: 'One, 420
One have I seen—that other, our liege lord,
The dread Pendragon,[6] Britain's King of kings,
Of whom the people talk mysteriously,
He will be there—then were I stricken blind
That minute, I might say that I had seen.' 425

So spake Lavaine, and when they reach'd the lists
By Camelot in the meadow, let his eyes
Run thro' the peopled gallery which half round

6. The title, denoting chief leader, given to ancient British or Welsh kings; their standard was the dragon. The word is derived from the Welsh *pen*, "head," and the Latin *draco*, "dragon." The title, according to Geoffrey of Monmouth, originated with Arthur's father, Uther Pendragon, who first carried the standard into battle.

Lay like a rainbow fallen upon the grass,
Until they found the clear-faced King, who sat   430
Robed in red samite, easily to be known,
Since to his crown the golden dragon clung,
And down his robe the dragon writhed in gold,
And from the carven-work behind him crept
Two dragons gilded, sloping down to make   435
Arms for his chair, while all the rest of them
Thro' knots and loops and folds innumerable
Fled ever thro' the woodwork, till they found
The new design wherein they lost themselves,
Yet with all ease, so tender was the work;   440
And, in the costly canopy o'er him set,
Blazed the last diamond of the nameless king.

Then Lancelot answer'd young Lavaine and said:
'Me you call great; mine is the firmer seat,
The truer lance; but there is many a youth   445
Now crescent, who will come to all I am
And overcome it; and in me there dwells
No greatness, save it be some far-off touch
Of greatness to know well I am not great.
There is the man.' And Lavaine gaped upon him   450
As on a thing miraculous, and anon
The trumpets blew; and then did either side,
They that assail'd, and they that held the lists,
Set lance in rest, strike spur, suddenly move,
Meet in the midst, and there so furiously   455
Shock that a man far-off might well perceive,
If any man that day were left afield,
The hard earth shake, and a low thunder of arms.
And Lancelot bode a little, till he saw
Which were the weaker; then he hurl'd into it   460
Against the stronger. Little need to speak
Of Lancelot in his glory! King, duke, earl,
Count, baron—whom he smote, he overthrew.

But in the field were Lancelot's kith and kin,
Ranged with the Table Round that held the lists,   465
Strong men, and wrathful that a stranger knight
Should do and almost overdo the deeds
Of Lancelot; and one said to the other, 'Lo!
What is he? I do not mean the force alone—
The grace and versatility of the man!   470
Is it not Lancelot?' 'When has Lancelot worn
Favor of any lady in the lists?
Not such his wont, as we that know him know.'
'How then? who then?' a fury seized them all,
A fiery family passion for the name   475
Of Lancelot, and a glory one with theirs.

They couch'd their spears and prick'd their steeds, and thus,
Their plumes driven backward by the wind they made
In moving, all together down upon him
Bare, as a wild wave in the wide North Sea,   480
Green-glimmering toward the summit, bears, with all
Its stormy crests that smoke against the skies,
Down on a bark, and overbears the bark
And him that helms it; so they overbore
Sir Lancelot and his charger, and a spear   485
Down-glancing lamed the charger, and a spear
Prick'd sharply his own cuirass, and the head
Pierced thro' his side, and there snapt and remain'd.

Then Sir Lavaine did well and worshipfully.
He bore a knight of old repute to the earth,   490
And brought his horse to Lancelot where he lay.
He up the side, sweating with agony, got,
But thought to do while he might yet endure,
And being lustily holpen by the rest,
His party,—tho' it seem'd half-miracle   495
To those he fought with,—drave his kith and kin,
And all the Table Round that held the lists,
Back to the barrier; then the trumpets blew
Proclaiming his the prize who wore the sleeve
Of scarlet and the pearls; and all the knights,   500
His party, cried, 'Advance and take thy prize
The diamond;' but he answer'd: 'Diamond me
No diamonds! for God's love, a little air!
Prize me no prizes, for my prize is death!
Hence will I, and I charge you, follow me not.'   505

He spoke, and vanish'd suddenly from the field
With young Lavaine into the poplar grove.
There from his charger down he slid, and sat,
Gasping to Sir Lavaine, 'Draw the lance-head.'
'Ah, my sweet lord Sir Lancelot,' said Lavaine,   510
'I dread me, if I draw it, you will die.'
But he, 'I die already with it; draw—
Draw,'—and Lavaine drew, and Sir Lancelot gave
A marvellous great shriek and ghastly groan,
And half his blood burst forth, and down he sank   515
For the pure pain, and wholly swoon'd away.
Then came the hermit out and bare him in,
There stanch'd his wound; and there, in daily doubt
Whether to live or die, for many a week
Hid from the wild world's rumor by the grove   520
Of poplars with their noise of falling showers,
And ever-tremulous aspen-trees, he lay.

But on that day when Lancelot fled the lists,
His party, knights of utmost North and West,

Lords of waste marshes, kings of desolate isles,   525
Came round their great Pendragon, saying to him,
'Lo, Sire, our knight, thro' whom we won the day,
Hath gone sore wounded, and hath left his prize
Untaken, crying that his prize is death.'
'Heaven hinder,' said the King, 'that such an one,   530
So great a knight as we have seen to-day—
He seem'd to me another Lancelot—
Yea, twenty times I thought him Lancelot—
He must not pass uncared for. Wherefore rise,
O Gawain, and ride forth and find the knight.   535
Wounded and wearied, needs must he be near.
I charge you that you get at once to horse.
And, knights and kings, there breathes not one of you
Will deem this prize of ours is rashly given;
His prowess was too wondrous. We will do him   540
No customary honor; since the knight
Came not to us, of us to claim the prize,
Ourselves will send it after. Rise and take
This diamond, and deliver it, and return,
And bring us where he is, and how he fares,   545
And cease not from your quest until ye find.'

   So saying, from the carven flower above,
To which it made a restless heart, he took
And gave the diamond. Then from where he sat
At Arthur's right, with smiling face arose,   550
With smiling face and frowning heart, a prince
In the mid might and flourish of his May,
Gawain, surnamed the Courteous, fair and strong,
And after Lancelot, Tristram, and Geraint,
And Gareth, a good knight, but therewithal   555
Sir Modred's brother, and the child of Lot,
Nor often loyal to his word,[7] and now
Wroth that the King's command to sally forth
In quest of whom he knew not, made him leave
The banquet and concourse of knights and kings.   560

   So all in wrath he got to horse and went;
While Arthur to the banquet, dark in mood,
Past, thinking, 'Is it Lancelot who hath come
Despite the wound he spake of, all for gain
Of glory, and hath added wound to wound,   565

---

7. In the older traditions, as in *Sir Gawain and the Green Knight,* Gawain is the knight of perfect courtesy; he was also probably the original hero of the Grail quest. Although Malory somewhat downgraded him, Gawain was still one of the most outstanding of the Round Table knights, whose loyalty was beyond question. In Malory, Sir Launcelot unknowingly kills Gawain's brother; Gawain forces Launcelot into a challenge, is mortally wounded, and later, from his deathbed, writes Launcelot a letter of reconciliation. But throughout Tennyson's poem, Gawain is a villainous figure, a self-serving opportunist like Tristram.

And ridden away to die?' So fear'd the King,
And, after two days' tarriance there, return'd.
Then when he saw the Queen, embracing ask'd,
'Love, are you yet so sick?' 'Nay, lord,' she said.
'And where is Lancelot?' Then the Queen amazed,   570
'Was he not with you? won he not your prize?'
'Nay, but one like him.' 'Why, that like was he.'
And when the King demanded how she knew,
Said: 'Lord, no sooner had ye parted from us
Than Lancelot told me of a common talk   575
That men went down before his spear at a touch,
But knowing he was Lancelot; his great name
Conquer'd; and therefore would he hide his name
From all men, even the King, and to this end
Had made the pretext of a hindering wound,   580
That he might joust unknown of all, and learn
If his old prowess were in aught decay'd;
And added, "Our true Arthur, when he learns,
Will well allow my pretext, as for gain
Of purer glory." '

           Then replied the King: 585
'Far lovelier in our Lancelot had it been,
In lieu of idly dallying with the truth,
To have trusted me as he hath trusted thee.
Surely his King and most familiar friend
Might well have kept his secret. True, indeed,   590
Albeit I know my knights fantastical,
So fine a fear in our large Lancelot
Must needs have moved my laughter; now remains
But little cause for laughter. His own kin—
Ill news, my Queen, for all who love him, this!—   595
His kith and kin, not knowing, set upon him;
So that he went sore wounded from the field.
Yet good news too; for goodly hopes are mine
That Lancelot is no more a lonely heart.
He wore, against his wont, upon his helm   600
A sleeve of scarlet, broider'd with great pearls,
Some gentle maiden's gift.'

               'Yea, lord,' she said,
'Thy hopes are mine,' and saying that, she choked,
And sharply turn'd about to hide her face,
Past to her chamber, and there flung herself   605
Down on the great King's couch, and writh'd upon it,
And clench'd her fingers till they bit the palm,
And shriek'd out 'Traitor!' to the unhearing wall,
Then flash'd into wild tears, and rose again,
And moved about her palace, proud and pale.   610

Gawain the while thro' all the region round
Rode with his diamond, wearied of the quest,
Touch'd at all points except the poplar grove,
And came at last, tho' late, to Astolat;
Whom glittering in enamell'd arms the maid   615
Glanced at, and cried, 'What news from Camelot, lord?
What of the knight with the red sleeve?' 'He won.'
'I knew it,' she said. 'But parted from the jousts
Hurt in the side;' whereat she caught her breath.
Thro' her own side she felt the sharp lance go.   620
Thereon she smote her hand; wellnigh she swoon'd.
And, while he gazed wonderingly at her, came
The Lord of Astolat out, to whom the prince
Reported who he was, and on what quest
Sent, that he bore the prize and could not find   625
The victor, but had ridden a random round
To seek him, and had wearied of the search.
To whom the Lord of Astolat: 'Bide with us,
And ride no more at random, noble prince!
Here was the knight, and here he left a shield;   630
This will he send or come for. Furthermore
Our son is with him; we shall hear anon,
Needs must we hear.' To this the courteous prince
Accorded with his wonted courtesy,
Courtesy with a touch of traitor in it,   635
And staid; and cast his eyes on fair Elaine;
Where could be found face daintier? then her shape
From forehead down to foot, perfect—again
From foot to forehead exquisitely turn'd.
'Well—if I bide, lo! this wild flower for me!'   640
And oft they met among the garden yews,
And there he set himself to play upon her
With sallying wit, free flashes from a height
Above her, graces of the court, and songs,
Sighs, and low smiles, and golden eloquence   645
And amorous adulation, till the maid
Rebell'd against it, saying to him: 'Prince,
O loyal nephew of our noble King,
Why ask you not to see the shield he left,
Whence you might learn his name? Why slight your King, 650
And lose the quest he sent you on, and prove
No surer than our falcon yesterday,
Who lost the hern we slipt her at, and went
To all the winds?' 'Nay, by mine head,' said he,
'I lose it, as we lose the lark in heaven,   655
O damsel, in the light of your blue eyes;
But an ye will it let me see the shield.'
And when the shield was brought, and Gawain saw
Sir Lancelot's azure lions, crown'd with gold,

Ramp in the field, he smote his thigh, and mock'd: 660
'Right was the King! our Lancelot! that true man!'
'And right was I,' she answer'd merrily, 'I,
Who dream'd my knight the greatest knight of all.'
'And if *I* dream'd,' said Gawain, 'that you love
This greatest knight, your pardon! lo, ye know it!   665
Speak therefore; shall I waste myself in vain?'
Full simple was her answer: 'What know I?
My brethren have been all my fellowship;
And I, when often they have talk'd of love,
Wish'd it had been my mother, for they talk'd,   670
Meseem'd, of what they knew not; so myself—
I know not if I know what true love is,
But if I know, then, if I love not him,
I know there is none other I can love.'
'Yea, by God's death,' said he, 'ye love him well,   675
But would not, knew ye what all others know,
And whom he loves.' 'So be it,' cried Elaine,
And lifted her fair face and moved away;
But he pursued her, calling, 'Stay a little!
One golden minute's grace! he wore your sleeve.   680
Would he break faith with one I may not name?
Must our true man change like a leaf at last?
Nay—like enow. Why then, far be it from me
To cross our mighty Lancelot in his loves!
And, damsel, for I deem you know full well   685
Where your great knight is hidden, let me leave
My quest with you; the diamond also—here!
For if you love, it will be sweet to give it;
And if he love, it will be sweet to have it
From your own hand; and whether he love or not,   690
A diamond is a diamond. Fare you well
A thousand times!—a thousand times farewell!
Yet, if he love, and his love hold, we two
May meet at court hereafter! there, I think,
So ye will learn the courtesies of the court,   695
We two shall know each other.'

               Then he gave,
And slightly kiss'd the hand to which he gave,
The diamond, and all wearied of the quest
Leapt on his horse, and carolling as he went
A true-love ballad, lightly rode away.   700

   Thence to the court he past; there told the King
What the King knew, 'Sir Lancelot is the knight.'
And added, 'Sire, my liege, so much I learnt,
But fail'd to find him, tho' I rode all round
The region; but I lighted on the maid   705
Whose sleeve he wore. She loves him; and to her,
Deeming our courtesy is the truest law,

I gave the diamond. She will render it;
For by mine head she knows his hiding-place.'

The seldom-frowning King frown'd, and replied,   710
'Too courteous truly! ye shall go no more
On quest of mine, seeing that ye forget
Obedience is the courtesy due to kings.'

He spake and parted. Wroth, but all in awe,
For twenty strokes of the blood, without a word,   715
Linger'd that other, staring after him;
Then shook his hair, strode off, and buzz'd abroad
About the maid of Astolat, and her love.
All ears were prick'd at once, all tongues were loosed:
'The maid of Astolat loves Sir Lancelot,   720
Sir Lancelot loves the maid of Astolat.'
Some read the King's face, some the Queen's, and all
Had marvel what the maid might be, but most
Predoom'd her as unworthy. One old dame
Came suddenly on the Queen with the sharp news.   725
She, that had heard the noise of it before,
But sorrowing Lancelot should have stoop'd so low,
Marr'd her friend's aim with pale tranquillity.
So ran the tale like fire about the court,
Fire in dry stubble a nine-days' wonder flared;   730
Till even the knights at banquet twice or thrice
Forgot to drink to Lancelot and the Queen,
And pledging Lancelot and the lily maid
Smiled at each other, while the Queen, who sat
With lips severely placid, felt the knot   735
Climb in her throat, and with her feet unseen
Crush'd the wild passion out against the floor
Beneath the banquet, where the meats became
As wormwood and she hated all who pledged.

But far away the maid in Astolat,   740
Her guiltless rival, she that ever kept
The one-day-seen Sir Lancelot in her heart,
Crept to her father, while he mused alone,
Sat on his knee, stroked his gray face and said:
'Father, you call me wilful, and the fault   745
Is yours who let me have my will, and now,
Sweet father, will you let me lose my wits?'
'Nay,' said he, 'surely.' 'Wherefore, let me hence,'
She answer'd, 'and find out our dear Lavaine.
'Ye will not lose your wits for dear Lavaine.   750
Bide,' answer'd he: 'we needs must hear anon
Of him, and of that other.' 'Ay,' she said,
'And of that other, for I needs must hence
And find that other, wheresoe'er he be,
And with mine own hand give his diamond to him,   755

Lest I be found as faithless in the quest
As yon proud prince who left the quest to me.
Sweet father, I behold him in my dreams
Gaunt as it were the skeleton of himself,
Death-pale, for the lack of gentle maiden's aid. 760
The gentler-born the maiden, the more bound,
My father, to be sweet and serviceable
To noble knights in sickness, as ye know,
When these have worn their tokens. Let me hence,
I pray you.' Then her father nodding said: 765
'Ay, ay, the diamond. Wit ye well, my child,
Right fain were I to learn this knight were whole,
Being our greatest. Yea, and you must give it—
And sure I think this fruit is hung too high
For any mouth to gape for save a queen's— 770
Nay, I mean nothing; so then, get you gone,
Being so very wilful you must go.'

 Lightly, her suit allow'd, she slipt away,
And while she made her ready for her ride
Her father's latest word humm'd in her ear, 775
'Being so very wilful you must go,'
And changed itself and echo'd in her heart,
'Being so very wilful you must die.'
But she was happy enough and shook it off,
As we shake off the bee that buzzes at us; 780
And in her heart she answer'd it and said,
'What matter, so I help him back to life?'
Then far away with good Sir Torre for guide
Rode o'er the long backs of the bushless downs
To Camelot, and before the city-gates 785
Came on her brother with a happy face
Making a roan horse caper and curvet[8]
For pleasure all about a field of flowers;
Whom when she saw, 'Lavaine,' she cried, 'Lavaine,
How fares my lord Sir Lancelot?' He amazed, 790
'Torre and Elaine! why here? Sir Lancelot!
How know ye my lord's name is Lancelot?'
But when the maid had told him all her tale,
Then turn'd Sir Torre, and being in his moods
Left them, and under the strange-statued gate, 795
Where Arthur's wars were render'd mystically,
Past up the still rich city to his kin,
His own far blood,[9] which dwelt at Camelot;
And her, Lavaine across the poplar grove
Led to the caves. There first she saw the casque 800
Of Lancelot on the wall; her scarlet sleeve,

8. A curvet is a leap in which the horse's forelegs are raised together and the hindlegs are raised up with a spring before the front legs touch the ground.
9. Distant relations.

Tho' carved and cut, and half the pearls away,
Stream'd from it still; and in her heart she laugh'd,
Because he had not loosed it from his helm,
But meant once more perchance to tourney in it.   805
And when they gain'd the cell wherein he slept,
His battle-writhen arms and mighty hands
Lay naked on the wolf-skin, and a dream
Of dragging down his enemy made them move.
Then she that saw him lying unsleek, unshorn,   810
Gaunt as it were the skeleton of himself,
Utter'd a little tender dolorous cry.
The sound not wonted in a place so still
Woke the sick knight, and while he roll'd his eyes
Yet blank from sleep, she started to him, saying,   815
'Your prize the diamond sent you by the King.'
His eyes glisten'd; she fancied, 'Is it for me?'
And when the maid had told him all the tale
Of king and prince, the diamond sent, the quest
Assign'd to her not worthy of it, she knelt   820
Full lowly by the corners of his bed,
And laid the diamond in his open hand.
Her face was near, and as we kiss the child
That does the task assign'd, he kiss'd her face.
At once she slipt like water to the floor.   825
'Alas,' he said, 'your ride hath wearied you.
Rest must you have.' 'No rest for me,' she said;
'Nay, for near you, fair lord, I am at rest.'
What might she mean by that? his large black eyes,
Yet larger thro' his leanness, dwelt upon her,   830
Till all her heart's sad secret blazed itself
In the heart's colors on her simple face;
And Lancelot look'd and was perplext in mind,
And being weak in body said no more,
But did not love the color; woman's love,   835
Save one, he not regarded, and so turn'd
Sighing, and feign'd a sleep until he slept.

     Then rose Elaine and glided thro' the fields,
And past beneath the weirdly-sculptured gates
Far up the dim rich city to her kin;   840
There bode the night, but woke with dawn, and past
Down thro' the dim rich city to the fields,
Thence to the cave. So day by day she past
In either twilight ghost-like to and fro
Gliding, and every day she tended him,   845
And likewise many a night; and Lancelot
Would, tho' he call'd his wound a little hurt
Whereof he should be quickly whole, at times
Brain-feverous in his heat and agony, seem
Uncourteous, even he. But the meek maid   850

Sweetly forbore him ever, being to him
Meeker than any child to a rough nurse,
Milder than any mother to a sick child,
And never woman yet, since man's first fall,
Did kindlier unto man, but her deep love   855
Upbore her; till the hermit, skill'd in all
The simples and the science of that time,
Told him that her fine care had saved his life.
And the sick man forgot her simple blush,
Would call her friend and sister, sweet Elaine,   860
Would listen for her coming and regret
Her parting step, and held her tenderly,
And loved her with all love except the love
Of man and woman when they love their best,
Closest and sweetest, and had died the death   865
In any knightly fashion for her sake.
And peradventure had he seen her first
She might have made this and that other world
Another world for the sick man; but now
The shackles of an old love straiten'd him,   870
His honor rooted in dishonor stood,
And faith unfaithful kept him falsely true.

　　Yet the great knight in his mid-sickness made
Full many a holy vow and pure resolve.
These, as but born of sickness, could not live;   875
For when the blood ran lustier in him again,
Full often the bright image of one face,
Making a treacherous quiet in his heart,
Dispersed his resolution like a cloud.
Then if the maiden, while that ghostly grace[1]   880
Beam'd on his fancy, spoke, he answer'd not,
Or short and coldly, and she knew right well
What the rough sickness meant, but what this meant
She knew not, and the sorrow dimm'd her sight,
And drave her ere her time across the fields   885
Far into the rich city, where alone
She murmur'd, 'Vain, in vain! it cannot be.
He will not love me. How then? must I die?'
Then as a little helpless innocent bird,
That has but one plain passage of few notes,   890
Will sing the simple passage o'er and o'er
For all an April morning, till the ear
Wearies to hear it, so the simple maid
Went half the night repeating, 'Must I die?'
And now to right she turn'd, and now to left,   895
And found no ease in turning or in rest;
And 'Him or death,' she mutter'd, 'death or him,'
Again and like a burthen, 'Him or death.'

1. Vision of Guinevere.

But when Sir Lancelot's deadly hurt was whole,
To Astolat returning rode the three.   900
There morn by morn, arraying her sweet self
In that wherein she deem'd she look'd her best,
She came before Sir Lancelot, for she thought,
'If I be loved, these are my festal robes,
If not, the victim's flowers before he fall.'   905
And Lancelot ever prest upon the maid
That she should ask some goodly gift of him
For her own self or hers: 'and do not shun
To speak the wish most near to your true heart;
Such service have ye done me that I make   910
My will of yours, and prince and lord am I
In mine own land, and what I will I can.'
Then like a ghost she lifted up her face,
But like a ghost without the power to speak.
And Lancelot saw that she withheld her wish,   915
And bode among them yet a little space
Till he should learn it; and one morn it chanced
He found her in among the garden yews,
And said, 'Delay no longer, speak your wish,
Seeing I go to-day.' Then out she brake: 920
'Going? and we shall never see you more.
And I must die for want of one bold word.'
'Speak; that I live to hear,' he said, 'is yours.'
Then suddenly and passionately she spoke:
'I have gone mad. I love you; let me die.'   925
'Ah, sister,' answer'd Lancelot, 'what is this?'
And innocently extending her white arms,
'Your love,' she said, 'your love—to be your wife.'
And Lancelot answer'd, 'Had I chosen to wed,
I had been wedded earlier, sweet Elaine;   930
But now there never will be wife of mine.'
'No, no,' she cried, 'I care not to be wife,
But to be with you still, to see your face,
To serve you, and to follow you thro' the world.'
And Lancelot answer'd: 'Nay, the world, the world,   935
All ear and eye, with such a stupid heart
To interpret ear and eye, and such a tongue
To blare its own interpretation—nay,
Full ill then should I quit your brother's love,
And your good father's kindness.' And she said,   940
'Not to be with you, not to see your face—
Alas for me then, my good days are done!'
'Nay, noble maid,' he answer'd, 'ten times nay!
This is not love, but love's first flash in youth,
Most common; yea, I know it of mine own self,   945
And you yourself will smile at your own self
Hereafter, when you yield your flower of life

To one more fitly yours, not thrice your age.
And then will I, for true you are and sweet
Beyond mine old belief in womanhood,
More specially should your good knight be poor,
Endow you with broad land and territory
Even to the half my realm beyond the seas,
So that would make you happy; furthermore,
Even to the death, as tho' ye were my blood,
In all your quarrels will I be your knight.
This will I do, dear damsel, for your sake,
And more than this I cannot.'

      While he spoke
She neither blush'd nor shook, but deathly-pale
Stood grasping what was nearest, then replied,
'Of all this will I nothing;' and so fell,
And thus they bore her swooning to her tower.

 Then spake, to whom thro' those black walls of yew
Their talk had pierced, her father: 'Ay, a flash,
I fear me, that will strike my blossom dead.
Too courteous are ye, fair Lord Lancelot.
I pray you, use some rough discourtesy
To blunt or break her passion.'

      Lancelot said,
'That were against me; what I can I will;'
And there that day remain'd, and toward even
Sent for his shield. Full meekly rose the maid,
Stript off the case, and gave the naked shield;
Then, when she heard his horse upon the stones,
Unclasping flung the casement back, and look'd
Down on his helm, from which her sleeve had gone.
And Lancelot knew the little clinking sound;
And she by tact of love was well aware
That Lancelot knew that she was looking at him.
And yet he glanced not up, nor waved his hand,
Nor bade farewell, but sadly rode away.
This was the one discourtesy that he used.

 So in her tower alone the maiden sat.
His very shield was gone; only the case,
Her own poor work, her empty labor, left.
But still she heard him, still his picture form'd
And grew between her and the pictured wall.
Then came her father, saying in low tones,
'Have comfort,' whom she greeted quietly.
Then came her brethren saying, 'Peace to thee,
Sweet sister,' whom she answer'd with all calm.
But when they left her to herself again,
Death, like a friend's voice from a distant field

Approaching thro' the darkness, call'd; the owls
Wailing had power upon her, and she mixt
Her fancies with the sallow-rifted glooms   995
Of evening and the moanings of the wind.

    And in those days she made a little song,
And call'd her song 'The Song of Love and Death,'
And sang it; sweetly could she make and sing.

        'Sweet is true love tho' given in vain, in vain;   1000
        And sweet is death who puts an end to pain.
        I know not which is sweeter, no, not I.

        'Love, art thou sweet? then bitter death must be.
        Love, thou are bitter; sweet is death to me.
        O Love, if death be sweeter, let me die.   1005

        'Sweet love, that seems not made to fade away;
        Sweet death, that seems to make us loveless clay;
        I know not which is sweeter, no, not I.

        'I fain would follow love, if that could be;
        I needs must follow death, who calls for me;   1010
        Call and I follow, I follow! let me die.'

    High with the last line scaled her voice, and this,
All in a fiery dawning wild with wind
That shook her tower, the brothers heard, and thought
With shuddering, 'Hark the Phantom[2] of the house   1015
That ever shrieks before a death,' and call'd
The father, and all three in hurry and fear
Ran to her, and lo! the blood-red light of dawn
Flared on her face, she shrilling, 'Let me die!'

    As when we dwell upon a word we know,   1020
Repeating, till the word we know so well
Becomes a wonder, and we know not why,
So dwelt the father on her face, and thought,
Is this Elaine?' till back the maiden fell,
Then gave a languid hand to each, and lay,   1025
Speaking a still good-morrow with her eyes.
At last she said: 'Sweet brothers, yester-night
I seem'd a curious little maid again,
As happy as when we dwelt among the woods,
And when ye used to take me with the flood   1030
Up the great river in the boatman's boat.
Only ye would not pass beyond the cape
That has the poplar on it; there ye fixt
Your limit, oft returning with the tide.
And yet I cried because ye would not pass   1035
Beyond it, and far up the shining flood
Until we found the palace of the King.

2. In Irish and Scottish folklore the under the windows of a house signal a
banshee, a female spirit whose wailings family member's approaching death.

And yet ye would not; but this night I dream'd
That I was all alone upon the flood,
And then I said, "Now shall I have my will;"   1040
And there I woke, but still the wish remain'd.
So let me hence that I may pass at last
Beyond the poplar and far up the flood,
Until I find the palace of the King.
There will I enter in among them all,   1045
And no man there will dare to mock at me;
But there the fine Gawain will wonder at me,
And there the great Sir Lancelot muse at me;
Gawain, who bade a thousand farewells to me,
Lancelot, who coldly went, nor bade me one.   1050
And there the King will know me and my love,
And there the Queen herself will pity me,
And all the gentle court will welcome me,
And after my long voyage I shall rest!'

   'Peace,' said her father, 'O my child, ye seem   1055
Light-headed, for what force is yours to go
So far, being sick? and wherefore would ye look
On this proud fellow again, who scorns us all?'

   Then the rough Torre began to heave and move,
And bluster into stormy sobs and say: 1060
'I never loved him; an I meet with him,
I care not howsoever great he be,
Then will I strike at him and strike him down.
Give me good fortune, I will strike him dead,
For this discomfort he hath done the house.'   1065

   To whom the gentle sister made reply:
'Fret not yourself, dear brother, nor be wroth,
Seeing it is no more Sir Lancelot's fault
Not to love me than it is mine to love
Him of all men who seems to me the highest.'   1070

   'Highest?' the father answer'd, echoing 'highest?'—
He meant to break the passion in her—'nay,
Daughter, I know not what you call the highest;
But this I know, for all the people know it,
He loves the Queen, and in an open shame,   1075
And she returns his love in open shame,
If this be high, what is it to be low?'

   Then spake the lily maid of Astolat:
'Sweet father, all too faint and sick am I
For anger. These are slanders; never yet   1080
Was noble man but made ignoble talk.
He makes no friend who never made a foe.
But now it is my glory to have loved
One peerless, without stain; so let me pass,

My father, howsoe'er I seem to you, 1085
Not all unhappy, having loved God's best
And greatest, tho' my love had no return.
Yet, seeing you desire your child to live,
Thanks, but you work against your own desire,
For if I could believe the things you say 1090
I should but die the sooner; wherefore cease,
Sweet father, and bid call the ghostly man³
Hither, and let me shrive me clean and die.'

 So when the ghostly man had come and gone,
She, with a face bright as for sin forgiven, 1095
Besought Lavaine to write as she devised
A letter, word for word; and when he ask'd,
'Is it for Lancelot, is it for my dear lord?
Then will I bear it gladly;' she replied,
'For Lancelot and the Queen and all the world, 1100
But I myself must bear it.' Then he wrote
The letter she devised; which being writ
And folded, 'O sweet father, tender and true,
Deny me not,' she said—'ye never yet
Denied my fancies—this, however strange, 1105
My latest. Lay the letter in my hand
A little ere I die, and close the hand
Upon it; I shall guard it even in death.
And when the heat has gone from out my heart,
Then take the little bed on which I died 1110
For Lancelot's love, and deck it like the Queen's
For richness, and me also like the Queen
In all I have of rich, and lay me on it.
And let there be prepared a chariot-bier
To take me to the river, and a barge 1115
Be ready on the river, clothed in black.
I go in state to court, to meet the Queen.
There surely I shall speak for mine own self,
And none of you can speak for me so well.
And therefore let our dumb old man alone 1120
Go with me; he can steer and row, and he
Will guide me to that palace, to the doors.'

 She ceased. Her father promised; whereupon
She grew so cheerful that they deem'd her death
Was rather in the fantasy than the blood. 1125
But ten slow mornings past, and on the eleventh
Her father laid the letter in her hand,
And closed the hand upon it, and she died.
So that day there was dole in Astolat.

 But when the next sun brake from underground, 1130
Then, those two brethren slowly with bent brows

3. A priest.

Accompanying, the sad chariot-bier
Past like a shadow thro' the field, that shone
Full-summer, to that stream whereon the barge,
Pall'd all its length in blackest samite, lay.   1135
There sat the lifelong creature of the house,
Loyal, the dumb old servitor, on deck,
Winking his eyes, and twisted all his face.
So those two brethren from the chariot took
And on the black decks laid her in her bed,   1140
Set in her hand a lily, o'er her hung
The silken case with braided blazonings,
And kiss'd her quiet brows, and saying to her,
'Sister, farewell forever,' and again,
'Farewell, sweet sister,' parted all in tears.   1145
Then rose the dumb old servitor, and the dead,
Oar'd by the dumb, went upward with the flood—
In her right hand the lily, in her left
The letter—all her bright hair streaming down—
And all the coverlid was cloth of gold   1150
Drawn to her waist, and she herself in white
All but her face, and that clear-featured face
Was lovely, for she did not seem as dead,
But fast asleep, and lay as tho' she smiled.

That day Sir Lancelot at the palace craved   1155
Audience of Guinevere, to give at last
The price of half a realm, his costly gift,
Hard-won and hardly won with bruise and blow,
With deaths of others, and almost his own,
The nine-years-fought-for diamonds; for he saw   1160
One of her house, and sent him to the Queen
Bearing his wish, whereto the Queen agreed
With such and so unmoved a majesty
She might have seem'd her statue, but that he,
Low-drooping till he wellnigh kiss'd her feet   1165
For loyal awe, saw with a sidelong eye
The shadow of some piece of pointed lace,
In the Queen's shadow, vibrate on the walls,
And parted, laughing in his courtly heart.

All in an oriel[4] on the summer side,   1170
Vine-clad, of Arthur's palace toward the stream,
They met, and Lancelot kneeling utter'd: 'Queen,
Lady, my liege, in whom I have my joy,
Take, what I had not won except for you,
These jewels, and make me happy, making them   1175
An armlet for the roundest arm on earth,
Or necklace for a neck to which the swan's
Is tawnier than her cygnet's.[5] These are words;

---

4. A room or recess with a bay-window, usually in an upper story.

5. An elaborate piece of flattery playing on a reversal of the fact that a

Your beauty is your beauty, and I sin
In speaking, yet O, grant my worship of it   1180
Words, as we grant grief tears. Such sin in words
Perchance, we both can pardon; but, my Queen,
I hear of rumors flying thro' your court.
Our bond, as not the bond of man and wife,
Should have in it an absoluter trust   1185
To make up that defect: let rumors be.
When did not rumors fly? these, as I trust
That you trust me in your own nobleness,
I may not well believe that you believe.'

      While thus he spoke, half turn'd away, the Queen   1190
Brake from the vast oriel-embowering vine
Leaf after leaf, and tore, and cast them off,
Till all the place whereon she stood was green;
Then, when he ceased, in one cold passive hand
Received at once and laid aside the gems   1195
There on a table near her, and replied:

      'It may be I am quicker of belief
Than you believe me, Lancelot of the Lake.
Our bond is not the bond of man and wife.
This good is in it, whatsoe'er of ill,   1200
It can be broken easier. I for you
This many a year have done despite and wrong
To one whom ever in my heart of hearts
I did acknowledge nobler. What are these?
Diamonds for me! they had been thrice their worth   1205
Being your gift, had you not lost your own.
To loyal hearts the value of all gifts
Must vary as the giver's. Not for me!
For her! for your new fancy. Only this
Grant me, I pray you; have your joys apart.   1210
I doubt not that, however changed, you keep
So much of what is graceful; and myself
Would shun to break those bounds of courtesy
In which as Arthur's Queen I move and rule,
So cannot speak my mind. An end to this!   1215
A strange one! yet I take it with Amen.
So pray you, add my diamonds to her pearls;
Deck her with these; tell her, she shines me down:
An armlet for an arm to which the Queen's
Is haggard, or a necklace for a neck   1220
O, as much fairer—as a faith once fair
Was richer than these diamonds—hers not mine—
Nay, by the mother of our Lord himself,
Or hers or mine, mine now to work my will—
She shall not have them.'

cygnet, or young swan, has a yellowish down, in contrast to the adult's pure white.

Saying which she seized,   1225
And, thro' the casement standing wide for heat,
Flung them, and down they flash'd, and smote the stream.
Then from the smitten surface flash'd, as it were,
Diamonds to meet them, and they past away.
Then while Sir Lancelot leant, in half disdain   1230
At love, life, all things, on the window ledge,
Close underneath his eyes, and right across
Where these had fallen, slowly past the barge
Whereon the lily maid of Astolat
Lay smiling, like a star in blackest night.   1235

But the wild Queen, who saw not, burst away
To weep and wail in secret; and the barge,
On to the palace-doorway sliding, paused.
There two stood arm'd, and kept the door; to whom,
All up the marble stair, tier over tier,   1240
Were added mouths that gaped, and eyes that ask'd,
'What is it?' but that oarsman's haggard face,
As hard and still as is the face that men
Shape to their fancy's eye from broken rocks
On some cliff-side, appall'd them, and they said: 1245
'He is enchanted, cannot speak—and she,
Look how she sleeps—the Fairy Queen, so fair!
Yea, but how pale! what are they? flesh and blood?
Or come to take the King to Fairyland?
For some do hold our Arthur cannot die,   1250
But that he passes into Fairyland.'

While thus they babbled of the King, the King
Came girt with knights. Then turn'd the tongueless man
From the half-face to the full eye, and rose
And pointed to the damsel and the doors.   1255
So Arthur bade the meek Sir Percivale
And pure Sir Galahad to uplift the maid;
And reverently they bore her into hall.
Then came the fine Gawain and wonder'd at her,
And Lancelot later came and mused at her,   1260
And last the Queen herself, and pitied her;
But Arthur spied the letter in her hand,
Stoopt, took, brake seal, and read it; this was all:

'Most noble lord, Sir Lancelot of the Lake,
I, sometime call'd the maid of Astolat,   1265
Come, for you left me taking no farewell,
Hither, to take my last farewell of you.
I loved you, and my love had no return,
And therefore my true love has been my death.
And therefore to our Lady Guinevere,   1270
And to all other ladies, I make moan:
Pray for my soul, and yield me burial.

Pray for my soul thou too, Sir Lancelot,
As thou art a knight peerless.'

      Thus he read;
And ever in the reading lords and dames   1275
Wept, looking often from his face who read
To hers which lay so silent, and at times,
So touch'd were they, half-thinking that her lips
Who had devised the letter moved again.

 Then freely spoke Sir Lancelot to them all: 1280
'My lord liege Arthur, and all ye that hear,
Know that for this most gentle maiden's death
Right heavy am I; for good she was and true,
But loved me with a love beyond all love
In women, whomsoever I have known.   1285
Yet to be loved makes not to love again;
Not at my years, however it hold in youth.
I swear by truth and knighthood that I gave
No cause, not willingly, for such a love.
To this I call my friends in testimony,   1290
Her brethren, and her father, who himself
Besought me to be plain and blunt, and use,
To break her passion, some discourtesy
Against my nature; what I could, I did.
I left her and I bade her no farewell;   1295
Tho', had I dreamt the damsel would have died,
I might have put my wits to some rough use,
And help'd her from herself.'

       Then said the Queen—
Sea was her wrath, yet working after storm:
'Ye might at least have done her so much grace,   1300
Fair lord, as would have help'd her from her death.'
He raised his head, their eyes met and hers fell,
He adding: 'Queen, she would not be content
Save that I wedded her, which could not be.
Then might she follow me thro' the world, she ask'd;   1305
It could not be. I told her that her love
Was but the flash of youth, would darken down,
To rise hereafter in a stiller flame
Toward one more worthy of her—then would I,
More specially were he she wedded poor,   1310
Estate them with large land and territory
In mine own realm beyond the narrow seas,
To keep them in all joyance. More than this
I could not; this she would not, and she died.'

 He pausing, Arthur answer'd: 'O my knight,   1315
It will be to thy worship, as my knight,
And mine, as head of all our Table Round,
To see that she be buried worshipfully.'

So toward that shrine which then in all the realm
Was richest, Arthur leading, slowly went   1320
The marshall'd Order of their Table Round,
And Lancelot sad beyond his wont, to see
The maiden buried, not as one unknown,
Nor meanly, but with gorgeous obsequies,
And mass, and rolling music, like a queen.   1325
And when the knights had laid her comely head
Low in the dust of half-forgotten kings,
Then Arthur spake among them: 'Let her tomb
Be costly, and her image thereupon,
And let the shield of Lancelot at her feet   1330
Be carven, and her lily in her hand.
And let the story of her dolorous voyage
For all true hearts be blazon'd on her tomb
In letters gold and azure!' which was wrought
Thereafter; but when now the lords and dames   1335
And people, from the high door streaming, brake
Disorderly, as homeward each, the Queen,
Who mark'd Sir Lancelot where he moved apart,
Drew near, and sigh'd in passing, 'Lancelot,
Forgive me; mine was jealousy in love.'   1340
He answer'd with his eyes upon the ground,
'That is love's curse; pass on, my Queen, forgiven.'
But Arthur, who beheld his cloudy brows,
Approach'd him, and with full affection said:

'Lancelot, my Lancelot, thou in whom I have   1345
Most joy and most affiance, for I know
What thou hast been in battle by my side,
And many a time have watch'd thee at the tilt
Strike down the lusty and long practised knight
And let the younger and unskill'd go by   1350
To win his honor and to make his name,
And loved thy courtesies and thee, a man
Made to be loved; but now I would to God,
Seeing the homeless trouble in thine eyes,
Thou couldst have loved this maiden, shaped, it seems,   1355
By God for thee alone, and from her face,
If one may judge the living by the dead,
Delicately pure and marvellously fair,
Who might have brought thee, now a lonely man
Wifeless and heirless, noble issue, sons   1360
Born to the glory of thy name and fame,
My knight, the great Sir Lancelot of the Lake.'

Then answer'd Lancelot: 'Fair she was, my King,
Pure, as you ever wish your knights to be.
To doubt her fairness were to want an eye,   1365
To doubt her pureness were to want a heart—

Yea, to be loved, if what is worthy love
Could bind him, but free love will not be bound.'

'Free love, so bound, were freest,' said the King.
'Let love be free; free love is for the best.   1370
And, after heaven, on our dull side of death,
What should be best, if not so pure a love
Clothed in so pure a loveliness? yet thee
She fail'd to bind, tho' being, as I think,
Unbound as yet, and gentle, as I know.'   1375

And Lancelot answer'd nothing, but he went,
And at the inrunning of a little brook
Sat by the river in a cove, and watch'd
The high reed wave, and lifted up his eyes
And saw the barge that brought her moving down,   1380
Far-off, a blot upon the stream, and said
Low in himself: 'Ah, simple heart and sweet,
Ye loved me, damsel, surely with a love
Far tenderer than my Queen's. Pray for thy soul?
Ay, that will I. Farewell too—now at last—   1385
Farewell, fair lily. "Jealousy in love?"
Not rather dead love's harsh heir, jealous pride?
Queen, if I grant the jealousy as of love,
May not your crescent fear for name and fame
Speak, as it waxes, of a love that wanes?   1390
Why did the King dwell on my name to me?
Mine own name shames me, seeming a reproach,
Lancelot, whom the Lady of the Lake
Caught from his mother's arms—the wondrous one
Who passes thro' the vision of the night—   1395
She chanted snatches of mysterious hymns
Heard on the winding waters, eve and morn
She kiss'd me saying, "Thou art fair, my child,
As a king's son," and often in her arms
She bare me, pacing on the dusky mere.   1400
Would she had drown'd me in it, where'er it be!
For what am I? what profits me my name
Of greatest knight? I fought for it, and have it.
Pleasure to have it, none; to lose it, pain;
Now grown a part of me; but what use in it?   1405
To make men worse by making my sin known?
Or sin seem less, the sinner seeming great?
Alas for Arthur's greatest knight, a man
Not after Arthur's heart! I needs must break
These bonds that so defame me. Not without   1410
She wills it—would I, if she will'd it? nay,
Who knows? but if I would not, then may God,
I pray him, send a sudden angel down
To seize me by the hair and bear me far,

And fling me deep in that forgotten mere,   1415
Among the tumbled fragments of the hills.'

So groan'd Sir Lancelot in remorseful pain,
Not knowing he should die a holy man.[6]

1859

The Holy Grail[7]

From noiseful arms, and acts of prowess done
In tournament or tilt, Sir Percivale
Whom Arthur and his knighthood call'd the Pure,
Had past into the silent life of prayer,
Praise, fast, and alms; and leaving for the cowl   5
The helmet in an abbey far away
From Camelot, there, and not long after, died.

And one, a fellow-monk among the rest,
Ambrosius, loved him much beyond the rest,
And honor'd him, and wrought into his heart   10
A way by love that waken'd love within,
To answer that which came; and as they sat
Beneath a world-old yew-tree, darkening half
The cloisters, on a gustful April morn
That puff'd the swaying branches into smoke[8]   15
Above them, ere the summer when he died,
The monk Ambrosius question'd Percivale:

"O brother, I have seen this yew-tree smoke,
Spring after spring, for half a hundred years;
For never have I known the world without,   20
Nor ever stray'd beyond the pale. But thee,
When first thou camest—such a courtesy

6. When asked by his son why he hadn't written an idyll on Lancelot's retirement into a hermitage and how he died a holy man, Tennyson replied, "Because it could not be done better than Malory."
7. One of several reasons Tennyson gave for pausing in the production of the *Idylls* after 1859 was: "I doubt whether such a subject as the San Graal could be handled in these days without incurring a charge of irreverence. It would be too much like playing with sacred things" (*Memoir*, II, 126). Although perhaps this is a valid excuse for procrastination, more likely he simply had been unable to devise a plan to incorporate the four earlier idylls. "The Holy Grail" was the first written of the new poems and became the central idyll in the work. It clearly shows the direction in which his thoughts are tending. The focus has moved from the relatively simplistic allegorical concern with true and false love to the much more complex matters of spiritualism and materialism. Indeed the subject of the Grail poem, showing that an excessively zealous pursuit after spiritual truth can be as destructive to social order as an indulgence in the materialistic qualities of life, suggests that Tennyson was a step ahead of himself in articulating his conception. For not until the following two idylls, "Pelleas and Ettarre" and "The Last Tournament," which were written later, does he seek to dramatize fully the consequences of a materialistic philosophy.

In Christian medieval legends, of which there are many, the Grail was the cup from which Christ drank at the Last Supper or the container in which Joseph of Arimathea caught some of the crucified Christ's blood; or it was one and the same vessel.
8. Clouds of pollen.

Spake thro' the limbs and in the voice—I knew
For one of those who eat in Arthur's hall;
For good ye are and bad, and like to coins, 25
Some true, some light, but every one of you
Stamp'd with the image of the King; and now
Tell me, what drove thee from the Table Round,
My brother? was it earthly passion crost?"

"Nay," said the knight; "for no such passion mine. 30
But the sweet vision of the Holy Grail
Drove me from all vainglories, rivalries,
And earthly heats that spring and sparkle out
Among us in the jousts, while women watch
Who wins, who falls, and waste the spiritual strength 35
Within us, better offer'd up to heaven."

To whom the monk: "The Holy Grail!—I trust
We are green in Heaven's eyes; but here too much
We moulder—as to things without I mean—
Yet one of your own knights, a guest of ours, 40
Told us of this in our refectory,
But spake with such a sadness and so low
We heard not half of what he said. What is it?
The phantom of a cup that comes and goes?"

"Nay, monk! what phantom?" answer'd Percivale. 45
"The cup, the cup itself, from which our Lord
Drank at the last sad supper with his own.
This, from the blessed land of Aromat[9]—
After the day of darkness, when the dead
Went wandering o'er Moriah[1]—the good saint 50
Arimathæan Joseph, journeying brought
To Glastonbury,[2] where the winter thorn
Blossoms at Christmas, mindful of our Lord.
And there awhile it bode; and if a man
Could touch or see it, he was heal'd at once, 55
By faith, of all his ills. But then the times
Grew to such evil that the holy cup
Was caught away to heaven, and disappear'd."

To whom the monk: "From our old books I know
That Joseph came of old to Glastonbury, 60
And there the heathen Prince, Arviragus,[3]
Gave him an isle of marsh whereon to build;
And there he built with wattles from the marsh
A little lonely church in days of yore,
For so they say, these books of ours, but seem 65

9. Poetic variation of *Arimathea*.
1. A mountain near Jerusalem.
2. An ancient town in Somerset where Joseph is said to have established the first Christian church in England.

There, supposedly, he planted his staff, from which sprouted the winter thorn.
3. In legend, the son of Cymbeline. His refusal to pay tribute supposedly precipitated another Roman invasion.

Mute of this miracle, far as I have read.
But who first saw the holy thing to-day?"

"A woman," answer'd Percivale, "a nun,
And one no further off in blood from me
Than sister; and if ever holy maid   70
With knees of adoration wore the stone,
A holy maid; tho' never maiden glow'd,
But that was in her earlier maidenhood,
With such a fervent flame of human love,
Which, being rudely blunted, glanced and shot   75
Only to holy things; to prayer and praise
She gave herself, to fast and alms. And yet,
Nun as she was, the scandal of the Court,
Sin against Arthur and the Table Round,
And the strange sound of an adulterous race,   80
Across the iron grating of her cell
Beat, and she pray'd and fasted all the more.

"And he to whom she told her sins, or what
Her all but utter whiteness held for sin,
A man wellnigh a hundred winters old,   85
Spake often with her of the Holy Grail,
A legend handed down thro' five or six,
And each of these a hundred winters old,
From our Lord's time. And when King Arthur made
His Table Round,[4] and all men's hearts became   90
Clean for a season, surely he had thought
That now the Holy Grail would come again;
But sin broke out. Ah, Christ, that it would come,
And heal the world of all their wickedness!
'O Father!' ask'd the maiden, 'might it come   95
To me by prayer and fasting?' 'Nay,' said he,
'I know not, for thy heart is pure as snow.'
And so she pray'd and fasted, till the sun
Shone, and the wind blew, thro' her, and I thought
She might have risen and floated when I saw her.   100

"For on a day she sent to speak with me.
And when she came to speak, behold her eyes
Beyond my knowing of them, beautiful,
Beyond all knowing of them, wonderful,
Beautiful in the light of holiness!   105
And 'O my brother Percivale,' she said,
'Sweet brother, I have seen the Holy Grail;
For, waked at dead of night, I heard a sound
As of a silver horn from o'er the hills
Blown, and I thought, "It is not Arthur's use   110

4. According to Malory, it seated 150 knights in a circle to avoid arguments over precedence. Merlin made it for Uther, who gave it to Leodogran, king of Cameliard (see "The Coming of Arthur"), who in turn gave it to Arthur when he married his daughter Guinevere—an account Tennyson omits.

To hunt by moonlight." And the slender sound
As from a distance beyond distance grew
Coming upon me—O never harp nor horn,
Nor aught we blow with breath, or touch with hand,
Was like that music as it came; and then   115
Stream'd thro' my cell a cold and silver beam,
And down the long beam stole the Holy Grail,
Rose-red with beatings in it, as if alive,
Till all the white walls of my cell were dyed
With rosy colors leaping on the wall;   120
And then the music faded, and the Grail
Past, and the beam decay'd, and from the walls
The rosy quiverings died into the night.
So now the Holy Thing is here again
Among us, brother, fast thou too and pray,   125
And tell thy brother knights to fast and pray,
That so perchance the vision may be seen
By thee and those, and all the world be heal'd.'

 "Then leaving the pale nun, I spake of this
To all men; and myself fasted and pray'd   130
Always, and many among us many a week
Fasted and pray'd even to the uttermost,
Expectant of the wonder that would be.

 "And one there was among us, ever moved
Among us in white armor, Galahad.   135
'God make thee good as thou art beautiful!'
Said Arthur, when he dubb'd him knight, and none
In so young youth was ever made a knight
Till Galahad; and this Galahad, when he heard
My sister's vision, fill'd me with amaze;   140
His eyes became so like her own, they seem'd
Hers, and himself her brother more than I.

 "Sister or brother none had he; but some
Call'd him a son of Lancelot,[5] and some said
Begotten by enchantment—chatterers they,   145
Like birds of passage piping up and down,
That gape for flies—we know not whence they come;
For when was Lancelot wanderingly lewd?

 "But she, the wan sweet maiden, shore away
Clean from her forehead all that wealth of hair   150
Which made a silken mat-work for her feet;
And out of this she plaited broad and long
A strong sword-belt, and wove with silver thread
And crimson in the belt a strange device,
A crimson grail within a silver beam;   155

5. In Malory, Launcelot dallies with several ladies, and Galahad, the last descendant of Joseph of Arimathea, is his illegitimate son by princess Elaine (not the lily maid of Astolat).

And saw the bright boy-knight, and bound it on him,
Saying: 'My knight, my love, my knight of heaven,
O thou, my love, whose love is one with mine,
I, maiden, round thee, maiden, bind my belt.
Go forth, for thou shalt see what I have seen,   160
And break thro' all, till one will crown thee king
Far in the spiritual city;' and as she spake
She sent the deathless passion in her eyes
Thro' him, and made him hers, and laid her mind
On him, and he believed in her belief.   165

"Then came a year of miracle. O brother,
In our great hall there stood a vacant chair,
Fashion'd by Merlin ere he past away,
And carven with strange figures; and in and out
The figures, like a serpent, ran a scroll   170
Of letters in a tongue no man could read.
And Merlin call'd it 'the Siege Perilous,'[6]
Perilous for good and ill; 'for there,' he said,
'No man could sit but he should lose himself.'
And once by misadvertence Merlin sat   175
In his own chair, and so was lost;[7] but he,
Galahad, when he heard of Merlin's doom,
Cried, 'If I lose myself, I save myself!'

"Then on a summer night it came to pass,
While the great banquet lay along the hall,   180
That Galahad would sit down in Merlin's chair.

"And all at once, as there we sat, we heard
A cracking and a riving of the roofs,
And rending, and a blast, and overhead
Thunder and in the thunder was a cry.   185
And in the blast there smote along the hall
A beam of light seven times more clear than day;
And down the long beam stole the Holy Grail
All over cover'd with a luminous cloud,
And none might see who bare it, and it past.   190
But every knight beheld his fellow's face
As in a glory, and all the knights arose,
And staring each at other like dumb men
Stood, till I found a voice and sware a vow.

"I sware a vow before them all, that I,   195
Because I had not seen the Grail, would ride
A twelvemonth and a day in quest of it,
Until I found and saw it, as the nun
My sister saw it; and Galahad sware the vow,

---

6. The vacant chair at the Round Table reserved for the knight who was destined to achieve the quest of the Grail. Tennyson said it "stands for the spiritual imagination."
7. Not according to Tennyson's "Merlin and Vivien" nor Malory.

And good Sir Bors, our Lancelot's cousin, sware,200
And Lancelot sware, and many among the knights,
And Gawain sware, and louder than the rest.'

Then spake the monk Ambrosius, asking him,
"What said the King? Did Arthur take the vow?"

"Nay, for my lord," said Percivale, "the King,205
Was not in hall; for early that same day,
Scaped thro' a cavern from a bandit hold,
An outraged maiden sprang into the hall
Crying on help; for all her shining hair
Was smear'd with earth, and either milky arm210
Red-rent with hooks of bramble, and all she wore
Torn as a sail that leaves the rope is torn
In tempest. So the King arose and went
To smoke the scandalous hive of those wild bees
That made such honey in his realm. Howbeit215
Some little of this marvel he too saw,
Returning o'er the plain that then began
To darken under Camelot; whence the King
Look'd up, calling aloud, 'Lo, there! the roofs
Of our great hall are roll'd in thunder-smoke!220
Pray heaven, they be not smitten by the bolt!'
For dear to Arthur was that hall of ours,
As having there so oft with all his knights
Feasted, and as the stateliest under heaven.

"O brother, had you known our mighty hall,225
Which Merlin built for Arthur long ago!
For all the sacred mount of Camelot,[8]
And all the dim rich city, roof by roof,
Tower after tower, spire beyond spire,
By grove, and garden-lawn, and rushing brook,230
Climbs to the mighty hall that Merlin built.
And four great zones[9] of sculpture, set betwixt
With many a mystic symbol, gird the hall;
And in the lowest beasts are slaying men,
And in the second men are slaying beasts,235
And on the third are warriors, perfect men,
And on the fourth are men with growing wings,

8. Of his "city of shadowy palaces," Tennyson said it is "everywhere symbolic of the gradual growth of human beliefs and institutions, and of the spiritual development of man" (*Memoir*, II, 127). Its decay, as described later in this idyll, obviously symbolizes the reverse.

9. The four zones represent human progress from bestiality to realization of the spiritual ideal. Throughout the *Idylls* Tennyson's use of the beast metaphor is, in part, a reflection of his continuing interest in Darwinism. But whereas earlier, in *In Memoriam* for example, he had conceived of progress toward the "one far-off divine event" as essentially linear, the *Idylls* stress the cyclical nature of history, with no guarantees that the human race will ever achieve an earthly utopia. Those, such as T. S. Eliot, who see no intellectual development from the ideas expressed in *In Memoriam*, should perhaps have read the later Tennyson more closely.

And over all one statue in the mould
Of Arthur, made by Merlin, with a crown,
And peak'd wings pointed to the Northern Star.   240
And eastward fronts the statue, and the crown
And both the wings are made of gold, and flame
At sunrise till the people in far fields,
Wasted so often by the heathen hordes,
Behold it, crying 'We have still a king.'   245

"And, brother had you known our hall within,
Broader and higher than any in all the lands!
Where twelve great windows blazon Arthur's wars,[1]
And all the light that falls upon the board
Streams thro' the twelve great battles of our King.   250
Nay, one there is, and at the eastern end,
Wealthy with wandering lines of mount and mere,
Where Arthur finds the brand Excalibur.
And also one to the west, and counter to it,
And blank; and who shall blazon it? when and how?—   255
O, there, perchance, when all our wars are done,
The brand Excalibur will be cast away!

"So to this hall full quickly rode the King,
In horror lest the work by Merlin wrought,
Dreamlike, should on the sudden vanish, wrapt   260
In unremorseful folds of rolling fire.
And in he rode, and up I glanced, and saw
The golden dragon sparkling over all;
And many of those who burnt the hold, their arms
Hack'd, and their foreheads grimed with smoke and sear'd,   265
Follow'd, and in among bright faces, ours,
Full of the vision, prest; and then the King
Spake to me, being nearest, 'Percivale,'—
Because the hall was all in tumult—some
Vowing, and some protesting,—'what is this?'   270

"O brother, when I told him what had chanced,
My sister's vision and the rest, his face
Darken'd, as I have seen it more than once,
When some brave deed seem'd to be done in vain,
Darken; and 'Woe is me, my knights,' he cried,   275
'Had I been here, ye had not sworn the vow.'
Bold was mine answer, 'Had thyself been here,
My King, thou wouldst have sworn.' 'Yea, yea,' said he,
'Art thou so bold and hast not seen the Grail?'

" 'Nay, lord, I heard the sound, I saw the light,   280
But since I did not see the holy thing,
I sware a vow to follow it till I saw.'

---

1. See "Launcelot and Elaine," lines 279 ff and note.

"Then when he ask'd us, knight by knight, if any
Had seen it, all their answers were as one:
'Nay, lord, and therefore have we sworn our vows.'   285

" 'Lo, now,' said Arthur, 'have ye seen a cloud?
What go ye into the wilderness to see?'[2]

"Then Galahad on the sudden, and in a voice
Shrilling along the hall to Arthur, call'd,
'But I, Sir Arthur, saw the Holy Grail,   290
I saw the Holy Grail and heard a cry—
"O Galahad, and O Galahad, follow me!" ' "

" 'Ah, Galahad, Galahad,' said the King, 'for such
As thou art is the vision, not for these.[3]
Thy holy nun and thou have seen a sign—   295
Holier is none, my Percivale, than she—
A sign to maim this Order which I made.
But ye that follow but the leader's bell,'—
Brother, the King was hard upon his knights,—
'Taliessin[4] is our fullest throat of song,   300
And one hath sung and all the dumb will sing.
Lancelot is Lancelot, and hath overborne
Five knights at once, and every younger knight,
Unproven, holds himself as Lancelot,
Till overborne by one, he learns—and ye,   305
What are ye? Galahads?—no, nor Percivales'—
For thus it pleased the King to range me close
After Sir Galahad;—'nay,' said he, 'but men
With strength and will to right the wrong'd, of power
To lay the sudden heads of violence flat,   310
Knights that in twelve great battles splash'd and dyed
The strong White Horse[5] in his own heathen blood—
But one hath seen, and all the blind will see.
Go, since your vows are sacred, being made.
Yet—for ye know the cries of all my realm   315
Pass thro' this hall—how often, O my knights,
Your places being vacant at my side,
This chance of noble deeds will come and go
Unchallenged, while ye follow wandering fires
Lost in the quagmire! Many of you, yea most,   320
Return no more. Ye think I show myself
Too dark a prophet. Come now, let us meet
The morrow morn once more in one full field
Of gracious pastime, that once more the King,
Before ye leave him for this quest, may count   325

2. See *Matthew*, 11:7: "What did you go out into the wilderness to behold? A reed shaken by the wind?"
3. In his note introducing this idyll, Tennyson said: "Faith declines, religion in many turns from practical goodness to the quest after the spiritual and marvellous and selfish religious excitement. Few are those for whom the quest is a source of spiritual strength."
4. A Welsh bard of the sixth century.
5. The Saxons' emblem.

The yet-unbroken strength of all his knights,
Rejoicing in that Order which he made.'

"So when the sun broke next from underground,
All the great Table of our Arthur closed
And clash'd in such a tourney and so full,   330
So many lances broken—never yet
Had Camelot seen the like since Arthur came;
And I myself and Galahad, for a strength
Was in us from the vision, overthrew
So many knights that all the people cried,   335
And almost burst the barriers in their heat,
Shouting, 'Sir Galahad and Sir Percivale!'

"But when the next day brake from underground—
O brother, had you known our Camelot,
Built by old kings, age after age, so old   340
The King himself had fears that it would fall,
So strange, and rich, and dim; for where the roofs
Totter'd toward each other in the sky,
Met foreheads all along the street of those
Who watch'd us pass; and lower, and where the long   345
Rich galleries, lady-laden, weigh'd the necks
Of dragons clinging to the crazy walls,
Thicker than drops from thunder, showers of flowers
Fell as we past; and men and boys astride
On wyvern,[6] lion, dragon, griffin, swan,   350
At all the corners, named us each by name,
Calling 'God speed!' but in the ways below
The knights and ladies wept, and rich and poor
Wept, and the King himself could hardly speak
For grief, and all in middle street the Queen,   355
Who rode by Lancelot, wail'd and shriek'd aloud,
'This madness has come on us for our sins.'
So to the Gate of the Three Queens[7] we came,
Where Arthur's wars are render'd mystically,
And thence departed every one his way.   360

"And I was lifted up in heart, and thought
Of all my late-shown prowess in the lists,
How my strong lance had beaten down the knights,
So many and famous names; and never yet
Had heaven appear'd so blue, nor earth so green,   365
For all my blood danced in me, and I knew
That I should light upon the Holy Grail.

"Thereafter, the dark warning of our King,
That most of us would follow wandering fires,
Came like a driving gloom across my mind.   370

6. A two-legged dragon; a griffin is   7. See "The Coming of Arthur," line
half lion and half eagle.   275 and note.

Then every evil word I had spoken once,
And every evil thought I had thought of old,
And every evil deed I ever did,
Awoke and cried, "This quest is not for thee.'
And lifting up mine eyes, I found myself   375
Alone, and in a land of sand and thorns,
And I was thirsty even unto death;
And I, too, cried, "This quest is not for thee.'

"And on I rode, and when I thought my thirst
Would slay me, saw deep lawns, and then a brook,   380
With one sharp rapid, where the crisping white
Play'd ever back upon the sloping wave
And took both ear and eye; and o'er the brook
Were apple-trees, and apples by the brook
Fallen, and on the lawns. 'I will rest here,'   385
I said, 'I am not worthy of the quest;'
But even while I drank the brook, and ate
The goodly apples, all these things at once
Fell into dust, and I was left alone
And thirsting in a land of sand and thorns.   390

"And then behold a woman at a door
Spinning; and fair the house whereby she sat.
And kind the woman's eyes and innocent,
And all her bearing gracious; and she rose
Opening her arms to meet me, as who should say,   395
'Rest here;' but when I touch'd her, lo! she, too,
Fell into dust and nothing, and the house
Became no better than a broken shed,
And in it a dead babe; and also this
Fell into dust, and I was left alone.   400

"And on I rode, and greater was my thirst.
Then flash'd a yellow gleam across the world,
And where it smote the plowshare in the field
The plowman left his plowing and fell down
Before it; where it glitter'd on her pail   405
The milkmaid left her milking and fell down
Before it, and I knew not why, but thought
'The sun is rising,' tho' the sun had risen.
Then was I ware of one that on me moved
In golden armor with a crown of gold   410
About a casque all jewels, and his horse
In golden armor jewelled everywhere;
And on the splendor came, flashing me blind,
And seem'd to me the lord of all the world,
Being so huge. But when I thought he meant   415
To crush me, moving on me, lo! he, too,
Open'd his arms to embrace me as he came,
And up I went and touch'd him, and he, too,

Fell into dust, and I was left alone
And wearying in a land of sand and thorns. 420

"And I rode on and found a mighty hill,
And on the top a city wall'd; the spires
Prick'd with incredible pinnacles into heaven.
And by the gateway stirr'd a crowd; and these
Cried to me climbing, 'Welcome, Percivale! 425
Thou mightiest and thou purest among men!'
And glad was I and clomb, but found at top
No man, nor any voice. And thence I past
Far thro' a ruinous city, and I saw
That man had once dwelt there; but there I found 430
Only one man of an exceeding age.
'Where is that goodly company,' said I,
'That so cried out upon me?' and he had
Scarce any voice to answer, and yet gasp'd,
'Whence and what art thou?' and even as he spoke 435
Fell into dust and disappear'd, and I
Was left alone once more and cried in grief,
'Lo, if I find the Holy Grail itself
And touch it, it will crumble into dust!'

"And thence I dropt into a lowly vale, 440
Low as the hill was high, and where the vale
Was lowest found a chapel, and thereby
A holy hermit in a hermitage,
To whom I told my phantoms, and he said:

" 'O son, thou hast not true humility, 445
The highest virtue, mother of them all;
For when the Lord of all things made Himself
Naked of glory for His mortal change,
"Take thou my robe," she said, "for all is thine,"
And all her form shone forth with sudden light 450
So that the angels were amazed, and she
Follow'd Him down, and like a flying star
Led on the gray-hair'd wisdom of the east.[8]
But her thou hast not known; for what is this
Thou thoughtest of thy prowess and thy sins? 455
Thou hast not lost thyself to save thyself
As Galahad.' When the hermit made an end,
In silver armor suddenly Galahad shone
Before us, and against the chapel door
Laid lance and enter'd, and we knelt in prayer. 460
And there the hermit slaked my burning thirst,
And at the sacring[9] of the mass I saw
The holy elements alone; but he,
'Say ye no more? I, Galahad, saw the Grail,
The Holy Grail, descend upon the shrine. 465

8. The Magi.   9. Consecration.

I saw the fiery face as of a child
That smote itself into the bread and went;
And hither am I come; and never yet
Hath what thy sister taught me first to see,
This holy thing, fail'd from my side, nor come   470
Cover'd, but moving with me night and day,
Fainter by day, but always in the night
Blood-red, and sliding down the blacken'd marsh
Blood-red, and on the naked mountain top
Blood-red, and in the sleeping mere below   475
Blood-red. And in the strength of this I rode,
Shattering all evil customs everywhere,
And past thro' Pagan realms, and made them mine,
And clash'd with Pagan hordes, and bore them down,
And broke thro' all, and in the strength of this   480
Come victor. But my time is hard at hand,
And hence I go, and one will crown me king
Far in the spiritual city; and come thou, too,
For thou shalt see the vision when I go.'

    "While thus he spake, his eye, dwelling on mine,   485
Drew me, with power upon me, till I grew
One with him, to believe as he believed.
Then, when the day began to wane, we went.

    "There rose a hill that none but man could climb,
Scarr'd with a hundred wintry watercourses—   490
Storm at the top, and when we gain'd it, storm
Round us and death; for every moment glanced
His silver arms and gloom'd, so quick and thick
The lightnings here and there to left and right
Struck, till the dry old trunks about us, dead,   495
Yea, rotten with a hundred years of death,
Sprang into fire. And at the base we found
On either hand, as far as eye could see,
A great black swamp and of an evil smell,
Part black, part whiten'd with the bones of men,   500
Not to be crost, save that some ancient king
Had built a way, where, link'd with many a bridge,
A thousand piers ran into the great Sea.
And Galahad fled along them bridge by bridge,
And every bridge as quickly as he crost   505
Sprang into fire and vanish'd, tho' I yearn'd
To follow; and thrice above him all the heavens
Open'd and blazed with thunder such as seem'd
Shoutings of all the sons of God. And first
At once I saw him far on the great Sea,   510
In silver-shining armor starry-clear;
And o'er his head the Holy Vessel hung
Clothed in white samite or a luminous cloud.

And with exceeding swiftness ran the boat,
If boat it were—I saw not whence it came. 515
And when the heavens open'd and blazed again
Roaring, I saw him like a silver star—
And had he set the sail, or had the boat
Become a living creature clad with wings?
And o'er his head the Holy Vessel hung 520
Redder than any rose, a joy to me,
For now I knew the veil had been withdrawn.
Then in a moment when they blazed again
Opening, I saw the least of little stars
Down on the waste, and straight beyond the star 525
I saw the spiritual city and all her spires
And gateways in a glory like one pearl—
No larger, tho' the goal of all the saints—
Strike from the sea; and from the star there shot
A rose-red sparkle to the city, and there 530
Dwelt, and I knew it was the Holy Grail,
Which never eyes on earth again shall see.
Then fell the floods of heaven drowning the deep,
And how my feet recrost the deathful ridge
No memory in me lives; but that I touch'd 535
The chapel-doors at dawn I know, and thence
Taking my war-horse from the holy man,
Glad that no phantom vext me more, return'd
To whence I came, the gate of Arthur's wars."

"O brother," ask'd Ambrosius,—"for in sooth 540
These ancient books—and they would win thee—teem,
Only I find not there this Holy Grail,
With miracles and marvels like to these,
Not all unlike; which oftentime I read,
Who read but on my breviary with ease, 545
Till my head swims, and then go forth and pass
Down to the little thorpe that lies so close,
And almost plaster'd like a martin's nest
To these old walls—and mingle with our folk;
And knowing every honest face of theirs 550
As well as ever shepherd knew his sheep,
And every homely secret in their hearts,
Delight myself with gossip and old wives,
And ills and aches, and teethings, lyings-in,
And mirthful sayings, children of the place, 555
That have no meaning half a league away;
Or lulling random squabbles when they rise,
Chafferings and chatterings at the market-cross,
Rejoice, small man, in this small world of mine,
Yea, even in their hens and in their eggs— 560
O brother, saving this Sir Galahad,

Came ye on none but phantoms in your quest,
No man, no woman?"

    Then Sir Percivale:
"All men, to one so bound by such a vow,
And women were as phantoms. O, my brother,   565
Why wilt thou shame me to confess to thee
How far I falter'd from my quest and vow?
For after I had lain so many nights,
A bed-mate of the snail and eft and snake,
In grass and burdock, I was changed to wan   570
And meagre, and the vision had not come;
And then I chanced upon a goodly town
With one great dwelling in the middle of it.
Thither I made, and there was I disarm'd
By maidens each as fair as any flower;   575
But when they led me into hall, behold,
The princess of that castle was the one,
Brother, and that one only, who had ever
Made my heart leap; for when I moved of old
A slender page about her father's hall,   580
And she a slender maiden, all my heart
Went after her with longing, yet we twain
Had never kiss'd a kiss or vow'd a vow.
And now I came upon her once again,
And one had wedded her, and he was dead,   585
And all his land and wealth and state were hers.
And while I tarried, every day she set
A banquet richer than the day before
By me, for all her longing and her will
Was toward me as of old; till one fair morn,   590
I walking to and fro beside a stream
That flash'd across her orchard underneath
Her castle-walls, she stole upon my walk,
And calling me the greatest of all knights,
Embraced me, and so kiss'd me the first time,   595
And gave herself and all her wealth to me.
Then I remember'd Arthur's warning word,
That most of us would follow wandering fires,
And the quest faded in my heart. Anon,
The heads of all her people drew to me,   600
With supplication both of knees and tongue:
'We have heard of thee; thou art our greatest knight,
Our Lady says it, and we well believe.
Wed thou our Lady, and rule over us,
And thou shalt be as Arthur in our land.'   605
O me, my brother! but one night my vow
Burnt me within, so that I rose and fled,
But wail'd and wept, and hated mine own self,

And even the holy quest, and all but her;
Then after I was join'd with Galahad   610
Cared not for her nor anything upon earth."

　　Then said the monk: "Poor men, when yule is cold,
Must be content to sit by little fires.
And this am I, so that ye care for me
Ever so little; yea, and blest be heaven   615
That brought thee here to this poor house of ours
Where all the brethren are so hard, to warm
My cold heart with a friend; but O the pity
To find thine own first love once more—to hold,
Hold her a wealthy bride within thine arms,   620
Or all but hold, and then—cast her aside,
Foregoing all her sweetness, like a weed!
For we that want the warmth of double life,
We that are plagued with dreams of something sweet
Beyond all sweetness in a life so rich,—   625
Ah, blessed Lord, I speak too earthly-wise,
Seeing I never stray'd beyond the cell,
But live like an old badger in his earth,
With earth about him everywhere, despite
All fast and penance. Saw ye none beside,   630
None of your knights?"

　　　　　　　　"Yea, so," said Percivale:
"One night my pathway swerving east, I saw
The pelican on the casque of our Sir Bors
All in the middle of the rising moon,
And toward him spurr'd, and hail'd him, and he me,   635
And each made joy of either. Then he ask'd:
Where is he? hast thou seen him—Lancelot?—Once,'
Said good Sir Bors, 'he dash'd across me—mad,
And maddening what he rode; and when I cried,
"Ridest thou then so hotly on a quest   640
So holy?" Lancelot shouted, "Stay me not!
I have been the sluggard, and I ride apace,
For now there is a lion in the way!"
So vanish'd.'

　　　　　　　　"Then Sir Bors had ridden on
Softly, and sorrowing for our Lancelot,   645
Because his former madness, once the talk
And scandal of our table, had return'd;
For Lancelot's kith and kin so worship him
That ill to him is ill to them, to Bors
Beyond the rest. He well had been content   650
Not to have seen, so Lancelot might have seen,
The Holy Cup of healing; and, indeed,
Being so clouded with his grief and love,
Small heart was his after the holy quest.

If God would send the vision, well; if not,　　　　655
The quest and he were in the hands of Heaven.

　　"And then, with small adventure met, Sir Bors
Rode to the lonest tract of all the realm,
And found a people there among their crags,
Our race and blood, a remnant that were left　　660
Paynim[1] amid their circles, and the stones
They pitch up straight to heaven; and their wise men
Were strong in that old magic which can trace
The wandering of the stars, and scoff'd at him
And this high quest as at a simple thing,　　665
Told him he follow'd—almost Arthur's words—
A mocking fire: 'what other fire than he[2]
Whereby the blood beats, and the blossom blows,
And the sea rolls, and all the world is warm'd?'
And when his answer chafed them, the rough crowd,　　670
Hearing he had a difference with their priests,
Seized him, and bound and plunged him into a cell
Of great piled stones; and lying bounden there
In darkness thro' innumerable hours
He heard the hollow-ringing heavens sweep　　675
Over him till by miracle—what else?—
Heavy as it was, a great stone slipt and fell,
Such as no wind could move; and thro' the gap
Glimmer'd the streaming scud. Then came a night
Still as the day was loud, and thro' the gap　　680
The seven clear stars[3] of Arthur's Table Round—
For, brother, so one night, because they roll
Thro' such a round in heaven, we named the stars,
Rejoicing in ourselves and in our King—
And these, like bright eyes of familiar friends,　　685
In on him shone: 'And then to me, to me,'
Said good Sir Bors, 'beyond all hopes of mine,
Who scarce had pray'd or ask'd it for myself—
Across the seven clear stars—O grace to me!—
In color like the fingers of a hand　　690
Before a burning taper, the sweet Grail
Glided and past, and close upon it peal'd
A sharp quick thunder.' Afterwards, a maid,
Who kept our holy faith among her kin
In secret, entering, loosed and let him go."　　695

　　To whom the monk: "And I remember now
That pelican on the casque. Sir Bors it was
Who spake so low and sadly at our board,
And mighty reverent at our grace was he;
A square-set man and honest, and his eyes,　　700

1. Pagans. Remnants of the ancient
Druids, whose mysterious rites were
held in stone circles, the most famous
remains of which are at Stonehenge.
2. The sun.
3. Ursa Major.

An outdoor sign of all the warmth within,
Smiled with his lips—a smile beneath a cloud,
But heaven had meant it for a sunny one.
Ay, ay, Sir Bors, who else? But when ye reach'd
The city, found ye all your knights return'd,   705
Or was there sooth in Arthur's prophecy,
Tell me, and what said each, and what the King?"

Then answer'd Percivale: "And that can I,
Brother, and truly; since the living words
Of so great men as Lancelot and our King   710
Pass not from door to door and out again,
But sit within the house. O, when we reach'd
The city, our horses stumbling as they trode
On heaps of ruin, hornless unicorns,
Crack'd basilisks,[4] and splinter'd cockatrices,   715
And shatter'd talbots, which had left the stones
Raw that they fell from, brought us to the hall.

"And there sat Arthur on the dais-throne,
And those that had gone out upon the quest,
Wasted and worn, and but a tithe of them,   720
And those that had not, stood before the King,
Who, when he saw me, rose and bade me hail,
Saying: 'A welfare in thine eyes reproves
Our fear of some disastrous chance for thee
On hill or plain, at sea or flooding ford.   725
So fierce a gale made havoc here of late
Among the strange devices of our kings,
Yea, shook this newer, stronger hall of ours,
And from the statue Merlin moulded for us
Half-wrench'd a golden wing; but now—the quest,   730
This vision—hast thou seen the Holy Cup
That Joseph brought of old to Glastonbury?'

"So when I told him all thyself hast heard,
Ambrosius, and my fresh but fixt resolve
To pass away into the quiet life,   735
He answer'd not, but, sharply turning, ask'd
Of Gawain, 'Gawain, was this quest for thee?'

" 'Nay, lord,' said Gawain, 'not for such as I.
Therefore I communed with a saintly man,
Who made me sure the quest was not for me;   740
For I was much a-wearied of the quest,
But found a silk pavilion in a field,
And merry maidens in it; and then this gale
Tore my pavilion from the tenting-pin,
And blew my merry maidens all about   745

---

4. The king of serpents, whose looks
were lethal to the gazer; cockatrices
were winged serpents; the talbot were
heraldic dogs.

With all discomfort; yea, and but for this,
My twelvemonth and a day were pleasant to me.'

"He ceased; and Arthur turn'd to whom at first
He saw not, for Sir Bors, on entering, push'd
Athwart the throng to Lancelot, caught his hand,   750
Held it, and there, half-hidden by him, stood,
Until the King espied him, saying to him,
'Hail, Bors! if ever loyal man and true
Could see it, thou hast seen the Grail;' and Bors,
'Ask me not, for I may not speak of it;   755
I saw it;' and the tears were in his eyes.

"Then there remain'd but Lancelot, for the rest
Spake but of sundry perils in the storm.
Perhaps, like him of Cana[5] in Holy Writ,
Our Arthur kept his best until the last;   760
'Thou, too, my Lancelot,' ask'd the King, 'my friend,
Our mightiest, hath this quest avail'd for thee?'

" 'Our mightiest!' answer'd Lancelot, with a groan;
'O King!'—and when he paused methought I spied
A dying fire of madness in his eyes—   765
'O King, my friend, if friend of thine I be,
Happier are those that welter in their sin,
Swine in the mud, that cannot see for slime,
Slime of the ditch; but in me lived a sin
So strange, of such a kind, that all of pure,   770
Noble, and knightly in me twined and clung
Round that one sin, until the wholesome flower
And poisonous grew together, each as each,
Not to be pluck'd asunder; and when thy knights
Sware, I sware with them only in the hope   775
That could I touch or see the Holy Grail
They might be pluck'd asunder. Then I spake
To one most holy saint, who wept and said
That, save they could be pluck'd asunder, all
My quest were but in vain; to whom I vow'd   780
That I would work according as he will'd.
And forth I went, and while I yearn'd and strove
To tear the twain asunder in my heart,
My madness came upon me as of old,
And whipt me into waste fields far away.   785
There was I beaten down by little men,
Mean knights, to whom the moving of my sword
And shadow of my spear had been enow
To scare them from me once; and then I came
All in my folly to the naked shore,   790

5. The first of Christ's miracles was the changing of water to wine at the marriage in Cana of Galilee. The governor of the feast praised the bridegroom for serving the best wine last. See *John,* 2:1–11.

Wide flats, where nothing but coarse grasses grew;
But such a blast, my King, began to blow,
So loud a blast along the shore and sea,
Ye could not hear the waters for the blast,
Tho' heapt in mounds and ridges all the sea   795
Drove like a cataract, and all the sand
Swept like a river, and the clouded heavens
Were shaken with the motion and the sound.
And blackening in the sea-foam sway'd a boat,
Half-swallow'd in it, anchor'd with a chain;   800
And in my madness to myself I said,
"I will embark and I will lose myself,
And in the great sea wash away my sin."
I burst the chain, I sprang into the boat.
Seven days I drove along the dreary deep,   805
And with me drove the moon and all the stars;
And the wind fell, and on the seventh night
I heard the shingle grinding in the surge,
And felt the boat shock earth, and looking up,
Behold, the enchanted towers of Carbonek,[6]   810
A castle like a rock upon a rock,
With chasm-like portals open to the sea,
And steps that met the breaker! There was none
Stood near it but a lion on each side
That kept the entry, and the moon was full.   815
Then from the boat I leapt, and up the stairs,
There drew my sword. With sudden-flaring manes
Those two great beasts rose upright like a man,
Each gript a shoulder, and I stood between,
And, when I would have smitten them, heard a voice,   820
"Doubt not, go forward; if thou doubt, the beasts
Will tear thee piecemeal." Then with violence
The sword was dash'd from out my hand, and fell.
And up into the sounding hall I past;
But nothing in the sounding hall I saw,   825
No bench nor table, painting on the wall
Or shield of knight, only the rounded moon
Thro' the tall oriel[7] on the rolling sea.
But always in the quiet house I heard,
Clear as a lark, high o'er me as a lark,   830
A sweet voice singing in the topmost tower
To the eastward. Up I climb'd a thousand steps
With pain; as in a dream I seem'd to climb
For ever; at the last I reach'd a door,
A light was in the crannies, and I heard,   835
"Glory and joy and honor to our Lord
And to the Holy Vessel of the Grail!"
Then in my madness I essay'd the door;

6. Malory located the Grail there.   7. Bay window.

It gave, an thro' a stormy glare, a heat
As from a seven-times-heated furnace, I, 840
Blasted and burnt, and blinded as I was,
With such a fierceness that I swoon'd away—
O, yet methought I saw the Holy Grail,
All pall'd in crimson samite, and around
Great angels, awful shapes, and wings and eyes! 845
And but for all my madness and my sin,
And then my swooning, I had sworn I saw
That which I saw; but what I saw was veil'd
And cover'd, and this quest was not for me.'

    "So speaking, and here ceasing, Lancelot left 850
The hall long silent, till Sir Gawain—nay,
Brother, I need not tell thee foolish words,—
A reckless and irreverent knight was he,
Now bolden'd by the silence of his King,—
Well, I will tell thee: 'O King, my liege,' he said, 855
'Hath Gawain fail'd in any quest of thine?
When have I stinted stroke in foughten field?
But as for thine, my good friend Percivale,
Thy holy nun and thou have driven men mad,
Yea, made our mightiest madder than our least. 860
But by mine eyes and by mine ears I swear,
I will be deafer than the blue-eyed cat,[8]
And thrice as blind as any noonday owl,
To holy virgins in their ecstasies,
Henceforward.'

    " 'Deafer,' said the blameless King, 865
'Gawain, and blinder unto holy things,
Hope not to make thyself by idle vows,
Being too blind to have desire to see.
But if indeed there came a sign from heaven,
Blessed are Bors, Lancelot, and Percivale, 870
For these have seen according to their sight.
For every fiery prophet in old times,
And all the sacred madness of the bard,
When God made music thro' them, could but speak
His music by the framework and the chord; 875
And as ye saw it ye have spoken truth.

    " 'Nay—but thou errest, Lancelot; never yet
Could all of true and noble in knight and man
Twine round one sin, whatever it might be,
With such a closeness but apart there grew, 880
Save that he were the swine thou spakest of,
Some root of knighthood and pure nobleness;
Whereto see thou, that it may bear its flower.

8. An allusion to the *Origin of Species* and Darwin's experimentations with cats. White, blue-eyed, male cats are generally deaf.

" 'And spake I not too truly, O my knights?
Was I too dark a prophet when I said   885
To those who went upon the Holy Quest,
That most of them would follow wandering fires,
Lost in the quagmire?—lost to me and gone,
And left me gazing at a barren board,
And a lean Order—scarce return'd a tithe—   890
And out of those to whom the vision came
My greatest hardly will believe he saw.
Another hath beheld it afar off,
And, leaving human wrongs to right themselves,
Cares but to pass into the silent life.   895
And one hath had the vision face to face,
And now his chair desires him here in vain,
However they may crown him otherwhere.

" 'And some among you held that if the King
Had seen the sight he would have sworn the vow.   900
Not easily, seeing that the King must guard
That which he rules, and is but as the hind
To whom a space of land is given to plow,
Who may not wander from the allotted field
Before his work be done, but, being done,   905
Let visions of the night or of the day
Come as they will; and many a time they come,
Until this earth he walks on seems not earth,
This light that strikes his eyeball is not light,
This air that smites his forehead is not air   910
But vision—yea, his very hand and foot—
In moments when he feels he cannot die,
And knows himself no vision to himself,
Nor the high God a vision,[9] nor that One
Who rose again. Ye have seen what ye have seen.'   915

"So spake the King; I knew not all he meant."

1869

Pelleas and Ettarre[1]

King Arthur made new knights to fill the gap
Left by the Holy Quest; and as he sat
In hall at old Caerleon, the high doors
Were softly sunder'd, and thro' these a youth,
Pelleas, and the sweet smell of the fields   5
Past, and the sunshine came along with him.

9. "I have expressed there my strong feelings as to the Reality of the Unseen. The end, where the king speaks of his work and of his visions, is intended to be the summing up of all in the highest note by the highest of human men.

These three lines [912–914] in Arthur's speech are the (spiritually) central lines of the Idylls" (*Memoir*, II, 90).
1. "Gareth and Lynette," which Tennyson started writing almost immediately after finishing "Pelleas and Ettarre,"

"Make me thy knight, because I know, Sir King,
All that belongs to knighthood, and I love."
Such was his cry; for having heard the King
Had let proclaim a tournament—the prize   10
A golden circlet and a knightly sword,
Full fain had Pelleas for his lady won
The golden circlet, for himself the sword.
And there were those who knew him near the King,
And promised for him; and Arthur made him knight.   15

And this new knight, Sir Pelleas of the Isles—
But lately come to his inheritance,
And lord of many a barren isle was he—
Riding at noon, a day or twain before,
Across the forest call'd of Dean,[2] to find   20
Caerleon and the King, had felt the sun
Beat like a strong knight on his helm and reel'd
Almost to falling from his horse, but saw
Near him a mound of even-sloping side
Whereon a hundred stately beeches grew,   25
And here and there great hollies under them;
But for a mile all round was open space
And fern and heath. And slowly Pelleas drew
To that dim day, then, binding his good horse
To a tree, cast himself down; and as he lay   30
At random looking over the brown earth
Thro' that green-glooming twilight of the grove,
It seem'd to Pelleas that the fern without
Burnt as a living fire of emeralds,
So that his eyes were dazzled looking at it.   35
Then o'er it crost the dimness of a cloud
Floating, and once the shadow of a bird
Flying, and then a fawn; and his eyes closed.
And since he loved all maidens, but no maid
In special, half-awake he whisper'd: "Where?   40
O, where? I love thee, tho' I know thee not.
For fair thou art and pure as Guinevere,
And I will make thee with my spear and sword
As famous—O my Queen, my Guinevere,
For I will be thine Arthur when we meet."   45

Suddenly waken'd with a sound of talk
And laughter at the limit of the wood,
And glancing thro' the hoary boles, he saw,

---

seems deliberately designed to contrast
the fortunes of two young knights.
Whereas Gareth's idealism prevails and
wins him Lynette, Pelleas' similar qual-
ities cannot possibly sustain him when
faced with Ettarre's lascivious conduct.
Although Tennyson had been praised
more than once in the last century for
never penning a line which could bring
a blush to the cheeks of an English
maiden, one can only postulate a rather
unimaginative reading of this idyll by
critic and maiden alike.
2. Dating from ancient times, an exten-
sive tract of country in Gloucestershire.

Strange as to some old prophet might have seem'd
A vision hovering on a sea of fire,   50
Damsels in divers colors like the cloud
Of sunset and sunrise, and all of them
On horses, and the horses richly trapt
Breast-high in that bright line of bracken stood;
And all the damsels talk'd confusedly,   55
And one was pointing this way and one that,
Because the way was lost.

                And Pelleas rose,
And loosed his horse, and led him to the light.
There she that seem'd the chief among them said:
"In happy time behold our pilot-star!   60
Youth, we are damsels-errant, and we ride,
Arm'd as ye see, to tilt against the knights
There at Caerleon, but have lost our way.
To right? to left? straight forward? back again?
Which? tell us quickly."

                Pelleas gazing thought,   65
"Is Guinevere herself so beautiful?"
For large her violet eyes look'd, and her bloom
A rosy dawn kindled in stainless heavens,
And round her limbs, mature in womanhood;
And slender was her hand and small her shape;   70
And but for those large eyes, the haunts of scorn,
She might have seem'd a toy to trifle with,
And pass and care no more. But while he gazed
The beauty of her flesh abash'd the boy,
As tho' it were the beauty of her soul;   75
For as the base man, judging of the good,
Puts his own baseness in him by default
Of will and nature, so did Pelleas lend
All the young beauty of his own soul to hers,
Believing her, and when she spake to him   80
Stammer'd, and could not make her a reply.
For out of the waste islands had he come,
Where saving his own sisters he had known
Scarce any but the woman of his isles,
Rough wives, that laugh'd and scream'd against the gulls,   85
Makers of nets, and living from the sea.

  Then with a slow smile turn'd the lady round
And look'd upon her people; and, as when
A stone is flung into some sleeping tarn
The circle widens till it lip the marge,   90
Spread the slow smile thro' all her company.
Three knights were thereamong, and they too smiled,
Scorning him; for the lady was Ettarre,
And she was a great lady in her land.

Again she said: "O wild and of the woods,   95
Knowest thou not the fashion of our speech?
Or have the Heavens but given thee a fair face,
Lacking a tongue?"

                "O damsel," answer'd he,
"I woke from dreams, and coming out of gloom
Was dazzled by the sudden light, and crave   100
Pardon; but will ye to Caerleon? I
Go likewise; shall I lead you to the King?"

   "Lead then," she said; and thro' the woods they went.
And while they rode, the meaning in his eyes,
His tenderness of manner, and chaste awe,   105
His broken utterances and bashfulness,
Were all a burthen to her, and in her heart
She mutter'd, "I have lighted on a fool,
Raw, yet so stale!" But since her mind was bent
On hearing, after trumpet blown, her name   110
And title, "Queen of Beauty," in the lists
Cried—and beholding him so strong she thought
That peradventure he will fight for me,
And win the circlet—therefore flatter'd him,
Being so gracious that he wellnigh deem'd   115
His wish by hers was echo'd; and her knights
And all her damsels too were gracious to him,
For she was a great lady.

               And when they reach'd
Caerleon, ere they past to lodging, she,
Taking his hand, "O the strong hand," she said,   120
"See! look at mine! but wilt thou fight for me,
And win this fine circlet, Pelleas,
That I may love thee?"

             Then his helpless heart
Leapt, and he cried, "Ay! wilt thou if I win?"
"Ay, that will I," she answer'd, and she laugh'd,   125
And straitly nipt the hand, and flung it from her;
Then glanced askew at those three knights of hers,
Till all her ladies laugh'd along with her.

   "O happy world," thought Pelleas, "all, meseems,
Are happy; I the happiest of them all!"   130
Nor slept that night for pleasure in his blood,
And green wood-ways, and eyes among the leaves;
Then being on the morrow knighted, sware
To love one only. And as he came away,
The men who met him rounded on their heels   135
And wonder'd after him, because his face
Shone like the countenance of a priest of old
Against the flame about a sacrifice
Kindled by fire from heaven; so glad was he.

Then Arthur made vast banquets, and strange knights   140
From the four winds came in; and each one sat,
Tho' served with choice from air, land, stream, and sea,
Oft in mid-banquet measuring with his eyes
His neighbor's make and might; and Pelleas look'd
Noble among the noble, for he dream'd   145
His lady loved him, and he knew himself
Loved of the King; and him his new-made knight
Worshipt, whose lightest whisper moved him more
Than all the ranged reasons of the world.

Then blush'd and brake the morning of the jousts,   150
And this was call'd "The Tournament of Youth;"
For Arthur, loving his young knight, withheld
His older and his mightier from the lists,
That Pelleas might obtain his lady's love,
According to her promise, and remain   155
Lord of the tourney. And Arthur had the jousts
Down in the flat field by the shore of Usk
Holden; the gilded parapets were crown'd
With faces, and the great tower fill'd with eyes
Up to the summit, and the trumpets blew.   160
There all day long Sir Pelleas kept the field
With honor; so by that strong hand of his
The sword and golden circlet were achieved.

Then rang the shout his lady loved; the heat
Of pride and glory fired her face, her eye   165
Sparkled; she caught the circlet from his lance,
And there before the people crown'd herself.
So for the last time she was gracious to him.

Then at Caerleon for a space—her look
Bright for all others, cloudier on her knight—   170
Linger'd Ettarre; and, seeing Pelleas droop,
Said Guinevere, "We marvel at thee much,
O damsel, wearing this unsunny face
To him who won thee glory!" And she said,
"Had ye not held your Lancelot in your bower,   175
My Queen, he had not won." Whereat the Queen,
As one whose foot is bitten by an ant,
Glanced down upon her, turn'd and went her way.[3]

But after, when her damsels, and herself,
And those three knights all set their faces home,   180
Sir Pelleas follow'd. She that saw him cried:
"Damsels—and yet I should be shamed to say it—
I cannot bide Sir Baby. Keep him back
Among yourselves. Would rather that we had
Some rough old knight who knew the worldly way,   185

3. A significant exchange in that the   previously had been only rumor.
Queen is openly confronted with what

Albeit grizzlier than a bear, to ride
And jest with! Take him to you, keep him off,
And pamper him with papmeat, if ye will,
Old milky fables of the wolf and sheep,
Such as the wholesome mothers tell their boys.   190
Nay, should ye try him with a merry one
To find his mettle, good; and if he fly us,
Small matter! let him." This her damsels heard,
And, mindful of her small and cruel hand,
They, closing round him thro' the journey home,   195
Acted her hest,[4] and always from her side
Restrain'd him with all manner of device,
So that he could not come to speech with her.
And when she gain'd her castle, upsprang the bridge,
Down rang the grate of iron thro' the groove,   200
And he was left alone in open field.

"These be the ways of ladies," Pelleas thought,
"To those who love them, trials of our faith.
Yea, let her prove me to the uttermost,
For loyal to the uttermost am I."   205
So made his moan, and, darkness falling, sought
A priory not far off, there lodged, but rose
With morning every day, and, moist or dry,
Full-arm'd upon his charger all day long
Sat by the walls, and no one open'd to him.   210

And this persistence turn'd her scorn to wrath.
Then, calling her three knights, she charged them, "Out!
And drive him from the walls." And out they came,
But Pelleas overthrew them as they dash'd
Against him one by one; and these return'd,   215
But still he kept his watch beneath the wall.

Thereon her wrath became a hate; and once,
A week beyond, while walking on the walls
With her three knights, she pointed downward, "Look,
He haunts me—I cannot breathe—besieges me!   220
Down! strike him! put my hate into your strokes,
And drive him from my walls." And down they went,
And Pelleas overthrew them one by one;
And from the tower above him cried Ettarre,
"Bind him, and bring him in."

He heard her voice;   225
Then let the strong hand, which had overthrown
Her minion-knights, by those he overthrew
Be bounden straight, and so they brought him in.

Then when he came before Ettarre, the sight
Of her rich beauty made him at one glance   230

4. Archaic for behest or bidding.

More bondsman in his heart than in his bonds.
Yet with good cheer he spake: "Behold me, lady,
A prisoner, and the vassal of thy will;
And if thou keep me in thy donjon here,
Content am I so that I see thy face   235
But once a day; for I have sworn my vows,
And thou hast given thy promise, and I know
That all these pains are trials of my faith,
And that thyself, when thou hast seen me strain'd
And sifted to the utmost, wilt at length   240
Yield me thy love and know me for thy knight."

Then she began to rail so bitterly,
With all her damsels, he was stricken mute,
But, when she mock'd his vows and the great King,
Lighted on words: "For pity of thine own self,   245
Peace, lady, peace; is he not thine and mine?"
"Thou fool," she said, "I never heard his voice
But long'd to break away. Unbind him now,
And thrust him out of doors; for save he be
Fool to the midmost marrow of his bones,   250
He will return no more." And those, her three,
Laugh'd, and unbound, and thrust him from the gate.

And after this, a week beyond, again
She call'd them, saying: "There he watches yet,
There like a dog before his master's door!   255
Kick'd, he returns; do ye not hate him, ye?
Ye know yourselves; how can ye bide at peace,
Affronted with his fulsome innocence?
Are ye but creatures of the board and bed.
No men to strike? Fall on him all at once,   260
And if ye slay him I reck not; if ye fail,
Give ye the slave mine order to be bound,
Bind him as heretofore, and bring him in.
It may be ye shall slay him in his bonds."

She spake, and at her will they couch'd their spears,   265
Three against one; and Gawain passing by,
Bound upon solitary adventure, saw
Low down beneath the shadow of those towers
A villainy, three to one; and thro' his heart
The fire of honor and all noble deeds   270
Flash'd, and he call'd, "I strike upon thy side—
The caitiffs!" "Nay," said Pelleas, "but forbear;
He needs no aid who doth his lady's will."

So Gawain, looking at the villainy done,
Forbore, but in his heat and eagerness   275
Trembled and quiver'd, as the dog, withheld
A moment from the vermin that he sees
Before him, shivers ere he springs and kills.

And Pelleas overthrew them, one to three;
And they rose up, and bound, and brought him in.   280
Then first her anger, leaving Pelleas, burn'd
Full on her knights in many an evil name
Of craven, weakling, and thrice-beaten hound:
"Yet, take him, ye that scarce are fit to touch,
Far less to bind, your victor, and thrust him out,   285
And let who will release him from his bonds.
And if he comes again"—there she brake short;
And Pelleas answer'd: "Lady, for indeed
I loved you and I deem'd you beautiful,
I cannot brook to see your beauty marr'd   290
Thro' evil spite; and if ye love me not,
I cannot bear to dream you so forsworn.
I had liefer ye were worthy of my love
Than to be loved again of you—farewell.
And tho' ye kill my hope, not yet my love,   295
Vex not yourself; ye will not see me more."

    While thus he spake, she gazed upon the man
Of princely bearing, tho' in bonds, and thought:
"Why have I push'd him from me? this man loves,
If love there be; yet him I loved not. Why?   300
I deem'd him fool? yea, so? or that in him
A something—was it nobler than myself?—
Seem'd my reproach? He is not of my kind.
He could not love me, did he know me well.
Nay, let him go—and quickly." And her knights   305
Laugh'd not, but thrust him bounden out of door.

    Forth sprang Gawain, and loosed him from his bonds,
And flung them o'er the walls; and afterward,
Shaking his hands, as from a lazar's rag,
"Faith of my body," he said, "and art thou not—   310
Yea thou art he, whom late our Arthur made
Knight of his table; yea, and he that won
The circlet? wherefore hast thou so defamed
Thy brotherhood in me and all the rest
As let these caitiffs on thee work their will?"   315

    And Pelleas answer'd: "O, their wills are hers
For whom I won the circlet; and mine, hers,
Thus to be bounden, so to see her face,
Marr'd tho' it be with spite and mockery now,
Other than when I found her in the woods;   320
And tho' she hath me bounden but in spite,
And all to flout me, when they bring me in,
Let me be bounden, I shall see her face;
Else must I die thro' mine unhappiness."

    And Gawain answer'd kindly tho' in scorn: 325
"Why, let my lady bind me if she will,

And let my lady beat me if she will;
But an she send her delegate to thrall
These fighting hands of mine—Christ kill me then
But I will slice him handless by the wrist,   330
And let my lady sear the stump for him,
Howl as he may! But hold me for your friend.
Come, ye know nothing; here I pledge my troth,
Yea, by the honor of the Table Round,
I will be leal[5] to thee and work thy work,   335
And tame thy jailing princess to thine hand.
Lend me thine horse and arms, and I will say
That I have slain thee. She will let me in
To hear the manner of thy fight and fall;
Then, when I come within her counsels, then   340
From prime to vespers will I chant thy praise
As prowest[6] knight and truest lover, more
Than any have sung thee living, till she long
To have thee back in lusty life again,
Not to be bound, save by white bonds and warm,   345
Dearer than freedom. Wherefore now thy horse
And armor; let me go; be comforted.
Give me three days to melt her fancy, and hope
The third night hence will bring thee news of gold."

       Then Pelleas lent his horse and all his arms,   350
Saving the goodly sword, his prize, and took
Gawain's, and said, "Betray me not, but help—
Art thou not he whom men call light-of-love?"

       "Ay," said Gawain, "for women be so light;"
Then bounded forward to the castle walls,   355
And raised a bugle hanging from his neck,
And winded it, and that so musically
That all the old echoes hidden in the wall
Rang out like hollow woods at huntingtide.

       Up ran a score of damsels to the tower;   360
"Avaunt," they cried, "our lady loves thee not!"
But Gawain lifting up his vizor said:
"Gawain am I, Gawain of Arthur's court,
And I have slain this Pelleas whom ye hate.
Behold his horse and armor. Open gates,   365
And I will make you merry."

                            And down they ran,
Her damsels, crying to their lady, "Lo!
Pelleas is dead—he told us—he that hath
His horse and armor; will ye let him in?
He slew him! Gawain, Gawain of the court,   370
Sir Gawain—there he waits below the wall,
Blowing his bugle as who should say him nay."

5. Loyal.   6. Noblest.

And so, leave given, straight on thro' open door
Rode Gawain, whom she greeted courteously.
"Dead, is it so?" she ask'd. "Ay, ay," said he, 375
"And oft in dying cried upon your name."
"Pity on him," she answer'd, "a good knight,
But never let me bide one hour at peace."
"Ay," thought Gawain, "and you be fair enow;
But I to your dead man have given my troth, 380
That whom ye loathe, him will I make you love."

So those three days, aimless about the land,
Lost in a doubt, Pelleas wandering
Waited, until the third night brought a moon
With promise of large light on woods and ways. 385

Hot was the night and silent; but a sound
Of Gawain ever coming, and this lay—
Which Pelleas had heard sung before the Queen,
And seen her sadden listening—vext his heart,
And marr'd his rest—"A worm within the rose." 390

   "A rose, but one, none other rose had I,
  A rose, one rose, and this was wondrous fair,
  One rose, a rose that gladden'd earth and sky,
  One rose, my rose, that sweeten'd all mine air—
  I cared not for the thorns; the thorns were there. 395

   "One rose, a rose to gather by and by,
  One rose, a rose, to gather and to wear,
  No rose but one—what other rose had I?
  One rose, my rose; a rose that will not die,—
  He dies who loves it,—if the worm be there." 400

This tender rhyme, and evermore the doubt,
"Why lingers Gawain with his golden news?"
So shook him that he could not rest, but rode
Ere midnight to her walls, and bound his horse
Hard by the gates. Wide open were the gates, 405
And no watch kept; and in thro' these he past,
And heard but his own steps, and his own heart
Beating, for nothing moved but his own self
And his own shadow. Then he crost the court,
And spied not any light in hall or bower, 410
But saw the postern portal also wide
Yawning; and up a slope of garden, all
Of roses white and red, and brambles mixt
And overgrowing them, went on, and found,
Here too, all hush'd below the mellow moon, 415
Save that one rivulet from a tiny cave
Came lightening downward, and so split itself
Among the roses and was lost again.

  Then was he ware of three pavilions rear'd
Above the bushes, gilden-peakt. In one, 420

Red after revel, droned her lurdane[7] knights
Slumbering, and their three squires across their feet;
In one, their malice on the placid lip
Frozen by sweet sleep, four of her damsels lay;
And in the third, the circlet of the jousts   425
Bound on her brow, were Gawain and Ettarre.

    Back, as a hand that pushes thro' the leaf
To find a nest and feels a snake, he drew;
Back, as a coward slinks from what he fears
To cope with, or a traitor proven, or hound   430
Beaten, did Pelleas in an utter shame
Creep with his shadow thro' the court again,
Fingering at his sword-handle until he stood
There on the castle-bridge once more, and thought,
"I will go back, and slay them where they lie."   435

    And so went back, and seeing them yet in sleep
Said, "Ye, that so dishallow the holy sleep,
Your sleep is death," and drew the sword, and thought,
"What! slay a sleeping knight? the King hath bound
And sworn me to this brotherhood;" again,   440
"Alas that ever a knight should be so false!"
Then turn'd, and so return'd, and groaning laid
The naked sword athwart their naked throats,
There left it, and them sleeping; and she lay,
The circlet of the tourney round her brows,   445
And the sword of the tourney across her throat.

    And forth he past, and mounting on his horse
Stared at her towers that, larger than themselves
In their own darkness, throng'd into the moon;
Then crush'd the saddle with his thighs, and clench'd   450
His hands, and madden'd with himself and moan'd:

    "Would they have risen against me in their blood
At the last day? I might have answer'd them
Even before high God. O towers so strong,
Huge, solid, would that even while I gaze   455
The crack of earthquake shivering to your base
Split you, and hell burst up your harlot roofs
Bellowing, and charr'd you thro' and thro' within,
Black as the harlot's heart—hollow as a skull!
Let the fierce east scream thro' your eyelet-holes,   460
And whirl the dust of harlots round and round
In dung and nettles! hiss, snake—I saw him there—
Let the fox bark, let the wolf yell! Who yells
Here in the still sweet summer night but I—
I, the poor Pelleas whom she call'd her fool?   465
Fool, beast—he, she, or I? myself most fool;

7. Sluggish and stupid.

Beast too, as lacking human wit—disgraced,
Dishonor'd all for trial of true love—
Love?—we be all alike; only the King
Hath made us fools and liars. O noble vows!   470
O great and sane and simple race of brutes
That own no lust because they have no law!
For why should I have loved her to my shame?
I loathe her, as I loved her to my shame.
I never loved her, I but lusted for her—   475
Away!"—

      He dash'd the rowel into his horse,
And bounded forth and vanish'd thro' the night.

  Then she, that felt the cold touch on her throat,
Awaking knew the sword, and turn'd herself
To Gawain: "Liar, for thou hast not slain   480
This Pelleas! here he stood, and might have slain
Me and thyself." And he that tells the tale
Says that her ever-veering fancy turn'd
To Pelleas, as the one true knight on earth
And only lover; and thro' her love her life   485
Wasted and pined, desiring him in vain.

  But he by wild and way, for half the night,
And over hard and soft, striking the sod
From out the soft, the spark from off the hard,
Rode till the star above the wakening sun,   490
Beside that tower where Percivale was cowl'd,
Glanced from the rosy forehead of the dawn.
For so the words were flash'd into his heart
He knew not whence or wherefore: "O sweet star,
Pure on the virgin forehead of the dawn!"   495
And there he would have wept, but felt his eyes
Harder and drier than a fountain bed
In summer. Thither came the village girls
And linger'd talking, and they come no more
Till the sweet heavens have fill'd it from the heights   500
Again with living waters in the change
Of seasons. Hard his eyes, harder his heart
Seem'd; but so weary were his limbs that he,
Gasping, "Of Arthur's hall am I, but here,
Here let me rest and die," cast himself down,   505
And gulf'd his griefs in inmost sleep; so lay,
Till shaken by a dream, that Gawain fired
The hall of Merlin, and the morning star
Reel'd in the smoke, brake into flame, and fell.

  He woke, and being ware of some one nigh,   510
Sent hands upon him, as to tear him, crying,
"False! and I held thee pure as Guinevere."

But Percivale stood near him and replied,
"Am I but false as Guinevere is pure?
Or art thou mazed with dreams? or being one   515
Of our free-spoken Table hast not heard
That Lancelot"—there he check'd himself and paused.

Then fared it with Sir Pelleas as with one
Who gets a wound in battle, and the sword
That made it plunges thro' the wound again,   520
And pricks it deeper; and he shrank and wail'd,
"Is the Queen false?" and Percivale was mute.
"Have any of our Round Table held their vows?"
And Percivale made answer not a word.
"Is the King true?" "The King!" said Percivale.   525
"Why, then let men couple at once with wolves.
What! art thou mad?"

                          But Pelleas, leaping up,
Ran thro' the doors and vaulted on his horse
And fled. Small pity upon his horse had he,
Or on himself, or any, and when he met   530
A cripple, one that held a hand for alms—
Hunch'd as he was, and like an old dwarf elm
That turns its back on the salt blast, the boy
Paused not, but overrode him, shouting, "False,
And false with Gawain!" and so left him bruised   535
And batter'd, and fled on, and hill and wood
Went ever streaming by him till the gloom
That follows on the turning of the world
Darken'd the common path. He twitch'd the reins,
And made his beast, that better knew it, swerve   540
Now off it and now on; but when he saw
High up in heaven the hall that Merlin built,
Blackening against the dead-green stripes of even,
"Black nest of rats," he groan'd, "ye build too high."

Not long thereafter from the city gates   545
Issued Sir Lancelot riding airily,
Warm with a gracious parting from the Queen,
Peace at his heart, and gazing at a star
And marvelling what it was; on whom the boy,
Across the silent seeded meadow-grass   550
Borne, clash'd; and Lancelot, saying, "What name hast thou
That ridest here so blindly and so hard?"
"No name, no name," he shouted, "a scourge am I
To lash the treasons of the Table Round."
"Yea, but thy name?" "I have many names," he cried: 555
"I am wrath and shame and hate and evil fame,
And like a poisonous wind I pass to blast
And blaze the crime of Lancelot and the Queen."
"First over me," said Lancelot, "shalt thou pass."

"Fight therefore," yell'd the youth, and either Knight   560
Drew back a space, and when they closed, at once
The weary steed of Pelleas floundering flung
His rider, who call'd out from the dark field,
"Thou art false as hell; slay me, I have no sword."
Then Lancelot, "Yea, between thy lips—and sharp;   565
But here will I disedge it by thy death."
"Slay then," he shriek'd, "my will is to be slain,"
And Lancelot, with his heel upon the fallen,
Rolling his eyes, a moment stood, then spake:
"Rise, weakling; I am Lancelot; say thy say."   570

    And Lancelot slowly rode his war-horse back
To Camelot, and Sir Pelleas in brief while
Caught his unbroken limbs from the dark field,
And follow'd to the city. It chanced that both
Brake into hall together, worn and pale.   575
There with her knights and dames was Guinevere.
Full wonderingly she gazed on Lancelot
So soon return'd, and then on Pelleas, him
Who had not greeted her, but cast himself
Down on a bench, hard-breathing. "Have ye fought?"   580
She ask'd of Lancelot. "Ay, my Queen," he said.
"And thou hast overthrown him?" "Ay, my Queen."
Then she, turning to Pelleas, "O young knight,
Hath the great heart of knighthood in thee fail'd
So far thou canst not bide, unfrowardly,   585
A fall from *him?*" Then, for he answer'd not,
"Or hast thou other griefs? If I, the Queen,
May help them, loose thy tongue, and let me know."
But Pelleas lifted up an eye so fierce
She quail'd; and he, hissing "I have no sword,"   590
Sprang from the door into the dark. The Queen
Look'd hard upon her lover, he on her,
And each foresaw the dolorous day to be;
And all talk died, as in a grove all song
Beneath the shadow of some bird of prey.   595
Then a long silence came upon the hall,
And Modred thought, "The time is hard at hand."

1869

The Last Tournament

Dagonet,[8] the fool, whom Gawain in his mood
Had made mock-knight of Arthur's Table Round,
At Camelot, high above the yellowing woods,
Danced like a wither'd leaf before the hall.
And toward him from the hall, with harp in hand,   5

8. Although he appears in Malory, the fool is largely of Tennyson's invention.

And from the crown thereof a carcanet[9]
Of ruby swaying to and fro, the prize
Of Tristram in the jousts of yesterday,
Came Tristram, saying, "Why skip ye so, Sir Fool?"

    For Arthur and Sir Lancelot riding once   10
Far down beneath a winding wall of rock
Heard a child wail. A stump of oak half-dead,
From roots like some black coil of carven snakes,
Clutch'd at the crag, and started thro' mid air
Bearing an eagle's nest; and thro' the tree   15
Rush'd ever a rainy wind, and thro' the wind
Pierced ever a child's cry; and crag and tree
Scaling, Sir Lancelot from the perilous nest,
This ruby necklace thrice around her neck,
And all unscarr'd from beak or talon, brought   20
A maiden babe, which Arthur pitying took,
Then gave it to his Queen to rear. The Queen,
But coldly acquiescing, in her white arms
Received, and after loved it tenderly,
And named it Nestling; so forgot herself   25
A moment, and her cares; till that young life
Being smitten in mid heaven with mortal cold
Past from her, and in time the carcanet
Vext her with plaintive memories of the child.
So she, delivering it to Arthur, said,   30
"Take thou the jewels of this dead innocence,
And make them, as thou wilt, a tourney-prize."

    To whom the King: "Peace to thine eagle-borne
Dead nestling, and this honor after death,
Following thy will! but, O my Queen, I muse   35
Why ye not wear on arm, or neck, or zone
Those diamonds that I rescued from the tarn,[1]
And Lancelot won, methought, for thee to wear."

    "Would rather you had let them fall," she cried,
"Plunge and be lost—ill-fated as they were,   40
A bitterness to me!—ye look amazed,
Not knowing they were lost as soon as given—
Slid from my hands when I was leaning out
Above the river—that unhappy child[2]
Past in her barge; but rosier luck will go   45
With these rich jewels, seeing that they came
Not from the skeleton of a brother-slayer,
But the sweet body of a maiden babe.
Perchance—who knows?—the purest of thy knights
May win them for the purest of my maids."   50

9. A necklace. The following story of its origin was apparently derived from a legendary incident in the life of King Alfred.

1. See "Lancelot and Elaine," lines 34 ff.
2. Elaine.

She ended, and the cry of a great jousts
With trumpet-blowings ran on all the ways
From Camelot in among the faded fields
To furthest towers; and everywhere the knights
Arm'd for a day of glory before the King.   55

But on the hither side of that loud morn
Into the hall stagger'd, his visage ribb'd
From ear to ear with dogwhip-weals,[3] his nose
Bridge-broken, one eye out, and one hand off,
And one with shatter'd fingers dangling lame,   60
A churl, to whom indignantly the King:

"My churl, for whom Christ died, what evil beast
Hath drawn his claws athwart thy face? or fiend?
Man was it who marr'd heaven's image in thee thus?"

Then, sputtering thro' the hedge of splinter'd teeth,   65
Yet strangers to the tongue, and with blunt stump
Pitch-blacken'd sawing the air, said the maim'd churl:

"He took them and he drave them to his tower—
Some hold he was a table-knight of thine—[4]
A hundred goodly ones—the Red Knight, he—   70
Lord, I was tending swine, and the Red Knight
Brake in upon me and drave them to his tower;
And when I call'd upon thy name as one
That doest right by gentle and by churl,
Maim'd me and maul'd, and would outright have slain,   75
Save that he sware me to a message, saying:
"Tell thou the King and all his liars that I
Have founded my Round Table in the North,
And whatsoever his own knights have sworn
My knights have sworn the counter to it—and say   80
My tower is full of harlots, like his court,
But mine are worthier, seeing they profess
To be none other than themselves—and say
My knights are all adulterers like his own,
But mine are truer, seeing they profess   85
To be none other; and say his hour is come,
The heathen are upon him, his long lance
Broken, and his Excalibur a straw.' "

Then Arthur turn'd to Kay the seneschal:
"Take thou my churl, and tend him curiously   90
Like a king's heir, till all his hurts be whole.
The heathen—but that ever-climbing wave,
Hurl'd back again so often in empty foam,
Hath lain for years at rest—and renegades,

3. Ridges raised on the flesh from lashing.
4. Tennyson said he is Pelleas, though here and later the text never makes the identity clear.

Thieves, bandits, leavings of confusion, whom 95
The wholesome realm is purged of otherwhere,
Friends, thro' your manhood and your fealty,—now
Make their last head like Satan in the North.[5]
My younger knights, new-made, in whom your flower
Waits to be solid fruit of golden deeds, 100
Move with me toward their quelling, which achieved,
The loneliest ways are safe from shore to shore.
But thou, Sir Lancelot, sitting in my place
Enchair'd to-morrow, arbitrate the field;
For wherefore shouldst thou care to mingle with it, 105
Only to yield my Queen her own again?
Speak, Lancelot, thou art silent; is it well?"

Thereto Sir Lancelot answer'd: "It is well;
Yet better if the King abide, and leave
The leading of his younger knights to me. 110
Else, for the King has will'd it, it is well."

Then Arthur rose and Lancelot follow'd him,
And while they stood without the doors, the King
Turn'd to him saying: "Is it then so well?
Or mine the blame that oft I seem as he 115
Of whom was written, 'A sound is in his ears'?
The foot that loiters, bidden go,—the glance
That only seems half-loyal to command,—
A manner somewhat fallen from reverence—
Or have I dream'd the bearing of our knights 120
Tells of a manhood ever less and lower?
Or whence the fear lest this my realm, uprear'd,
By noble deeds at one with noble vows,
From flat confusion and brute violences,
Reel back into the beast, and be no more?" 125

He spoke, and taking all his younger knights,
Down the slope city rode, and sharply turn'd
North by the gate. In her high bower the Queen,
Working a tapestry, lifted up her head,
Watch'd her lord pass, and knew not that she sigh'd. 130
Then ran across her memory the strange rhyme
Of bygone Merlin, "Where is he who knows?
From the great deep to the great deep he goes."[6]

But when the morning of a tournament,
By these in earnest those in mockery call'd 135
The Tournament of the Dead Innocence,
Brake with a wet wind blowing, Lancelot,
Round whose sick head all night, like birds of prey,
The words of Arthur flying shriek'd, arose,

---

5. Satan mustered his rebellious forces
in the north of Heaven. See *Isaiah,*
14:12–14.

6. From Merlin's song in "The Coming
of Arthur," lines 409–410.

And down a streetway hung with folds of pure   140
White samite, and by fountains running wine,
Where children sat in white with cups of gold,
Moved to the lists, and there, with slow sad steps
Ascending, fill'd his double-dragon'd chair.

    He glanced and saw the stately galleries,   145
Dame, damsel, each thro' worship of their Queen
White-robed in honor of the stainless child,
And some with scatter'd jewels, like a bank
Of maiden snow mingled with sparks of fire.
He look'd but once, and vail'd[7] his eyes again.   150

    The sudden trumpet sounded as in a dream
To ears but half-awaked, then one low roll
Of Autumn thunder, and the jousts began;
And ever the wind blew, and yellowing leaf,
And gloom and gleam, and shower and shorn plume   155
Went down it. Sighing weariedly, as one
Who sits and gazes on a faded fire,
When all the goodlier guests are past away,
Sat their great umpire looking o'er the lists.
He saw the laws that ruled the tournament   160
Broken, but spake not; once, a knight cast down
Before his throne of arbitration cursed
The dead babe and the follies of the King;
And once the laces of a helmet crack'd,
And show'd him, like a vermin in its hole,   165
Modred, a narrow face. Anon he heard
The voice that billow'd round the barriers roar
An ocean-sounding welcome to one knight,
But newly-enter'd, taller than the rest,
And armor'd all in forest green, whereon   170
There tript a hundred tiny silver deer,
And wearing but a holly-spray for crest,
With ever-scattering berries, and on shield
A spear, a harp, a bugle—Tristram—late
From over-seas in Brittany return'd,   175
And marriage with a princess of that realm,
Isolt the White—Sir Tristram[8] of the Woods—
Whom Lancelot knew, had held sometime with pain
His own against him, and now yearn'd to shake
The burthen off his heart in one full shock   180
With Tristram even to death. His strong hands gript
And dinted the gilt dragons right and left,

7. Lowered, not veiled.
8. With Tristram, as with Gawain, Tennyson has drastically altered personalities to suit his own purposes. The chief exponent of free love, Tristram becomes a cynical materialist whose affair with Mark's wife is meant to parallel the Lancelot-Guinevere-Arthur triangle. In Malory, Tristram was a knight of the Round Table second only to Launcelot, and in legends generally Tristram was the quintessence of the romantic lover.

Until he groan'd for wrath—so many of those
That ware their ladies' colors on the casque
Drew from before Sir Tristram to the bounds,   185
And there with gibes and flickering mockeries
Stood, while he mutter'd, "Craven crests! O shame!
What faith have these in whom they sware to love?
The glory of our Round Table is no more."

    So Tristram won, and Lancelot gave, the gems,   190
Not speaking other word than, "Hast thou won?
Art thou the purest, brother? See, the hand
Wherewith thou takest this is red!" to whom
Tristram, half plagued by Lancelot's languorous mood,
Made answer: "Ay, but wherefore toss me this   195
Like a dry bone cast to some hungry hound?
Let be thy fair Queen's fantasy. Strength of heart
And might of limb, but mainly use and skill,
Are winners in this pastime of our King.
My hand—belike the lance hath dript upon it—   200
No blood of mine, I trow; but O chief knight,
Right arm of Arthur in the battle-field,
Great brother, thou nor I have made the world;
Be happy in thy fair Queen as I in mine."

    And Tristram round the gallery made his horse   205
Caracole;[9] then bow'd his homage, bluntly saying,
"Fair damsels, each to him who worships each
Sole Queen of Beauty and of love, behold
This day my Queen of Beauty is not here."
And most of these were mute, some anger'd, one   210
Murmuring, "All courtesy is dead," and one,
"The glory of our Round Table is no more."[1]

    Then fell thick rain, plume droopt and mantle clung,
And pettish cries awoke, and the wan day
Went glooming down in wet and weariness;   215
But under her black brows a swarthy one
Laugh'd shrilly, crying: "Praise the patient saints,
Our one white day of Innocence hath past,
Tho' somewhat draggled at the skirt. So be it.
The snowdrop only, flowering thro' the year,   220
Would make the world as blank as winter-tide.
Come—let us gladden their sad eyes, our Queen's
And Lancelot's, at this night's solemnity
With all the kindlier colors of the field."

    So dame and damsel glitter'd at the feast   225
Variously gay; for he[2] that tells the tale

9. In horsemanship, to execute half-
turns to the right or left.
1. The laws of the joust required the
prize to be given to some lady present

on the field, but here all rules are
broken, even those of common courtesy.
2. Tennyson.

Liken'd them, saying, as when an hour of cold
Falls on the mountain in midsummer snows,
And all the purple slopes of mountain flowers
Pass under white, till the warm hour returns   230
With veer of wind and all are flowers again,
So dame and damsel cast the simple white,
And glowing in all colors, the live grass,
Rose-campion, bluebell, kingcup, poppy, glanced
About the revels, and with mirth so loud   235
Beyond all use, that, half-amazed, the Queen,
And wroth at Tristram and the lawless jousts,
Brake up their sports, then slowly to her bower
Parted, and in her bosom pain was lord.

    And little Dagonet on the morrow morn,   240
High over all the yellowing autumn-tide,
Danced like a wither'd leaf before the hall.
Then Tristram saying, "Why skip ye so, Sir Fool?"
Wheel'd round on either heel, Dagonet replied,
"Belike for lack of wiser company;   245
Or being fool, and seeing too much wit
Makes the world rotten, why, belike I skip
To know myself the wisest knight of all."
"Ay, fool," said Tristram, "but 't is eating dry
To dance without a catch, a roundelay   250
To dance to." Then he twangled on his harp,
And while he twangled little Dagonet stood
Quiet as any water-sodden log
Stay'd in the wandering warble of a brook,
But when the twangling ended, skipt again;   255
And being ask'd, "Why skipt ye not, Sir Fool?"
Made answer, "I had liefer twenty years
Skip to the broken music of my brains
Than any broken music thou canst make."
Then Tristram, waiting for the quip to come,   260
"Good now, what music have I broken, fool?"
And little Dagonet, skipping, "Arthur, the King's;
For when thou playest that air with Queen Isolt,
Thou makest broken music with thy bride,
Her daintier namesake[3] down in Brittany—   265
And so thou breakest Arthur's music too."
"Save for that broken music in thy brains,
Sir Fool," said Tristram, "I would break thy head.
Fool, I came late, the heathen wars were o'er,
The life had flown, we sware but by the shell—   270
I am but a fool to reason with a fool—
Come, thou art crabb'd and sour; but lean me down,
Sir Dagonet, one of thy long asses' ears,
And harken if my music be not true.

3. Isolt of the White Hands.

" 'Free love—free field—we love but while we may.   275
The woods are hush'd, their music is no more;
The leaf is dead, the yearning past away.
New leaf, new life—the days of frost are o'er;
New life, new love, to suit the newer day;
New loves are sweet as those that went before.   280
Free love—free field—we love but while we may.'

"Ye might have moved slow-measure to my tune,
Not stood stock-still. I made it in the woods,
And heard it ring as true as tested gold."

But Dagonet with one foot poised in his hand: 285
"Friend, did ye mark that fountain yesterday,
Made to run wine?—but this had run itself
All out like a long life to a sour end—
And them that round it sat with golden cups
To hand the wine to whosoever came—   290
The twelve small damosels white as Innocence,
In honor of poor Innocence the babe,
Who left the gems which Innocence the Queen
Lent to the King, and Innocence the King
Gave for a prize—and one of those white slips   295
Handed her cup and piped, the pretty one,
'Drink, drink, Sir Fool,' and thereupon I drank,
Spat—pish—the cup was gold, the draught was mud."

And Tristram: "Was it muddier than thy gibes?
Is all the laughter gone dead out of thee?—   300
Not marking how the knighthood mock thee, fool—
'Fear God: honor the King—his one true knight—
Sole follower of the vows'—for here be they
Who knew thee swine enow before I came,
Smuttier than blasted grain. But when the King   305
Had made thee fool, thy vanity so shot up
It frighted all free fool from out thy heart;
Which left thee less than fool, and less than swine,
A naked aught—yet swine I hold thee still,
For I have flung thee pearls and find thee swine."   310

And little Dagonet mincing with his feet:
"Knight, an ye fling those rubies round my neck
In lieu of hers, I'll hold thou hast some touch
Of music, since I care not for thy pearls.
Swine? I have wallow'd, I have wash'd—the world   315
Is flesh and shadow—I have had my day.
The dirty nurse, Experience, in her kind
Hath foul'd me—an I wallow'd, then I wash'd—
I have had my day and my philosophies—
And thank the Lord I am King Arthur's fool.   320
Swine, say ye? swine, goats, asses, rams, and geese

Troop'd round a Paynim harper[4] once, who thrumm'd
On such a wire as musically as thou
Some such fine song—but never a king's fool."

And Tristram, "Then were swine, goats, asses, geese   325
The wiser fools, seeing thy Paynim bard
Had such a mastery of his mystery
That he could harp his wife up out of hell."

Then Dagonet, turning on the ball of his foot,
"And whither harp'st thou thine? down! and thyself   330
Down! and two more; a helpful harper thou,
That harpest downward! Dost thou know the star
We call the Harp of Arthur[5] up in heaven?"

And Tristram, "Ay, Sir Fool, for when our King
Was victor wellnigh day by day, the knights,   335
Glorying in each new glory, set his name
High on all hills and in the signs of heaven."

And Dagonet answer'd: "Ay, and when the land
Was freed, and the Queen false, ye set yourself
To babble about him, all to show your wit—   340
And whether he were king by courtesy,
Or king by right—and so went harping down
The black king's[6] highway, got so far and grew
So witty that ye play'd at ducks and drakes
With Arthur's vows on the great lake of fire.   345
Tuwhoo! do ye see it? do ye see the star?"[7]

"Nay, fool," said Tristram, "not in open day."
And Dagonet: "Nay, nor will; I see it and hear.
It makes a silent music up in heaven,
And I and Arthur and the angels hear,   350
And then we skip." "Lo, fool," he said, "ye talk
Fool's treason; is the King thy brother fool?"
Then little Dagonet clapt his hands and shrill'd:
"Ay, ay, my brother fool, the king of fools!
Conceits himself as God that he can make   355
Figs out of thistles, silk from bristles, milk
From burning spurge,[8] honey from hornet-combs,
And men from beasts—Long live the king of fools!"

And down the city Dagonet danced away;
But thro' the slowly-mellowing avenues   360
And solitary passes of the wood
Rode Tristram toward Lyonnesse and the west.
Before him fled the face of Queen Isolt

---

4. Orpheus.
5. Lyra, a northern constellation.
6. The devil's. "Enter by the narrow gate; for the gate is wide and the way is easy, that leads to destruction"
(*Matthew*, 7:13).
7. Either the constellation Lyra, or perhaps Vega, the first magnitude and brightest star in it.
8. It contains an acrid, milky juice.

With ruby-circled neck, but evermore
Past, as a rustle or twitter in the wood   365
Made dull his inner, keen his outer eye
For all that walk'd, or crept, or perch'd, or flew.
Anon the face, as, when a gust hath blown,
Unruffling waters re-collect the shape
Of one that in them sees himself, return'd;   370
But at the slot or fewmets[9] of a deer,
Or even a fallen feather, vanish'd again.

So on for all that day from lawn to lawn
Thro' many a league-long bower he rode. At length
A lodge of intertwisted beechen-boughs,   375
Furze-cramm'd and bracken-rooft, the which himself
Built for a summer day with Queen Isolt
Against a shower, dark in the golden grove
Appearing, sent his fancy back to where
She lived a moon in that low lodge with him;   380
Till Mark her lord had past, the Cornish King,
With six or seven, when Tristram was away,
And snatch'd her thence, yet, dreading worse than shame
Her warrior Tristram, spake not any word,
But bode his hour, devising wretchedness.   385

And now that desert lodge to Tristram lookt
So sweet that, halting, in he past and sank
Down on a drift of foliage random-blown;
But could not rest for musing how to smooth
And sleek his marriage over to the queen.   390
Perchance in lone Tintagil far from all
The tonguesters of the court she had not heard.
But then what folly had sent him over-seas
After she left him lonely here? a name?
Was it the name of one in Brittany,   395
Isolt, the daughter of the king? "Isolt
Of the White Hands" they call'd her: the sweet name
Allured him first, and then the maid herself,
Who served him well with those white hands of hers,[1]
And loved him well, until himself had thought   400
He loved her also, wedded easily,
But left her all as easily, and return'd.
The black-blue Irish hair and Irish eyes
Had drawn him home—what marvel? then he laid
His brows upon the drifted leaf and dream'd.   405

9. Droppings; the "slot" is a footprint or tracks.
1. She had cured Tristram of a wound from a poisoned arrow. Previously Tristram had been healed of another wound by Isolt of Ireland. When he told King Mark of her beauty, he sent Tristram to bring her for his wife. On the return voyage, they unknowingly drank in each other's presence the love philtre reserved for Isolt's first meeting with Mark. In Malory, the effects of the philtre wear off by the time Tristram marries Isolt of Brittany; in other versions, its effect is permanent.

He seem'd to pace the strand of Brittany
Between Isolt of Britain and his bride,
And show'd them both the ruby-chain, and both
Began to struggle for it, till his queen
Graspt it so hard that all her hand was red.   410
Then cried the Breton, "Look, her hand is red!
These be no rubies, this is frozen blood,
And melts within her hand—her hand is hot
With ill desires, but this I gave thee, look,
Is all as cool and white as any flower."   415
Follow'd a rush of eagle's wings, and then
A whimpering of the spirit of the child,
Because the twain had spoil'd her carcanet.

He dream'd; but Arthur with a hundred spears
Rode far, till o'er the illimitable reed,   420
And many a glancing plash and sallowy isle,
The wide-wing'd sunset of the misty marsh
Glared on a huge machicolated[2] tower
That stood with open doors, whereout was roll'd
A roar of riot, as from men secure   425
Amid their marshes, ruffians at their ease
Among their harlot-brides, an evil song.
"Lo there," said one of Arthur's youth, for there,
High on a grim dead tree before the tower,
A goodly brother of the Table Round   430
Swung by the neck; and on the boughs a shield
Showing a shower of blood in a field noir,
And therebeside a horn, inflamed the knights
At that dishonor done the gilded spur,
Till each would clash the shield and blow the horn.   435
But Arthur waved them back. Alone he rode.
Then at the dry harsh roar of the great horn,
That sent the face of all the marsh aloft
An ever upward-rushing storm and cloud
Of shriek and plume, the Red Knight heard, and all,   440
Even to tipmost lance and topmost helm,
In blood-red armor sallying, howl'd to the King:

"The teeth of Hell flay bare and gnash thee flat!—
Lo! art thou not that eunuch-hearted king
Who fain had clipt free manhood from the world—   445
The woman-worshipper? Yea, God's curse, and I,
Slain was the brother of my paramour
By a knight of thine, and I that heard her whine
And snivel, being eunuch-hearted too,
Sware by the scorpion-worm[3] that twists in hell   450

2. A tower with openings between the corbels, the supports for a projecting parapet, through which molten lead, stones, etc., were dropped upon assailants.

3. In legend, the scorpion, when surrounded by fire, stings itself to death.

And stings itself to everlasting death,
To hang whatever knight of thine I fought
And tumbled. Art thou king?—Look to thy life!"

He ended. Arthur knew the voice; the face
Wellnigh was helmet-hidden, and the name[4]   455
Went wandering somewhere darkling in his mind.
And Arthur deign'd not use of word or sword,
But let the drunkard, as he stretch'd from horse
To strike him, overbalancing his bulk,
Down from the causeway heavily to the swamp   460
Fall, as the crest of some slow-arching wave,
Heard in dead night along that table-shore,
Drops flat, and after the great waters break
Whitening for half a league, and thin themselves,
Far over sands marbled with moon and cloud,   465
From less and less to nothing; thus he fell
Head-heavy. Then the knights, who watch'd him, roar'd
And shouted and leapt down upon the fallen,
There trampled out his face from being known,
And sank his head in mire, and slimed themselves;   470
Nor heard the King for their own cries, but sprang
Thro' open doors, and swording right and left
Men, women, on their sodden faces, hurl'd
The tables over and the wines, and slew
Till all the rafters rang with woman-yells,   475
And all the pavement stream'd with massacre.[5]
Then, echoing yell with yell, they fired the tower,
Which half that autumn night, like the live North,[6]
Red-pulsing up thro' Alioth and Alcor,[7]
Made all above it, and a hundred meres   480
About it, as the water Moab[8] saw
Come round by the east, and out beyond them flush'd
The long low dune and lazy-plunging sea.

So all the ways were safe from shore to shore,
But in the heart of Arthur pain was lord.   485

Then, out of Tristram waking, the red dream
Fled with a shout, and that low lodge return'd,
Mid-forest, and the wind among the boughs.
He whistled his good war-horse left to graze
Among the forest greens, vaulted upon him,   490
And rode beneath an ever-showering leaf,
Till one lone woman, weeping near a cross,
Stay'd him. "Why weep ye?" "Lord," she said, "my man
Hath left me or is dead;" whereon he thought—

---

4. Pelleas.
5. Contrast "The Coming of Arthur,"
lines 119 ff.
6. The Northern Lights.

7. Two of the stars in Ursa Major.
8. Alludes to the Moabites, who saw
water as red as blood. See II *Kings*,
3:22.

"What, if she[9] hate me now? I would not this.   495
What, if she love me still? I would not that.
I know not what I would"—but said to her,
"Yet weep not thou, lest, if thy mate return,
He find thy favor changed and love thee not"—
Then pressing day by day thro' Lyonnesse   500
Last in a roky[1] hollow, belling, heard
The hounds of Mark, and felt the goodly hounds
Yelp at his heart,[2] but, turning, past and gain'd
Tintagil,[3] half in sea and high on land,
A crown of towers.

               Down in a casement sat,   505
A low sea-sunset glorying round her hair
And glossy-throated grace, Isolt the queen.
And when she heard the feet of Tristram grind
The spiring stone[4] that scaled about her tower,
Flush'd, started, met him at the doors, and there   510
Belted his body with her white embrace,
Crying aloud: "Not Mark—not Mark, my soul!
The footstep flutter'd me at first—not he!
Catlike thro' his own castle steals my Mark,
But warrior-wise thou stridest thro' his halls   515
Who hates thee, as I him—even to the death.
My soul, I felt my hatred for my Mark
Quicken within me, and knew that thou wert nigh."
To whom Sir Tristram smiling, "I am here;
Let be thy Mark, seeing he is not thine."   520

   And drawing somewhat backward she replied:
"Can he be wrong'd who is not even his own,
But save for dread of thee had beaten me,
Scratch'd, bitten, blinded, marr'd me somehow—Mark?
What rights are his that dare not strike for them?   525
Not lift a hand—not, tho' he found me thus!
But harken! have ye met him? hence he went
To-day for three days' hunting—as he said—
And so returns belike within an hour.
Mark's way, my soul!—but eat not thou with Mark,   530
Because he hates thee even more than fears,
Nor drink; and when thou passest any wood
Close vizor, lest an arrow from the bush
Should leave me all alone with Mark and hell.
My God, the measure of my hate for Mark   535
Is as the measure of my love for thee!"

9. His wife, Isolt.
1. Misty, foggy; "belling" means bay-
ing in unison, like chiming bells.
2. Either a premonition of approaching
doom or, since Tristram was a famous
hunter, a momentary diversion.

3. The ruins of the castle by the Cor-
nish Sea are still visible. See *Memoir*,
II, 340–341, for Tennyson's last visit
there.
4. A spiral stone stairway.

So, pluck'd one way by hate and one by love,
Drain'd of her force, again she sat, and spake
To Tristram, as he knelt before her, saying:
"O hunter, and O blower of the horn,   540
Harper, and thou hast been a rover too,
For, ere I mated with my shambling king,
Ye twain had fallen out about the bride
Of one—his name is out of me—the prize,
If prize she were—what marvel?—she could see—   545
Thine, friend; and ever since my craven seeks
To wreck thee villainously—but, O Sir Knight,
What dame or damsel have ye kneel'd to last?"

And Tristram, "Last to my Queen Paramount,
Here now to my queen paramount of love   550
And loveliness—ay, lovelier than when first
Her light feet fell on our rough Lyonnesse,
Sailing from Ireland."

                              Softly laugh'd Isolt:
"Flatter me not, for hath not our great Queen
My dole of beauty trebled?" and he said: 555
"Her beauty is her beauty, and thine thine,
And thine is more to me—soft, gracious, kind—
Save when thy Mark is kindled on thy lips
Most gracious; but she, haughty, even to him,
Lancelot, for I have seen him wan enow   560
To make one doubt if ever the great Queen
Have yielded him her love."

                              To whom Isolt:
"Ah, then, false hunter and false harper, thou
Who brakest thro' the scruple of my bond,
Calling me they white hind, and saying to me   565
That Guinevere had sinn'd against the highest,
And I—misyoked with such a want of man—
That I could hardly sin against the lowest."

He answer'd: "O my soul, be comforted!
If this be sweet, to sin in leading-strings,   570
If here be comfort, and if ours be sin,
Crown'd warrant had we for the crowning sin
That made us happy; but how ye greet me—fear
And fault and doubt—no word of that fond tale—
Thy deep heart-yearnings, thy sweet memories   575
Of Tristram in that year he was away."

And, saddening on the sudden, spake Isolt:
"I had forgotten all in my strong joy
To see thee—yearnings?—ay! for, hour by hour,
Here in the never-ended afternoon,   580
O, sweeter than all memories of thee,

Deeper than any yearnings after thee
Seem'd those far-rolling, westward-smiling seas,
Watch'd from this tower. Isolt of Britain dash'd
Before Isolt of Brittany on the strand,   585
Would that have chill'd her bride-kiss? Wedded her?
Fought in her father's battles? wounded there?
The King was all fulfill'd with gratefulness,
And she, my namesake of the hands, that heal'd
Thy hurt and heart with unguent and caress—   590
Well—can I wish her any huger wrong
Than having known thee? her too hast thou left
To pine and waste in those sweet memories.
O, were I not my Mark's, by whom all men
Are noble, I should hate thee more than love."   595

And Tristram, fondling her light hands, replied:
"Grace, queen, for being loved; she loved me well.
Did I love her? the name at least I loved.
Isolt?—I fought his battles, for Isolt!
The night was dark; the true star set. Isolt!   600
The name was ruler of the dark—Isolt?
Care not for her! patient, and prayerful, meek,
Pale-blooded, she will yield herself to God."

And Isolt answer'd: "Yea, and why not I?
Mine is the larger need, who am not meek,   605
Pale-blooded, prayerful. Let me tell thee now.
Here one black, mute midsummer night I sat,
Lonely, but musing on thee, wondering where,
Murmuring a light song I had heard thee sing,
And once or twice I spake thy name aloud.   610
Then flash'd a levin-brand;[5] and near me stood,
In fuming sulphur blue and green, a fiend—
Mark's way to steal behind one in the dark—
For there was Mark: 'He has wedded her,' he said,
Not said, but hiss'd it; then this crown of towers   615
So shook to such a roar of all the sky,
That here in utter dark I swoon'd away,
And woke again in utter dark, and cried,
'I will flee hence and give myself to God'—
And thou wert lying in thy new leman's[6] arms."   620

Then Tristram, ever dallying with her hand,
"May God be with thee, sweet, when old and gray,
And past desire!" a saying that anger'd her.
" 'May God be with thee, sweet, when thou art old,
And sweet no more to me!' I need Him now.   625
For when had Lancelot utter'd aught so gross
Even to the swineherd's malkin in the mast?[7]

---

5. Flash of lightning.
6. Lover's.

7. Acorns, chestnuts, etc.; hence, a slut among the swine's food.

The greater man the greater courtesy.
Far other was the Tristram, Arthur's knight!
But thou, thro' ever harrying thy wild beasts—   630
Save that to touch a harp, tilt with a lance
Becomes thee well—art grown wild beast thyself.
How darest thou, if lover, push me even
In fancy from thy side, and set me far
In the gray distance, half a life away.   635
Her to be loved no more? Unsay it, unswear!
Flatter me rather, seeing me so weak,
Broken with Mark and hate and solitude,
Thy marriage and mine own, that I should suck
Lies like sweet wines. Lie to me; I believe.   640
Will ye not lie? not swear, as there ye kneel,
And solemnly as when ye sware to him,
The man of men, our King—My God, the power
Was once in vows when men believed the King!
They lied not then who sware, and thro' their vows   645
The King prevailing made his realm—I say,
Swear to me thou wilt love me even when old,
Gray-hair'd, and past desire, and in despair."

        Then Tristram, pacing moodily up and down:
"Vows! did you keep the vow you made to Mark   650
More than I mine? Lied, say ye? Nay, but learnt,
The vow that binds too strictly snaps itself—
My knighthood taught me this—ay, being snapt—
We run more counter to the soul thereof
Than had we never sworn. I swear no more.   655
I swore to the great King, and am forsworn.
For once—even to the height—I honor'd him.
'Man, is he man at all?' methought, when first
I rode from our rough Lyonnesse, and beheld
That victor of the Pagan throned in hall—   660
His hair, a sun that ray'd from off a brow
Like hill-snow high in heaven, the steel-blue eyes,
The golden beard that clothed his lips with light—
Moreover, that weird legend of his birth,
With Merlin's mystic babble about his end   665
Amazed me; then, his foot was on a stool
Shaped as a dragon; he seem'd to me no man,
But Michael trampling Satan; so I sware,
Being amazed. But this went by—The vows!
O, ay—the wholesome madness of an hour—   670
They served their use, their time; for every knight
Believed himself a greater than himself,
And every follower eyed him as a God;
Till he, being lifted up beyond himself,
Did mightier deeds than elsewise he had done,   675

And so the realm was made.[8] But then their vows—
First mainly thro' that sullying of our Queen—
Began to gall the knighthood, asking whence
Had Arthur right to bind them to himself?
Dropt down from heaven? wash'd up from out the deep?   680
They fail'd to trace him thro' the flesh and blood
Of our old kings. Whence then? a doubtful lord
To bind them by inviolable vows,
Which flesh and blood perforce would violate;
For feel this arm of mine—the tide within   685
Red with free chase and heather-scented air,
Pulsing full man. Can Arthur make me pure
As any maiden child? lock up my tongue
From uttering freely what I freely hear?
Bind me to one? The wide world laughs at it.   690
And worldling of the world am I, and know
The ptarmigan[9] that whitens ere his hour
Woos his own end; we are not angels here
Nor shall be. Vows—I am woodman of the woods,
And hear the garnet-headed yaffingale[1]   695
Mock them—my soul, we love but while we may;
And therefore is my love so large for thee,
Seeing it is not bounded save by love."

   Here ending, he moved toward her, and she said:
"Good; an I turn'd away my love for thee   700
To some one thrice as courteous as thyself—
For courtesy wins woman all as well
As valor may, but he that closes both
Is perfect, he is Lancelot—taller indeed,
Rosier and comelier, thou—but say I loved   705
This knightliest of all knights, and cast thee back
Thine own small saw, 'We love but while we may,'
Well then, what answer?"

               He that while she spake,
Mindful of what he brought to adorn her with,
The jewels, had let one finger lightly touch   710
The warm white apple of her throat, replied,
"Press this a little closer, sweet, until—
Come, I am hunger'd and half-anger'd—meat,
Wine, wine—and I will love thee to the death,
And out beyond into the dream to come."   715

   So then, when both were brought to full accord,
She rose, and set before him all he will'd;

---

8. "My father felt strongly that only under the inspiration of ideals, and with his 'sword bathed in heaven,' can a man combat the cynical indifference, the intellectual selfishness, the sloth of will, the utilitarian materialism of a transition age" (*Memoir*, II, 129). Tristram manifests all these negative qualities.
9. A bird of the grouse family whose feathers change from brown to white for camouflage in winter.
1. A green, red-headed woodpecker.

And after these had comforted the blood
With meats and wines, and satiated their hearts—
Now talking of their woodland paradise,   720
The deer, the dews, the fern, the founts, the lawns;
Now mocking at the much ungainliness,
And craven shifts, and long crane legs of Mark—
Then Tristram laughing caught the harp and sang:

    "Ay, ay, O, ay—the winds that bend the brier!   725
    A star in heaven, a star within the mere!
    Ay, ay, O, ay—a star was my desire,
    And one was far apart and one was near.
    Ay, ay, O, ay—the winds that bow the grass!
    And one was water and one star was fire,   730
    And one will ever shine and one will pass.
    Ay, ay, O, ay—the winds that move the mere!"

Then in the light's last glimmer Tristram show'd
And swung the ruby carcanet. She cried,
"The collar of some Order, which our King   735
Hath newly founded, all for thee, my soul,
For thee, to yield thee grace beyond thy peers."

"Not so, my queen," he said, "but the red fruit
Grown on a magic oak-tree in mid-heaven,
And won by Tristram as a tourney-prize,   740
And hither brought by Tristram for his last
Love-offering and peace-offering unto thee."

He spoke, he turn'd, then, flinging round her neck,
Claspt it, and cried, "Thine Order, O my queen!"
But, while he bow'd to kiss the jewell'd throat,   745
Out of the dark, just as the lips had touch'd,
Behind him rose a shadow and a shriek—
"Mark's way," said Mark, and clove him thro' the brain.

That night came Arthur home, and while he climb'd,
All in a death-dumb autumn-dripping gloom,   750
The stairway to the hall, and look'd and saw
The great Queen's bower was dark,[2]—about his feet
A voice clung sobbing till he question'd it,
"What art thou?" and the voice about his feet
Sent up an answer, sobbing, "I am thy fool,   755
And I shall never make thee smile again."

1871

Guinevere[3]

Queen Guinevere had fled the court, and sat
There in the holy house at Almesbury[4]

---

2. As the next idyll makes clear, Guine-
vere has fled with Lancelot.
3. The idyll draws very little on

Malory or any other source except the
poet's imagination.
4. Amesbury, near Stonehenge.

Weeping, none with her save a little maid,
A novice. One low light betwixt them burn'd
Blurr'd by the creeping mist, for all abroad,   5
Beneath a moon unseen albeit at full,
The white mist, like a face-cloth to the face,
Clung to the dead earth, and the land was still.

   For hither had she fled, her cause of flight
Sir Modred;[5] he that like a subtle beast   10
Lay couchant with his eyes upon the throne,
Ready to spring, waiting a chance. For this
He chill'd the popular praises of the King
With silent smiles of slow disparagement;
And tamper'd with the Lords of the White Horse,   15
Heathen, the brood by Hengist[6] left; and sought
To make disruption in the Table Round
Of Arthur, and to splinter it into feuds
Serving his traitorous end; and all his aims
Were sharpen'd by strong hate for Lancelot.   20

   For thus it chanced one morn when all the court,
Green-suited, but with plumes that mock'd the may,[7]
Had been—their wont—a-maying and return'd,
That Modred still in green, all ear and eye,
Climb'd to the high top of the garden-wall   25
To spy some secret scandal if he might,
And saw the Queen who sat betwixt her best
Enid and lissome Vivien, of her court
The wiliest and the worst; and more than this
He saw not, for Sir Lancelot passing by   30
Spied where he couch'd, and as the gardener's hand
Picks from the colewort[8] a green caterpillar,
So from the high wall and the flowering grove
Of grasses Lancelot pluck'd him by the heel,
And cast him as a worm upon the way;   35
But when he knew the prince tho' marr'd with dust,
He, reverencing king's blood in a bad man,
Made such excuses as he might, and these
Full knightly without scorn. For in those days
No knight of Arthur's noblest dealt in scorn;   40
But, if a man were halt,[9] or hunch'd, in him
By those who God had made full-limb'd and tall,

---

5. In Malory, Sir Mordred usurps the throne and attempts to marry Guinevere while the King is off fighting in France. Upon Arthur's return, they mortally wound each other. Although Modred makes several brief appearances in the *Idylls*, Tennyson never attempts to develop his character fully. He is a minor villain whose chief function is to expose Guinevere's liaison with Lancelot.

6. The Saxons' emblem was the White Horse; Hengist and his brother Horsa, according to Geoffrey of Monmouth's *History of the Kings of Britain*, were Jute invaders of England (c. 449). Hengist was said to have ruled the kingdom of Kent until 488.
7. I.e., as white as hawthorn blossoms.
8. Cabbage.
9. Crippled.

Scorn was allow'd as part of his defect,
And he was answer'd softly by the King
And all his Table. So Sir Lancelot holp   45
To raise the prince, who rising twice or thrice
Full sharply smote his knees, and smiled, and went;
But, ever after, the small violence done
Rankled in him and ruffled all his heart,
As the sharp wind that ruffles all day long   50
A little bitter pool about a stone
On the bare coast.

              But when Sir Lancelot told
This matter to the Queen, at first she laugh'd
Lightly, to think of Modred's dusty fall,
Then shudder'd, as the village wife who cries,   55
"I shudder, some one steps across my grave;"
Then laugh'd again, but faintlier, for indeed
She half-foresaw that he, the subtle beast,
Would track her guilt until he found, and hers
Would be for evermore a name of scorn.   60
Henceforward rarely could she front in hall,
Or elsewhere, Modred's narrow foxy face,
Heart-hiding smile, and gray persistent eye.
Henceforward too, the Powers that tend the soul,
To help it from the death that cannot die,   65
And save it even in extremes, began
To vex and plague her. Many a time for hours,
Beside the placid breathings of the King,
In the dead night, grim faces came and went
Before her, or a vague spiritual fear—   70
Like to some doubtful noise of creaking doors,
Heard by the watcher in a haunted house,
That keeps the rust of murder on the walls—
Held her awake; or if she slept she dream'd
An awful dream, for then she seem'd to stand   75
On some vast plain before a setting sun,
And from the sun there swiftly made at her
A ghastly something, and its shadow flew
Before it till it touch'd her, and she turn'd—
When lo! her own, that broadening from her feet,   80
And blackening, swallow'd all the land, and in it
Far cities burnt, and with a cry she woke.
And all this trouble did not pass but grew,
Till even the clear face of the guileless King,
And trustful courtesies of household life,   85
Became her bane; and at the last she said:
"O Lancelot, get thee hence to thine own land,
For if thou tarry we shall meet again,
And if we meet again some evil chance
Will make the smouldering scandal break and blaze   90

Before the people and our lord the King."
And Lancelot ever promised, but remain'd,
And still they met and met. Again she said,
"O Lancelot, if thou love me get thee hence."
And then they were agreed upon a night—   95
When the good King should not be there—to meet
And part for ever. Vivien, lurking, heard.
She told Sir Modred. Passion-pale they met
And greeted. Hands in hands, and eye to eye,
Low on the border of her couch they sat   100
Stammering and staring. It was their last hour,
A madness of farewells. And Modred brought
His creatures to the basement of the tower
For testimony; and crying with full voice,
"Traitor, come out, ye are trapt at last," aroused   105
Lancelot, who rushing outward lionlike
Leapt on him, and hurl'd him headlong, and he fell
Stunn'd, and his creatures took and bare him off,
And all was still. Then she, "The end is come,
And I am shamed for ever;" and he said: 110
"Mine be the shame, mine was the sin; but rise,
And fly to my strong castle over-seas.
There will I hide thee till my life shall end,
There hold thee with my life against the world."
She answer'd: "Lancelot, wilt thou hold me so?   115
Nay, friend, for we have taken our farewells.
Would God that thou couldst hide me from myself!
Mine is the shame, for I was wife, and thou
Unwedded; yet rise now, and let us fly,
For I will draw me into sanctuary,   120
And bide my doom." So Lancelot got her horse,
Set her thereon, and mounted on his own,
And then they rode to the divided way,
There kiss'd and parted weeping; for he past,
Love-loyal to the least wish of the Queen,   125
Back to his land; but she to Almesbury
Fled all night long by glimmering waste and weald,
And heard the spirits of the waste and weald
Moan as she fled, or thought she heard them moan.
And in herself she moan'd, "Too late, too late!"   130
Till in the cold wind that foreruns the morn,
A blot in heaven, the raven, flying high,
Croak'd, and she thought, "He spies a field of death;
For now the heathen of the Northern Sea,
Lured by the crimes and frailties of the court,   135
Begin to slay the folk and spoil the land."

    And when she came to Almesbury she spake
There to the nuns, and said, "Mine enemies
Pursue me, but, O peaceful Sisterhood,

Receive and yield me sanctuary, nor ask   140
Her name to whom ye yield it till her time
To tell you;" and her beauty, grace, and power
Wrought as a charm upon them, and they spared
To ask it.

       So the stately Queen abode
For many a week, unknown, among the nuns,   145
Nor with them mix'd, nor told her name, nor sought,
Wrapt in her grief, for housel[1] or for shrift
But communed only with the little maid,
Who pleased her with a babbling heedlessness
Which often lured her from herself; but now,   150
This night, a rumor wildly blown about
Came that Sir Modred had usurp'd the realm
And leagued him with the heathen, while the King
Was waging war on Lancelot. Then she thought,
"With what a hate the people and the King   155
Must hate me," and bow'd down upon her hands
Silent, until the little maid, who brook'd
No silence, brake it, uttering "Late! so late!
What hour, I wonder now?" and when she drew
No answer, by and by began to hum   160
An air the nuns had taught her: "Late, so late!"
Which when she heard, the Queen look'd up, and said,
"O maiden, if indeed ye list to sing,
Sing, and unbind my heart that I may weep."
Whereat full willingly sang the little maid.   165

       "Late, late, so late! and dark the night and chill!
       Late, late, so late! but we can enter still.
       Too late, too late! ye cannot enter now.

       "No light had we; for that we do repent,
       And learning this, the bridegroom will relent.   170
       Too late, too late! yet cannot enter now.

       "No light! so late! and dark and chill the night!
       O, let us in, that we may find the light!
       Too late, too late! ye cannot enter now.

       "Have we not heard the bridegroom is so sweet?   175
       O, let us in, tho' late, to kiss his feet!
       No, no, too late! ye cannot enter now."[2]

So sang the novice,[3] while full passionately,
Her head upon her hands, remembering
Her thought when first she came, wept the sad Queen.   180
Then said the little novice prattling to her:

---

1. Reception of the Holy Communion; "shrift" is confession.
2. See the parable of the wise and foolish virgins, *Matthew*, 25.
3. There is something to be said for Littledale's observation that "the child's talk that follows is a recapitulation of the story of the Coming of Arthur, as it may be supposed to have settled itself in the popular imagination."

"O pray you, noble lady, weep no more:
But let my words—the words of one so small,
Who knowing nothing knows but to obey,
And if I do not there is penance given—   185
Comfort your sorrows, for they do not flow
From evil done; right sure am I of that,
Who see your tender grace and stateliness.
But weigh your sorrows with our lord the King's,
And weighing find them less; for gone is he   190
To wage grim war against Sir Lancelot there,
Round that strong castle where he holds the Queen;
And Modred whom he left in charge of all,
The traitor—Ah, sweet lady, the King's grief
For his own self, and his own Queen, and realm,   195
Must needs be thrice as great as any of ours!
For me, I thank the saints, I am not great;
For if there ever come a grief to me
I cry my cry in silence, and have done;
None knows it, and my tears have brought me good.   200
But even were the griefs of little ones
As great as those of great ones, yet this grief
Is added to the griefs the great must bear,
That, howsoever much they desire
Silence, they cannot weep behind a cloud;   205
As even here they talk at Almesbury
About the good King and his wicked Queen,
And were I such a King with such a Queen,
Well might I wish to veil her wickedness,
But were I such a King it could not be."   210

    Then to her own sad heart mutter'd the Queen,
"Will the child kill me with her innocent talk?"
But openly she answer'd, "Must not I,
If this false traitor have displaced his lord,
Grieve with the common grief of all the realm?"   215

    "Yea," said the maid, "this all is woman's grief,
That *she* is woman, whose disloyal life
Hath wrought confusion in the Table Round
Which good King Arthur founded, years ago,
With signs and miracles and wonders, there   220
At Camelot, ere the coming of the Queen."

    Then thought the Queen within herself again,
"Will the child kill me with her foolish prate?"
But openly she spake and said to her,
"O little maid, shut in by nunnery walls,   225
What canst thou know of Kings and Tables Round,
Or what of signs and wonders, but the signs
And simple miracles of thy nunnery?"

To whom the little novice garrulously:
"Yea, but I know; the land was full of signs   230
And wonders.ere the coming of the Queen.
So said my father, and himself was knight
Of the great Table—at the founding of it,
And rode thereto from Lyonnesse; and he said
That as he rode, an hour or maybe twain   235
After the sunset, down the coast, he heard
Strange music, and he paused, and turning—there,
All down the lonely coast of Lyonnesse,
Each with a beacon-star upon his head,
And with a wild sea-light about his feet,   240
He saw them—headland after headland flame
Far on into the rich heart of the west.
And in the light the white mermaiden swam,
And strong man-breasted things stood from the the sea,
And sent a deep sea-voice thro' all the land,   245
To which the little elves of chasm and cleft
Made answer, sounding like a distant horn.
So said my father—yea, and furthermore,
Next morning, while he past the dim-lit woods
Himself beheld three spirits mad with joy   250
Come dashing down on a tall wayside flower,
That shook beneath them as the thistle shakes
When three gray linnets wrangle for the seed.
And still at evenings on before his horse
The flickering fairy-circle wheel'd and broke   255
Flying, and link'd again, and wheel'd and broke
Flying, for all the land was full of life.
And when at last he came to Camelot,
A wreath of airy dancers hand-in-hand
Swung round the lighted lantern of the hall;   260
And in the hall itself was such a feast
As never man had dream'd; for every knight
Had whatsoever meat he long'd for served
By hands unseen; and even as he said
Down in the cellars merry bloated things   265
Shoulder'd the spigot,[4] straddling on the butts
While the wine ran; so glad were spirits and men
Before the coming of the sinful Queen."

    Then spake the Queen and somewhat bitterly,
"Were they so glad? ill prophets were they all,   270
Spirits and men. Could none of them foresee,
Not even thy wise father with his signs
And wonders, what has fallen upon the realm?"

    To whom the novice garrulously again:
"Yea, one, a bard, of whom my father said,   275

---

4. The stopper for the mouth of the cask or butt.

Full many a noble war-song had he sung,
Even in the presence of an enemy's fleet,
Between the steep cliff and the coming wave;
And many a mystic lay of life and death
Had chanted on the smoky mountain-tops,   280
When round him bent the spirits of the hills
With all their dewy hair blown back like flame.
So said my father—and that night the bard
Sang Arthur's glorious wars, and sang the King
As wellnigh more than man, and rail'd at those   285
Who call'd him the false son of Gorloïs.[5]
For there was no man knew from whence he came;
But after tempest, when the long wave broke
All down the thundering shores of Bude and Bos,[6]
There came a day as still as heaven, and then   290
They found a naked child upon the sands
Of dark Tintagil by the Cornish sea,
And that was Arthur, and they foster'd him
Till he by miracle was approven King;
And that his grave should be a mystery   295
From all men, like his birth; and could he find
A woman in her womanhood as great
As he was in his manhood, then, he sang,
The twain together well might change the world.
But even in the middle of his song   300
He falter'd, and his hand fell from the harp,
And pale he turn'd, and reel'd, and would have fallen,
But that they stay'd him up; nor would he tell
His vision; but what doubt that he foresaw
This evil work of Lancelot and the Queen?"   305

    Then thought the Queen, "Lo! they have set her on,
Our simple-seeming abbess and her nuns,
To play upon me," and bow'd her head nor spake.
Whereat the novice crying, with clasp'd hands,
Shame on her own garrulity garrulously,   310
Said the good nuns would check her gadding[7] tongue
Full often, "and, sweet lady, if I seem
To vex an ear too sad to listen to me,
Unmannerly, with prattling and the tales
Which my good father told me, check me too   315
Nor let me shame my father's memory, one
Of noblest manners, tho' himself would say
Sir Lancelot had the noblest; and he died,
Kill'd in a tilt, come next, five summers back,
And left me; but of others who remain,   320
And of the two first-famed for courtesy—

---

5. See "The Coming of Arthur," lines 67–73, for the beginning of the extensive discussion about Arthur's origins.
6. Areas of Cornwall, north of Tintagil.
7. Rambling.

And pray you check me if I ask amiss—
But pray you, which had noblest, while you moved
Among them, Lancelot or our lord the King?"

Then the pale Queen look'd up and answer'd her: 325
"Sir Lancelot, as became a noble knight,
Was gracious to all ladies, and the same
In open battle or the tilting-field
Forbore his own advantage, and the King
In open battle or the tilting-field   330
Forbore his own advantage, and these two
Were the most nobly-manner'd men of all;
For manners are not idle, but the fruit
Of loyal nature and of noble mind."

"Yea," said the maid, "be manners such fair fruit?   335
Then Lancelot's needs must be a thousand fold
Less noble, being, as all rumor runs,
The most disloyal friend in all the world."

To which a mournful answer made the Queen:
"O, closed about by narrowing nunnery-walls,   340
What knowest thou of the world and all its lights
And shadows, all the wealth and all the woe?
If ever Lancelot, that most noble knight,
Were for one hour less noble than himself,
Pray for him that he scape the doom of fire,   345
And weep for her who drew him to his doom."

"Yea," said the little novice, "I pray for both;
But I should all as soon believe that his,
Sir Lancelot's, were as noble as the King's,
As I could think, sweet lady, yours would be   350
Such as they are, were you the sinful Queen."

So she, like many another babbler, hurt
Whom she would soothe, and harm'd where she would heal;
For here a sudden flush of wrathful heat
Fired all the pale face of the Queen, who cried: 355
"Such as thou art be never maiden more
For ever! thou their tool, set on to plague
And play upon and harry me, petty spy
And traitress!" When that storm of anger brake
From Guinevere, aghast the maiden rose,   360
White as her veil, and stood before the Queen
As tremulously as foam upon the beach
Stands in a wind, ready to break and fly,
And when the Queen had added, "Get thee hence!"
Fled frighted. Then that other left alone   365
Sigh'd, and began to gather heart again,
Saying in herself: "The simple, fearful child
Meant nothing, but my own too-fearful guilt,

Simpler than any child, betrays itself.
But help me, Heaven, for surely I repent!   370
For what is true repentance but in thought—
Not even in inmost thought to think again
The sins that made the past so pleasant to us?
And I have sworn never to see him more,
To see him more."

     And even in saying this,   375
Her memory from old habit of the mind
Went slipping back upon the golden days
In which she saw him first, when Lancelot came,
Reputed the best knight and goodliest man,
Ambassador, to yield her to his lord   380
Arthur, and led her forth, and far ahead
Of his and her retinue moving, they,
Rapt in sweet talk or lively, all on love
And sport and tilts and pleasure,—for the time
Was may-time, and as yet no sin was dream'd,—   385
Rode under groves that look'd a paradise
Of blossom, over sheets of hyacinth
That seem'd the heavens upbreaking thro' the earth,
And on from hill to hill, and every day
Beheld at noon in some delicious dale   390
The silk pavilions of King Arthur raised
For brief repast or afternoon repose
By couriers gone before; and on again,
Till yet once more ere set of sun they saw
The Dragon of the great Pendragonship,[8]   395
That crown'd the state pavilion of the King,
Blaze by the rushing brook or silent well.

 But when the Queen immersed in such a trance,
And moving thro' the past unconsciously,
Came to that point where first she saw the King   400
Ride toward her from the city, sigh'd to find
Her journey done, glanced at him, thought him cold,
High, self-contain'd, and passionless, not like him,
"Not like my Lancelot"—while she brooded thus
And grew half-guilty in her thoughts again,   405
There rode an armed warrior to the doors.
A murmuring whisper thro' the nunnery ran,
Then on a sudden a cry, "The King!" She sat
Stiff-stricken, listening; but when armed feet
Thro' the long gallery from the outer doors   410
Rang coming, prone from off her seat she fell,
And grovell'd with her face against the floor.
There with her milk-white arms and shadowy hair
She made her face a darkness from the King,

---

8. See "Lancelot and Elaine," line 422 and note.

And in the darkness heard his armed feet   415
Pause by her; then came silence, then a voice,
Monotonous and hollow like a ghost's
Denouncing judgment, but, tho' changed, the King's:

"Liest thou here so low, the child of one
I honor'd, happy, dead before thy shame?   420
Well is it that no child is born of thee.
The children born of thee are sword and fire,
Red ruin, and the breaking up of laws,
The craft of kindred and the godless hosts
Of heathen swarming o'er the Northern Sea;   425
Whom I, while yet Sir Lancelot, my right arm,
The mightiest of my knights, abode with me,
Have everywhere about this land of Christ
In twelve great battles ruining overthrown.
And knowest thou now from whence I come—from him,   430
From waging bitter war with him; and he,
That did not shun to smite me in worse way,
Had yet that grace of courtesy in him left,
He spared to lift his hand against the King
Who made him knight. But many a knight was slain;   435
And many more and all his kith and kin
Clave to him, and abode in his own land.
And many more when Modred raised revolt,
Forgetful of their troth and fealty, clave
To Modred, and a remnant stays with me.   440
And of this remnant will I leave a part,
True men who love me still, for whom I live,
To guard thee in the wild hour coming on,
Lest but a hair of this low head be harm'd.
Fear not; thou shalt be guarded till my death.   445
Howbeit I know, if ancient prophecies
Have err'd not, that I march to meet my doom.
Thou hast not made my life so sweet to me,
That I the King should greatly care to live;
For thou hast spoilt the purpose of my life.   450
Bear with me for the last time while I show,
Even for thy sake, the sin which thou hast sinn'd.
For when the Roman left us, and their law
Relax'd its hold upon us, and the ways
Were fill'd with rapine, here and there a deed   455
Of prowess done redress'd a random wrong.
But I was first of all the kings who drew
The knighthood-errant of this realm and all
The realms together under me, their Head,
In that fair Order of my Table Round,   460
A glorious company, the flower of men,
To serve as model for the mighty world,
And be the fair beginning of a time.

I made them lay their hands in mine and swear
To reverence the King, as if he were   465
Their conscience, and their conscience as their King,
To break the heathen and uphold the Christ,
To ride abroad redressing human wrongs,
To speak no slander, no, nor listen to it,
To honor his own word as if his God's,   470
To lead sweet lives in purest chastity,
To love one maiden only, cleave to her,
And worship her by years of noble deeds,
Until they won her; for indeed I knew
Of no more subtle master under heaven   475
Than is the maiden passion for a maid,
Not only to keep down the base in man,
But teach high thought, and amiable words
And courtliness, and the desire of fame,
And love of truth, and all that makes a man.   480
And all this throve before I wedded thee,
Believing, 'Lo, mine helpmate, one to feel
My purpose and rejoicing in my joy!'
Then came thy shameful sin with Lancelot;
Then came the sin of Tristram and Isolt;   485
Then others, following these my mightiest knights,
And drawing foul ensample from fair names,
Sinn'd also, till the loathsome opposite
Of all my heart had destined did obtain,
And all thro' thee! so that this life of mine   490
I guard as God's high gift from scathe and wrong,
Not greatly care to lose; but rather think
How sad it were for Arthur, should he live,
To sit once more within his lonely hall,
And miss the wonted number of my knights,   495
And miss to hear high talk of noble deeds
As in the golden days before thy sin.
For which of us who might be left could speak
Of the pure heart, nor seem to glance at thee?
And in thy bowers of Camelot or of Usk   500
Thy shadow still would glide from room to room,
And I should evermore be vext with thee
In hanging robe or vacant ornament,
Or ghostly footfall echoing on the stair.
For think not, tho' thou wouldst not love thy lord,   505
Thy lord has wholly lost his love for thee.
I am not made of so slight elements.
Yet must I leave thee, woman, to thy shame.
I hold that man the worst of public foes
Who either for his own or children's sake,   510
To save his blood from scandal, lets the wife
Whom he knows false abide and rule the house:

For being thro' his cowardice allow'd
Her station, taken everywhere for pure,
She like a new disease, unknown to men,   515
Creeps, no precaution used, among the crowd,
Makes wicked lightnings of her eyes, and saps
The fealty of our friends, and stirs the pulse
With devil's leaps, and poisons half the young.
Worst of the worst were that man he that reigns!   520
Better the King's waste hearth and aching heart
Than thou reseated in thy place of light,
The mockery of my people and their bane!"

    He paused, and in the pause she crept an inch
Nearer, and laid her hands about his feet.   525
Far off a solitary trumpet blew.
Then waiting by the doors the war-horse neigh'd
As at a friend's voice, and he spake again:

    "Yet think not that I come to urge thy crimes;
I did not come to curse thee, Guinevere,   530
I, whose vast pity almost makes me die
To see thee, laying there thy golden head,
My pride in happier summers, at my feet.
The wrath of which forced my thoughts on that fierce law,
The doom of treason and the flaming death,[9]—   535
When first I learnt thee hidden here,—is past.
The pang—which, while I weigh'd thy heart with one
Too wholly true to dream untruth in thee,
Made my tears burn—is also past—in part.
And all is past, the sin is sinn'd, and I,   540
Lo, I forgive thee, as Eternal God
Forgives! do thou for thine own soul the rest.
But how to take last leave of all I loved?
O golden hair, with which I used to play
Not knowing! O imperial-moulded form,   545
And beauty such as never woman wore,
Until it came a kingdom's curse with thee—
I cannot touch thy lips, they are not mine,
But Lancelot's; nay, they never were the King's.
I cannot take thy hand; that too is flesh,   550
And in the flesh thou hast sinn'd; and mine own flesh,
Here looking down on thine polluted, cries,
'I loathe thee;' yet not less, O Guinevere,
For I was ever virgin save for thee,
My love thro' flesh hath wrought into my life   555
So far that my doom is, I love thee still.
Let no man dream but that I love thee still.
Perchance, and so thou purify thy soul,
And so thou lean on our fair father Christ,

9. In Malory, Guinevere is condemned by Launcelot at the last minute.
to be burnt at the stake and is rescued

Hereafter in that world where all are pure   560
We two may meet before high God, and thou
Wilt spring to me, and claim me thine, and know
I am thine husband—not a smaller soul,
Nor Lancelot, nor another. Leave me that,
I charge thee, my last hope. Now must I hence.   565
Thro' the thick night I hear the trumpet blow.
They summon me their King to lead mine hosts
Far down to that great battle in the west,
Where I must strike against the man they call
My sister's son—no kin of mine, who leagues   570
With Lords of the White Horse, heathen, and knights,
Traitors—and strike him dead, and meet myself
Death, or I know not what mysterious doom.
And thou remaining here wilt learn the event;
But hither shall I never come again,   575
Never lie by thy side, see thee no more—
Farewell!"

        And while she grovell'd at his feet,[1]
She felt the King's breath wander o'er her neck,
And in the darkness o'er her fallen head
Perceived the waving of his hands that blest.   580

   Then, listening till those armed steps were gone,
Rose the pale Queen, and in her anguish found
The casement: "peradventure," so she thought,
"If I might see his face, and not be seen."
And lo, he sat on horseback at the door!   585
And near him the sad nuns with each a light
Stood, and he gave them charge about the Queen,
To guard and foster her for evermore.
And while she spake to these his helm was lower'd,
To which for crest the golden dragon clung   590
Of Britain; so she did not see the face,
Which then was as an angel's, but she saw,
Wet with the mists and smitten by the lights,
The Dragon of the great Pendragonship
Blaze, making all the night a steam of fire.   595
And even then he turn'd; and more and more
The moony vapor rolling round the King,
Who seem'd the phantom of a giant in it,
Enwound him fold by fold, and made him gray
And grayer, till himself became as mist   600
Before her, moving ghostlike to his doom.[2]

---

1. The Queen's posture and Arthur's conduct towards her have often been used in arguments to show the King's priggishness. Although perhaps he does uncomfortably resemble our stereotyped notion of the Victorian patriarch indignant over his wife's infidelity, I have never seen a convincing alternative offered to explain how Tennyson should have conducted the scene.

2. In part accounting for the pause in writing the *Idylls,* Tennyson said of these lines: "I could hardly light upon a finer close than that ghost-like passing away of the King" (*Memoir,* II, 126). In this instance, Tennyson's estimate of his own poetry was certainly sound.

Then she stretch'd out her arms and cried aloud,
"O Arthur!" there her voice brake suddenly,
Then—as a stream that spouting from a cliff
Fails in mid air, but gathering at the base   605
Re-makes itself, and flashes down the vale—
Went on in passionate utterance:

                              "Gone—my lord!
Gone thro' my sin to slay and to be slain!
And he forgave me, and I could not speak.
Farewell? I should have answer'd his farewell.   610
His mercy choked me. Gone, my lord the King,
My own true lord! how dare I call him mine?
The shadow of another cleaves to me,
And makes me one pollution. He, the King,
Call'd me polluted. Shall I kill myself?   615
What help in that? I cannot kill my sin,
If soul be soul, nor can I kill my shame;
No, nor by living can I live it down.
The days will grow to weeks, the weeks to months,
The months will add themselves and make the years,   620
The years will roll into the centuries,
And mine will ever be a name of scorn.
I must not dwell on that defeat of fame.
Let the world be; that is but of the world—
What else? what hope? I think there was a hope,   625
Except he mock'd me when he spake of hope;
His hope he call'd it; but he never mocks,
For mockery is the fume of little hearts.
And blessed be the King, who hath forgiven
My wickedness to him, and left me hope   630
That in mine own heart I can live down sin
And be his mate hereafter in the heavens
Before high God! Ah great and gentle lord,
Who wast, as is the conscience of a saint
Among his warring senses, to thy knights—   635
To whom my false voluptuous pride, that took
Full easily all impressions from below,
Would not look up, or half-despised the height
To which I would not or I could not climb—
I thought I could not breathe in that fine air,   640
That pure severity of perfect light—
I yearn'd for warmth and color which I found
In Lancelot—now I see thee what thou art,
Thou art the highest and most human too,
Not Lancelot, nor another. Is there none   645
Will tell the King I love him tho' so late?
Now—ere he goes to the great battle? none!
Myself must tell him in that purer life,
But now it were too daring. Ah my God,

What might I not have made of thy fair world,   650
Had I but loved thy highest creature here?
It was my duty to have loved the highest;
It surely was my profit had I known;
It would have been my pleasure had I seen.
We needs must love the highest when we see it,   655
Not Lancelot, nor another."

               Here her hand
Grasp'd made her vail[3] her eyes. She look'd and saw
The novice, weeping, suppliant, and said to her,
"Yea, little maid, for am *I* not forgiven?"
Then glancing up beheld the holy nuns   660
All round her, weeping; and her heart was loosed
Within her, and she wept with these and said:

  "Ye know me then, that wicked one, who broke
The vast design and purpose of the King.
O, shut me round with narrowing nunnery-walls,   665
Meek maidens, from the voices crying, 'Shame!'
I must not scorn myself; he loves me still.
Let no one dream but that he loves me still.
So let me, if you do not shudder at me,
Nor shun to call me sister, dwell with you;   670
Wear black and white, and be a nun like you,
Fast with your fasts, not feasting with your feasts;
Grieve with your griefs, not grieving at your joys,
But not rejoicing; mingle with your rites;
Pray and be pray'd for; lie before your shrines;   675
Do each low office of your holy house;
Walk your dim cloister, and distribute dole
To poor sick people, richer in His eyes
Who ransom'd us, and haler too than I;
And treat their loathsome hurts and heal mine own;   680
And so wear out in alms-deed and in prayer
The sombre close of that voluptuous day
Which wrought the ruin of my lord the King."

  She said. They took her to themselves; and she
Still hoping, fearing "Is it yet too late?"   685
Dwelt with them, till in time their abbess died.
Then she, for her good deeds and her pure life,
And for the power of ministration in her,
And likewise for the high rank she had borne,
Was chosen abbess, there, an abbess, lived   690
For three brief years, and there, an abbess, past
To where beyond these voices there is peace.

1859

3. Lower.

The Passing of Arthur[4]

That story which the bold Sir Bedivere,
First made and latest left of all the knights,
Told, when the man was no more than a voice
In the white winter of his age, to those
With whom he dwelt, new faces, other minds.   5

For on their march to westward, Bedivere,
Who slowly paced among the slumbering host,
Heard in his tent the moanings of the King:

"I found Him in the shining of the stars,
I mark'd Him in the flowering of His fields,   10
But in His ways with men I find Him not.
I waged His wars, and now I pass and die.
O me! for why is all around us here
As if some lesser god had made the world,
But had not force to shape it as he would,   15
Till the High God behold it from beyond,
And enter it, and make it beautiful?
Or else as if the world were wholly fair,
But that these eyes of men are dense and dim,
And have not power to see it as it is—   20
Perchance, because we see not to the close;—
For I, being simple, thought to work His will,
And have but stricken with the sword in vain,
And all whereon I lean'd in wife and friend
Is traitor to my peace, and all my realm   25
Reels back into the beast, and is no more.
My God, thou hast forgotten me in my death!
Nay—God my Christ—I pass but shall not die."

Then, ere that last weird battle in the west,
There came on Arthur sleeping, Gawain kill'd   30
In Lancelot's war, the ghost of Gawain blown
Along a wandering wind, and past his ear
Went shrilling: "Hollow, hollow all delight!
Hail, King! to-morrow thou shalt pass away.
Farewell! there is an isle of rest for thee.   35
And I am blown along a wandering wind,
And hollow, hollow, hollow all delight!"
And fainter onward, like wild birds that change
Their season in the night and wail their way
From cloud to cloud, down the long wind the dream   40

4. The first-written of the *Idylls*, the earlier "Morte d'Arthur" (see "The Epic," p. 81), was expanded by adding an introduction (lines 1–169) and a conclusion (lines 441–469) for publication in 1869. "The form of the 'Coming of Arthur' and of the 'Pass-ing,' " Tennyson said, "is purposely more archaic than that of the other 'Idylls,' " adding elsewhere that they "are simpler and more severe in style, as dealing with the awfulness of Birth and Death" (*Memoir*, II, 133, and I, 483 n.).

Shrill'd; but in going mingled with dim cries
Far in the moonlit haze among the hills,
As of some lonely city sack'd by night,
When all is lost, and wife and child with wail
Pass to new lords; and Arthur woke and call'd: 45
"Who spake? A dream. O, light upon the wind,
Thine, Gawain, was the voice—are these dim cries
Thine? or doth all that haunts the waste and wild
Mourn, knowing it will go along with me?"

    This heard the bold Sir Bedivere and spake: 50
"O me, my King, let pass whatever will,
Elves, and the harmless glamour of the field;
But in their stead thy name and glory cling
To all high places like a golden cloud
For ever; but as yet thou shalt not pass.   55
Light was Gawain in life, and light in death
Is Gawain, for the ghost is as the man;
And care not thou for dreams from him, but rise—
I hear the steps of Modred in the west,
And with him many of thy people, and knights   60
Once thine, whom thou hast loved, but grosser grown
Than heathen, spitting at their vows and thee.
Right well in heart they know thee for the King.
Arise, go forth and conquer as of old."

    Then spake King Arthur to Sir Bedivere: 65
"Far other is this battle in the west
Whereto we move than when we strove in youth,
And brake the petty kings, and fought with Rome,
Or thrust the heathen from the Roman wall,
And shook him thro' the north. Ill doom is mine   70
To war against my people and my knights.
The king who fights his people fights himself.
And they my knights, who loved me once, the stroke
That strikes them dead is as my death to me.
Yet let us hence, and find or feel a way   75
Thro' this blind haze which, ever since I saw
One[5] lying in the dust at Almesbury,
Hath folded in the passes of the world."

    Then rose the King and moved his host by night,
And ever push'd Sir Modred, league by league,   80
Back to the sunset bound of Lyonnesse[6]—
A land of old upheaven from the abyss
By fire, to sink into the abyss again;
Where fragments of forgotten peoples dwelt,
And the long mountains ended in a coast   85
Of ever-shifting sand, and far away

5. Guinevere.
6. In fable, the land that sank into the sea. See "Lancelot and Elaine," line 35 and note.

The phantom circle of a moaning sea.
There the pursuer could pursue no more,
And he that fled no further fly the King;
And there, that day when the great light of heaven   90
Burn'd at his lowest in the rolling year,
On the waste sand by the waste sea they closed.
Nor ever yet had Arthur fought a fight
Like this last, dim, weird battle of the west.
A death-white mist slept over sand and sea,   95
Whereof the chill, to him who breathed it, drew
Down with his blood, till all his heart was cold
With formless fear; and even on Arthur fell
Confusion, since he saw not whom he fought.
For friend and foe were shadows in the mist,   100
And friend slew friend not knowing whom he slew;
And some had visions out of golden youth,
And some beheld the faces of old ghosts·
Look in upon the battle; and in the mist
Was many a noble deed, many a base,   105
And chance and craft and strength in single fights,
And ever and anon with host to host
Shocks, and the splintering spear, the hard mail hewn,
Shield-breakings, and the clash of brands, the crash
Of battle-axes on shatter'd helms, and shrieks   110
After the Christ, of those who falling down
Look'd up for heaven, and only saw the mist;
And shouts of heathen and the traitor knights,
Oaths, insult, filth, and monstrous blasphemies,[7]
Sweat, writhings, anguish, laboring of the lungs   115
In that close mist, and cryings for the light,
Moans of the dying, and voices of the dead.

    Last, as by some one death-bed after wail
Of suffering, silence follows, or thro' death
Or death-like swoon, thus over all that shore,   120
Save for some whisper of the seething seas,
A dead hush fell; but when the dolorous day
Grew drearier toward twilight falling, came
A bitter wind, clear from the north, and blew
The mist aside, and with that wind the tide   125
Rose, and the pale King glanced across the field
Of battle. But no man was moving there;
Nor any cry of Christian heard thereon,
Nor yet of heathen; only the wan wave
Brake in among dead faces, to and fro   130
Swaying the helpless hands, and up and down
Tumbling the hollow helmets of the fallen,
And shiver'd brands that once had fought with Rome,
And rolling far along the gloomy shores
The voice of days of old and days to be.   135

7. See *Revelation*, 16.

Then spake King Arthur to Sir Bedivere,
And whiter than the mist that all day long
Had held the field of battle was the King:

"Hearest thou this great voice that shakes the world,
And wastes the narrow realm whereon we move,　　　140
And beats upon the faces of the dead,
My dead, as tho' they had not died for me?—
O Bedivere, for on my heart hath fallen
Confusion, till I know not what I am,
Nor whence I am, nor whether I be king;　　　145
Behold, I seem but king among the dead."

Then spoke the bold Sir Bedivere: "My King!
King everywhere! and so the dead have kings,
There also will I worship thee as king.
Yet still thy life is whole, and still I live　　　150
Who love thee; but who hates thee, he that brought
The heathen back among us, yonder stands,
Modred, unharm'd, the traitor of thine house."

Then spake the King: "My house hath been my doom.
But call not thou this traitor of my house　　　155
Who hath but dwelt beneath one roof with me.
My house are rather they who sware my vows,
Yea, even while they brake them, own'd me king.
And well for thee, saying in my dark hour,
When all the purport of my throne hath fail'd,　　　160
That quick or dead thou holdest me for king.
King am I, whatsoever be their cry;
And one last act of kinghood shalt thou see
Yet, ere I pass." And uttering this the King
Made at the man. Then Modred smote his liege　　　165
Hard on that helm which many a heathen sword
Had beaten thin; while Arthur at one blow,
Striking the last stroke with Excalibur,
Slew him, and, all but slain himself, he fell.

So all day long the noise of battle roll'd　　　170
Among the mountains by the winter sea,
Until King Arthur's Table, man by man,
Had fallen in Lyonnesse about their lord,
King Arthur; then, because his wound was deep,
The bold Sir Bedivere uplifted him,　　　175
And bore him to a chapel nigh the field,
A broken chancel with a broken cross,
That stood on a dark strait of barren land.
On one side lay the Ocean, and on one
Lay a great water, and the moon was full.　　　180

Then spake King Arthur to Sir Bedivere:
"The sequel of to-day unsolders all
The goodliest fellowship of famous knights

Whereof this world holds record. Such a sleep
They sleep—the men I loved. I think that we   185
Shall never more, at any future time,
Delight our souls with talk of knightly deeds,
Walking about the gardens and the halls
Of Camelot, as in the days that were.
I perish by this people which I made,—   190
Tho' Merlin sware that I should come again
To rule once more—but let what will be be,
I am so deeply smitten thro' the helm
That without help I cannot last till morn.
Thou therefore take my brand Excalibur,   195
Which was my pride; for thou rememberest how
In those old days, on summer noon, an arm
Rose up from out the bosom of the lake,
Clothed in white samite, mystic, wonderful,
Holding the sword—and how I row'd across   200
And took it, and have worn it, like a king;
And, wheresoever I am sung or told
In aftertime, this also shall be known.
But now delay not; take Excalibur,
And fling him far into the middle mere;   205
Watch what thou seest, and lightly[8] bring me word."

To him replied the bold Sir Bedivere:
"It is not meet, Sir King, to leave thee thus,
Aidless, alone, and smitten thro' the helm—
A little thing may harm a wounded man;   210
Yet I thy hest will all perform at full,
Watch what I see, and lightly bring thee word."

So saying, from the ruin'd shrine he stept,
And in the moon athwart the place of tombs,
Where lay the mighty bones of ancient men,   215
Old knights, and over them the sea-wind sang
Shrill, chill, with flakes of foam. He, stepping down
By zigzag paths and juts of pointed rock,
Came on the shining levels of the lake.

There drew he forth the brand Excalibur,   220
And o'er him, drawing it, the winter moon,
Brightening the skirts of a long cloud, ran forth
And sparkled keen with frost against the hilt;
For all the haft[9] twinkled with diamond sparks,
Myriads of topaz-lights, and jacinth-work   225
Of subtlest jewellery. He gazed so long
That both his eyes were dazzled as he stood,
This way and that dividing the swift mind,

8. Quickly.
9. Hilt; a "jacinth" in ancient usage was a gem of blue color, probably the sapphire. In modern use it is a reddish-orange gem.

In act to throw; but at the last it seem'd
Better to leave Excalibur conceal'd   230
There in the many-knotted water-flags,
That whistled stiff and dry about the marge.
So strode he back slow to the wounded King.

Then spake King Arthur to Sir Bedivere:
"Hast thou perform'd my mission which I gave?   235
What is it thou hast seen? or what hast heard?"

And answer made the bold Sir Bedivere:
"I heard the ripple washing in the reeds,
And the wild water lapping on the crag."

To whom replied King Arthur, faint and pale: 240
"Thou hast betray'd thy nature and thy name,
Not rendering true answer, as beseem'd
Thy fealty, nor like a noble knight;
For surer sign had follow'd, either hand,
Or voice, or else a motion of the mere.   245
This is a shameful thing for men to lie.
Yet now, I charge thee, quickly go again,
As thou art lief[1] and dear, and do the thing
I bade thee, watch, and lightly bring me word."

Then went Sir Bedivere the second time   250
Across the ridge, and paced beside the mere,
Counting the dewy pebbles, fixt in thought;
But when he saw the wonder of the hilt,
How curiously and strangely chased, he smote
His palms together, and he cried aloud: 255

"And if indeed I cast the brand away,
Surely a precious thing, one worthy note,
Should thus be lost for ever from the earth,
Which might have pleased the eyes of many men.
What good should follow this, if this were done?   260
What harm, undone? Deep harm to disobey,
Seeing obedience is the bond of rule.
Were it well to obey then, if a king demand
An act unprofitable, against himself?
The King is sick, and knows not what he does.   265
What record or what relic of my lord
Should be to aftertime, but empty breath
And rumors of a doubt? But were this kept,
Stored in some treasure-house of mighty kings,
Some one might show it at a joust of arms,   270
Saying: 'King Arthur's sword, Excalibur,
Wrought by the lonely Maiden of the Lake.
Nine years she wrought it, sitting in the deeps
Upon the hidden bases of the hills.'

1. Beloved.

So might some old man speak in the aftertime   275
To all the people, winning reverence.
But now much honor and much fame were lost."

So spake he, clouded with his own conceit,
And hid Excalibur the second time,
And so strode back slow to the wounded King.   280

Then spoke King Arthur, breathing heavily:
"What is it thou hast seen? or what hast heard?"

And answer made the bold Sir Bedivere:
"I heard the water lapping on the crag,
And the long ripple washing in the reeds."   285

To whom replied King Arthur, much in wrath:
"Ah miserable, and unkind, untrue,
Unknightly, traitor-hearted! Woe is me!
Authority forgets a dying king,
Laid widow'd of the power in his eye   290
That bow'd the will. I see thee what thou art,
For thou, the latest-left of all my knights,
In whom should meet the offices of all,
Thou wouldst betray me for the precious hilt;
Either from lust of gold, or like a girl   295
Valuing the giddy pleasure of the eyes.
Yet, for a man may fail in duty twice,
And the third time may prosper, get thee hence;
But, if thou spare to fling Excalibur,
I will arise and slay thee with my hands."   300

Then quickly rose Sir Bedivere, and ran,
And, leaping down the ridges lightly, plunged
Among the bulrush beds, and clutch'd the sword,
And strongly wheel'd and threw it. The great brand
Made lightnings in the splendor of the moon,   305
And flashing round and round, and whirl'd in an arch,
Shot like a streamer[2] of the northern morn,
Seen where the moving isles[3] of winter shock
By night, with noises of the Northern sea.
So flash'd and fell the brand Excalibur;   310
But ere he dipt the surface, rose an arm
Clothed in white samite, mystic, wonderful,
And caught him by the hilt, and brandish'd him
Three times, and drew him under in the mere.
And lightly went the other to the King.   315

Then spoke King Arthur, drawing thicker breath:
"Now see I by thine eyes that this is done.
Speak out; what is it thou hast heard, or seen?"

---

2. The Northern Lights.   3. Icebergs.

And answer made the bold Sir Bedivere:
"Sir King, I closed mine eyelids, lest the gems   320
Should blind my purpose, for I never saw,
Nor shall see, here or elsewhere, till I die,
Not tho' I live three lives of mortal men,
So great a miracle as yonder hilt.
Then with both hands I flung him, wheeling him;   325
But when I look'd again, behold an arm,
Clothed in white samite, mystic, wonderful,
That caught him by the hilt, and brandish'd him
Three times, and drew him under in the mere."

And answer made King Arthur, breathing hard: 330
"My end draws nigh; 't is time that I were gone.
Make broad thy shoulders to receive my weight,
And bear me to the margin; yet I fear
My wound hath taken cold, and I shall die."

So saying, from the pavement he half rose,   335
Slowly, with pain, reclining on his arm,
And looking wistfully with wide blue eyes
As in a picture. Him Sir Bedivere
Remorsefully regarded thro' his tears,
And would have spoken, but he found not words;   340
Then took with care, and kneeling on one knee,
O'er both his shoulders drew the languid hands,
And rising bore him thro' the place of tombs.

But, as he walk'd, King Arthur panted hard,
Like one that feels a nightmare on his bed   345
When all the house is mute. So sigh'd the King,
Muttering and murmuring at his ear, "Quick, quick!
I fear it is too late, and I shall die."
But the other swiftly strode from ridge to ridge,
Clothed with his breath, and looking, as he walk'd,   350
Larger than human on the frozen hills.
He heard the deep behind him, and a cry
Before. His own thought drove him like a goad.
Dry clash'd his harness in the icy caves
And barren chasms, and all to left and right   355
The bare black cliff clang'd round him, as he based
His feet on juts of slippery crag that rang
Sharp-smitten with the dint of armed heels—
And on a sudden, lo, the level lake,
And the long glories of the winter moon!   360

Then saw they how there hove a dusky barge,
Dark as a funeral scarf from stem to stern,
Beneath them; and descending they were ware
That all the decks were dense with stately forms,
Black-stoled, black-hooded, like a dream—by these   365

Three queens[4] with crowns of gold—and from them rose
A cry that shiver'd to the tingling stars,
And, as it were one voice, an agony
Of lamentation, like a wind that shrills
All night in a waste land, where no one comes,   370
Or hath come, since the making of the world.

Then murmur'd Arthur, "Place me in the barge."
So to the barge they came. There those three queens
Put forth their hands, and took the King, and wept.
But she that rose the tallest of them all   375
And fairest laid his head upon her lap,
And loosed the shatter'd casque,[5] and chafed his hands,
And call'd him by his name, complaining loud,
And dropping bitter tears against a brow
Striped with dark blood; for all his face was white   380
And colorless, and like the wither'd moon
Smote by the fresh beam of the springing east;
And all his greaves[6] and cuisses dash'd with drops
Of onset;[7] and the light and lustrous curls—
That made his forehead like a rising sun   385
High from the dais-throne—were parch'd with dust,
Or, clotted into points and hanging loose,
Mixt with the knightly growth that fringed his lips.
So like a shatter'd column lay the King;
Not like that Arthur who, with lance in rest,   390
From spur to plume a star of tournament,
Shot thro' the lists at Camelot, and charged
Before the eyes of ladies and of kings.

Then loudly cried the bold Sir Bedivere:
"Ah! my Lord Arthur, whither shall I go?   395
Where shall I hide my forehead and my eyes?
For now I see the true old times are dead,
When every morning brought a noble chance,
And every chance brought out a noble knight.
Such times have been not since the light[8] that led   400
The holy Elders with the gift of myrrh.
But now the whole Round Table is dissolved
Which was an image of the mighty world;
And I, the last, go forth companionless,
And the days darken round me, and the years,   405
Among new men, strange faces, other minds."

And slowly answer'd Arthur from the barge:
"The old order changeth yielding place to new,
And God fulfils himself in many ways,

---

4. They may represent Faith, Hope, and Charity. See "The Coming of Arthur," line 275 and note.
5. Helmet.
6. Armor for the shins; "cuisses" were
guards for protecting the front of the thighs.
7. Blood from the battle.
8. The star of Bethlehem.

Lest one good custom should corrupt the world.   410
Comfort thyself; what comfort is in me?
I have lived my life, and that which I have done
May He within himself make pure! but thou,
If thou shouldst never see my face again,
Pray for my soul. More things are wrought by prayer   415
Than this world dreams of. Wherefore, let thy voice
Rise like a fountain for me night and day.
For what are men better than sheep or goats
That nourish a blind life within the brain,
If, knowing God, they lift not hands of prayer   420
Both for themselves and those who call them friend?
For so the whole round earth is every way
Bound by gold chains about the feet of God.
But now farewell. I am going a long way
With these thou seest—if indeed I go—   425
For all my mind is clouded with a doubt—
To the island-valley of Avilion;[9]
Where falls not hail, or rain, or any snow,
Nor ever wind blows loudly; but it lies
Deep-meadow'd, happy, fair with orchard lawns   430
And bowery hollows crown'd with summer sea,
Where I will heal me of my grievous wound."

So said he, and the barge with oar and sail
Moved from the brink, like some full-breasted swan
That, fluting a wild carol ere her death,   435
Ruffles her pure cold plume, and takes the flood
With swarthy webs. Long stood Sir Bedivere
Revolving many memories, till the hull
Look'd one black dot against the verge of dawn,
And on the mere the wailing died away.   440

But when that moan had past for evermore,
The stillness of the dead world's winter dawn
Amazed him, and he groan'd, "The King is gone."
And therewithal came on him the weird rhyme,
"From the great deep to the great deep he goes."   445

Whereat he slowly turn'd and slowly clomb
The last hard footstep of that iron crag,
Thence mark'd the black hull moving yet, and cried:
"He passes to be king among the dead,
And after healing of his grievous wound   450
He comes again; but—if he come no more—
O me, be yon dark queens in yon black boat,
Who shriek'd and wail'd, the three whereat we gazed
On that high day, when, clothed with living light,
They stood before his throne in silence, friends   455
Of Arthur, who should help him at his need?"

9. In Celtic mythology, Avalon was the   paradise in the Western seas.
Island of Blessed Souls, an earthly

Then from the dawn it seem'd there came, but faint
As from beyond the limit of the world,
Like the last echo born of a great cry,
Sounds, as if some fair city were one voice   460
Around a king returning from his wars.

Thereat once more he moved about, and clomb
Even to the highest he could climb, and saw,
Straining his eyes beneath an arch of hand,
Or thought he saw, the speck that bare the King,   465
Down that long water opening on the deep
Somewhere far off, pass on and on, and go
From less to less and vanish into light.
And the new sun rose bringing the new year.

1833–35; 1842 (1869)

To the Queen

O loyal to the royal in thyself,
And loyal to thy land, as this to thee—
Bear witness, that rememberable day,[1]
When, pale as yet and fever-worn, the Prince
Who scarce had pluck'd his flickering life again   5
From halfway down the shadow of the grave
Past with thee thro' thy people and their love,
And London roll'd one tide of joy thro' all
Her trebled millions, and loud leagues of man
And welcome! witness, too, the silent cry,   10
The prayer of many a race and creed, and clime—
Thunderless lightnings[2] striking under sea
From sunset and sunrise of all thy realm,
And that true North,[3] whereof we lately heard
A strain to shame us, "Keep you to yourselves;   15
So loyal is too costly! friends—your love
Is but a burthen; loose the bond, and go."
Is this the tone of empire? here the faith
That made us rulers? this, indeed, her voice
And meaning whom the roar of Hougoumont[4]   20
Left mightiest of all peoples under heaven?
What shock has fool'd her since, that she should speak
So feebly? wealthier—wealthier—hour by hour!
The voice of Britain, or a sinking land,
Some third-rate isle half-lost among her seas?   25
There rang her voice, when the full city peal'd

---

1. In February 1872, when Queen Victoria and her son Edward, Prince of Wales, who had been dangerously ill with typhoid fever, made a public appearance at St. Paul's.
2. Messages by transatlantic cable.
3. A response to the proposition that the recently confederated Dominion of Canada was too costly for the Empire to maintain.
4. In the battle of Waterloo, this castle or fortified chateau had been the key to the British position; it was successfully defended against severe attack.

Thee and thy Prince! The loyal to their crown
Are loyal to their own far sons, who love
Our ocean-empire with her boundless homes
For ever-broadening England, and her throne   30
In our vast Orient, and one isle, one isle,
That knows not her own greatness; if she knows
And dreads it we are fallen.—But thou, my Queen,
Not for itself, but thro' thy living love
For one[5] to whom I made it o'er his grave   35
Sacred, accept this old imperfect tale,
New-old, and shadowing Sense at war with Soul,
Ideal manhood closed in real man,[6]
Rather than that gray king whose name, a ghost,
Streams like a cloud, man-shaped, from mountain peak,   40
And cleaves to cairn[7] and cromlech still; or him
Of Geoffrey's book, or him of Malleor's,[8] one
Touch'd by the adulterous finger of a time
That hover'd between war and wantonness,
And crownings and dethronements. Take withal   45
Thy poet's blessing, and his trust that Heaven
Will blow the tempest in the distance back
From thine and ours; for some are scared, who mark,
Or wisely or unwisely, signs of storm,
Waverings of every vane with every wind,   50
And wordy trucklings to the transient hour,
And fierce or careless looseners of the faith,
And Softness breeding scorn of simple life,
Or Cowardice, the child of lust for gold,
Or Labor, with a groan and not a voice,   55
Or Art with poisonous honey stolen from France,
And that which knows, but careful for itself,
And that which knows not, ruling that which knows
To its own harm. The goal of this great world
Lies beyond sight; yet—if our slowly-grown   60
And crown'd Republic's crowning common-sense,
That sav'd her many times, not fail—their fears
Are morning shadows[9] huger than the shapes
That cast them, not those gloomier which forego[1]
The darkness of that battle in the west   65
Where all of high and holy dies away.

1872

5. Prince Albert, to whom the *Idylls* were dedicated in 1862.
6. This line was inserted in 1891 as Tennyson's last correction, because, according to his son, he felt that "he had not made the real humanity of the King sufficiently clear in his epilogue" (*Memoir*, II, 129).
7. A pyramid of stones raised as a memorial or landmark; a "cromlech" is an ancient structure consisting of a large flat stone resting horizontally on three or more upright stones.
8. Geoffrey of Monmouth's *History of the Kings of Britain* (c. 1137). Malory's name is variously spelled Maleorye, Maleore, and Malleor.
9. The epilogue's optimism certainly jars with the grim allegorical implications of the last idylls.
1. Precede.

The Late Period
(1872—1892)

The Voice and the Peak[1]

1

The voice and the Peak
    Far over summit and lawn,
The lone glow and long roar
    Green-rushing from the rosy thrones of dawn!

2

All night have I heard the voice   5
    Rave over the rocky bar,
But thou wert silent in heaven,
    Above thee glided the star.

3

Hast thou no voice, O Peak,
    That standest high above all?   10
"I am the voice of the Peak,
    I roar and rave, for I fall.

4

"A thousand voices go
    To North, South, East, and West;
They leave the heights and are troubled,   15
    And moan and sink to their rest.

5

"The fields are fair beside them,
    The chestnut towers in his bloom;
But they—they feel the desire of the deep—
    Fall, and follow their doom.   20

6

"The deep has power on the height,
    And the height has power on the deep;
They are raised for ever and ever,
    And sink again into sleep."

7

Not raised for ever and ever,   25
    But when their cycle is o'er,
The valley, the voice, the peak, the star
    Pass, and are found no more.

1. Composed in the Val d'Anzasca, in the Alps, during a tour of Italy in the summer and fall of 1873, the poem seeks to embody "the thought which was so often in his mind during these years—that the spirit of man is more real and more enduring than the most awe-inspiring features of the material universe" (*Alfred Tennyson*, p. 407). Compare "The Higher Pantheism."

8

The Peak is high and flush'd
    At his highest with sunrise fire;   30
The Peak is high, and the stars are high,
    And the thought of a man is higher.

9

A deep below the deep,
    And a height beyond the height!
Our hearing is not hearing,   35
    And our seeing is not sight.

10

The voice and the Peak
    Far into heaven withdrawn,
The lone glow and long roar
    Green-rushing from the rosy thrones of dawn!   40

1874

The Revenge[2]

A BALLAD OF THE FLEET

1

At Flores in the Azores Sir Richard Grenville lay,
And a pinnace, like a flutter'd bird, came flying from far away:[3]
"Spanish ships of war at sea! we have sighted fifty-three!"
Then sware Lord Thomas Howard: " 'Fore God I am no coward;
But I cannot meet them here, for my ships are out of gear,   5
And the half my men are sick. I must fly, but follow quick.
We are six ships of the line; can we fight with fifty-three?"

2

Then spake Sir Richard Grenville: "I know you are no coward;
You fly them for a moment to fight with them again.

2. Both the ship and Sir Richard Grenville had been famous before the engagement which was to immortalize them. In 1588 Drake had commanded the *Revenge* against the Spanish Armada, and in 1585 Grenville, under Sir Walter Raleigh, had led the first colonizing expedition to Roanoke Island, Virginia. In 1591 Lord Howard was sent to the Azores with 16 ships to intercept Spanish treasure-vessels returning from the West Indies. A Spanish fleet of 53 warships was sent out against Howard, who escaped with five ships, but Grenville remained to take his sick men aboard. In the battle, Grenville alone attempted to run through the entire Spanish fleet, and surrendered after 15 hours, when he had been mortally wounded and his ship's complement had been reduced to only 20 able-bodied men.

    Tennyson had wanted to write a poem about the *Revenge* since 1852, when he read J. A. Froude's article "England's Forgotten Worthies" in the July issue of the *Westminster Review*. Although the action of a single ship, the story, Froude said, had struck a "deeper terror into the hearts of the Spanish people" than the fate of the Armada (*Memoir*, II, 251). But not until 1877, when Tennyson saw Edward Arber's reprint of all available information about the *Revenge*, was he moved or did he feel sufficiently knowledgeable to write his poem. (See *Alfred Tennyson*, p. 438.) The ballad was instantly popular, but perhaps the sweetest praise of all came from Carlyle, who had found little enough to his liking in Tennyson's poetry after 1842: "Eh! Alfred, you have got the grip of it," he said after the poet read him the poem (*Memoir*, II, 234).
3. From the coast of Portugal, where the Earl of Cumberland had sighted the enemy fleet.

But I've ninety men and more that are lying sick ashore.   10
I should count myself the coward if I left them, my Lord Howard,
To these Inquisition dogs and the devildoms of Spain."

3
So Lord Howard past away with five ships of war that day,
Till he melted like a cloud in the silent summer heaven;
But Sir Richard bore in hand all his sick men from the land   15
Very carefully and slow,
Men of Bideford in Devon,
And we laid them on the ballast down below;
For we brought them all aboard,
An they blest him in their pain, that they were not left to Spain,   20
To the thumb-screw and the stake, for the glory of the Lord.

4
He had only a hundred seamen to work the ship and to fight,
And he sailed away from Flores till the Spaniard came in sight,
With his huge sea-castles heaving upon the weather bow.
"Shall we fight or shall we fly?   25
Good Sir Richard, tell us now,
For to fight is but to die!
There 'll be little of us left by the time this sun be set."
And Sir Richard said again: "We be all good English men.
Let us bang these dogs of Seville, the children of the devil,   30
For I never turn'd my back upon Don or devil yet."

5
Sir Richard spoke and he laugh'd and we roar'd a hurrah, and so
The little Revenge ran on sheer into the heart of the foe,
With her hundred fighters on deck, and her ninety sick below;
For half of their fleet to the right and half to the left were seen,   35
And the little Revenge ran on thro' the long sea-lane between.

6
Thousands of their soldiers look'd down from their decks and
                    laugh'd,
Thousands of their seamen made mock at the mad little craft
Running on and on, till delay'd
By their mountain-like San Philip that, of fifteen hundred tons,   40
And up-shadowing high above us with her yawning tiers of guns,
Took the breath from our sails, and we stay'd.

7
And while now the great San Philip hung above us like a cloud
Whence the thunderbolt will fall
Long and loud,   45
Four galleons drew away
From the Spanish fleet that day,
And two upon the larboard and two upon the starboard lay,
And the battle-thunder broke from them all.

8

But anon the great San Philip, she bethought herself and went,   50
Having that within her womb that had left her ill content;
And the rest they came aboard us, and they fought us hand to hand,
For a dozen times they came with their pikes and musqueteers,
And a dozen times we shook 'em off as a dog that shakes his ears
When he leaps from the water to the land.   55

9

An the sun went down, and the stars came out far above the summer sea,
But never a moment ceased the fight of the one and the fifty-three.
Ship after ship, the whole night long, their high-built galleons came,
Ship after ship, the whole night long, with her battle-thunder and flame;
Ship after ship, the whole night long, drew back with her dead and her shame.   60
For some were sunk and many were shatter'd, and so could fight us no more—
God of battles, was ever a battle like this in the world before?

10

For he said, "Fight on! fight on!"
Tho' his vessel was all but a wreck;
And it chanced that, when half of the short summer night was gone,   65
With a grisly wound to be drest he had left the deck,
But a bullet struck him that was dressing it suddenly dead,
And himself he was wounded again in the side and the head,
And he said, "Fight on! fight on!"

11

And the night went down, and the sun smiled out far over the summer sea,   70
And the Spanish fleet with broken sides lay round us all in a ring;
But they dared not touch us again, for they fear'd that we still could sting,
So they watch'd what the end would be.
And we had not fought them in vain,
But in perilous plight were we.   75
Seeing forty of our poor hundred were slain,
And half of the rest of us maim'd for life
In the crash of the cannonades and the desperate strife;
And the sick men down in the hold were most of them stark and cold,
And the pikes were all broken or bent, and the powder was all of it spent;   80
And the masts and the rigging were lying over the side;
But Sir Richard cried in his English pride:

"We have fought such a fight for a day and a night
As may never be fought again!
We have won great glory, my men!   85
And a day less or more
At sea or ashore,
We die—does it matter when?
Sink me the ship, Master Gunner—sink her, split her in twain.[4]
Fall into the hands of God, not into the hands of Spain!"   90

12

And the gunner said, "Ay, ay," but the seamen made reply:
"We have children, we have wives,
And the Lord hath spared our lives.
We will make the Spaniard promise, if we yield, to let us go;
We shall live to fight again and to strike another blow."   95
And the lion there lay dying, and they yielded to the foe.

13

And the stately Spanish men to their flagship[5] bore him then,
Where they laid him by the mast, old Sir Richard caught at last,
And they praised him to his face with their courtly foreign grace;
But he rose upon their decks, and he cried: 100
"I have fought for Queen and Faith like a valiant man and true;
I have only done my duty as a man is bound to do.
With a joyful spirit I Sir Richard Grenville die!"
And he fell upon their decks, and he died.

14

And they stared at the dead that had been so valiant and true,   105
And had holden the power and glory of Spain so cheap
That he dared her with one little ship and his English few;
Was he devil or man? He was devil for aught they knew,
But they sank his body with honor down into the deep,
And they mann'd the Revenge with a swarthier alien crew,   110
And away she sail'd with her loss and long'd for her own;
When a wind from the lands they had ruin'd awoke from sleep,
And the water began to heave and the weather to moan,
And or ever that evening ended a great gale blew,
And a wave like the wave that is raised by an earthquake grew,   115
Till it smote on their hulls and their sails and their masts and their
                    flags,
And the whole sea plunged and fell on the shot-shatter'd navy of
                    Spain,
And the little Revenge herself went down by the island crags
To be lost evermore in the main.

1878

---

4. According to Sir Walter Raleigh's account, Grenville "commanded the master gunner, whom he knew to be a most resolute man, to split and sink the ship, that thereby nothing might remain of glory in victory to the Spaniards, seeing in so many hours they were not able to take her, having had fifteen hours' time, fifteen thousand men, and fifty-three sail of men of war to perform it withal" (*Memoir*, II, 251).

5. The *San Pablo*.

The Voyage of Maeldune[6]

FOUNDED ON AN IRISH LEGEND A.D. 700

1

I was the chief of the race—he had stricken my father dead—
But I gather'd my fellows together, I swore I would strike off his
    head.
Each of them look'd like a king, and was noble in birth as in worth,
And each of them boasted he sprang from the oldest race upon earth.
Each was as brave in the fight as the bravest hero of our song,   5
And each of them liefer had died than have done one another a
    wrong.
He lived on an isle in the ocean—we sail'd on a Friday morn—
He that had slain my father the day before I was born.

2

And we came to the isle in the ocean, and there on the shore was he.
But a sudden blast blew us out and away thro' a boundless sea.   10

3

And we came to the Silent Isle that we never had touch'd at before,
Where a silent ocean always broke on a silent shore,
And the brooks glitter'd on in the light without sound, and the long
    waterfalls
Pour'd in a thunderless plunge to the base of the mountain walls,
And the poplar and cypress unshaken by storm flourish'd up beyond
    sight,   15
And the pine shot aloft from the crag to an unbelievable height,
And high in the heaven above it there flicker'd a songless lark,
And the cock could n't crow, and the bull could n't low, and the dog
    could n't bark.
And round it we went, and thro' it, but never a murmur, a breath—
It was all of it fair as life, it was all of it quiet as death,   20
And we hated the beautiful isle, for whenever we strove to speak
Our voices were thinner and fainter than any flittermouse[7]-shriek;
And the men that were mighty of tongue and could raise such a bat-
    tle-cry
That a hundred who heard it would rush on a thousand lances and
    die—
O, they to be dumb'd by the charm!—so fluster'd with anger were
    they   25
They almost fell on each other; but after we sail'd away.

4

And we came to the Isle of Shouting; we landed, a score of wild
    birds
Cried from the topmost summit with human voices and words.
Once in an hour they cried, and whenever their voices peal'd

6. "I read the legend in Joyce's *Cel-
tic Legends* [*Old Celtic Romances*
(1879)]," Tennyson noted, "but most
of the details are mine" (*Memoir*, II,
255).
7. A bat.

The steer fell down at the plow and the harvest died from the
    field,   30
And the men dropt dead in the valleys and half of the cattle went
    lame,
And the roof sank in on the hearth, and the dwelling broke into
    flame;
And the shouting of these wild birds ran into the hearts of my crew,
Till they shouted along with the shouting and seized one another
    and slew.
But I drew them the one from the other; I saw that we could not
    stay,   35
And we left the dead to the birds, and we sail'd with our wounded
    away.

5

And we came to the Isle of Flowers; their breath met us out on the
    seas,
For the Spring and the middle Summer sat each on the lap of the
    breeze;
And the red passion-flower to the cliffs, and the dark-blue clematis
    clung,
And starr'd with a myriad blossom the long convolvulus hung;   40
And the topmost spire of the mountain was lilies in lieu of snow,
And the lilies like glaciers winded down, running out below
Thro' the fire of the tulip and poppy, the blaze of gorse, and the
    blush
Of millions of roses that sprang without leaf or a thorn from the
    bush;
And the whole isle-side flashing down from the peak without ever
    a tree   45
Swept like a torrent of gems from the sky to the blue of the sea.
And we roll'd upon capes of crocus and vaunted our kith and our
    kin,
And we wallow'd in beds of lilies, and chanted the triumph of Finn,[8]
Till each like a golden image was pollen'd from head to feet
And each was as dry as a cricket, with thirst in the middle-day
    heat.   50
Blossom and blossom, and promise of blossom, but never a fruit!
And we hated the Flowering Isle, as we hated the isle that was
    mute,
And we tore up the flowers by the million and flung them in bight
    and bay,
And we left but a naked rock, and in anger sail'd away.

6

And we came to the Isle of Fruits; all round from the cliffs and the
    capes,   55
Purple or amber, dangled a hundred fathom of grapes,
And the warm melon lay like a little sun on the tawny sand,
And the fig ran up from the beach and rioted over the land,

8. The father of Ossian and the greatest of legendary Irish heroes.

And the mountain arose like a jewell'd throne thro' the fragrant air,
Glowing with all-color'd plums and with golden masses of pear,   60
And the the crimson and scarlet of berries that flamed upon bine
     and vine,
But every berry and fruit was the poisonous pleasure of wine;
And the peak of the mountain was apples, the hugest that ever were
     seen,
And they prest, as they grew, on each other, with hardly a leaflet
     between,
And all of them redder than rosiest health or than utterest shame, 65
And setting, when Even descended, the very sunset aflame.
And we stay'd three days, and we gorged and we madden'd, till
     every one drew
His sword on his fellow to slay him, and ever they struck and they
     slew;
And myself, I had eaten but sparely, and fought till I sunder'd the
     fray,
Then I bade them remember my father's death, and we sail'd
     away.   70

7

And we came to the Isle of Fire; we were lured by the light from
     afar,
For the peak sent up one league of fire to the Northern Star;
Lured by the glare and the blare, but scarcely could stand upright,
For the whole isle shudder'd and shook like a man in a mortal af-
     fright.
We were giddy besides with the fruits we had gorged, and so crazed
     that at last   75
There were some leap'd into the fire; and away we sail'd, and we
     past
Over that undersea isle, where the water is clearer than air.
Down we look'd—what a garden! O bliss, what a Paradise there!
Towers of a happier time, low down in a rainbow deep
Silent palaces, quiet fields of eternal sleep!   80
And three of the gentlest and best of my people, whate'er I could
     say,
Plunged head-down in the sea, and the Paradise trembled away.

8

And we came to the Bounteous Isle, where the heavens lean low on
     the land,
And ever at dawn from the cloud glitter'd o'er us a sun-bright hand,
Then it open'd and dropt at the side of each man, as he rose from
     his rest,   85
Bread enough for his need till the laborless day dipt under the west;
And we wander'd about it and thro' it. O, never was time so good!
And we sang of the triumphs of Finn, and the boast of our ancient
     blood,
And we gazed at the wandering wave as we sat by the gurgle of
     springs,

And we chanted the songs of the Bards and the glories of fairy
    kings.   90
But at length we began to be weary, to sigh, and to stretch and yawn,
Till we hated the Bounteous Isle and the sun-bright hand of the
    dawn,
For there was not an enemy near, but the whole green isle was our
    own,
And we took to playing at ball, and we took to throwing the stone,
And we took to playing at battle, but that was a perilous play,   95
For the passion of battle was in us, we slew and we sail'd away.

9

And we came to the Isle of Witches and heard their musical cry—
"Come to us, O, come, come!" in the stormy red of a sky
Dashing the fires and the shadows of dawn on the beautiful shapes,
For a wild witch naked as heaven stood on each of the loftiest
    capes,   100
And a hundred ranged on the rock like white sea-birds in a row,
And a hundred gamboll'd and pranced on the wrecks in the sand
    below,
And a hundred splash'd from the ledges, and bosom'd the burst of
    the spray;
But I knew we should fall on each other, and hastily sail'd away.

10[9]

And we came in an evil time to the Isle of the Double Towers,   105
One was of smooth-cut stone, one carved all over with flowers,
But an earthquake always moved in the hollows under the dells,
And they shock'd on each other and butted each other with clashing
    of bells,
And the daws flew out of the towers and jangled and wrangled in
    vain,
And the clash and boom of the bells rang into the heart and the
    brain,   110
Till the passion of battle was on us, and all took sides with the
    towers,
There were some for the clean-cut stone, there were more for the
    carven flowers,
And the wrathful thunder of God peal'd over us all the day,
For the one half slew the other, and after we sail'd away.

11

And we came to the Isle of a Saint who had sail'd with Saint
    Brendan[1] of yore,   115
He had lived ever since on the isle and his winters were fifteen score,
And his voice was low as from other worlds, and his eyes were
    sweet,

---

9. According to the poet's son, the
stanza is "symbolical of the contest
between Roman Catholics and Protes-
tants."
1. A sixth-century sailor who was sup-
posed to have sailed from Kerry west-
ward into the Atlantic and to have
landed on the North American conti-
nent.

And his white hair sank to his heels, and his white beard fell to his
    feet,
And he spake to me: "O Maeldune, let be this purpose of thine!
Remember the words of the Lord when he told us, 'Vengeance is
    mine!'   120
His fathers have slain thy fathers in war or in single strife,
Thy fathers have slain his fathers, each taken a life for a life,
Thy father had slain his father, how long shall the murder last?
Go back to the Isle of Finn and suffer the Past to be Past."
And we kiss'd the fringe of his beard, and we pray'd as we heard him
    pray,   125
And the holy man he assoil'd[2] us, and sadly we sail'd away.

12

And we came to the isle we were blown from, and there on the
    shore was he,
The man that had slain my father. I saw him and let him be.
O, weary was I of the travel, the trouble, the strife, and the sin,
When I landed again with a tithe of my men, on the Isle of
    Finn!   130

1880

Battle of Brunanburh[3]

1

    Athelstan King,[4]
    Lord among Earls,
    Bracelet-bestower and
    Baron of Barons,
    He with his brother,   5
    Edmund Atheling,
    Gaining a lifelong
    Glory in battle,
    Slew with the sword-edge
    There by Brunanburh,   10
    Brake the shield-wall,
    Hew'd the linden-wood,[5]
    Hack'd the battle-shield,
Sons of Edward with hammer'd brands.

2

    Theirs was a greatness   15
    Got from their grandsires—
    Theirs that so often in

2. Absolved.
3. A translation from the Anglo-Saxon, printed in 1880 with the following prefatory note: "Constantinus, King of the Scots, after having sworn allegiance to Athelstan, allied himself with the Danes of Ireland under Aulaf, and invading England, was defeated by Athelstan and his brother Edmund with great slaughter at Brunanburh in the year 937." (Notes in quotation marks are Tennyson's, and were published with the poem.)
4. "I have more or less availed myself of my son's prose translation of this poem in the 'Contemporary Review' (November, 1876)."
5. "Shields of lindenwood."

Strife with their enemies
Struck for their hoards and their hearts and their homes.

3

Bow'd the spoiler,   20
Bent the Scotsman,
Fell the ship-crews
Doom'd to the death.
All the field with blood of the fighters
Flow'd, from when first the great   25
Sun-star of morning-tide,
Lamp of the Lord God
Lord everlasting,
Glode over earth till the glorious creature
Sank to his setting.   30

4

There lay many a man
Marr'd by the javelin,
Men of the Northland
Shot over shield.
There was the Scotsman   35
Weary of war.

5

We the West-Saxons,
Long as the daylight
Lasted, in companies
Troubled the track of the host that we hated;   40
Grimly with swords that were sharp from the grindstone,
Fiercely we hack'd at the flyers before us.

6

Mighty the Mercian,[6]
Hard was his hand-play,
Sparing not any of   45
Those that with Anlaf,
Warriors over the
Weltering waters
Borne in the bark's-bosom,
Drew to this island—   50
Doom'd to the death.

7

Five young kings put asleep by the sword-stroke,
Seven strong earls of the army of Anlaf
Fell on the war-field, numberless numbers,
Shipmen and Scotsmen.   55

8

Then the Norse leader—
Dire was his need of it,
Few were his following—

---

6. Mercia was the ancient Anglican kingdom in central England and included London.

Fled to his war-ship;
Fleeted his vessel to sea with the king in it,   60
Saving his life on the fallow flood.

9

Also the crafty one,
Constantinus,
Crept to his North again,
Hoar-headed hero!   65

10

Slender warrant had
He to be proud of
The welcome of war-knives—
He that was reft of his
Folk and his friends that had   70
Fallen in conflict,
Leaving his son too
Lost in the carnage,
Mangled to morsels,
A youngster in war!   75

11

Slender reason had
He to be glad of
The clash of the war-glaive—
Traitor and trickster
And spurner of treaties—   80
He nor had Anlaf
With armies so broken
A reason for bragging
That they had the better
In perils of battle   85
On places of slaughter—
The struggle of standards,
The rush of the javelins,
The crash of the charges,[7]
The wielding of weapons—   90
The play that they play'd with
The children of Edward.

12

Then with their nail'd prows
Parted the Norsemen, a
Blood-redden'd relic of   95
Javelins over
The jarring breaker, the deep-sea billow,
Shaping their way toward Dyflen[8] again,
    Shamed in their souls.

13

Also the brethren,   100
King and Atheling,

---

7. "Lit. 'the gathering of men.' "   8. "Dublin."

Each in his glory,
Went to his own in his own West-Saxon-land,
Glad of the war.

14

Many a carcase they left to be carrion,   105
Many a livid one, many a sallow-skin—
Left for the white-tail'd eagle to tear it, and
Left for the horny-nibb'd raven to rend it, and
Gave to the garbaging war-hawk to gorge it, and
That gray beast, the wolf of the weald.   110

15

Never had huger
Slaughter of heroes
Slain by the sword-edge—
Such as old writers
Have writ of in histories—   115
Hapt in this isle, since
Up from the East hither
Saxon and Angle from
Over the broad billow
Broke into Britain with   120
Haughty war-workers who
Harried the Welshman, when
Earls that were lured by the
Hunger of glory gat
Hold of the land.   125

1880

Rizpah[9]

17—

1

Wailing, wailing, wailing, the wind over land and sea—
And Willy's voice in the wind, "O mother, come out to me!"

9. Tennyson founded his poem on an incident "related in some penny magazine called *Old Brighton*." For the account, see *Memoir*, II, 249–251. The late-eighteenth-century tale involved two young men, Rooke and Howell, who robbed a mail coach and, according to the justice of the day, were hanged on the spot where the crime was committed. As was customary, their chained bodies were left on the gallows to rot. Rooke's old mother collected her son's bones as they dropped from the decaying flesh and finally buried them in Old Shoreham Churchyard's hallowed ground, denied to executed criminals. Although Tennyson first titled his poem "Bones," before publication he took his title from II *Samuel*, 21:8–11. Rizpah's two sons were hanged by the Gibeonites, and she stood guard over their bodies warding off birds and beasts.

Tennyson cast his poem as a dramatic monologue spoken by the dying old mother from her hospital bed to a rather dense, visiting charity-worker. Swinburne, whose response to the *Idylls of the King* had seldom been less than vicious, pleaded that language failed him in expressing the depth of his feelings about "Rizpah." If it alone survived of all the poet's work, he said, it would be "proof positive . . . that in the author of this single poem a truly great poet had been born." The statement indirectly reminds us that Tennyson was seventy when he wrote the poem.

Why should he call me to-night, when he knows that I cannot go?
For the downs are as bright as day, and the full moon stares at the
     snow.

2

We should be seen, my dear; they would spy us out of the town.   5
The loud black nights for us, and the storm rushing over the down,
When I cannot see my own hand, but am led by the creak of the
     chain,
And grovel and grope for my son till I find myself drenched with the
     rain.

3

Anything fallen again? nay—what was there left to fall?
I have taken them home, I have number'd the bones, I have hidden
     them all.   10
What am I saying? and what are *you*? do you come as a spy?
Falls? what falls? who knows? As the tree falls so must it lie.

4

Who let her in? how long has she been? you—what have you heard?
Why did you sit so quiet? you never have spoken a word.
O—to pray with me—yes—a lady—none of their spies—   15
But the night has crept into my heart, and begun to darken my eyes.

5

Ah—you, that have lived so soft, what should *you* know of the
     night,
The blast and the burning shame and the bitter frost and the fright?
I have done it, while you were asleep—you were only made for the
     day.
I have gather'd my baby together—and now you may go your way. 20

6

Nay—for it 's kind of you, madam, to sit by an old dying wife.
But say nothing hard of my boy, I have only an hour of life.
I kiss'd my boy in the prison, before he went out to die.
"They dared me to do it," he said, and he never has told me a lie.
I whipt him for robbing an orchard once when he was but a
     child—   25
"The farmer dared me to do it," he said; he was always so wild—
And idle—and could n't be idle—my Willy—he never could rest.
The King should have made him a soldier, he would have been
     one of his best.

7

But he lived with a lot of wild mates, and they never would let him
     be good;
They swore that he dare not rob the mail, and he swore that he
     would;   30
And he took no life, but he took one purse, and when all was done
He flung it among his fellows—"I 'll none of it," said my son.

8

I came into court to the judge and the lawyers. I told them my tale,
God's own truth—but they kill'd him, they kill'd him for robbing
     the mail.

They hang'd him in chains for a show—we had always borne a good
     name—   35
To be hang'd for a thief—and then put away—is n't that enough
     shame?
Dust to dust—low down—let us hide! but they set him so high
That all the ships of the world could stare at him, passing by.
God 'ill pardon the hell-black raven and horrible fowls of the air,
But not the black heart of the lawyer who kill'd him and hang'd him
     there.   40

9

And the jailer forced me away. I had bid him my last good-bye;
They had fasten'd the door of his cell. "O mother!" I heard him cry.
I could n't get back tho' I tried, he had something further to say,
And now I never shall know it. The jailer forced me away.

10

Then since I could n't but hear that cry of my boy that was dead, 45
They seized me and shut me up: they fasten'd me down on my bed.
"Mother, O mother!"—he call'd in the dark to me year after year—
They beat me for that, they beat me—you know that I could n't
     but hear;
And then at the last they found I had grown so stupid and still
They let me abroad again—but the creatures had worked their
     will.   50

11

Flesh of my flesh was gone, but bone of my bone was left—
I stole them all from the lawyers—and you, will you call it a
     theft?—
My baby, the bones that had suck'd me, the bones that had
     laughed and had cried—
Theirs? O, no! they are mine—not theirs—they had moved in my
     side.

12

Do you think I was scared by the bones? I kiss'd 'em, I buried 'em
     all—   55
I can't dig deep, I am old—in the night by the churchyard wall.
My Willy 'ill rise up whole when the trumpet of judgment 'ill
     sound,
But I charge you never to say that I laid him in holy ground.

13

They would scratch him up—they would hang him again on the
     cursed tree.
Sin? O, yes, we are sinners, I know—let all that be,   60
And read me a Bible verse of the Lord's goodwill toward men—
"Full of compassion and mercy, the Lord"[1]—let me hear it again;
"Full of compassion and mercy—long-suffering." Yes, O, yes!
For the lawyer is born but to murder—the Saviour lives but to bless.
He 'll never put on the black cap[2] except for the worst of the
     worst,   65

1. See *Psalms*, 86:15.
2. Put on by the judge when he passed the death sentence.

And the first may be last—I have heard it in church—and the last
      may be first.[3]
Suffering—O, long-suffering—yes, as the Lord must know,
Year after year in the mist and the wind and the shower and the
      snow.

14

Heard, have you? what? they have told you he never repented his
      sin.
How do they know it? are *they* his mother? are *you* of his kin?   70
Heard! have you ever heard, when the storm on the downs began,
The wind that 'ill wail like a child and the sea that 'ill moan like
      a man?

15

Election, Election, and Reprobation[4]—it 's all very well.
But I go to-night to my boy, and I shall not find him in hell.
For I cared so much for my boy that the Lord has look'd into my
      care,   75
And He means me I'm sure to be happy with Willy, I know not
      where.

16

And if *he* be lost—but to save *my* soul, that is all your desire—
Do you think that I care for *my* soul if my boy be gone to the fire?
I have been with God in the dark—go, go, you may leave me
      alone—
You never have borne a child—you are just as hard as a stone.   80

17

Madam, I beg your pardon! I think that you mean to be kind,
But I cannot hear what you say for my Willy's voice in the wind—
The snow and the sky so bright—he used but to call in the dark,
And he calls to me now from the church and not from the gibbet—
      for hark!
Nay—you can hear it yourself—it is coming—shaking the walls— 85
Willy—the moon 's in a cloud——Good-night. I am going. He
      calls.

1880

In the Children's Hospital[5]

EMMIE

1

Our doctor had call'd in another, I never had seen him before,
But he sent a chill to my heart when I saw him come in at the door,

---

3. See *Matthew*, 19:30.
4. Alludes to the Calvinistic doctrine of predestination; regardless of the apparent quality of a man's life, he has been saved or damned.
5. "A true story told me by Mary Gladstone. The doctors and hospital are unknown to me. The two children

are the only characters taken from life in this little dramatic poem, in which the hospital nurse and not the poet is speaking throughout" (Tennyson's note; see *Memoir*, II, 253–254, for the story). Tennyson was susceptible to most, if not all, of the weaknesses apparent in Victorian sentimental lit-

Fresh from the surgery-schools of France[6] and of other lands—
Harsh red hair, big voice, big chest, big merciless hands!
Wonderful cures he had done, O, yes, but they said too of him   5
He was happier using the knife than in trying to save the limb,
And that I can well believe, for he look'd so coarse and so red,
I could think he was one of those who would break their jests on the
     dead,
And mangle the living dog that had loved him and fawn'd at his
     knee—
Drench'd with the hellish oorali[7]—that ever such things should
     be!   10

2

Here was a boy—I am sure that some of our children would die
But for the voice of love, and the smile, and the comforting eye—
Here was a boy in the ward, every bone seem'd out of its place—
Caught in a mill and crush'd—it was all but a hopeless case:
And he handled him gently enough; but his voice and his face were
     not kind,   15
And it was but a hopeless case, he had seen it and made up his
     mind,
And he said to me roughly, 'The lad will need little more of your
     care.'
'All the more need,' I told him, 'to seek the Lord Jesus in prayer;
They are all His children here, and I pray for them all as my own.'
But he turn'd to me, 'Ay, good woman, can prayer set a broken
     bone?'   20
Then he mutter'd half to himself, but I know that I heard him say,
'All very well—but the good Lord Jesus has had his day.'

3

Had? has it come? It has only dawn'd. It will come by and by.
O, how could I serve in the wards if the hope of the world were a
     lie?
How could I bear with the sights and the loathsome smells of
     disease   25
But that He said, 'Ye do it to me, when ye do it to these'?

4

So he went. And we past to this ward where the younger children
     are laid.
Here is the cot of our orphan, our darling, our meek little maid;
Empty, you see, just now! We have lost her who loved her so
     much—

---

erature, and this poem, with its par-
ticularly unbelievable nurse, shows
enough of them. There is a good deal
of truth in the saying that if one wants
fully to understand the Victorian
period, one must read the third-rate
literature. The same may hold for the
individual poet.
6. Tennyson could seldom resist the
opportunity to cast aspersions on the
French.
7. A poison used chiefly in physiolog-
ical experiments. When injected into
the blood, it arrests the action of the
motor nerves but does not kill pain.
Tennyson was strongly against vivi-
section, which, at the time, was cer-
tainly in need of regulatory laws.

Patient of pain tho' as quick as a sensitive plant to the touch.   30
Hers was the prettiest prattle, it often moved me to tears,
Hers was the gratefullest heart I have found in a child of her years—
Nay you remember our Emmie; you used to send her the flowers.
How she would smile at 'em, play with 'em, talk to 'em hours after
      hours!
They that can wander at will where the works of the Lord are
      reveal'd   35
Little guess what joy can be got from a cowslip out of the field;
Flowers to these 'spirits in prison' are all they can know of the
      spring,
They freshen and sweeten the wards like the waft of an angel's wing.
And she lay with a flower in one hand and her thin hands crost on
      her breast—
Wan, but as pretty as heart can desire, and we thought her at rest,   40
Quietly sleeping—so quiet, our doctor said, 'Poor little dear,
Nurse, I must do it to-morrow; she 'll never live thro' it, I fear.'

5

I walk'd with our kindly old doctor as far as the head of the stair,
Then I return'd to the ward; the child did n't see I was there.

6

Never since I was nurse had I been so grieved and so vext!   45
Emmie had heard him. Softly she call'd from her cot to the next,
'He says I shall never live thro' it; O Annie, what shall I do?'
Annie consider'd. 'If I,' said the wise little Annie, 'was you,
I should cry to the dear Lord Jesus to help me, for, Emmie, you see,
It 's all in the picture there: "Little children should come to
      me" '—   50
Meaning the print that you gave us, I find that it always can please
Our children, the dear Lord Jesus with children about his knees.
'Yes, and I will,' said Emmie, 'but then if I call to the Lord,
How should he know that it 's me? such a lot of beds in the ward!'
That was a puzzle for Annie. Again she consider'd and said: 55
'Emmie, you put out your arms, and you leave 'em outside on the
      bed—
The Lord has so *much* to see to! but, Emmie, you tell it him plain,
It 's the little girl with her arms lying out on the counterpane.'

7

I had sat three nights by the child—I could not watch her for
      four—
My brain had begun to reel—I felt I could do it no more.   60
That was my sleeping-night, but I thought that it never would pass.
There was a thunderclap once, and a clatter of hail on the glass,
And there was a phantom cry that I heard as I tost about,
The motherless bleat of a lamb in the storm and the darkness
      without;
My sleep was broken besides with dreams of the dreadful knife   65
And fears for our delicate Emmie who scarce would escape with her
      life;

Then in the gray of the morning it seem'd she stood by me and
     smiled,
And the doctor came at his hour, and we went to see to the child.

8

He had brought his ghastly tools; we believed her asleep again—
Her dear, long, lean, little arms lying out on the counterpane—   70
Say that His day is done! Ah, why should we care what they say?
The Lord of the children had heard her, and Emmie had past away.

1880

"Frater Ave Atque Vale"[8]

Row us out from Desenzano,[9] to your Sirmione row!
So they row'd, and there we landed—"O venusta Sirmio!"[1]
There to me thro' all the groves of olive in the summer glow,
There beneath the Roman ruin where the purple flowers grow,
Came that "Ave atque Vale" of the Poet's hopeless woe,   5
Tenderest of Roman poets nineteen hundred years ago,
"Frater Ave atque Vale"—as we wander'd to and fro
Gazing at the Lydian laughter of the Garda Lake below
Sweet Catullus's all-but-island,[2] olive-silvery Sirmio!

1880; 1883

Despair[3]

1

Is it you,[4] that preach'd in the chapel there looking over the sand?
Follow'd us too that night, and dogg'd us, and drew me to land?

8. The death of Tennyson's brother Charles in April 1879 was clearly in the poet's mind when he wrote these lines during the summer of 1880 while visiting Sirmione, the peninsula in Lake Garda where Catullus (c. 87–54 B.C.) had maintained his country villa. The words of the title, "Brother, hail and farewell," are from Catullus' elegiac lament for his brother (see *In Memoriam*, 57, 4, and note).
9. A town at the southern end of Lake Garda, about three miles from Sirmione.
1. "O lovely Sirmione."
2. I.e., the peninsula.
3. When the poem was published in 1881, Tennyson included the following prefatory note: "A man and his wife having lost faith in a God, and hope of a life to come, and being utterly miserable in this, resolve to end themselves by drowning. The woman is drowned, but the man is rescued by a minister of the sect he had abandoned." At the end of his poem he wrote: "In my boyhood

I came across the Calvinist Creed, and assuredly however unfathomable the mystery, if one cannot believe in the freedom of the human will as of the Divine, life is hardly worth having" (*Memoir*, I, 317). (See Tennyson's early poem "Remorse" and notes, p. 522.) Predictably, the poem provoked vigorous protest, from both freethinkers and Evangelicals. (See *Alfred Tennyson*, pp. 460–461.) Although by no means as clever as Browning's "Caliban upon Setebos" (1864) in its attack upon Calvinist dogma, the poem is nonetheless important to an understanding of the late Tennyson. His deepening pessimism occasionally led him into inarticulate hectorings against the dark times he saw resulting from widespread acceptance of materialistic doctrines. In "Despair" as in "Locksley Hall Sixty Years After," one suspects that the speakers' views and the poet's are very close.
4. The Calvinist minister.

2

What did I feel that night? You are curious. How should I tell?
Does it matter so much what I felt? You rescued me—yet—was it
    well
That you came unwish'd for, uncall'd, between me and the deep
    and my doom,   5
Three days since, three more dark days of the Godless gloom
Of a life without sun, without health, without hope, without any
    delight
In anything here upon earth? but, ah, God! that night, that night
When the rolling eyes of the lighthouse there on the fatal neck
Of land running out into rock—they had saved many hundreds
    from wreck—   10
Glared on our way toward death, I remember I thought, as we past,
Does it matter how many they saved? we are all of us wreck'd at
    last—
'Do you fear?' and there came thro' the roar of the breaker a
    whisper, a breath,
'Fear? am I not with you? I am frighted at life, not death.'[5]

3

And the suns of the limitless universe sparkled and shone in the
    sky,   15
Flashing with fires as of God, but we knew that their light was a
    lie—
Bright as with deathless hope—but, however they sparkled and
    shone,
The dark little worlds running round them were worlds of woe like
    our own—
No soul in the heaven above, no soul on the earth below,
A fiery scroll written over with lamentation and woe.   20

4

See, we were nursed in the drear nightfold of your fatalist creed,
And we turn'd to the growing dawn, we had hoped for a dawn
    indeed,
When the light of a sun that was coming would scatter the ghosts
    of the past,
And the cramping creeds that had madden'd the peoples would
    vanish at last,
And we broke away from the Christ, our human brother and
    friend,   25
For He spoke, or it seem'd that He spoke, of a hell without help,
    without end.

5

Hoped for a dawn, and it came, but the promise had faded away;
We had past from a cheerless night to the glare of a drearier day;
He is only a cloud and a smoke who was once a pillar of fire,
The guess of a worm in the dust and the shadow of its desire—   30

5. Insofar as the speaker's views may reflect the poet's, this is perhaps truer of Tennyson than he ever fully realized.

Of a worm as it writhes in a world of the weak trodden down by the
 strong,
Of a dying worm in a world, all massacre, murder, and wrong.[6]

6

O, we poor orphans of nothing—alone on that lonely shore—
Born of the brainless Nature who knew not that which she bore!
Trusting no longer that earthly flower would be heavenly fruit— 35
Come from the brute, poor souls—no souls—and to die with the
 brute[7]—

7

Nay, but I am not claiming your pity; I know you of old—
Small pity for those that have ranged from the narrow warmth of
 your fold,
Where you bawl'd the dark side of your faith and a God of eternal
 rage,
Till you flung us back on ourselves, and the human heart, and the
 Age. 40

8

But pity—the Pagan held it a vice—was in her and in me,
Helpless, taking the place of the pitying God that should be!
Pity for all that aches in the grasp of an idiot power,
And pity for our own selves on an earth that bore not a flower;
Pity for all that suffers on land or in air or the deep, 45
And pity for our own selves till we long'd for eternal sleep.

9

'Lightly step over the sands! the waters—you hear them call!
Life with its anguish, and horrors, and errors—away with it all!'
And she laid her hand in my own—she was always loyal and sweet—
Till the points of the foam in the dusk came playing about our
 feet. 50
There was a strong sea-current would sweep us out to the main.
'Ah, God!' tho' I felt as I spoke I was taking the name in vain—
'Ah, God!' and we turn'd to each other, we kiss'd, we embraced,
 she and I,
Knowing the love we were used to believe everlasting would die.
We had read their know-nothing books, and we lean'd to the
 darker side— 55
Ah, God, should we find Him, perhaps, perhaps, if we died, if we
 died;
We never had found Him on earth,[8] this earth is a fatherless hell—
'Dear love, for ever and ever, for ever and ever farewell!'
Never a cry so desolate, not since the world began,
Never a kiss so sad, no, not since the coming of man! 60

10

But the blind wave cast me ashore, and you saved me, a valueless
 life.
Not a grain of gratitude mine! You have parted the man from the
 wife.

---

6. Compare *Maud,* Part 1, IV, 4, lines
120 ff.

7. Compare *In Memoriam,* 56.

8. See *In Memoriam,* 124.

I am left alone on the land, she is all alone in the sea;
If a curse meant aught, I would curse you for not having let me be.

11

Visions of youth—for my brain was drunk with the water, it
    seems; 65
I had past into perfect quiet at length out of pleasant dreams,
And the transient trouble of drowning—what was it when match'd
    with the pains
Of the hellish heat of a wretched life rushing back thro' the veins?

12

Why should I live? one son had forged on his father and fled,
And if I believed in a God, I would thank Him, the other is dead, 70
And there was a baby-girl, that had never look'd on the light;
Happiest she of us all, for she past from the night to the night.

13

But the crime, if a crime, of her eldest-born, her glory, her boast,
Struck hard at the tender heart of the mother, and broke it almost;
Tho', glory and shame dying out for ever in endless time, 75
Does it matter so much whether crown'd for a virtue, or hang'd for
    a crime?

14

And ruin'd by *him*, by *him*, I stood there, naked, amazed
In a world of arrogant opulence, fear'd myself turning crazed,
And I would not be mock'd in a mad-house! and she, the delicate
    wife,
With a grief that could only be cured, if cured, by the surgeon's
    knife,— 80

15

Why should we bear with an hour of torture, a moment of pain,
If every man die for ever, if all his griefs are in vain,
And the homeless planet at length will be wheel'd thro' the silence
    of space,
Motherless evermore of an ever-vanishing race,
When the worm shall have writhed its last, and its last brother-
    worm will have fled 85
From the dead fossil skull that is left in the rocks of an earth that
    is dead?

16

Have I crazed myself over their horrible infidel writings? O, yes,
For these are the new dark ages, you see, of the popular press,
When the bat comes out of his cave, and the owls are whooping
    at noon,
And Doubt is the lord of this dunghill and crows to the sun and the
    moon, 90
Till the sun and the moon of our science are both of them turn'd
    into blood,
And Hope will have broken her heart, running after a shadow of
    good;
For their knowing and know-nothing books are scatter'd from hand
    to hand—
W*e* have knelt in your know-all chapel too, looking over the sand.

17

What! I should call on that Infinite Love that has served us so
    well?   95
Infinite cruelty rather that made everlasting hell,
Made us, foreknew us, foredoom'd us, and does what he will with
    his own;
Better our dead brute mother who never has heard us groan!

18

Hell? if the souls of men were immortal, as men have been told,
The lecher would cleave to his lusts, and the miser would yearn for
    his gold,   100
And so there were hell for ever! but were there a God, as you say,
His love would have power over hell till it utterly vanish'd away.

19

Ah, yet—I have had some glimmer, at times, in my gloomiest woe,
Of a God behind all—after all—the great God, for aught that I
    know;
But the God of love and of hell together—they cannot be
    thought,   105
If there be such a God, may the Great God curse him and bring
    him to nought!

20

Blasphemy! whose is the fault? is it mine? for why would you save
A madman to vex you with wretched words, who is best in his
    grave?
Blasphemy! ay, why not, being damn'd beyond hope of grace?
O, would I were yonder with her, and away from your faith and
    your face!   110
Blasphemy! true! I have scared you pale with my scandalous talk,
But the blasphemy to *my* mind lies all in the way that you walk.

21

Hence! she is gone! can I stay? can I breathe divorced from the
    past?
You needs must have good lynx-eyes if I do not escape you at last.
Our orthodox coroner doubtless will find it a felo-de-se,   115
And the stake and the cross-road, fool, if you will, does it matter
    to me?

1881

To Virgil[9]

WRITTEN AT THE REQUEST OF THE MANTUANS FOR THE
NINETEENTH CENTENARY OF VIRGIL'S DEATH

1

Roman Virgil, thou that singest
    Ilion's lofty temples robed in fire,

9. This flawless and beautiful poem alone could testify that Tennyson in his seventies had not lost his touch. Virgil, to whom he had always looked as the master artist, was born on a farm near Mantua in 70 B.C. and died in 19 B.C. making this celebration of the nineteenth centenary a year late.

Ilion falling, Rome arising,
    wars, and filial faith, and Dido's pyre;[1]

2

Landscape-lover, lord of language   5
    more than he[2] that sang the "Works and Days,"
All the chosen coin of fancy
    flashing out from many a golden phrase;

3

Thou that singest wheat and woodland,
    tilth and vineyard, hive and horse and herd;   10
All the charm of all the Muses
    often flowering in a lonely word;

4

Poet of the happy Tityrus[3]
    piping underneath his beechen bowers;
Poet of the poet-satyr[4]   15
    whom the laughing shepherd bound with flowers;

5

Chanter of the Pollio,[5] glorying
    in the blissful years again to be,
Summers of the snakeless meadow,
    unlaborious earth and oarless sea;   20

6

Thou that seest Universal
    Nature moved by Universal Mind;
Thou majestic in thy sadness
    at the doubtful doom of human kind;

7

Light among the vanish'd ages;   25
    star that gildest yet this phantom shore;
Golden branch[6] amid the shadows,
    kings and realms that pass to rise no more;

8

Now thy Forum roars no longer,
    fallen every purple Cæsar's dome—   30
Tho' thine ocean-roll of rhythm
    sound forever of Imperial Rome—

9

Now the Rome of slaves hath perish'd,
    and the Rome of freemen[7] holds her place,
I, from out the Northern Island   35
    sunder'd once from all the human race,

---

1. The allusions are to the *Aeneid*, the burning of Troy (Ilion) and Dido's suicide after Aeneas abandoned her in Carthage.
2. Hesiod, the eighth-century-B.C. Greek poet whose *Works and Days* contained moral maxims and precepts on farming which anticipated Virgil's *Georgics*.
3. A shepherd in Virgil's *Eclogue* I.
4. Silenus, in *Eclogue* VI.
5. Virgil's patron, mentioned in *Eclogue* IV, in which the prophecy of a golden age has been frequently read as anticipating Christ's birth.
6. The golden bough, with which Aeneas gained access to the underworld. See *Aeneid*, VI, 206 ff.
7. Alludes to Rome's liberation from Austria and the Vatican in 1870.

10

I salute thee, Mantovano,[8]
    I that loved thee since my day began,
Wielder of the stateliest measure
    ever moulded by the lips of man.   40

1882

The Ancient Sage[9]

A thousand summers ere the time of Christ,
From out his ancient city came a Seer[1]
Whom one that loved and honor'd him, and yet
Was no disciple, richly garb'd, but worn
From wasteful living, follow'd—in his hand   5
A scroll of verse—till that old man before
A cavern whence an affluent fountain pour'd
From darkness into daylight, turn'd and spoke:

    "This wealth of waters might but seem to draw
From yon dark cave, but, son, the source is higher,   10
Yon summit half-a-league in air—and higher
The cloud that hides it—higher still the heavens
Whereby the cloud was moulded, and whereout
The cloud descended. Force is from the heights.
I am wearied of our city, son, and go   15
To spend my one last year among the hills.
What hast thou there? Some death-song for the Ghouls
To make their banquet relish? let me read.

        " 'How far thro' all the bloom and brake
            That nightingale is heard!   20
        What power but the bird's could make
            This music in the bird?
        How summer-bright are yonder skies,
            And earth as fair in hue!
        And yet what sign of aught that lies   25
            Behind the green and blue?
        But man to-day is fancy's fool
            As man hath ever been.
        The nameless Power, or Powers that rule
            Were never heard or seen.'   30

---

8. Mantuan.
9. A synthesis of Tennyson's lifelong concern with the problems of faith, free will, immortality, and mysticism, "The Ancient Sage" embodies nearly all of the poet's more idealistic assumptions about life and death. "The whole poem," he said, "is very personal. The passages about 'Faith' and the 'Passion of the Past' were more especially my own personal feelings. This 'Passion of the Past' I used to feel when a boy" (*Memoir*, II, 319). Tennyson had been reading of Lao-tse, a seventh-century-B.C. Chinese philosopher, and noted that the poem expressed "what I might have believed about the deeper problems of life 'A thousand summers ere the birth of Christ.' "
1. Lao-tse's name means "Old Philosopher."

If thou wouldst hear the Nameless, and wilt dive
Into the temple-cave of thine own self,[2]
There, brooding by the central altar, thou
Mayst haply learn the Nameless hath a voice,
By which thou wilt abide, if thou be wise,   35
As if thou knewest, tho' thou canst not know;
For Knowledge[3] is the swallow on the lake
That sees and stirs the surface-shadow there
But never yet hath dipt into the abysm,
The abysm of all abysms, beneath, within   40
The blue of sky and sea, the green of earth,
And in the million-millionth of a grain
Which cleft and cleft again for evermore,
And ever vanishing, never vanishes,
To me, my son, more mystic than myself,   45
Or even than the Nameless is to me.
    "And when thou sendest thy free soul thro' heaven,
Nor understandest bound nor boundlessness,
Thou seest the Nameless of the hundred names.
    "And if the Nameless should withdraw from all   50
Thy frailty counts most real, all thy world
Might vanish like thy shadow in the dark.

            "'And since—from when this earth began—
                The Nameless never came
                Among us, never spake with man,   55
                And never named the Name'—

Thou canst not prove the Nameless, O my son,
Nor canst thou prove the world thou movest in,
Thou canst not prove that thou art body alone,
Nor canst thou prove that thou art spirit alone,   60
Nor canst thou prove that thou art both in one.
Thou canst not prove thou art immortal, no,
Nor yet that thou art mortal—nay, my son,
Thou canst not prove that I, who speak with thee,
Am not thyself in converse with thyself,   65
For nothing worthy proving can be proven,
Nor yet disproven.[4] Wherefore thou be wise,
Cleave ever to the sunnier side of doubt,
And cling to Faith beyond the forms of Faith!
She reels not in the storm of warring words,   70
She brightens at the clash of 'Yes' and 'No,'
She sees the best that glimmers thro' the worst,
She feels the sun is hid but for a night,
She spies the summer thro' the winter bud,
She tastes the fruit before the blossom falls,   75
She hears the lark within the songless egg,
She finds the fountain where they wail'd 'Mirage!'

2. Compare *In Memoriam,* 124, 4.
3. Compare *In Memoriam,* "Prologue,"
6.

4. Essentially the same reasoning was
used in "The Two Voices" to defeat
the arguments of the negative voice.

" 'What Power? aught akin to Mind,
    The mind in me and you?
  Or power as of the Gods gone blind   80
    Who see not what they do?'

But some in yonder city hold, my son,
That none but gods could build this house of ours,
So beautiful, vast, various, so beyond
All work of man, yet, like all work of man,   85
A beauty with defect—till That which knows,
And is not known, but felt thro' what we feel
Within ourselves is highest, shall descend
On this half-deed, and shape it at the last
According to the Highest in the Highest.   90

" 'What Power but the Years that make
    And break the vase of clay,
  And stir the sleeping earth, and wake
    The bloom that fades away?
  What rulers but the Days and Hours   95
    That cancel weal with woe,
  And wind the front of youth with flowers,
    And cap our age with snow?'

The days and hours are ever glancing by,
And seem to flicker past thro' sun and shade,   100
Or short, or long, as Pleasure leads, or Pain,
But with the Nameless is nor day nor hour;
Tho' we, thin minds, who creep from thought to thought,
Break into 'Thens' and 'Whens' the Eternal Now—
This double seeming of the single world!—   105
My words are like the babblings in a dream
Of nightmare, when the babblings break the dream.
But thou be wise in this dream-world of ours,
Nor take thy dial for thy deity,
But make the passing shadow serve thy will.   110

" 'The years that made the stripling wise
    Undo their work again,
  And leave him, blind of heart and eyes,
    The last and least of men;
  Who clings to earth, and once would dare   115
    Hell-heat or Arctic cold,
  And now one breath of cooler air
    Would loose him from his hold.
  His winter chills him to the root,
    He withers marrow and mind;   120
  The kernel of the shrivell'd fruit
    Is jutting thro' the rind;
  The tiger spasms tear his chest,
    The palsy wags his head;
  The wife, the sons, who love him best   125
    Would fain that he were dead;
  The griefs by which he once was wrung
    Were never worth the while'—

Who knows? or whether this earth-narrow life
Be yet but yolk, and forming in the shell?   130

    " 'The shaft of scorn that once had stung
        But wakes a dotard smile.'

The placid gleam of sunset after storm!

    " 'The statesman's brain that sway'd the past
        Is feebler than his knees;   135
    The passive sailor wrecks at last
        In ever-silent seas;
    The warrior hath forgot his arms,
        The learned all his lore;
    The changing market frets or charms   140
        The merchant's hope no more:
    The prophet's beacon burn'd in vain,
        And now is lost in cloud;
    The plowman passes, bent with pain,
        To mix with what he plow'd;   145
    The poet whom his age would quote
        As heir of endless fame—
    He knows not even the book he wrote,
        Not even his own name.
    For man has overlived his day,   150
        And, darkening in the light,
    Scarce feels the senses break away
        To mix with ancient Night.'

The shell must break before the bird can fly.

    " 'The years that when my youth began   155
        Had set the lily and rose
    By all my ways where'er they ran,
        Have ended mortal foes;
    My rose of love for ever gone,
        My lily of truth and trust—   160
    They made her lily and rose in one,
        And changed her into dust.
    O rose-tree planted in my grief,
        And growing on her tomb,
    Her dust is greening in your leaf,   165
        Her blood is in your bloom.
    O slender lily waving there,
        And laughing back the light,
    In vain you tell me "Earth is fair"
        When all is dark as night.'   170

My son, the world is dark with griefs and graves,
So dark that men cry out against the heavens.
Who knows but that the darkness is in man?
The doors of Night may be the gates of Light;
For wert thou born or blind or deaf, and then   175
Suddenly heal'd, how wouldst thou glory in all
The splendors and the voices of the world!
And we, the poor earth's dying race, and yet

No phantoms, watching from a phantom shore
Await the last and largest sense to make   180
The phantom walls of this illusion fade,
And show us that the world is wholly fair.

    " 'But vain the tears for darken'd years
        As laughter over wine,
    And vain the laughter as the tears,   185
        O brother, mine or thine,
    For all that laugh, and all that weep
        And all that breathe are one
    Slight ripple on the boundless deep
        That moves, and all is gone.'   190

But that one ripple on the boundless deep
Feels that the deep is boundless, and itself
For ever changing form, but evermore
One with the boundless motion of the deep.

    " 'Yet wine and laughter, friends! and set   195
        The lamps alight, and call
      For golden music, and forget
        The darkness of the pall.'

If utter darkness closed the day, my son—
But earth's dark forehead flings athwart the heavens   200
Her shadow crown'd with stars—and yonder—out
To northward—some that never set, but pass
From sight and night to lose themselves in day.
I hate the black negation of the bier,
And wish the dead, as happier than ourselves   205
And higher, having climb'd one step beyond
Our village miseries, might be borne in white
To burial or to burning, hymn'd from hence
With songs in praise of death, and crown'd with flowers!

    " 'O worms and maggots of to-day   210
        Without their hope of wings!'"

But louder than thy rhyme the silent Word
Of that world-prophet in the heart of man.

    " 'Tho' some have gleams, or so they say,
        Of more than mortal things.'   215

To-day? but what of yesterday? for oft
On me, when boy, there came what then I call'd,
Who knew no books and no philosophies,
In my boy-phrase, 'The Passion of the Past.'
The first gray streak of earliest summer-dawn,   220
The last long stripe of waning crimson gloom,
As if the late and early were but one—
A height, a broken grange, a grove, a flower
Had murmurs, 'Lost and gone, and lost and gone!'
A breath, a whisper—some divine farewell[5]—   225

5. Compare "Tears, Idle Tears."

Desolate sweetness—far and far away—
What had he loved, what had he lost, the boy?
I know not, and I speak of what has been.
 "And more, my son! for more than once when I
Sat all alone, revolving in myself   230
The word that is the symbol of myself,
The mortal limit of the Self was loosed,
And past into the Nameless, as a cloud
Melts into heaven. I touch'd my limbs, the limbs
Were strange, not mine—and yet no shade of doubt, 235
But utter clearness, and thro' loss of self
The gain of such large life as match'd with ours
Were sun to spark—unshadowable in words,
Themselves but shadows of a shadow-world.[6]

    " 'And idle gleams will come and go, 240
     But still the clouds remain;'

The clouds themselves are children of the Sun.

    " 'And Night and Shadow rule below
     When only Day should reign.'

And Day and Night are children of the Sun,   245
And idle gleams to thee are light to me.
Some say, the Light was father of the Night,
And some, the Night was father of the Light,
No night, no day!—I touch thy world again—
No ill, no good! such counter-terms, my son,   250
Are border-races, holding each its own
By endless war. But night enough is there
In yon dark city. Get thee back; and since
The key to that weird casket, which for thee
But holds a skull, is neither thine nor mine,   255
But in the hand of what is more than man,
Or in man's hand when man is more than man,
Let be thy wail, and help thy fellow-men,
And make thy gold thy vassal, not thy king,
And fling free alms into the beggar's bowl,   260
And send the day into the darken'd heart;
Nor list for guerdon in the voice of men,
A dying echo from a falling wall;
Nor care—for Hunger hath the evil eye—
To vex the noon with fiery gems, or fold   265

6. Compare "The Mystic" for one of Tennyson's earliest statements about such transcendental experience. "There are moments," he said "when the flesh is nothing to me, when I feel and know the flesh to be the vision, God and the Spiritual the only real and true. Depend upon it, the Spiritual *is* the real: it belongs to one more than the hand and the foot. You may tell me that my hand and my foot are only imaginary symbols of my existence, I could believe you; but you never, never can convince me that the *I* is not an eternal Reality, and that the Spiritual is not the true and real part of me" (*Memoir*, II, 90). See also *Memoir*, I, 320; *In Memoriam*, 95; and King Arthur's speech in "The Holy Grail," lines 906–915.

Thy presence in the silk of sumptuous looms;
Nor roll thy viands on a luscious tongue,
Nor drown thyself with flies in honeyed wine;
Nor thou be rageful, like a handled bee,
And lose thy life by usage of thy sting;   270
Nor harm an adder thro' the lust for harm,
Nor make a snail's horn shrink for wantonness.
And more—think well! Do-well will follow thought,
And in the fatal sequence of this world
An evil thought may soil thy children's blood;   275
But curb the beast would cast thee in the mire,[7]
And leave the hot swamp of voluptuousness,
A cloud between the Nameless and thyself,
And lay thine uphill shoulder to the wheel,
And climb the Mount of Blessing, whence, if thou   280
Look higher, then—perchance—thou mayest—beyond
A hundred ever-rising mountain lines,
And past the range of Night and Shadow—see
The high-heaven dawn of more than mortal day
Strike on the Mount of Vision!
                   So, farewell."   285

1885

Poets and Their Bibliographies

Old poets foster'd under friendlier skies,[8]
    Old Virgil who would write ten lines, they say,
    At dawn, and lavish all the golden day
To make them wealthier in his reader's eyes;
And you, old popular Horace, you the wise   5
    Adviser of the nine-years-ponder'd lay,
    And you, that wear a wreath of sweeter bay,
Catullus, whose dead songster never dies;
If, glancing downward on the kindly sphere
    That once had roll'd you round and round the sun,   10
You see your Art still shrined in human shelves,
You should be jubilant that you flourish'd here
    Before the Love of Letters, overdone,
Had swampt the sacred poets with themselves.

1885

---

7. In *In Memoriam* and throughout *Idylls of the King* the use of the beast metaphor expresses Tennyson's preoccupation with scientific materialism and its consequences following acceptance of the Darwinian hypothesis. Although the application of the metaphor underwent little change from the 1840's, the ideas informing it were not static. One may notice that in the late poems the city, which earlier had been rendered as the locus of all that is high and holy, is no longer the corrective metaphor it once was. Usually far more tough-minded than Dickens, Tennyson toward the end of his life adopts a Blakean view of the city.
8. Compare the early poem "The Poet" (1830), p. 8.

The Dead Prophet[9]

182–

1

Dead!
   And the Muses cried with a stormy cry,
'Send them no more, for evermore
   Let the people die.'

2

Dead!   5
   'Is it *he* then brought so low?'
And a careless people flock'd from the fields
   With a purse to pay for the show.

3

Dead, who had served his time,
   Was one of the people's kings,   10
Had labor'd in lifting them out of slime,
   And showing them, souls have wings!

4

Dumb on the winter heath he lay.
   His friends had stript him bare,
And roll'd his nakedness everyway   15
   That all the crowd might stare.

5

A storm-worn signpost not to be read,
   And a tree with a moulder'd nest
On its barkless bones, stood stark by the dead;
   And behind him, low in the West,   20

6

With shifting ladders of shadow and light,
   And blurr'd in color and form,
The sun hung over the gates of night,
   And glared at a coming storm.

7

Then glided a vulturous beldam forth,   25
   That on dumb death had thriven;
They call'd her 'Reverence' here upon earth,
   And 'The Curse of the Prophet' in heaven.

9. Although the date "182–" has led to speculation, Tennyson said his poem was "about no particular prophet." As his much earlier poem "To ——, After Reading a Life and Letters" may have been in response to the publication of Keats's correspondence with Fanny Brawne, so "The Dead Prophet" may have been prompted by Froude's disclosure of the bickerings in the private life of Jane and Thomas Carlyle. "I am sure that Froude is wrong," Tennyson said. "I saw a great deal of them. They were always 'chaffing' one another, and they could not have done that if they had got on so 'badly together' as Froude thinks." Tennyson always believed a writer's work should stand for his life (see *Memoir*, II, 165), and a measure of his dread of biography is given in his son's remark that, when writing "The Dead Prophet," the poet chanted:
   While I live the OWLS!
   When I die the GHOULS!!

8

She knelt—'We worship him'—all but wept—
    'So great, so noble, was he!'   30
She clear'd her sight, she arose, she swept
    The dust of earth from her knee.

9

'Great! for he spoke and the people heard,
    And his eloquence caught like a flame
From zone to zone of the world, till his word   35
    Had won him a noble name.

10

'Noble! he sung, and the sweet sound ran
    Thro' palace and cottage door,
For he touch'd on the whole sad planet of man,
    The kings and the rich and the poor;   40

11

'And he sung not alone of an old sun set,
    But a sun coming up in his youth!
Great and noble—O, yes—but yet—
    For man is a lover of truth,

12

'And bound to follow, wherever she go   45
    Stark-naked, and up or down,
Thro' her high hill-passes of stainless snow,
    Or the foulest sewer of the town—

13

'Noble and great—O, ay—but then,
    Tho' a prophet should have his due,   50
Was he noblier-fashion'd than other men?
    Shall we see to it, I and you?

14

'For since he would sit on a prophet's seat,
    As a lord of the human soul,
We needs must scan him from head to feet,   55
    Were it but for a wart or a mole?'

15

His wife and his child stood by him in tears,
    But she—she push'd them aside.
'Tho' a name may last for a thousand years,
    Yet a truth is a truth,' she cried.   60

16

And she that had haunted his pathway still,
    Had often truckled and cower'd
When he rose in his wrath, and had yielded her will
    To the master, as overpower'd,

17

She tumbled his helpless corpse about.   65
    'Small blemish upon the skin!
But I think we know what is fair without
    Is often as foul within.'

18

She crouch'd, she tore him part from part,
    And out of his body she drew   70
The red 'blood-eagle'[1] of liver and heart;
    She held them up to the view;

19

She gabbled, as she groped in the dead,
    And all the people were pleased;
'See, what a little heart,' she said,   75
    'And the liver is half-diseased!'

20

She tore the prophet after death,
    And the people paid her well.
Lightnings flicker'd along the heath;
    One shriek'd, 'The fires of hell!'   80

1885

Vastness[2]

1

Many a hearth upon our dark globe sighs after many a vanish'd face.
Many a planet by many a sun may roll with the dust of a vanish'd
        race.

2

Raving politics, never at rest—as this poor earth's pale history
        runs,—
What is it all but a trouble of ants in the gleam of a million million
        of suns?

3

Lies upon this side, lies upon that side, truthless violence mourn'd
        by the wise,   5
Thousands of voices drowning his own in a popular torrent of lies
        upon lies;

4

Stately purposes, valor in battle, glorious annals of army and fleet,
Death for the right cause, death for the wrong cause, trumpets of
        victory, groans of defeat;

5

Innocence seethed in her mother's milk, and Charity setting the
        martyr aflame;

---

1. "Old Viking term for lungs, liver, etc., when torn by the conqueror out of the body of the conquered" (Tennyson's note).
2. Although "The Ancient Sage" expresses the poet's optimistic beliefs, "Vastness" shows the mood of delusion more characteristic of his last years. In an atempt at objectivity lacking in "Locksley Hall, Sixty Years After," he asks yet once more the question which had so deeply concerned him throughout his life: "Hast Thou made all this for naught! Is all this trouble of life worth undergoing if we only end in our own corpse-coffins at last? If you allow a God, and God allows this strong instinct and universal yearning for another life, surely that is in a measure a presumption of its truth" (*Memoir,* I, 321).

Thraldom who walks with the banner of Freedom, and recks not to
    ruin a realm in her name.   10

6

Faith at her zenith, or all but lost in the gloom of doubts that
    darken the schools;
Craft with a bunch of all-heal[3] in her hand, follow'd up by her vassal
    legion of fools;

7

Trade flying over a thousand seas with her spice and her vintage,
    her silk and her corn;
Desolate offing, sailorless harbors, famishing populace, wharves for-
    lorn;

8

Star of the morning, Hope in the sunrise; gloom of the evening,
    Life at a close;   15
Pleasure who flaunts on her wide downway with her flying robe and
    her poison'd rose;

9

Pain, that has crawl'd from the corpse of Pleasure, a worm which
    writhes all day, and at night
Stirs up again in the heart of the sleeper, and stings him back to the
    curse of the light;

10

Wealth with his wines and his wedded harlots; honest Poverty, bare
    to the bone;
Opulent Avarice, lean as Poverty; Flattery gilding the rift in a
    throne;   20

11

Fame blowing out from her golden trumpet a jubilant challenge to
    Time and to Fate;
Slander, her shadow, sowing the nettle on all the laurell'd graves of
    the great;

12

Love for the maiden, crown'd with marriage, no regrets for aught
    that has been,
Household happiness, gracious children, debtless competence,
    golden mean;

13

National hatreds of whole generations, and pigmy spites of the vil-
    lage spire;   25
Vows that will last to the last death-ruckle, and vows that are snapt
    in a moment of fire;

14

He that has lived for the lust of the minute, and died in the doing
    it, flesh without mind;
He that has nail'd all flesh to the Cross, till Self died out in the love
    of his kind;

---

3. An herb for all maladies, generally associated with rustics' remedies.

15

Spring and Summer and Autumn and Winter, and all these old rev-
olutions of earth;
All new-old revolutions of Empire—change of the tide—what is all
of it worth?   30

16

What the philosophies, all the sciences, poesy, varying voices of
prayer,
All that is noblest, all that is basest, all that is filthy with all that is
fair?

17

What is it all, if we all of us end but in being our own corpse-coffins
at last?
Swallow'd in Vastness, lost in Silence, drown'd in the deeps of a
meaningless Past?

18

What but a murmur of gnats in the gloom, or a moment's anger of
bees in their hive?—   35

.   .   .   .

Peace, let it be! for I loved him, and love him for ever: the dead are
not dead but alive.[4]

1885

Locksley Hall Sixty Years After[5]

Late, my grandson! half the morning have I paced these sandy
tracts,
Watch'd again the hollow ridges roaring into cataracts,

Wander'd back to living boyhood while I heard the curlews call,
I myself so close on death, and death itself in Locksley Hall.

So—your happy suit was blasted—she the faultless, the divine;   5
And you liken—boyish babble—this boy-love of yours with mine.

I myself have often babbled doubtless of a foolish past;
Babble, babble; our old England may go down in babble at last.

4. Tennyson glossed: "The last line means 'What matters anything in this world without faith in the immortality of the soul and of Love?' " The "him" is usually taken to be Arthur Hallam, but, as Jerome Buckley has convincingly argued from earlier drafts which mention a brother, the reference is probably to Charles. See *Tennyson,* pp. 231–232.

5. Contrary to Tennyson's assertion that he had written "a dramatic poem, and the Dramatis Personae are imaginary," the views of the speaker are very close to the poet's own. Published forty-four years after "Locksley Hall," the sequel thunders forth the opinions of an old man looking back in disillusionment at his youthful optimism and faith in progress. "It seemed to my father," Hallam noted, "that the two *Locksley Halls* were likely to be in the future two of the most historically interesting of his poems, as descriptive of the tone of the age at two distinct periods of his life." But the tone of the late poem is too hysterical to reflect "the age"; it tells us much more about the poet.

'Curse him!' curse your fellow-victim? call him dotard in your rage?
Eyes that lured a doting boyhood well might fool a dotard's age.   10

Jilted for a wealthier! wealthier? yet perhaps she was not wise;
I remember how you kiss'd the miniature with those sweet eyes.

In the hall there hangs a painting—Amy's arms about my neck—
Happy children in a sunbeam sitting on the ribs of wreck.

In my life there was a picture, she that clasp'd my neck had flown;   15
I was left within the shadow sitting on the wreck alone.[6]

Yours has been a slighter ailment, will you sicken for her sake?
You, not you! your modern amorist is of easier, earthlier make.

Amy loved me, Amy fail'd me, Amy was a timid child;
But your Judith—but your worldling—*she* had never driven me
          wild.   20

She that holds the diamond necklace dearer than the golden ring,
She that finds a winter sunset[7] fairer than a morn of spring.

She that in her heart is brooding on his briefer lease of life,
While she vows 'till death shall part us,' she the would-be-widow
          wife.

She the worldling born of worldlings—father, mother—be content,[25]
Even the homely farm can teach us there is something in descent.

Yonder in that chapel, slowly sinking now into the ground,
Lies the warrior, my forefather, with his feet upon the hound.

Cross'd![8] for once he sail'd the sea to crush the Moslem in his pride;
Dead the warrior, dead his glory, dead the cause in which he died.   30

Yet how often I and Amy in the mouldering aisle have stood,
Gazing for one pensive moment on that founder of our blood.

There again I stood to-day, and where of old we knelt in prayer,
Close beneath the casement crimson with the shield of Locksley—
          there,

All in white Italian marble, looking still as if she smiled,   35
Lies my Amy dead in childbirth, dead the mother, dead the child.

Dead—and sixty years ago, and dead her aged husband now—
I, this old white-headed dreamer, stoopt and kiss'd her marble brow.

Gone the fires of youth, the follies, furies, curses, passionate tears,
Gone like fires and floods and earthquakes of the planet's dawning
          years.   40

Fires that shook me once, but now to silent ashes fallen away.
Cold upon the dead volcano sleeps the gleam of dying day.

6. Lines 13–16, Tennyson said, "were
the nucleus of the poem, and were
written fifty years ago."

7. I.e., marriage to the older man.
8. The statue's crossed feet indicate
that he had been a crusader.

Gone the tyrant[9] of my youth, and mute below the chancel stones,
All his virtues—I forgive them—black in white[1] above his bones.

Gone the comrades of my bivouac, some in fight against the foe,   45
Some thro' age and slow diseases, gone as all on earth will go.

Gone with whom for forty years my life in golden sequence ran,
She with all the charm of woman, she with all the breadth of man,

Strong in will and rich in wisdom, Edith, yet so lowly-sweet,
Woman to her inmost heart, and woman to her tender feet,   50

Very woman of very woman, nurse of ailing body and mind,
She that link'd again the broken chain that bound me to my kind.

Here to-day was Amy with me, while I wander'd down the coast,
Near us Edith's holy shadow, smiling at the slighter ghost.

Gone our sailor son thy father, Leonard early lost at sea;   55
Thou alone, my boy, or Amy's kin and mine art left to me.

Gone thy tender-natured mother, wearying to be left alone,
Pining for the stronger heart that once had beat beside her own.

Truth, for truth is truth, he worshipt, being true as he was brave;
Good, for good is good, he follow'd, yet he look'd beyond the
       grave,[2]   60

Wiser there than you, that crowning barren Death as lord of all,
Deem this over-tragic drama's closing curtain is the pall!

Beautiful was death in him, who saw the death, but kept the deck,
Saving women and their babes, and sinking with the sinking wreck,

Gone for ever! Ever? no—for since our dying race began,   65
Ever, ever, and for ever was the leading light of man.

Those that in barbarian burials kill'd the slave, and slew the wife
Felt within themselves the sacred passion of the second life.

Indian warriors dream of ampler hunting grounds beyond the night;
Even the black Australian dying hopes he shall return, a white.   70

Truth for truth, and good for good! The good, the true, the pure, the
       just—
Take the charm 'For ever' from them, and they crumble into dust.

Gone the cry of 'Forward, Forward,' lost within a growing gloom;
Lost, or only heard in silence from the silence of a tomb.

Half the marvels of my morning, triumphs over time and space,   75
Staled by frequence, shrunk by usage into commonest commonplace!

'Forward' rang the voices then, and of the many mine was one.
Let us hush this cry of 'Forward' till ten thousand years have gone.

---

9. The "selfish uncle" (see "Locksley
Hall," line 156), whose ward he became
after his father's death.
1. The inscription, lettered in black,
has been carved in a white stone slab.

2. This couplet and lines 71–72 were
written in April 1886, just after Tenny-
son learned that his son Lionel had
died while returning home from India.

Far among the vanish'd races, old Assyrian kings would flay
Captives whom they caught in battle—iron-hearted victors they.   80

Ages after, while in Asia, he that led the wild Moguls,
Timur[3] built his ghastly tower of eighty thousand human skulls;

Then, and here in Edward's time,[4] an age of noblest English names,
Christian conquerors took and flung the conquer'd Christian into
                    flames.

Love your enemy, bless your haters, said the Greatest of the great; 85
Christian love among the Churches look'd the twin of heathen hate.

From the golden alms of Blessing man had coin'd himself a curse:
Rome of Cæsar, Rome of Peter, which was crueller? which was
                    worse?

France had shown a light to all men, preach'd a Gospel, all men's
                    good;
Celtic Demos rose a Demon, shriek'd and slaked the light with
                    blood.[5]
                                                                    90

Hope was ever on her mountain, watching till the day begun—
Crown'd with sunlight—over darkness—from the still unrisen sun.

Have we grown at last beyond the passions of the primal clan?
'Kill your enemy, for you hate him,' still, 'your enemy' was a man.

Have we sunk below them? peasants maim the helpless horse, and
                    drive
                                                                    95
Innocent cattle under thatch, and burn the kindlier brutes alive.[6]

Brutes, the brutes are not your wrongers—burnt at midnight, found
                    at morn,
Twisted hard in mortal agony with their offspring, born-unborn,

Clinging to the silent mother! Are we devils? are we men?
Sweet Saint Francis[7] of Assisi, would that he were here again,   100

He that in his Catholic wholeness used to call the very flowers
Sisters, brothers—and the beasts—whose pains are hardly less than
                    ours!

Chaos, Cosmos! Cosmos, Chaos! who can tell how all will end?
Read the wide world's annals, you, and take their wisdom for your
                    friend.

Hope the best, but hold the Present fatal daughter of the Past,   105
Shape your heart to front the hour, but dream not that the hour will
                    last.

---

3. Tamerlane (1336–1405), whose Asian conquests resulted in several massive slaughters.
4. Alludes to the reign of Edward VI (1547–53), when the Catholics were persecuted; his successor, Bloody Mary (1553–58), persecuted the Protestants.
5. Alludes to the French Revolution of 1789 and the Reign of Terror in 1793–94; "Demos" means common people.
6. In the 1880's there were peasant uprisings over the issue of Home Rule.
7. Chiefly known for his tenderness toward all living creatures.

Ay, if dynamite and revolver leave you courage to be wise—
When was age so cramm'd with menace? madness? written, spoken
    lies?

Envy wears the mask of Love, and, laughing sober fact to scorn,
Cries to weakest as to strongest, 'Ye are equals, equal-born.'   110

Equal-born? O, yes, if yonder hill be level with the flat.
Charm us, orator, till the lion took no larger than the cat,

Till the cat thro' that mirage of overheated language loom
Larger than the lion,—Demos end in working its own doom.

Russia bursts our Indian barrier,[8] shall we fight her? shall we
    yield?   115
Pause ! before you sound the trumpet, hear the voices from the field.

Those three hundred millions under one Imperial sceptre now,
Shall we hold them? shall we loose them? take the suffrage of the
    plow.[9]

Nay, but these would feel and follow Truth if only you and you,
Rivals of realm-ruining party, when you speak were wholly true.   120

Plowmen, shepherds, have I found, and more than once, and still
    could find,
Sons of God, and kings of men in utter nobleness of mind,

Truthful, trustful, looking upward to the practised hustings-liar;[1]
So the higher wields the lower, while the lower is the higher.

Here and there a cotter's babe is royal-born by right divine;   125
Here and there my lord is lower than his oxen or his swine.

Chaos, Cosmos! Cosmos, Chaos! once again the sickening game;
Freedom, free to slay herself, and dying while they shout her name.

Step by step we gain'd a freedom known to Europe, known to all;
Step by step we rose to greatness,—thro' the tonguesters we may
    fall.   130

You that woo the Voices[2]—tell them 'old experience is a fool,'
Teach your flatter'd kings that only those who cannot read can rule.

Pluck the mighty from their seat, but set no meek ones in their
    place;
Pillory Wisdom in your markets, pelt your offal at her face.

Tumble Nature heel o'er head, and, yelling with the yelling street, 135
Set the feet above the brain and swear the brain is in the feet.

Bring the old dark ages back without the faith, without the hope,
Break the State, the Church, the Throne, and roll their ruins down
    the slope.

8. The Panjdeh incident of 1885 involved another of Russia's periodic attempts to gain entry into India through Afghanistan, which the British regarded as a buffer zone.
9. I.e., let the farm laborers' vote (a right granted by Parliament in 1884) decide the fate of India, which had become part of the Empire in 1877.
1. A lying political campaigner.
2. Votes.

Authors—essayist, atheist, novelist, realist, rhymester, play your part,
Paint the mortal shame of nature with the living hues of art.   140

Rip your brothers' vices open, strip your own foul passions bare;
Down with Reticence, down with Reverence—forward—naked—let
    them stare.

Feed the budding rose of boyhood with the drainage of your sewer;
Send the drain into the fountain, lest the stream should issue pure.

Set the maiden fancies wallowing in the troughs of Zolaism,[3]—   145
Forward, forward, ay, and backward, downward too into the abysm!

Do your best to charm the worst, to lower the rising race of men;
Have we risen from out the beast, then back into the beast again?

Only 'dust to dust' for me that sicken at your lawless din,
Dust in wholesome old-world dust before the newer world begin.   150

Heated am I? you—you wonder—well, it scarce becomes mine age—
Patience! let the dying actor mouth his last upon the stage.

Cries of unprogressive dotage ere the dotard fall asleep?
Noises or a current narrowing, not the music of a deep?

Ay, for doubtless I am old, and think gray thoughts, for I am gray;   155
After all the stormy changes shall we find a changeless May?

After madness, after massacre, Jacobinism and Jacquerie,[4]
Some diviner force to guide us thro' the days I shall not see?

When the schemes and all the systems, kingdoms and republics fall,
Something kindlier, higher, holier—all for each and each for all?   160

All the full-brain, half-brain races, led by Justice, Love, and Truth;
All the millions one at length with all the visions of my youth?

All diseases quench'd by Science, no man halt, or deaf, or blind;
Stronger ever born of weaker, lustier body, larger mind?

Earth at last a warless world, a single race, a single tongue—   165
I have seen her far away—for is not Earth as yet so young?—

Every tiger madness muzzled, every serpent passion kill'd,
Every grim ravine a garden, every blazing desert till'd,

Robed in universal harvest up to either pole she smiles,
Universal ocean softly washing all her warless isles.   170

Warless? when her tens are thousands, and her thousands millions,
    then—
All her harvest all too narrow—who can fancy warless men?

3. The popularity of Emile Zola, whose naturalistic novels such as *Nana* (1880) dealt openly with prostitution and dissipation, was to Tennyson symptomatic of England's susceptibility to the cultural decadence he had long associated with France.
4. The Jacobins were originally liberal members of the National Assembly (1789) and became increasingly radical and played a major role in the Reign of Terror. A "Jacquerie," named for an unsuccessful insurrection (1358) of French peasants against the nobles, is a term for any mob uprising.

Warless? war will die out late then. Will it ever? late or soon?
Can it, till this outworn earth be dead as yon dead world the moon?

Dead the new astronomy calls her.—On this day and at this hour, 175
In this gap between the sandhills, whence you see the Locksley
    tower,

Here we met, our latest meeting—Amy—sixty years ago—
She and I—the moon was falling greenish thro' a rosy glow,

Just above the gateway tower, and even where you see her now—
Here we stood and claspt each other, swore the seeming-deathless
    vow.— 180

Dead, but how her living glory lights the hall, the dune, the grass!
Yet the moonlight is the sunlight, and the sun himself will pass.

Venus near her! smiling downward at this earthlier earth of ours,
Closer on the sun, perhaps a world of never fading flowers.

Hesper, whom the poet[5] call'd the Bringer home of all good
    things— 185
All good things may move in Hesper, perfect peoples, perfect kings.

Hesper—Venus—were we native to that splendor or in Mars,
We should see the globe we groan in, fairest of their evening stars.

Could we dream of wars and carnage, craft and madness, lust and
    spite,
Roaring London, raving Paris, in that point of peaceful light? 190

Might we not in glancing heavenward on a star so silver-fair,
Yearn, and clasp the hands and murmur, 'Would to God that we
    were there'?

Forward, backward, backward, forward, in the immeasurable sea,
Sway'd by vaster ebbs and flows than can be known to you or me.

All the suns—are these but symbols of innumerable man, 195
Man or Mind that sees a shadow of the planner or the plan?

Is there evil but on earth? or pain in every peopled sphere?
Well, be grateful for the sounding watchword 'Evolution' here,

Evolution ever climbing after some ideal good,
And Reversion ever dragging Evolution[6] in the mud. 200

What are men that He should heed us? cried the king[7] of sacred
    song;
Insects of an hour, that hourly work their brother insect wrong,

5. Sappho, in the line, "Oh, Hesperus! Thou bringest all things home."
6. Even before publication of Darwin's *Origin of Species* (1859), the idea of evolution seemed to promise scientific support to the popular notion of society's inevitable progress toward an earthly utopia (see "Locksley Hall," lines 119 ff). But as the real implica-tions of the Darwinian hypothesis were assimilated during the seventies and eighties—notably, that the process involved almost incredibly long periods of time and that survival of the ethically best in human terms had nothing to do with natural laws—the "myth of Evolution" gradually lost its adherents.
7. David. See *Psalms*, 8:4.

While the silent heavens roll, and suns along their fiery way,
All their planets whirling round them, flash a million miles a day.

Many an æon moulded earth before her highest, man, was born,   205
Many an æon too may pass when earth is manless and forlorn,

Earth so huge, and yet so bounded—pools of salt, and plots of
        land—
Shallow skin of green and azure—chains of mountain, grains of
        sand!

Only That which made us meant us to be mightier by and by,
Set the sphere of all the boundless heavens within the human
        eye,   210

Sent the shadow of Himself, the boundless, thro' the human soul;
Boundless inward in the atom, boundless outward in the Whole.

        .   .   .   .

Here is Locksley Hall, my grandson, here the lion-guarded gate.
Not to-night in Locksley Hall—to-morrow—you, you come so late.

Wreck'd—your train—or all but wreck'd? a shatter'd wheel? a
        vicious boy!   215
Good, this forward, you that preach it, is it well to wish you joy?

Is it well that while we range with Science, glorying in the Time,
City children soak and blacken soul and sense in city slime?

There among the glooming alleys Progress halts on palsied feet,
Crime and hunger cast our maidens by the thousand on the
        street.   220

There the master scrimps his haggard sempstress of her daily bread,
There a single sordid attic holds the living and the dead.

There the smouldering fire of fever creeps across the rotted floor,
And the crowded couch of incest in the warrens of the poor.[8]

Nay, your pardon, cry your 'Forward,' yours are hope and youth, but
        I—   225
Eighty winters leave the dog too lame to follow with the cry,

Lame and old, and past his time, and passing now into the night;
Yet I would the rising race were half as eager for the light.

Light the fading gleam of even? light the glimmer of the dawn?
Aged eyes may take the growing glimmer for the gleam with-
        drawn.   230

Far away beyond her myriad coming changes earth will be
Something other than the wildest modern guess of you and me.

---

8. Throughout most of his life, Tenny-
son's associations with the city were
predominately positive. Here, as in
much of the late poetry, he reverts to
a Blakean view of the city as a product
of the bad effects of the Industrial
Revolution.

Earth may reach her earthly-worst, or if she gain her earthly-best,
Would she find her human offspring this ideal man at rest?

Forward then, but still remember how the course of Time will
   swerve,   235
Crook and turn upon itself in many a backward streaming curve.

Not the Hall to-night, my grandson! Death and Silence hold their
   own.
Leave the master[9] in the first dark hour of his last sleep alone.

Worthier soul was he than I am, sound and honest, rustic Squire,
Kindly landlord, boon companion—youthful jealousy is a liar. 240

Cast the poison from your bosom, oust the madness from your brain.
Let the trampled serpent show you that you have not lived in vain.

Youthful! youth and age are scholars yet but in the lower school,
Nor is he the wisest man who never proved himself a fool.

Yonder lies our young sea-village—Art and Grace are less and
   less: 245
Science grows and Beauty dwindles—roofs of slated hideousness!

There is one old hostel left us where they swing the Locksley shield,
Till the peasant cow shall butt the 'lion passant' from his field.[1]

Poor old Heraldry, poor old History, poor old Poetry, passing hence,
In the common deluge drowning old political common-sense! 250

Poor old voice of eighty crying after voices that have fled!
All I loved are vanish'd voices, all my steps are on the dead.

All the world is ghost to me, and as the phantom disappears,
Forward far and far from here is all the hope of eighty years.

  · · · · · · · · · · · ·

In this hostel—I remember—I repent it o'er his grave—   255
Like a clown—by chance he met me—I refused the hand he gave.

From that casement where the trailer mantles all the mouldering
   bricks—
I was then in early boyhood, Edith but a child of six—

While I shelter'd in this archway from a day of driving showers—
Peept the winsome face of Edith like a flower among the flowers. 260

Here to-night! the Hall to-morrow, when they toll the chapel bell!
Shall I hear in one dark room a wailing, 'I have loved thee well'?

Then a peal that shakes the portal—one has come to claim his
   bride,
Her that shrank, and put me from her, shriek'd, and started from
   my side—

9. Amy's husband and the speaker's
rival, maligned in the first "Locksley
Hall."

1. The surface of the Locksley shield,
on which the coat-of-arms showed a
running lion.

Silent echoes! You, my Leonard, use and not abuse your day,   265
Move among your people, know them, follow him who led the way,

Strove for sixty widow'd years to help his homelier brother men,
Served the poor, and built the cottage, raised the school, and drain'd
       the fen.

Hears he now the voice that wrong'd him? who shall swear it
       cannot be?
Earth would never touch her worst, were one in fifty such as he.   270

Ere she gain her heavenly-best, a God must mingle with the game.
Nay, there may be those about us whom we neither see nor name,

Felt within us as ourselves, the Powers of Good, the Powers of Ill,
Strowing balm, or shedding poison in the fountains of the will.

Follow you the star that lights a desert pathway, yours or mine.   275
Forward, till you see the Highest Human Nature is divine.

Follow Light, and do the Right—for man can half-control his
       doom—
Till you find the deathless Angel[2] seated in the vacant tomb.

Forward, let the stormy moment fly and mingle with the past.
I that loathed have come to love him. Love will conquer at the
       last.   280

Gone at eighty, mine own age, and I and you will bear the pall;
Then I leave thee lord and master, latest lord of Locksley Hall.

1886

Demeter and Persephone[3]

(IN ENNA)

Faint as a climate-changing bird that flies
All night across the darkness, and at dawn
Falls on the threshold of her native land,

2. The angel who rolled away the stone from Christ's tomb. See *Matthew*, 28:1–7.
3. From boyhood Tennyson had shown interest in this myth, and indeed his earliest extant poem in his "Translation from Claudian's 'Proserpine.'" At the request of his son for a poem about Demeter, he said: "I will write it, but when I write an antique like this I must put it into a frame—something modern about it. It is no use giving a mere *réchauffé* of old legends" (*Memoir*, II, 364). The illusive "something modern" is, however, never obtrusive, as it often is in *Idylls of the King*, and adds an enriching complexity to the poem. Robert Stange has provocatively said: "Since the story of Persephone is a

myth of generation, the poet includes in his treatment of it not only the fertility of the soil and the creation of new life, but his definition of the attributes of the artist—imperial, disimpassioned, who moves between divided and distinguished worlds."

Among Tennyson's sources were the Homeric *Hymn to Demeter* and Ovid's *Metamorphoses*. The earth goddess Demeter abandons her care of the crops while vainly searching for her daughter Persephone, who, when gathering flowers in the field of Enna, had been carried off by Dis, or Pluto, to be queen of Hades. To ensure the resumption of nature's productivity, Zeus finally arranges to have Persephone returned to her mother for nine months

And can no more, thou camest, O my child,
Led upward by the God[4] of ghosts and dreams,   5
Who laid thee at Eleusis,[5] dazed and dumb
With passing thro' at once from state to state,
Until I brought thee hither, that the day,
When here thy hands let fall the gather'd flower,
Might break thro' clouded memories once again   10
On thy lost self. A sudden nightingale
Saw thee, and flash'd into a frolic of song
And welcome; and a gleam as of the moon,
When first she peers along the tremulous deep,
Fled wavering o'er thy face, and chased away   15
That shadow of a likeness to the king
Of shadows, thy dark mate. Persephone!
Queen of the dead no more—my child! Thine eyes
Again were human-godlike, and the Sun
Burst from a swimming fleece of winter gray,   20
And robed thee in his day from head to feet—
"Mother!" and I was folded in thine arms.

    Child, those imperial, disimpassion'd eyes
Awed even me at first, thy mother—eyes
That oft had seen the serpent-wanded power   25
Draw downward into Hades with his drift
Of flickering spectres, lighted from below
By the red race of fiery Phlegethon;[6]
But when before have Gods or men beheld
The Life that had descended re-arise,   30
And lighted from above him by the Sun?
So mighty was the mother's childless cry,
A cry that rang thro' Hades, Earth, and Heaven!

    So in this pleasant vale we stand again,
The field of Enna, now once more ablaze   35
With flowers that brighten as thy footstep falls,
All flowers—but for one black blur of earth
Left by that closing chasm, thro' which the car
Of dark Aïdoneus[7] rising rapt thee hence.
And here, my child, tho' folded in thine arms,   40
I feel the deathless heart of motherhood
Within me shudder, lest the naked glebe
Should yawn once more into the gulf, and thence
The shrilly whinnyings of the team of Hell,
Ascending, pierce the glad and songful air,   45
And all at once their arch'd necks, midnight-maned,

---

of every year. Sir James Frazer in *The Golden Bough* (the first volume of which appeared in 1890) observes that the origin of the myth was clearly an attempt to account for the seasonal cycles.

4. Hermes, the messenger of the gods.
5. A town near Athens where Demeter was worshipped.
6. In Hades, the river of fire.
7. Dis.

Jet upward thro' the midday blossom. No!
For, see, thy foot has touch'd it; all the space
Of blank earth-baldness clothes itself afresh,
And breaks into the crocus-purple hour   50
That saw thee vanish.[8]

                             Child, when thou wert gone,
I envied human wives, and nested birds,
Yea, the cubb'd lioness; went in search of thee
Thro' many a palace, many a cot, and gave
Thy breast[9] to ailing infants in the night,   55
And set the mother waking in a maze
To find her sick one whole; and forth again
Among the wail of midnight winds, and cried,
"Where is my loved one? Wherefore do ye wail?"
And out from all the night an answer shrill'd,   60
"We know not, and we know not why we wail."
I climb'd on all the cliffs of all the seas,
And ask'd the waves that moan about the world,
"Where? do ye make your moaning for my child?"
And round from all the world the voices came,   65
"We know not, and we know not why we moan."
"Where?" and I stared from every eagle-peak,
I thridded[1] the black heart of all the woods,
I peer'd thro' tomb and cave, and in the storms
Of autumn swept across the city, and heard   70
The murmur of their temples chanting me,
Me, me, the desolate mother! "Where?"—and turn'd,
And fled by many a waste, forlorn of man,
And grieved for man thro' all my grief for thee,—
The jungle rooted in his shatter'd hearth,   75
The serpent coil'd about his broken shaft,
The scorpion crawling over naked skulls;—
I saw the tiger in the ruin'd fane
Spring from his fallen God, but trace of thee
I saw not; and far on, and, following out   80
A league of labyrinthine darkness, came
On three gray heads[2] beneath a gleaming rift.
"Where?" and I heard one voice from all the three,
"We know not, for we spin the lives of men,
And not of Gods, and know not why we spin!   85
There is a Fate beyond us." Nothing knew.

---

8. Lines 34–51 seem consciously to echo Milton's simile describing Eden in *Paradise Lost*, Book IV, lines 268 ff:

         Not that faire field
Of *Enna*, where *Proserpin* gathring flours
Her self a fairer Floure by gloomie *Dis*

Was gatherd, which cost *Ceres* all that pain
To seek her through the world . . .
. . . might with this Paradise
Of Eden strive.

9. Demeter's breast, which had suckled Persephone.
1. Threaded.
2. The Fates.

Last as the likeness of a dying man,
Without his knowledge, from him flits to warn
A far-off friendship that he comes no more,
So he, the God of dreams, who heard my cry,   90
Drew from thyself the likeness of thyself
Without thy knowledge, and thy shadow past
Before me, crying, "The Bright one in the highest
Is brother of the Dark one in the lowest,
And Bright and Dark have sworn that I, the child   95
Of thee, the great Earth-Mother, thee, the Power
That lifts her buried life from gloom to bloom,
Should be for ever and for evermore
The Bride of Darkness."

                 So the Shadow wail'd.
Then I, Earth-Goddess, cursed the Gods of heaven.   100
I would not mingle with their feasts; to me
Their nectar smack'd of hemlock on the lips,
Their rich ambrosia tasted aconite.[3]
That man, that only lives and loves an hour,
Seem'd nobler than their hard eternities.   105
My quick tears kill'd the flower, my ravings hush'd
The bird, and lost in utter grief I fail'd
To send my life thro' olive-yard and vine
And golden-grain, my gift to helpless man.
Rain-rotten died the wheat, the barley-spears   110
Were hollow-husk'd, the leaf fell, and the Sun,
Pale at my grief, drew down before his time
Sickening, and Ætna kept her winter snow.

Then He,[4] the brother of this Darkness, He
Who still is highest, glancing from his height   115
On earth a fruitless fallow, when he miss'd
The wonted steam of sacrifice, the praise
And prayer of men, decreed that thou shouldst dwell
For nine white moons of each whole year with me,
Three dark ones in the shadow with thy king.   120

Once more the reaper in the gleam of dawn
Will see me by the landmark far away,
Blessing his field, or seated in the dusk
Of even, by the lonely threshing-floor,
Rejoicing in the harvest and the grange.   125

Yet I, Earth-Goddess, am but ill-content
With them who still are highest. Those gray heads,
What meant they by their "Fate beyond the Fates"
But younger kindlier Gods to bear us down,[5]
As we bore down the Gods before us? Gods,   130

---

3. A deadly poison.   5. Recalls   Aeschylus' *Prometheus*
4. Zeus.   *Bound.*

To quench, not hurl the thunderbolt, to stay,
Not spread the plague, the famine; Gods indeed,
To send the noon into the night and break
The sunless halls of Hades into Heaven?
Till thy dark lord accept and love the Sun,   135
And all the Shadow die into the Light,[6]
When thou shalt dwell the whole bright year with me,
And souls of men, who grew beyond their race,
And made themselves as Gods against the fear
Of Death and Hell; and thou that hast from men,   140
As Queen of Death, that worship which is Fear,
Henceforth, as having risen from out the dead,
Shalt ever send thy life along with mine
From buried grain thro' springing blade, and bless
Their garner'd autumn also, reap with me,
Earth-mother, in the harvest hymns of Earth
The worship which is Love, and see no more
The Stone, the Wheel,[7] the dimly-glimmering lawns
Of that Elysium, all the hateful fires
Of torment, and the shadowy warrior glide   150
Along the silent field of Asphodel.[8]

1887; 1889

The Oak[9]

Live thy Life,
    Young and old,
Like yon oak,
Bright in spring,
    Living gold;   5

Summer-rich
    Then; and then
Autumn-changed,
Soberer-hued
    Gold again.   10

All his leaves
    Fallen at length,
Look, he stands,
Trunk and bough,
    Naked strength.   15

1889

---

6. A line Tennyson cited as reflecting the "modern frame" (*Memoir*, II, 364).
7. The stone of Sisyphus and Ixion's wheel, Greek conceptions of eternal torment.
8. The immortal flowers which covered the Elysian fields.

9. Tennyson liked to think his poem could be called "clean cut like a Greek epigram" (*Memoir*, II, 366), and indeed it does show elements of the best in his late style; spare and sharply focused, there is not a trace of the over-refinement which Douglas Bush has called Tennyson's "besetting sin."

Parnassus[1]

Exegi monumentum . . .
Quod non . . .
Possit diruere . . .
. . . innumerabilis
Annorum series et fuga temporum.
—HORACE

1

What be those crown'd forms high over the sacred fountain?
Bards, that the mighty Muses have raised to the heights of the
mountain,
And over the flight of the Ages! O Goddesses, help me up thither!
Lightning may shrivel the laurel of Cæsar, but mine would not
wither.
Steep is the mountain, but you, will help me to overcome it, 5
And stand with my head in the zenith, and roll my voice from the
summit,
Sounding for ever and ever thro' Earth and her listening nations,
And mixt with the great sphere-music of stars and of constellations.

2

What be those two shapes high over the sacred fountain,
Taller than all the Muses, and huger than all the mountain? 10
On those two known peaks they stand ever spreading and height-
ening;
Poet, that evergreen laurel is blasted by more than lightning!
Look, in their deep double shadow the crown'd ones all disappear-
ing!
Sing like a bird and be happy, nor hope for a deathless hearing!
"Sounding for ever and ever?" pass on! the sight confuses— 15
These are Astronomy and Geology, terrible Muses!

3

If the lips were touch'd with fire from off a pure Pierian[2] altar,
Tho' their music here be mortal need the singer greatly care?
Other songs for other worlds! the fire within him would not falter;
Let the golden Iliad vanish, Homer here is Homer there. 20

1889

Merlin and the Gleam[3]

O young Mariner,
You from the haven
Under the sea-cliff,

1. The epigraph from Horace, *Odes*, III, xxx, 1–5, means: "I have constructed a monument which the passage of uncounted years cannot destroy." As with a late poem of Yeats, one must have read the poet in some depth to appreciate this poem. For most of his mature life, Tennyson had been struggling with the "terrible Muses" of Astronomy and Geology, concepts of infinite space and measureless time which forced upon the sensitive Victorian mind such a difficult revaluation of the human condition.
2. Of Pieria in Thessaly, the reputed home of the Muses.
3. "The 'Gleam,'" Tennyson noted, "signifies in my poem the higher poetic imagination." Although he conceived the poem as a poetic autobiography, he takes some license with chronology.

You that are watching
The gray Magician
With eyes of wonder,
I am Merlin,
And I am dying,
I am Merlin
Who follow the Gleam.

2
Mighty the Wizard
Who found me at sunrise
Sleeping, and woke me
And learn'd me Magic!
Great the Master,
And sweet the Magic,
When over the valley,
In early summers,
Over the mountain,
On human faces,
And all around me,
Moving to melody,[4]
Floated the Gleam.

3
Once at the croak of a Raven[5] who crost it
A barbarous people,
Blind to the magic
And deaf to the melody,
Snarl'd at and cursed me,
A demon vext me,
The light retreated,
The landskip darken'd,
The melody deaden'd,
The Master whisper'd,
"Follow the Gleam."

4
Then to the melody,[6]
Over a wilderness
Gliding, and glancing at
Elf of the woodland,

5

10

15

20

25

30

35

---

4. Perhaps alludes to the poetry of the 1830 and 1832 volumes, much of which was composed from his impressions in and around the Somersby countryside.
5. Hallam says his father meant "the harsh voices of those who were unsympathetic." One thinks first of John Wilson Croker's nasty review in 1833 and next of John Wilson's (Christopher North's) hostile response in 1832. In a not wholly successful effort to reconcile the rest of the poem with the actual course of the poet's career, Sir Charles Tennyson believes the reference is to "the family troubles which followed Dr. Tennyson's death in 1831"

and the several attempts of Tennyson's grandfather "to divert Alfred from his determination to devote himself to poetry" (*Alfred Tennyson*, p. 517 n).
6. According to Sir Charles's assumption about the "Raven," sections 4, 5, and 6 would refer to "the poet's development during the years of closest friendship with Arthur Hallam (1832 and 1833)." More likely, section 4 describes the "romantic" poems of 1842. Section 5 would then refer to the English Idyls first published in 1842, as, it seems to me, the almost inescapable allusions to the rural domestic life pictured in them would demand.

Gnome of the cavern,
Griffin and Giant, 40
And dancing of Fairies
In desolate hollows,
And wraiths of the mountain,
And rolling of dragons
By warble of water, 45
Or cataract music
Of falling torrents,
Flitted the Gleam.

5

Down from the mountain
And over the level, 50
And streaming and shining on
Silent river,
Silvery willow,
Pasture and plowland,
Innocent maidens, 55
Garrulous children,
Homestead and harvest,
Reaper and gleaner,
And rough-ruddy faces
Of lowly labor, 60
Slided the Gleam—

6

Then, with a melody
Stronger and statelier,
Led me at length
To the city and palace 65
Of Arthur the King;[7]
Touch'd at the golden
Cross of the churches,
Flash'd on the tournament,
Flicker'd and bicker'd 70
From helmet to helmet,
And last on the forehead
Of Arthur the blameless
Rested the Gleam.

7[8]

Clouds and darkness 75
Closed upon Camelot;
Arthur had vanish'd
I knew not whither,
The king who loved me,

7. The "Morte d'Arthur" was written between 1833 and 1835, first appearing in the 1842 volumes. Although a violation of the rigid chronological interpretation, Tennyson had, I believe, the whole of *Idylls of the King* in mind. 8. This section obviously looks back to Hallam's death and the composition of the elegies for *In Memoriam* (1833–50; published 1850). The identification of Arthur Hallam with King Arthur strongly suggests that Tennyson did not feel himself constrained to follow a literal sequence of events.

And cannot die; 80
For out of the darkness
Silent and slowly
The Gleam, that had waned to a wintry glimmer
On icy fallow
And faded forest, 85
Drew to the valley
Named of the shadow,
And slowly brightening
Out of the glimmer,
And slowly moving again to a melody 90
Yearningly tender,
Fell on the shadow,
No longer a shadow,
But clothed with the Gleam.

8⁹

And broader and brighter 95
The Gleam flying onward,
Wed to the melody,
Sang thro' the world;
And slower and fainter,
Old and weary, 100
But eager to follow,
I saw, whenever
In passing it glanced upon
Hamlet or city,
That under the Crosses 105
The dead man's garden,
The mortal hillock,
Would break into blossom;
And so to the land's
Last limit I came— 110
And can no longer,
But die rejoicing,
For thro' the Magic
Of Him the Mighty,
Who taught me in childhood, 115
There on the border
Of boundless Ocean,
And all but in Heaven
Hovers the Gleam.

9

Not of the sunlight, 120
Not of the moonlight,
Not of the starlight!
O young Mariner,

9. This and the following section ex- press the poet's final acceptance of death as he comes to terms with the achievements of his literary life. He reasserts a faith and idealism seldom so unequivocally embraced in the late poems.

Down to the haven,
Call your companions,   125
Launch your vessel
And crowd your canvas,
And, ere it vanishes
Over the margin,
After it, follow it,   130
Follow the Gleam.

1889

Far—Far—Away[1]

(FOR MUSIC)

What sight so lured him thro' the fields he knew
As where earth's green stole into heaven's own hue,
          Far—far—away?

What sound was dearest in his native dells?
The mellow lin-lan-lone of evening bells   5
          Far—far—away.

What vague world-whisper, mystic pain or joy,
Thro' those three words would haunt him when a boy,
          Far—far—away?

A whisper from his dawn of life? a breath   10
From some fair dawn beyond the doors of death
          Far—far—away?

Far, far, how far? from o'er the gates of birth,
The faint horizons, all the bounds of earth,
          Far—far—away?   15

What charm in words, a charm no words could give?
O dying words, can Music make you live
          Far—far—away?

1889

By an Evolutionist[2]

The Lord let the house of a brute to the soul of a man,
   And the man said, 'Am I your debtor?'

1. "Before I could read I was in the habit on a stormy day of spreading my arms to the wind and crying out, 'I hear a voice that's speaking in the wind,' and the words 'far, far away' had always a strange charm for me." In 1888, Tennyson was seriously ill; according to his doctor "he had been as near death as a man could be without dying" (*Memoir,* II, 508). Hallam adds to his father's note: "He said that he had wonderful thoughts about God and the Universe, and felt as if looking into the other world." This and the following poem are attempts to express these thoughts.
2. Although nowhere in Tennyson does one find any direct reference to the transmutation of species, he generally accepts the theory that man evolved from some lower form of life. Tennyson reacted strongly, however, against those who, he felt, "exaggerated Darwinism" —i.e., used the hypothesis to deny the existence of God and the immortality of the soul.

And the Lord—'Not yet; but make it as clean as you can,
 And then I will let you a better.'

1

If my body come from brutes, my soul uncertain or a fable, 5
 Why not bask amid the senses while the sun of morning shines,
I, the finer brute rejoicing in my hounds, and in my stable,
 Youth and health, and birth and wealth, and choice of women
  and of wines?[3]

2

What hast thou done for me, grim Old Age, save breaking my
  bones on the rack?
 Would I had past in the morning that looks so bright from
  afar! 10

Old Age

Done for thee? starved the wild beast that was linkt with thee eighty
  years back.
 Less weight now for the ladder-of-heaven that hangs on a star.

I

If my body come from brutes, tho' somewhat finer than their own,
 I am heir, and this my kingdom. Shall the royal voice be mute?
No, but if the rebel subject seek to drag me from the throne, 15
 Hold the sceptre, Human Soul, and rule thy province of the brute.

II

I have climb'd to the snows of Age, and I gaze at a field in the Past,
 Where I sank with the body at times in the sloughs of a low
  desire,
But I hear no yelp of the beast, and the Man is quiet at last,
 As he stands on the heights of his life with a glimpse of a height
  that is higher. 20

1889

To Ulysses[4]

1

 Ulysses, much-experienced man,
  Whose eyes have known this globe of ours,
  Her tribes of men, and trees, and flowers,
 From Corrientes[5] to Japan,

2

 To you that bask below the Line, 5
  I soaking here in winter wet—
  The century's three strong eights have met
 To drag me down to seventy-nine

---

3. Compare *In Memoriam,* 35 and 118.
4. Addressed to W. G. Palgrave, whose varied career as soldier, Jesuit priest, missionary, and diplomat justifies his identification with Ulysses. "*Ulysses* was the title of a volume of Palgrave's essays. He died at Monte Video before seeing my poem." (Notes in quotation marks are Tennyson's.)
5. Capital of an Argentine province of the same name.

3

In summer if I reach my day—
    To you, yet young, who breathe the balm   10
    Of summer-winters by the palm
And orange grove of Paraguay,

4

I, tolerant of the colder time,
    Who love the winter woods, to trace
    On paler heavens the branching grace   15
Of leafless elm, or naked lime,

5

And see my cedar green, and there
    My giant ilex[6] keeping leaf
    When frost is keen and days are brief—
Or marvel how in English air   20

6

My yucca, which no winter quells,
    Altho' the months have scarce begun,
    Has push'd toward our faintest sun
A spike of half-accomplish'd bells—

7

Or watch the waving pine which here   25
    The warrior[7] of Caprera set,
    A name that earth will not forget
Till earth has roll'd her latest year—

8

I, once half-crazed for larger light
    On broader zones beyond the foam,   30
    But chaining fancy now at home
Among the quarried downs of Wight,

9

Not less would yield full thanks to you
    For your rich gift, your tale of lands
    I know not,[8] your Arabian sands;   35
Your cane, your palm, tree-fern, bamboo,

10

The wealth of tropic bower and brake;
    Your Oriental Eden-isles,[9]
    Where man, nor only Nature smiles;
Your wonder of the boiling lake;[1]   40

11

Phra-Chai, the Shadow of the Best,[2]
    Phra-bat[3] the step; your Pontic coast;

6. An evergreen oak.
7. Garibaldi, the Italian patriot, who visited Tennyson at Farringford in 1864 and planted the "waving pine." See *Memoir*, II, 1–4. "Garibaldi said to me, alluding to his barren island, 'I wish I had your trees.' "
8. "The Tale of Nejd." Palgrave published his *Narrative of a Year's Journey through Central and Eastern Arabia* in 1865.

9. "The Philippines."
1. "In Dominica."
2. "The Shadow of the Lord. Certain obscure markings on a rock in Siam, which express the image of Buddha to the Buddhist more or less distinctly according to his faith and his moral worth."
3. "The footstep of the Lord on another rock."

Crag-cloister[4]; Anatolian Ghost;[5]
Hong-Kong,[6] Karnac,[7] and all the rest;

1 2

Thro' which I follow'd line by line   45
    Your leading hand, and came, my friend,
    To prize your various book, and send
A gift of slenderer value, mine.

1889

To One Who Ran Down the English

You make our faults too gross, and thence maintain
Our darker future. May your fears be vain!
At times the small black fly upon the pane
May seem the black ox of the distant plain.[8]

1889

To Mary Boyle[9]

WITH THE FOLLOWING POEM

1

'Spring-flowers'! While you still delay to take
    Your leave of town,
Our elm-tree's ruddy-hearted blossom-flake
    Is fluttering down.

2

Be truer to your promise. There! I heard   5
    Our cuckoo call.
Be needle to the magnet of your word,
    Nor wait, till all

3

Our vernal bloom from every vale and plain
    And garden pass,   10
And all the gold from each laburnum chain
    Drop to the grass.

4

Is memory with your Marian gone to rest,
    Dead with the dead?
For ere she left us, when we met, you prest   15
    My hand, and said

4. "The monastery of Sumelas."
5. "Anatolian spectre stories."
6. "The three cities."
7. "Travels in Egypt."
8. Compare "Epilogue" to *Idylls of the King,* line 63.

9. Tennyson first met Mary Boyle, the aunt of Hallam Tennyson's wife, in 1882 (see *Memoir,* II, 294) and dedicated to her "The Progress of Spring," a rediscovered piece written in the thirties. See p. 87.

5

'I come with your spring-flowers.' You came not, friend;
      My birds would sing,
You heard not. Take then this spring-flower I send,
      This song of spring,   20

6

Found yesterday—forgotten mine own rhyme
      By mine old self,
As I shall be forgotten by old Time,
      Laid on the shelf—

7

A rhyme that flower'd betwixt the whitening sloe   25
      And kingcup blaze,
And more than half a hundred years ago,
      In rick-fire days,[1]

8

When Dives loathed the times, and paced his land
      In fear of worse,   30
And sanguine Lazarus felt a vacant hand
      Fill with *his* purse.[2]

9

For lowly minds were madden'd to the height
      By tonguester tricks,
And once—I well remember that red night   35
      When thirty ricks,

10

All flaming, made an English homestead hell—
      These hands of mine
Have helpt to pass a bucket from the well
      Along the line,   40

11

When this bare dome had not begun to gleam
      Thro' youthful curls,
And you were then a lover's fairy dream,
      His girl of girls;

12

And you, that now are lonely, and with Grief   45
      Sit face to face,
Might find a flickering glimmer of relief
      In change of place.

13

What use to brood? This life of mingled pains
      And joys to me,   50
Despite of every Faith and Creed, remains
      The Mystery.

1. The early 1830's, when farmers burned their haystacks and sometimes their barns in protest against their landlords.

2. For the parable of the rich man (Dives) and Lazarus see *Luke*, 16:19–31.

14

Let golden youth bewail the friend, the wife,
  For ever gone.
He dreams of that long walk thro' desert life   55
  Without the one.

15

The silver year should cease to mourn and sigh—
  Not long to wait—
So close are we, dear Mary, you and I
  To that dim gate.   60

16

Take, read! and be the faults your Poet makes
  Or many or few,
He rests content, if his young music wakes
  A wish in you

17

To change our dark Queen-city, all her realm   65
  Of sound and smoke,
For his clear heaven, and these few lanes of elm
  And whispering oak.

1889

Beautiful City

Beautiful city,[3] the centre and crater of European confusion,
O you with your passionate shriek for the rights of an equal
  humanity,
How often your Re-volution has proven but E-volution
Roll'd again back on itself in the tides of a civic insanity!
1889

June Bracken and Heather

TO ———[4]

There on the top of the down,
The wild heather round me and over me June's high blue,
When I look'd at the bracken so bright and the heather so brown,
I thought to myself I would offer this book to you,
This, and my love together,   5
To you that are seventy-seven,
With a faith as clear as the heights of the June-blue heaven,

3. A heavy-handed ironic attack on Paris, in keeping with the poet's worst efforts in his lifelong, obsessive hostility toward the French.

4. Addressed to Tennyson's wife Emily and serving as the dedication to her of his last volume of poems.

And a fancy as summer-new
As the green of the bracken amid the gloom of the heather.

1892

The Death of Œnone[5]

Œnone sat within the cave from out
Whose ivy-matted mouth she used to gaze
Down at the Troad;[6] but the goodly view
Was now one blank, and all the serpent vines
Which on the touch of heavenly feet had risen,   5
And gliding thro' the branches overbower'd
The naked Three,[7] were wither'd long ago,
And thro' the sunless winter morning-mist
In silence wept upon the flowerless earth.
   And while she stared at those dead cords that ran   10
Dark thro' the mist, and linking tree to tree,
But once were gayer than a dawning sky
With many a pendent bell and fragrant star,
Her Past became her Present, and she saw
Him, climbing toward her with the golden fruit,   15
Him, happy to be chosen Judge of Gods,
Her husband in the flush of youth and dawn,
Paris, himself as beauteous as a God.
   Anon from out the long ravine below,
She heard a wailing cry, that seem'd at first   20
Thin as the batlike shrillings of the Dead
When driven to Hades, but, in coming near,
Across the downward thunder of the brook
Sounded "Œnone"; and on a sudden he,
Paris, no longer beauteous as a God,   25
Struck by a poison'd arrow in the fight,
Lame, crooked, reeling, livid, thro' the mist
Rose, like the wraith of his dead self, and moan'd:
   "Œnone, *my* Œnone, while we dwelt
Together in this valley—happy then—   30
Too happy had I died within thine arms,
Before the feud of Gods had marr'd our peace,
And sunder'd each from each. I am dying now
Pierced by a poison'd dart. Save me. Thou knowest,
Taught by some God, whatever herb or balm   35
May clear the blood from poison, and thy fame

---

5. A sequel to "Œnone" (see p. 20), the poem dramatizes Œnone's revenge against Paris for his desertion of her for Helen years earlier. Wounded by Philoctetes' poisoned arrow, he must seek out Œnone, who alone has the power to heal him. Tennyson said of his poem that "he considered it even more strictly classical in form and language than the old 'Œnone'" (*Memoir*, II, 386).
6. The district of Troy.
7. Hera, Athene, and Aphrodite. See "Œnone," lines 92 ff.

Is blown thro' all the Troad, and to thee
The shepherd brings his adder-bitten lamb,
The wounded warrior climbs from Troy to thee.
My life and death are in thy hand. The Gods   40
Avenge on stony hearts a fruitless prayer
For pity. Let me owe my life to thee.
I wrought thee bitter wrong, but thou forgive,
Forget it. Man is but the slave of Fate.
Œnone, by thy love which once was mine,   45
Help, heal me. I am poison'd to the heart."
"And I to mine," she said. "Adulterer,
Go back to thine adulteress and die!"

    He groan'd, he turn'd, and in the mist at once
Became a shadow, sank and disappear'd,   50
But, ere the mountain rolls into the plain,
Fell headlong dead; and of the shepherds one
Their oldest, and the same who first had found
Paris, a naked babe, among the woods
Of Ida, following lighted on him there,   55
And shouted, and the shepherds heard and came.

    One raised the Prince, one sleek'd the squalid hair,
One kiss'd his hand, another closed his eyes,
And then, remembering the gay playmate rear'd
Among them, and forgetful of the man,   60
Whose crime had half unpeopled Ilion, these
All that day long labour'd, hewing the pines,
And built their shepherd-prince a funeral pile;
And, while the star of eve was drawing light
From the dead sun, kindled the pyre, and all   65
Stood round it, hush'd, or calling on his name.

    But when the white fog vanish'd like a ghost
Before the day, and every topmost pine
Spired into bluest heaven, still in her cave,
Amazed, and ever seeming stared upon   70
By ghastlier than the Gorgon[8] head, a face,—
His face deform'd by lurid blotch and blain—
There, like a creature frozen to the heart
Beyond all hope of warmth, Œnone sat
Not moving, till in front of that ravine   75
Which drowsed in gloom, self-darken'd from the west,
The sunset blazed along the wall of Troy.

    Then her head sank, she slept, and thro' her dream
A ghostly murmur floated, "Come to me,
Œnone! I can wrong thee now no more,   80
Œnone, my Œnone," and the dream
Wail'd in her, when she woke beneath the stars.

---

8. Her hideous face turned to stone anyone who gazed upon it.

What star could burn so low? not Ilion yet.
What light was there? She rose and slowly down,
By the long torrent's ever-deepen'd roar,   85
Paced, following, as in a trance, the silent cry.
She waked a bird of prey that scream'd and past;
She roused a snake that hissing writhed away;
A panther sprang across her path, she heard
The shriek of some lost life among the pines,   90
But when she gain'd the broader vale, and saw
The ring of faces redden'd by the flames
Enfolding the dark body which had lain
Of old in her embrace, paused—and then ask'd
Falteringly, "Who lies on yonder pyre?"   95
But every man was mute for reverence.
Then moving quickly forward till the heat
Smote on her brow, she lifted up a voice
Of shrill command, "Who burns upon the pyre?"
Whereon their oldest and their boldest said,   100
"He, whom thou wouldst not heal!" and all at once
The morning light of happy marriage broke
Thro' all the clouded years of widowhood,
And muffling up her comely head, and crying
"Husband!" she leapt upon the funeral pile,   105
And mixt herself with *him* and past in fire.

1892

Poets and Critics

This thing, that thing is the rage,
Helter-skelter runs the age;
Minds on this round earth of ours
Vary like the leaves and flowers,
   Fashion'd after certain laws;   5
Sing thou low or loud or sweet,
All at all points thou canst not meet,
   Some will pass and some will pause.

What is true at last will tell:
Few at first will place thee well;   10
Some too low would have thee shine,
Some too high—no fault of thine—
   Hold thine own, and work thy will!
Year will graze the heel of year,
But seldom comes the poet here,   15
   And the Critic's rarer still.

1892

The Dawn[9]

1
Red of the Dawn!
Screams of a babe in the red-hot palms of a Moloch[1] of Tyre,
    Man with his brotherless dinner on man in the tropical wood,
    Priests in the name of the Lord passing souls thro' fire to the fire,
Head-hunters and boats of Dahomey[2] that float upon human
        blood!   5

2
Red of the Dawn!
Godless fury of peoples, and Christless frolic of kings,
    And the bolt of war dashing down upon cities and blazing farms,
    For Babylon was a child new-born, and Rome was a babe in arms,
And London and Paris and all the rest are as yet but in leading-
        strings.   10

3
Dawn not Day,
While scandal is mouthing a bloodless name at *her* cannibal feast,
    And rake-ruin'd bodies and souls go down in a common wreck,
    And the Press of a thousand cities is prized for it smells of the
        beast,
Or easily violates virgin Truth for a coin or a cheque.   15

4
Dawn not Day!
Is it Shame, so few should have climb'd from the dens in the level
        below,
    Men, with a heart and a soul, no slaves of a four-footed will?
    But if twenty million of summers are stored in the sunlight still,
We are far from the noon of man, there is time for the race to
        grow.   20

5
Red of the Dawn!
Is it turning a fainter red? so be it, but when shall we lay
    The Ghost of the Brute that is walking and haunting us yet, and
        be free?
    In a hundred, a thousand winters? Ah, what will *our* children be,
The men of a hundred thousand, a million summers away?   25

1892

9. This and the following two poems fairly represent Tennyson's thoughts at the end of his life on the future of the human race. Resigned, insofar as possible, to the implications of geological time and the all but limitless space of the new astronomy, he clings with guarded optimism to the hope that man may eventually resolve his human problems.

1. A Canaanite idol to whom children, especially the first-born, were sacrificed as burnt offerings.

2. A West African territory notorious for persisting in human sacrifice.

The Making of Man

Where is one that, born of woman, altogether can escape
From the lower world within him, moods of tiger, or of ape?
   Man as yet is being made, and ere the crowning Age of ages,
Shall not æon after æon pass and touch him into shape?

All about him shadow still, but, while the races flower and fade,   5
Prophet-eyes may catch a glory slowly gaining on the shade,
   Till the peoples all are one, and all their voices blend in choric
Hallelujah to the Maker 'It is finish'd. Man is made.'

1892

God and the Universe

1

Will my tiny spark of being wholly vanish in your deeps and
      heights?
Must my day be dark by reason, O ye Heavens, of your boundless
      nights,
Rush of Suns, and roll of systems, and your fiery clash of meteorites?

2

'Spirit, nearing yon dark portal at the limit of thy human state,
Fear not thou the hidden purpose of that Power which alone is
      great,   5
Not the myriad world, His shadow, nor the silent Opener of the
      Gate.'

1892

The Silent Voices[3]

    When the dumb Hour, clothed in black,
    Brings the Dreams about my bed,
    Call me not so often back,
    Silent Voices of the dead,
    Toward the lowland ways behind me,   5
    And the sunlight that is gone!
    Call me rather, silent voices,
    Forward to the starry track
    Glimmering up the heights beyond me
    On, and always on!   10

1892

---

3. Set to music by Tennyson's wife, this and "Crossing the Bar" were the two anthems sung at the poet's funeral in Westminster Abbey. See *Memoir,* II, 430.

Crossing the Bar[4]

Sunset and evening star,
    And one clear call for me!
And may there be no moaning of the bar,
    When I put out to sea,

But such a tide as moving seems asleep,   5
    Too full for sound and foam,
When that which drew from out the boundless deep
    Turns again home.

Twilight and evening bell,
    And after that the dark!   10
And may there be no sadness of farewell,
    When I embark;

For tho' from out our bourne[5] of Time and Place
    The flood may bear me far,
I hope to see my Pilot face to face   15
    When I have crost the bar.

1889

4. Written after a serious illness while crossing the Solent from Aldworth to Farringford on the Isle of Wight, the poem, Tennyson said, "came in a moment." In answer to the questions about the Pilot's presence, why he should remain on board when the ship reaches open sea or why the speaker only sees him then, Tennyson explained: "The Pilot has been on board all the while, but in the dark I have not seen him." He is, he said, "that Divine and Unseen Who is always guiding us" (*Memoir,* II, 367). A few days before he died, Tennyson instructed his son to "put 'Crossing the Bar' at the end of all editions of my poems"—a request all editors have honored.

5. Boundary.

Juvenilia and
Early Responses

(1820 – 1835)

Juvenilia

FROM *UNPUBLISHED EARLY POEMS* (1931)
AND *THE DEVIL AND THE LADY* (1930)

Translation from Claudian's "Proserpine"[1]

The gloomy chariot of the God of night,
And the wan stars that sicken'd at the sight,
And the dark nuptials of th' infernal King,[2]
With senses rapt in holy thought, I sing.
Away! away! profane ones! ye whose days   5
Are spent in endless sin and error's maze,
Seraphic transports through my bosom roll,
All Phoebus[3] fills my heart and fires my soul.
Lo! the shrines tremble and a heavenly light
Streams from their vaulted roofs serenely bright,   10
The God! the God, appears! the yawning ground
Moans at the view, the temples quake around,
And high in air the Eleusinians[4] raise
The sacred torch with undulating blaze;
Hiss the green snakes to sacred rapture giv'n   15
And meekly lift their scaly necks to heav'n,
With easy lapse they win their gentle way
And rear their rosy crests and listen to my lay.
See! see! where triform Hecate[5] dimly stands,
And mild Iacchus[6] leads the tuneful bands!   20
Immortal glories round his temples shine,
And flow'ring ivy wreaths his brows entwine;
From Parthia's[7] land he clasps beneath his chin
The speckled honours of the tiger's skin;
A vine-clad thyrsus with celestial grace   25
Sustains his reeling feet and props his falling pace.
Ye mighty demons, whose tremendous sway

1. Tennyson's earliest extant poem, perhaps written when he was eleven. Although a translation of the first 93 lines of Claudian's "De Raptu Proserpinae," it contains a number of original lines and phrases. Of his debt to Pope, Tennyson later said, at "about ten or eleven Pope's *Homer's Iliad* became a favourite of mine and I wrote hundreds and hundreds of lines in the regular Popeian metre" (*Memoir,* I, 11).
2. Pluto, who carried Proserpine off to the underworld while she was gathering flowers in Sicily.
3. Apollo, the sun god; also god of music and poets, invoked to illuminate the speaker's vision of the underworld.
4. Those practicing the Eleusinian mysteries, in ancient Greece the secret rites celebrated every spring at Eleusis in honor of Demeter and Persephone.
5. Patroness of witches and magicians.
6. Dionysus, god of fertility and wine.
7. An ancient kingdom southeast of the Caspian Sea.

The shadowy tribes of airy ghosts obey,
To whose insatiate portion ever fall
All things that perish on this earthly ball, 30
Whom livid Styx with lurid torrent bounds
And fiery Phlegethon for aye surrounds,
Dark, deep and whirling round his flaming caves
The braying vortex of his breathless waves,
Eternal spirits! to your bard explain 35
The dread Arcana[8] of the Stygian reign,
How that stern Deity, Infernal Jove,
First felt the power, and own'd the force of love;
How Hell's fair Empress first was snatch'd away
From Earth's bright regions, and the face of day; 40
How anxious Ceres[9] wander'd far and near
Now torn by grief and tortur'd now by fear,
Whence laws to man are giv'n, and acorns yield
To the rich produce of the golden field.
Hell's haughty Lord in times of old began 45
To rouse 'gainst Heav'n the terrors of his clan;
Stern fury shook his soul—that he alone
Of every God upon his glitt'ring throne,
Should lead a dull and melancholy life,
Without the fond endearments of a wife— 50
Wretch that he was, who knew not how to claim
A consort's or a father's dearer name!
Now Hell's misshapen monsters rush to arms
And fill the wide abyss with loud alarms;
The haggard train of midnight Furies meet 55
To shake the Thunderer from his starry seat,
And pale Tisiphone,[1] with baleful breath
Calls the thin Ghosts within the Camp of Death;
High in her hand amid the shades of night
The gleaming pine shoots forth a dismal light, 60
Around her head the snaky volumes rise
And dart their tongues of flame and roll their gory eyes.
Now had all nature gone to wrack again
And Earth's fell offspring burst their brazen chain,
And from the deep recesses where they lay 65
Uprisen in wrath to view the beam of day,
Now had the fierce Aegaeon[2] thrown aside
The adamantine limits of his pride,
Uprear'd his hundred-handed form on high
And dar'd the forkéd terrors of the sky; 70
But the dire Parcae[3] with a piercing yell

8. Secrets or mysteries beyond the perception of ordinary men.
9. Mother of Proserpine and Roman goddess of agriculture equivalent to Greek Demeter (see note 4 above). In search of her lost daughter, Ceres vainly roamed the earth at last appealing to Zeus, who decreed that Proserpine should be Queen of Hades for three months of the year and live the other nine months on earth.
1. One of the three Furies.
2. A giant son of Uranus by Gaea.
3. Latin name for the three Fates.

Before the throne of gloomy Pluto fell,
Around his knees their suppliant hands were thrown,
Those awful hands which make the world their own,
Whose dreadful power the shades of Hades fear   75
And men on earth, and Gods in Heav'n revere,
Which mark the lot of fate's unerring page
And ply their iron tasks through every age.
First Lachesis[4] began (while all around
Hell's hollow caverns shudder'd at the sound),   80
"Dark Power of night and God of Hell, for whom
We draw the fated threads of human doom,
Thou end and origin of all on earth,
Redeeming death below by human birth!
Thou Lord of life and dissolution! King   85
Of all that live! (for first from thee they spring
And to thee they return, and in thy reign
Take other shapes and seek the world again)
Break not, ah! break not with unholy deed
That peace our laws have fix'd, our threats decreed.   90
Oh, wake not thou the trumpet's impious swell
Nor raise thy standard in the gulph of Hell
Nor rouse the Titans[5] from their dread abode,
The hideous Titans, foes to man and God.
Jove,—Jove himself shall grant thine ardent wish   95
And some fond wife shall crown thy nuptial bliss."
She spake—the God was struck with sudden shame
And his wild fury lost its former flame.
So when with whirlwinds in his icy train
Stern Boreas[6] sweeps along the sounding plain,   100
Bright o'er his wings the glittering frost is spread
And deathless winters crown his hoary head,
Then bow the groves, the woods his breath obey,
The heaving Ocean tosses either way.
But lo! if chance on far Aeolia's shores   105
The God of winds[7] should close his brazen doors,
With sudden pause the jarring tumults cease,
And Earth, Air, Ocean, find one common peace.
Then Maia's[8] son he calls, in haste to bear
His fix'd commands through all the deep of air;   110
Prompt at the word Cyllenius is at hand
Adorn'd with pinion'd brow and magic wand.
Himself the God of terrors, rear'd on high,
Sits thron'd in shades of midnight majesty,
Dim wreaths of mist his mighty sceptre shroud,   115
He veils his horrors in a viewless cloud.

4. The Fate who measured the length of the thread of life. Atropos cut the thread, Clotho spun it.
5. The giant gods who warred against Zeus and were thrown into Hades.
6. God of the north wind.
7. Aeolus, who confined the winds in a cave in the Aeolian Islands.
8. Mother of Hermes, Cyllenius of line 111, the messenger of the gods.

Then thus in haughty tone the God began
(Through Hell's wide halls the echoing accents ran,
The bellowing beast[9] that guards the gates of Hell
Repress'd the thunder of his triple yell,   120
And sad Cocytus[1] at the sudden cry
Recall'd his wailing stream of misery.
From Acheron's banks no sullen murmurs spread,
His hoarse waves slumbered on his noiseless bed,
'Gan Phlegethon in surly haste retire   125
And still his whirling waves and check his flood of fire),
"Grandson of Atlas, thou whose footsteps stray
Through Hell's deep shadows, and the realms of day,
To whom alone of all the Gods 'tis giv'n
To tread the shores of Styx and halls of Heav'n,   130
Chain of each world and link of either sphere,
Whom Tegea's[2] sons in silent awe revere,
Go, cleave the winds and bear my will to Jove,
That haughty God who sways the realms above. . . .

1820–23; 1931

From The Devil and the Lady[3]

From Act 1, Scene 4

AMORET   Go thy ways![4]
Thou yellowest leaf on Autumn's wither'd tree!
Thou sickliest ear of all the sheaf! thou clod!
Thou fireless mixture of Earth's coldest clay!
Thou crazy dotard, crusted o'er with age[5]   5
As thick as ice upon a standing pool!
Thou shrunken, sapless, wizen Grasshopper,[6]
Consuming the green promise of my youth!
Go, get thee gone, and evil winds attend thee,
Thou antidote to love! thou bane of Hope,   10

9. Cerberus, the three-headed dog guarding the entrance to the underworld.
1. Cocytus, Acheron, Phlegethon, Styx are rivers of Hades.
2. A city of Arcadia founded by Tegeus and noted for the exceptional bravery of its inhabitants.
3. This curious "Elizabethan" comedy in blank verse, strongly influenced by extensive reading in Shakespeare, Beaumont and Fletcher, and perhaps Ben Jonson, is the longest and most carefully written work of the juvenilia. An incredible achievement for a boy fourteen years old, the unfinished play is about an aged necromancer called Magus who leaves his young and wanton bride Amoret in the care of the Devil, conjured from the underworld. The Devil summarily sends Amoret off to bed and, disguised in her clothes, meets the inevitable troop of suitors who appear during the husband's absence. The play ends abruptly in the third scene of Act 3, when Magus returns, and one can only guess how the poet intended to finish it.
4. The magician has departed on some mysterious journey, and in this soliloquy Amoret reveals her true feelings, the nature but hardly the intensity of which Magus had suspected.
5. Magus is in his eighties and Amoret is just twenty, one of several interesting parallels to Merlin and Vivien in *Idylls of the King*.
6. Tithonus, to whom Jupiter granted immortality but not eternal youth, withered away and was turned into a cicada. See Tennyson's "Tithonus."

Which like the float o' th' fisher's rod buoys up
The sinking line and by its fluctuations
Shows when the pang of Disappointment gnaws
Beneath it! But to me are both unknown:
I never more can hope and therefore never   15
Can suffer Disappointment.
He bears a charmed life and will outlast me
In mustiness of dry longevity,
Like some tough mummy wither'd, not decay'd—
His years are countless as the dusty race   20
That people an old Cheese and flourish only
In the unsoundest parts on't.
The big waves shatter thy frail skiff! the winds
Sing anything but lullabies unto thee!
The dark-hair'd Midnight grant no ray to thee,   25
But that of lightning, or the dreadful splendour
Of the conflicting wave! the red bolt scathe thee!
Why was I link'd with such a frowzy mate,
With such a fusty partner of my days?

From Act 2, Scene 1[7]

[MAGUS's *cottage with the wood and lake in the distance.
      Enter* DEVIL *and takes his station before the cot-
      tage door attired in a cap and gown.*]

DEVIL   The starry fires of yon Chrystalline vault
      Are waning,[8] and the airy-footed Night
      Will soon withdraw the dismal solitude
      Of her capacious pall, wherewith she clouds
      Yon mighty and illimitable sky,   5
      Placing a death-like colour in all things,
      Monopolizing all the varied Earth
      With her dim mantle—

                                          [A *pause*
                  Oh! ye eyes of Heaven,
      Ye glorious inextinguishable lights,
      High blazing mid the lone solemnity   10
      Of night and silence, shall the poor worm, Man,
      The creature of this solitary earth,
      Presume to think his destiny enroll'd
      In your almighty everlasting fires?
      Shall this poor thing of melancholy clay,   15
      This lone ephemeris of one small hour,
      Proudly suppose his little fate inscribed

---

7. Here, as elsewhere in the play, the Devil becomes the young Tennyson's mouthpiece as he speculates upon the nature of human existence and the illusory qualities of the visible universe. The passage is especially important be-

cause many of the questions foreshadow the concerns of the late poetry.
8. The time, as established at the end of Act 1, is "half after midnight" and not, as one might suspect, before dawn.

In the magnificent stars? What have the worlds
Of yon o'er arching Heav'n—the ample spheres
Of never-ending space, to do with Man?[9]   20
And some romantick visionaries have deem'd
This petty clod the centre of all worlds.
Nay—even the Sun himself, the gorgeous Sun,
Pays homage to it. Ha! Ha! Ha! Poor Man,
Thou summer midge![1]—Oh, ye shine bravely now   25
Through the deep purple of the summer sky,
I know that ye are Earths as fair and fairer
And mightier than this I tread upon—
For I have scaled your mountains, to whose cones
Of most insuperable altitude   30
This Earth's most glorious Eminences and heights
All pil'd and heap'd upon each other's brows,
And massed and kneaded to one common substance,
Were but a molehill.
And I have swum your boundless seas, whose waves   35
Were each an ocean of this little orb,
Yet know I not your natures, or if that
Which we call palpable and visible
Is condensation of firm particles.
O suns and spheres and stars and belts and systems,[2]   40
Are ye or are ye not?
Are ye realities or semblances
Of that which men call real?
Are ye true substance? are ye anything
Except delusive shows and physical points   45
Endow'd with some repulsive potency?
Could the Omnipotent fill all space, if ye
Or the least atom in ye or the least
Division of that atom (if least can dwell
In infinite divisibility) should be impenetrable?   50
I have some doubt if ye exist when none
Are by to view ye; if your Being alone
Be in the mind and the intelligence
Of the created? should some great decree
Annihilate the sentient principle   55

9. A question at the center of several sections of *In Memoriam* and of such late pieces as "Despair" and "Vastness."
1. Two manuscript versions of the play exist. The earlier version contained in notebook #1 in the Harvard collection ends with "midge," and what follows, perhaps added one or two years later, is from the so-called Trinity Manuscript from which Sir Charles Tennyson had the play printed.
2. Lines 40–57 anticipate some of Tennyson's later metaphysical speculations. "There are moments when the flesh is

nothing to me," he said in 1869, "when I feel and know the flesh to be the vision, God and the Spiritual the only real and true. Depend upon it, the Spiritual *is* the real" (*Memoir*, II, 90). Frederick Locker-Lampson reported that in the same year Tennyson told him in a discussion about the Materialists, "I think it [matter] is merely the shadow of something greater than itself, and which we poor shortsighted creatures cannot see" (*Memoir*, II, 69). For similar views expressed in poetry see, for example, King Arthur's speech in "The Holy Grail," lines 906–915.

Would ye or would ye not be non-existent?
'Tis a shrewd doubt—

From Act 3, Scene 2[3]

MAGUS Half the powers o' th' other world
Were leagued against my journeying: but had not
The irresistible and lawless might
Of brazen-handed fix'd Fatality[4]
Oppos'd me, I had done it. The black storm,   5
From out whose mass of volum'd vapour sprang
The lively curling thunderbolt had ceas'd
Long ere from out the dewy depth of Pines
Emerging on the hollow'd banks, that bound
The leapings of the saucy tide, I stood—   10
The mighty waste of moaning waters lay
So goldenly in moonlight, whose clear lamp
With its long line of vibratory lustre
Trembled on the dun surface, that my Spirit
Was buoyant with rejoicings. Each hoar wave   15
With crisped undulation arching rose,
Thence falling in white ridge with sinuous slope
Dash'd headlong to the shore and spread along
The sands its tender fringe of creamy spray.[5]
Thereat my shallop lightly I unbound,   20
Spread my white sail and rode exulting on
The placid murmurings of each feathery wave
That hurried into sparkles round the cleaving
Of my dark Prow; but scarcely had I past
The third white line of breakers when a squall   25
Fell on me from the North, an inky Congress
O' the Republican clouds unto the zenith
Rush'd from th' horizon upwards with the speed
Of their own thunder-bolts.
The seas divided and dim Phantasies   30
Came thronging thickly round me, with hot eyes
Unutterable things came flitting by me;
Semblance of palpability was in them,
Albeit the wavering lightnings glitter'd thro'
Their shadow'd immaterialities.   35
Black shapes clung to my boat; a sullen owl[6]

3. Magus is back home outside his cottage, now filled with the suitors. He is explaining to the Devil the reasons for his untimely return. "The powers o' th' other world" are apparently from Heaven, though the spirits Magus describes as having thwarted his passage seem hardly to have come from there.
4. Like Milton's Satan after his defeat in Heaven, Magus ascribes the cause of his failure to Fate not God—a compari-son Tennyson may have had in mind. The influence of *Paradise Lost* is clearly evident throughout this passage, which draws upon Milton's description of Satan's journey through Chaos to Eden.
5. Tennyson, one of the great landscape painters in verse, shows in these five lines the precise visual detail and care-ful choice of adjectives which will char-acterize his mature art.
6. Here a bird of ill omen.

Perch'd on the Prow, and overhead the hum
As of infernal Spirits in mid Heaven
Holding aerial council caught mine ear.
Then came a band of melancholy sprites,   40
White as their shrouds and motionlessly pale
Like some young Ashwood when the argent[7] Moon
Looks in upon its many silver stems.
And thrice my name was syllabled i' th' air
And thrice upon the wave, like that loud voice   45
Which thro' the deep dark night i' th' olden time
Came sounding o'er the lone Ionian.
Thereat I girded round my loins the scarf
Thy Mother Hecate gave me and withstood
The violent tempest: the insulting surge   50
Rode over me in glassy arch but dar'd not
Sprinkle one drop of its nefarious spray
Upon my charméd person: the red heralds
O' th' heavy footed thunder glanc'd beside me,
Kiss'd my bar'd front and curl'd around my brow   55
In lambent wreaths of circling fire, but could not
Singe one loose lock of vagrant grey, that floated
To the wind's dalliance. But nor magic spells
Vigour of heart or vigilance of hand,
Could back the Ocean's spumy menacings,   60
Which drove my leaky skiff upon the sands.
Soon as I touch'd firm Earth, each mounting billow
Fell laxly back into its windless bed,
And all the moon-lit Ocean slumber'd still.
Thrice with bold prow I breasted the rough spume   65
But thrice a vitreous wall of waves up sprung
Ridging the level sea—so far'd it with me
Foil'd of my purpose. Some unwholesome star,
Some spells of darker Gramarie[8] than mine,
Rul'd the dim night and would not grant me passage.   70

*   *   *

MAGUS[9]   'Tis even thus—
And they[1] would pluck from th' casket the sole gem
Of mine affections, taint its innocent lustre,
And give it back dishonour'd, they would canker
My brightest flower, would muddy the clear source   5
Whence flows my only stream of early bliss;
Would let the foul consuming worm into
The garner of my love. O Earthliness!
Man clambers over the high battlements

---

7. Silver.
8. Magic.
9. The Devil has told Magus about the situation at the cottage, and the magician is left alone to speculate on sex and morality. These lines also appear

only in the Trinity Manuscript, were therefore probably written when Tennyson was 15 or 16, and chiefly reflect the poet's views, not the character's.
1. The suitors, the gem being Amoret.

That part the principalities of good 10
And ill—perchance a few hot tears, and then
The sear'd heart yields to 't and Crime's signet stamps
Her burning image there. The summer fly
That skims the surface of the deep black pool
Knows not the gulf beneath its slippery path. 15
Man sees,[2] but plunges madly into it.
We follow thro' a night of crime and care
The voice of soft Temptation, still it calls,
And still we follow onwards, till we find
She is a Phantom and—we follow still. 20
When couched in Boyhood's passionless tranquillity,
The natural mind of man is warm and yielding,
Fit to receive the best impressions,
But raise it to the atmosphere of manhood
And the rude breath of dissipation 25
Will harden it to stone. 'Tis like the seaplant
Which in its parent and unshaken depths
Is mouldable as clay, but when rude hands
Have pluck'd it from its billowless Abyss
Unto the breathings of Heaven's airs, each gust 30
Which blows upon 't will fix it into hardness.
I'll to the Northern casement which looks over
The shrubby banks o' th' mountain Lake, for thence
The slightest whisper from within may reach me.

1823–24; 1930

Armageddon[3]

Spirit of Prophecy whose mighty grasp
Enfoldeth all things, whose capacious soul
Can people the illimitable abyss
Of vast and fathomless futurity
With all the Giant Figures that shall pace 5
The dimness of its stage,—whose subtle ken
Can throng the doubly-darkened firmament
Of Time to come with all its burning stars
At awful intervals. I thank thy power,[4]

2. Because, unlike animals, man has a moral sense and can perceive evil.
3. The plain of Megiddo, where, according to the Bible (*Revelation,* 16:16), the final decisive battle between the forces of good and evil will be fought before the Day of Judgment. This very early fragmentary dream-vision in Miltonic blank verse later became the basis for Tennyson's Prize Poem "Timbuctoo," for which he won the Chancellor's Medal at Cambridge in 1829.
4. The first nine lines are from the Trinity College manuscripts, recently made available. They are reprinted by permission of the Lord Tennyson Trustees, Trinity College, Cambridge. In the Harvard manuscript, in which words are obliterated, the first nine lines read:

. . . . Prophecy whose mighty grasp
. . . . . . ings whose capacious soul
. . . . illimitable abyss
. . . . bottomless futurity
. . . . . giant figures that shall pace
. . . of its stage—whose subtle ken
. . . the doubly darkened firmament
. . . to come with all its burning stars
. . . erful intervals. I thank thy power,

Whose wondrous emanation hath poured 10
Bright light on what was darkest, and removed
The cloud that from my mortal faculties
Barred out the knowledge of the Latter Times.

I stood upon the mountain which o'erlooks
The valley of destruction and I saw 15
Things strange, surpassing wonder; but to give
Utterance to things unutterable, to paint
In dignity of language suitable
The majesty of what I then beheld,
Were past the power of man. No fabled Muse 20
Could breathe into my soul such influence
Of her seraphic nature, as to express
Deeds inexpressible by loftiest rhyme.

I stood upon the mountain which o'erlooks
The valley of Megiddo.—Broad before me 25
Lay a huge plain whereon the wandering eye,
Weary with gazing, found no resting-place,
Unbroken by the ridge of mound or hill
Or far-off cone of some aerial mount
Varying the horizon's sameness.
                      Eve came down 30
Upon the valleys and the sun was setting;
Never set sun with such portentous glare
Since he arose on that gay morn, when Earth
First drunk the light of his prolific ray.
Strange figures thickly thronged his burning orb, 35
Spirits of discord seem'd to weave across
His fiery disk a web of bloody haze,
Thro' whose reticulations struggled forth
His ineffectual, intercepted beams,
Curtaining in one dark terrific pall 40
Of dun-red light heaven's azure and earth's green.

The beasts fled to their dens; the little birds
All wing'd their way home shrieking: fitful gusts
Of violent tempest shook the scanty palm
That cloth'd the mountain ridge whereon I stood: 45
And in the red and murky Even light,
Black, formless, unclean things came flitting by;
Some seemed of bestial similitude
And some half human, yet so horrible,
So shadowy, indistinct and undefin'd, 50
It were a mockery to call them ought
Save unrealities, which took the form
And fashioning of such ill-omened things
That it were sin almost to look on them.[5]

5. Tennyson was most probably already familiar with Dante, and the above verse-paragraph may have been influenced by the Francesca episode, *Inferno*, V, lines 121 ff.

There was a mingling too of such strange sounds   55
(Which came at times upon my startled hearing)
Half wailing and half laughter; such a dissonance
Of jarring confus'd voices, part of which
Seem'd hellish and part heavenly, whisperings,
Low chauntings, strangled screams, and other notes   60
Which I may liken unto nothing which
I ever heard on Earth, but seem'd most like
A mixture of the voice of man and beast;
And then again throughout the lurid waste
Of air, a breathless stillness reigned, so deep,   65
So deathlike, so appalling, that I shrunk
Into myself again, and almost wish'd
For the recurrence of those deadly sounds,
Which fix'd my senses into stone, and drove
The buoyant life-drops back into my heart.   70

Nor did the glittering of white wings escape
My notice far within the East, which caught
Ruddy reflection from the ensanguin'd West;
Nor, ever and anon, the shrill clear sound
Of some aerial trumpet, solemnly   75
Pealing throughout the Empyrean void.

Thus to some wakeful hind who on the heights
Outwatches the wan planet, comes the sound
Of some far horn along the distant hills
Echoing, in some beleaguer'd country, where   80
The pitiless Enemy by night hath made
Sudden incursion and unsafe inroad.

The streams, whose imperceptible advance
Lingering in slow meanders, once was wont
To fertilize the plain beneath—whose course   85
Was barely mark'd save by the lazy straws
That wandered down them—now, as instinct with life,
Ran like the lightning's wing, and dash'd upon
The curvature of their green banks a wreath
Of lengthen'd foam; and yet, although they rush'd   90
Incalculably swift and fring'd with spray
The pointed crags, whose wave-worn slippery height
Parted their glassy channels, there awoke
No murmurs round them—but their sapphire depths
Of light were changed to crimson, as the sky   95
Glow'd like a fiery furnace.
                              In the East
Broad rose the moon, first like a beacon flame
Seen on the far horizon's utmost verge,
Of red eruption from the fissur'd cone
Of Cotopaxi's[6] cloud-cap't altitude;   100

6. An active volcano in the Andes, probably the world's highest (19,347 feet)
live volcano.

Then with dilated orb and mark'd with lines
Of mazy red athwart her shadowy face,
Sickly, as though her secret eyes beheld
Witchcrafts, abominations, and the spells
Of sorcerers, what time they summon up   105
From out the stilly chambers of the earth
Obscene, inutterable phantasies.

The sun went down; the hot and feverish night
Succeeded; but the parch'd, unwholesome air
Was unrecruited by the tears of heaven.   110
There was a windless calm, a dismal pause,
A dreary interval, wherein I held
My breath and heard the beatings of my heart.
The moon show'd clearer yet, with deadlier gleam,
Her ridgéd and uneven surface stain'd   115
With crosses, fiery streaks, and wandering lines—
Bloody impressions! and a star or two
Peer'd through the thick and smoky atmosphere.

Strange was that lunar light: the rock which stood
Fronting her sanguine ray, seem'd chang'd unto   120
A pillar of crimson, while the other half
Averted, and whatever else around
Stood not in opposition to her beams,
Was shrouded in the densest pall of night
And darkness almost palpable.
                                        Deep fear   125
And trembling came upon me, when I saw
In the remotest chambers of the East
Ranges of silver tents beside the moon,
Clear, but at distance so ineffable,
That save when keenly view'd, they else might seem   130
But little shining points or galaxies,
The blending of the beams of many stars.

Full opposite within the lurid West,
In clear relief against the long rich vein
Of melancholy red that fring'd the sky,   135
A suite of dark pavilions met mine eyes,
That covered half the western tide of Heaven,
Far stretching, in the midst of which tower'd one
Pre-eminent, which bore aloft in air
A standard, round whose staff a mighty snake   140
Twin'd his black folds, the while his ardent crest
And glossy neck were swaying to and fro.
                    2[7]
The rustling of white wings! The bright descent
Of a young seraph! and he stood beside me

7. Tennyson drew most heavily on sec-   into "Timbuctoo."
tions 2 and 3 when reworking this poem

In the wide foldings of his argent robes   145
There on the ridge, and look'd into my face
With his unutterable shining eyes,
So that with hasty motion I did veil
My vision with both hands, and saw before me
Such coloured spots as dance before the eyes   150
Of those that gaze upon the noonday sun.

   "O Son of Man, why stand you here alone
Upon the mountain, knowing not the things
Which will be, and the gathering of the nations
Unto the mighty battle of the Lord?   155
Thy sense is clogg'd with dull Mortality,[8]
Thy spirit fetter'd with the bond of clay—
Open thine eyes and see!"
                              I look'd, but not
Upon his face, for it was wonderful
With its exceeding brightness, and the light   160
Of the great Angel Mind that look'd from out
The starry glowing of his restless eyes.
I felt my soul grow godlike, and my spirit[9]
With supernatural excitation bound
Within me, and my mental eye grew large   165
With such a vast circumference of thought,
That, in my vanity, I seem'd to stand
Upon the outward verge and bound alone
Of God's omniscience. Each failing sense,
As with a momentary flash of light,   170
Grew thrillingly distinct and keen.[1] I saw
The smallest grain that dappled the dark Earth,
The indistinctest atom in deep air,
The Moon's white cities, and the opal width
Of her small, glowing lakes, her silver heights   175
Unvisited with dew of vagrant cloud,
And the unsounded, undescended depth
Of her black hollows. Nay—the hum of men
Or other things talking in unknown tongues,
And notes of busy Life in distant worlds,   180
Beat, like a far wave, on my anxious ear.

   I wondered with deep wonder at myself:
My mind seem'd wing'd with knowledge and the strength
Of holy musings and immense Ideas,

---

8. A phrase probably from Beaumont and Fletcher's *The Faithful Shepherdess*, I, ii, 104–105: ". . . so to make thee free / From dying flesh and dull mortality." Also compare this passage and the following to Tennyson's "The Ancient Sage," lines 229–232.
9. Lines 167 ff record a mystical experience which in some respects resembles Wordsworth's in "Ode: Intimations of Immortality," especially ". . . Those obstinate questionings / Of sense and outward things, / Falling from us, vanishings" (lines 141–143).
1. In "The Coming of Arthur" Tennyson speaks of the King's enlightenment in similar terms: "The world / Was all so clear about him that he saw / The smallest rock far on the faintest hill" (lines 96–98).

Even to Infinitude.[2] All sense of Time 185
And Being and Place was swallowed up and lost
Within a victory of boundless thought.
I was a part of the Unchangeable,
A scintillation of Eternal Mind,
Remix'd and burning with its parent fire. 190
Yea! in that hour I could have fallen down
Before my own strong soul and worshipp'd it.

Highly and holily the Angel look'd.
Immeasurable Solicitude and Awe,
And solemn Adoration and high Faith, 195
Were trac'd on his imperishable front—
Then with a mournful and ineffable smile,
Which but to look on for a moment fill'd
My eyes with irresistible sweet tears,
In accents of majestic melody, 200
Like a swollen river's gushings in still night
Mingled with floating music, thus he spoke.

3
"O Everlasting God, and thou not less
The Everlasting Man (since that great spirit
Which permeates and informs thine inward sense, 205
Though limited in action, capable
Of the extreme of knowledge—whether join'd
Unto thee in conception or confin'd
From former wanderings in other shapes
I know not—deathless as its God's own life, 210
Burns on with inextinguishable strength),
O Lords of Earth and Tyrannies of Hell,
And thrones of Heaven, whose triple pride shall clash
In the annihilating anarchy
Of unimaginable war, a day 215
Of darkness riseth on ye, a thick day,
Pall'd with dun wreaths of dusky fight, a day
Of many thunders and confuséd noise,
Of bloody grapplings in the interval
Of the opposéd Battle, a great day 220
Of wonderful revealings and vast sights
And inconceivable visions, such as yet
Have never shone into the heart of Man—
THE DAY of the Lord God!"
His voice grew deep
With volumes of strong sound, which made the rock 225
To throb beneath me, and his parted locks
Of spiral light fell raylike, as he mov'd,

2. An expression recalling the young Keats's remark in his early poem "Sleep and Poetry": "There ever rolls a vast idea before me / And I glean therefrom my liberty" (lines 290–292). Although a number of passages in "Armageddon" and others in the very early poetry beg comparison with Keats, Tennyson probably had not read either Keats or Wordsworth until after he entered Cambridge in February 1828.

On each white shoulder: his ambrosial lip
Was beautifully curv'd, as in the pride
And power of his mid Prophecy: his nostril   230
Dilated with Expression; half upturn'd
The broad beneficence of his clear brow
Into the smoky sky; his sunlike eyes
With tenfold glory lit; his mighty arm
Outstretch'd described half-circles; small thin flashes   235
Of intense lustre followed it.

4

            I look'd,
And lo! the vision of the night was chang'd.
The sooty mantle of infernal smoke
Whose blank, obliterating, dewless cloud
Had made the plain like some vast crater, rose   240
Distinct from Earth and gather'd to itself
In one dense, dry, interminable mass
Sailing far Northward, as it were the shadow
Of this round Planet cast upon the face
Of the bleak air. But this was wonderful,   245
To see how full it was of living things,
Strange shapings, and anomalies of Hell,
And dusky faces, and protruded arms
Of hairy strength, and white and garish eyes,
And silent intertwisted thunderbolts,   250
Wreathing and sparkling restlessly like snakes
Within their grassy depths. I watch'd it till
Its latest margin sank beneath the sweep
Of the horizon.
            All the crimson streaks
And bloody dapplings faded from the disk   255
Of the immaculate morn.
              An icy veil
Of pale, weak, lifeless, thin, unnatural blue
Wrapt up the rich varieties of things
In grim and ghastly sameness.
              The clear stars
Shone out with keen but fix'd intensity,   260
All-silence, looking steadfast consciousness
Upon the dark and windy waste of Earth.
There was a beating in the atmosphere,
An indefinable pulsation
Inaudible to outward sense, but felt   265
Thro' the deep heart of every living thing,
As if the great soul of the Universe
Heav'd with tumultuous throbbings on the vast
Suspense of some grand issue. . . .[3]

1824?; 1931

3. The poet's sense of the unity among all living things again suggests Wordsworth. In Book II of *The Prelude* he celebrates his awakening power during his seventeenth year to see relationships among objects "By observation of affi-

Memory[4]

Ay me! those childish lispings roll
As thunder thro' my heart and soul,
Those fair eyes in my inmost frame
Are subtle shafts of pierceant[5] flame.

Blesséd, curséd, Memory,   5
Shadow, Spirit as thou may'st be,
Why hast thou become to me
A conscience dropping tears of fire
On the heart, which vain desire
Vexeth all too bitterly?   10
When the wand of circumstance
All at once hath bid thee glance,
From the body of the Past,
Like a wandering ghost aghast,
Why wearest thou, mad Memory,   15
Lip and lip and hair and eye,[6]
Life—life without life or breath,
Death forth issuing from Death?

May goes not before dark December,
Nor doth the year change suddenly;   20
Wherefore do I so remember
That Hope is born of Memory
Nightly in the house of dreams?
But when I wake, at once she seems
The faery changeling wan Despair,   25
Who laughs all day and never speaks—
O dark of bright! O foul of fair!
A frightful child with shrivelled cheeks.

Why at break of cheerful day[7]
Doth my spirit faint away   30

nities / In objects where no brotherhood exists / To passive minds" (lines 382–402). Tennyson's phrase "outward sense" seems almost equivalent in meaning to Wordsworth's "passive minds."

4. Sir Charles Tennyson believes this and the following poem belong to the Somersby-Cambridge transition period. In some form they were probably written early enough to be considered for publication in *Poems by Two Brothers* (1827). The reason Tennyson gave for excluding such pieces was that they were "too much out of the common for the public taste" (*Memoir*, I, 23). More likely the Jacksons, publishers of the volume, wanted to safeguard their already risky venture by printing poems visibly indebted to the fashionable

poets, particularly Byron, Gray, Moore, and Scott. But, as Sir Charles suggests, Alfred may have been reticent to include poetry which revealed his personal thoughts and feelings. See *Alfred Tennyson*, p. 52.

5. Piercing. Tennyson probably confused the two obsolete forms: piercent and perceant.

6. "The first word of this line is very hard to decipher and I cannot guarantee the text" (Sir Charles Tennyson's note).

7. See the epigraph to the other poem entitled "Memory," on page 520. The epigraph, curiously, has almost nothing to do with that poem but perhaps partially helps to explain lines 29 ff of this poem. Tennyson may have been seeking to articulate his own longing for new experience through the image of the "hungry serpent" which had consumed

Like a wanderer in the night?
Why in visions of the night
Am I shaken with delight
Like a lark at dawn of day?
As a hungry serpent coiled   35
Round a palm tree in the wild,
When his bakéd jaws are bare
Burning in the burning air,
And his corky tongue is black
With the raging famine-crack,   40
If perchance afar he sees
Winding up among the trees,
Lordly-headed buffaloes,
Or but hears their distant lows,
With the fierce remembrance drunk   45
He crushes all the stalwart trunk
Round which his fainting folds are prest,
With delirium-causing throes
Of anticipated zest.

1826–27?; 1931

Perdidi Diem[8]

And thou[9] hast lost a day! Oh mighty boast!
Dost thou miss one day only? I have lost
A life, perchance an immortality;
I never *liv'd* a day, but daily die,
    I have no real breath;   5
My being is a vacant worthlessness,
A carcase in the coffin of this flesh,
    Pierc'd thro' with loathly worms of utter Death.
My soul is but th' eternal mystic lamp,
Lighting that charnel damp,   10
Wounding with dreadful days that solid gloom,
And shadowing forth th' unutterable tomb,
Making a 'darkness visible'[1]
Of that which without thee we had not felt
As darkness, dark ourselves and loving night,   15

its "stores of food" and was not satisfied by "remembrance." The metaphor, however, is not fully under control, nor is the poem itself clear at all points. Its interest lies in what it reveals of a young poet's efforts at self-expression, his attempt to resolve in poetry his conflicting feelings of hope and despair, desire and revulsion during the difficult period of adolescence.
8. Clearly a piece which draws heavily on Milton and Dante for structure and imagery, the poem is characteristic of Tennyson's mordant, introspective

moods. In fits of despondency, the boy more than once "went out through the black night, and threw himself on a grave in the churchyard, praying to be beneath the sod himself" (*Memoir*, I, 15).
9. The voice in the title, "I have lost the day." The poem, which may have been originally conceived as a dialogue between selves, anticipates in mood and form the longer, more carefully worked piece "The Two Voices."
1. See Milton's description of Hell in Book I of *Paradise Lost*, especially lines 56–69.

Night-bats into the filtering crevices
Hook'd, clinging, darkness-fed, at ease:
Night-owls whose organs were not made for light.
I must needs pore upon the mysteries
Of my own infinite Nature and torment   20
My Spirit with a fruitless discontent:
As in the malignant light
Of a dim, dripping, moon-enfolding night,
Young ravens fallen from their cherishing nest
On the elm-summit, flutter in agony   25
With a continual cry
About its roots, and fluttering trail and spoil
Their new plumes on the misty soil,
But not the more for this
Shall the loved mother minister   30
Aerial food, and to their wonted rest
Win them upon the topmost branch in air
With sleep-compelling down of her most glossy breast.
In chill discomfort still they cry—
What is the death of life if this be not to die?   35

2

You tell me that to me a Power is given,
An effluence of serenest fire from Heaven,
Pure, vapourless, and white,
As God himself in kind, a spirit-guiding light,
Fed from each self-originating spring   40
Of most inviolate Godhead, issuing
From underneath the shuddering stairs which climb
The throne,
Where each intense pulsation
And going-on o' th' heart of God's great life,   45
Out of the sphere of Time,
As from an actual centre is heard to beat,
And to the thrilling mass communicate,
Goes through and through with musical fire and through
The spiritual nerves and arteries   50
Of those first spirits, which round the incorruptible base
Bow, with furl'd pinions veiling their immortal eyes,
As not enduring, face to face,
Eye-combat with th' unutterable gaze.
These are the highest few: 55
Thence to the lower, broader circle runs
The sovran subtil impulse on and on,
Until all Heaven, an inconceivable cone
Of vision-shadowing vans and claspéd palms,
Of circle below circle, file below   60
File, one life, one heart, one glow,[2]

2. The imagery throughout Section 2, particularly in this and the lines just above, recall Dante's ascent to the Em-pyrean and vision of Heaven as described in Cantos 30–33 of the *Paradiso*.

Even to the latest range which tramples on the highest suns,
With every infinite pulsation
Brightens and darkens; downward, downward still
The mighty pulses thrill   65
With wreathéd light and sound,
Thro' the rare web-work woven round
The highest spheres,
Prompting the audible growth of great harmonious years.
Base of the cone,   70
Last of the link,
Each rolling sun and hornéd moon,
All the awful and surpassing lights
Which we from every zone
Of th' orbed Earth survey on summer nights,   75
(When nights are deepest and most clear)
Are in their station cold;
The latest energies of light they drink:
The latest fiat of Divine Art,
Our Planets, slumbering in their swiftness, hear   80
The last beat of the thunder of God's heart. . . .

1826–28; 1931

FROM *POEMS BY TWO BROTHERS* (1827)

On Sublimity[1]

The sublime always dwells on great objects and terrible.
—BURKE

O tell me not of vales in tenderest green,
    The poplar's shade, the plantane's graceful tree;
Give me the wild cascade, the rugged scene.

1. This poem and the eight following are from *Poems by Two Brothers*. Since the dates of publication, 1826 and 1827, have been used indiscriminately, confusion exists over the actual date the volume appeared. As Tennyson himself tells us, "The book was issued late in 1826, but *ante*-dated (as is the fashion of publishers) as coming out in 1827. . . . When the poems were published Charles was eighteen, I was seventeen." See the 1898 edition of the *Memoir*, I, 22–23. For dates of composition, which cannot be precisely known, the advertisement explains: "The following Poems were written from the ages of fifteen to eighteen." And in the preface to his facsimile edition of 1893, Hallam Tennyson notes: "My father writes, 'The Preface states "written from 15 to 18." I was between 15 and 17, Charles between 15 and 18.' " When originally published the volume contained no references anywhere to the authors' names. In the 1893 edition Hallam, working with the publishers' manuscript and the help of Frederick Tennyson, Alfred's other older brother, then in his late eighties, assigned initials to the poems. Alfred had contributed over half the volume, and Frederick, it turned out, had written three or four of the poems. The authorship of several pieces, however, remains in doubt.

For these nine poems, the notes in quotation marks are Alfred Tennyson's; a few of them have been shortened. I have not tried to trace the extensive literary indebtedness nor attempted to provide notes for all the numerous proper names.

The loud surge bursting o'er the purple sea:
On such sad views my soul delights to pore,   5
　　By Teneriffe's peak, or Kilda's giant height,
Or dark Loffoden's melancholy shore,[2]
　　What time grey eve is fading into night;
When by that twilight beam I scarce descry
The mingled shades of earth and sea and sky.   10

Give me to wander at midnight alone,
　　Through some august cathedral, where, from high,
The cold, clear moon on the mosaic stone
　　Comes glancing in gay colours gloriously,
Through windows rich with gorgeous blazonry,   15
　　Gilding the niches dim, where, side by side,
Stand antique mitred prelates, whose bones lie
　　Beneath the pavement, where their deeds of pride
Were graven, but long since are worn away
By constant feet of ages day by day.   20

Then, as Imagination aids, I hear
　　Wild heavenly voices sounding from the quoir,
And more than mortal music meets mine ear,
　　Whose long, long notes among the tombs expire,
With solemn rustling of cherubic wings,   25
　　Round those vast columns which the roof upbear;
While sad and undistinguishable things
　　Do flit athwart the moonlit windows there;
And my blood curdles at the chilling sound
Of lone, unearthly steps, that pace the hallow'd ground!   30

I love the starry spangled heav'n, resembling
　　A canopy with fiery gems o'erspread,
When the wide loch[3] with silvery sheen is trembling,
　　Far stretch'd beneath the mountain's hoary head.
But most I love that sky, when, dark with storms,   35
　　It frowns teriffic o'er this wilder'd earth,
While the black clouds, in strange and uncouth[4] forms,
　　Come hurrying onward in their ruinous wrath;
And shrouding in their deep and gloomy robe
The burning eyes of heav'n and Dian's lucid globe!   40

I love your voice, ye echoing winds, that sweep
　　Thro' the wide womb of midnight, when the veil
Of darkness rests upon the mighty deep,
　　The labouring vessel, and the shatter'd sail—
Save when the forked bolts of lightning leap   45
　　On flashing pinions, and the mariner pale
Raises his eyes to heaven. Oh! who would sleep
　　What time the rushing of the angry gale

---

2. Teneriffe, largest of the Canary Is-　3. Here, apparently, a lake.
lands.　4. Strange.

Is loud upon the waters?—Hail, all hail!
Tempest and clouds and night and thunder's rending peal!   50

All hail, Sublimity! thou lofty one,
   For thou dost walk upon the blast, and gird
Thy majesty with terrors, and thy throne
   Is on the whirlwind, and thy voice is heard
In thunders and in shakings: thy delight   55
   Is in the secret wood, the blasted heath,
The ruin'd fortress, and the dizzy height,
   The grave, the ghastly charnel-house of death,
In vaults, in cloisters, and in gloomy piles,
Long corridors and towers and solitary aisles!   60

Thy joy is in obscurity, and plain
   Is nought with thee; and on thy steps attend
Shadows but half-distinguish'd; the thin train
   Of hovering spirits round thy pathway bend,
With their low tremulous voice and airy tread,[5]   65
   What time the tomb above them yawns and gapes:
For thou dost hold communion with the dead
   Phantoms and phantasies and grisly shapes;
And shades and headless spectres of Saint Mark,[6]
Seen by a lurid light, formless and still and dark!   70

What joy to view the varied rainbow smile
   On Niagara's flood of matchless might,
Where all around the melancholy isle[7]
   The billows sparkle with their hues of light!
While, as the restless surges roar and rave,   75
   The arrowy stream descends with awful sound,
Wheeling and whirling with each breathless wave,[8]
   Immense, sublime, magificent, profound!
If thou hast seen all this, and could'st not feel,
Then know, thine heart is fram'd of marble or of steel.   80

The hurricane fair earth to darkness changing,
   Kentucky's chambers of eternal gloom,[9]
The swift pac'd columns of the desert ranging
   Th' uneven waste, the violent Simoom,[1]
Thy snow-clad peaks, stupendous Gungotree!   85
   Whence springs the hallow'd Jumna's echoing tide,
Hoar Cotopaxi's cloud-clapt majesty,

---

5. "According to Burke, a low tremulous intermitted sound is conductive to the sublime."

6. "It is received opinion, that on St. Mark's Eve all the persons who are to die on the following year make their appearances without their heads in the churches of their respective parishes.—See Dr. Langhorne's *Notes to Collins*."

7. "This island, on both sides of which the waters rush with astonishing swiftness, is 900 or 800 feet long, and its lower edge is just at the perpendicular edge of the fall."

8. " 'Undis Phlegethon perlustrat AN-HELIS.'—Claudian."

9. "See Dr. Nahum Ward's account of the great Kentucky Cavern, in the *Monthly Magazine,* October 1816."

1. Violent sandstorms in Arabia and neighboring areas.

Enormous Chimborazo's naked pride,
The dizzy Cape of winds that cleaves the sky,[2]
Whence we look down into eternity,   90

The pillar'd cave of Morven's giant king,[3]
    The Yanar,[4] and the Geyser's boiling fountain,
The deep volcano's inward murmuring,
    The shadowy Colossus of the mountain;[5]
Antiparos, where sun-beams never enter;   95
    Loud Stromboli, amid the quaking isles;
The terrible Maelstroom, around his centre
    Wheeling his circuit of unnumber'd miles:
These, these are sights and sounds that freeze the blood,
Yet charm the awe-struck soul which doats on solitude.   100

Blest be the bard, whose willing feet rejoice
    To tread the emerald green of Fancy's vales,
Who hears the music of her heavenly voice,
    And breathes the rapture of her nectar'd gales!
Blest be the bard, whom golden Fancy loves,   105
    He strays for ever thro' her blooming bowers,
Amid the rich profusion of her groves,
    And wreathes his forehead with her spicy flowers
Of sunny radiance; but how blest is he
Who feels the genuine force of high Sublimity!   110

1827

Memory[6]

The memory is perpetually looking back when we have nothing present to entertain us: it is like those repositories in animals that are filled with stores of food, on which they may ruminate when their present pasture fails.   —ADDISON

Memory! dear enchanter!
    Why bring back to view
Dreams of youth, which banter
    All that e'er was true?

Why present before me   5
    Thoughts of years gone by,
Which, like shadows o'er me,
    Dim in distance fly?

Days of youth, now shaded
    By twilight of long years,[7]   10

2. "In the Ukraine."
3. "Fingal's Cave in the Island of Staffa."
4. "Or, perpetual fire."
5. "Alias, the Spectre of the Broken."
6. Although Hallam Tennyson tentatively assigned authorship of the poem to Charles, later editors have tended to ascribe it to Alfred. The poem's relationship to the other "Memory" and to "Ode to Memory," as well as its length and content, strongly link it to Alfred.
7. Often in *Poems by Two Brothers* Tennyson adopts the mask of an older man, as in the opening lines of the following poem, "Remorse."

Flowers of youth, now faded,
   Though bathed in sorrow's tears:

Thoughts of youth, which waken
   Mournful feelings now,
Fruits which time hath shaken   15
   From off their parent bough:

Memory! why, oh why,
   This fond heart consuming,
Shew me years gone by,
   When those hopes were blooming.   20

Hopes which now are parted,
   Hopes which then I priz'd,
Which this world, cold-hearted,
   Ne'er has realiz'd?

I knew not then its strife,   25
   I knew not then its rancour;
In every rose of life,
   Alas! there lurks a canker.

Round every palm-tree, springing
   With bright fruit in the waste,   30
A mournful asp[8] is clinging,
   Which sours it to our taste.

O'er every fountain, pouring
   Its waters thro' the wild,
Which man imbibes, adoring,   35
   And deems it undefil'd,

The poison-shrubs are dropping
   Their dark dews day by day;
And Care is hourly lopping
   Our greenest boughs away!   40

Ah! these are thoughts that grieve me
   Then, when others rest.
Memory! why deceive me
   By thy visions blest?

Why lift the veil, dividing   45
   The brilliant courts of spring—
Where gilded shapes are gliding
   In fairy colouring—

From age's frosty mansion,
   So cheerless and so chill?   50
Why bid the bleak expansion
   Of past life meet us still?

8. A perplexing image. The word "mournful" qualifies the conventional association of serpents with evil. Tennyson had read Shakespeare's *Antony and Cleopatra* and perhaps was thinking of that asp too. For an interesting discussion of the imagery in the early work, W. D. Paden's psychologically inclined *Tennyson in Egypt* is well worth consulting.

Where's now that peace of mind
   O'er youth's pure bosom stealing
So sweet and so refin'd,   55
   So exquisite a feeling?

Where's now the heart exulting
   In pleasure's buoyant sense,
And gaiety, resulting
   From conscious innocence?   60

All, all have past and fled,
   And left me lorn and lonely;
All those dear hopes are dead,
   Remembrance wakes them only!

I stand like some lone tower   65
   Of former days remaining,
Within whose place of power
   The midnight owl is plaining;—

Like oak-tree old and grey,
   Whose trunk with age is failing,   70
Thro' whose dark boughs for aye
   The winter winds are wailing.

Thus, Memory, thus thy light
   O'er this worn soul is gleaming,
Like some far fire at night   75
   Along the dun deep streaming.

1827

Remorse

—sudant tacita præcordia culpa[9]
—JUVENAL

Oh! 't is a fearful thing to glance
   Back on the gloom of mis-spent years:[1]
What shadowy forms of guilt advance,
   And fill me with a thousand fears!
The vices of my life arise,   5
   Pourtray'd in shapes, alas! too true;
   And not one beam of hope breaks through,
To cheer my old and aching eyes,
T' illume my night of wretchedness,
My age of anguish and distress.   10
If I am damn'd, why find I not
Some comfort in this earthly spot?
But no! this world and that to come

9. The hearts sweat in unspeaking guilt.
1. Compare the last stanza from the Prologue to *In Memoriam,* "Forgive these wild and wandering cries, / Confusions of a wasted youth . . ."

Are both to me one scene of gloom!
Lest ought of solace I should see,   15
   Or lose the thoughts of what I do,
Remorse, with soul-felt agony,
   Holds up the mirror to my view.
And I was cursed from my birth,
A reptile made to creep on earth,   20
An hopeless outcast, born to die
A living death eternally![2]
With too much conscience to have rest,
Too little to be ever blest,
To you vast world of endless woe,   25
   Unlighted by the cheerful day,
   My soul shall wing her weary way;
      To those dread depths where aye the same,
Throughout the waste of darkness, glow
      The glimmerings of the boundless flame.   30
And yet I cannot here below
Take my full cup of guilt, as some,
And laugh away my doom to come.
I would I'd been all-heartless! then
I might have sinn'd like other men;   35
But all this side the grave is fear,
A wilderness so dank and drear,
That never wholesome plant would spring;
   And all behind—I dare not think!
I would not risk th' imagining—   40
   From the full view my spirits shrink;
And starting backwards, yet I cling
To life, whose every hour to me
Hath been increase of misery.
But yet I cling to it, for well   45
   I know the pangs that rack me now
Are trifles, to the endless hell
   That waits me, when my burning brow
And my wrung eyes shall hope in vain
For one small drop to cool the pain,   50
The fury of that madd'ning flame
That then shall scorch my writhing frame!
Fiends! who have goaded me to ill!
Distracting fiends, who goad me still!
If e'er I work'd a sinful deed,   55

2. One suspects the influence of Tennyson's Aunt Mary Bourne in such passages. A rigid Calvinist of the hellfire and damnation school, she would weep for hours over God's infinite goodness. " 'Has He not damned,' she cried, 'most of my friends? But *me, me* He has picked out for eternal salvation, *me* who am no better than my neighbors.' One day she said to her nephew, 'Alfred, Alfred, when I look at you, I think of the words of Holy Scripture— "Depart from me, ye cursed, into everlasting fire" ' " (*Memoir*, I, 15). Whatever Aunt Mary's effect on Tennyson may have been, he probably took his Byron more seriously.

Ye know how bitter was the draught;
Ye know my inmost soul would bleed,
    And ye have look'd at me and laugh'd,
Triumphing that I could not free
My spirit from your slavery!   60
Yet is there that in me which says,
    Should these old feet their course retread
From out the portal of my days,
    That I should lead the life I've led:
My agony, my torturing shame,   65
My guilt, my errors all the same!
Oh, God! that thou wouldst grant that ne'er
    My soul its clay-cold bed forsake,
    That I might sleep, and never wake
Unto the thrill of conscious fear;[3]   70
    For when the trumpet's piercing cry[4]
Shall burst upon my slumb'ring ear,
    And countless seraphs throng the sky,
How shall I cast my shroud away,
And come into the blaze of day?   75
How shall I brook to hear each crime,
    Here veil'd by secrecy and time,
Read out from thine eternal book?
    How shall I stand before thy throne,
        While earth shall like a furnace burn?   80
How shall I bear the with'ring look
        Of men and angels, who will turn
    Their dreadful gaze on me alone?

1827

The Passions[5]

You have passions in your heart—scorpions; they sleep now—beware
how you awaken them! they will sting you even to death!
                                —*Mysteries of Udolpho,* vol. iii

Beware, beware, ere thou takest
    The draught of misery!
Beware, beware, e'er thou wakest
    The scorpions that sleep in thee!

3. An inchoate expression of the tension between desiring the escape offered by unconsciousness and accepting the burdens of consciousness, a tension at the center of Tennyson's thought in his mature poetry. "Supposed Confessions" will be his first concerted effort to work out the dilemma which also becomes the subject of "The Lotos-Eaters" and numerous other poems.

4. On the Day of Judgment.

5. Like a number of other pieces in *Poems by Two Brothers,* this Byronic effusion should not be dismissed as a mere exercise in mimicry. Tennyson was keenly sensitive to the sexual dilemmas of adolescence, and, as he said, "Byron expressed what I felt" (*Memoir,* I, 16). On the day he learned of Byron's death, Tennyson, then fourteen, went out and carved on a rock, "Byron is dead"; he later recalled that it was "a day when the whole world seemed to be darkened for me" (*Memoir,* I, 4). The epigraph from Ann Radcliffe's gothic novel is but one of many instances where Tennyson shows his early fascination with that literary genre.

The woes which thou canst not number,   5
    As yet are wrapt in sleep;
Yet oh! yet they slumber,
    But their slumbers are not deep.

Yet oh! yet while the rancour
    Of hate has no place in thee,   10
While thy buoyant soul has an anchor
    In youth's bright tranquil sea:

Yet oh! yet while the blossom
    Of hope is blooming fair,
While the beam of bliss lights thy bosom—   15
    O! rouse not the serpent there!

For bitter thy tears will trickle
    'Neath misery's heavy load,
When the world has put in its sickle
    To the crop which fancy sow'd.   20

When the world has rent the cable
    That bound thee to the shore,
And launched thee weak and unable
    To bear the billow's roar;

Then the slightest touch will waken   25
    Those pangs that will always grieve thee,
And thy soul will be fiercely shaken
    With storms that will never leave thee!

So beware, beware, ere thou takest
    The draught of misery!   30
Beware, beware, ere thou wakest
    The scorpions that sleep in thee!

1827

Love[6]

1

Almighty Love! whose nameless power
    This glowing heart defines too well,
Whose presence cheers each fleeting hour,
    Whose silken bonds our souls compel,
    Diffusing such a sainted spell,   5

As gilds our being with the light
    Of transport and of rapturous bliss,
And almost seeming to unite

---

6. Although of absolutely no literary merit, the poem suggests the order of Tennyson's early interest in natural science and shows the eighteenth-century deistic quality of his thought at this period. Later he completely repudiated the notion that God's existence could be known through any argument based on design and reason. Cf. *In Memoriam*, 124, 2.

The joys of other worlds to this,
    The heavenly smile, the rosy kiss;— 10

Before whose blaze my spirits shrink,
    My senses all are wrapt in thee,
Thy force I own too much, to think
    (So full, so great thine ecstacy)
    That thou are less than deity! 15

Thy golden chains embrace the land,
    The starry sky, the dark blue main;
And at the voice of thy command,
    (So vast, so boundless is thy reign)
    All nature springs to life again! 20

2

The glittering fly, the wondrous things
    That microscopic art descries;
The lion of the waste, which springs,
    Bounding upon his enemies;
The mighty sea-snake of the storm, 25
The vorticella's viewless form,[7]

The vast leviathan, which takes
    His pastime in the sounding floods;
The crafty elephant, which makes
    His haunts in Ceylon's spicy woods— 30
Alike confess thy magic sway,
Thy soul-enchanting voice obey!

O! whether thou, as bards have said,
    Of bliss or pain the partial giver,
Wingest thy shaft of pleasing dread 35
    From out thy well-stor'd golden quiver,
O'er earth thy cherub wings extending,
Thy sea-born mother's side attending;—

Or else, as Indian fables say,
    Upon thine emerald lory riding, 40
Through gardens, mid the restless play
    Of fountains, in the moon-beam gliding,
Mid sylph-like shapes of maidens dancing,
Thy scarlet standard high advancing;—

Thy fragrant bow of cane thou bendest,[8] 45
    Twanging the string of honey'd bees,
And thence the flower-tipp'd arrow sendest,

7. "See BAKER on Animalculae." The single-celled vorticella is viewless, i.e., visible only through a microscope.
8. "See Sir William Jones's Works, vol. vi, p. 313.
    'He bends the luscious cane, and twists the string;
With bees how sweet, but ah! how keen the sting!
He with five flowrets tips thy ruthless darts,
Which thro' five senses pierce enraptur'd hearts.' "

Which gives or robs the heart of ease;
    Camdeo, or Cupid, O be near,
To listen, and to grant my prayer!   50

1827

"And Ask Ye Why These Sad Tears Stream?"[9]

Te somnia nostra reducunt.[1]
—Ovid

And ask ye why these sad tears stream?
    Why these wan eyes are dim with weeping?
I had a dream—a lovely dream,
    Of her that in the grave is sleeping.

I saw her as 't was yesterday,   5
    The bloom upon her cheek still glowing;
And round her play'd a golden ray,
    And on her brows were gay flowers blowing.

With angel-hand she swept a lyre,
    A garland red with roses bound it;   10
Its strings were wreath'd with lambent fire
    And amaranth was woven round it.

I saw her mid the realms of light,
    In everlasting radiance gleaming;
Co-equal with the seraphs bright,   15
    Mid thousand thousand angels beaming.

I strove to reach her, when, behold,
    Those fairy forms of bliss Elysian,
And all that rich scene wrapt in gold,
    Faded in air—a lovely vision!   20

And I awoke, but oh! to me
    That waking hour was doubly weary;
And yet I could not envy thee,
    Although so blest, and I so dreary.

1827

"I Wander in Darkness and Sorrow"

I wander in darkness and sorrow,
    Unfriended, and cold, and alone,
As dismally gurgles beside me

---

9. The influence of Thomas Moore's *Irish Melodies* (1808–1834) is dominant here and in the next poem. Since the debt lies in mood more than content, it is hard to know which of Moore's poems Tennyson may have read and drawn upon. In that effort, however, I have discovered only that a number of poems published too late for Tennyson's access seemed the most likely sources.

1. Our dreams bring you back.

The bleak river's desolate moan.
The rise of the volleying thunder   5
    The mountain's lone echoes repeat:
The roar of the wind is around me,
    The leaves of the year at my feet.

I wander in darkness and sorrow,
    Uncheer'd by the moon's placid ray;   10
Not a friend that I lov'd but is dead,
    Not a hope but has faded away!
Oh! when shall I rest in the tomb,
    Wrapt about with the chill winding sheet?
For the roar of the wind is around me,   15
    The leaves of the year at my feet.

I heed not the blasts that sweep o'er me,
    I blame not the tempests of night;
They are not the foes who have banish'd
    The visions of youthful delight: 20
I hail the wild sound of their raving,
    Their merciless presence I greet;
Though the roar of the wind be around me,
    The leaves of the year at my feet.

In this waste of existence, for solace,   25
    On whom shall my lone spirit call?
Shall I fly to the friends of my bosom?
    My God! I have buried them all![2]
They are dead, they are gone, they are cold,
    My embraces no longer they meet;   30
Let the roar of the wind be around me,
    The leaves of the year at my feet!

Those eyes that glanc'd love unto mine,
    With motionless slumbers are prest;
Those hearts which once throbb'd but for me,   35
    Are chill as the earth where they rest.
Then around on my wan wither'd form
    Let the pitiless hurricanes beat;
Let the roar of the wind be around me,
    The leaves of the year at my feet!   40

Like the voice of the owl in the hall,
    Where the song and the banquet have ceas'd,
Where the green weeds have mantled the hearth,
    Whence arose the proud flame of the feast;
So I cry to the storm, whose dark wing   45

2. As noted above, a not infrequent posture. The degree to which Tennyson was aware of the incongruities in the pose of a boy of 17 speaking out on a wasted youth filled with vice and mortal sin is open to speculation. One can, of course, poke fun at such seriousness, calling it, as some have, "hopelessly out of place in the mouth of a boy." A more charitable, if not more intelligent, view is to see it as the attempt, however awkward, to create a dramatic voice.

Scatters on me the wild-driving sleet—
'Let the roar of the wind be around me,
The fall of the leaves at my feet!'

1827

"Thou Camest to Thy Bower, My Love, across the Musky Grove"[3]

Virgo egregia forma.[4]
—TERENCE

Thou camest to thy bower, my love, across the musky grove,
To fan thy blooming charms within the coolness of the shade;
Thy locks were like a midnight cloud with silver moon-beams wove,[5]
And o'er thy face the varying tints of youthful passion play'd.

Thy breath was like the sandal-wood that casts a rich perfume,   5
Thy blue eyes mock'd the lotos in the noon-day of his bloom;
Thy cheeks were like the beamy flush that gilds the breaking day,
And in th' ambrosia of thy smiles the god of rapture lay.[6]

Fair as the cairba-stone art thou, that stone of dazzling white,[7]
Ere yet unholy fingers chang'd its milk-white hue to night;   10
And lovelier than the loveliest glance from Even's placid star,[8]
And brighter than the sea of gold,[9] the gorgeous Himsagar.

In high Mohammed's boundless heaven Al Cawthor's stream may
     play,
The fount of youth may sparkling gush beneath the western ray;[1]
And Tasnim's wave in chrystal cups may glow with musk and
     wine,   15
But oh! their lustre could not match one beauteous tear of thine!

1827

The Expedition of Nadir Shah into Hindostan[2]

Quoi! vous allez combattre un roi, dont la puissance
Semble forcer le ciel de prendre sa défense,
Sous qui toute l'Asie a vu tomber ses rois
Et qui tient la fortune attachée à ses lois![3]
—RACINE'S *Alexandre*

Squallent populatibus agri.[4]
—CLAUDIAN

As the host of the locusts in numbers, in might
As the flames of the forest that redden the night,

3. In contrast to "The Passions" or "Remorse," this almost Keatsian indulgence in sensuous experience for its own sake is unique among Alfred's contributions and is happily at odds with the moralizing temper of the volume as a whole.

4. A girl of outstanding beauty.
5. "A simile elicited from the songs of Jayadeva, the Horace of India."
6. "Vide Horace's ODE—'Pulchris EXCUBAT in genis.'"
7. "Vide Sale's *Koran.*"
8. Venus, the evening star.

They approach: but the eye may not dwell on the glare
Of standard and sabre that sparkle in air.

Like the fiends of destruction they rush on their way,   5
The vulture behind them is wild for his prey;
And the spirits of death, and the demons of wrath,
Wave the gloom of their wings o'er their desolate path.

Earth trembles beneath them, the dauntless, the bold.
Oh! weep for thy children, thou region of gold;[5]   10
For thy thousands are bow'd to the dust of the plain,
And all Delhi runs red with the blood of her slain.

For thy glory is past, and thy splendour is dim,
And the cup of thy sorrow is full to the brim;
And where is the chief in thy realms to abide,   15
The 'Monarch of Nations,'[6] the strength of his pride?

Like a thousand dark streams from the mountain they throng,
With the fife and the horn and the war-beating gong:
The land like an Eden before them is fair,
But behind them a wilderness dreary and bare.[7]   20

The shrieks of the orphan, the lone widow's wail,
The groans of the childless, are loud on the gale;
For the star of thy glory is blasted and wan,
And wither'd the flower of thy fame, Hindostan!

1827

FROM *POEMS, CHIEFLY LYRICAL* (1830)

Ode to Memory[1]

ADDRESSED TO ———.

1

Thou who stealest fire,
From the fountains of the past,

---

9. "See Sir William Jones on Eastern Plants."
1. "The fabled fountain of youth in the Bahamas, in search of which Juan Ponce de Leon discovered Florida."
2. A poem characteristic of a number of Alfred's pieces most visibly indebted to Byron and Scott for style and subject.
3. What! You are going to fight a king, whose power seems to force the heavens to defend him, under whom all Asia has seen her kings fall and whose force of conquest finds strength in his laws.
4. The fields lie wasted with devastation.
5. "This invader required as a ransom for Mohammed Shah no less than thirty millions, and amassed in the rich city of Delhi the enormous sum of two hundred and thirty-one milions sterling. Others, however, differ considerably in their account of this treasure."
6. "Such pompous epithets the Oriental writers are accustomed to bestow on their monarchs; of which sufficient specimens may be seen in Sir William Jones's translation of the History of Nadir Shah."
7. " 'The land is as the garden of Eden before them, and behind them a desolate wilderness.' JOEL."
1. First published in the 1830 volume with the subtitle "Written very Early in Life" which subsequently became "Addressed to ———" with Arthur Hallam in mind.

To glorify the present, O, haste,
    Visit my low desire!
Strengthen me, enlighten me!   5
I faint in this obscurity,
Thou dewy dawn of memory.

2

    Come not as thou camest of late,
    Flinging the gloom of yesternight
On the white day, but robed in soften'd light   10
    Of orient state.
Whilome thou camest with the morning mist,
    Even as a maid, whose stately brow
The dew-impearled winds of dawn have kiss'd,
        When she, as thou,   15
Stays on her floating locks the lovely freight
Of overflowing blooms, and earliest shoots
Of orient green, giving safe pledge of fruits,
    Which in wintertide shall star
    The black earth with brilliance rare.   20

3

Whilome thou camest with the morning mist,
    And with the evening cloud,
Showering thy gleaned wealth into my open breast;
Those peerless flowers which in the rudest wind
       Never grow sere,   25
When rooted in the garden of the mind,
    Because they are the earliest of the year.
       Nor was the night thy shroud.
In sweet dreams softer than unbroken rest
Thou leddest by the hand thine infant Hope.   30
The eddying of her garments caught from thee
The light of thy great presence; and the cope[2]
    Of the half-attain'd futurity,
    Tho' deep not fathomless,
Was cloven with the million stars which tremble   35
O'er the deep mind of dauntless infancy.
Small thought was there of life's distress;
For sure she deem'd no mist of earth could dull
Those spirit-thrilling eyes so keen and beautiful;
Sure she was nigher to heaven's spheres,   40
Listening the lordly music flowing from
       The illimitable years.
    O, strengthen me, enlighten me!
    I faint in this obscurity,
    Thou dewy dawn of memory.   45

4

Come forth, I charge thee, arise,
Thou of the many tongues, the myriad eyes!

---

2. Cloak.

Thou comest not with shows of flaunting vines
  Unto mine inner eye,
  Divinest Memory!   50
 Thou wert not nursed by the waterfall
Which ever sounds and shines
 A pillar of white light upon the wall
Of purple cliffs, aloof descried:
Come from the woods that belt the gray hillside,[3]   55
The seven elms, the poplars four
That stand beside my father's door,
And chiefly from the brook that loves
To purl o'er matted cress and ribbed sand,
Or dimple in the dark of rushy coves,   60
Drawing into his narrow earthen urn,
  In every elbow and turn,
The filter'd tribute of the rough woodland;
  O, hither lead thy feet!
Pour round mine ears the livelong bleat   65
Of the thick-fleeced sheep from wattled folds,
  Upon the ridgéd wolds,
When the first matin-song hath waken'd loud
Over the dark dewy earth forlorn,
What time the amber morn   70
Forth gushes from beneath a low-hung cloud.

5

Large dowries doth the raptured eye
 To the young spirit present
  When first she is wed,
   And like a bride of old   75
  In triumph led,
   With music and sweet showers
   Of festal flowers,
 Unto the dwelling she must sway.
Well hast thou done, great artist Memory,   80
 In setting round thy first experiment
  With royal framework of wrought gold;
Needs must thou dearly love thy first essay,
And foremost in thy various gallery
  Place it, where sweetest sunlight falls   85
   Upon the storied walls;
   For the discovery
And newness of thine art so pleased thee

---

3. The following lines describe in some detail the landscape about the Somersby rectory, the family home until 1837. Tennyson would draw throughout his life upon his memories of the Lincolnshire countryside as a source for natural imagery, and Arthur Hallam's romanticized notion of Somersby is essentially accurate in stressing its centrality in the moulding of the young poet's mind. "Many years perhaps, or shall I say many ages, after we all have been laid in dust," Hallam wrote to Alfred's sister Emily in 1831, "young lovers of the beautiful and the true may seek in faithful pilgrimage the spot where Alfred's mind was moulded in silent sympathy with the everlasting forms of nature" (*Memoir*, I, 74).

That all which thou hast drawn of fairest
Or boldest since but lightly weighs   90
With thee unto the love thou bearest
The first-born of thy genius. Artist-like,
Ever retiring thou dost gaze
On the prime labor of thine early days,
No matter what the sketch might be: 95
Whether the high field on the bushless pike,[4]
Or even a sand-built ridge[5]
Of heaped hills that mound the sea,
Overblown with murmurs harsh,
Or even a lowly cottage whence we see   100
Stretch'd wide and wild the waste enormous marsh,
Where from the frequent bridge,
Like emblems of infinity,
The trenched waters run from sky to sky;
Or a garden bower'd close   105
With plaited alleys of the trailing rose,
Long alleys falling down to twilight grots,
Or opening upon level plots
Of crowned lilies, standing near
Purple-spiked lavender: 110
Whither in after life retired
From brawling storms,
From weary wind,
With youthful fancy re-inspired,
We may hold converse with all forms   115
Of the many-sided mind,
And those whom passion hath not blinded,
Subtle-thoughted, myriad-minded.

My friend, with you to live alone[6]
Were how much better than to own   120
A crown, a sceptre, and a throne!
O, strengthen me, enlighten me!
I faint in this obscurity,
Thou dewy dawn of memory.

1826?; 1830

---

4. A Cumberland word for "peak."
5. Here follows a description of the seaside on the North Sea at Mable-thorpe where the family regularly went during the summer. "I used to stand on this sand-built ridge . . . and think that it was the spine-bone of the world" (*Memoir*, I, 20). A fragment of a poem about Mablethorpe composed in 1837 provides an interesting gloss.

> Here often when a child I lay re-clined:
>   I took delight in this fair strand and free;
> Here stood the infant Ilion of the mind,
>   And here the Grecian ships all seem'd to be.
> And here again I come, and only find
>   The drain-cut level of the marshy lea,
> Gray sand-banks, and pale sunsets, dreary wind,
>   Dim shores, dense rains, and heavy-clouded sea.
>   (*Memoir*, I, 161.)

6. These lines to Arthur Hallam were probably added just before the poem was published.

Song[7]

1

A spirit haunts the year's last hours
Dwelling amid these yellowing bowers.
    To himself he talks;
For at eventide, listening earnestly,
At his work you may hear him sob and sigh   5
    In the walks;
  Earthward he boweth the heavy stalks
Of the mouldering flowers.
      Heavily hangs the broad sunflower
        Over its grave i' the earth so chilly;   10
      Heavily hangs the hollyhock,
        Heavily hangs the tiger-lily.

2

The air is damp, and hush'd, and close,
As a sick man's room when he taketh repose
    An hour before death;[8]   15
My very heart faints and my whole soul grieves
At the moist rich smell of the rotting leaves,
    And the breath
Of the fading edges of box beneath,
And the year's last rose.   20
      Heavily hangs the broad sunflower
        Over its grave i' the earth so chilly;
      Heavily hangs the hollyhock,
        Heavily hangs the tiger-lily.

1830

Sonnet[9]

Could I outwear my present state of woe
With one brief winter, and indue i' the spring
Hues of fresh youth, and mightily outgrow
The wan dark coil of faded suffering—
Forth in the pride of beauty issuing   5
A sheeny snake, the light of vernal bowers,
Moving his crest to all sweet plots of flowers
And watered valleys where the young birds sing;

---

7. Written on the lawn outside the rectory at Somersby, this poem, like "Ode to Memory," shows clearly that Tennyson's most accomplished early work derived from firsthand experiences. As direct as anything may well be in reporting sensations, the hauntingly evocative picture of autumnal decay especially appealed to Edgar Allan Poe. One thinks of Keats's "Ode to Autumn," although there the notion of decay is implicit.

8. Compare the opening of T. S. Eliot's "The Love Song of J. Alfred Prufrock," in which ". . . the evening is spread out against the sky / Like a patient etherized upon a table."

9. Appearing in the edition of 1830 but omitted later, this sonnet is included here to indicate the uneven quality of the poetry in that volume.

Could I thus hope my lost delight's renewing,
I straightly would command the tears to creep   10
From my charged lids; but inwardly I weep;
Some vital heat as yet my heart is wooing:
That to itself hath drawn the frozen rain
From my cold eyes, and melted it again.

1830

The Mystic[1]

Angels have talked with him, and showed him thrones:
Ye knew him not; he was not one of ye,
Ye scorned him with an undiscerning scorn:
Ye could not read the marvel in his eye,
The still serene abstraction: he hath felt   5
The vanities of after and before;
Albeit, his spirit and his secret heart
The stern experiences of converse lives,
The linkéd woes of many a fiery change
Had purified, and chastened, and made free.   10
Always there stood before him, night and day,
Of wayward vary-colored circumstance
The imperishable presences serene,
Colossal, without form, or sense, or sound,
Dim shadows but unwaning presences   15
Fourfacéd to four corners of the sky:
And yet again, three shadows, fronting one,
One forward, one respectant, three but one;
And yet again, again and evermore,
For the two first were not, but only seemed.   20
One shadow in the midst of a great light,
One reflex from eternity on time,
One mighty countenance of perfect calm,
Awful with most invariable eyes.
For him the silent congregated hours,   25
Daughters of time, divinely tall, beneath
Severe and youthful brows, with shining eyes
Smiling a godlike smile (the innocent light

---

1. Suppressed after 1830, this poem does not reappear in an authorized edition. Hallam Tennyson reprinted "The Mystic" in his notes to "The Ancient Sage" (1885), observing the poet's "early intimations, or indistinct visions of the mind's power to pass beyond the shadows of the world—to pierce beyond the enveloping clouds of ignorance and illusion, and to search some region of pure light and untroubled calm, where perfect knowledge shall have extinguished doubt." Tennyson himself wrote: "A kind of waking trance I have frequently had, quite up from boyhood, when I have been all alone. This has generally come upon me thro' repeating my own name two or three times to myself silently, till all at once, as it were out of the intensity of the consciousness of individuality, the individuality itself seemed to dissolve and fade away into boundless being" (*Memoir*, I, 320). "The Mystic" may be compared with "Armageddon," a more personal expression of similar mystic experience, and to passages from *The Devil and the Lady*. See note 2, p. 504.

Of earliest youth pierced through and through with all
Keen knowledges of low-embowéd eld)   30
Upheld, and ever hold aloft the cloud
Which droops low-hung on either gate of life,
Both birth and death: he in the centre fixt,
Saw far on each side through the grated gates
Most pale and clear and lovely distances.   35
He often lying broad awake, and yet
Remaining from the body, and apart
In intellect and power and will,[2] hath heard
Time flowing in the middle of the night,
And all things creeping to a day of doom.   40
How could ye know him?[3] Ye were yet within
The narrower circle: he had wellnigh reached
The last, which with a region of white flame,
Pure without heat, into a larger air
Upburning, and an ether of black blue,   45
Investeth and ingirds all other lives.

1830

Love[4]

1

Thou, from the first, unborn, undying Love,
Albeit we gaze not on thy glories near,
Before the face of God didst breathe and move,
Though night and pain and ruin and death reign here.
Thou foldest, like a golden atmosphere,   5
The very throne of the eternal God:
Passing through thee the edicts of his fear
Are mellowed into music, borne abroad
By the loud winds, though they uprend the sea,
Even from its central deeps: thine empery   10
Is over all; thou wilt not brook eclipse;
Thou goest and returnest to His lips
Like lightning: thou dost ever brood above
The silence of all hearts, unutterable Love.

2

To know thee is all wisdom, and old age   15
Is but to know thee: dimly we behold thee
Athwart the veils of evils which infold thee.

2. Of the experience in general Tennyson said, "This might be the state which St. Paul describes, 'Whether in the body I cannot tell, or whether out of the body I cannot tell' " (*Memoir*, I, 320). Compare *In Memoriam*, 95, 5–11.

3. See "The Poet" and "The Poet's Mind" for the notion of the prophet-poet as similarly detached from society.

4. Suppressed after its appearance in 1830, this sonnet series, like passages in *The Devil and the Lady*, concerns the theme of transcendent love, later more fully developed in *In Memoriam*. Similar use of the serpent figure appears in the sonnet "Could I outwear my present state of woe." Also see note 7 to "Memory," p. 514, and note 8 to the other "Memory," p. 521.

We beat upon our aching hearts in rage;
We cry for thee; we deem the world thy tomb.
As dwellers in lone planets look upon   20
The mighty disk of their majestic sun,
Hollowed in awful chasms of wheeling gloom,
Making their day dim, so we gaze on thee.
Come, thou of many crowns, white-robéd Love,
Oh! rend the veil in twain: all men adore thee;   25
Heaven crieth after thee; earth waiteth for thee;
Breathe on thy wingéd throne, and it shall move
In music and in light o'er land and sea.

3
And now—methinks I gaze upon thee now,
As on a serpent in his agonies   30
Awe-stricken Indians; what time laid low
And crushing the thick fragrant reeds he lies,
When the new year warm-breathéd on the Earth,
Waiting to light him with her purple skies,
Calls to him by the fountain to uprise.   35
Already with the pangs of a new birth
Strain the hot spheres of his convulséd eyes,
And in his writhings awful hues begin
To wander down his sable-sheeny sides.[5]
Like light on troubled waters: from within   40
Anon he rusheth forth with merry din.
And in him light and joy and strength abides;
And from his brows a crown of living light
Looks through the thick-stemmed woods by day and night.

1830

The Dying Swan

1
The plain was grassy, wild and bare,
Wide, wild, and open to the air,
Which had built up everywhere
    An under-roof of doleful gray.
With an inner voice the river ran,   5
Adown it floated a dying swan,
    And loudly did lament.
    It was the middle of the day.
Ever the weary wind went on,
    And took the reed-tops as it went.   10

---

5. As elsewhere in the early poems, these lines show Tennyson's struggle to render his notion of passion in the ill-suited snake metaphor. In *Tennyson in Egypt*, pp. 48 ff, W. D. Paden has an interesting, if at times far-fetched, psychoanalytic interpretation in which he sees Tennyson's identification with the snake as a surrogate for sexual experience.

2

Some blue peaks in the distance rose,
And white against the cold-white sky
Shone out their crowning snows.
  One willow over the river wept,
And shook the wave as the wind did sigh;   15
Above in the wind was the swallow,
    Chasing itself at its own wild will,[6]
    And far thro' the marish green and still
    The tangled water-courses slept,
Shot over with purple, and green, and yellow.   20

3

The wild swan's death-hymn took the soul
Of that waste place with joy
Hidden in sorrow. At first to the ear
The warble was low, and full and clear;
And floating about the under-sky,   25
Prevailing in weakness, the coronach[7] stole
Sometimes afar, and sometimes anear;
But anon her awful jubilant voice,
With a music strange and manifold,
Flow'd forth on a carol free and bold;   30
As when a mighty people rejoice
With shawms,[8] and with cymbals, and harps of gold,
And the tumult of their acclaim is roll'd
Thro' the open gates of the city afar,
To the shepherd who watcheth the evening star.   35
And the creeping mosses and clambering weeds,
And the willow-branches hoar and dank,
And the wavy swell of the soughing[9] reeds,
And the wave-worn horns of the echoing bank,
And the silvery marish-flowers that throng   40
The desolate creeks and pools among,
Were flooded over with eddying song.[1]

1830

The Deserted House

1

Life and Thought have gone away
    Side by side,
    Leaving door and windows wide;
Careless tenants they!

---

6. Compare Wordsworth's line, "The river glideth at his own sweet will," from "Composed upon Westminster Bridge."
7. A dirge.
8. A kind of oboe.

9. A murmuring, sighing sound.
1. As in "The Ode to Memory" and "A Spirit Haunts the Year's Last Hours," the imagery of section 3 particularly seems to be drawn from the Rectory garden at Somersby.

2

All within is dark as night: 5
In the windows is no light;
And no murmur at the door,
So frequent on its hinge before.

3

Close the door, the shutters close,
    Or thro' the windows we shall see   10
    The nakedness and vacancy
Of the dark deserted house.[2]

4

Come away; no more of mirth
    Is here or merry-making sound.
The house was builded of the earth,   15
    And shall fall again to ground.

5

Come away; for Life and Thought
    Here no longer dwell,
But in a city glorious—
A great and distant city[3]—have bought   20
    A mansion incorruptible.
Would they could have stayed with us!

1830

The Grasshopper[4]

1

Voice of the summer wind,
Joy of the summer plain,
Life of the summer hours,
Carol clearly, bound along.
No Tithon[5] thou as poets feign   5
(Shame fall 'em, they are deaf and blind),
But an insect lithe and strong,
Bowing the seeded summer flowers.
Prove their falsehood and thy quarrel,
    Vaulting on thine airy feet.   10
Clap thy shielded sides and carol,
    Carol clearly, chirrup sweet.

2. Allegorically, the human body.
3. Here, as in the preceding poem, the city as contrasted to the wastelands assumes positive connotations. The conclusion of "The Palace of Art" contains a similar vision of the city as the locus of social values and dimly foreshadows the poet's much later conception of Camelot in *Idylls of the King* in which the city temporarily becomes the center of all which is "high and holy."
4. Suppressed after 1830, the poem does not reappear in an authorized text.

Typical of the juvenilia, with such minor affectations as the sounded "éd" in "floweréd," perhaps the poem's chief interest lies in contrasting it to the far superior 'Tithonus,' begun as early as 1833.
5. Tithonus, granted eternal life but not eternal youth, was turned into a grasshopper. The piece is an ingenuous attempt to divest the grasshopper of the mythological identity imposed upon him.

Thou art a mailéd warrior in youth and strength complete;
      Armed cap-a-pie[6]
      Full fair to see;   15
      Unknowing fear,
      Undreading loss,
  A gallant cavalier,
  Sans peur et sans reproche,
  In sunlight and in shadow,   20
  The Bayard[7] of the meadow.

2

I would dwell with thee,
  Merry grasshopper,
 Thou art so glad and free,
  And as light as air;   25
Thou hast no sorrow or tears,
Thou hast no compt of years,
No withered immortality,
But a short youth sunny and free.
Carol clearly, bound along,   30
  Soon thy joy is over,
A summer of loud song,
  And slumbers in the clover.
What hast thou to do with evil
In thine hour of love and revel,   35
  In thy heat of summer pride,
Pushing the thick roots aside
Of the singing floweréd grasses,
That brush thee with their silken tresses?
What hast thou to do with evil,[8]   40
Shooting, singing, ever springing
  In and out the emerald glooms,
Ever leaping, ever singing,
  Lighting on the golden blooms?

1830

Recollections of the Arabian Nights[9]

When the breeze of a joyful dawn blew free
In the silken sail of infancy,
The tide of time flow'd back with me,
  The forward-flowing tide of time;
And many a sheeny summer-morn,   5

---

6. From head to foot.
7. Chevalier Bayard (c. 1473–1524), known as the knight "without fear and without reproach."
8. In the poem the question seems irrelevant, but it is familiar enough in the context of the juvenilia. See, for example, *The Devil and the Lady,* note

2, p. 507, for a similar concern with animals and their lack of a moral sense.
9. Reflecting Tennyson's early interest in exotic Eastern literature, the poem is reminiscent of a number of pieces in *Poems by Two Brothers.*

Adown the Tigris I was borne,
By Bagdat's shrines of fretted gold,
High-walled gardens green and old;
True Mussulman was I and sworn,
   For it was in the golden prime   10
      Of good Haroun Alraschid.[1]

Anight my shallop, rustling thro'
The low and bloomed foliage, drove
The fragrant, glistening deeps, and clove
The citron-shadows in the blue;   15
By garden porches on the brim,
The costly doors flung open wide,
Gold glittering thro' lamplight dim,
And broider'd sofas on each side.
   In sooth it was a goodly time,   20
      For it was in the golden prime
      Of good Haroun Alraschid.

Often, where clear-stemm'd platans guard
The outlet, did I turn away
The boat-head down a broad canal   25
From the main river sluiced, where all
The sloping of the moonlit sward
Was damask-work, and deep inlay
Of braided blooms unmown, which crept
Adown to where the water slept.   30
   A goodly place, a goodly time,
      For it was in the golden prime
      Of good Haroun Alraschid.

A motion from the river won
Ridged the smooth level, bearing on   35
My shallop thro' the star-strown calm,
Until another night in night
I enter'd, from the clearer light,
Imbower'd vaults of pillar'd palm,
Imprisoning sweets, which, as they clomb   40
Heavenward, were stay'd beneath the dome
   Of hollow boughs. A goodly time,
      For it was in the golden prime
      Of good Haroun Alraschid.[2]

Still onward; and the clear canal   45
Is rounded to as clear a lake.
From the green rivage[3] many a fall
Of diamond rillets musical,
Thro' little crystal arches low

1. A Caliph of Bagdad (763–809), patron of the arts, and hero of the *Arabian Nights* stories, Tennyson's source in Galland's French translation.
2. A stanza which clearly shows a stylistic indebtedness to Coleridge's "Kubla Khan," a poem Tennyson especially admired.
3. The riverbank.

Down from the central fountain's flow   50
Fallen silver-chiming, seemed to shake
The sparkling flints beneath the prow.
   A goodly place, a goodly time,
   For it was in the golden prime
      Of good Haroun Alraschid.   55

Above thro' many a bowery turn
A walk with vari-colored shells
Wander'd engrain'd. On either side
All round about the fragrant marge
From fluted vase, and brazen urn   60
In order, eastern flowers large,
Some dropping low their crimson bells
Half-closed, and others studded wide
   With disks and tiars, fed the time
   With odor in the golden prime   65
      Of good Haroun Alraschid.

Far off, and where the lemon grove
In closest coverture upsprung,
The living airs of middle night
Died round the bulbul[4] as he sung;   70
Not he, but something which possess'd
The darkness of the world, delight,
Life, anguish, death, immortal love,
Ceasing not, mingled, unrepress'd,
   Apart from place, withholding time,   75
   But flattering the golden prime
      Of good Haroun Alraschid.

Black the garden-bowers and grots
Slumber'd; the solemn palms were ranged
Above, unwoo'd of summer wind;   80
A sudden splendor from behind
Flush'd all the leaves with rich gold-green,
And, flowing rapidly between
Their interspaces, counterchanged
The level lake with diamond-plots   85
   Of dark and bright. A lovely time,
   For it was in the golden prime
      Of good Haroun Alraschid.

Dark-blue the deep sphere overhead,
Distinct with vivid stars inlaid,   90
Grew darker from that under-flame;
So, leaping lightly from the boat,
With silver anchor left afloat,
In marvel whence that glory came
Upon me, as in sleep I sank   95

---

4. Persian name for the nightingale.

In cool soft turf upon the bank,
   Entranced with that place and time,
   So worthy of the golden prime
     Of good Haroun Alraschid.

Thence thro' the garden I was drawn—   100
A realm of pleasance, many a mound,
And many a shadow-chequer'd lawn
Full of the city's stilly sound,
And deep myrrh-thickets blowing round
The stately cedar, tamarisks,[5]   105
Thick rosaries of scented thorn,
Tall orient shrubs, and obelisks
   Graven with emblems of the time,
   In honor of the golden prime
     Of good Haroun Alraschid.   110

With dazed vision unawares
From the long alley's latticed shade
Emerged, I came upon the great
Pavilion of the Caliphat.
Right to the carven cedarn doors,   115
Flung inward over spangled floors,
Broad-based flights of marble stairs
Ran up with golden balustrade,
   After the fashion of the time,
   And humor of the golden prime   120
     Of good Haroun Alraschid.

The fourscore windows all alight
As with the quintessence of flame,
A million tapers flaring bright
From twisted silvers look'd to shame   125
The hollow-vaulted dark, and stream'd
Upon the mooned[6] domes aloof
In inmost Bagdat, till there seem'd
Hundreds of crescents on the roof
   Of night new-risen, that marvellous time   130
   To celebrate the golden prime
     Of good Haroun Alraschid.

Then stole I up, and trancedly
Gazed on the Persian girl[7] alone,
Serene with argent-lidded eyes   135
Amorous, and lashes like to rays
Of darkness, and a brow of pearl
Tressed with redolent ebony,

---

5. Desert shrubs with white or pink flowers.
6. The crescent of the Turkish emblem, and not Arabian.
7. Noureddin, the "fair Persian" in the *Arabian Nights*. The episode shows a new sense of freedom to indulge in a Keatsian vision of sensuous experience. See note 3 to "Thou Camest to Thy Bower," p. 529.

In many a dark delicious curl,
Flowing beneath her rose-hued zone;   140
   The sweetest lady of the time,
    Well worthy of the golden prime
     Of good Haroun Alraschid.

Six columns, three on either side,
Pure silver, underpropt a rich   145
Throne of the massive ore, from which
Down-droop'd, in many a floating fold,
Engarlanded and diaper'd[8]
With inwrought flowers, a cloth of gold.
Thereon, his deep eye laughter-stirr'd   150
With merriment of kingly pride,
   Sole star of all that place and time,
   I saw him—in his golden prime,
    The Good Haroun Alraschid.

1830

The Sleeping Beauty[9]

1

Year after year unto her feet,
   She lying on her couch alone,
Across the purple coverlet
   The maiden's jet-black hair has grown,
On either side her tranced form   5
   Forth streaming from a braid of pearl;
The slumbrous light is rich and warm,
   And moves not on the rounded curl.

2

The silk star-broider'd coverlid
   Unto her limbs itself doth mould   10
Languidly ever; and, amid
   Her full black ringlets downward roll'd,
Glows forth each softly-shadow'd arm
   With bracelets of the diamond bright.
Her constant beauty doth inform   15
   Stillness with love, and day with light.

3

She sleeps; her breathings are not heard
   In palace chambers far apart.
The fragrant tresses are not stirr'd
   That lie upon her charmed heart.   20
She sleeps; on either hand upswells

8. Patterned with the shapes of diamonds.
9. Altered slightly from the 1830 version, the piece reappears in 1842 as the third section of the much longer and elaborately wrought poem, "The Day-Dream."

The gold-fringed pillow lightly prest;
She sleeps, nor dreams, but ever dwells
A perfect form in perfect rest.

1830

A Character[1]

With a half-glance upon the sky
At night he said, "The wanderings
Of this most intricate Universe
Teach me the nothingness of things;"
Yet could not all creation pierce   5
Beyond the bottom of his eye.

He spake of beauty: that the dull
Saw no divinity in grass,
Life in dead stones, or spirit in air;
Then looking as 't were in a glass,   10
He smooth'd his chin and sleek'd his hair,
And said the earth was beautiful.

He spake of virtue: not the gods
More purely when they wish to charm
Pallas and Juno sitting by;   15
And with a sweeping of the arm,
And a lack-lustre dead-blue eye,
Devolved his rounded periods.[2]

Most delicately hour by hour
He canvass'd human mysteries,   20
And trod on silk, as if the winds
Blew his own praises in his eyes,
And stood aloof from other minds
In impotence of fancied power.

With lips depress'd as he were meek,   25
Himself unto himself he sold:
Upon himself himself did feed;
Quiet, dispassionate, and cold,
And other than his form of creed,
With chisell'd features clear and sleek.   30

1830

1. Sunderland, the most able and most brilliant speaker in the Cambridge Union Debating Society, has been identified as the character in the poem, one of Tennyson's few attempts at satire. When showed the lines and told Tennyson was the author, Sunderland reportedly asked, "Which Tennyson? The slovenly one?" Edward FitzGerald called Sunderland "a very plausible, parliament-like, self-satisfied speaker" (*Memoir*, I, 37).
2. Sunderland apparently spoke in a cold drawl which Tennyson found particularly obnoxious.

Early Responses[*]

ARTHUR HENRY HALLAM

On Some of the Characteristics of Modern Poetry, and on the Lyrical Poems of Alfred Tennyson[†]

When Mr. Wordsworth, in his celebrated Preface to the "Lyrical Ballads," asserted that immediate or rapid popularity was not the test of poetry, great was the consternation and clamour among those farmers of public favour, the established critics. Never had so audacious an attack been made upon their undoubted privileges and hereditary charter of oppression. * * * They could not put down Mr. Wordsworth by clamour, or prevent his doctrine, once uttered, and enforced by his example, from awakening the minds of men, and giving a fresh impulse to art. It was the truth, and it prevailed; not only against the exasperation of that hydra, the Reading Public, whose vanity was hurt, and the blustering of its keepers, whose delusion was exposed, but even against the false glosses and narrow apprehensions of the Wordsworthians themselves. It is the madness of all who loosen some great principle, long buried under a snow-heap of custom and superstition, to imagine that they can restrain its operation, or circumscribe it by their purposes. But the right of private judgment was stronger than the will of Luther; and even the genius of Wordsworth cannot expand itself to the full periphery of poetic art.

It is not true, as his exclusive admirers would have it, that the highest species of poetry is the reflective: it is a gross fallacy, that, because certain opinions are acute or profound, the expression of them by the imagination must be eminently beautiful. Whenever the mind of the artist suffers itself to be occupied, during its periods of creation, by any other predominant motive than the desire of beauty, the result is false in art. Now there is undoubtedly no reason, why he may not find beauty in those moods of emotion, which arise from the combinations of reflective thought, and it is possible that he may delineate these with fidelity, and not be led astray by any suggestions of an unpoetical mood. But, though

[*] In the following commentaries, including those in the Criticism section, the footnotes of the originals have been retained, with additional notes by the present editor marked [*Editor*].
[†] From the *Englishman's Magazine*, I (August 1831), pp. 616–628.

possible, it is hardly probable: for a man, whose reveries take a reasoning turn, and who is accustomed to measure his ideas by their logical relations rather than the congruity of the sentiments to which they refer, will be apt to mistake the pleasure he has in knowing a thing to be true, for the pleasure he would have in knowing it to be beautiful, and so will pile his thoughts in a rhetorical battery, that they may convince, instead of letting them glow in the natural course of contemplation, that they may enrapture. It would not be difficult to shew, by reference to the most admired poems of Wordsworth, that he is frequently chargeable with this error, and that much has been said by him which is good as philosophy, powerful as rhetoric, but false as poetry. Perhaps this very distortion of the truth did more in the peculiar juncture of our literary affairs to enlarge and liberalize the genius of our age, than could have been effected by a less sectarian temper. However this may be, a new school of reformers soon began to attract attention, who, professing the same independence of immediate favour, took their stand on a different region of Parnassus from that occupied by the Lakers, and one, in our opinion, much less liable to perturbing currents of air from ungenial climates. We shall not hesitate to express our conviction, that the Cockney school (as it was termed in derision, from a cursory view of its accidental circumstances) contained more genuine inspiration, and adhered more speedily to that portion of truth which it embraced, than any *form* of art that has existed in this country since the day of Milton. Their *caposetta* was Mr. Leigh Hunt, who did little more than point the way, and was diverted from his aim by a thousand personal predilections and political habits of thought. But he was followed by two men of a very superior make; men who were born poets, lived poets, and went poets to their untimely graves. Shelley and Keats were, indeed, of opposite genius; that of the one was vast, impetuous, and sublime: the other seemed to be "fed with honey-dew," and to have "drunk the milk of Paradise." Even the softness of Shelley comes out in bold, rapid, comprehensive strokes; he has no patience for minute beauties, unless they can be massed into a general effect of grandeur. On the other hand, the tenderness of Keats cannot sustain a lofty flight; he does not generalize or allegorize Nature; his imagination works with few symbols, and reposes willingly on what is given freely. Yet in this formal opposition of character there is, it seems to us, a ground-work of similarity sufficient for the purposes of classification, and constituting a remarkable point in the progress of literature. They are both poets of sensation rather than reflection. * * * But the age in which we live comes late in our national progress. That first raciness, and juvenile vigour of literature, when nature "wantoned as in her prime, and played at will her virgin fancies," is gone, never to return. Since that day we have undergone a period of degradation. "Every handicraftsman has worn the mark of Poesy." It would be tedious to repeat the tale, so often related, of French contagion, and the heresies of the Popian school. With the close of the last century came an era of reaction, an era of painful struggle, to bring our overcivilised condition of thought into union with the fresh productive spirit that brightened the morning of our literature. But repentance is unlike innocence: the laborious endeavour to restore has more complicated methods of action, than the freedom of untainted nature. Those different powers of poetic disposition, the energies of Sensitive, of Reflective, of Passionate Emotion, which in former times were intermingled, and derived from mutual support an extensive empire over the feelings of men, were now restrained within separate spheres of agency. The whole system no longer worked harmoniously, and by intrinsic harmony acquired external freedom; but there arose a violent and unusual action in the several component functions, each for itself, all striving to reproduce the regular power which the whole had once enjoyed. Hence the melancholy, which so evidently characterises the spirit of modern poetry; hence that return of the mind upon itself, and the habit of seeking relief in idiosyncracies rather than community of interest. In the old times the poetic impulse went along with the general impulse of the nation; in these, it is a reaction against it, a check acting for conservation against a propulsion towards change. We have indeed seen it urged in some of our fashionable publications, that the diffusion of poetry must necessarily be in the direct ratio of the diffusion of machinery, because a highly civilized people must have new objects of interest, and thus a new field will be opened to description. But this notable argument forgets that against this *objective* amelioration may be set the decrease of *subjective* power, arising from a prevalence of social activity, and a continual absorption of the higher feelings into the palpable interests of ordinary life. The French Revolution may be a finer theme than the war of Troy; but it does not so evidently follow that Homer is to find his superior. Our inference, therefore, from this change in the relative position of artists to the rest of the community is, that modern poetry, in proportion to its depth and truth, is likely to have little immediate authority over public opinion. Admirers it will have; sects consequently it will form; and these strong under-currents will in time sensibly affect the principal stream. Those writers, whose genius, though great, is not strictly and essentially poetic, become mediators between the votaries of art and the careless cravers for excitement. Art herself, less manifestly glorious than in her periods of undisputed supremacy, retains her essential prerogatives, and forgets not to raise up chosen spirits, who may minister to her state, and vindicate her title.

One of this faithful Islam, a poet in the truest and highest sense, we are anxious to present to our readers. He has yet written little, and published less; but in these "preludes of a loftier strain," we recognise the inspiring god. Mr. Tennyson belongs decidedly to the class we have already described as Poets of Sensation. He sees all the forms of nature with the *"eruditus oculus,"* and his ear has a fairy fineness. There is a strange earnestness in his worship of beauty, which throws a charm over his impassioned song, more easily felt than described, and not to be escaped by those who have once felt it. We think he has more definiteness, and soundness of general conception, than the late Mr. Keats, and is much more free from blemishes of diction, and hasty capriccios of fancy. He has also this advantage over that poet, and his friend Shelley, that he comes before the public, unconnected with any political party, or peculiar system of opinions. Nevertheless, true to the theory we have stated, we believe his participation in their characteristic excellencies is sufficient to secure him a share in their unpopularity. The volume of "Poems, chiefly Lyrical," does not contain above 154 pages; but it shews us much more of the character of its parent mind, than many books we have known of much larger compass, and more boastful pretensions. The features of original genius are clearly and strongly marked. The author imitates nobody; we recognise the spirit of his age, but not the individual form of this or that writer. His thoughts bear no more resemblance to Byron or Scott, Shelley or Coleridge, than to Homer or Calderon, Ferdusi or Calidas. We have remarked five distinctive excellencies of his own manner. First, his luxuriance of imagination, and at the same time his control over it. Secondly, his power of embodying himself in ideal characters, or rather moods of character, with such extreme accuracy of adjustment, that the circumstances of the narration seem to have a natural correspondence with the predominant feeling, and, as it were, to be evolved from it by assimilative force. Thirdly, his vivid, picturesque delineation of objects, and the peculiar skill with which he holds all of them *fused*, to borrow a metaphor from science, in a medium of strong emotion. Fourthly, the variety of his lyrical measures, and exquisite modulation of harmonious words and cadences to the swell and fall of the feelings expressed. Fifthly, the elevated habits of thought, *implied* in these compositions, and imparting a mellow soberness of tone, more impressive, to our minds, than if the author had drawn up a set of opinions in verse, and sought to instruct the understanding, rather than to communicate the love of beauty to the heart. We shall proceed to give our readers some specimens in illustration of these remarks, and, if possible, we will give them entire; for no poet can fairly be judged of by fragments, least of all a poet, like Mr. Tennyson, whose mind conceives nothing isolated, nothing abrupt, but every part with reference to some other part, and in subservience to the idea of the whole.

"Recollections of the Arabian Nights!" What a delightful, endearing title! How we pity those to whom it calls up no reminiscence of early enjoyment, no sentiment of kindliness as towards one who sings a song they have loved, or mentions with affection a departed friend! But let nobody expect a multifarious enumeration of Viziers, Barmecides, Fireworshippers, and Cadis; trees that sing, horses that fly, and Goules that eat rice pudding! Our author knows what he is about: he has, with great judgment, selected our old acquaintance, "the good Haroun Alraschid," as the most prominent object of our childish interest, and with him has called up one of those luxurious garden scenes, the account of which, in plain prose, used to make our mouths water for sherbet, since luckily we were too young to think much about Zobeide! We think this poem will be the favourite among Mr. Tennyson's admirers; perhaps upon the whole it is our own; at least we find ourselves recurring to it oftener than to any other, and every time we read it, we feel the freshness of its beauty increase. * * *

Criticism will sound but poorly after this; yet we cannot give silent votes. The first stanza, we beg leave to observe, places us at once in the position of feeling, which the poem requires. This scene is before us, around us; we cannot mistake its localities, or blind ourselves to its colours. That happy ductility of childhood returns for the moment; "true Mussulmans are we, and sworn," and yet there is a latent knowledge, which heightens the pleasure, that to our change from really childish thought we owe the capacities by which we enjoy the recollection. As the poem proceeds, all is in perfect keeping. There is a solemn distinctness in every image, a majesty of slow motion in every cadence, that aids the illusion of thought, and steadies its contemplation of the complete picture. Originality of observation seems to cost nothing to our author's liberal genius; he lavishes images of exquisite accuracy and elaborate splendour, as a common writer throws about metaphysical truisms, and exhausted tropes. Amidst all the varied luxuriance of the sensations described, we are never permitted to lose sight of the idea which gives unity to this variety, and by the recurrence of which, as a sort of mysterious influence, at the close of every stanza, the mind is wrought up, with consummate art, to the final disclosure. This poem is a perfect gallery of pictures; and the concise boldness, with which in a few words an object is clearly painted, is sometimes (see the 6th stanza) majestic as Milton, sometimes (see the 12th) sublime as Æschylus. We have not, however, so far forgot our vocation as critics, that we would leave without notice the slight faults which adhere to this precious work. In the 8th stanza, we doubt the propriety of using the bold compound "black-green," at least in such close vicinity to "gold-green:" nor is it perfectly clear by the term, although indicated by the context, that "diamond plots" relates to shape rather than colour. We are perhaps very stupid, but "vivid stars unrayed" does not convey to us a very precise notion. "*Rosaries* of scented thorn," in the 10th stanza, is, we believe, an entirely unauthorized use of the word. Would our author translate "*biferique rosaria Pæsti.*"—"And *rosaries* of Pæstum, twice in bloom?" To the beautiful 13th stanza, we are sorry to find any objection: but even the bewitching loveliness of that "Persian girl" shall not prevent our performing the rigid duty we have undertaken, and we must hint to Mr. Tennyson, that "redolent" is no synonyme for "fragrant." Bees may be redolent *of* honey: spring may be "redolent *of* youth and love," but the absolute use of the word has, we fear, neither in Latin nor English, any better authority than the monastic epitaph on Fair Rosamond. "*Hic jacet in tombâ Rosa Mundi, non Rosa Munda, non redolet, sed olet, quæ redolere solet.*"

We are disposed to agree with Mr. Coleridge, when he says "no adequate compensation can be made for the mischief a writer does by confounding the distinct senses of words." At the same time our feelings in this instance rebel strongly in behalf of "redolent;" for the melody of the passage, as it stands, is beyond the possibility of improvement, and unless he should chance to light upon a word very nearly resembling this in consonants and vowels, we can hardly quarrel with Mr. Tennyson if, in spite of our judgment, he retains the offender in his service.

One word more, before we have done, and it shall be a word of praise. The language of this book, with one or two rare exceptions, is thorough and sterling English. A little more respect, perhaps, was due to the "*jus et norma loquendi*," but we are inclined to consider as venial a fault arising from generous enthusiasm for the principles of sound analogy, and for that Saxon element, which constitutes the intrinsic freedom and nervousness of our native tongue. We see no signs in what Mr. Tennyson has written of the Quixotic spirit which has led some persons to desire the reduction of English to a single form, by excluding nearly the whole of Latin and Roman derivatives. Ours is necessarily a compound language; as such alone it can flourish and increase; nor will the author of the poems we have extracted be likely to barter for a barren appearance of symmetrical structure that fertility of expression, and variety of harmony, which "the speech, that Shakespeare spoke," derived from the sources of southern phraseology.

In presenting this young poet to the public, as one not studious of instant popularity, nor likely to obtain it, we may be thought to play the part of a fashionable lady, who deludes her refractory mate into doing what she chooses, by pretending to wish the exact contrary, or of a cunning pedagogue, who practises a similar manœuvre on some self-willed Flibbertigibbet of the schoolroom. But the supposition would do us wrong. We have spoken in good faith, commending this volume to feeling hearts and imaginative tempers, not to the stupid readers, or the voracious readers, or the malignant readers, or the readers after dinner! We confess, indeed, we never knew an instance in which the theoretical abjurers of popularity have shewn themselves very reluctant to admit its actual advances; so much virtue is not, perhaps, in human nature; and if the world should take a fancy to buy up these poems, in order to be revenged on the ENGLISHMAN'S MAGAZINE, who knows whether even we might not disappoint its malice by a cheerful adaptation of our theory to "existing circumstances?"

JOHN WILSON ["Christopher North"]

Tennyson's Poems†

* * *

But we are getting into the clouds, and our wish is to keep jogging along the turnpike road. So let all this pass for an introduction to our Article—and let us abruptly join company with the gentleman whose name stands at the head of it, Mr Alfred Tennyson, of whom the world, we presume, yet knows but little or nothing, whom his friends call a Phœnix, but who, we hope, will not be dissatisfied with us, should we designate him merely a Swan.

One of the saddest misfortunes that can befall a young poet, is to be the Pet of a Coterie; and the very saddest of all, if in Cockneydom. Such has been the unlucky lot of Alfred Tennyson. He has been elevated to the throne of Little Britain, and sonnets were showered over his coronation from the most remote regions of his empire, even from Hampstead Hill. Eulogies more elaborate than the architecture of the costliest gingerbread, have been built up into panegyrical piles, in commemoration of the Birth-day; and 'twould be a pity indeed with one's crutch to smash the gilt battlements, white too with sugar as with frost, and begemmed with comfits. The besetting sin of all periodical criticism, and now-a-days

† From *Blackwood's Edinburgh Magazine*, XXXI (May 1832), pp. 721–741.

there is no other, is boundless extravagance of praise; but none splash it on like the trowel-men who have been bedaubing Mr Tennyson. There is something wrong, however, with the compost. It won't stick; unseemly cracks deform the surface; it falls off piece by piece ere it has dried in the sun, or it hardens into blotches; and the worshippers have but discoloured and disfigured their Idol. The worst of it is, that they make the Bespattered not only feel, but look ridiculous; he seems as absurd as an Image in a tea-garden; and, bedizened with faded and fantastic garlands, the public cough on being told he is a Poet, for he has much more the appearance of a Post.

The Englishman's Magazine ought not to have died; for it threatened to be a very pleasant periodical. An Essay[1] "on the Genius of Alfred Tennyson," sent it to the grave. The superhuman —nay, supernatural—pomposity of that one paper, incapacitated the whole work for living one day longer in this unceremonious world. The solemnity with which the critic approached the object of his adoration, and the sanctity with which he laid his offerings on the shrine, were too much for our irreligious age. The Essay "on the genius of Alfred Tennyson," awoke a general guffaw, and it expired in convulsions. Yet the Essay was exceedingly well-written —as well as if it had been "on the Genius of Sir Isaac Newton." Therein lay the mistake. Sir Isaac discovered the law of gravitation; Alfred had but written some pretty verses, and mankind were not prepared to set him among the stars. But that he has genius is proved by his being at this moment alive; for had he not, he must have breathed his last under that critique. The spirit of life must indeed be strong within him; for he has outlived a narcotic dose administered to him by a crazy charlatan in the Westminster,[2] and after that he may sleep in safety with a pan of charcoal.

But the Old Man must see justice done to this ingenious lad, and save him from his worst enemies, his friends. Never are we so happy—nay, 'tis now almost our only happiness—as when scattering flowers in the sunshine that falls from the yet unclouded sky on the green path prepared by gracious Nature for the feet of enthusiastic youth. Yet we scatter them not in too lavish profusion; and we take care that the young poet shall see, along with the shadow of the spirit that cheers him on, that, too, of the accompanying crutch. Were we not afraid that our style might be thought to wax too figurative, we should say that Alfred is a promising plant; and that the day may come when, beneath sun and shower, his genius may grow up and expand into a stately tree, embower-

1. Hallam's review [*Editor*].
2. Alludes to a panegyrical review of *Poems, Chiefly Lyrical* in the *West-* *minster Review*, XIV (January 1831), pp. 210–224, probably by William Johnson Fox [*Editor*].

ing a solemn shade within its wide circumference, while the daylight lies gorgeously on its crest, seen from afar in glory—itself a grove.

But that day will never come, if he hearken not to our advice, and, as far as his own nature will permit, regulate by it the movements of his genius. This may perhaps appear, at first sight or hearing, not a little unreasonable on our part; but not so, if Alfred will but lay our words to heart, and meditate on their spirit. We desire to see him prosper; and we predict fame as the fruit of obedience. If he disobey, he assuredly goes to oblivion.

* * *

Shakspeare—Spenser—Milton—Wordsworth—Coleridge—The Ettrick Shepherd—Allan Cunninghame, and some others, have loved, and been beloved by mermaidens, sirens, sea and land fairies, and revealed to the eyes of us who live in the thick atmosphere of this "dim spot which men call earth," all the beautiful wonders of subterranean and submarine climes—and of the climes of Nowhere, lovelier than them all. It pains us to think, that with such names we cannot yet rank that of Alfred Tennyson. We shall soon see that he possesses feeling, fancy, imagination, genius. But in the preternatural lies not the sphere in which he excels. Much disappointed were we to find him weak where we expected him strong; yet we are willing to believe that his failure has been from "affectations." In place of trusting to the natural flow of his own fancies, he has followed some vague abstract idea, thin and delusive, which has escaped in mere words—words—words. Yet the Young Tailor in the Westminster thinks he could take the measure of the merman, and even make a riding-habit for the sirens to wear on gala days, when disposed for "some horseback." 'Tis indeed a jewel of a Snip. His protégee has indited two feeble and fantastic strains entitled "Nothing will Die," "All things will Die." And them, Parsnip Junior, without the fear of the shears before his eyes, compares with L'Allegro and Il Penseroso of Milton, saying, that in Alfred's "there is not less truth, and perhaps more refined observation!" That comes of sitting from childhood cross-legged on a board beneath a skylight.

The Young Tailor can with difficulty keep his seat with delight, when talking of Mr Tennyson's descriptions of the sea. " 'Tis barbarous," quoth he, "to break such a piece of coral for a specimen;" and would fain cabbage the whole lump, with the view of placing it among other rarities, such as bits of Derbyshire spar and a brace of mandarins, on the chimney-piece of the shew-parlour in which he notches the dimensions of his visitors. So fired is his imagination, that he beholds in a shred of green fustian a swatch of the multitudinous sea; and on tearing a skreed, thinks he hears him roaring. But Mr Tennyson should speak of the sea so as to rouse the souls of sailors, rather than the soles of tailors—the enthusiasm of the deck, rather than of the board. Unfortunately, he seems never to have seen a ship, or, if he did, to have forgotten it. The vessel in which the landlubbers were drifting, when the Sea-Fairies salute them with a song, must have been an old tub of a thing, unfit even for a transport. Such a jib! In the cut of her mainsail you smoke the old table-cloth. To be solemn—Alfred Tennyson is as poor on the sea as Barry Cornwall—and, of course, calls him a serpent. They both write like people who, on venturing upon the world of waters in a bathing machine, would ensure their lives by a cork-jacket. Barry swims on the surface of the Great Deep like a feather; Alfred dives less after the fashion of a duck than a bell; but the one sees few lights, the other few shadows, that are not seen just as well by an oyster-dredger. But the soul of the true sea-poet doth undergo a sea-change, soon as he sees Blue Peter; and is off in the gig,

> While bending back, away they pull,
> With measured strokes most beautiful—

There goes the Commodore!
"Our author having the secret of the transmigration of the soul," passes, like Indur, into the bodies of various animals, and

> Three will I mention dearer than the rest,

the Swan, the Grashopper, and the Owl. The Swan is dying; and as we remember hearing Hartley Coleridge praise the lines, they must be fine; though their full meaning be to us like the moon "hid in her vacant interlunar cave." But Hartley, who is like the river Wye, a wanderer through the woods, is aye haunted with visions of the beautiful; and let Alfred console himself by that reflection, for the absent sympathy of Christopher. As for the Grashopper, Alfred, in that green grig, is for a while merry as a cricket, and chirps and chirrups, though with less meaning, with more monotony, than that hearth-loving insect, who is never so happy, you know, as when in the neighbourhood of a baker's oven. He says to himself as Tithon, though he disclaims that patronymic,

> Thou art a mailed warrior, in youth and strength complete.

a line liable to two faults; first, absurdity, and, second, theft; for the mind is unprepared for the exaggeration of a grashopper into a Templar; and Wordsworth, looking at a beetle through the wonder-working glass of a wizard, beheld

> A mailed angel on a battle-day.

But Tennyson out-Wordsworths Wordsworth, and pursues the knight, surnamed Longshanks, into the fields of chivalry.

> Arm'd cap-a-pie,
> Full fain to see;
> Unknowing fear,
> Undreading loss,
> A gallant cavalier,
> *Sans peur et sans reproche*,
> In sunlight and in shadow,
> THE BAYARD OF THE MEADOW!!

Conceived and executed in the spirit of the celebrated imitation—
"Dilly—dilly Duckling! Come and be killed!" But Alfred is greatest
as an Owl.

SONG.—THE OWL.

> When the cats run home and light is come,
>   And dew is cold upon the ground,
> And the far-off stream is dumb,
>   And the whirring sail goes round,
>   And the whirring sail goes round;
>   Alone and warming his five wits,
>   The white owl in the belfry sits.
>
> When merry milkmaids click the latch,
>   And rarely smells the new mown hay,
> And the cock hath sung beneath the thatch
>   Twice or thrice his roundelay:
>   Twice or thrice his roundelay:
>   Alone and warming his five wits,
>   The white owl in the belfry sits.

SECOND SONG.—TO THE SAME

> Thy tuwhits are lulled, I wot,
>   Thy tuwhoos of yesternight,
> Which upon the dark afloat,
>   So took echo with delight,
>   So took echo with delight,
>   That her voice untuneful grown,
>   Wears all day a fainter tone.
>
> I would mock thy chant anew;
>   But I cannot mimic it,
> Not a whit of thy tuwhoo,
>   Thee to woo to thy tuwhit,
>   Thee to woo to thy tuwhit,
>   With a lengthened loud halloo,
>   Tuwhoo, tuwhit, tuwhit, tuwhoo-o-o.

All that he wants is to be shot, stuffed, and stuck into a glass-
case, to be made immortal in a museum.

But, mercy on us! Alfred becomes a—Kraken! Leviathan, "wallowing unwieldy, enormous in his gait," he despises, as we would a minnow; his huge ambition will not suffer him to be "very like a whale;" he must be a—Kraken. And such a Kraken, too, as would have astounded Pontoppidan.

* * *

Our critique is near its conclusion; and in correcting it for press, we see that its whole merit, which is great, consists in the extracts, which are "beautiful exceedingly." Perhaps, in the first part of our article, we may have exaggerated Mr Tennyson's not unfrequent silliness, for we are apt to be carried away by the whim of the moment, and in our humorous moods, many things wear a queer look to our aged eyes, which fill young pupils with tears; but we feel assured that in the second part we have not exaggerated his strength—that we have done no more than justice to his fine faculties—and that the millions who delight in Maga[3] will, with one voice, confirm our judgment—that Alfred Tennyson is a poet.

But, though it might be a mistake of ours, were we to say that he has much to learn, it can be no mistake to say that he has not a little to unlearn, and more to bring into practice, before his genius can achieve its destined triumphs. A puerile partiality for particular forms of expression, nay, modes of spelling and of pronunciation, may be easily overlooked in one whom *we* must look on as yet a mere boy; but if he carry it with him, and indulge it in manhood, why it will make him seem silly as his sheep; and should he continue to bleat so when his head and beard are as grey as ours, he will be truly a laughable old ram, and the ewes will care no more for him than if he were a wether.

* * *

JOHN WILSON CROKER

Poems by Alfred Tennyson†

This is, as some of his marginal notes intimate, Mr. Tennyson's second appearance. By some strange chance we have never seen his first publication, which, if it at all resembles its younger brother, must be by this time so popular that any notice of it on our part would seem idle and presumptuous; but we gladly seize this opportunity of repairing an unintentional neglect, and of introducing to the admiration of our more sequestered readers a new prodigy of genius—another and a brighter star of that galaxy or *milky way*

---

3. I.e., *Blackwood's Edinburgh Magazine* [*Editor*].

† From *Quarterly Review,* XLIX (April 1833), pp. 81–96.

of poetry of which the lamented Keats was the harbinger; and let us take this occasion to sing our palinode on the subject of 'Endymion.' We certainly did not discover in that poem the same degree of merit that its more clear-sighted and prophetic admirers did. We did not foresee the unbounded popularity which has carried it through we know not how many editions; which has placed it on every table; and, what is still more unequivocal, familiarized it in every mouth. All this splendour of fame, however, though we had not the sagacity to anticipate, we have the candour to acknowledge; and we request that the publisher of the new and beautiful edition of Keats's works now in the press, with graphic illustrations by Calcott and Turner, will do us the favour and the justice to notice our conversion in his prolegomena.

Warned by our former mishap, wiser by experience, and improved, as we hope, in taste, we have to offer Mr. Tennyson our tribute of unmingled approbation, and it is very agreeable to us, as well as to our readers, that our present task will be little more than the selection, for their delight, of a few specimens of Mr. Tennyson's singular genius, and the venturing to point out, now and then, the peculiar brilliancy of some of the gems that irradiate his poetical crown. * * *

The 'Lotuseaters'—a kind of classical opium-eaters—are Ulysses and his crew. They land on the 'charmèd island,' and eat of the 'charmèd root,' and then they sing—

> 'Long enough the winedark wave our weary bark did carry.
> This is lovelier and sweeter,
> Men of Ithaca, this is meeter,
> In the hollow rosy vale to tarry,
> Like a dreamy Lotuseater—a delicious Lotuseater!
> We will eat the Lotus, sweet
> As the yellow honeycomb;
> In the valley some, and some
> On the ancient heights divine,
> And no more roam,
> On the loud hoar foam,
> To the melancholy home,
> At the limits of the brine,
> The little isle of Ithaca, beneath the day's decline.'—p. 116.

Our readers will, we think, agree that this is admirably characteristic, and that the singers of this song must have made pretty free with the intoxicating fruit. How they got home you must read in Homer:—Mr. Tennyson—himself, we presume, a dreamy lotus-eater, a delicious lotus-eater—leaves them in full song.

Next comes another class of poems,—Visions. The first is the 'Palace of Art,' or a fine house, in which the poet *dreams* that he sees a very fine collection of well-known pictures. An ordinary versifier would, no doubt, have followed the old routine, and dully described himself as walking into the Louvre, or Buckingham Palace, and there seeing certain masterpieces of painting:—a true poet dreams it. We have not room to hang many of these *chefs-d'œuvre*, but for a few we must find space.—'The Madonna'—

> 'The maid mother by a crucifix,
>   In yellow pastures sunny warm,
> Beneath branch work of costly sardonyx
>   Sat smiling—*babe in arm*.'—p. 72.

The use of this latter, apparently, colloquial phrase is a deep stroke of art. The form of expression is always used to express an habitual and characteristic action. A knight is described *'lance in rest'*—a dragoon, *'sword in hand'*—so, as the idea of the Virgin is inseparably connected with her child, Mr. Tennyson reverently describes her conventional position—*'babe in arm.'*

His gallery of illustrious portraits is thus admirably arranged:— The Madonna—Ganymede—St. Cecilia—Europa—Deep-haired Milton—Shakspeare—Grim Dante—Michael Angelo—Luther— Lord Bacon—Cervantes—Calderon—King David—'the Halicarnassëan' (*quære*, which of them?)—Alfred, (not Alfred Tennyson, though no doubt in any other man's gallery *he* would have had a place) and finally—

> 'Isaïah, with fierce Ezekiel,
>   Swarth Moses by the Coptic sea,
> Plato, *Petrarca*, Livy, and Raphaël,
>   And eastern Confutzee!'

We can hardly suspect the very original mind of Mr. Tennyson to have harboured any recollections of that celebrated Doric idyll, 'The groves of Blarney,' but certainly there is a strong likeness between Mr. Tennyson's list of pictures and the Blarney collection of statues—

> 'Statues growing that noble place in,
>   All heathen goddesses most rare,
> Homer, Plutarch, and Nebuchadnezzar,
>   All standing naked in the open air!'

In this poem we first observed a stroke of art (repeated afterwards) which we think very ingenious. No one who has ever written verse but must have felt the pain of erasing some happy line, some striking stanza, which, however excellent in itself, did not exactly suit the place for which it was destined. How curiously does an author mould and remould the plastic verse in order to fit in the favourite thought; and when he finds that he cannot introduce it, as Corporal Trim says, *any how*, with what reluctance does he at last reject the intractable, but still cherished offspring of his brain! Mr. Tennyson manages this delicate matter in a new and better way; he says, with great candour and simplicity, 'If this poem were not already too long, *I should have added* the following stanzas,' and *then he adds them*, (p. 84;)—or, 'the following lines are manifestly superfluous, as a part of the text, but they may be allowed to stand as a separate poem,' (p. 121,) *which they do;*—or, 'I intended to have added something on statuary, but I found it very difficult;'—(he had, moreover, as we have seen, been anticipated in this line by the Blarney poet)—'but I had finished the statues of *Elijah* and *Olympias*—judge whether I have succeeded,' (p. 73)—and then we have these two statues. This is certainly the most ingenious device that has ever come under our observation, for reconciling the rigour of criticism with the indulgence of parental partiality. It is economical too, and to the reader profitable, as by these means

> 'We lose no drop of the immortal man.'

The other vision is 'A Dream of Fair Women,' in which the heroines of all ages—some, indeed, that belong to the times of 'heathen goddesses most rare'—pass before his view. We have not time to notice them all, but the second, whom we take to be Iphigenia, touches the heart with a stroke of nature more powerful than even the veil that the Grecian painter threw over the head of her father.

> ————'dimly I could descry
> The stern blackbearded kings with wolfish eyes,
>   Watching to see me die.
> The tall masts quivered as they lay afloat;
>   The temples, and the people, and the shore;
> One drew a sharp knife through my tender throat—
>   Slowly,—and *nothing more!*'

What touching simplicity—what pathetic resignation—he cut my throat—'*nothing more!*' One might indeed ask, 'what *more*' she would have?

But we must hasten on; and to tranquillize the reader's mind after the last affecting scene, shall notice the only two pieces of a lighter strain which the volume affords. The first is elegant and playful; it is a description of the author's study, which he affectionately calls his *Darling Room.*

> 'O darling room, my heart's delight;
> Dear room, the apple of my sight;
> With thy two couches, soft and white,

There is no room so exqui*site*;
No little room so warm and bright,
Wherein to read, wherein to write.'

We entreat our readers to note how, even in this little trifle, the singular taste and genius of Mr. Tennyson break forth. In such a dear *little* room a narrow-minded scribbler would have been content with *one* sofa, and that one he would probably have covered with black mohair, or red cloth, or a good striped chintz; how infinitely more characteristic is white dimity!—'tis as it were a type of the purity of the poet's mind. * * *

The second of the lighter pieces, and the last with which we shall delight our readers, is a severe retaliation on the editor of the Edinburgh Magazine, who, it seems, had not treated the first volume of Mr. Tennyson with the same respect that we have, we trust, evinced for the second.

'TO CHRISTOPHER NORTH.
You did late review my lays,
    Crusty Christopher;
You did mingle blame and praise,
    Rusty Christopher.

When I learnt from whom it came
I forgave you all the blame,
    Musty Christopher;
I could *not* forgive the praise,
    Fusty Christopher.'—p. 153.

Was there ever anything so genteelly turned—so terse—so sharp —and the point so stinging and *so true?*

* * *

JOHN STUART MILL

Tennyson's Poems†

* * *

Of all the capacities of a poet, that which seems to have arisen earliest in Mr. Tennyson, and in which he most excels, is that of scene-painting, in the higher sense of the term: not the mere power of producing that rather vapid species of composition usually termed descriptive poetry—for there is not in these volumes one passage of pure description; but the power of *creating* scenery, in

† From *London Review*, I (July 1835), pp. 402–424.

keeping with some state of human feeling; so fitted to it as to be the embodied symbol of it, and to summon up the state of feeling itself, with a force not to be surpassed by anything but reality. Our first specimen, selected from the earlier of the two volumes, will illustrate chiefly this quality of Mr. Tennyson's productions. We do not anticipate that this little poem will be equally relished at first by all lovers of poetry: and, indeed, if it were, its merit could be but of the humblest kind; for sentiments and imagery which can be received at once, and with equal ease, into every mind, must necessarily be trite. Nevertheless, we do not hesitate to quote it at full length. The subject is Mariana, the Mariana of "Measure for Measure," living deserted and in solitude in the "moated grange." The ideas which these two words suggest, impregnated with the feelings of the supposed inhabitant, have given rise to the following picture: [Mill here reproduced the text of "Mariana."]

In the one peculiar and rare quality which we intended to illustrate by it, this poem appears to us to be preeminent. We do not, indeed, defend all the expressions in it, some of which seem to have been extorted from the author by the tyranny of rhyme; and we might find much more to say against the poem, if we insisted upon judging it by a wrong standard. The nominal subject excites anticipations which the poem does not even attempt to fulfil. The humblest poet who is a poet at all, could make more than is here made of the situation of a maiden abandoned by her lover. But that was not Mr. Tennyson's idea. The love-story is secondary in his mind. The words, "he cometh not," are almost the only words which allude to it at all. To place ourselves at the right point of view, we must drop the conception of Shakespeare's Mariana, and retain only that of a "moated grange," and a solitary dweller within it, forgotten by mankind. And now see whether poetic imagery ever conveyed a more intense conception of such a place, or of the feeling of such an inmate. From the very first line, the rust of age and the solitude of desertion are on the whole picture. Words surely never excited a more vivid feeling of physical and spiritual dreariness: and not dreariness alone—for that might be felt under many other circumstances of solitude—but the dreariness which speaks not merely of being far from human converse and sympathy, but of being *deserted* by it.

* * *

If every one approached poetry in the spirit in which it ought to be approached, willing to feel it first and examine it afterwards, we should not premise another word. But there is a class of readers (a class, too, on whose verdict the early success of a young poet mainly depends), who dare not enjoy until they have felt satisfied themselves that they have a warrant for enjoying; who read a poem with the critical understanding first, and only when they are convinced that it is right to be delighted, are willing to give their spontaneous feelings fair play. The consequence is that they lose the general effect, while they higgle about the details, and never place themselves in the position in which, even with their mere understandings, they can estimate the poem as a whole. For the benefit of such readers, we tell them beforehand, that this is a tale of enchantment, and that they will never enter into the spirit of it unless they surrender their imagination to the guidance of the poet, with the same easy credulity with which they would read the "Arabian Nights," or what this story more resembles, the tales of magic of the Middle Ages.

Though the agency is supernatural, the scenery, as will be perceived, belongs to the actual world. No reader of any imagination will complain, that the precise nature of the enchantment is left in mystery.

*　　*　　*

In powers of narrative and scene-painting combined, this poem must be ranked among the very first of its class. The delineation of outward objects, as in the greater number of Mr. Tennyson's poems, is, not picturesque, but (if we may use the term) statuesque; with brilliancy of colour superadded. The forms are not as in painting, of unequal degrees of definiteness; the tints do not melt gradually into each other, but each individual object stands out in bold relief, with a clear decided outline. This statue-like precision and distinctness few artists have been able to give to so essentially vague a language as that of words: but if once this difficulty be got over, scene-painting by words has a wider range than either painting or sculpture; for it can represent (as the reader must have seen in the foregoing poem), not only with the vividness and strength of the one, but with the clearness and definiteness of the other, objects in motion. Along with all this there is in the poem all that power of making a few touches do the whole work, which excites our admiration in Coleridge. Every line suggests so much more than it says, that much may be left unsaid: the concentration, which is the soul of narrative, is obtained without the sacrifice of reality and life. Where the march of the story requires that the mind shall pause, details are specified; where rapidity is necessary, they are all brought before us at a flash. Except that the versification is less exquisite, the "Lady of Shalott" is entitled to a place by the side of "The Ancient Mariner" and "Christabel."

*　　*　　*

The poems which we have quoted from Mr. Tennyson prove incontestably that he possesses, in an eminent degree, the natural endowment of a poet—the poetic temperament. And it appears clearly not only from a comparison of the two volumes, but of different poems in the same volume, that, with him, the other element of poetic excellence—intellectual culture—is advancing both steadily and rapidly; that he is not destined like so many others, to be remembered for what he might have done, rather than for what he did; that he will not remain a poet of mere temperament, but is ripening into a true artist. Mr. Tennyson may not be conscious of the wide difference in maturity of intellect, which is apparent in his various poems. Though he now writes from greater fulness and clearness of thought, it by no means follows that he has learnt to detect the absence of those qualities in some of his earlier effusions. Indeed, he himself in one of the most beautiful poems of his first volume (though, as a work of art, very imperfect), the "Ode to Memory," confesses a parental predilection for the "first born" of his genius. But to us it is evident, not only that his second volume differs from his first as early manhood from youth, but that the various poems of the first volume belong to different, and even distant stages of intellectual development;—distant, not perhaps in years—for a mind like Mr. Tennyson's advances rapidly—but corresponding to very different states of the intellectual powers, both in respect of their strength and of their proportions.

From the very first, like all writers of his natural gifts, he luxuriates in sensuous imagery; his nominal subject sometimes lies buried in a heap of it. From the first, too, we see his intellect, with every successive dgree of strength, struggling upwards to shape this sensuous imagery to a spiritual meaning, to bring the materials which sense supplies, and fancy summons up, under the command of a central and controlling thought or feeling. We have seen by the poem of "Mariana" with what success he could occasionally do this, even in the period which answers to his first volume; but that volume contains various instances in which he has attempted the same thing and failed.

* * *

Some of the smaller poems have a fault which in any but a very juvenile production would be the worse fault of all: they are altogether without meaning: none, at least, that can be discerned in them by persons otherwise competent judges of poetry; if the author had any meaning, he has not been able to express it. Such, for instance are the two songs on the Owl; such, also, are the verses headed "The How and the Why," in the first volume, and the lines on "To-day and Yesterday," in the second. In the former of these productions Mr. Tennyson aimed at shadowing forth the vague aspirations to a knowledge beyond the reach of man—the yearnings for a solution of all questions, soluble or insoluble, which concern our nature and destiny—the impatience under the insufficiency of the human faculties to penetrate the secret of our being here, and being what we are—which are natural in a certain state of the human mind; if this was what he sought to typify, he has only proved that he knows not the feeling—that he has neither experienced it, nor realized it in imagination. The questions which a Faust calls upon earth and heaven, and all powers supernal and infernal, to resolve for him, are not the ridiculous ones which Mr. Tennyson asks himself in these verses.

But enough of faults which the poet has almost entirely thrown off merely by the natural expansion of his intellect. We have alluded to them chiefly to show how rapidly progressive that intellect has been. There are traces, we think, of a continuance of the same progression throughout the second as well as the first volume.

In the art of painting a picture to the inward eye, the improvement is not so conspicuous as in other qualities; so high a degree of excellence having been already attained in the first volume. Besides the poems which we have quoted, we may refer, in that volume, to those entitled, "Recollections of the Arabian Nights," "The Dying Swan," "The Kraken," "The Sleeping Beauty," the beautiful poems (songs they are called, but are not), "In the glooming light," and "A spirit haunts the year's last hours," are (like the "Mariana") not mere pictures, but states of emotion, embodied in sensuous imagery. From these, however, to the command over the materials of outward sense for the purpose of bodying forth states of feeling, evinced by some of the poems in the second volume, especially "The Lady of Shalott" and "The Lotos Eaters," there is a considerable distance; and Mr. Tennyson seems, as he proceeded to have raised his aims still higher, to have aspired to render his poems not only vivid representations of spiritual states, but symbolical of spiritual truths. His longest poem, "The Palace of Art," is an attempt of this sort. As such we do not think it wholly successful, though rich in beauties of detail; but we deem it of the most favourable augury for Mr. Tennyson's future achievements, since it proves a continually increasing endeavour towards the highest excellence, and a constantly rising standard of it.

We predict, that as Mr. Tennyson advances in general spiritual culture, these higher aims will become more and more predominant in his writings, that he will strive more and more diligently, and, even without striving, will be more and more impelled by the natural tendencies of an expanding character, towards what has been described as the highest object of poetry, "to incorporate the everlasting reason of man in forms visible to his sense, and suitable to it." For the fulfilment of this exalted purpose, what we have already seen of him authorizes us to foretell with confidence that powers of execution will not fail him; it rests with himself to see that his powers of thought may keep pace with them. To render his poetic endowment the means of giving impressiveness to important truths, he must by continual study and meditation strengthen his intellect for the discrimination of such truths; he must see that his theory of life and the world be no chimera of the brain, but the well-grounded result of solid and mature thinking;—he must culti-vate, and with no half-devotion, philosophy as well as poetry.

* * *

JOHN STERLING

Poems by Alfred Tennyson†

What poetry might be in our time and land, if a man of the highest powers and most complete cultivation exercised the art among us, will be hard to say until after the fact of such a man's existence. Waiting for this desirable event, we may at least see that poetry, to be for us what it has sometimes been among mankind, must wear a new form, and probably comprise elements hardly found in our recent writings, and impossible in former ones.

Of verses, indeed, of every sort but the excellent there is no want: almost all, however, so helpless in skill, so faint in meaning, that one might almost fancy the authors wrote metre from mere in-capacity of expressing themselves at all in prose—as boys at school sometimes make nonsense-verses before they can construct a rational sentence. Yet it is plain that even our magazine stanzas, album sonnets, and rhymes in corners of newspapers aim at the forms of emotion, and use some of the words in which men of genius have symbolized profound thoughts. The whole, indeed, is generally a lump of blunder and imbecility, but in the midst there is often some turn of cadence, some attempt at an epithet of more signifi-cance and beauty than perhaps a much finer mind would have hit on a hundred years ago. The crowds of stammering children are yet the offspring of an age that would fain teach them—if it knew how—a richer, clearer language than they can learn to speak.

It is hard in this state of things not to conceive that the time, among us at least, is an essentially unpoetic one—one which, what-ever may be the worth of its feelings, finds no utterance for them in melodious words.

* * * Now, strangely as our time is racked and torn, haunted by ghosts, and errant in search of lost realities, poor in genuine culture, incoherent among its own chief elements, untrained to social facility and epicurean quiet, yet unable to unite its means in pursuit of any lofty blessing, half-sick, half-dreaming, and whole confused—he would be not only misanthropic, but ignorant, who

† From *Quarterly Review*, LXX (September 1842), pp. 385–416.

should maintain it to be a poor, dull, and altogether helpless age, and not rather one full of great though conflicting energies, seething with high feelings, and struggling towards the light with piercing though still hooded eyes. The fierce, too often mad force, that wars itself away among the labouring poor, the manifold skill and talent and unwearied patience of the middle classes, and the still unshaken solidity of domestic life among them—these are facts open to all, though by none perhaps sufficiently estimated. And over and among all society the wealth of our richer people is gathered and diffused as it has never been before anywhere else, shaping itself into a thousand arts of luxury, a million modes of social pleasure, which the moralist may have much to object against, but which the poet, had we a truly great one now rising among us, would well know how to employ for his own purposes.

Then, too, if we reflect that the empire and nation seated here as in its centre, and at home so moving and multifarious, spreads its dominions all round the globe, daily sending forth its children to mix in the life of every race of man, seek adventures in every climate, and fit themselves to every form of polity, or it to them— whereafter they return in body, or at least reflect their mental influences among us—it cannot be in point of diversity and meaning that Britain disappoints any one capable of handling what it supplies.

*   *   *

Little therefore as is all that has been done towards the poetic representation of our time—even in the looser and readier form of prose romance—it is hard to suppose that it is incapable of such treatment. The still unadulterated purity of home among large circles of the nation presents an endless abundance of the feelings and characters, the want of which nothing else in existence can supply even to a poet. And these soft and steady lights strike an observer all the more from the restless activity and freedom of social ambition, the shifting changes of station, and the wealth gathered on one hand and spent on the other with an intenseness and amplitude of will to which there is at least nothing now comparable among mankind. The power of self-subjection combined with almost boundless liberty, indeed necessitated by it, and the habit of self-denial with wealth beyond all calculation—these are indubitable facts in modern England. But while recognised as facts, how far do they still remain from that development as thoughts which philosophy desires, or that vividness as images which is the aim of poetry! It is easy to say that the severity of conscience in the best minds checks all play of fancy, and the fierceness of the outward struggle for power and riches absorbs the energies that would otherwise exert themselves in shapeful melody. But had we minds full of the idea and the strength requisite for such work, they would find in this huge, harassed, and luxurious national existence the nourishment, not the poison, of creative art. The death-struggle of commercial and political rivalry, the brooding doubt and remorse, the gas-jet flame of faith irradiating its own coal-mine darkness—in a word, our overwrought materialism fevered by its own excess into spiritual dreams—all this might serve the purposes of a bold imagination, no less than the creed of the antipoetic Puritans became poetry in the mind of Milton, and all bigotries, superstitions, and gore-dyed horrors were flames that kindled steady light in Shakespeare's humane and meditative song.

* * *

In thus pointing to the problem which poetry now holds out, and maintaining that it has been but partially solved by our most illustrious writers, there is no design of setting up an unattainable standard, and then blaming any one in particular for inevitably falling short of it. Out of an age so diversified and as yet so unshapely, he who draws forth any graceful and expressive forms is well entitled to high praise. Turning into fixed beauty any part of the shifting and mingled matter of our time, he does what in itself is very difficult, and affords very valuable help to all his future fellow-labourers. If he has not given us back our age as a whole transmuted into crystalline clearness and lustre, a work accomplished only by a few of the greatest minds under the happiest circumstances for their art, yet we scarce know to whom we should be equally grateful as to him who has enriched us with any shapes of lasting loveliness 'won from the vague and formless infinite.'

Mr. Tennyson has done more of this kind than almost any one that has appeared among us during the last twenty years. And in such a task of alchemy a really successful experiment, even on a small scale, is of great worth compared with the thousands of fruitless efforts or pretences on the largest plan, which are daily clamouring for all men's admiration of their nothingness.

* * *

JAMES SPEDDING

Tennyson's Poems†

* * * The decade during which Mr Tennyson has remained silent has wrought a great improvement. The handling in his later pieces is much lighter and freer; the interest deeper and purer;— there is more humanity with less imagery and drapery; a closer

† From *Edinburgh Review*, LXXVII (April 1843), pp. 373–391.

adherence to truth; a greater reliance for effect upon the simplicity of nature. Moral and spiritual traits of character are more dwelt upon, in place of external scenery and circumstance. He addresses himself more to the heart, and less to the ear and eye. This change, which is felt in its results throughout the second volume, may in the latter half of the first be traced in its process. The poems originally published in 1832, are many of them largely altered; generally with great judgment, and always with a view to strip off redundancies—to make the expression simpler and clearer, to substitute thought for imagery, and substance for shadow. * * * All that is of true and lasting worth in poetry, must have its root in a sound view of human life and the condition of man in the world; a just feeling with regard to the things in which we are all concerned. Where this is not, the most consummate art can produce nothing which men will long care for—where it is, the rudest will never want audience; for then nothing is trivial—the most ordinary incidents of daily life are invested with an interest as deep as the springs of emotion in the heart—as deep as pity, and love, and fear, and awe. In this requisite Mr Tennyson will not be found wanting. The human soul, in its infinite variety of moods and trials, is his favourite haunt; nor can he dwell long upon any subject, however apparently remote from the scenes and objects of modern sympathy, without touching some string which brings it within the range of our common life. His moral views, whether directly or indirectly conveyed, are healthy, manly, and simple; and the truth and delicacy of his sentiments is attested by the depth of the pathos which he can evoke from the commonest incidents, told in the simplest manner, yet deriving all their interest from the manner of telling. * * * There are four poems in which Mr Tennyson has expressly treated of certain morbid states of the mind; and from these we may gather, not indeed his creed, but some hints concerning his moral theory of life and its issues, and of that which constitutes a sound condition of the soul. These are the 'Palace of Art,' the 'St Simeon Stylites,' the 'Two Voices,' and the 'Vision of Sin.' The 'Palace of Art' represents allegorically the condition of a mind which, in the love of beauty and the triumphant consciousness of knowledge and intellectual supremacy, in the intense enjoyment of its own power and glory has lost sight of its relation to man and to God.

* * *

As the 'Palace of Art' represents the pride of voluptuous enjoyment in its noblest form, the 'St Simeon Stylites' represents the pride of asceticism in its basest. To shadow forth dramatically the faith, the feelings, and the hopes, which support the man who, being taught that the rewards of another life will be proportioned to the misery voluntarily undergone in this, is best on qualifying himself for the best place—appears to be the design, or the running idea, of the poem. It is done with great force and effect; and, as far as we can guess, with great fidelity to nature. Of this, however, we must confess that we are not competent judges. Holding, as we do, that all self-torment inflicted for its own sake—all mortification beyond what is necessary to keep the powers of self-command and self-restraint in exercise, and the lower parts of our nature in due subjection to the higher—is a thing unblest; and that the man who thinks to propitiate God by degrading his image and making his temple loathsome, must have his whole heart out of tune, and be in the right way to the wrong place—we must confess that we cannot so expand our human sympathy as to reach the case of St Simeon. We notice the poem for the light it throws on Mr Tennyson's feeling with regard to this disease of the mind; which, if we collect it rightly—(for, as the saint has all the talk to himself, it cannot of course be conveyed directly)—is, that selfishness, sensuality, and carnal pride, are really at the bottom of it; and this, however paradoxical it may appear, we believe to be quite true.

In the 'Two Voices' we have a history of the agitations, the suggestions, and counter-suggestions, of a mind sunk in hopeless despondency, and meditating self-destruction; together with the manner of its recovery to a more healthy condition. Though not one of the most perfect, it is one of the most remarkable of Mr Tennyson's productions. An analysis of the arguments urged on either side, would present nothing very new or striking; and in point of poetical management—though rising occasionally into passages of great power and beauty, and though indicating throughout a subtle and comprehensive intellect, well fitted for handling such questions—it appears to us to be too long drawn out, and too full of a certain tender and passionate eloquence, hardly compatible with that dreary and barren misery in which the mind is supposed to be languishing. The dry and severe style with which the poem begins, should have been kept up, we think, through the greater portion of the dialogue, especially on the part of the 'dull and bitter' voice, which sustains the character of a tempting Mephistopheles. These, however, are points of minute criticism, into which we have not room to enter. What we are at present concerned with, is the moral bearing of the poem. The disease is familiar; but where are we to look for the remedy? Many persons would have thought it enough to administer a little religious consolation to the diseased mind; but unfortunately despondency is no more like ignorance than atrophy is like hunger; and as the most nutritious food will not nourish the latter, so the most comfortable doctrine will not refresh the former. Not the want of consoling topics, but the incapacity to receive consolation, constitutes the disease. Others would have been content to give the bad voice the worst of the argument; but, unhappily, all moral reasoning must ultimately rest on the internal evidence of the moral sense; and where this is disordered, the most unquestionable logic can conclude nothing, because it is the first principles which are at issue;—the *major* is not admitted. Mr Tennyson's treatment of the case is more scientific. We quote it, not indeed as new or original,—(it has been anticipated, and may perhaps have been suggested, by Mr Wordsworth, in the memorable passage at the close of the fourth book of the 'Excursion,')— but for the soundness of the philosophy, and the poetic beauty of the handling. The dialogue ends, (as such a dialogue, if truly reported, must always do,) leaving every thing unsettled, and nothing concluded. * * *

The 'Vision of Sin' touches upon a more awful subject than any of these;—the end, here and hereafter, of the merely sensual man:—

> 'I had a vision when the night was late:
> A youth came riding toward a palace-gate.
> He rode a horse with wings, that would have flown,
> But that his heavy rider kept him down.
> And from the palace came a child of sin,
> And took him by the curls, and led him in.'

Then follows a passage of great lyrical power, representing, under the figure of Music, the gradual yielding up of the soul to sensual excitement, in its successive stages of languor, luxury, agitation, madness, and triumph:—

> 'Till, kill'd with some luxurious agony,
> The nerve-dissolving melody
> Flutter'd headlong from the sky.'

This is the sensual life to which the youth is supposed to be given up. Meantime, the inevitable, irrevocable judgment comes slowly on,—not without due token and warning, but without regard:—

> 'And then I look'd up toward a mountain-tract,
> That girt the region with high cliff and lawn:
> I saw that every morning, far withdrawn
> Beyond the darkness and the cataract,
> God made Himself an awful rose of dawn,
> Unheeded: and detaching, fold by fold,
> From those still heights, and, slowly drawing near,
> A vapour heavy, hueless, formless, cold,
> Came floating on for many a month and year,

> Unheeded; and I thought I would have spoken,
> And warn'd that madman ere it grew too late:
> But, as in dreams, I could not. Mine was broken,
> When that cold vapour touch'd the palace-gate,
> And link'd again. I saw within my head
> A grey and gap-tooth'd man as lean as death,
> Who slowly rode across a wither'd heath,
> And lighted at a ruin'd inn——'

This is the youth, the winged steed, and the palace—the warm blood, the mounting spirit, and the lustful body—now chilled, jaded, and ruined; the cup of pleasure drained to the dregs; the senses exhausted of their power to enjoy, the spirit of its wish to aspire: nothing left but 'loathing, craving, and rottenness.'[1] His mental and moral state is developed in a song, or rather a lyric speech, too long to quote; and of which, without quoting, we cannot attempt to convey an idea;—a ghastly picture (lightened only by a seasoning of wild inhuman humour) of misery and mockery, impotent malice and impenitent regret; 'languid enjoyment of evil with utter incapacity to 'good.'[2] Such is his end on earth. But the end of all?

> 'The voice grew faint: there came a further change;
> Again arose the mystic mountain-range:
> Below were men and horses pierced with worms,
> And slowly quickening into lower forms;
> By shards and scurf of salt, and scum of dross,
> Old plash of rains and refuse patch'd with moss.
> Then some one said, "Behold! it was a crime
> Of sense avenged by sense that wore with time."
> Another said, "The crime of sense became
> The crime of malice, and is equal blame."
> And one: "He had not wholly quench'd his power;
> A little grain of conscience made him sour."
> At last I heard a voice upon the slope
> Cry to the summit—"Is there any hope!"
> To which an answer peal'd from that high land,
> But in a tongue no man could understand;
> And on the glimmering limit, far-withdrawn,
> God made Himself an awful rose of dawn.'

Into the final mysteries of judgment and of mercy let no man presume to enquire further. Enough for us to know what for us is evil. Be the rest left to Him with whom nothing is impossible!

We have dwelt longer on these four poems than either their prominence or their relative poetic merit would have led us to do; because, though they may not show the author's art in its most

---

1. Berkeley.   2. Lamb.

perfect or most attractive form, they show the depth from which it springs; they show that it is no trick of these versifying times—born of a superficial sensibility to beauty and a turn for setting to music the current doctrines and fashionable feelings of the day; but a genuine growth of nature, having its root deep in the pensive heart —a heart accustomed to meditate earnestly, and feel truly, upon the prime duties and interests of man.

We cannot conclude without reminding Mr Tennyson, that highly as we value the Poems which he has produced, we cannot accept them as a satisfactory account of the gifts which they show that he possesses; any more than we could take a painter's collection of *studies* for a picture, in place of the picture itself. Powers are displayed in these volumes, adequate, if we do not deceive ourselves, to the production of a great work; at least we should find it difficult to say which of the requisite powers is wanting. But they are displayed in fragments and snatches, having no connexion, and therefore deriving no light or fresh interest the one from the other. By this their effective value is incalculably diminished. Take the very best scenes in Shakspeare—detach them from the context— and suppose all the rest to have perished, or never to have been written—where would be the evidence of the power which created Lear and Hamlet? Yet, perhaps, not one of those scenes could have been produced by a man who was not capable of producing the whole. If Mr Tennyson can find a subject large enough to take the entire impress of his mind, and energy persevering enough to work it faithfully out as one whole, we are convinced that he may produce a work, which, though occupying no larger space than the contents of these volumes, shall as much exceed them in value, as a series of quantities multiplied into each other exceeds in value the same series simply added together.

JAMES KNOWLES

A Personal Reminiscence†

If in the following pages I can contribute a few touches to the portrait of Lord Tennyson which his contemporaries alone can paint, my object in writing them will be accomplished. Of Tennyson the Poet his Poems will remain a 'monument more lasting than brass' to the remotest future. But of the man himself 'in his habit as he lived' the likeness can only be portrayed by those who knew him personally, and only now, while their memory of him is fresh, and

† From *The Nineteenth Century*, XXXIII (January 1893), pp. 164–188.

before it passes away with them into oblivion. What would the world not give for such a picture of Shakespeare by his friends as may now be made of Tennyson?

In a letter of his which lies before me he draws a distinction between personal things which may be told of a man before and after his death, and complains of the neglect of that distinction during his life. He recognised that after death a Memoir of him was inevitable, and left the charge of it in its fulness to his son. What follow are but slight contributions towards any such complete biography, for only upon the few occasions which are here recorded did I make any note in writing of all Tennyson's talk heard and enjoyed for nearly thirty years. His own words I have printed always in italics.

More than thirty years ago I had the happiness of making his acquaintance. I was about to publish a little book on King Arthur, chiefly compiled from Sir Thomas Malory, and, as a stranger, had written to ask leave to dedicate it to him—a leave which was directly granted.

For some time afterwards I knew him merely by correspondence, but being in the Isle of Wight one autumn I called to thank him personally for what he had written to me, and then first saw him face to face. I found him even kinder than his letters, and from that time our acquaintance grew gradually closer until it became intimate.

Before long he asked me to become his architect for the new house he proposed to build near Haslemere ('Aldworth' as it was finally called), and the consultations and calculations which naturally followed as to his way of living, the plans, and the cost of building, led to much business confidence. This presently extended to the field of his own business transactions with his publishers, and from these in time to confidences about his Work and Art; until at length he came to tell me of Poems not yet in being, but contemplated, and to talk about them and show me their progress.

Then, and for many years after, under his roof or under mine, it was my great privilege to see and know him intimately; and the more he was known the more impressive were his greatness, tenderness, and truth. The simplicity, sensitiveness, freshness, and almost divine insight of a child were joined in him, as in no other man, to the dignity, sagacity, humour, and knowledge of age at its noblest. An immense sanity underlay the whole—the perfection of common-sense—and over all was the perpetual glamour of supreme genius.

Affectation was so alien from him that he spoke and acted exactly as he felt and thought everywhere and about everything. This at times would perplex and bewilder strangers. The shy were frightened at it; the affected took it for affectation (for, as he was fond of saying, '*every man imputes himself*'), the rough for roughness, the bears for bearishness; whereas it was but simple straightforward honesty, and as such of the deepest interest to all who could watch and learn in it the ways of Nature with her greatest men.

The little affectations and insincerities of life so troubled him, and his natural shyness, increased by his disabling short sight, so fought with his innate courtesy to all, that general society was always an effort and a burden to him. His fame increased the trouble, and he often told me how he wished he could have had all the money which his books had made without the notoriety. Even a single stranger was, as such and at first, always a trial to him, and his instinctive desire was to hide as much of himself as possible from observation until he found his companion sympathetic. Then he expanded as a flower does in the sunshine, and he never hoarded or kept back any of the profuse riches and splendour of his mind. When Frederick Robertson of Brighton—the great preacher, who had written much and admirably about his poems, and for whom he had a high regard—first called upon him, '*I felt*,' said Tennyson, '*as if he had come to pluck out the heart of my mystery—so I talked to him about nothing but beer.*' He could not help it; it was impossible for him to wear his heart upon his sleeve.

The shortness of his sight, which was extreme, tormented him always. When he was looking at any object he seemed to be smelling it. He said that he had '*never seen the two pointers of the Great Bear except as two intersecting circles, like the first proposition in Euclid*,' and at my first visit to him he warned me, as I left, to come up and speak to him wherever I next met him, '*for if not*,' he said, '*I shouldn't know you though I rubbed against you in the street.*' His hearing, on the other hand, was exceptionally keen, and he held it as a sort of compensation for his blurred sight; he could hear '*the shriek of a bat*,' which he always said was the test of a quick ear. Its real compensation, however, was in the quickness of his mental vision, which made more out of the imperfect indications of his bodily eyes than most men with perfect sight would see. I remember his telling me (in explanation of a passage in 'Maud') —'*If you tread on daisies they turn up underfoot and get rosy.*' He could read a man through and through in a flash even from his face, and it was wonderful to hear him sum up a complex character in some single phrase. He told me that he was once travelling with an unknown person whose countenance he caught but for an instant from behind a newspaper, but whom he set down, from that flying glimpse, as a rogue. To his surprise he turned out to be somebody of the highest local standing and repute, but he nevertheless held by his impression and in the end was justified; for presently the man fled from justice and the country, leaving hundreds ruined who had trusted him.

His judgment of men was the more terrible because so naturally charitable and tender. Seldom, if ever, did he carry beyond words his anger even with those who had gravely injured him. '*I eat my heart with silent rage at*——' he said one day of such a one. How different in this from Carlyle, whose open rage with mankind was so glaring! '*Ha! ye don't know*,' he cried out to me one day, '*ye don't know what d——d beasts men are*.' Tennyson, quite otherwise, had the tenderest thought and hope for all men individually, however much he loathed that 'many-headed beast' the mob. '*I feel ashamed to see misery and guilt*,' he said as he came out from going over Wandsworth Gaol; '*I can't look it in the face*.' Yet he had no love for milksops. '*The only fault of So-and-so*,' he said, '*is that he has no fault at all*.'

It was touching to see his playfulness with children, and how he would win them from their nervousness of his big voice and rather awful presence. I have seen him hopping about on the floor like a great bird, enveloped in his big cloak and flapping hat, in a game of pursuing a little band of them until they shrieked with laughter. It reminded me of a scene in his Cambridge days which he had described to me when he, '*Charles Tennyson, Spedding, and Thompson of Trinity, danced a quadrille together in the upper room of a house opposite the "Bull."* ' There was a great abundance of playfulness under the grimness of his exterior, and as to humour, that was all-pervading and flavoured every day with salt. It was habitual with him, and seemed a sort of counteraction and relief to the intense solemnity of his also habitual gaze at life in its deeper aspects, which else would almost have overwhelmed him with awe. He had a marvellous fund of good stories which he loved to recount after dinner and over his 'bottle of port.' In later life he gave up the port, but not the stories. He used to say there ought to be a collection of the hundred best ones in the world chosen from different countries so as to show the national diversities, and he would give illustrations of such, declaring that for true and piercing wit the French beat all the others. Could they have been reported *verbatim* as he gave them, they would have been models of English prose. More serious narratives he told thrillingly—one especially of how his own father escaped from Russia as a young man after an incautious speech about the recent murder of the Emperor Paul; how he wandered for months in the Crimea, where 'the wild people of the country came about him' and explained to him that twice a year only, at uncertain times, a courier passed through the place blowing a horn before him, and that then was his only chance of safety; how he lay waiting and listening through the nights until the weird sound came, and how he fared through all the hair-breadth 'scapes that followed.

He would pretend to look upon his bottle of port as a sort of counsellor to be heard sometimes before finally making up his mind upon moot-points, and after the varying moods of the day about them. For instance, he told me: *'The night before I was asked to take the Laureateship, which was offered to me through Prince Albert's liking for my "In Memoriam," I dreamed that he came to me and kissed me on the cheek. I said, in my dream, "Very kind, but very German." In the morning the letter about the Laureateship was brought to me and laid upon my bed. I thought about it through the day, but could not make up my mind whether to take it or refuse it, and at the last I wrote two letters, one accepting and one declining, and threw them on the table, and settled to decide which I would send after my dinner and bottle of port.'*

A notable thing was his comparative indifference to music as a separate art: it almost seemed as if the extreme fineness of his hearing was *too* fine for the enjoyment of its usual intervals and effects and craved the subtler and multitudinous distinctions and inflections and variations of sound, which only the instrument of language can produce. Certainly I hardly ever knew him to care greatly for any 'setting' of his own songs, which he justly felt had already their own music that was confused by the 'setting.' It is curious that Browning, whose music is so rare in his verse, was a masterly musician outside of it, while Tennyson, whose every line was music, cared so little for it except in poetry.

His way of working was much less like 'work' than inspiration. *'I can always write,'* he said, *'when I see my subject, though sometimes I spend three-quarters of a year without putting pen to paper.'* When he did 'see' it, his mind dwelt on it at all times and seasons, possessing him until he possessed and perfected it. Sparkles and gleams might flash out at any moments from the anvil where his genius was beating his subject into shape, but the main creative process, where the vision was condensed into art, went on when he had shut himself up in his room with his pipe. He would do this two or three times a day—his *'most valuable hour,'* as he often told me, being the hour after dinner—and then with his pipe in his mouth and over the fire he would weave into music what things *'came to him;'* for he never accounted for his Poetry in any other way than that *'it came.'* *'Many thousand fine lines go up the chimney,'* he said to me, and indeed the mechanical toil of writing them down, made heavier by his short sight, was so great that it was easy to believe in the sublime waste—the characteristic profuseness of genius. When he came out from his room at such seasons, he would often have a sort of dazed and far-off dreamy look about him, as if seeing 'beyond this ignorant present,' and such as Millais alone has caught in his great portrait, where he looks like the Prophet and Bard that he was. And then he might perhaps say aloud, and almost as it were to himself, some passage he had just made, but seldom twice in the same words, and, unless written down at once, the first and original form of it was often lost or 'improved.' This was the beginning of that process of refinement by art until absolute perfection was attained which he always carried on—the cutting and polishing of the native diamonds into complete and brilliant beauty. If interrupted during his hours of seclusion—which of course never happened except upon emergency —his look of 'sensitiveness' was surprising. He seemed ready to quiver at the faintest breath, or sound, or movement, and as though suddenly waked up out of a dream.

After his hour of privacy he would often ask his friends to come to his room with him, and then would talk of present, past, and future in a way which was, in the Arab phrase, like 'the opening of many gates.'

Many personal things he told me at such times when alone with him, which are of course sacred from repetition; but of many other things he spoke openly to whomsoever might be there, and especially he loved to speculate freely on theological and metaphysical subjects.

He formulated once and quite deliberately his own religious creed in these words: 'THERE'S A SOMETHING THAT WATCHES OVER US; AND OUR INDIVIDUALITY ENDURES: THAT'S MY FAITH, AND THAT'S ALL MY FAITH.' This he said with such a calm emphasis that I wrote it down (with the date) exactly and at once. But he was by no means always so calm. His belief in personal immortality was passionate—I think almost the strongest passion that he had. I have heard him thunder out against an opponent of it: '*If there be a God that has made the earth and put this hope and passion into us, it must foreshow the truth. If it be not true, then no God, but a mocking fiend, created us, and*' (growing crimson with excitement) '*I'd shake my fist in his almighty face, and tell him that I cursed him! I'd sink my head tonight in a chloroformed handkerchief and have done with it all.*'

To one who said, 'My dearest object in life, when at my best, is to leave the world, by however little, better than I found it—what is yours?' he answered: '*My greatest wish is to have a clearer vision of God.*'

He said: '*Men have generally taken God for the devil. . . . The majority of Englishmen think of Him as an immeasurable clergyman in a white tie.*'

He inclined somewhat to the theory of a Demiurge with whom alone man comes into direct contact, saying that this was perhaps 'the nearest explanation of the facts of the world which we can get;' and this he put into the mouth of the King in the 'Passing of Arthur,' where he cries:

> O me! for why is all around us here
> As if some lesser God had made the world,
> But had not force to shape it as he would,
> Till the High God behold it from beyond,
> And enter it and make it beautiful?

He was disposed to doubt the real existence of a material world, and frequently adduced the infinite divisibility of matter as a difficulty which made it unthinkable. He leaned to the idealism of Berkeley, and in physical science preferred the term 'centres of force' to 'atoms' as not involving the idea of matter. He said to me one day: *'Sometimes as I sit here alone in this great room I get carried away out of sense and body, and rapt into mere existence, till the accidental touch or movement of one of my own fingers is like a great shock and blow and brings the body back with a terrible start.'*

All such subjects moved him profoundly, and to an immense curiosity and interests about them. He told me that 'Tears, idle tears' was written as an expression of such longings. *'It is in a way like St. Paul's "groanings which cannot be uttered." It was written at Tintern when the woods were all yellowing with autumn seen through the ruined windows. It is what I have always felt even from a boy, and what as a boy I called the "passion of the past." And it is so always with me now; it is the distance that charms me in the landscape, the picture and the past, and not the immediate to-day in which I move.'*

*   *   *

A frequent subject of his talk in the evenings, or in the long afternoon walks which were his habit, was, as might be expected, Poetry and the Poets. His acquaintance with all previous poetry was unlimited, and his memory of it amazing. He would quote again and again with complete delight the passages which were his favourites, stopping and calling upon his hearer to consider the beauty of this or that line, and repeating it to admire it the more.

His reading was always in a grand, deep, measured voice, and was rather intoning on a few notes than speaking. It was like a sort of musical thunder, far off or near—loud-rolling or 'sweet and low'—according to the subject, and once heard could never be forgotten.

It made no difference whence a fine line or passage came; it struck him equally with pleasure, when he heard or came across it, whether it were another man's or his own. He would pause in precisely the same way to call out 'That's magnificent,' 'What a line!' 'Isn't that splendid?' whether reading Shakespeare, Milton, Wordsworth, or himself. He was struck by the beauty of the art without thinking for one moment of the artist. The shallow-pated, hearing him thus apostrophise his own work, which they may have begged him to read to them, might think in their vain hearts 'How vain!' But vanity had no more to do with it than they had; he was thinking solely of the subject and the music, and only cried out to his hearers for the sake of an echo to his own absorbing pleasure.

He often insisted that the grandest music in the English language was in Milton, and especially in the first book of *Paradise Lost*, and he would repeatedly chant out with the deepest admiration, as the finest of all, the passage—

> Thammuz came next behind,
> Whose annual wound to Lebanon allured
> The Syrian damsels to lament his fate
> In amorous ditties all a summer's day;
> While smooth Adonis from his native rock
> Ran purple to the sea, supposed with blood
> Of Thammuz yearly wounded; the love-tale
> Infected Sion's daughters with like heat,
> Whose wanton passions in the sacred porch
> Ezekiel saw, when, by the vision led,
> His eye surveyed the dark idolatries
> Of alienated Judah.

As a single line he said he knew hardly any to exceed for charm

> Of Abbana and Pharphar, lucid streams,

unless it were Wordsworth's great line in Tintern Abbey—

> Whose dwelling is the light of setting suns.

'Poetry,' he would say at such times, '*is a great deal truer than fact.*'

His own poetry, he declared, was easy enough to read aloud, if people would only read it just as it was written and not try to scan it or to force the accent. Some few passages, he admitted however, were difficult, such as that in 'Maud' beginning

> O, that 'twere possible,

but this because '*it ought to be read all through without taking breath:*' the 'bugle song' in the 'Princess' was another.

The first thing I ever heard him read was his 'Boadicea,' for I said 'I never can tell how to scan it.' '*Read it like prose,*' he said, '*just as it is written, and it will come all right.*' And then, as if to confute himself, he began it, and in his weird and deep intoning, which was as unlike ordinary prose as possible, sang the terrible war song, until the little attic at Farringford melted out of sight and one *saw* the far-off fields of early Britain, thronged with the maddened warriors of the maddened queen, and heard the clashing of the brands upon the shields, and the cries which

Roar'd as when the rolling breakers boom and blanch on the precipices.

The image of some ancient bard rose up before one as he might have sung the story by the watch-fires of an army the day before a battle. It was perhaps from some such association of ideas that his name among his intimates became 'The Bard'—a way of recognising in one word and in ordinary talk his mingled characters of Singer, Poet, and Prophet.

When building Aldworth he desired to have, whenever the room was finally decorated, the following names of his six favourite poets carved and painted on the six stone shields which I had designed as part of the chimney-piece in his study, and in front of which he always sat and smoked—namely, *Shakespeare, Chaucer, Milton, Wordsworth, Dante, and Goethe.*

He used to say '*Keats, if he had lived, would have been the greatest of all of us;*' he considered Goethe '*the greatest artist of the nineteenth century, and Scott its greatest man of letters;*' and he said of Swinburne, '*He's a tube through which all things blow into music.*' He said '*Wordsworth would have been much finer if he had written much less,*' and he told Browning in my presence that '*if he got rid of two-thirds, the remaining third would be much finer.*' After saying that, and when Browning had left us, he enlarged on the imperative necessity of restraint in art. '*It is necessary to respect the limits,*' he said; '*an artist is one who recognises bounds to his work as a necessity, and does not overflow illimitably to all extent about a matter. I soon found that if I meant to make any mark at all it must be by shortness, for all the men before me had been so diffuse, and all the big things had been done. To get the workmanship as nearly perfect as possible is the best chance for going down the stream of time. A small vessel on fine lines is likely to float further than a great raft.*'

Once, as we stood looking at Aldworth just after its completion, he turned to me and said, '*You will live longer than I shall. That house will last five hundred years.*' I answered him, 'I think the English language will last longer.'

Another frequent subject of his talk was the criticism on his own work, *when unfavourable.* All the mass of eulogy he took comparatively little notice of, but he never could forget an unfriendly word, even from the most obscure and insignificant and unknown quarter. He was hurt by it as a sensitive child might be hurt by the cross look of a passing stranger; or rather as a supersensitive skin is hurt by the sting of an invisible midge. He knew it was a weakness in him, and could be laughed out of it for a time, but it soon returned upon him, and had given him from his early youth exaggerated vexation. When remonstrated with for the Hogarth's perspective he thus made, he would grimly smile and say, '*Oh yes, I know. I'm black-blooded like all the Tennysons—I remember everything that has been said against me, and forget all the rest.*' It was his temperament, and showed itself in other matters besides criticism. For instance, the last time I went with him to the oculist, he was most heartily reassured about his eyes by the great expert after a careful and detailed inspection. But as we left the door he turned to me and said with utter gloom, '*No man shall persuade me that I'm not going blind.*' Few things were more delightful than to help chase away such clouds and see and feel the sunshine come out again, responsive to the call of cheerfulness. To one who had so cheered him he said: '*You certainly are a jolly good fellow, you do encourage me so much.*' And at another time:'*I'm very glad to have known you. It has been a sort of lift in my life.*' The clouds would gather on him most in the solitude of the country, and he often told me it was needful for him to come from time to time to London to rub the rust from off him. It must be added that so soon as ever the rust was rubbed off he hastened to be back among the woods and hills.

Criticism

The Reaction Against
Tennyson and Its Corrective

A. C. BRADLEY

The Reaction Against Tennyson†

When he died, in 1870, Dickens was still at the height of his fame. The public idolized him, and critical readers, though they had a good deal to say against him, did not question his greatness. Some twenty years later, however, a decided change was visible, chiefly among such readers and especially among the younger men of letters. It was more than a cooling of enthusiasm: it was a strong reaction. Certain defects of the novelist were keenly felt, and all the more keenly because it seemed that his immense popularity had been largely due to them. To decry Dickens, even to protest that you could not read him, became a fashion and a mark of being up to date. And in this reaction two curious traits might be noticed. One was the belief that Dickens's faults were a new discovery and had never been suspected in his lifetime. The other was still stranger, and much more important. The dislike of his faults appeared often to kill the power of perceiving and enjoying his virtues. Because you could not abide the death of Paul Dombey or Little Nell, you listened to Sam Weller and Mrs. Gamp without a smile.

This was the nadir of Dickens's star. After a time it rose again. The wholesome work of reaction was finished. In the more literary sections of the public, and among men of letters, there is now a fairly general agreement about him. His defects are simply taken for granted; but his astonishing genius is fully recognized, and his almost inexhaustible creations are as keenly enjoyed as they were fifty years ago. The best critique of his works written in the first decade of this century came, not from an old stager, but from Mr. Chesterton. And now, if you are unable to read Dickens and yet wish to be in the literary swim, you must either hold your tongue about him or tell lies about yourself.

† From A. C. Bradley, *A Miscellany* (London: Macmillan & Co., Ltd., 1929), pp. 1–4, 7–14, 27–31. Reprinted by permission of the publisher. (The essay was first given as a lecture in 1914.)

This story, down to a certain stage in it, has exactly repeated itself in the case of Tennyson—a writer less astonishing in genius and much less faulty in art. At the time of his death, nearly a quarter of a century ago, he was immensely popular; and of a large part of the public it may fairly be said that it did not recognize his weaknesses and even liked them. After a while, in small circles, the reaction began, and it has spread, and, so far as it has spread, is now intense. The nadir of his fame may not quite be reached, but it can hardly be far off. To care for his poetry is to be old-fashioned, and to belittle it is to be in the movement. And those curious traits of the Dickens reaction have reappeared, the first of them in a more amusing shape. The mid-Victorian, a figure amply proving the creative energy of Georgian imagination, is supposed to have been blind to Tennyson's defects, though the actual surviving mid-Victorian rarely hears a sane word about them which was not familiar to him in his youth. And—what really matters—the antipathy to these defects seems in some cases to have so atrophied the power of enjoyment that Tennyson's weakest poems and his best meet with the same indifference or contempt, and a reader will remain unmoved by lines which, if he were ignorant of their authorship, he would hail with delight.

The loss of such delight is a heavy one, and ingratitude is not a pretty vice; but otherwise the reaction against Tennyson is not, on the whole, a matter for regret. It was necessary, for one thing, in the interests of poetry itself. For the formal characteristics of his style were easily caught, and Tennysonian minor poetry, if less absurd than Byronic minor poetry, was quite as sickening; so that those who admire him most can only rejoice that no trace of his influence remains in the poetry of the present day. Besides, his popularity in the last twenty or thirty years of his life made the public unjust to other living poets, and he was over-estimated even by some good critics; and in such cases (George Eliot's is another) some reaction is both natural and wholesome. It hastens, also, that sifting process to which the works of all poets have to submit (unless, like Sappho's, they are almost all lost). The result of that process is that a part of the works is separated out and continues to be widely read or, as we say, to "live," while the remainder passes more or less from public view and is explored only by lovers of the poet or students of literary history. This has already happened to Tennyson's immediate predecessors, and it is happening to him now. When the process is complete nobody troubles to dwell on the poet's defects, nobody is blinded by them to his merits, and it is possible to form a comparative estimate of his worth. The time for this has not yet come in Tennyson's case, and it will hardly come in my lifetime; but, if only for your entertainment, I will hazard a brief prophecy. I believe he will be considered the best poet of his own age, though not so much the best as his own age supposed; and, while I have never thought that in native endowment he was quite the equal of the best of the preceding age, yet the distance, as it seems to me, is not wide; and, as he was blessed with long life, made (like Pope) the most of his gift, and in a wonderful degree retained and even developed it to the end, I do not doubt that his place will be beside them, and expect that the surviving portion of his work will not be smaller than what survives of theirs. * * * The root of the reaction against Tennyson among capable readers of the new generation is, we are told, that his ideas do not appeal to them—neither the more explicit ideas, sometimes called the "philosophy," found in *In Memoriam* and elsewhere, nor the ideas or way of regarding life implicit in many other poems. This is probably true, and, if this were all, there would be little or nothing in the fact to cause surprise or regret. The statement would hold good of the ideas of Carlyle, and, with some modification, of those of Ruskin and Browning. They all permeated, more or less, the minds of several generations, and, doubtless losing something in the process, became an atmosphere surrounding the mind of the present; and an atmosphere, however wholesome, cannot well have the charm of novelty. But every generation naturally asks for novelty; and, further, the ideas and the literature of times immediately preceding its own are apt to be the least interesting of all to it, because they have less novelty for it than those of periods more distant, and may even be felt, as those more distant ideas are not, to be a prison from which it is necessary to escape. This, no doubt, is a wise provision of Nature to ensure progress, and it would be foolish to complain of it, even though its result is that the full meaning of the ideas in question is lost for a time and remains to be re-discovered when they are no longer familiar.

There is little I need say about the attitude of the reaction towards Tennyson's "philosophical" ideas, but I cannot say it without interposing a word of protest. Harm has been done by those who have spoken of his "philosophy," whether to exalt or to belittle it. He was not a philosopher, any more than Wordsworth was, or Browning, or Meredith, though he shows, I think, more signs than they do of the gift that makes a philosopher. And he, like them, is happier when he simply expresses his ideas, with the emotions that accompany them, than when he argues about them, or attempts to systematize them; happier in *The Ancient Sage* and *The Higher Pantheism* and certain passionate sections of *In Memoriam* than in certain other sections of that poem, just as Wordsworth is happier in *Tintern Abbey* than in the most analytical passages of *The Prelude*. Coleridge might perhaps have discussed with profit, in prose, the question whether that which Wordsworth found in Nature was found there or put there; but, even if this question were suitable for verse at all, Wordsworth was not competent to discuss it. Neither Tennyson nor Browning offers, I believe, any argument for personal immortality that had not been stated in preciser terms and more complete connexion by philosophers; but their passion for this belief made fine poetry, and far more impressive to me than their arguments in support of it is the bare fact (whatever it may point to) that two minds so much superior to my own could make no sense of the world without it.

I come now to the "philosophical" ideas, as distinguished from the arguments, that lay nearest to Tennyson's heart. One of them was that just mentioned. A second was the idea of human progress on the earth—the faith that man, through a process lasting for thousands or millions of years, is developing into something infinitely greater than he was at first, and even that "the whole creation" is moving to "some divine event." Of this second idea I shall say nothing, because, whatever the attitude of the "reaction" may be in regard to it, Tennyson's attitude does not appear to be a source of irritation. The third may be called the idea of God; but it would be better, I think, to call it the idea of the ultimate power, because the main source of Tennyson's interest in this idea seems to me to have lain in its bearing on the other two. The main source, that is to say, was not so much the strictly religious impulse to adore as the need to be satisfied that, since the ultimate power in the universe is clearly not man, this power,

> He, They, One, All; within, without;
> The Power in darkness whom we guess,

is of such a nature as to value highest what man at his best values highest, and therefore to ensure his progress both on earth and elsewhere. And that need, we should observe, was for Tennyson peculiarly imperative. Like his great predecessors, he may be called a poet of Nature, but with a difference. For Wordsworth and Shelley the spirit of Nature, we may roughly say,[1] is wholly beautiful, good, and unhampered, while in man this same spirit is thwarted, and struggles against ugliness and evil; and so Nature is, for them, a promise, and almost a pledge, of man's ultimate victory. But it could not be so for Tennyson. Though he wrote *In Memoriam* before the days of Darwin, he had fully realized and keenly felt the conflict, pain, and waste in Nature; so that it presented to him not a solution, but the same problem as man's life, and required the same further guarantee. Then (to look for a moment beyond *In Memoriam*), as years went by, this need became still more

1. As regards Shelley the statement is not quite accurate.

insistent, because the advance of science and the theory of evolution (both of which he welcomed) had, however unjustifiably, made materialism a popular magazine-philosophy, and this philosophy again, in Tennyson's view, was in part responsible for moral phenomena which he detested. This was unfortunate for him, partly because it alarmed and exasperated him and touched some of his poetry with the spirit of ephemeral controversy, and partly because it led unwise opponents to regard him as a reactionary, and unwise admirers to make claims for him as a philosophic teacher which he never made for himself.

To return to the reaction. I quite understand that *In Memoriam*, as regards its ideas, cannot appeal to readers now as it did to thousands in the generation before mine, or even in mine or the next after mine. But why *In Memoriam* and other poems, because of these ideas, should lose all interest for those who share in the reaction, I do *not* understand; and still less how any one can offer the explanation that these ideas, one or all, are so alien to his own that he cannot read the poems with enjoyment or even with patience. That explanation, it seems to me, implies an altogether perverse attitude towards poetry or, for that matter, any other product of imagination.

I do not mean merely that a reader who is indifferent or hostile to the main ideas used in a poem ought to be able, in spite of this, to enjoy the beauty of its style and music. I mean that, for the time being, he ought to be able to adopt these ideas, to identify himself imaginatively with them, to feel as his own the emotions that accompany them; and, further, that unless he has done this he cannot fully appreciate the poem or, in the full sense of the word, read it. If, as I read Browning's *Cavalier Tunes*, my Roundhead sympathies prevent my feeling like a Cavalier, how can I read the *Tunes* with any gusto; and, read without gusto, are they themselves? Are the Jolly Beggars to me what they are in the poem, if I refuse to be a Jolly Beggar for the moment and insist on remaining a member of a Charity Organization Committee? And if this holds of poems like these, equally, or if possible even more, it holds of a poem like *In Memoriam*, which is concerned not with a past political conflict or a minor form of free enjoyment, but with something which has been, is, and always must be, the centre of men's doubts, fears, hopes, or convictions about themselves and the world, and which, in a variety of shapes, may even be said to form the ultimate subject of all great philosophies and religions and of most of the greatest poems. In *In Memoriam* it takes a particular shape. There is a large and beautiful soul—for all who know it, a pre-eminently large and beautiful soul; for them, therefore, something of the highest value: and suddenly, with all its promise unfulfilled, it appears to vanish like the rainbow of a minute, and therefore to have no more value than the rainbow for the ultimate power. Can this be really so? Again: this power, as Job believes, is the friend of the man who tries to do his will; yet Job, who knows—and, for the author of the poem, truly knows—that, imperfect as he is, he has tried with all his heart to do that will, is treated like a defiant rebel: how can this be? Again: God is perfect goodness and power; how is it, then, that Satan and his host exist, and that man, who was made in God's image, has lost his Paradise; and how, once more, that countless images of God appear to walk their way to Purgatory or to Hell? And, whether visibly or no, the same mystery haunts all great tragedy and even great works not tragic. Was ever soul nobler than Antigone's or Othello's; yet what becomes of them? And if Don Quixote's soul was no less noble, why was it the prey of delusions and a butt for vulgar insult? Well, then, when I read the *Book of Job*, the *Divine Comedy*, or the *Antigone*, surely I do not say, "These ideas about God or Zeus or Heaven and Hell are not my ideas and clash with mine, and therefore I cannot enter into them." On the contrary, I do enter into them and feel in them the same problem and the same passion that belong to my own ideas, truer perhaps than they, but unlikely to be the unveiled truth. And if I did anything else, what would you call me? Either a man with no literary education, or else a man with a literary education, but— stupid.

* * *

After all this balancing and distinguishing, it would be a relief to me, as well as to you, if I ended with mere praise of what is greatest and highest in Tennyson's poetry. But that would take too long, and I will end with praise of a minor merit, which I think as indisputable as any poetical merit can be. It appears, though not solely, in his treatment of Nature. As regards that particular treatment of Nature which we associate with the name of Wordsworth, I should not think of comparing Tennyson either with Wordsworth or with Shelley; but I believe he is unsurpassed, and I suspect he is unequalled, among English poets in two things—one, the accuracy and delicacy of his perceptions; and the other, the felicity of his translation into language of that which he perceives. The first of these things is not specially distinctive of a poet; the second, though not by itself enough to make a poet great, is *the* distinction of a poet from other artists. Poetry is an art of language; and the born poet, of whatever size, is a person who has a peculiar gift for translating his experiences—whatever he sees, hears, feels, imagines, thinks—into metrical language, a special necessity in his nature to do this, and a unique joy in doing it well. The universe, we may say, is for him an invitation or a challenge to such expression. Well, just now we are concerned with sense-experiences, and especially those that come from Nature; and I repeat that here Tennyson seems to me unsurpassed and perhaps unequalled among our poets in the accuracy and delicacy of his perceptions, and in the felicity of his translation into language of that which he perceives.[2] As to the latter you may perhaps recall Ruskin's emphatic statement: "Tennyson's 'Rivulet' [he means *The Brook*] is far beyond anything I ever did, or could have done, in beauty of description." As to the former you will certainly remember how attention was called in *Cranford* to the line,

> More black than ash-buds in the front of March,

and how, since then, this line has been quoted *ad nauseam* as though it were something exceptional. In reality it is an example, and not a remarkable one, of something ubiquitous in Tennyson. If a man who had derived great happiness from the observation of nature were stricken with blindness or confined for the rest of his life to a sick-room, and if he were condemned to lose his recollection of all poets but one, Tennyson's is the poetry he should choose to keep. There, for example, he could follow the progress of spring, from the beginning when

> Once more the Heavenly Power
> Makes all things new,
> And domes the red-plowed hills
> With loving blue;

when rosy plumelets tuft the larch, and a million emeralds break from the ruby-budded lime, and the ruddy-hearted blossom-flakes flutter down from the elm in tens of thousands; when the satin-shining palms appear on sallows in the windy gleams, and, later, a gust strikes the yew and puffs the swaying branches into smoke, and all the wood stands in a mist of green, till, later still, as you cross the wood you pass through a green gloom. Or, again, Tennyson will bring back to him the coming of the storm; its green malignant light near the horizon; then the ragged rims of thunder brooding low, with shadow-streaks of rain; and then the blasts that blow the poplar white and lash with storm the streaming pane; the stammering cracks and claps, the bellowing of the tempest, and at last the sounds of its retreat into the distance, moaning and calling out of other lands. Or, if he has loved the sea, with Tennyson he may still watch, on a windless day, the crisping ripples on the beach, and tender curving lines of creamy spray; or, on a windy one, crisp foam-

2. Since this lecture was first given, two excellent papers by Mr. Morton Luce on *Nature in Tennyson* (Birds and Trees) have appeared in the *British Review* (1915).

flakes scudding along the level sand; or may recall from memories of the open sea a huge wave, green-glimmering towards the summit, with all its stormy crests that smoke against the skies. It will be just the same with him if he thinks of sunrise and sunset; of the nightingale or the thrush (whose voice has so become speech in *The Throstle* that, as he remembers it, he will laugh for amusement and joy); or of the mother-dog with her blind and shuddering puppies, or the rabbit fondling his own harmless face. And, as our invalid lies awake through the night in his sick-room, he may remember Tennyson when the grandfather clocks in rooms beneath throb thunder through the floors, and may remember Tennyson again as the dawn approaches and the casement slowly grows a glimmering square.

These are a few examples[3] of what I mean, out of hundreds. Well, my friend of the reaction will not find in the poetic virtue shown in them the deepest and highest that poetry can reach or that this poet can reach; but he will not belittle it if he loves nature and knows what poetry is. Let him enjoy it, if he can enjoy nothing else in Tennyson. And if he enjoys and reveres science too (from a closer acquaintance, I hope, than mine), perhaps he will consider favourably the last claim that I urge on behalf of this poet. We live, and civilized man must continue to live, in an age of science. But, with the partial exception of Shelley, Tennyson is the only one of our great poets whose attitude towards the sciences of Nature was what a modern poet's attitude ought to be; the only one whose words constantly come to your mind as you read, if you can get no farther, your manual of astronomy[4] or geology; the only one to whose habitual way of seeing, imagining, or thinking, it makes any real difference that Laplace, or for that matter Copernicus, ever lived. He gazed too, without flinching, on aspects of Nature which Wordsworth did not face; and in this also the poetry of the future must surely follow him. One may hope that courage and faithfulness like his will not prevent it, as it prevented him, from sharing Wordsworth's intuition of

> A central peace, subsisting at the heart
> Of endless agitation.

But, however that may be, when we have again a poetry of Nature equal to Wordsworth's, it will have to be, in his own phrase, "the inspired expression that is in the countenance of all science," and it will look back with gratitude to Tennyson.

---

3. I have not thought it necessary to give references to the poems and passages where these "examples" occur.
4. Readers who may be interested in Tennyson's very numerous astronomical passages will find a full treatment of the subject by Mr. C. T. Whitmell in the *Journal and Transactions of the Leeds Astronomical Society* for 1906.

HAROLD NICOLSON

The Tennyson Legend†

* * *

There are several alternative devices by which Tennyson might be rendered almost palatable to modern readers: I have worked out the several theses which could potentially be adopted. One might embark, for instance, on the theory that the real Tennyson, the poet Tennyson, was not a Victorian at all but a later Georgian. This contention could be elaborated and maintained with more detail and conviction than might be supposed: one can see the general outlines and the few high lights on which such a composition would be based. As frontispiece, of course, there would be the fierce and adventurous Tennyson of the Sam Lawrence portrait—the fine brown forehead, the brown, defiant eyelids, the ugly, ill-tempered mouth, the huge stock and collar. Much would be made of his youth and boyhood: of George III, of the Regency, of George IV, of press-gangs and crimping, of cock-fights and professional boxers, of Hessian boots and the smugglers' stories at Mablethorpe. Circumstantial detail would be provided by the drinking parsons who would ride across Lincolnshire to dine at 5 p.m. with his father in the Rectory hall, by the Bishop of Lincoln in his wig, by his father's knee-breeches and silver buckles, by the cake and negus in the parlour, by his sisters playing bilbo or embroidering fire-screens in Berlin wool, by the tinder-box and tallow dip at his bedside, by the thieves swinging in chains against the sunset on Gibbet Hill. The Cambridge period would be dated (perhaps ante-dated) by similar touches: there would be a picture of the fireworks at the accession of William IV, of the mulled claret, the rat hunts and the churchwarden pipes, of the port-besotted dons in Trinity Common room, of Sunderland's kerseymere breeches and of the Byronic manner in which Arthur Hallam discarded his stock. London would come with a reference to the haymakers in Bays-water, the stile into the fields at the end of Portland Place, and the snipe-shooting in Kensington; Tom Moore and Rogers would figure prominently, and Leigh Hunt would flit contemporaneously through the picture; there would be much about curiously shaped bottles of heavy port at the Cock Tavern, and Government lottery tickets, and M. Dubourg's cork models of Roman antiquities at his exposition in Bond Street. One would thus arrive in a rich Han-

† From Harold Nicolson, *Tennyson: Aspects of His Life, Character and Poetry* (London, Constable & Co., Ltd., 1923), pp. 6–10, 25–29. Reprinted by permission of Nigel Nicolson.

overian atmosphere at the volumes of 1830 and 1832, at the composition of all that is most valuable in the 1842 volume, at the earlier versions of *In Memoriam*, and one could emerge triumphantly in 1837 having proved that all the most durable of Tennyson's work was either published or composed before the accession of Queen Victoria. If determined still further to prove such a contention, one might extend the time limit a few years by maintaining that the first decade of the young Queen's reign had still a dash about it of the old Brunswick hilarity, and that the real Victorian fog did not settle upon England till close on 1850. One would, by such a paradox, gain *The Princess* for the theory, and even the final version of *In Memoriam*, and could kill Tennyson off fairly securely by the date of the first Exhibition.

A great many people would doubtless be angered and stimulated by such a thesis: I doubt whether very many would be convinced.

Another and even more alluring performance would be to work backwards. To start from Mr. Gosse and Swinburne and struggle back to the Pre-Raphaelites, and thus to the 1842 volume. In other words, to drape Tennyson in the fabric of the middle 'eighties, and to ignore the less effervescent period from 1842 to 1866. But such a contention would, after all, get seriously out of hand.

One can but mention such possible theses: their elaboration might be entertaining, and would serve at least to remove many current misconceptions and prejudices, would serve to startle the average reader out of his accepted assumptions of Tennyson, and to correct what is obviously a false perspective; as a negative business, the process might be valuable enough.

If, however, any practical zest for Tennyson is to revive in this generation, some more positive theory will be required; some formula such as will enable the modern reader, while accepting with kindly resignation Tennyson's undoubted deficiencies, to come upon his virtues with a shock of sudden and delighted surprise. Such a formula will not be attained by the negative processes which I have adumbrated; still less will it be attained by the comparative method, always dangerous, but in the case of Tennyson actually deceptive. I have carefully eschewed the temptation of emphasising obvious differences or of drawing far-fetched resemblances between Tennyson and his contemporaries; and indeed to seek, as some have sought, analogies between Tennyson and Browning, or Tennyson and Clough, or Tennyson and Patmore, or Tennyson and Swinburne, or Tennyson and the now popular Morris appears of all tasks the most mistaken and unremunerative.

The formula, moreover, will not be attained by suppressing or ignoring the Victorian element in Tennyson's poetry: it will be attained only by analysing and defining that element with a view to isolate it from the central lyrical throb which pulsates through his work. It can only be discovered and conveyed by following the thread of Tennyson's life and work from his unhappy and puzzled boyhood to his puzzled and prosperous old age; and by examining, and endeavouring at times to disentangle, the diverse strands which are interwoven so curiously as to give to the superficial observer a mistaken impression of uniformity. For the secret of Tennyson is to be sought not in the apparent harmony between his work and character, but in the essential conflict between the two: in the conflict, that is, between the remarkable depth and originality of his poetic temperament and the shallowness and timidity of his practical intelligence.

Temperamentally Tennyson possessed all the qualities which should have rendered him one of the greatest and most original of our lyric poets. With the strong, full blood of his yeoman forebears mingled the black and bitter strain of some obscurer ancestry; through the arteries of an athlete fluttered the frightened, sensitive pulses of a mystic; and under the scent and music of delicate and tender things pierced the coarse salt savour of the wold and marsh.

That Tennyson's genius was essentially of a subjective, and not of an objective, quality will, I suppose, be now generally admitted; it is tempting even to consider how his genius would have developed had not the force and passion of his poetic temperament been hushed by quite ephemeral considerations. For had his lot fallen among other circumstances, or in a less cloying age; had that unfortunate element of caution been absent from his character; had some whim of fate let loose the vast reserves of emotion which were in him, and had he realised that what he *felt* was infinitely more important than what he *thought*, we might well have had a greater Francis Thompson, or maybe—for who can tell?—an earlier Swinburne. I am not so illiterate as to suggest that Tennyson would have been a better poet had he been a less reputable man and citizen. Yet even if he had retained his austerity, even if he had lost nothing of the sombre stateliness of his manner, a little more emotion, a little less accuracy, might well have rendered him our supreme poet of despair—a broader and more human Alfred de Vigny. He was intended to be a subjective poet, and was forced by circumstances into fifty years of unnatural objectivity. He chose the easier and more prosperous course: he became the Laureate of his age; he subordinated the lyric to the instructional. And his poetry thereby has lost one half of its potential value.

* * *

We must realise that against the insidious influence of his age, against the sheer misfortune of having been born at exactly the wrong moment, Tennyson had, in fact, but little chance. He was by no means the only writer of that time who so succumbed. Had he arrived a generation earlier, he would have been a great Romantic; had he delayed a generation later, he would have been greater than any of the pre-Raphaelites; even as it was, he might well have emerged an immortal had his intelligence been equal to his poetic temperament. But it was not equal. And there is a great deal, therefore, which needs to be explained away.

It avails, I recognise, but little to contend that it was the fault of the age, and not of the poet, that Tennyson was thus or thus. It would be easy, indeed, to show that those characteristics of Tennyson which estrange him the most from modern readers are but the passing reflection of the thoughts and manners of his time—that his sentimentality, his commonplace morals, his caution, his shallow thought, his maddening accuracy, are merely incidentals which should not affect our estimate of his poetry. It avails still less to indicate what a very remarkable poet Tennyson would have become had he been different in himself or had he fallen upon other circumstances. If an impression is to be made by any advocacy of Tennyson, it is necessary at the outset to diagnose the real nature of the aversion with which he is now regarded, and, having done so, to examine whether this aversion is superficial only or profound.

It may be assumed that every generation, and indeed every individual, will evolve their own particular definition of what constitutes the highest poetry. Such definitions are entertaining, and may even be useful so long as they are advanced as relative only, and not as absolute. The most that one may hazard is that the scattered individual definitions of any given generation, if fused together into a composite formula, do actually constitute an indication of the particular aspect upon poetry which is prevalent in, or natural to, that generation. And I think it may be said without fear of contradiction that what the early twentieth century primarily demands from poetry is a reality of emotional impulse. One can amplify this formula if desired: one may exact, with Mr. Drinkwater, that poetry should be the "announcement of spiritual discovery"; one may demand "a coincidence of unfettered imaginative ecstasy with superb mental poise"; one may apply to it the definition which Mr. Middleton Murry applies to style—"a combination of the maximum of personality with the maximum of impersonality; . . . a concentration of peculiar and personal emotion . . . a complete projection of this personal emotion into the created thing." We may do all this, and more; but we shall come back, I think, to the simple conclusion that what people look for to-day is this reality of emotional impulse. They look for it in Tennyson, and they find, or think they find, little reality, less emotion and scarcely any impulse at all. They accuse him, therefore, of being no true poet; and this accusation, I contend, rests on a complete misconception of his peculiar genius.

For although the great mass of Tennyson's poetry, however skilful it may be in form, appears in substance to be lacking in these important qualities of impulse, reality and emotion; although one must admit that his prosperous assurance, his laborious and careful revisions, his accuracy and caution, lead one at times to doubt the compelling force of his inspiration, and even, perhaps, to question his sincerity; although he was apt on all occasions to exploit sentiments and situations which were certainly superficial and perhaps unreal; although he flinched alike before the flame of passion and the cold nakedness of truth, yet there are sudden panting moments when the frightened soul of the man cries out to one like some wild animal caught in the fens at night-time—moments when he lies moaning in the half-light in an agony of fear. And at such moments the mystical genius of Tennyson comes upon one in a flash, and there can be no question of the reality of his emotion and his impulse.

I advance this theory not as a paradox but, for what it is worth, as an absolute personal conviction. For me, the essential Tennyson is a morbid and unhappy mystic. He is the hero of *The Sensitive Mind* [*sic*], of *The Two Voices* and above all of *Maud*. He is a spirit for whom there was an "ever-moaning battle in the mist"—a soul whose fancies mingled

> "with the sallow-rifted glooms
> Of evening, and the moanings of the wind";

and thus at times there comes

> "A cry that shiver'd to the tingling stars,
> And, as it were one voice, an agony
> Of lamentation, like a wind, that shrills
> All night in a waste land, where no one comes
> Or hath come, since the making of the world."

For those who accept this theory no great difficulty will arise in reconciling the essential Tennyson with the Tennyson of the legend. One would prefer not to fall back upon the jargon of the psychoanalysts, but the application of the Freudian system to the case of Tennyson is quite illuminating. For Tennyson was afraid of a great many things: predominantly he was afraid of death, and sex, and God. And in all these matters he endeavoured instinctively to sublimate his terrors by enunciating the beliefs which he desired to feel, by dwelling upon the solutions by which he would like to be convinced. The point does not require further elaboration: my contention is merely that once one accepts the realisation of Tennyson, and particularly the younger Tennyson, as a man who was morbidly afraid, one must admit that the processes by which he conquered his afflictions cannot by any possibility be described as consciously insincere. And once one is able to dispose of this fatal suspicion of insincerity, the real beauty of Tennyson's poetry will triumph of itself.

I have endeavoured in this introductory chapter to indicate some of the reasons for which Tennyson is so little esteemed by the present generation, and to suggest the processes by which an interest in his poetry might be encouraged to revive. I have explained that to some extent the reaction against him is to be attributed to the exaggerated adulation accorded to him by the Victorian age; and I have admitted that a contributory cause of this reaction is the fact that so subjective a poet should have been forced, however justifiably, into a perpetual straining after objective expression. I have urged, as an excuse for this, the peculiar circumstances of the period when Tennyson first appeared as a poet and the unfortunate condition of contemporary literary taste. I have contended that, if we still desire to be fair to Tennyson, it is necessary to realise the duality which exists between his temperament and his intelligence, between his lyrical genius and the peculiar qualities which were imposed upon him by his age; and I have concluded with the theory that the essential inspiration of Tennyson was the inspiration of fear, and that, if once this view is accepted and realised, the most damaging criticism against him—the criticism that he was both morally and intellectually insincere—will cease to trouble or to disconcert.

I do not imagine that I have at this stage convinced anyone by this thesis: it is a theory at which I have arrived myself only after much doubt and hesitation. I ask only that it may be accepted as a working basis for what follows, and that it will be allowed to give a certain thread of consistency to the chapters, otherwise inchoate, in which the development of the poet is traced from his childhood days at Somersby to the final dignity of his old age.

And in the end, as always with any poet of value, it matters little what theories are propounded or what discoveries are made. In the end Tennyson will be appreciated, not in the least because the ingenious critic has toyed for an hour or two with some fresh or forgotten aspect of his genius. He will be appreciated because he wrote *Ulysses* and *The Lotos-Eaters*; because he wrote *Tithonus*; because he wrote *The Two Voices*; because he wrote *Maud*; because he wrote:—

"Now lies the Earth all Danaë to the stars,"

and *Crossing the Bar*.

And, after all, *In Memoriam*.

DOUGLAS BUSH

Tennyson†

Of late years, very happily, sniffs or sneers at Tennyson have ceased to be proof of a modern critical intelligence. The reaction of the earlier twentieth century against the Laureate was not in itself entirely modern. Some of our complaints had been made by Wilson and Lockhart, and, as the Victorian era advanced, most of the others were added; even the years of relative security after 1850 were not altogether a green lawn "where Alf, the sacred river, ran." As that great era receded into the past hostile voices increased in volume and shrillness, for the white light of truth heated as well as illuminated the modern mind. Victorian literature could be damned outright as "pink pills for pale people," and its most complete and revered representative was the chief sufferer. The reaction was of course inevitable, and, in cutting Tennyson loose from a mass of dubious writing, from a partly adventitious and spurious reputation, it has left an indubitable poet standing on a smaller but firmer pedestal. Much of his work is dead beyond recall, but we still hear the wind sweep and the plover cry, and the sea breaking on the cold gray stones. For he lives mainly as a painter of landscape and water, as a poet of lyrical, especially elegiac, moments, and, within limits, as a superb artist in words, a maker of golden lines.

Tennyson's mind and career, some modern critics have thought, are paradoxical, and they have tried to find a formula which explains apparent changes in him. The common pattern of interpretation is something like this. Tennyson began as a genuine romantic poet and ended as a Laureate, a British minister for divine affairs, who aspired to see his Pilot face to face, "as gentleman to gentleman." The real poetic fire that he possessed was gradually extinguished, it seems, by a number of causes—native timidity and morbid sensitiveness to both praise and blame; the Apostles' contagious zeal for uplift; hostile reviewers; the thrusting, by misguided friends and pious public, of the rôle of *vates* or preacher upon a born singer; the paralyzing result of accepting and expounding the Victorian compromise; the taming influence of a wife who ruled his spirit from her sofa; prosperity and familiar acquaintance with Royalty.

Doubtless all these deleterious agencies and more were in operation, and some of them certainly left their mark, but the formula

† From Douglas Bush, *Mythology and the Romantic Tradition in English Poetry* (Cambridge, Mass.: Harvard University Press, 1937; W. W. Norton & Co., Inc., 1963), pp. 197–202. Copyright © 1937 by the President and Fellows of Harvard College; 1965 by Douglas Bush. Reprinted by permission of the Harvard University Press.

of the frustrated artist has been so widely used by modern biograph-
ical writers that one may grow suspicious of a well-worn pass-key.
A complete survey of Tennyson's life from Somersby to West-
minster Abbey does not suggest that he was notably warped, that
he took or was pushed into the wrong road. Surely his temperament,
his parentage, his early training and environment, made his future
course almost certain. There are paradoxes in the mature Tennyson,
but there are paradoxes in little Alfred, who was a combination of
normal boy, scholar, poet, melancholist and mystic. In that aston-
ishing play, *The Devil and the Lady*, which he wrote at the age of
fourteen, in the midst of boyish high jinks and Elizabethan robust-
iousness (and Tennysonian landscape-painting), we have specula-
tions about the mystery of evil and about "suns and spheres and
stars and belts and systems."[1] If we must have a formula, a glance
at the Tennysonian table of contents will furnish one that is far
from novel. From the juvenilia to *Crossing the Bar* Tennyson was
sometimes a poet, sometimes a preacher. Nor was the preacher
wholly an encumbrance; if it was he who modulated "the last de-
liberate snuffle of 'the blameless king,' " he also gave strength to
Ulysses and *In Memoriam*. We may wish that Tennyson had been,
like Keats, a "natural man," so to speak, who had to make himself
and his own spiritual world, instead of finding both ready made,
but we must take him as he is. If one allows for the normal mel-
lowing of maturity, Tennyson was at the end what he was at the
beginning, an artist who had consummate powers of expression
and not very much, except as an emotional poet, to say.

I

The earliest poem that we have shows Tennyson in the capacity
of translator. Between his eleventh and fourteenth years he trans-
lated the first ninety-three lines of Claudian's *De Raptu Prosperinae*
into a hundred and thirty-three lines of regular and often antitheti-
cal couplets. It was the work of a boy saturated in Pope's *Homer*,
and it not unworthily inaugurated the long career of a poet who,
whatever flickering lights sometimes misled him, never wavered in
his loyalty to the ancients. Nearly threescore and ten years later
we shall find him returning to the vale of Enna, and apparently to
Claudian too.[2] Classical influence was much less potent in *Poems
by Two Brothers* than the pseudo-orientalism of Byron and Moore.

1. *The Devil and the Lady*, ed. Charles
Tennyson (London, 1930), pp. 65, 24.
2. See the discussion of *Demeter and
Persephone*. The juvenile paraphrase is
in *Unpublished Early Poems by Alfred
Tennyson*, ed. Charles Tennyson
(1931). For an early Ovidian poem see
Alfred Lord Tennyson: A Memoir
(1897), I, 40, note. This biography by
the poet's son is henceforth cited as
Memoir.

In the volume of 1830, along with much decorative and melodious romanticism—and the gloomy *Supposed Confessions* and the original *Mariana* and *The Kraken*—appeared two classical pieces, *Hero to Leander* and *The Sea Fairies*. The speech of Hero to her departing lover has the long tradition of the *aubade* behind it; the immediate suggestion may have come from Hood's *Hero and Leander*, which opens with a similar situation.[3] The passion is partly Shelleyan, but a little more authentic than in the earlier *Antony to Cleopatra*.

The Sea-Fairies is linked in theme and manner with the inferior *Merman* and *Mermaid* and with the remarkable *Hesperides* of 1833. The first three are light-hearted poems of escape; they show the only kind of audacity that remained with Tennyson to the end, metrical audacity. *The Sea-Fairies* is the first of his variations on Homeric motives, though the connection with Homer is slight;[4] these sirens are innocent creatures, almost angels in appearance, who invite, not to sin, but to a carefree holiday. If the later *Lotos-Eaters* has gained much in its long-drawn languors and inlaid gold of phrase, it has also lost something, the untroubled play of youthful fancy and the relative naturalness of lyrical style. The romanticism of *The Sea-Fairies* is quite external; *The Hesperides* is the purest piece of magic and mystery, and perhaps the only piece of myth-making, that Tennyson ever wrote. What opium was for the author of *Kubla Khan*, two lines of *Comus* were for our sober young bard; he did not reprint the result, though he later wished he had done so—and though he reprinted *The Lord of Burleigh* and *The May Queen*. Nowhere else in his poetry is such strangeness added to beauty as in this weird mythological incantation. But it is hardly the work of "The Poet," and with such words Freedom could not shake the world.[5]

So far in this slight sketch we have seen Tennyson as a conscious and not altogether unworthy heir of the romantic poets. But his

3. For the text, see W. J. Rolfe's edition of Tennyson's *Works* (Boston, 1898), p. 782, and *Early Poems of Alfred Lord Tennyson*, ed. J. Churton Collins (1900), p. 286. There does not seem to be any specific debt to the versions of Marlowe or Leigh Hunt.
4. See *Odyssey*, xii. 39 ff., 181 ff. The early text is in Rolfe, p. 786, and Collins, p. 29. The revised text is in the standard editions, such as the one-volume *Works*, ed. Hallam, Lord Tennyson (1913). This edition, in the impression of 1931, is henceforth cited as *Works*.

I should mention *Ilion, Ilion*, apparently written in Tennyson's Cambridge days (*Unpublished Early Poems*, p. 47). Like most English poems in quan-

tity, it has the air of a cat picking its way along the top of a fence, yet it does deserve the threadbare adjective "haunting."
5. The poem is printed in *Works*, p. 873; *Memoir*, I, 61; Rolfe, p. 787; Collins, p. 301. The specific allusions in the introductory stanza are based on the *Periplus* of Hanno; see the translation by Wilfred H. Schoff (Philadelphia, 1912).

A reviewer, probably Bulwer, described *The Hesperides* and *Œnone* as "of the best Cockney classic," and Keatesian [*sic*] to the marrow" (*New Monthly Magazine*, XXXVII [1833], 72). *The Hesperides* has lately been praised by Mr. Eliot (*Essays Ancient and Modern*, 1936, pp. 176–78).

voluminous juvenilia reveal two instincts likely to impair the flow of lyrical emotion, one moralistic and one stylistic; both might be taken as symptoms of lower poetic vitality than the romantics possessed. The romantics, to be sure, had been both teachers and artists, but they had lived more fully than Tennyson, had earned a more valid right to expound what truth they had attained; further, however ornate they might be, style remained a means, it did not become an end in itself. In *The Palace of Art*, for instance, Tennyson poses much the same question that had troubled Shelley and Keats: can the individual live in an intellectual and artistic world of his own, or does he need the nourishment of ordinary human life and sympathy with the common lot?[6] In spite of the artistic faults of *Alastor* and *Endymion*, no one can doubt that Shelley and Keats are stirred to their depths by the problem they try to solve. Tennyson is more palpably didactic—instead of Platonic idealism he has the religious inheritance of Somersby and the "Apostles' Creed"— but he is not struggling toward a glimpse of truth, he has apparently always known it. His poem, as a poem, does not move us at all, partly because it seems to have cost so little, partly because, as the endless revision testifies, the author is mainly concerned with the framing of exquisite panel pictures and the subtle arrangement of vowels and consonants.

These paragraphs, intended as a preface, have grown much too long, but one needs to emphasize the fact that all the elements, good and bad, of the mature and the aged Tennyson appear in his early work. If he was a poet *manqué*, the spoiling process had begun at a date too early for critical analysis; it was indeed partly pre-natal. At any rate there is probably no group of poems, outside of the great lyrics, so sure of a place in any Tennyson anthology as most of the long series of classical pieces.[7] In the verse of classical inspiration—and that includes hundreds of scattered lines and phrases—we have less of Tennyson's weakness and more of his strength than in any other part of his work, except, as I said, the small body of perfect lyrics. For the classical themes generally banished from his mind what was timid, parochial, sentimental, inadequately philosophical, and evoked his special gifts and his most authentic emotions, his rich and wistful sense of the past, his love of nature, and his power of style.

6. Without disputing this traditional interpretation, which was that of Spedding and the poet's other friends, Mr. A. C. Howell argues that Tennyson, compelled to leave Cambridge for "the world," was finding compensation in the thought of his university as a beautiful home of sterile pedantry. This may well be one of the "lesser meanings," though Mr. Howell seems inclined to make it more than that. In any case, while the suggestion enriches the poem as a personal document, it does not, I think, give the poem as a poem any more moving reality than it had before. See *S.P.*, XXXIII (1936), 507–22.

7. Since, as in my other volume, I am not discussing stage plays, I omit *The Cup*.

ARTHUR J. CARR

Tennyson as a Modern Poet†

'Modern fame is nothing,' said Tennyson to William Allingham. 'I'd rather have an acre of land. I shall go down, down! I'm up now. Action and reaction.'

'Action and reaction' only partly account for Tennyson's fall. We cannot help feeling in the bard of Farringford and Aldworth, in the author of 'The May Queen', *Enoch Arden*, and 'The Promise of May', that depressing sense of imagination 'more saved than spent', which made Henry James breathe, 'Oh, dear, oh, dear', upon discovering that Tennyson himself 'was not Tennysonian'.

Not until after the great dividing years of 1914–18 was it possible to view the dead laureate with some composure and to wish to retrieve at least the part of his work that was not official and 'Victorian'. For an age that demanded of poetry 'reality of emotional impulse,' Harold Nicolson boiled the essential Tennyson down to 'a morbid and unhappy mystic', 'afraid of death, and sex, and God'. A little later, T. S. Eliot boldly called him 'a great poet', because of his 'abundance, variety, and complete competence'. When W. H. Auden made up a selection of Tennyson's poetry very much as Nicolson had specified, he conceded that Tennyson 'had the finest ear, perhaps, of any English Poet'; then he added, 'he was undoubtedly the stupidest; there was little about melancholia that he didn't know; there was little else that he did'.

In the presence of such a figure it is no wonder that critics who are also poets grow nervous and exasperated. They see in Tennyson not an open but a covert capitulation, perhaps involuntary though not altogether unconscious. Yet he is our true precursor. He shows and hides, as if in embryo, a master theme of Joyce's *Ulysses*—the accentuated and moody self-consciousness and the sense of loss that mark Stephen Dedalus. He forecasts Yeats's interest in the private myth. He apprehended in advance of Aldous Huxley the uses of mysticism to castigate materialistic culture. And in *Maud*, at least, he prepared the way for the verse of Eliot's 'Preludes' and 'Prufrock'. At some crucial points Tennyson is a modern poet, and there are compelling reasons why we should try to comprehend him. Our uneasiness, our reluctance to acknowledge the relationship is understandable, and it explains how little we advance towards seeing what Tennyson's poetry is like.

† From *University of Toronto Quarterly*, XIX (1949), pp. 361–382. Reprinted by permission of the author and the publisher, University of Toronto Press.

Seeing what it is like, discerning the essentials without 'essentializing', as Kenneth Burke would ask, demands that criticism breathe a mixed atmosphere, neither wholly aesthetic nor wholly biographical. It is not a question of choosing to consult biography in order to chart the poem or of preferring to ignore the private reference. In Tennyson's poetry the private and public worlds are fused. In the presence of such poetry, criticism must act upon life as well as upon art. Tennyson's double nature does not divide itself between the poet and the man; his poetry has a double nature and reveals not only itself but the poet. This is the truth that Hallam Tennyson confessed in his preface to the *Memoir* of his father's life: '. . . but besides the letters of my father and of his friends there are his poems, and in them we must look for the innermost sanctuary of his being. For my own part, I feel strongly that no biographer could so truly give him as he gives himself in his own works'. Although we must look to the man to find the poet, we shall find the man in his poems.

The artistic and cultural crisis which underlies the swervings and sudden drops in his long career was clearly sketched for Tennyson while he was at Cambridge, from 1828 to 1831. It was the protean question that the members of the Apostles Club debated, and that some of them attempted to resolve in action. The ill-fated Torrijos expedition, vigorously recounted by Carlyle in his *Life of John Sterling*, was a point of focus. With a handful of exiled Spaniards around General Torrijos, a few of 'the young Cambridge democrats' joined in a pitifully brave and futile attempt to restore constitutional monarchy to Spain by simultaneous uprisings in the north and south. In the summer of 1830 Alfred Tennyson and Arthur Hallam carried messages through southern France to leaders of the northern conspiracy. At the same moment Torrijos and his compatriots were landing at Gibraltar with Tennyson's friends John Mitchell Kemble (later the editor of *Beowulf*) and Richard Chenevix Trench (later the Archbishop of Dublin).

Perhaps more lucidly than the other English youths, Trench saw it as a desperate venture of sensibility that charged the external political motives and the physical danger with symbolic drama concerning the role of the individual in society and the role of the artist in a disordered culture. To another of the Apostles, W. B. Donne, Trench wrote on the eve of his departure from England:

> But the future, the future—who shall question that? What will one be? What will this age be? Must one end in a worldling; and our age, will it prove the decrepitude of the world? Are we not gathering up the knowledge of past generations because we are adding nothing ourselves? Do we not place the glory of our century in the understanding of past ages, because our individual

energy is extinct, and we are ourselves nothing? After one or two revolutions in thought and opinion, all our boasted poetry, all, or nearly all, of Keats and Shelley and Wordsworth and Byron, will become unintelligible. When except in our times, did men seek to build up their poetry on their own individual experiences, instead of some objective foundations common to all men?[1]

The question of 'objective foundations' permeates Tennyson's career and binds his poetry to the crisis of the arts in our century. Tennyson took in the sickening fact that the continental areas of common values were breaking up. Myths, rituals, slogans, accustomed loyalties and animosities, the classic procedures of politics and warfare, the classic mysteries of philosophies, the groundwork of rational history and rational science, the themes and modes of art —all cemented by hallowed ethical and economic traditions—were coming loose fast. The sense of this fact is the atmosphere of his poetry and is present everywhere. It is evident in his exploitation of a multitude of traditional poetic forms, in the question of electing a tradition and in the desperate virtuosity of his style; in his private use of the public domain of myth and legend as he turns from the formal and familiar elements to the inward and particular. We may trace it in his anxiety to keep up with the thought of his day and to draw it—drag it, if necessary—into his poetry; in his quest for symbols; in his perplexity over the artist's involvement in affairs ('The Palace of Art' sprang from Trench's ultimatum, 'Tennyson, we cannot live in art'); and in his sad conviction that his work would fail.

Only a little altered in the fashion of their dress, these questions still pace our critical reviews and galleries of art. Tennyson's awareness of these issues, which the century since the publication of *In Memoriam* has tiresomely expounded, was never lucidly conceived. His ideas flow in the current of his melancholic sensibility. When that sensibility was fed, enormously, by such a loss as the death of Arthur Hallam, Tennyson's poetry swept the entire range of crisis.

The theme of loss appeared very early in Tennyson's poetry as the talisman of imaginative energy. Whenever this theme reappears, even after *In Memoriam*, it works its magic. This fact may explain why Tennyson often seems to force himself to remember the loss of Hallam, enclosing him in the figure of King Arthur in *Idylls of the King*, performing again the ritual of loss and recovery in 'Vastness', 'In the Valley of Cauteretz', 'Merlin and the Gleam', and 'Crossing the Bar', and implicitly in many other poems. When the private sensibility was not stirred, the awareness was wanting, and 'stupid' 'Alfred Lawn Tennyson', the Victorian, wrote masterly bathos.

1. M. Trench, *Richard Chenevix Trench, Archbishop; Letters and Memorials* (1888), i, 73.

Tennyson is the most 'occasional' of poets, but the occasions were not public, even when he made them so. His imagination rose only to its own promptings or to the lure of an event that suggested or reproduced the subjective drama of loss, defeat, and disappointment. Then manner and matter would unite, and even in the placid years he could write the 'Ode on the Death of the Duke of Wellington', of a man who reminded Tennyson of the statesman latent in Arthur Hallam, and *Idylls of the King*, which broods over the disintegration of an ideal society and the fall of a heroic lay-figure. Such a survival of imagination in spite of all that was wasted taught Henry James to observe: 'As a didactic creation I do not greatly care for King Arthur; but as a fantastic one he is infinitely remunerative.' As Trench saw, there is a romantic entanglement of poet and poem. The concinnity of Tennyson's art rests on his 'individual experiences', rather than upon 'some objective foundations common to all men.'

* * *

The Tennysonian theme is frustration, and his poetry offers an analysis of its symptoms rather than the cure. What is overcome through the elaborate strategies of dream and vision is not the frustration but the disappointment that follows it. It is a poetry of illusions, some painful, some happy, none of them wearing the ultimate authority of reality. The recurrent pattern is a transition through death, loss, or dream towards ideal moods that dissolve the edges of thought and appetite. Under such illusions, Tennyson sometimes mistakes the sense of relief for the signs of truth. But because the sources of his poetry lay, finally, beyond his control, he could not get free of what is genuine as well as painful.

What saved him, at last, was that he felt his predicament even if he did not thoroughly comprehend it. He saw the crisis of art and society as a war of values, a matter of conscience. He does not theorize about it nor arrive at systematic principles. Yet in viewing the function and origin of conscience, he offers a more complex and subtler insight than T. H. Huxley, who supposed conscience to be merely a social monitor, the inner voice of social obligations. For Tennyson, it is more primitive and more powerful, arising in partly unconscious levels of the mind and presenting to the reason and the will an ambiguous scene of unreconciled motives and values. In Tennyson's anatomy of conscience, our human action upon nature and society meets a crisis of the divided will, which cannot be healed until it frees itself from fantasy and despair. That freedom Tennyson could not really win. His failure accurately represents the continuing crisis of our culture.

Walt Whitman, who liked Tennyson, discerned that 'his very doubts, swervings, doublings upon himself, have been typical of our age'. The price that Tennyson pays for being a 'representative' poet is great. He suffers our disease and our confusion. He triumphs not as a master but as a victim. It is a vicarious role, and upon him we heap our detested sins. If the circumstances of his breeding, his generation, and his temperament had made him a convert to Catholicism, socialism, or theosophy, he might have written more interestingly to us. He might have been admired to the extent that he escaped the general malaise. But he kept to the mid-stream of his culture. As a result, he works out remorselessly the fatal consequences of the romantic tradition, bankrupts its style by his lavish expenditures, and reduces its intellectual ambitions to the accidents of individual perceptions and personal blindness. After him the deluge, the spreading chaos of 'modern art'. He is one of its makers.

There is no Tennyson tragedy. The themes of frustration can scarcely amount to that, and the tragic order of values is lacking. Besides, the victim himself, though not our father, turns out to be a well-remembered uncle, and no hero. Yet there was in him, as Hawthorne instantly perceived, 'the something not to be meddled with', as he moved with the shuffling gait of a man whose injury cannot be healed and who makes of it, by force of will, the secret of his strength.

ROBERT W. HILL, JR.

In Defense of Reading Tennyson

In 1923, during a period when it was fashionable to condemn the Victorians, Harold Nicolson proposed that "of all poets, Tennyson should be read very carelessly or not at all." Contrary to the persuasive urgings of the poet's more recent defenders, who insist upon the rewards which repay close attention to the poetry, Nicolson's advice is still followed. For if the real truth be known, Tennyson is read carelessly. Apparently few modern readers have the inclination or stamina to ponder very long the *Idylls of the King* or to linger willingly over *In Memoriam*. Unlike Keats or Yeats, Tennyson wrote poetry which seldom lends itself to the critical methods of close textual analysis. Indeed, as Cleanth Brooks has argued, "Tears, Idle Tears" is possibly the only poem which does, and the ambiguities there may very well have been unintentional. Complexity in Tennyson can prove to be the result of muddled thinking rather than conscious design, and Paull F. Baum has amply shown how that discovery simply provides easy access to further prejudice. Yet a poet, especially a poet in his seventies, who can write of Persephone's return in spring from the underworld,

> Faint as a climate-changing bird that flies
> All night across the darkness, and at dawn
> Falls on the threshold of her native land,
> And can no more . . . ,

deserves more attention than Mr. Nicolson's remark allows. The over-refinement which Douglas Bush calls Tennyson's besetting sin is singularly absent from that language. The image is precisely right, the adjectives sure, the mood—perhaps the most illusive quality in poetry and most difficult to discuss—somehow mysteriously enchanting. Tennyson does not have an agile mind. He lacks Keats's penetrating insights, Wordsworth's profundity, Yeats's breadth of vision. He is, to use his own words in praise of Virgil, a "lord of language." A modern reader must have some love of language for its own sake, must like to listen and respond to the sound of words to care much about Tennyson. Otherwise he had best take the second half of Mr. Nicolson's advice.

As one who cares about how Tennyson is read, my problem, however, is not with the deaf or the inchoate sloppy mind, nor am I anxious to argue at length with the kind of familiar response which goes, "I don't like *Antony and Cleopatra*; I can't relate to Shakespeare." What does concern me is the less than sensitive response often evoked by Tennyson from among those who bring to their reading an active intelligence and initial enthusiasm. I wonder why certain sections of *In Memoriam*, section 95 for example, do not move readers as I am moved. A bright student once wrote for me in a seminar introducing a rather smart discussion of *In Memoriam*: "Armed with these weapons [hopeful grief, inability to understand God by the reasoning power (the power of language), faith and trust, and love] Tennyson plunges into the depths of 131 sections of single-meter iambic tetrameter to later emerge the victor over evil nature, deceiving reason, and crippling despair." I am less concerned that he has got the whole poem wrong than I am with the tone of voice, the dismissive attitude, the precipitous tough-mindedness which refuses to share vicariously in valid emotional experience. Perhaps such a response, however characteristic, is but a vagary of the times, and certainly Tennyson has withstood his share of shifting tastes and various moralistic critical sensibilities. But I am inclined to blame also the lasting, deleterious influence of the new criticism—the insistence that a poem exists in and of itself and that a reading of it should be free of all biographical or historical encumbrance. A full access to Tennyson, I am saying, must arise through a determined effort to learn and understand something about the times in which he wrote. He must be read in depth over a long period, for, as Jerome Buckley has put it, "His poetry deals typically not with the great action seen as an object in itself but with the search through situation and symbol for meaning and the sudden illuminating discovery of purpose." The meaning and discovery of which Buckley speaks simply cannot be divorced from the intellectual climate which gave them content. The impact of Tennyson's poetry, so often achieved through symbolic overtones, simply does not emerge from a slipshod reading.

Tennyson's literary output spans a remarkably long period of time. Unlike Wordsworth, he continued to produce poetry of lasting value right up to the end of his life, in 1892. He was born in 1809, began composing verse practically as soon as he could write, and by the age of fourteen had drafted the incomplete play *The Devil and the Lady*. Here and in much of the other juvenilia his precociousness and sensitivity are extraordinary by any standards. In conjunction with his older brother Charles, he was in print by 1827 with *Poems by Two Brothers*. In 1830 and again in 1832 he published volumes which, though pompously and hostilely reviewed, clearly showed the signs of poetic genius. The scars from the rough treatment given many of these poems contributed to his lifelong distrust of critics, but at the time his friend Arthur Hallam urged him to put petty grievances in a proper perspective. Hallam's sudden death in the fall of 1833 was a staggering blow from which Tennyson never fully recovered. His natural tendencies toward gloom and melancholy took on proportions which were sometimes suicidal. Left, as he believed, very much alone in the world, he had to construct out of what he felt were the shambles of his life some sense of direction. Nine years passed before he again ventured into print with some new pieces and many reworked poems from the preceding two volumes. But in the seventeen years after Hallam's death, he was primarily engaged in composing and assembling the elegies which were published anonymously as *In Memoriam A. H. H.* in 1850, the year he became poet laureate and finally married Emily Sellwood. T. S. Eliot, among others, finds that after 1850, "Tennyson seems to have reached the end of his spiritual development." This notion, along with the "two-Tennyson" theory, that there is a central division in the poet between the public moral voice speaking out on national issues to the largest audience ever commanded by any poet and the private lyric voice which acknowledges doubt and despair, have contributed, I believe, to serious misconceptions. Many of the poems after 1850—*Maud*, idylls such as "The Holy Grail," "The Ancient Sage," "Demeter and Persephone," or "To Virgil," to name only a few—simply do not reflect a static sensibility or stagnant intellect. Nor, as a responsible reading of the poetry before 1850 will show, did Tennyson simultaneously put on his laureate's robes and adopt a split personality.

Yet in reading Tennyson one is inevitably brought to question the source of the tension between conflicting impulses which prevails in nearly every subject he seriously addressed. Early in his career he sought to understand the poet's place in a world which seemed increasingly alien to the artist. In "The Hesperides" and in "The Poet's Mind" he explored the possibilities open to the retired aesthete enjoying art for its own sake. "The Lady of Shalott," "The Palace of Art," and "The Lotos-Eaters" approach from various angles the dangers inherent in that posture. The issue, in sharper perspective, reemerges in *In Memoriam* and becomes one of its central themes. Tennyson's mind was often disposed to explore incompatible modes of thought, to consider alternative courses of action. Whereas he was impelled, like his own Ulysses "to strive, to seek, to find and not to yield," he was similarly drawn toward a life of Wordsworthian seclusion—perhaps even to the indolent, mindless ease of the lotos-eater. An examination of Tennyson's childhood reveals an alternately tortured and happy relationship with his father; the lingering presence of a Calvinistic background in conflict with the emerging sexual desires of adolescence; the quotidian practicalities of life among a large family set against the rich, imaginative world of a child who could lose himself in books; the sometimes smothering closeness of a tightly knit family life contrasted to the still wild, natural world of the Somersby countryside. The list could be much extended. No manipulation of its details, however, would account for the schizophrenia which the "two-Tennyson" notion sometimes implies. We have to move to the Victorian period itself to discover the source of the conflicting impulses at the center of Tennyson's mature being.

In *Science and the Modern World* Alfred North Whitehead wrote that "the history of thought in the eighteenth and nineteenth centuries is governed by the fact that the world had got hold of a general idea which it could neither live with nor live without." The idea is the mechanistic theory of nature. "The stars," the voice of Sorrow whispers in *In Memoriam*, "blindly run." If there is order in the physical universe, it is the product of natural laws over which man has no control. God is not in his heaven, and what is right with the world is purely a matter of human invention. Tennyson's lifelong interest in science has been acknowledged. As A. C. Bradley observed many years ago, "with the partial exception of Shelley, Tennyson is the only one of our great poets whose attitude towards the sciences of Nature was what a modern poet's attitude ought to be . . . the only one to whose habitual way of seeing, imagining, or thinking, it makes any real difference that Laplace, or for that matter Copernicus, ever lived." But the implications of a concern with science in the nineteenth century can be difficult for us to imagine. How are we to measure on our own pulses what it was like to read Lyell's *Principles of Geology* (1830–33) and be forced to acknowledge that the Biblical interpretation of the Creation, accepted through nineteen centuries of stony thought, was at the very best metaphorical? We have almost endless records of the responses to Darwinism, but when Henry Adams says of the years 1867–68 that "at that moment Darwin was convulsing society," how, really, are we to measure those convulsions in the "night of fear" that every man had to live through privately? In Tennyson's resort to a belief beyond proof, in his acceptance of God by faith and faith alone, Whitehead sees the weakness and muddle which typified the period's dilemma and divided the individual against himself. The rational, objective mind had to admit that science tended to deny the existence of God, at least as conventionally understood, and, consequently, the immortality of the soul was no more than myth or fable. The feelings rebelled. Tennyson could do no more than proclaim, "I have felt." In response to the imagined speculation of physicists on the vastness of the universe and possibility of life on other planets, Robert Frost wrote, "I have it in me so much nearer home/To scare myself with my own desert places." The newness of nineteenth-century discoveries in geology and astronomy did not admit such tough-minded choices. The terror existed, from within and from without. To see in Tennyson a bifurcated intellect is, in the last and fair analysis, merely to acknowledge that he was inextricably caught up in and by the dichotomy which characterized the age in which he lived.

After 1855 with the publication of *Maud*, Tennyson devoted much of his energy to the composition of the *Idylls of the King*. Carlyle dismissed the first four idylls which appeared in 1859 as "lollipops." A decade later Robert Browning considered "The Holy Grail" but "more moonlight on the castle." Ruskin said he felt the art and finish more than he should have liked. Matthew Arnold criticized Tennyson for lacking the intellectual abilities to work out such a vast project. But from 1859 to 1888, when the complete edition of twelve poems was assembled, the favorable responses far outweighed the hostile. After Tennyson's death, and well into the twentieth century, the *Idylls* came in for a storm of criticism, by a ratio very nearly the reverse of what it had been. Although today there is by no means a consensus on the poem's worth, F. E. L. Priestley surely has defined the governing impulse behind the poem when he says that the *Idylls* "represent one of Tennyson's most earnest and important efforts to deal with major problems of his time." The poem as a whole may not succeed because it tries and fails to dramatize what the acceptance of materialistic values means to society. But to conclude that Tennyson's spiritual development ceased after *In Memoriam*—to say, as Eliot does, that he "turned aside from the journey through the dark night, to become the surface flatterer of his own time"—is seriously to misread the *Idylls*. Tennyson said every reader must find his own meaning in the poem, a statement which is both a poet's dodge and a challenge. Jerome Buckley implicitly faults the poem's detractors when he says, "In final effect, then, the *Idylls*, which traces the rise of a purposeful order and the gradual catastrophic betrayal of its sustaining idealism, stands as an oblique warning, if not a direct ultimatum, to nineteenth-century England."

Perhaps we accept neither view. But to read the *Idylls* carelessly or not at all is not merely to deny ourselves pleasure—the pleasure of listening to another voice of a "lord of language"—but to deny ourselves one opportunity to understand a society in crisis. However doomed we are to repeat our mistakes, we have in Tennyson's poetry the best single record of a sensitive mind trying to come to terms with issues which, though seemingly remote in time, are hardly foreign to men's minds in any age.

Interpretations of the Major Poems

T. S. ELIOT

In Memoriam†

Tennyson is a great poet, for reasons that are perfectly clear. He has three qualities which are seldom found together except in the greatest poets: abundance, variety, and complete competence. We therefore cannot appreciate his work unless we read a good deal of it. We may not admire his aims: but whatever he sets out to do, he succeeds in doing, with a mastery which gives us the sense of confidence that is one of the major pleasures of poetry. His variety of metrical accomplishment is astonishing. Without making the mistake of trying to write Latin verse in English, he knew everything about Latin versification that an English poet could use; and he said of himself that he thought he knew the quantity of the sounds of every English word except perhaps *scissors*. He had the finest ear of any English poet since Milton. He was the master of Swinburne; and the versification of Swinburne, himself a classical scholar, is often crude and sometimes cheap, in comparison with Tennyson's. Tennyson extended very widely the range of active metrical forms in English: in *Maud* alone the variety is prodigious. But innovation in metric is not to be measured solely by the width of the deviation from accepted practice. It is a matter of the historical situation: at some moments a more violent change may be necessary than at others. The problem differs at every period. At some times, a violent revolution may be neither possible nor desirable; at such times, a change which may appear very slight, is the change which the important poet will make. The innovation of Pope, after Dryden, may not seem very great; but it is the mark of the master to be able to make small changes which will be highly significant, as at another time to make radical changes, through which poetry will curve back again to its norm.

† From T. S. Eliot, *Selected Essays of T. S. Eliot,* New Edition (New York: Harcourt Brace Jovanovich, Inc.; London: Faber and Faber Ltd., 1932), pp. 286–295. Copyright 1932, 1936, 1950 by Harcourt Brace Jovanovich, Inc.; renewed, 1960, 1964 by T. S. Eliot. Reprinted by permission of the publishers.

There is an early poem, only published in the official biography, which already exhibits Tennyson as a master. According to a note, Tennyson later expressed regret that he had removed the poem from his Juvenilia; it is a fragmentary *Hesperides*, in which only the 'Song of the Three Sisters' is complete. The poem illustrates Tennyson's classical learning and his mastery of metre. The first stanza of 'The Song of the Three Sisters' is as follows:

> The Golden Apple, the Golden Apple, the hallow'd fruit,
> Guard it well, guard it warily,
> Singing airily,
> Standing about the charmèd root.
> Round about all is mute,
> As the snowfield on the mountain peaks,
> As the sandfield at the mountain-foot.
> Crocodiles in briny creeks
> Sleep and stir not; all is mute.
> If ye sing not, if ye make false measure,
> We shall lose eternal pleasure,
> Worth eternal want of rest.
> Laugh not loudly: watch the treasure
> Of the wisdom of the West.
> In a corner wisdom whispers. Five and three
> (Let it not be preach'd abroad) make an awful mystery:
> For the blossom unto threefold music bloweth;
> Evermore it is born anew,
> And the sap to threefold music floweth,
> From the root,
> Drawn in the dark,
> Up to the fruit,
> Creeping under the fragrant bark,
> Liquid gold, honeysweet through and through.
> Keen-eyed Sisters, singing airily,
> Looking warily
> Every way,
> Guard the apple night and day,
> Lest one from the East come and take it away.

A young man who can write like that has not much to learn about metric; and the young man who wrote these lines somewhere between 1828 and 1830 was doing something new. There is something not derived from any of his predecessors. In some of Tennyson's early verse the influence of Keats is visible—in songs and in blank verse; and less successfully, there is the influence of Wordsworth, as in *Dora*. But in the lines I have just quoted, and in the two Mariana poems, 'The Sea-Fairies', 'The Lotos-Eaters', 'The Lady of Shalott', and elsewhere, there is something wholly new.

> All day within the dreamy house,
>   The doors upon their hinges creak'd;
> The blue fly sung in the pane; the mouse
>   Behind the mouldering wainscot shriek'd,
> Or from the crevice peer'd about.

The blue fly sung in the pane (the line would be ruined if you substituted *sang for sung*) is enough to tell us that something important has happened.

The reading of long poems is not nowadays much practised: in the age of Tennyson it appears to have been easier. For a good many long poems were not only written but widely circulated; and the level was high: even the second-rate long poems of that time, like *The Light of Asia*, are better worth reading than most long modern novels. But Tennyson's long poems are not long poems in quite the same sense as those of his contemporaries. They are very different in kind from *Sordello* or *The Ring and the Book*, to name the greatest by the greatest of his contemporary poets. *Maud* and *In Memoriam* are each a series of poems, given form by the greatest lyrical resourcefulness that a poet has ever shown. The *Idylls of the King* have merits and defects similar to those of *The Princess*. An *idyll* is a 'short poem descriptive of some picturesque scene or incident'; in choosing the name Tennyson perhaps showed an appreciation of his limitations. For his poems are always descriptive, and always picturesque; they are never really narrative. The *Idylls of the King* are no different in kind from some of his early poems; the *Morte d'Arthur* is in fact an early poem. *The Princess* is still an idyll, but an idyll that is too long. Tennyson's versification in this poem is as masterly as elsewhere: it is a poem which we must read, but which we excuse ourselves from reading twice. And it is worth while recognizing the reason why we return again and again, and are always stirred by the lyrics which intersperse it, and which are among the greatest of all poetry of their kind, and yet avoid the poem itself. It is not, as we may think while reading, the outmoded attitude towards the relations of the sexes, the exasperating views on the subjects of matrimony, celibacy, and female education, that make us recoil from *The Princess*.[1] We can swallow the most antipathetic doctrines if we are given an exciting narrative. But for narrative Tennyson had no gift at all. For a static poem, and a moving poem, on the same subject, you have only to compare his 'Ulysses' with the condensed and intensely exciting narrative of that hero in the XXVIth Canto of Dante's *Inferno*. Dante is telling a

---

1. For a revelation of the Victorian mind on these matters, and of opinions to which Tennyson would probably have subscribed, see the Introduction by Sir Edward Strachey, Bt., to his emasculated edition of the *Morte D' Arthur* of Malory, still current. Sir Edward admired the *Idylls of the King*.

story. Tennyson is only stating an elegiac mood. The very greatest poets set before you real men talking, carry you on in real events moving. Tennyson could not tell a story at all. It is not that in *The Princess* he tries to tell a story and failed: it is rather that an idyll protracted to such length becomes unreadable. So *The Princess* is a dull poem; one of the poems of which we may say, that they are beautiful but dull.

But in *Maud* and in *In Memoriam*, Tennyson is doing what every conscious artist does, turning his limitations to good purpose. Of the content of *Maud*, I cannot think so highly as does Mr. Humbert Wolfe, in his interesting essay on Tennyson which is largely defence of the supremacy of that poem. For me, *Maud* consists of a few very beautiful lyrics, such as 'O let the solid ground', 'Birds in the high Hall-garden', and 'Go not, happy day', around which the semblance of a dramatic situation has been constructed with the greatest metrical virtuosity. The whole situation is unreal; the ravings of the lover on the edge of insanity sound false, and fail, as do the bellicose bellowings, to make one's flesh creep with sincerity. It would be foolish to suggest that Tennyson ought to have gone through some experience similar to that described: for a poet with dramatic gifts, a situation quite remote from his personal experience may release the strongest emotion. And I do not believe for a moment that Tennyson was a man of mild feelings or weak passions. There is no evidence in his poetry that he knew the experience of violent passion for a woman; but there is plenty of evidence of emotional intensity and violence—but of emotion so deeply suppressed, even from himself, as to tend rather towards the blackest melancholia than towards dramatic action. And it is emotion which, so far as my reading of the poems can discover, attained no ultimate clear purgation. I should reproach Tennyson not for mildness, or tepidity, but rather for lack of serenity.

> Of love that never found his earthly close,
> What sequel?

The fury of *Maud* is shrill rather than deep, though one feels in every passage what exquisite adaptation of metre to the mood Tennyson is attempting to express. I think that the effect of feeble violence, which the poem as a whole produces, is the result of a fundamental error of form. A poet can express his feelings as fully through a dramatic, as through a lyrical form; but *Maud* is neither one thing nor the other: just as *The Princess* is more than an idyll, and less than a narrative. In *Maud*, Tennyson neither identifies himself with the lover, nor identifies the lover with himself: consequently, the real feelings of Tennyson, profound and tumultuous as they are, never arrive at expression.

It is, in my opinion, in *In Memoriam,* that Tennyson finds full expression. Its technical merit alone is enough to ensure its perpetuity. While Tennyson's technical competence is everywhere masterly and satisfying, *In Memoriam* is the most unapproachable of all his poems. Here are one hundred and thirty-two passages, each of several quatrains in the same form, and never monotony or repetition. And the poem has to be comprehended as a whole. We may not memorize a few passages, we cannot find a 'fair sample'; we have to comprehend the whole of a poem which is essentially the length that it is. We may choose to remember:

> Dark house, by which once more I stand
>> Here in the long unlovely street,
>> Doors, where my heart was used to beat
> So quickly, waiting for a hand,
>
> A hand that can be clasp'd no more—
>> Behold me, for I cannot sleep,
>> And like a guilty thing I creep
> At earliest morning to the door.
>
> He is not here; but far away
>> The noise of life begins again,
>> And ghastly thro' the drizzling rain
> On the bald street breaks the blank day.

This is great poetry, economical of words, a universal emotion in what could only be an English town: and it gives me the shudder that I fail to get from anything in *Maud.* But such a passage, by itself, is not *In Memoriam*: *In Memoriam* is the whole poem. It is unique: it is a long poem made by putting together lyrics, which have only the unity and continuity of a diary, the concentrated diary of a man confessing himself. It is a diary of which we have to read every word.

Apparently Tennyson's contemporaries, once they had accepted *In Memoriam,* regarded it as a message of hope and reassurance to their rather fading Christian faith. It happens now and then that a poet by some strange accident expresses the mood of his generation, at the same time that he is expressing a mood of his own which is quite remote from that of his generation. This is not a question of insincerity: there is an amalgam of yielding and opposition below the level of consciousness. Tennyson himself, on the conscious level of the man who talks to reporters and poses for photographers, to judge from remarks made in conversation and recorded in his son's *Memoir,* consistently asserted a convinced, if somewhat sketchy, Christian belief. And he was a friend of Frederick Denison Maurice —nothing seems odder about that age than the respect which its eminent people felt for each other. Nevertheless, I get a very different impression from *In Memoriam* from that which Tennyson's contemporaries seem to have got. It is of a very much more interesting and tragic Tennyson. His biographers have not failed to remark that he had a good deal of the temperament of the mystic—certainly not at all the mind of the theologian. He was desperately anxious to hold the faith of the believer, without being very clear about what he wanted to believe: he was capable of illumination which he was incapable of understanding. The 'Strong Son of God, immortal Love', with an invocation of whom the poem opens, has only a hazy connection with the Logos, or the Incarnate God. Tennyson is distressed by the idea of a mechanical universe; he is naturally, in lamenting his friend, teased by the hope of immortality and reunion beyond death. Yet the renewal craved for seems at best but a continuance, or a substitute for the joys of friendship upon earth. His desire for immortality never is quite the desire for Eternal Life; his concern is for the loss of man rather than for the gain of God.

> shall he,
>
> Man, her last work, who seem'd so fair,
>   Such splendid purpose in his eyes,
>   Who roll'd the psalm to wintry skies,
> Who built him fanes of fruitless prayer,
>
> Who trusted God was love indeed
>   And love Creation's final law—
>   Tho' Nature, red in tooth and claw
> With ravine, shriek'd against his creed—
>
> Who loved, who suffer'd countless ills,
>   Who battled for the True, the Just,
>   Be blown about the desert dust,
> Or seal'd within the iron hills?

That strange abstraction, 'Nature', becomes a real god or goddess, perhaps more real, at moments, to Tennyson than God ('Are God and Nature then at strife?'). The hope of immortality is confused (typically of the period) with the hope of the gradual and steady improvement of this world. Much has been said of Tennyson's interest in contemporary science, and of the impression of Darwin. *In Memoriam*, in any case, antedates *The Origin of Species* by several years, and the belief in social progress by democracy antedates it by many more; and I suspect that the faith of Tennyson's age in human progress would have been quite as strong even had the discoveries of Darwin been postponed by fifty years. And after all, there is no logical connection: the belief in progress being current already, the discoveries of Darwin were harnessed to it:

No longer half-akin to brute,
    For all we thought and loved and did,
    And hoped, and suffer'd, is but seed
Of what in them is flower and fruit;

Whereof the man, that with me trod
    This planet, was a noble type
    Appearing ere the times were ripe,
That friend of mine who lives in God,

That God, which ever lives and loves,
    One God, one law, one element,
    And one far-off divine event,
To which the whole creation moves.

These lines show an interesting compromise between the religious attitude and, what is quite a different thing, the belief in human perfectibility; but the contrast was not so apparent to Tennyson's contemporaries. They may have been taken in by it, but I don't think that Tennyson himself was, quite: his feelings were more honest than his mind. There is evidence elsewhere—even in an early poem, 'Locksley Hall', for example—that Tennyson by no means regarded with complacency all the changes that were going on about him in the progress of industrialism and the rise of the mercantile and manufacturing and banking classes; and he may have contemplated the future of England, as his years drew out, with increasing gloom. Temperamentally, he was opposed to the doctrine that he was moved to accept and to praise.[2]

Tennyson's feelings, I have said, were honest; but they were usually a good way below the surface. *In Memoriam* can, I think, justly be called a religious poem, but for another reason than that which made it seem religious to his contemporaries. It is not religious because of the quality of its faith, but because of the quality of its doubt. Its faith is a poor thing, but its doubt is a very intense experience. *In Memoriam* is a poem of despair, but of despair of a religious kind. And to qualify its despair with the adjective 're-ligious' is to elevate it above most of its derivatives. For *The City of Dreadful Night*, and the *Shropshire Lad*, and the poems of Thomas Hardy, are small work in comparison with *In Memoriam*: it is greater than they and comprehends them.[3]

In ending we must go back to the beginning and remember that *In Memoriam* would not be a great poem, or Tennyson a great

2. See, in Harold Nicolson's admirable *Tennyson*, pp. 252 ff.
3. There are other kinds of despair. Davidson's great poem, *Thirty Bob a Week*, is not derivative from Tennyson. On the other hand, there are other things derivative from Tennyson be-sides *Atalanta in Calydon*. Compare the poems of William Morris with *The Voyage of Maeldune*, and *Barrack Room Ballads* with several of Tenny-son's later poems.

poet, without the technical accomplishment. Tennyson is the great master of metric as well as of melancholia; I do not think any poet in English has ever had a finer ear for vowel sound, as well as a subtler feeling for some moods of anguish:

> Dear as remember'd kisses after death,
> And sweet as those by hopeless fancy feign'd
> On lips that are for others; deep as love,
> Deep as first love, and wild with all regret.

And this technical gift of Tennyson's is no slight thing. Tennyson lived in a time which was already acutely time-conscious: a great many things seemed to be happening, railways were being built, discoveries were being made, the face of the world was changing. That was a time busy in keeping up to date. It had, for the most part, no hold on permanent things, on permanent truths about man and God and life and death. The surface of Tennyson stirred about with his time; and he had nothing to which to hold fast except his unique and unerring feeling for the sounds of words. But in this he had something that no one else had. Tennyson's surface, his technical accomplishment, is intimate with his depths: what we most quickly see about Tennyson is that which moves between the surface and the depths, that which is of slight importance. By looking innocently at the surface we are most likely to come to the depths, to the abyss of sorrow. Tennyson is not only a minor Virgil, he is also with Virgil as Dante saw him, a Virgil among the Shades, the saddest of all English poets, among the Great in Limbo, the most instinctive rebel against the society in which he was the most perfect conformist.

Tennyson seems to have reached the end of his spiritual development with *In Memoriam*; there followed no reconciliation, no resolution.

> And now no sacred staff shall break in blossom,
> No choral salutation lure to light
> A spirit sick with perfume and sweet night,

or rather with twilight, for Tennyson faced neither the darkness nor the light, in his later years. The genius, the technical power, persisted to the end, but the spirit had surrendered. A gloomier end than that of Baudelaire: Tennyson had no *singulier avertissement*. And having turned aside from the journey through the dark night, to become the surface flatterer of his own time, he has been rewarded with the despite of an age that succeeds his own in shallowness.

PAULL F. BAUM

'In Memoriam'†

*   *   *

According to the poet himself, 'In Memoriam' "begins with a funeral and ends with a marriage"; the Epilogue is therefore integral. And Miss Chapman, with Tennyson's approval, says: "such a marriage is the very type and hope of all things fair and bright and good, seeming to bring us nearer to . . . that crowning race, that Christ that is to be." Tennyson's favorite solvent of all hard questions, the little child, very plain at the end of 'The Two Voices'—

> And in their double love secure,
> The little maiden walk'd demure,
> Pacing with downward eyelids pure,

and still plainer through the latter half of 'The Princess,' here functions in more delicately allusive form as the soul which is to "draw from out the vast" and so as a symbol of our racial progress towards the divine event of which Hallam has now become an anticipatory "noble type." Thus the elegy ends on the cheerful note of reproduction and our racial hopes remain in the Tennyson family.

These poems or 'sections' were composed, as is well known, over a period of sixteen or seventeen years, the earliest probably soon after Hallam's death in September 1833 and the latest (cxxi) not long before publication in June 1850. Some twenty more may be approximately dated from various kinds of external and internal evidence; the others cannot now be assigned to a particular time. It is not even possible to say certainly that most of them were composed in the thirties or in the forties. Moreover, the poet himself makes record that "The sections were written at many different places [as well as times], and as the phases of our intercourse came to memory and suggested them." And since he added: "I did not write them with any view of weaving them into a whole, or for publication, until I found I had written so many," we are not justified in looking for unity of tone or plan. In truth, it is greatly to be regretted that, whenever it was that he decided to publish, he ever made the effort to superinduce an appearance of arrangement upon the various sections; for the two anniversary and the three Christ-

---

† From Paull F. Baum, *Tennyson Sixty Years After* (Chapel Hill: The University of North Carolina Press, 1948), pp. 114–124. Reprinted by permission of the publisher.

mas poems produce only an illusion of order and have led incautious readers to assume (and somehow find) more method than actually exists. It would have been better to leave them as a miscellany, like the Psalms or the sonnet-sequences of Shakespeare and others, with only the most general order of emotional development. But Tennyson made the initial error, and no doubt the anxious commentators may be forgiven their exceeding zeal; though both they and he may have prejudiced their case by undertaking too much.

At the moment when Tennyson perceived that he had on hand a collection of elegies or, as he called them, "memorial poems," which might be worked up for publication as parts of a single long poem, just what (one may ask) was the state of his artistic conscience, if he submitted it to a rigid examen? The earliest-written sections were certainly the spontaneous overflow of real and immediate feeling and the later-written sections a somewhat idealized projection of the first experience, in which Hallam became less the deceased friend and more and more the symbol of personal loss. In this way, which would be entirely natural and in no sense impugn the poet's sincerity, the original loss would become depersonalized, a generalized loss used for artistic purpose as the basis for reflection on death and the future life. Somewhere in this gradual extension of a personal feeling into an impersonal situation, however, there may well arise the danger of—not so much insincerity as—artificiality. Remembering Tennyson's habitual search for poetic material, we may be permitted to wonder if sometimes in the passage of seventeen years the composition of these elegies did not become a kind of habit and the death of Hallam a kind of convenience to the muse.[1]

In different ways and in different degrees this is one of the dangers of all artistic work. There is the impulse, the motion of the spirit disciplined by craftsmanship, and when the impulse flags, as it always must, the craftsman takes over. Only the most skilful and most gifted can surmount the danger; the others resort to artificial stimuli to re-beat the flame. Tennyson was exposed to this danger from two directions. What began as an intense private experience, recorded in some of the opening sections of the poem, became confessedly a mere starting-point for the expression of feelings and

1. This is not exactly the "sad mechanic exercise" of v. There is a suggestion of it, however, in one of the grumbling letters of FitzGerald, 28 February 1845, who had seen part of the manuscript: "If one could have good lyrics, I think the World wants them as much as ever. Tennyson's are good: but not of the *kind* wanted. We have surely had enough of men reporting their sorrows: especially when one is aware all the time that the poet wilfully protracts what he complains of . . . and yet we are to condole with him, and be taught to ruminate our losses & sorrows in the same way. I felt that if Tennyson had got on a horse and ridden 20 miles, instead of moaning over his pipe, he would have been cured of his sorrows in half the time" (*A FitzGerald Friendship being Hitherto Unpublished Letters from Edward Fitz-Gerald to William Bodham Donne*, ed. N. C. Hannay, New York, 1932, p. 10).

ideas which were intended to be of 'universal' significance ("the way of the soul"); and 'In Memoriam' in its final arrangement of parts does not seem to be or pretend to be a continuous development from the personal to the general, but rather an intermingling of the two kinds. The question would not present itself if the whole poem were dramatic, if the personal loss of the poet were from the outset submerged or sublimated into a general grief whence spring the reflections on death and immortality. And secondly, this danger is the more acute and obvious when the poet is trying to add from without a structure which is admittedly inorganic to a number of lyrics which have accumulated in his notebooks.

Another result of the irregular composition of 'In Memoriam' is its variations in style—not the inequalities of poetic merit or the unevenness which is inevitable in any long poem, but the mixture of incompatible styles. This is in part a concomitant of the different sorts of subject matter, but it is more. It might be amusing to classify the sections from this point of view. About 70 per cent of them are 'simple' in the sense that they are readily understood and not markedly ornate; and these could be subdivided into three nearly equal groups, according to degree, as fairly simple, simple, and too simple. In contrast some twenty-five sections are either cryptic or obscure, and the rest elaborate or rhetorical in style (sometimes in the good sense, sometimes in the bad sense). The so-called Epilogue contains illustrations of all these manners, but some other examples will serve better. Put the third stanza of LIX beside the last stanza of CXXII or the third of CV:

> My centred passion cannot move,
>   Nor will it lessen from to-day;
>   But I'll have leave at times to play
> As with the creature of my love. . . .
>
> And all the breeze of Fancy blows,
>   And every dew-drop paints a bow,
>   The wizard lightnings deeply glow,
> And every thought breaks out a rose. . . .
>
> No more shall wayward grief abuse
>   The genial hour with mask and mime;
>   For change of place, like growth of time,
> Has broke the bond of dying use.

Or read consecutively the soaring ecstatic LXXXVI (which has been called the climax of the poem)—

> Sweet after showers, ambrosial air,
>   That rollest from the gorgeous gloom
>   Of evening over brake and bloom
> And meadow, slowly breathing bare
>   The round of space

and the following section (of whose ten stanzas I quote only the first and fifth)—

> I past beside the reverend walls
> In which of old I wore the gown;
> I roved at random thro' the town,
> And saw the tumult of the halls; . . .

> Another name was on the door:
> I linger'd; all within was noise
> Of songs, and clapping hands, and boys
> That crash'd the glass and beat the floor.

"That crash'd the glass" is one thing; the "gorgeous gloom of evening" is quite another. Or take the last stanza (plain) of xc with the first (colored) of the next section—

> Ah dear, but come thou back to me:
> Whatever change the years have wrought,
> I find not yet one lonely thought
> That cries against my wish for thee. . . .

> When rosy plumelets tuft the larch,
> And rarely pipes the mounted thrush;
> Or underneath the barren bush
> Flits by the sea-blue bird of March.

And finally read xliv, to which Bradley devotes eleven pages of inconclusive exegesis, alongside the too easy transparency of lx. Sometimes, of course, the style is aspiring and difficult because the matter is difficult and cannot be communicated in simple language; and sometimes it seems just needlessly cryptic (as in i). The opening and closing stanzas of xcv illustrate the old-fashioned descriptive technique of the best eighteenth-century; xv the newer romantic style which became Tennyson's staple. And so on. It is only natural that during seventeen years a poet's style should vary, and should vary with the different kinds of subject, but at a sacrifice of unity; in this poem, however, the variations are not so much due to Tennyson's maturing as to his choice of manners. In 'In Memoriam' which predominates, uniformity or variety?

But these are secondary questions. Even if faults of artistic insincerity and of unevenness are fully admitted, they would damage but not seriously undermine 'In Memoriam.' The primary question is: is it a true poem, a poetical treatment of its chosen subject?

The subject of 'In Memoriam' is twofold: Alfred Tennyson's grief for the death of Arthur Hallam (or the poet's grief for the loss of his friend) and Tennyson's battle with doubt, ending with victory (or the poet's reflections on death and immortality, the "way of the soul"). 'In Memoriam' is therefore both an elegy and a philosophical poem; and each aspect, sorrow and consolation, has a double meaning, the personal and the impersonal, which cannot be evaded in spite of Tennyson's warning. "It must be remembered," said he,

that this is a poem, *not* an actual biography. It is founded on our friendship, on the engagement of Arthur Hallam to my sister, on his sudden death at Vienna, just before the time fixed for their marriage, and on the burial at Clevedon Church. The poem concludes with the marriage of my youngest sister Cecilia. It was meant to be a kind of *Divina Commedia*, ending with happiness. . . . The different moods of sorrow as in a drama are dramatically given, and my conviction that fear, doubts, and suffering will find answer and relief only through Faith in a God of Love. 'I' is not always the author speaking of himself, but the voice of the human race speaking thro' him. . . .

A few points here demand annotation. Cecilia is of course not the sister who was to marry Arthur Hallam. The meaning of "It" in "It was meant to be a kind of *Divina Commedia*" is not entirely perspicuous. The reference might be vaguely to the epithalamic epilogue. But Tennyson seems to have meant that his whole poem was like the *Divine Comedy* in that both works end happily. Surely he did not wish to imply comparison with Dante's poem in any other respect. Further, "was meant to" must refer to a time after he decided to arrange the elegies for publication. The dramatic effect of the different moods is not obvious. The cardinal 'teaching' of the poem, a belief in personal immortality, is not hinted as part of his "conviction." And finally, the "always" should be underscored.[2] In a word, the poem is, on the poet's own testimony, partly personal and partly impersonal—"the voice of the human race"; but it is left for our own tact to distinguish the two voices.

The form of the poem *as elegy* is well fitted both to the subject and to Tennyson's genius. For a record of sorrowing moments and personal memories the method—short lyrics without noticeable connection—is well chosen. But for a long philosophic poem it cannot be maintained that this method is a happy one. Moreover, the mixture of personal elements and universalizing elements is an 'inconvenience' (as Bacon would say) troublesome both to the poet and to the reader. There is a good deal in 'In Memoriam' about the private and domestic relations of Arthur Hallam and Alfred Tennyson, some of which is poetically unmanageable. Although there is never any doubt, biographically, of Tennyson's sincerity, there is a question whether he has made his personal suffering in-

2. The whole paragaph is so filled with confusion that one hesitates to confront the poet with it; but it is set forth without qualification in the *Memoir* (I, 304–305). Tennyson was often unfortunate in commenting on his own work.

teresting, sufficiently real to the reader and therefore worthy of such protracted mourning. It is a question if parts of the poem are not too personal and intimate, and therefore if our attention is not drawn so specifically to Arthur Hallam and Alfred Tennyson (to say nothing of the poet's sisters and their marriages) that we cannot easily accept the data as a basis for generalizing the "way of the soul." The autobiographic and the speculative are side by side: they may "cleave" but do they "incorporate"?

Though the direct celebration of Hallam occupies relatively small space in the whole poem, and that chiefly towards the end, his presence is felt in many sections where he is not even mentioned. We receive, nevertheless, no clear conception of him as an individual; and in LXXV the poet says expressly: "by the measure of my grief I leave thy greatness to be guess'd." This grief is itself rather implied than portrayed, except in a few early sections, and is accordingly less powerful dramatically, that is, less likely to move our sympathy and secure our understanding of the poet's argument which is founded upon his grief.[3] Yet, paradoxically, his grief is rendered poetically effective by virtue of the skill and beauty of the language. The number of sections in which this is true is not large, but it is large enough. The distinction is quite simple and fairly significant. His private sorrow, which was the starting point of his poem, has failed to stir us deeply, although he exhibited it freely, with realistic details. His accomplishment is due to his art, and not at all to the personal impulse towards composition; and the personal impulse becomes therefore irrelevant, intrusive, wrong. To put the paradox in another way: 'In Memoriam' would have been just as impressive as a lament if the sorrow had been 'dramatic' rather than 'real,' and such an imagined sorrow would have been equally powerful as a basis for the philosophical or religious 'teaching' which Tennyson develops from his private emotion.[4]

'In Memoriam' is not only a monument to Arthur Hallam and a record of Tennyson's personal suffering at Hallam's early death, it is also the "way of the soul"—a somewhat pretentious phrase, but Tennyson's own—his representation of everyman's pain when con-

---

3. Possibly the dispersion of expressions of grief through a long poem has something to do with this. If they were all brought together and read consecutively the effect might be greater. But note Andrew Lang's comment: "in *In Memoriam* sympathy and relief have been found, and will be found, by many. Another, we feel, has trodden our dark and stony path," and so on (p. 71).

4. This view is interestingly supported by the English elegiac parallels. Although each one is very different from the other, the personal element has been remarkably slight in our great elegies. In Gray's it is almost nil, so far as we are aware; in Milton's nearly nil, and so also in Swinburne's; in Shelley's certainly not strong; and in Arnold's it was a distraction. One cannot quite say that the poetry varies in inverse ratio to the personal concern of the poet, yet there is a hint of this. Sentimental readers may well have been affected by Tennyson's baring of his own heart to their view; but while he won readers at the outset he has lost them in the sequel.

fronted with death, the struggle with doubt, and the triumphant assertion of God's love. The poet is at first overcome with his own loss, questions the ways of God to man, seeks consolation for himself, and in fighting his own fight reveals the grounds of consolation and hope for all mankind.

What, now, is Tennyson's answer? Put in the briefest form, Tennyson's answer to the problem of human existence is the belief in personal immortality. "His belief in personal immortality," said Knowles, "was passionate—I think almost the strongest passion he had"; and outside of 'In Memoriam,' in the *Memoir* and in other records of conversations with the poet, there is abundant substantiation of this statement.[5] "The chief consideration which induced Tennyson to cling to faith in immortality," says Masterman, "and the argument which he asserts almost defiantly throughout the remainder of his poetical career, is the impossibility of the deliberate acceptance of the negative belief." For to Tennyson as to many others "life, regarded simply as life terminating in death, yields no meaning whatever." As a corollary to this, he clings to a belief in the possibility of communion with the dead. Thence he proceeds, relying on the then undeveloped theories of evolution, to a belief in the gradual improvement of the human race. Accepting the doctrine of development from the inanimate to animate life, or at least of the development of brute into man and man into superior man, he found it repugnant to think that this development should stop abruptly with death. And further, in order that this view should yield its fullest meaning and satisfaction, there must be the concomitant development of the spiritual element, already latent in man, into the highest and ultimate realization, its absorption into the divine—though in consistency with his belief that "individuality endures" he was obliged sometimes (as in XLVII) to deny absolute absorption or to speak with oracular ambiguity.

Such, crudely stated, is Tennyson's position in 'In Memoriam.' It is certainly incomplete and not inexpugnable. But *that* is not our concern. We do not now read *Paradise Lost* and the *Divine Comedy* for their doctrinal content; we do not read the Oedipus plays or *Hamlet* with anxious concern over the ethical principles underlying them; we do read Chaucer's *Troilus* and Byron's *Don Juan* without distress at their 'immorality.' And so we are now able to read 'In Memoriam,' as our fathers and grandfathers were un-

5. Tennyson is reported once as saying: "I'll shake my fist in God Almighty's face and say it isn't fair, if I find there is no immortality" (D. A. Wilson, *Carlyle on Cromwell and Others*, p. 325). The vehemence betrays a want of confidence. Said Tennyson to Carlyle: "Your traveller comes to an inn and lies down in his bed almost with the certainty that he will go on his journey rejoicing the next morning." Carlyle only grunted in reply. Afterwards FitzGerald remarked to Tennyson: "You had him there"; but Tennyson admitted later to Miss Thackeray (Lady Ritchie) that it only proved "how dangerous an illustration is."

able to read it, without being swayed by the religious value of its central 'argument.' It has been said, with some exaggeration perhaps, that to-day the belief in personal immortality is a matter of taste. It is at any rate not a burning question.[6]

It would be tempting, but profitless, to pursue some of the awkward puzzles which spring to most modern readers' minds when they seriously consider the 'theology and philosophy' of the poem—Tennyson's infirmity in the face of doubt; his failure as Seer and Prophet to speak forth with the confidence of Faith; his admission (privately to Knowles) that the conclusion reached in the poem is "too hopeful";[7] his seeming helplessness before simple logical processes (not that one expects a poem to be a syllogism), and his reliance upon "Short swallow-flights of song" in preference to a reasoned progress of ideas when he is working in the domain of reason; his rejection of the standard ontological and teleological arguments as well as Christian revelation; the only half-hidden spiritual pride of his exaltation of personality and his insistence on self; his apparent surprise at finding that certain points cannot be "proved"; his unwillingness to admit, with Pascal, that "Le cœur a ses raisons, que la raison ne connaît pas" and proceed accordingly, or with St. Augustine that faith depends upon the will as much as upon the reason, and advance from there; and beyond all, the illogical conclusion, the happy ending wherein the immortality of mankind through evolution is substituted for the immortality of the individual soul, and, Hallam having died without issue, the future of the race is entrusted to the poet's sister. But of course a poem may be "somehow good" in spite of such handicaps.

The real charge, however, against 'In Memoriam' is of course not that it is Victorian in theology and social ideas or that its an-

6. There used to be debate whether this position had anything novel or original in it. The case for the negative was cogently put by Frederic Harrison, who might be expected to take issue with a branch of the evangelical creed. Cf. *Tennyson, Ruskin, Mill*, 1900, pp. 10–11. For the other side, see Andrew Lang's *Tennyson*, pp. 63 ff. Professor H. V. Routh (*Towards the Twentieth Century*, 1937, pp. 86–88), without mentioning either Harrison or Lang has answered them both. "The influence of *In Memoriam* has steadily declined. By the end of the century it was valued only as a phrase-book, a metrical triumph, a masterpiece of poetic expressiveness, and as such, generally relegated to schools and colleges.

"In one sense the poems deserved this fate because their author (through no fault of his own) did not face the spiritual problem of the nineteenth century; he only appeared to do so." In 1902 Churton Collins had said much the same thing. "As a contribution to theological thought and philosophy—and on its first appearance it was hailed as a momentous contribution to both—*In Memoriam* has a very wasting hold on life. . . . We may perhaps think that its power is not equal to its charm, that it practically leaves us where it found us, that it furnishes faith with no new supports and truth with no new documents" (ed. *In Memoriam, The Princess, and Maud*, p. 20).

7. "More than I am myself," said Tennyson (*Nineteenth Century*, XXXIII (1893), 182). And then he continued: "I am thinking of adding another to it, a speculative one. . . . showing that all the arguments are about as good on one side as the other, and thus throw man back more on the primitive impulses and feelings." Luckily he abandoned the purpose.

swers to the doubts which spring from intense sorrow are not the answers which we of another generation desire—not, in a word, in the *thought* of the poem at all (though largely in the *thinking*), but rather that it does not satisfy what Arnold called "the laws of poetic truth and poetic beauty." Arnold never quite explained what these laws are, nor has anyone else, but we have a general idea. 'In Memoriam' is certainly a criticism of life and it has plenty of high seriousness—though many of the sections are seriously deficient in this quality—but it lacks form and coherence (what Arnold called, after Goethe, architectonics) and it lacks that clearness and sureness of treatment which its subject emphatically demands.

JOHN KILLHAM

Tennyson's *Maud*—The Function of the Imagery[†]

Shall I weep if a Poland fall? shall I shriek if a Hungary fail?
Or an infant civilization be ruled with rod or with knout?

This is the despairing question which posed itself to one of the literary outsiders of a century ago—to the speaker in Tennyson's *Maud*. It is this sort of allusion to contemporary political and social affairs which makes the poem so difficult to grasp as an artistic unity. From its first appearance until today readers have been embarrassed too by the conclusion wherein the speaker sails to the Crimea:

And I stood on a giant deck and mixt my breath
With a loyal people shouting a battle cry.[1]

The modern historical view of the Crimean venture does not coincide with that in the poem, that Nicholas I was a 'giant liar', and that the cause was 'pure and true'. Moreover, the modern experience of the horrors of war forces us hopefully to seek for an alternative to the view that Tennyson was a Jingoist and to argue that the conclusion is to be read strictly in terms of a mind still disordered, finding in war the only solution adequate to its needs.[2] The historical objections to the poem can thus be conveniently turned aside by arguing for psychological relativism being part of Tennyson's intention from the very beginning. Smaller objections can equally easily be disposed of in this way. For instance the com-

† From John Killham, ed., *Critical Essays on the Poetry of Tennyson* (New York: Barnes & Noble, Inc.; London: Routledge & Kegan Paul Ltd., 1960), pp. 219–224. Reprinted by permission of the publishers.

1. See, e.g., E. D. H. Johnson, *The Alien Vision of Victorian Poetry* (Princeton, 1952), p. 31.
2. This is the view of Roy P. Basler in *Sex, Symbolism, and Psychology in Literature* (1945), p. 87 f.

plaint, forcefully uttered soon after the poem was published, that even if one admitted that the war was ethically justifiable it could hardly be expected to end the commercial malpractices against which the speaker rails at the beginning of the poem, cannot be sustained if one pleads that he is incapable of thinking logically.

One of the difficulties arising from using psychological concepts to counter historical ones is, whatever side we take, to cause us to consider the poem very largely in ideological terms—as propaganda or as a case-study. This is not to say that the issue can go unresolved. The poem, after all, deals directly with matters falling within the province of both history and psychology. But from the literary critic's point of view one important thing to emphasize is the dramatic nature of the poem: it deals with character and action. The historian's objections to the conclusion can be ruled out by simply asserting that the speaker's actions are governed by the beliefs he is shown to hold, and not by what other people may believe. The psychoanalytic view of the conclusion, which at first sight seems to resemble this, really bases itself upon the analyst's own feelings about war rather than upon those of the protagonist (if such a term is admissible in relation to a 'monodrama'). For it is not difficult to see that the conclusion, though perhaps not as inevitable as one would wish, is carefully prepared for throughout the poem. The hero's mind, as a result of the shock given it in childhood by the frightening circumstances of his father's death in the 'dreadful hollow behind the little wood', is obsessed by violence and death. He sees commercial competition to have led to a state resembling civil war, the spirit of Cain being paramount—an age

> When only the ledger lives, and when only not all men lie.

All about him

> . . . nature is one with rapine, a harm no preacher can heal;

> The Mayfly is torn by the swallow, the sparrow spear'd by the shrike,
> And the whole little wood where I sit is a world of plunder and prey.

The whole universe, in fact, seems to move without a conscience or an aim: animal species die and are superseded: a 'sad astrology' teaches that even the stars are tyrants,

> Innumerable, pitiless, passionless eyes,
> Cold fires, yet with power to burn and brand
> His nothingness into man.

What wonder that his whole desire is for withdrawal! He is cowed by life and regrets that he ever came to possess the consciousness which causes him to believe that life involves an unremitting re-sort to either violence or cunning, the struggle inevitably culmi-nating in death.

Quite naturally introduced into the first part of the poem are references to the war to come. The cruel suppression of Poland and Hungary by Russia and Austria undertaken in 1848 and 1849 justifies his general mood of despair and quietism. International affairs are seemingly conducted upon the same ruthless pattern of violence, the suppression of the weak by the strong. Colonialism too is but disguised tyranny. The mendacity of Czar Nicholas I over the 'sick man of Europe' is no better than the petty untruth-fulness of any working man:

> And Jack on his ale-bench has as many lies as a Czar.

Even those of the anti-war party seem to him to be motivated by an ignoble self-interest, a concern for their profits:

> Last week came one to the country town,
> To preach our poor little army down,
> And play the game of the despot kings,
> Tho' the state has done it and thrice as well.
> This broad-brimm'd hawker of holy things,
> Whose ear is cramm'd with his cotton, and rings
> Even in dreams to the chink of his pence,
> This huckster put down war! can he tell
> Whether war be a cause or a consequence?

Ironically one of his earliest encounters with Maud is on the occa-sion of his passing near her unseen while she is singing,

> Singing of men that in battle array,
> Ready in heart and ready in hand,
> March with banner and bugle and fife
> To the death, for their native land.

This does not, as might have been expected, create in him a sense of revulsion against her, but rather a recognition that it is his own, and his age's baseness that is highlighted by her confident trust, as expressed by the words of the passionate ballad, that violent death for one's country in the cause of honour is not without posi-tive value. As his love for Maud deepens his attitude towards vio-lence and death changes: he is able to see that in some circum-stances a resort to violence may not be without ethical justifica-tion. As his reasons for finding pleasure in life increase with his love, he paradoxically comes to see that death is not fearful and that the good may have to be defended by force. For Maud, for instance, he would die,

> for sullen-seeming Death may give
> More life to Love than ever is or was
> In our low world, where yet 'tis sweet to live;

though his aim now is to live,

> Not die, but live a life of truest breath,
> And teach true life to fight with mortal wrongs.

In Part II of the poem his killing of Maud's brother causes him to revert quickly to the mood of the opening lines, and it seems that he is again utterly revolted by violence. He sees the explosion of his pistol to have

> thunder'd up into heaven the Christless code
> That must have life for a blow,

and that the heavens are justified in destroying men who are but

> The feeble vassals of wine and anger and lust,
> The little hearts that know not how to forgive.

But even when he has succumbed to madness he sees clearly what he should have remembered before engaging in the duel: that violence, though never justified in the sphere of personal relations is permissible in defence of the *public* good:

> Friend, to be struck by the public foe,
> Then to strike him and lay him low,
> There were a public merit, far,
> Whatever the Quaker holds, from sin;
> But the red life spilt for a private blow—
> I swear to you, lawful and lawless war
> Are scarcely even akin.

From this position it is a reasonably natural development to Part III wherein, exactly a year after, his mental disturbance righted, and his actions seemingly directed by a dream of Maud (some time dead), he faces the issue of imminent war. It appears to him as fulfilling the conditions which he earlier saw made a resort to force not merely justifiable but even an obligation imposed upon men who seek to direct their lives into good courses by upholding what they take to be right:

> . . . it lighten'd my despair
> When I thought that a war would arise in defence of the right,
> That an iron tyranny now should bend or cease,
>
> . . . .
>
> For I cleaved to a cause that I felt to be pure and true.

We should not allow our historical judgement of the merits of the Crimean War to enter here. The problem of what attitude we should take in face of tyranny can be related to any war which strikes the reader as offering the issue Tennyson presents. In other words, the rigidly historical approach can injure the poem if it takes no account of the dramatic development. On the other hand we should not attempt to disregard this dramatic development in another way by introducing the concept of psychological relativism as the proper counter to the historical approach. The high destructiveness of modern warfare makes us recoil from the use of violence, but unfortunately the basic problem is thereby made only more acute. Indeed it is a pity that the discussion of *Maud* turns so often upon such ideological problems; for its real value as a poem is consequently only partially considered. The historical and psychological aspects of the action have to be related to the work considered both as drama and a series of lyrics. Taken simply as a sort of drama it has admittedly to be recognized that it deals with a psychological-cum-philosophical theme in an historical setting. This theme is reducible ultimately to the notion that a psychic balance in man, who is obliged to accept that violence and death have to be faced as part of his lot on earth, is attainable through the experience of love, which with maturity can take the form of sexual love. (The various fantasy-worlds of each of the patients in the asylum is explicitly stated to be meant to

> . . . wheedle a world that loves him not.)

To body forth this theme (which is touched upon in the early (1830) poem 'Love and Death'), Tennyson devised the plot of *Maud*, a plot which, more than fifty years ago, Andrew Lang showed to resemble that of *The Bride of Lammermoor*.

But although the role of the dramatic plot is to develop this overall theme, it must not be forgotten that it was devised at the suggestion of Sir John Simeon as a setting for the poem 'O that 'twere possible' published long before in 1837, now forming (with slight changes) the fourth section of Part II. In addition, the poem as we now have it is not really a regular drama at all, but a series of lyrics and dramatic monologues. In fact, it is truer on the whole to say that the drama is subordinate to the lyrics, rather than the reverse; and this means that the critical techniques used to show the way in which a reader's response to lyric poems is controlled are just as applicable to *Maud* as are those used in relation to drama. In other words, the imagery is as important as the themes, and the portrayal of character in action serves Tennyson's lyric interests equally with his thematic ones.

* * *

F. E. L. PRIESTLEY

Tennyson's *Idylls*†

One of the most persistent heresies in Tennyson criticism is the belief that the *Idylls* are literature of escape. Ever since Carlyle, with his usual vigour and not unusual critical myopia, greeted the first group with remarks about 'finely elaborated execution', 'inward perfection of vacancy', and 'the lollipops were so superlative', the myth has persisted that the poems are mere tapestry-work, 'skilfully wrought of high imaginings, faery spells, fantastic legends, and mediaeval splendours . . . suffused with the Tennysonian glamour of golden mist, . . . like a chronicle illuminated by saintly hands . . .'; 'a refuge from life'; 'a mediaeval arras' behind which Tennyson fled from 'the horrors of the Industrial Revolution'.

The *Idylls* are so far from being escape that they represent one of Tennyson's most earnest and important efforts to deal with major problems of his time. Their proper significance can only be grasped by a careful reading, not of separate idylls, but of the complete group in its final form. The misunderstandings by critics have, I think, arisen largely from the reading of detached idylls, a habit encouraged by Tennyson's mode of composition and publication.

The real deficiency of the *Idylls* grows out of their piece-meal composition; quite clearly Tennyson's intention, and with it his treatment, passed through three stages, introducing inconsistencies which only complete revision and a larger measure of rewriting of the earlier idylls could have removed. Tennyson began in the eighteen-thirties with 'Morte d'Arthur', which is conscientiously epic in style, and follows Malory very closely. But even at this stage he was not content merely to 'remodel models', and recognized that only the finding of a modern significance in the Arthurian material would redeem his poem 'from the charge of nothingness'. It seems evident, however, that he could see at this time no satisfactory way of continuing the epic treatment, and his next step was to abandon the 'epyllion' for the 'idyll'. The titles, *Enid and Nimuë: The True and the False*, of 1857, and 'The True and the False: Four Idylls of the King', in the proof-sheets of 1859, suggest a development of intention. The title of 1859 gives primacy to the exemplary and didactic function of the stories, with Enid and Elaine as types of fidelity, Nimuë (Vivien) and Guinevere as types of the false and unchaste. The moral message is, however, very general, and the treatment is for the most part

† From *University of Toronto Quarterly*, XIX (1949), pp. 35–49. Reprinted by permission of the author and the publisher, University of Toronto Press.

rather like that of the 'English Idyls'; 'Nimuë' in particular offers a convincing portrayal of ordinary human psychology. Critics who approach these poems as typical of the *Idylls* may perhaps be forgiven for believing that the poet is concerned chiefly with a translation of the Arthurian material into a poetical variety of realistic fiction. But the style retains reminiscences of the epic, and 'Enid' and 'Nimuë' often suggest symbolic overtones, especially in Earl Doorm. Tennyson's final intention appears ten years later, with the provision of the main framework of symbolic allegory in 'The Coming of Arthur', 'The Holy Grail', and 'The Passing of Arthur'. 'Pelleas and Ettarre' and the later poems complete the pattern, but however unified the total structure has been made thematically, the treatment remains heterogeneous. 'Lancelot and Elaine' belong quite clearly to a different *genre* from 'The Holy Grail'—to the *genre* of 'Enoch Arden' or 'Aylmer's Field', not to that of 'The Vision of Sin.'

Nevertheless, the twelve poems do in fact form a pattern, and this pattern is best appreciated by interpreting the whole in terms of Tennyson's last intention, and recognizing that it is not his primary purpose to re-vivify Malory's story in a dramatic narrative, but to use the Arthurian cycle as a medium for the discussion of problems which are both contemporary and perennial. The *Idylls* are primarily allegorical, or (as Tennyson preferred to put it) parabolic. It is important to remember that the allegory is not simple. Tennyson himself, after reading reviews of the 1869 volume, complained: 'They have taken my hobby, and ridden it too hard, and have explained some things too allegorically, although there is an allegorical or perhaps rather a parabolic drift in the poem. . . . I hate to be tied down to say, *"This* means *that,"* because the thought within the image is much more than any one interpretation.' Professor Cleanth Brooks's comment on *The Waste Land* applies with very little modification to the *Idylls:* 'The symbols resist complete equation with a simple meaning. . . . The poem would undoubtedly be "clearer" if every symbol had one, unequivocal meaning; but the poem would be thinner, and less honest. For the poet has not been content to develop a didactic allegory in which the symbols are two-dimensional items adding up directly to the sum of the general scheme.'[1] As Tennyson says elsewhere, 'liberal applications lie In Art like Nature.'

Tennyson himself tells us something. His earliest note identifies Arthur with religious faith, and the Round Table with liberal institutions. Much later, in conversation with Knowles, he said, 'By Arthur I always meant the soul, and by the Round Table the

1. *T. S. Eliot: A Study of His Writings by Several Hands,* ed. B. Rajan (London, 1947), pp. 34–5.

passions and capacities of a man.' Arthur's relationship to his knights is likened by Guinevere to that of the 'conscience of a saint' to his 'warring senses'. And again, Tennyson is quoted in the *Memoir* as saying, 'The whole is the dream of a man coming into practical life and ruined by one sin. Birth is a mystery and death is a mystery, and in the midst lies the tableland of life, and its struggles and performances. It is not the history of one man or of one generation but of a whole cycle of generations.' According to his son, Tennyson 'felt strongly that only under the inspiration of ideals, and with his "sword bathed in heaven", can a man combat the cynical indifference, the intellectual selfishness, the sloth of will, the utilitarian materialism of a transition age. . . . If Epic unity is looked for in the *Idylls*, we find it . . . in the unending war of humanity in all ages—the world-wide war of sense and soul, typified in individuals. . . .'[2]

Arthur is, then, in the most general sense, soul or spirit in action. It is significant that he is constantly associated with the bringing of order out of chaos, harmony out of discord. His city is ever being built to music, 'therefore never built at all. And therefore built for ever'. The life of man, the life of society—each depends upon a principle of order, upon the recognition of a set of spiritual values to which all is harmonized. Arthur as soul is a symbol of these spiritual values, ideals, aspirations, and is consequently for Tennyson identified with the religious faith which must animate man, society, and nation. The Round Table is the symbol of the order, individual or social, which the values create. It is 'an image of the mighty world', the cosmos created by spirit. The tragic collapse of Arthur's work in the *Idylls* is an allegory of the collapse of society, of nation, and of individual, which must follow the rejection of spiritual values.

But Tennyson is not so naïve as to think that the problem of retaining spiritual values is a simple one. From the first, we are faced with the most fundamental doubt of all: that of the validity of the values. What are the origins of our ideals? Some give to Arthur a naturalistic origin, saying that he is the son of Uther by Gorlois' wife; but Uther and Ygerve were both dark in hair and eyes, and 'this king is fair Beyond the race of Britons and of men'. Nevertheless many, among them Modred, deny the supernatural origin of Arthur, 'some there be that hold the King a shadow, and the city real'. Those who accept Arthur accept him in one of two ways. Bellicent, by knowing Arthur, has felt the power and attraction of his personality, and intuitively has known his kingship. (Arthur has comforted her in her sorrow; 'being a child with me',

2. *Memoir*, ii, pp. 127, 129–30.

as she grew greater he grew with her, was stern at times, and sad at times, 'but sweet again, and then I loved him well'.) Gareth, on the other hand, accepts Arthur as proved by his works: to his mother's objection that Arthur is 'not wholly proven king' he replies,

'Not proven, who swept the dust of ruin'd Rome
From off the threshold of the realm and crush'd
The idolaters, and made the people free?
Who should be king save him who makes us free?'

But the difficulty remains: the authenticity of Arthur's kingship is not established so that all *must* accept him. And even over those who acknowledge him king his power is not complete nor permanent. At the institution of the Order of the Round Table, a momentary likeness of the king flashes over the faces of the knights as they have the brief clear vision of Arthur's divine authority, but soon some are thinking of Arthur as merely human, others are recognizing his authority while they defy it, others are starting to complain that his system of vows is too strict for human nature to observe. Bound up in this fundamental problem of Arthur's authority is the whole set of fundamental problems of moral philosophy: the origin of our moral ideals, the sanctions attached to them, the nature of obligation, and so on.

Further problems are brought out by Arthur's marriage to Guinevere. Soul must act through Body; Thought must wed Fact; the Spirit must mix himself with Life; the Idea must be actualized:

'. . . for saving I be join'd
To her that is the fairest under heaven,
I seem as nothing in the mighty world,
And cannot will my will nor work my work
Wholly, nor make myself in mine own realm
Victor and lord. But were I join'd with her,
Then might we live together as one life,
And reigning with one will in everything,
Have power on this dark land to lighten it,
And power on this dead world to make it live.'

It is only through alliance with the temporal that the eternal can work in the temporal, and since for Tennyson the prime function of an ideal is to work in the temporal, the alliance is necessary. It nevertheless brings the inevitable danger of separation and of conflict.

From the start, then, the stability of Arthur's realm, of the reign of spirit, is threatened in two ways; its collapse occurs when the challenge to Arthur's authority becomes more widespread and open, and the rebellion of the flesh within the realm becomes more violent. The defection of Guinevere is by no means the sole, or perhaps the chief, cause of the failure of Arthur's plans. It is, to be sure, important, since it tends constantly to reinforce other influences operating towards the catastrophe. But the activities of Vivien, her capture of Merlin, the revolt against the vows typified by Tristram, the effects of the Grail quest, and the stealthy work of Modred are all profoundly significant.

Vivien and Tristram are both associated with the court of Mark, a court of active and irreconcilable evil. When Mark tries to bribe his way into the Order, he has his gift burned by Arthur and his petition indignantly rejected: 'More like are we to reave him of his crown Than make him knight because men call him king.' Mark, inasmuch as men *do* call him king, stands for a set of values accepted by many but absolutely opposed to the Christian values Arthur stands for. Mark's values are defined by Vivien and Tristram. Vivien's whole being is dedicated to one purpose, the destruction of the Order; she has no fleshly motive for her wickedness, nor does she need any; her motive is essentially the hate felt by evil for the good.

> 'As love, if love be perfect, casts out fear,
> So hate, if hate be perfect, casts out fear.
> My father died in battle against the King,
> My mother on his corpse in open field;
>   . . . born from death was I
> Among the dead and sown upon the wind. . . .'

Her song, 'The fire of heaven is not the flame of hell,' echoes Lucretian themes of materialist naturalism, and at once recalls the similar songs in 'The Vision of Sin' and 'The Ancient Sage'. Her values are thoroughly hedonist. 'I better prize the living dog than the dead lion.' 'What shame in love, So love be true.' Her weapons are slander and seduction. But it is to be noted that she succeeds only where some weakness already exists for her to exploit. She vanquishes Merlin only because he is already prey to 'a great melancholy', a sense of 'doom that poised itself to fall', a premonition of

> World-war of dying flesh against the life,
> Death in all life and lying in all love,
> The meanest having power upon the highest,
> And the high purpose broken by the worm.

He is overcome finally by weariness and Vivien's feigned repentance.

Merlin's surrender seems to signify more than the mere defeat of Reason by Passion, although this is undoubtedly in part what is meant. But Merlin, we are told, knew the range of all arts, was the king's chief builder, 'was also Bard, and knew the starry heavens'. His charm, the secret of his power and the preserver of his authority and indeed of his function, came to him from a seer to whom 'the wall That sunders ghosts and shadow-casting men Became a crystal'. If Merlin represents Reason, then, it is quite clearly not Reason in its empirical or even discursive sense; he is endowed with what Tennyson would call Wisdom, rather than Knowledge; like the poet, he threads 'the secretest walks of fame', and sees 'thro' life and death, thro' good and ill'. It is Vivien's complaint that he does not belong wholly to her; it is her boast finally that she has made Merlin's glory hers. The authority belonging properly to the intuitive reason, which is not bound to sensation and phenomena, but can penetrate to ideal reality, has been usurped by the senses. Reason has been reduced to 'empirical verification', and 'closed in the four walls of a hollow tower, From which was no escape for evermore'. The overthrow of Merlin means the rejection of that faculty which perceives the ideal, the faculty of the poet and seer.

With his removal, the task of Vivien becomes much simpler, for Merlin has been the chief support of Arthur's system, the chief witness of Arthur's kingship. After he is gone, the reality of the ideal, the validity of Arthur's kingship, is judged by other standards. Even Guinevere can question the value of the Round Table; she resorts to the false but comforting doctrine of the fallen: 'He is all fault who hath no fault at all', and glibly attributes to Arthur her own defection: 'A moral child without the craft to rule, Else had he not lost me.' The cause Vivien represents has won: Guinevere values imperfection and evil (since they are natural) above perfection and good; she admires craft more than virtue; and she judges worth by success in craft. These are the ethics of materialism, naturalism, utilitarianism. Once the higher ethical system is undermined, all codes go. The last virtues to be discarded are the merely barbarian 'sporting' virtues; Gawain breaks an oath readily, even when sworn by the honour of the Table Round, but it still stirs him to see three attacking one. Yet even these, when become a mere code of sportsmanship not based upon any deeper ideal, are abandoned, and the last tournament is simply a struggle for prizes. The change in attitude is symbolized by the absence of Arthur as president, and by the victory of Tristram, who now replaces Vivien as a symbol of 'Mark's way'.

In him the naturalist philosophy of the court of Mark has become more conscious and rationalized. He repeats the doctrines of hedonism, but his motivation is different from Vivien's. He is a sceptic. Vivien has always recognized the value of what she is attacking; she knows that Arthur is right, and that her own life is wrong and evil. But Tristram is prepared to defend by argument his own rejection of the vows: 'The vow that binds too strictly snaps itself— . . . ay, being snapt—We run more counter to the soul thereof Than had we never sworn.' He questions the foundation of Arthur's authority, of the authority of spiritual values, by an appeal to the 'natural':

> 'The vows!
> O, ay—the wholesome madness of an hour—
> They served their use, their time; for every knight . . .
> Did mightier deeds than elsewise he had done,
> And so the realm was made. But then their vows . . .
> Began to gall the knighthood, asking when
> Had Arthur right to bind them to himself?
> Dropt down from heaven? Wash'd up from out the deep?
> They fail'd to trace him thro' the flesh and blood
> Of our old kings. Whence then? a doubtful lord
> To bind them by inviolable vows,
> Which flesh and blood perforce would violate. . . .'

The only validity Tristram grants at any time to the vows is a pragmatic one: they served their use. He challenges their permanent validity by a naturalistic argument—Arthur cannot be traced 'thro' the flesh and blood Of our old kings', i.e., the spiritual values Arthur represents are not derived from the ruling elements of our physical nature. The morality Tristram seeks is one founded in those elements; he is the type of those who talk about making morality 'conform to the facts of human nature'. What he would advocate is an attitude which accepts the good and evil of human nature indifferently, which recognizes the naturalness of man's frailties, and which, making 'naturalness' the norm, gives free play to the passions. It is worth noting that Guinevere's sin occupies a subordinate place in Tristram's argument; he attributes the downfall of the Round Table primarily to the impossible strictness of the vows.

Guinevere had at one point also drawn comfort in her error from the belief (or hope) that goodness was impossible for ordinary human nature; she had spoken scornfully of Arthur,

> 'Rapt in this fancy of his Table Round,
> And swearing men to vows impossible,
> To make them like himself.'

Even the faithful fool Dagonet is moved to cry out bitterly that Arthur is the king of fools, who

> 'Conceits himself as God that he can make
> Figs out of thistles, silk from bristles, milk
> From burning spurge, honey from hornet-combs,
> And men from beasts.'

All of these characters give strong expression to the naturalistic argument and challenge the authority of religion and of systems of ethics from the point of view of evolutionary naturalism.

But the problem is wider; it involves the whole difficulty of the relationship of the ethical ideal to the humanly possible. And Tennyson undertakes a solution. In the first place, he argues that the vows are brought into disrepute, and indeed are made almost impossible to follow, if they are exaggerated into an excessive asceticism. Mark and Vivien recognize their first opportunity when they hear that a few of the younger knights have renounced marriage,

> So passionate for an utter purity
> Beyond the limit of their bond are these,
> For Arthur bound them not to singleness.

Sir Pellam shows another aspect of asceticism which has its dangers: he holds that heavenly things must not be defiled with earthly uses; his heir is Garlon, the poisonous vessel of scorn and slander. Some of the meaning of the Grail poem is to the same general effect; ideals are for application to life, to human nature. If they involve a turning of the back upon life, they are barren at best, destructive at worst. The strict vow is for the exceptional, for Galahads or perhaps even Percivales. But, asks Arthur,

> 'What are ye? Galahads?—no, nor Percivales
>   . . . but men
> With strength and will to right the wrong'd, of power
> To lay the sudden heads of violence flat. . . .
> Your places being vacant at my side,
> This chance of noble deeds will come and go,
> Unchallenged. . . .'

There is a special significance, perhaps, in the fact that the chance of noble deeds was not being seized *before* the Grail vision. Percivale's decision to pursue the Grail arose out of dissatisfaction with the condition of the court,

> 'vainglories, rivalries,
> And earthly heats that spring and sparkle out
> Among us in the jousts, while women watch
> Who wins, who falls, and waste the spiritual strength
> Within us, better offer'd up to heav'n.'

The society is already pervaded with a sense of spiritual frustration; the ideal of service is already lost; the old order is already vastly changed. And the turning to the Grail quest marks for most of the knights a withdrawal from the everyday problems involved in Arthur's original purpose, to 'have power on this dead world to make it live', to inform the real with the ideal. For those who find the revelation, it is well, but few find it.

The Grail poem undoubtedly expresses, as most critics recognize, Tennyson's rejection of the ascetic way of life, at least as a normal vocation. But I think there is more in it. 'One has seen,' says Arthur, 'and all the blind will see.' And when the knights return, each has seen according to his sight.

> 'And out of those to whom the vision came
> · My greatest hardly will believe he saw.
> Another hath beheld it afar off,
> And, leaving human wrongs to right themselves,
> Cares but to pass into the silent life.'

Quite clearly, the true purposes of ordinary life are not served at all by the Grail quest. Galahad, in his success, is as much 'lost to life and use' as Merlin; he has passed out on to the great Sea, beyond the limits of human life; he has been willing to lose himself to save himself. But the others, while wishing to stay in life, are seeking an easy way to spiritual certitude in the shift and clash of moral values. Without having any deep inward conviction, they insist on seeing the unseen. Arthur is content to let the visions come, and many a time they come. Not directly and deliberately seeking the vision, he sees more than most of the Grail adventurers. The restless quest for religious certainty, for most an inevitably fruitless quest, brings a paralysis of the will, as Tennyson had known as he wrote 'Supposed Confessions', and 'The Two Voices', and as Carlyle and Arnold had known. If man's proper task is undertaken, that of establishing the kingdom of the highest ideal on earth, then the 'visions' will come as a deep and passionate conviction that all pertaining to the flesh is vision, and 'God and the Spiritual the only real and true', and then will come to man the

> moments when he feels he cannot die,
> And knows himself no vision to himself,
> Nor the high God a vision, nor that One
> Who rose again.

(These lines, said Tennyson, are the central lines of the *Idylls*.) The proper way to faith is through works.

It is thoroughly consistent that those who seek to *know* Arthur's origins find no certainty. Arthur's royalty and holiness, and the holiness of the vows, are not to be empirically proved, 'Thou canst not prove the Nameless'; they are either recognized immediately, or not at all. Guinevere is for long blind to them; at the end it is as if a veil has been lifted:

> 'Thou art the highest and most human too,
> Not Lancelot, nor another. Is there none
> Will tell the King I love him tho' so late?

Now—ere he goes to the great battle? None!
Myself must tell him in that purer life. . . .
                                      Ah my God,
What might I not have made of thy fair world,
Had I but loved thy highest creature here?
It was my duty to have loved the highest;
It surely was my profit had I known;
It would have been my pleasure had I seen.'

The whole problem appears in that 'had I known', 'had I seen'.
What had prevented her from knowing, and seeing?

'False voluptuous pride, that took
Full easily all impressions from below,
Would not look up, or half-despised the height
To which I would not or I could not climb.'

The defect of recognition proceeds from a defect of will.

In Guinevere's repentant insight we are also given Tennyson's
second answer to the naturalistic argument. The vows present the
paradox: The highest is the most human too. A morality which
merely conforms to our nature is based upon less than the highest
possibility of our nature; we are most human when we transcend
our ordinary selves. The ideal must not, like the ascetic ideal, be
so remote that it seems obviously unattainable; nor must it, like
the naturalistic ideal, be so close that it seems obviously attained.
But it is the essence of ethics to be not descriptive, but normative;
not to tell us how we behave, but how we ought to behave. The
ethics of naturalism confuse the prescriptive end of ethics with the
descriptive end of science.

The causes of Arthur's failure, then, are many. All round are the
powers of the wasteland, powers of violence, hate, and lust. How
far these and the powers of the North represent an active diabolic
spirit of evil, and how far primitive atavistic forces within the
individual soul and within society, does not matter—nor, I think,
would Tennyson have felt it necessary to decide. Assisting them are
the false philosophies represented by Mark, Vivien, and Tristram.
These operate at two levels: as rationalizations in the individual,
and as popular modes of thought in society. Both society and
individual are secure against these powers of disintegration as long
as there is a clear recognition of the spiritual values which give
coherence to society and individual. This clear recognition is
threatened in three ways: by doubts of the foundation and validity
of the ideals; by a separation of the ideals from the actual, either in
an exaggerated asceticism or in a withdrawal; and by the ignoring
of the primary importance of action, and the abandonment of
ethical problems in the quest for religious certainty.

The failure of Arthur's work presents the basic problem of the moral order. And here, in the last of the poems, whether deliberately or forced by the earlier pattern established in 'Morte d'Arthur', Tennyson changes the relationship of the king to the theme. He is no longer so much a symbol of Soul, or of the Ideal, as of defeated mankind asking a question. The poems have hitherto displayed how evil triumphs, how 'bright things come to confusion'; now Arthur asks the deeper question why.

> 'I found Him in the shining of the stars,
> I mark'd Him in the flowering of His fields,
> But in His ways with men I find Him not.'

God's hand is visible in the physical order, but not in the moral; the history of the stars and of the flowers shows a pattern, but not the history of man. The problem of evil is an urgent one for Arthur. His whole work has been based upon belief in an ultimate moral order, in a system wherein good must finally prevail—and yet, as he looks back upon the history of his Round Table, he sees the Cosmos which he created out of Chaos succeeded merely by a new Chaos. And with the final doubt of the moral order, Arthur doubts himself: 'I know not what I am, Nor whence I am, nor whether I be king.' But as he prepares for death by the surrender of Excalibur, symbol of his kingship, the 'arm, clothed in white samite, mystic, wonderful', which catches the flung sword, by its very appearance and action proclaims again the reality of his kingship, and by its repetition of the beginning affirms the pattern. What the pattern is, Arthur cannot see; but that his life began with a solemn arming and ends with a solemn disarming suggests the completion of a cycle, a cycle whose meaning may not be clear to Arthur, but is clear to those who armed him.

With the reassurance thus established, Arthur is able to affirm a faith in the order of the historical process. The flux of events is not a blind flux; the growth and decay of institutions, of societies, is not a mere mechanical sequence of phenomena. Nor does the fact of change carry implications of moral relativity. Every new order is a mode of actualization of the ideal: 'God fulfils himself in many ways, Lest one good custom should corrupt the world.' The ultimate truth is the paradox of the permanence of the ideal which underlies the transitory shifting phenomena. The history of Arthur 'is not the history of one man or of one generation but of a whole cycle of generations'. The war of Sense and Soul is an 'unending war of humanity in all ages'. The Ideal which Arthur symbolizes has found embodiment in many forms, in many ages, in many places; it has fought its battles and has, in each form, yielded place to new. It passes but never dies. As Bedivere watches the speck of Arthur's barge, it vanishes 'into light, And the new sun rose bringing the new year'.

Tennyson is asserting through the *Idylls* the primacy of the Unseen, the ultimate reality of the Spiritual, which is manifested in a constant succession of phenomena, and gives permanent meaning to them. The phenomena are not merely shadows or illusions; they are 'real' in that they are the temporal actualization of the ideal. Man's task is not to pierce through the evil of appearances and brush it aside; it is to recognize the relationship of appearance to an ideal reality which he cannot fully know, and to work in the realm of phenomena towards more complete actualization of the ideal in so far as he knows it. And Tennyson believes that the activity of working itself brings fuller knowledge. His idealism, in short, serves to guarantee the religious and ethical values (both for the individual and for society), while not permitting a retreat into contemplative passivity; the temporal aspects of individual and social problems are the aspects under which we are bound to see, and bound to attack them. The Creed of Creeds must be worked out by human hands; the watchword is 'Do Well'. The task is not to be fulfilled by a denial of human nature and of human problems; asceticism is a retreat. Nor is it to be fulfilled by the search for personal intellectual certainty of the Unseen; this again is a retreat from the real duty.

Man's proper task is that of securing order and harmony in all phases of human activity: in the individual, the harmony of senses, passions, reason, ordered by conscience; in society, harmony of individuals, and of social groups in their relations to each other, ordered again by conscience operating as a sense of justice, loyalty, duty or responsibility, and love. The threats to order come from within and without. Within there are crimes of sense: lust, pride, anger, gluttony; and crimes of malice: slander, wilful breach of trust, envy of the lost good, and so on. Without there are active powers of malevolence and brutality, symbolized traditionally in the poem by the powers in the North. These have success only against those already weakened internally.

When the real nature of the *Idylls* is properly understood, it is possible to appreciate their quality, which is essentially that of dramatic allegory. The twelve poems fall naturally into three groups of four, corresponding closely to the three acts of modern drama. The first act opens with the highly symbolic 'Coming of Arthur', and closes with 'Geraint and Enid'. Each of the four poems it includes has what can be considered a happy ending, and the general theme of all is the establishing of order and the victory of good over evil. Arthur is characterized by sharp clarity of vision; Gareth shows similar sureness and fixity of purpose. Gareth knows from the first his end in life, and recognizes easily Arthur's kingship. He finds freedom in service, and resolutely overcomes the Star Knights and the Knight of the Castle Perilous. He and Enid provide exemplars of the ideals of Arthur. Geraint and Lynette, in their perverse obstinacy and reluctant recognition of values represent internal obstacles to be overcome, rather than external forces threatening the good. But we are kept aware, during the triumphs, of the threats to Arthur's reign. The knights are few, and include slothful officers, mean-spirited knights like Sir Kay. Outside the court lie the waste-land and the dark powers of the North, violent and brutal, denying Arthur's kingship and doubting his origin. And already there is suggestion of falseness at the very heart of the realm; it is a rumour about Guinevere that leads Geraint to mistrust Enid. All these elements moderate the pattern of success and prepare for the second act.

This opens powerfully with the grim 'Balin and Balan', and ends with the climax of 'The Holy Grail'. The forces of disruption move suddenly into sharp focus: the illicit love of Lancelot and Guine-vere, formerly an uncertain and shadowy rumour, becomes a hard certainty; evil emerges, conscious, deliberate, and triumphant, in Vivien and Garlon. The fierce and tragic opening is modulated through the 'Merlin and Vivien' to the pathetic involvement of the innocent Elaine, and finally to the complex pattern of splendid holiness, shameful sin, glorious achievement, and foolish futility of 'The Holy Grail'. Arthur, who in the first act is shown presiding at the Hall of Justice, is left at the end of the second 'gazing at a barren board, And a lean Order—scarce return'd a tithe'.

The last act opens with the bitterly ironic 'Pelleas and Ettarre'. Pelleas is reminiscent of Gareth, particularly in his youthful eager-ness and zeal, but he has none of Gareth's clarity, and his concep-tion of knighthood is not, like Gareth's, one of religious service; it is wholly secular. His is the ideal of the courtly lover, seeking fame for a lady. He is abashed by the fleshly beauty of the harlot Ettarre, 'as tho' it were the beauty of her soul'. Ettarre is no Lynette or Enid; she values experienced worldliness, not young enthusiasm. And when Pelleas, betrayed by Ettarre and Gawain, goes half mad with disillusionment, it is significant that he turns against Arthur and the vows. 'The Last Tournament' completes the theme of cor-ruption by presenting the form which the spirit has left. The irony becomes deeper and all-pervading, in the title of the tournament, the prize offered, and the winner. Victory goes merely to the most experienced, who is also the most open repudiator of all that Arthur stands for. The defence of Arthur is given to Dagonet, the fool, the sad and lonely remnant of the king's following. All that remains is for the form to collapse. The last two idylls present the *dénoue-*

ment, and in the repentance of Guinevere a final statement, now tragic, of the worth of what has decayed. The choric comment by Arthur in the last poem sets the whole action in cosmic perspective, with a levelling off of emotion, and an affirmation of faith in order. The total dramatic effect seems to me to have considerable power.

That Tennyson sees a particular relevance for his own time in what he is saying is clear enough. The *Idylls* present in allegory the philosophy which pervades the whole of Tennyson's poetry, the philosophy which he felt it necessary to assert throughout his poetic lifetime. Penetrating all his poetry is the strong faith in the eternal world of spirit, expressed particularly in 'The Higher Pantheism', 'De Profundis', 'The Ancient Sage', at the end of 'Locksley Hall Sixty Years After', and in 'Merlin and the Gleam'. The assertion of the validity and necessity of idealism is reinforced by continual warnings of the dangers of materialism: 'The Vision of Sin', *Maud*, 'Aylmer's Field', 'Despair', and 'Lucretius' are the chief vehicles for these warnings. Like most sensitive thinkers of his day, Tennyson was deeply concerned with the growing materialism, with the new hedonism, with the utilitarian ethic with its relativism and naturalism, with the attack on the religious foundation of the Christian ethic not merely by the higher critics but particularly by those who were applying evolutionary principles to show the 'natural' origin of moral ideas. He was concerned with the apparent decay of ethical principles in commercial, political, and social life, and with the growing tendency to defend all sensual gratification as 'natural'. He saw that religious leaders were not always effective in combating these tendencies, since they were on the defensive, and were busy trying to 'demonstrate', to 'prove' Christianity. The expenditure of effort against Huxley over the Gadarene swine is significant and symptomatic. The laity could hardly be blamed for thinking that Christian doctrine ought to be susceptible of the same kind of verification as scientific fact; they either wearied and perplexed themselves in the search for certainty, or sank into agnosticism. Tennyson is asserting in the *Idylls* that Christianity is not so much a set of facts to be argued about as a system of principles to be lived by; that the proof of these principles is to be established not by external empirical evidence, but by the power with which they unify and give stability and meaning to the life of man and of societies. He wants to make the reader understand how these principles become neglected, and what must happen to individuals and societies who neglect them. He is voicing a warning to his own age and nation, and to all ages and nations. He is consistently opposing a revival of the Lucretian philosophy, with its materialism, its naturalism, and its secularism. To him it is the philosophy of pessimism and despair, of defeat and social destruction.

Against the Lucretian spirit Tennyson upholds the Vergilian. The two have been well characterized by the late Professor C. N. Cochrane:

> The one holds up an ideal of repose and refined sensual enjoyment; the other, one of restless effort and activity. Lucretius urges the recognition that men are limited as the dust; that the pursuit of their aspirations is as vain and futile as are the impulses of religion, pride, ambition which ceaselessly urge them on. The purpose of Vergil is to vindicate those obscure forces within the self by which mankind is impelled to material achievement and inhibited from destroying the work of his own hands. . . . The one . . . accepts the intellectual assurance of futility, the other . . . , like all enlightened men, is beset by the problem of finding a reasonable ground for his faith.[3]

The last line of Tennyson's 'Lucretius' presents acutely the implications of the Lucretian philosophy: 'Thy duty? What is duty?' The man or society who can find no answer must perish.

FRANCIS GOLFFING

Tennyson's Last Phase: The Poet as Seer†

Any mention of Tennyson today, even in advanced circles, is likely to draw a rather blank response. Those who remember him at all evoke the image of an extremely suave, mellifluous poet, technically expert or at any rate very versatile in point of prosody; as far as ideas are concerned, pretty conformist, a towering monument to Victorian complacency. The intellectual challenge of his verse has never been considered very great: Tennyson had none of the dialectical skill and driving force of Browning, his nearest compeer in the estimation of his contemporaries, and was far less given to worrying abstract ideas than Matthew Arnold, with whom he shared, or is said to have shared, the peculiarly Victorian spiritual malaise. My own view of Tennyson's contribution to poetry differs very sharply from the accepted one.

Although Tennyson strikes me as an interesting poet throughout his career I want to focus on his final phase: the verse written between 1880 and 1890, when Tennyson was a very old man. I need not rehearse here Tennyson's poetic progress in detail: the main stages of that progress are familiar to all. The publication, in 1830, of his *Poems, Chiefly Lyrical* put Tennyson on the literary

---

3. 'The Latin Spirit in Literature' (*Univ. of Toronto Quarterly*, ii. pp. 330–1).

† From *The Southern Review*, II (1966), pp. 264–285. Reprinted by permission of the author.

map, on which he was to stay pretty securely for the next fifty years. This early collection was a stunning performance, which revolutionized the language of English poetry no less thoroughly than Wordsworth's *Lyrical Ballads* had done one generation earlier. Tennyson maintained the momentum of his first effort in his next four collections, right up to *In Memoriam*, which was published in 1850, and which still ranks as one of the chief examples of meditative poetry in English, though its lustre is now somewhat dimmed. After 1850 Tennyson began to decline somewhat in poetic power and sureness of touch, while his prestige continued to soar. This is the period marked by the publication in 1855 of *Maud*, an experimental novel in verse, and of the *Idylls of the King*, whose composition was begun in 1856, though it took Tennyson another thirty years to complete that ambitious project. The decline I spoke of is relative, to be sure; Tennyson's lyrical impulse was far from exhausted. Some of his most poignant lyrics date from his middle period, that of the fifties and early sixties—witness such famous anthology pieces as "The Splendor Falls on Castle Walls," "Tears, Idle Tears," "Now Sleeps the Crimson Petal, Now the White,"—all of which are marked by a melting melodiousness quite peculiar to him, by great subtlety of cadence, and a refinement or delicacy of feeling which might best be described by the Italian term *morbidezza*. *Maud*, too, contains a number of exquisite lyrics. But Tennyson clearly underwent a crisis during these decades, which was both psychological and technical. I am only concerned here with his artistic crisis, and I shall attempt briefly to characterize its nature.

For over twenty years Tennyson had worked within an extremely restricted range of feeling as well as language, and he was fully aware of this—as aware as Yeats was when around 1910 he made a resolute attempt to get beyond the Celtic twilight into the full light of day. Tennyson understood that he had to develop new resources of style as well as new subject matter if he was to avoid becoming a prisoner of his refined inwardness; he did not wish to modulate endlessly on a few tonal combinations, however exquisite these might be. He accepted the challenge, which is greatly to his credit, but he miscalculated his powers rather drastically, and in the eyes of many critics disastrously took the wrong turn.

Tennyson's prestige with the public continued to rise, right up to and beyond the publication of *The Holy Grail*; but as regards his prestige with the critics and cognoscenti, the case is quite different. After the appearance in 1872 of *Gareth and Lynette* critical plaudits sharply declined and finally ceased altogether. Critics felt that he had had his say, and was not likely to add to his stature henceforward. The evidence certainly seemed to corroborate that prediction: the critics of the day could not know that Tennyson still had another ace up his sleeve. During the seventies and eighties he was concentrating his efforts as a poet on drama and heroic narrative, in flagrant misjudgment of his peculiar talent, which was lyrical in an unusually wide sense, but *purely* lyrical and not at all dramatic or heroic. He might have become a distinguished writer of prose, had he chosen to do so, but he could never have written a viable tragedy, for the reason—to put it very simply—that he lacked any real sense of tragic guilt. He was a meliorist, of a very complex sort, a little like Goethe in that respect, and his plays fail for the same reason that Goethe's *Tasso* and *Iphigenia in Tauris* fail as tragedies. But though he did give much of his time to the composition of plays during that period, Tennyson continued to write lyric and meditative verse, the best of which didn't appear in print until after his death. It is in these poems, uneven as is all his work, but often quite extraordinary, that Tennyson tried to embody his new vision of the world. It cannot be shown that Tennyson suppressed the poems which came out posthumously, in *The Death of Oenone*, the way he had suppressed so much of his earlier material all through his career, but there is evidence that he was slow and rather reluctant to publish them. His biographers tell us that from about 1880 onward Tennyson frequently complained about being misunderstood, not just as a dramatist but in his basic poetic intentions. A close look at these intentions suggests that they were quite unfashionable: Tennyson was beginning to be out of tune with his time. It is my contention that many of the poems written between 1880 and 1892 present a radical departure from the thought models current in his day. That departure is intimately bound up with the issue of the two cultures (C. P. Snow's famous phrase for the increasing bifurcation of the humanistic and scientific world views in Western civilization); so, to set the scene, allow me to briefly characterize the stage that hiatus had reached in England about 1880.

At this time we find two intellectual elites in sharp confrontation: the scientific, represented most impressively by T. H. Huxley, and that of the traditional humanists, whose chief spokesman was Matthew Arnold, insisting vigorously on the redemptive virtues of the Graeco-Judaic-Christian heritage. The two camps were ranged on either side of a fence across which they glared at each other, trying I suppose to stare each other down, for there were really no common terms of discourse by which they could have composed their differences. Tennyson, so far as I know, was the only major figure on the scene who refused to play the game, not by *sitting* on the fence but by attempting to set a fuse to it and blast it out of existence.

Now this sort of thing does not go over very well in any context, for a variety of reasons; and perhaps least well in England, the country most thoroughly committed to sportsmanship and gentleman's agreements, and by the same token most impatient of saboteurs and other spoilsports. Here was a game set up in perfectly good faith, which could be played according to rules which were clearly worded: the fact that it could be played indefinitely—and so perhaps wasn't a true game at all, but something much more frustrating, and possibly sinister—occurred to very few of the Victorian thinkers. But it did occur to some, Ruskin for example, and also to a flagrant nonthinker like Tennyson. Tennyson did not have it in him to try for a change in the rules of the game—say, by a conceptual or vocabulary reform—but he tackled the job in his own way, which for the sake of convenience I shall call the utopian or visionary way. He proposed, late in life, something that was quite unheard of and drew a stare of blank incomprehension from both parties: that they stop sparring and get down to business. And by business he meant neither more nor less than the future of the human race. Tennyson imagined that future to lie at the convergence of both mandates—the humanist and the scientific—in their stage of final perfection. And he assumed, very boldly, that a conceptual vehicle common to both these concerns could eventually be found, though as I have said he had no talent for providing such a vehicle; neither did he claim to.

These convictions Tennyson expressed in a series of very curious poems. The attitude they embodied was novel at the time of their appearance, almost without precedent in English verse, if one excepts certain poems by William Morris, George Meredith, and James Thomson, at least some of which antedate Tennyson's departure by a few years. The attitude is frankly naturalistic, this-worldly; supernaturalism of any kind is rejected, and attention centered upon man's mandate on this earth. James Thomson's couplet "Life liveth but in Life and does not roam/To other realms if all be well at home" might serve as an epigraph for the entire cycle. But Tennyson's man-centeredness differs in many important respects from that of Morris, Thomson, or Meredith. Morris, we all know, was in outlook a preindustrial utopist, who rejected science and technology out of hand, and harked back to the medieval economics of the artisan guilds. Meredith worshipped nature in the manner of Hegel or Schelling, as the matrix of spirituality, but though a progressive in politics paid little attention to the human commonwealth as a whole. His interest in science, moreover, was minimal. Thomson was a thoroughgoing monist and evolutionist, in the Lucretian tradition, but the view he took of humanity was so desperate that he would never allow himself to speculate about the future of the species. Tennyson is unique, so far as I know, among the poets of his period in envisaging a social order which would embrace all of mankind, and which would be based on a rational technology and a thoroughly humanized science.

This may sound like a rather dreary program for a poet to tackle —stated in this way it suggests preachment and versified tracts rather than imaginative vision. But Tennyson redeems the program by using every poetic resource at his command for its effective articulation. Even so, today's reader may find a certain excess of eloquence over sheer poetic substance in these poems; but the substance is there, and the eloquence, or rhetoric, is of a very high order—never hackneyed and free from any trace of special pleading. The program, as I have said, is essentially rational, even rationalistic; yet the role the poet assumes is frankly Dionysiac, in sharp contrast to the role of mellow sage which Tennyson had adopted during the sixties and seventies. And his imagery keeps pace with his developing vision. It describes the world as seen by one who is very much part of the human scene and yet in a sense above the melee; by turns stocktaking and prophetic, but never censorious, never ill-tempered or petty. The key terms become increasingly those of astrophysics; if not astronautics; Tennyson's avatar [is] a planet which exhibits certain features of the earth, orbiting around the sun as its ultimate center of energy and reference. The master image is always that of a new world in the making, finding its identity as it whirls through the lonely cosmic spaces—in the hope that eventually itself, and the traversed vastnesses, may be made less lonely by being consolidated, humanized, made rational, and productive at—the phrase is Tennyson's—"the limit of the human state." Here is the earth speaking, as it speaks so often in Tennyson's late poetry, wistfully but not at all despairingly: "Must my day be dark by reason, O ye Heavens, of your boundless nights,/Rush of Suns, and roll of systems, and your fiery clash of meteorites?" The answer is that this need not be; that man can reach his true estate by bending every effort to the achievement of his planetary mission, to self-creation without benefit of dogma, till he can exclaim, with justified pride, "It is finished. Man is made"—meaning man's evolution as a rational species.

What are some of the assumptions behind this remarkable transformation—the moody and somewhat haughty recluse re-emerging as a kind of Zarathustra, offering mankind the tablets of a new and essentially naturalistic covenant?

Tennyson holds that notwithstanding his incredibly long career, man is still at the beginning of his planetary mandate. Like Teilhard de Chardin, he envisages a noosphere eventually growing out of the biosphere: a specifically human, social order enveloping the random evolution of the lower species, among whom man as he is now is included; and man's eventual triumph would consist, not in lording it over all of nature but in extending the realm of nature by adding to it the dimension of a perfected human society, which takes strict account of the demands made by the so-called lower orders of creation. The conflict between nature and culture which so exercised his contemporaries—in both of the camps I have mentioned—has no fundamental meaning for Tennyson.

Remember that the only traffic between the two cultures the age could recognize was compromise: an attempt to reconcile Deism with Darwinism, as Agassiz, Dana, and many other scientists as well as distinguished laymen had done. These men were not playing the game either, but at least they were operating within the accepted terms, which everybody could understand. They were bad sports, in that they wanted the game to come to a rapid conclusion, but they were still sports. Tennyson, like Nietzsche a generation later, showed no interest in the dialectic of reason versus faith. As it happened, he confessed himself a Christian, of a somewhat pantheistic cast, but this fact and that other fact of his being a well-wisher and ardent admirer of the advancing scientific technology provide no matter for conflict in his poetry. It would appear from the biographical record that he saw no real conflict here; not, I submit, because he was too stupid to see it but because he was not especially interested in personal redemption. Tennyson's later poetry has become curiously depersonalized and focuses almost entirely on one single issue: the happiness of the human race, conceived on a global scale. That problem assumes an ever increasing urgency for him, and he handles it with remarkable subtlety. Tennyson is not openly optimistic about the prospects of the species, as Browning was; neither is he apprehensive or fainthearted about these prospects, in the manner of Matthew Arnold. He remains perfectly matter of fact in presenting what scientists would call the data, and reserves such passion or pathos as he can muster for his future projection—his vision of what we might become if we tried, concertedly and unremittingly, to realize our human substance. To achieve that end, every legitimate human power and ability must be invoked, and this means that technology and morality must move in harness, that there must be an end to the squabble between the advocates of empiricism and rationalism, rationalism and faith. It also means that a common denominator can, and must, be found for the poetic imagination, on the one hand, and the scientific, technical, and economic imagination, on the other. More clear-headed than most poets of his age—and, I may add, most poets of our own—Tennyson realized that the only conceivable issue to a schizophrenic civilization is a new age of barbarism, more terrible than the old barbarism because of the instruments of large-scale destruction it is able to wield. Science and poetry must learn to live with one another; the poetic imagination must temper and control the scientific, and vice versa, lest both soar off into irrelevance, or possibly into something far worse than mere irrelevance.

* * *

Now I am not claiming that Tennyson, in his old age, came up with an authoritative answer to these tough, excruciating questions. I merely claim that he had begun to view them in their full complexity, and was now in a position to frame possible, utopian, visionary answers, which moreover were infused with deep passion—the kind of passion born of absolute conviction—and with an equally profound honesty. Poems like "Locksley Hall" had still exhibited a certain amount of cant, or wishful thinking, or meliorist cliché. The later poems are free from these vices; when they are flawed—and they often are—the flaws are flaws of style, and in some cases Tennyson was unhappy in his choice of meter. The late Tennyson is often awkward, with the awkwardness arising from untried materials, but I for one am not at all unhappy to see him fail in this way. Having been troubled, like so many readers of Tennyson, by a kind of meretricious bravura in the earlier work, I discover this kind of stumbling comes as a relief, almost.

There is awkwardness in some of the late poems, along with much that is brilliant and exciting; and there is something else—not always to be sure but fairly frequently—which might offend the tidy mind. As I have said earlier, Tennyson could not fully conceptualize his unitary vision of man. The tenor of his late poetry is frankly naturalistic, concerned with man's self-realization and nothing else; yet he cannot altogether dispense with old-time teleology, nor with God as the traditional master image. It is fascinating to watch how theology creeps into the poetry whenever there is an empty place on Tennyson's conceptual map which he doesn't quite know how to fill by legitimate means. I am not much bothered by these lapses, perhaps because my own mind is rather untidy, and because I know how difficult it is to elaborate a consistent vocabulary when you are dealing with uncharted territories. What matters is that these deistic vestiges do not seriously infringe the completeness of Tennyson's vision, or its authenticity. Let the purist, if he likes, substitute the proper conceptual counters for the offending terms: I personally would rather watch the poet derail on occasion than the nonpoet stay on the track, at all hazards.

I have made out a case for Tennyson as a genuine seer, as a poet who tried with variable but on the whole impressive success to pierce the mists of the future, project a state of rational happiness in which all humanity could share. Before I present my examples from his works to support my case, I wish to specify a little more closely what I consider to be Tennyson's scope as a visionary poet, and I also want to say something about his method.

First, his scope. Tennyson's range of poetic comprehension was unusually wide, not just by Victorian standards but by any standard you might want to apply. He could fix on both near and distant objectives with unerring aim, always on the wing as it were. But compared with Blake, or John Clare, or Christopher Smart—the visionary poets par excellence—he seems somewhat shallow, for he rarely succeeds in making his objectives yield up their whole meaning. Tennyson was a triple victim: of the Victorian temper, of his tremendous versatility, and of his public role as poet laureate. One feels that he rarely stays with his subject quite long enough to encompass it wholly; and looking over his entire body of work one notices a shying away from radical solutions, though the questions he asks are radical enough. It is very characteristic of the poet that he suppressed most of the poems which dealt with the extremes of the human spectrum, or else refused to have them reprinted after they had appeared in periodicals. Victorian decorum frowned equally on the slough of despond and on the beatific vision: Tennyson had experienced them both, and possessed the means of rendering them memorably, but he had to watch his step and, at least within sight of the public, tried to keep to the middle range. But the damage goes deeper: Tennyson's uneasiness about his audience so cramped his style that even those poems which were never meant for public consumption were liable to suffer from a certain inhibition—as though he didn't dare to speak his whole mind. There are exceptions of course, both among the published and suppressed poems. Indeed my presentation will be concerned with the exceptions only. The fact remains that for the most part both terror and exultation, both curse and good tidings, are somewhat muted in Tennyson's verse; he will rarely let himself go, come what may, the way Blake does. I am not at all sure that he saw less, or less deeply, than Blake or, say, Hopkins, or that he was inferior to either of these men in power of expression, but what comes through in the end is less, and the fault lies with the strangling combination of outer and inner censorship.

There is still another factor which must have had a muting effect on Tennyson's expression of his deepest convictions. He had before him, in the person of Browning, a poet with a narrow but powerful, almost cocky vision of the world—a poet specializing in prophecy and heady asseverations about the human lot, always ready with an answer to every cosmic or psychological conundrum. Tennyson could not but be appalled by so much certainty and seems to have tried for an equally massive concentration of doubt, hesitancy, questioning, as a counterweight. This makes his verse look paler, if subtler, than Browning's. It also makes it more honest; and whenever Tennyson does come up with a strong affirmation, the impact is likely to be much greater than the impact we get from Browning's steady battering ram.

The over-all movement of Tennyson's vision is from blank despair, the experience of unmeaning, to an adumbration of total meaning, man at the height of his powers, the earthly paradise. My first example—promptly suppressed by Tennyson, after its publication in a magazine—may be said to render the zero point of total unmeaning. The date is 1865.

> I stood on a tower in the wet,
> And new year and old year met,
> And winds were roaring and blowing;
> And I said, "O years, that meet in tears,
> Have you aught that is worth the Knowing?
> Science enough and exploring,
> Wanderers coming and going,
> Matter enough for deploring,
> But aught that is worth the Knowing?"
> Seas from my feet were flowing,
> Waves on the shingle pouring,
> Old year roaring and blowing,
> And new year blowing and roaring.

Here the experience is one of seesawing nothingness. The gap between science and knowing is presented as desperate; the melioristic solution is flatly rejected: science is on the march, very well, but what good does it do? how can it ever hope to illustrate, or illuminate, man's predicament? Yet the poem remains open. The question the poet addresses to the years conveys stubborn hope: perhaps the meaning is there, after all, hidden underneath the monotonous tumult of sea motion and roaring wind, and if we are patient enough the years may yield it up in the end.

A tentative answer to this piece is found in Tennyson's last volume (1892): a riddling, somewhat Yeatsian poem, written in the same meter. On the face of it, this is no answer at all but merely another question, but perhaps I am not wholly wrong in viewing the poem as a breakthrough to the visionary position.

> A voice spake out of the skies
> To a just man and wise—
> "The world and all within it
> Will only last a minute!"
> And a beggar began to cry
> "Food, food, or I die!"
> Is it worth his while to eat,
> Or mine to give him meat,
> If the world and all within it
> Were nothing the next minute?

I read this poem as follows: assuming an imminent cataclysm, what is the just and wise man to do? Sit still and wait for the disaster, totally oblivious of his fellows who are, presumably, neither just nor wise, and who lack the necessities of life which he still possesses? What do justice and wisdom mean if they remain un-exercised or are exercised only in the service of self-perfection? The crucial concept of this poem, it seems to me, is that of the existen-tial, Kierkegaardian *moment*. The moment for right action always exists, it is now or never, and the fact that the world may crumble to nothing in the next minute has no bearing on one's decision. There is also an implication here that the prophecy may be false, a temptation, again in Kierkegaard's sense: somebody is being tested for his stamina, his convictions; it is made very easy for the just and wise man to back out at the crucial moment, if he is told that there is going to be no future either for himself or the beggar. Why trouble under these circumstances? And yet, the trouble must be taken.

The poem, to be sure, does not say this; it ends with a question, presents merely a neat dilemma. But there is little doubt in my mind that Tennyson meant the question to be answered by the reader, and answered in the way I have indicated.

Tennyson, I said, had to make his mind a tabula rasa before he could go on to the task of constructing, or reconstructing. There is another transitional poem, as extreme in its rejections as was my first example, but the target is quite different. It presents yet another jumping-off place into utopianism, and one the reader is least likely to expect. This poem, entitled "Cambridge," was never pub-lished in Tennyson's lifetime, which should hardly come as a sur-prise.

> Therefore your halls, your ancient colleges,
> Your portals statued with old kings and queens,
> Your bridges and your busted libraries,
> Wax-lighted chapels and rich carvéd screens,
> Your doctors and your proctors and your deans
> Shall not avail you when the day-beam sports
> New-risen over awakened Albion—No,
> Nor yet your solemn organ-pipes that blow
> Melodious thunders through your vacant courts
> At morn and even; for your manner sorts
> Not with this age, nor with the thoughts that roll,
> Because the words of little children preach
> Against you,—ye that did profess to teach
> And have taught nothing, feeding on the soul.

Tennyson has taken the measure of traditional learning and good breeding and found them utterly wanting. Cambridge here stands for the Establishment, worldly power, pomp and circumstance; and it is sharply confronted with the new world that is dawning, which is the world of science, of enlightenment, and happiness for all, but also a world in which the voices of children will have more power, more resonance, than those of dons and pundits. The reference is evidently taken from the gospel: "Suffer the little children to come unto me, and forbid them not, for of such is the kingdom of God"; or perhaps Tennyson was thinking of a passage from the psalms: "Instead of thy fathers shall be thy children, whom thou mayest make princes in all the earth." Yet the tenor of this poem is clearly not theological but very much of this earth: anti-institutional and emphatic about the innocence of primary perception as a necessary precondition for the earthly paradise.

There are four poems which, in different ways and with varying degrees of success, show Tennyson's fully matured utopian views. All are taken from the poet's posthumous volume, *The Death of Oenone*. The first poem, "The Dawn," still employs very liberally the mode of question but observe how forceful the questions have become, and how specific; how much territory of human experience is compassed and how urgent and relevant are the answers that flow from the questions the poet asks. I am quoting these poems not as indubitable masterpieces but rather as intense experiments in vision, flawed but quite magnificent in places, and as honest and straightforward as Tennyson, given the limitations I have mentioned, could make them.

* * *

Like the poem, "The Dawn," this ["The Making of Man"] is a poem about cultural evolution, or rather about what might be called cultural "hominization," for man is still essentially unfinished, Tennyson holds, merely the shadow of what he might eventually become. The view is close to that of Teilhard de Chardin and also to that of many Marxist philosophers; a view fostered by the pain of seeing the sharp discrepancy between man's social potentialities and his actual ineptitude in building a social order of global scope. Tennyson envisages a self-made and self-regulating society in which all peoples and races would share equally, and though he renders homage to God at the end of the poem, this can hardly be taken for more than an act of courtesy. For it is man, not God, who has been the instrument of this utopian evolution; Tennyson makes that quite clear in the body of the poem, and there is no cogent reason why God should have been brought in to watch mankind perfect himself, or why he should receive thanks after the process is finished. Be that as it may, the inconsistency here is no worse than it is in Teilhard de Chardin, and the accent should be placed where it belongs: on the anthropological triumph of man, incarnating himself at last in a global community, after millennia of severalty and mutual hatred or contempt. The poem's laconic ending, "Man is made," has, for me, great power, and helps justify the meter which makes it possible; though I would hold no brief for the meter itself, for which, ever since he wrote "Locksley Hall," Tennyson maintained an inexplicable fondness.

The last poem I am going to discuss—and the last poem Tennyson wrote, at the age of 83—is called "The Dreamer." This is a curious dialogue between the poet and the orbiting earth on the point of despairing of its destiny. The poet seeks to hearten the faint-hearted planet, himself a son of the earth and yet gifted with the gift of prophecy. Again, there is some trouble here of a metrical sort, but I would ask you to concentrate on the pitch of the poet's answer, at once serene and ecstatic, much closer to the mood of Shakespeare's *Tempest* than, say, to Browning's flights of optimistic affirmation.

On a midnight in midwinter when all but the winds were dead,
"The meek shall inherit the earth" was a Scripture that rang thro'
      his head,
Till he dream'd that a Voice of the Earth went wailingly past him
      and said:

    "I am losing the light of my Youth
    And the Vision that led me of old,
    And I clash with an iron Truth,
    When I make for an Age of gold,
    And I would that my race were run,
    For teeming with liars, and madmen, and knaves,
    And wearied of Autocrats, Anarchs, and Slaves,
    And darken'd with doubts of a Faith that saves,
    And crimson with battles, and hollow with graves,
    To the wail of my winds, and the moan of my waves
    I whirl, and follow the Sun."

Was it only the wind of the Night shrilling out Desolation and
      wrong
Thro' a dream of the dark? Yet he thought that he answer'd her
      wail with a song—

    Moaning your losses, O Earth,
      Heart-weary and overdone!
    But all's well that ends well,
      Whirl, and follow the Sun!

    He is racing from heaven to heaven
      And less will be lost than won,
    For all's well that ends well,
      Whirl, and follow the Sun!

    The reign of the Meek upon earth,
      O weary one, has it begun?
    But all's well that ends well,
      Whirl, and follow the Sun!

For moans will have grown sphere-music
  Or ever your race be run!
And all's well that ends well,
  Whirl, and follow the Sun!

I don't know whether this is a great poem or not. To a reader coming to it cold, without having traced the whole course of Tennyson's poetic career, it may seem facile, almost glib; and the rushing rhythms may easily numb him to what the poet is actually saying. But I think he is saying a great deal, and saying it both subtly and movingly. The affirmative stance of the poet is not at all facile, but hard-won; and the dialectic which actuates the piece is authentic, for both the voice of the earth—wailing, despairing—and that of the poet—realistic yet at the same time strangely exultant—say all they mean, and mean all they say. Both, in short, tell the truth; or, rather, each tells that aspect of the truth it thoroughly knows. What the earth knows, and tells, is the shame of sameness, the eternal return of iniquity, war, nagging doubt, and despair; what the poet knows of a certainty is that horror and sameness can be transcended in the end. The dialectic is acted out between a universe that is merely revolving, unable to peer beyond its own rim, and an evolving universe capable of receiving intimations of novelty. The fact that any emergent novelty would still be bounded by the limits of the human condition does not detract from its value; it simply provides the authenticating hallmark of realism.

Perhaps some will feel that this is not enough, or else too much; that it is the office of the poet either to dramatize the world as we all know it, or to counter it with another world, compact of imagination and not at all resembling our painful, struggling planet—the kind of world Wallace Stevens constructs for us with such splendor. Tennyson is not the kind of poet to satisfy either hunger. His method is extrapolation, moving outward from the known to the unknown; his lens telescopic, not microscopic. He could not render the fine structure of events, nor could he answer this world with an autonomous world of his own. But he could do what not many poets have done: widen the horizon of the future by radically extending the limits of human perception and sympathy. And he could view this earth in a cosmic perspective, without trickery and without renouncing his allegiance to the earth. His vision may not have been profound, but it touches on the sublime; not only in its physical scale but also in the degree of understanding and final acceptance it implies. And if a poet can see as far as Tennyson did, and report as honestly what he has seen—the shape of things to come, truly and literally—I do not think that we can deny him the title of seer.

Tennyson and the
Theory of Evolution

GEORG ROPPEN

The Crowning Race†

To his contemporaries, Tennyson early became 'the poet of Evolution', and it was taken for granted that certain passages of *In Memoriam* anticipated both *Vestiges of Creation* and Darwin's work of 1859.[1] Tennyson himself stated that he had written 'many a poem' about the subject of *Vestiges of Creation* when he wrote to Moxon for it in 1844.[2] At that time, however, it seems improbable that evolution meant to him what it meant to Chambers and to Darwin, i. e. transmutation of species; at least there is some agreement among scholars at present that it is evolution in the idealistic, Hegelian sense which is reflected in the early poetry of Tennyson, as in that of Browning.[3] The doctrine of 'Progression' which they found in contemporary science described an ascent of organic existence in terms of intelligent, purposive creation, and the *modus operandi* in this process was to them unimportant compared with its moral meaning and the chiliastic promise it held out to humanity. Because their interest is focused on the underlying Divine power manifested in life, and on its future goal, there is an easy transition from this belief in *natura naturans* to their later acceptance of a teleological theory of transmutation. The visions of progressive, aspiring life in *In Memoriam*, in Browning's *Paracelsus* (1835) and in Hugh Clough's *Natura Naturans* (1849) might, in their general descriptive terminology, express either theory, and this accounts for

---

† From Georg Roppen, *Evolution and Poetic Belief: A Study in Some Victorian and Modern Writers*, no. 5 in *Norwegian Studies in English* (Oslo: Universitetsforlaget, 1965), pp. 83–112. Reprinted by permission of the publisher.

1. 'In *In Memoriam* Tennyson noted the fact, and a few years later Darwin supplied the explanation'; Romanes, *Darwin and After Darwin; op. cit. A Memoir*, I, p. 223.
2. *Ibid.*, I, p. 223.—His son notes that Tennyson had read the 'sections about Evolution' in *In Memoriam* some time before 1844.
3. Cf. J. Warren Beach, *The Concept of Nature in Nineteenth Century English Poetry*, p. 330; G. R. Potter, 'Tennyson and the Biological Theory of Mutability of Species', *Philological Quarterly*, 1937.

the favour which their 'evolutionary' poetry enjoyed on both sides.[4] In the following, therefore, the terms 'evolution' and 'evolutionary' will be used also of Tennyson's poetry before 1859.

In the early poems there are no certain traces of ideas referring to biological progress.[5] At Cambridge Tennyson is said to have toyed with the notion that 'the development of the human body might possibly be traced from the radiated, vermicular, molluscous and vertebrate organisms'.[6] This suggestion appears to reflect the current doctrine of 'Archetypal plan', in which the idea of progress was a central aspect. Two rejected stanzas from *The Palace of Art* (included in the 1833 and 1844 volumes) have also been quoted as evidence of Tennyson's interest in foetal development, from which he may have arrived at a belief in evolution:

> 'From shape to shape at first within the womb,
>   The brain is modelled', she began,
> 'And through all phases of all thought I come
>   Into the perfect man.
>
> All Nature widens upwards. Evermore
>   The simpler essence lower lies:
> More complex is more perfect, owning more
>   Discourse, more widely wise.'

We have seen that Tennyson's world, as it emerges from the poems, is permeated by change and natural process, from the primordial amorphous state—the 'regions of lucid matter', 'haze of light' and 'tracts of fluent heat' into the 'clusters and beds of worlds'. In *The Princess* this cosmic development is continued in a perspective reaching from 'monster' to 'man'. Similarly, *The Two Voices* outlines a historical process reminiscent of Cuvier and his theory of 'Special Creations':

> I said, "When first the world began,
> Young Nature through five cycles ran,
> And in the sixth she moulded man.

This is a reinterpretation of Genesis in terms of natural law, 'Nature' here taking the place of God. In both poems the human being is closely related to the evolving natural scheme, though he is not stated to have descended from animal species. In the eighteenth century one heard frequently of man as a 'link in being's endless chain',[7] and this idea persisted in the first half of the nineteenth as

4. On reading *The Two Voices*, Spencer sent Tennyson a copy of his *Principles of Psychology*, which, he claimed, expounded the same 'hypothesis'; cf. *A Memoir*, I, p. 411.

5. G. R. Potter rightly, it seems, denies importance to the unpublished poem from boyhood, *The Quick-wing'd Gnat*, *A Memoir*, I, p. 44, in opposition to

Lionel Stevenson's opinion in *Darwin Among the Poets*.

6. *A Memoir*, I, p. 44.—Potter here sees an influence of Von Baer's embryology, yet it is doubtful whether Tennyson knew of this at the time.

7. Cf. Young, *Night Thoughts*, 'Night the Ninth'.

embryologists and comparative anatomists continued to reconstruct the 'archetypal plan'. And as man became more definitely fitted into the organic pattern of this plan, his dualistic nature was increasingly emphasized, by the idealists in particular, since his soul could only derive from a Divine source. In *The Two Voices* the poet clings to the assumption of man's spiritual origin as an argument of cosmic purpose, while the voice of despair cynically wields the eighteenth-century argument of plenitude: Man is too imperfect to be the last goal of creation. To Pope (and to Browning) this idea was proof of sufficient reason, but to Tennyson it implies the absurdity of human existence. Man is the central fact in Tennyson's world, and every individual matters infinitely in the cosmic scheme.

In *The Two Voices* Tennyson, in his effort to explore life as a phase of spiritual existence, surveys three possibilities: The soul might have 'lapsed from nobler place', or first have been 'naked essence'; or

> ". . . if through lower lives I came—
> Though all experience past became
> Consolidate in mind and frame—

The boundaries of life are expanded through a notion of unconscious memory which somehow persists from one embodiment to another.[8] This spiritual continuity is, moreover, associated with phases of organic growth suggesting, though vaguely, a physical continuity as well.

The same expansion of life through the idea of metempsychosis is, in *In Memoriam*, given a more definite direction:

> I held it truth, with him who sings
> To one clear harp in divers tones,
> That men may rise on stepping-stones
> Of their dead selves to higher things.[9]

The spirit walks from 'state to state' in an 'eternal process', leaving behind the 'shatter'd stalks' of its mortal abode.[1] Here the insistence on man's spiritual destiny excludes a closer interest in the development of physical aspects. In *The Princess*, however, we are told that 'the brain was like the hand, and grew with using', and this Lamarckian idea refers not, it would seem, to the individual, but to the human race as a whole. Physical growth here, as in the omitted stanzas from *The Palace of Art*, illustrates mental development. Lady Psyche's lecture expounds in an impersonal manner a view of cosmic evolution such as a contemporary naturalist might have

8. It is probable, as Potter suggests, that this idea refers to the transmigration of souls, recurrent in Tennyson's poetry.
9. i.
1. lxxxii.

stated it without reference to final causes: Man is a link in the great chain of being, and testifies to the universal progress. Later, as the problem of man's place in Nature becomes all-important and moves into the tormented world of *In Memoriam*, this confident view dissolves into a perplexed question:

> And he, shall, he,
>
> > Man, her last work, who seem'd so fair,
> > > Such splendid purpose in his eyes,
> > > Who roll'd the psalm to wintry skies,
> > Who built him fanes of fruitless prayer,
>
> > Who trusted God was love indeed,
> > > And love Creation's final law—
> > > Though Nature, red in tooth and claw
> > With ravine, shriek'd against his creed—
>
> > Who loved, who suffer'd countless ills,
> > > Who battled for the True, the Just,
> > > Be blown about the desert dust,
> > Or seal'd within the iron hills?[2]

Man represents a distinctly new adventure in the predatory animal world. Yet is he altogether different? Is he primarily an immortal soul? Or is he merely a being mocked by his aspirations and doomed to perish utterly like the fossils of former life? The poet turns away from this vision of 'discord' and does not face the enigma again until the purgatory of grief lies behind him. As peace comes to his mind, the vision changes,[3] Man is still seen as the work of Nature and of Time, but his spiritual being is vindicated with a new assurance:

> > Contemplate all this work of Time,
> > > The giant labouring in his youth;
> > > Nor dream of human love and truth,
> > As dying Nature's earth and lime;
>
> > But trust that those we call the dead
> > > Are breathers of an ampler day
> > > For ever nobler ends. They say
> > The solid earth whereon we tread
>
> > In tracts of fluent heat began,
> > > And grew to seeming-random forms,
> > > The seeming prey of cyclic storms,
> > Till at the last arose the man;
>
> > Who throve and branch'd from clime to clime,
> > > The herald of a higher race,

2. lvi.
3. In section ciii two evolutionary ideas occur, casually thrown in: that of the 'great race, which is to be', and the 'shaping of a star'.

And of himself in higher place,
If so he type this work of time

Within himself, from more to more;
    Or, crown'd with attributes of woe
    Like glories, move his course, and show
That life is not as idle ore,

But iron dug from central gloom,
    And heated hot with burning fears,
    And dipt in baths of hissing tears,
And batter'd with the shocks of doom

To shape and use. Arise, and fly
    The reeling Faun, the sensual feast;
    Move upward, working out the beast,
And let the ape and tiger die.[4]

The idea of cosmic evolution is here implicitly accepted. It is traced, as in *The Princess*, from stellar phases of development, and emphasis is throughout on progress in Nature and in man. Though efficient and final causes are not involved, the poet sheds, in the first stanzas, an indirect light on the evolutionary process: existence is the working out of a seminal principle of spirit, manifesting itself as striving, ascent—a purposive urge towards nobler life.

The Nebular Hypothesis and the theory of Catastrophism have left traces in the third stanza, in a pattern balanced between the enigma of: chance or direction? Physical nature yields no answer. Yet as man enters the scene, this ambiguity ceases, and even the 'seeming-random forms' become part of a creative purpose. Again man is seen as the last work of Nature, though how he 'arose' is not explained, probably because to Tennyson, as to Lyell, it remained a mystery. Man, however, gives to the evolutionary perspective a clear direction: he is the crowning evidence that life has a meaning, he is the shaft of light sunk to its dim origins beyond our knowledge, and he points our race to a greater future, which will be the fulfilment of his noblest aspirations. This is a historical process; but likewise in eternity the human soul will rise to higher levels of existence in an ascent that continues and completes the progress in time. The fourth stanza builds up and connects the transcendence-structure of the second stanza with that of evolution in the third.

The attainment of this double goal depends on man's moral effort. He must 'type' or re-enact the cosmic development in himself, from 'more to more'. The poet sees him as a microcosm capable of repeating the universal and phylogenetic progress, by conscious striving, and by turning to good account the emotional purgatory

4. cxviii.

of his existence.[5] The ambiguities of the fourth and fifth stanzas do not impede the general unity of tone and argument: Existence is a real, historical development, though at the same time it is but a phase in the universal ascent of spirit, and man partakes in this, body and soul. Man is the outcome of a catharsis purifying life and elevating it from its lowest levels, its 'central gloom', to the highest values that man is capable of enjoying: love and truth. The universal law, as manifested in evolution, is 'from more to more', and if man conforms to this law on earth, his effort will shape out a 'higher race' in the future, and enable him to ascend in eternity to a 'higher place'. The two goals are thus seen as different aspects of the way of the soul, one racial and one individual, interacting with one another in a mutual advance.

In the fifth stanza the distinctive 'Or' seems to break the thought-structure by implying these alternatives: *either* man should follow the course of Nature, which appears as predetermined, *or* be guided by his suffering.[6] In the context of the poem, however, no such opposition between the two courses exists, and it is reasonable to see the function of 'Or' as an emphasis, rather than as a choice. At this point a greater awareness of human suffering forces the poet's vision in a new direction, so that the development is felt to be, above all, a purgatory of man's emotional nature. Thus with man, evil and pain receive a new significance, as instruments of working out his animal, baser self. The central experience of *In Memoriam*, here condensed into the words 'fears' and 'tears' and the imagery of plastic and purifying process, moves from the individual stance into the universal destiny of the human race, through a clearer perception of teleological development. In the final stanza, the reconciliation of man with his purpose takes the form of a direct moral exhortation, and its dynamic, vertical movement built up on 'Arise', 'fly' and 'move upward', visualizes an ultimate evolutionary liberation from the animal chain.

This poem (cxviii.) shows clearly the meaning which Tennyson reads into the idea of evolution, and how it effects his vision of the world. It does not disperse his Chaos, for only his faith, or hope,

5. A. C. Bradley comments on the difficulties of this passage, beginning with 'if so he type', and suggests that 'type' means 'repeat': there are 'two possible ways by which man can repeat the work of time within himself and so advance on earth and elsewhere,—the one is steady thriving and adding more to more; . . the other painful struggle'; *Commentary on Tennyson's In Memoriam*, p. 215. J. C. Collins reads 're-produce' for 'type', and agrees in the main with the interpretation of Bradley; *In Memoriam, The Princess, Maud*, p. 127. G. R. Potter claims that 'type' means 'parallel': man may parallel the cosmic process, but he is not part of it, since the evolution is a *natura naturans; op. cit.*—This distinction would seem to be somewhat artificial in view of the place occupied by man in the evolutionary pattern in the third stanza, and the purgatory structure, including all life, of the three final ones.

6. A. C. Bradley notes that 'Or' reads 'And' in the first edition, which indicates that Tennyson originally had no sharp distinction in mind; *Commentary*, p. 214.

that love is Creation's final law, can reassure him of the purpose and significance of life. Yet, having achieved this certainty, as far as he is able to, evolution offers strong evidence of a Divine plan in the ordered and progressive growth of life to higher levels. It speaks, moreover, of the triumph of life over death, of the glory of human effort and endurance, of fulfilment in life and in eternity. Now that Chaos has ceased, the force of evolution in the poet's cosmos is seen as an impetus thrown out towards two great goals of human aspiration. Within the framework of this idealistic and mystical belief, the question whether the idea expressed by Tennyson in *In Memoriam* is transmutation or *natura naturans* would seem to be of minor consequence.[7]

The recurrence of the evolution-theme in the Epilogue is an indication that it is beginning to assume a profounder and more vital significance in Tennyson's belief. Here the moral exhortation in the final stanza of section cxviii is developed into a prophecy of the new human life, in which the individual soul participates as a creative energy, and illumines the destiny of the race:

> A soul shall draw from out the vast
> And strike his being into bounds,
>
> And, moved through life of lower phase,
>   Result in man, be born and think,
>   And act and love, a closer link
> Betwixt us and the crowning race
>
> Of those that, eye to eye, shall look
>   On knowledge; under whose command
>   Is Earth and Earth's, and in their hand
> Is Nature like an open book;
>
> No longer half-akin to brute,
>   For all we thought, and loved, and did,
>   And hoped, and suffer'd, is but seed
> Of what in them is flower and fruit;
>
> Whereof the man, that with me trod
>   This planet, was a noble type
>   Appearing ere the times were ripe,
> That friend of mine who lives in God—
>
> That God, which ever lives and loves,
>   One God, one law, one element,
>   And one far-off divine event,
> To which the whole creation moves.[8]

7. G. Hough suspects the influence of *Vestiges of Creation* on this poem, and points out the contrast between this section and liv—lvi, which he explains by the transition in Tennyson's reading from Lyell to Chambers; 'The Natural Theology of *In Memoriam*', *Review of English Studies*, 1947–8.
8. W. Rutland thinks that *Vestiges of Creation* may have influenced Tennyson

In 'life of lower phase' there is probably a statement of Von Baer's 'Recapitulation'-theory: the ontogenesis repeats the phylogenesis.[9] The predominant trend is, however, the Platonic idea of spirit or soul flowing into matter and urging life upwards through various phases of growth. Through the connective action of 'link', the word which stands, as it were, at the centre of the thought-structure, the universal progress of life is seen moving from its 'lower phase', through man, towards the crowning race of the future.[1] It is a historical, cumulative process: Man as yet is half-akin to brute, but through his intellectual effort and emotional purgatory, he will be freed in the future from the animal chain. The form and content of Tennyson's 'crowning race' prophecy is dictated partly by his emotional and intellectual aspiration, partly by the grief for his friend, who, as he elsewhere states—'bore without abuse/The grand old name of gentleman . . .' who was 'Seraphic intellect', and 'High nature amorous of the good'[2]. This 'noble type' predicts a fulfilment of the best features in man. In the final stanza, however, the prophecy points beyond this 'crowning race' to a transcendent goal in which all existence will find consummation. The idea appears to be a development of the corresponding pattern in section cxviii, in that it foreshadows not only an ascent to a 'higher place' in eternity, but an ultimate arrival.

In *De Profundis*, written in 1852 and published in the *Ballads* volume of 1880, Tennyson returns to the evolutionary theme of the Epilogue:

> Out of the deep, my child, out of the deep,
> Where all that was to be, in all that was,
> Whirl'd for a million æons thro' the vast
> Waste dawn of multitudinous-eddying light—
> Out of the deep, my child, out of the deep,
> Thro' all this changing world of changeless law,
> And every phase of ever-heightening life,
> And nine long months of antenatal gloom,
> With this last moon, this crescent—her dark orb
> Touch'd with earth's light—thou comest, darling boy;

here, and discusses the chronological problem; 'Tennyson and the Theory of Evolution', *Essays and Studies*, 1940, vol. xxvi. The same view is argued by G. Hough, who finds in these stanzas an impact stronger even than in cxviii; *op. cit.* It would appear, however, that in supposing *Vestiges* to have relieved Tennyson of the pessimism, due, it is thought, to Lyell's *Principles of Geology*, one pays scant heed to the deeper and more personal experience through which the poet lived while at work on

In Memoriam.
9. Thus A. C. Bradley, *op. cit.*, p. 239, and G. R. Potter, on the authority of W. North Price, *op. cit.*
1. W. Rutland sees a striking resemblance between the 'crowning race' and a similar prophecy in *Vestiges of Creation*, p. 276: 'Is our race but the initial of the grand crowning type?' Yet Tennyson had used 'great race' already in ciii, dated by Bradley to 1837, *Commentary*, p. 15.
2. cxi, cix.

Our own; a babe in lineament and limb
Perfect, and prophet of the perfect man . . .

Cosmic evolution, in a pattern composed of Platonism, modern
cosmogony (Nebular Hypothesis) and biological 'Progression' again
forms the background of the embryological growth of an individual
which repeats this evolution through phases of 'ever-heightening
life'. Both processes stem from a common source, and the passage
through 'this changing world of changeless law' does not necessarily
imply a historical, organic transmutation, but certainly, seen in
connexion with the following line, implies progressive development.
It either means that the child achieves existence in the spiritual
world, the 'deep', in a process analogous to that of cosmic evolution,
which it merely reflects, in an ideal sense, or it may mean that the
child has a double origin, the 'deep' from which the soul directly
emerges, and the physical, organic process which brings forth the
human body from lower forms. In this last reading Tennyson's out-
look would approach to the views of organic evolution later held by
Wallace and Lyell.

The poem is vague in its blending of transcendent and im-
manent aspects, and the general impact is that of *natura naturans*.
It is probable however, that the idea of 'ever-heightening life'
should be connected with the 'perfect man' anticipation in a
coherent evolutionary structure, similar to that in the Epilogue. In
the perspective here opened up the process of ascending life assumes
a real and historical meaning. Yet, clearly, the question whether it
takes place through special creations or transmutation is not in-
volved.

Tennyson's treatment of the theme of cosmic evolution in *The
Two Voices, The Princess, In Memoriam* and *De Profundis* shows
that to him it contains less of directive metaphysical thought than
of spiritual aspiration and quest for life. If it confirms his belief in
purposive and providential creation, and a universal principle of
love, it is largely because the development reveals an increasing
presence of mind and moral consciousness in the world. In these
realities, too, he sees the strongest proof of the immortality of the
soul: of the 'ever nobler ends' for which man is bound. Conversely,
these are also evidence against the 'cunning casts in clay' that
materialistic science makes of human beings. Hence his exhortation
to moral effort; for the working out of the beast, the attainment to
the perfect man and finally to the 'full new life', whether in time
or in eternity, depends in no small degree on human striving. This
tendency to charge the evolutionary theme with a moral content is
explicit already in *In Memoriam*, and is next woven into the medita-
tion of the young man in *Maud:*

A monstrous eft was of old the Lord and Master of Earth,
For him did his high sun flame, and his river billowing ran,
And he felt himself in his force to be Nature's crowning race.
As nine months go to the shaping an infant ripe for his birth,
So many a million of ages have gone to the making of man:
He now is first, but is he the last? is he not too base?[3]

In this poem Tennyson finds more precise use for the Recapitulation theory: it now works as an analogy defining and limiting the concept of growth as applied directly to the evolution of the human race. Possibly by this year (1855) he had come to adopt the ideas expounded in V*estiges of Creation*, and at the same time Spencer's bold defence of the 'Development Hypothesis' in *The Leader* (1852) might have been known to him and helped to clarify his own belief.[4] Man is seen as the outcome of a slow and continuous process; the ontogenesis repeats the phylogenesis in a millionth fraction of time, and testifies clearly to the progressive direction in organic development. In *Maud* the ambiguity which still remains is due to the uncertain meaning of the 'eft'-image. If 'monstrous eft' means literally a prehistoric animal, then the poet implies that man has actually developed from such a creature, and the pre-natal growth of the foetus illustrates in a real sense the various stages of his evolution. In that case, Tennyson's outlook has become more 'naturalistic' since he wrote in *The Princess* of the successive appearances of 'then the monster, then the man'. If, on the other hand, 'eft' is merely a symbol of the brutish amoral nature of primitive man, the development is one of emotional and intellectual faculties within the human species. This reading, however, would surrender the analogy of foetal growth, which is here the very clue to the creative mystery, and it is reasonable to think that in *Maud* Tennyson for the first time has consciously expressed a belief in the transmutation of species. Yet his main interest, here as in the earlier poems, is focused on the moral nature of man capable of improvement. While *In Memoriam* derives from cosmic evolution, from the increasing presence of soul in the world, and from the effects of emotional purgatory, a promise of the 'higher race', *Maud* is a negative approach, and its tone and feeling lend to the argument an aspect of nausea with existing things, and a contempt for man: Man is too *base* to remain the crowning achievement in Nature. The same idea emerged as a theme of despair in *The Two Voices*, rooted in a different emotional experience. Here the young soliloquist in his universal spleen judges man by eighteenth-century

3. IV, vi.
4. W. Rutland finds in *Maud* a direct influence from *Vestiges* in the idea of the 'crowning race'; *op. cit.—Vestiges* *of Creation*, it will be remembered, used the Recapitulation theory as a defence of transmutation and as an argument to overcome emotional prejudice.

principles of sufficient reason and plenitude: If the human being is bound to develop, it is not only because he has, in fact, greatly changed in the past, but because he falls short of an ideal of perfection inherent in the cosmic scheme. This ideal, seen through the word 'base', is essentially a moral destination. As a corollary, an important directive principle in evolution is ethical necessity.[5]

After *Origin of Species* had appeared, and Tennyson got the reassuring answer from its author to his question: 'Your theory of Evolution does not make against Christianity?', it was still this moral and spiritual significance of the evolutionary process which held his interest.[6] He remained, on the whole, undisturbed by the remoter philosophical implications of Darwin's thesis, and did not take part in the controversy, though in one or two of his later poems there are oblique references to it. Much in the same spirit as F. D. Maurice and Charles Kingsley, Tennyson adapted the new doctrine to his fundamental idealistic belief:

> That makes no difference to me, even if the Darwinians did not, as they do, exaggerate Darwinism. To God all is present. He sees present, past, and future as one.[7]

Like Lyell, he moved naturally from a progressionist standpoint to one of teleological evolution, convinced that in cosmic and organic process works a power from which the individual soul emanates and of which it is an imperishable part. He saw

> Life of Nature as a lower stage in the manifestation of a principle which is more fully manifested in the spiritual life of man, with the idea that in this process of Evolution the lower is to be regarded as a means to the higher.[8]

Tennyson's attitude to the problem of man's place in Nature is stamped by the spiritual, idealistic meaning he reads into the evolutionary process, and he states it also in negative terms similar to those of Lyell and the neo-Lamarckians:

> No evolutionist is able to explain the mind of Man or how any possible physiological change of tissue can produce conscious thought.[9]

---

5. Cf. *A Memoir*, I, p. 324: 'The answer he would give to this query ['He now is first, but is he the last?'] was: "No, mankind is as yet on one of the lowest rungs of the ladder, although every man has and has had from everlasting his true and perfect being in the Divine Consciousness."

6. *Loc. cit.*, *A Memoir*, II, p. 57. It is not probable that, as G. R. Potter contends, Tennyson's question proves that he was unfamiliar with the idea before Darwin's publication. He knew of evolutionary ideas even before *Vestiges of Creation*, and his question implies merely: 'Your *specific*, or *new* theory' . . etc.

7. *A Memoir*, I, p. 322; Cf. also: 'Darwinism, Man from Ape, would that really make any difference?', *ibid.* p. 514. See the striking parallelism with Browning's attitude.

8. *Ibid.*, p. 323.

9. *Ibid.*, p. 323.

The human soul derives its existence from a non-material, supra-natural source, and man thus, as the poet had vaguely indicated in *De Profundis*, has a double origin, which is merely two different facets of the Divine creative power. Evolution is the gradual fulfilment of the striving of the soul after perfection and fuller life, and it takes place in time as well as in eternity.[1] On the issue of man Tennyson deplored the standpoint of the extreme Darwinians, and he voiced, in *Despair* (1881), the sad perplexity which their denial of man's immortal soul had thrust upon his age, and perhaps, sometimes, upon himself:

> O, we poor orphans of nothing—alone on that lonely shore—
> Born of the brainless Nature who knew not that which she
>   bore!
>
> . . . .
>
> Come from the brute, poor souls—no souls—and to die with
>   the brute—

Though the statement, one feels, has no deep personal root, it is related to the emotional tension which elsewhere makes Chaos in the poet's universe. It is again the horror of a blind, clock-work process in Nature, and this time under the impact of that principle of chance—Natural Selection. The final conclusion is reached through an in-flowing of Darwinian doctrine upon his fear of death, and tinged with the pervading pessimism of the 70's and 80's. In Thomas Hardy, as we shall see, similar visions, derived from the same sources of despair, had already from 1866 (*Hap*) formed integral parts of his consistently fatalistic belief.

The attack on Darwinism in *Despair* is levelled against the agnostic and materialistic formulation of the theory which tended to banish soul and intelligent plan from the universe. In general, however, evolution, in the sense of expansion and progress of life, remained to Tennyson a source of optimism, and a buttress to his Cosmos. It becomes a theme of life-assertive prophecy, as when *The Ancient Sage* (*Tiresias* volume 1885) anticipates that the creative power—'That which knows',

>   shall descend
> On this half-deed, and shape it at the last
> According to the Highest in the Highest.

In evolution there is a proof that the human race is bound, by law of Nature, to ascend to higher levels of life. It does not, indeed, explain evil and imperfection, but it reveals man as participator in a great cosmic enterprise, a pilgrimage upwards through the ages,

---

1. Cf. *A Memoir*, I, p. 321: 'I can hardly understand, how any great, imaginative man, who has deeply lived, suffered, thought and wrought, can doubt of the Soul's continuous progress in the after-life'.

and a future bright with promise. It sanctions, moreover, the belief in social and material progress so dear to the age. Tennyson wanted to share this faith, yet here too his attitude is often one of doubt and vacillation. He was, temperamentally, a troubadour of the past, of *In Memoriam*, of King Arthur and Ulysses. His delight in the gains of industrial and material progress suffered intrusion from regrets of things ancient and treasured which were, or would be, swept away. The world he loved was in danger of sinking, like Arthur's Lyonesse, into the abyss for ever.

It has been observed that Tennyson's conservative bent was not just this loyalty to the past, but a distrust in truths untried which might lead to strange gods and dead ends of anarchy. However, to dispel this threat of chaos, the idea of evolution points the movement to the 'crowning race' and reassures him that the world is 'wholly fair'. In the first *Locksley Hall* Tennyson is in search of a directive principle:

> Yet I doubt not through the ages one increasing purpose runs,
> And the thoughts of men are widen'd with the process of the
>   suns.

In the bewilderment of the second *Locksley Hall*, as in *In Memoriam*, the principle is seen emerging despite evil and pain:

> Is there evil but on earth? or pain in every peopled sphere?
> Well be grateful for the sounding watchword 'Evolution' here.

Yet, if the general direction is clear, human progress is often thwarted and apparently futile. It is again the drama of Cosmos and Chaos:

> Evolution ever climbing after some ideal good,
> And Reversion ever dragging Evolution in the mud.

In this poem as in *The Ancient Sage*, the Divine power is invoked to assert its purpose: 'A God must mingle with the game.' Thus Tennyson's evolutionary belief continues to interact with his religion as with his ethics. His prophetic vision ranges forward to a 'warless world, a single race, a single tongue' when man has outgrown his base nature:

> Every tiger madness muzzled, every serpent passion kill'd.

This moral message is the sole theme of *By An Evolutionist* (1888). It visualizes a conflict between man and animal, spirit and flesh:

> The Lord let the house of a brute to the soul of a man,
>   And the man said 'Am I your debtor?'
> And the Lord—'Not yet: but make it as clean as you can,
>   And then I will let you a better.'

The stanza illustrates well Tennyson's moral reading of evolution. It is a variation on the purgatory theme of *In Memoriam* (cxviii) which marks a significant change of psychological emphasis in that it, contrary to the naturalistic doctrine, dwells on man's dualistic nature and the widening cleavage between his physical and spiritual instincts. Evolution, in Darwin's theory, implied an integration of all faculties and instincts with man's animal past and with his physical nature: man is a purely natural being. As this integration threatened to swamp the reality of his soul, it was counteracted by Christians and neo-Lamarckian scholars who offered an alternative teleological formulation of the theory. It seems to be this religious effort that makes its impact on Tennyson's frank sermon on Evolution. The second stanza of the poem adduces an argument for the pleasures of the 'brute'—a kind of Epicurean logic drawn from the possibility that the life of the flesh is the only one, so: eat and drink, for to-morrow we die!

> If my body come from brutes, my soul uncertain or a fable,
>   Why not bask amid the senses while the sun of morning shines.

For creatures that are nothing but mechanical products of Natural Selection, nothing but 'cunning casts in clay', extreme materialism and sensualism seems indeed the rational way of life. Few of the naturalists, and least of all Darwin and Huxley had accepted this as a corollary of the biological facts, and they repeatedly asserted that the instincts of man, though 'natural', are not all of them necessarily 'good'. Yet evolutionary ideas were increasingly adopted in the utilitarian and naturalistic doctrines of ethics and furnished some of the main arguments to those who sought to establish a code of conduct, and a theory of values, on a scientific and sociological basis. This aggressive materialism, Tennyson feared, would lead to a disintegration of moral consciousness and brutalize man. In *The Promise of May* (1884) Edgar, the villain, personifies the cynical modern sophist who makes his 'natural' instincts and the new scientific theory an excuse for licentious living:

> And when the man,
> The child of evolution, flings aside
> His swaddling-bands, the morals of the tribe,
> He, following his own instincts as his God,
> Will enter on the larger golden age;
> No pleasure there taboo'd . . .

To fight this vicious attitude, human experience, wisdom, Old Age in *By An Evolutionist*, assures us that the moral effort of a life-time is not futile: it is necessary to starve the 'wild beast' with which we are 'linkt' in a youth of reckless cravings, for only thus can we reach our spiritual destination, and fulfil our great task:

If my body come from brutes, tho' somewhat finer than their
own,
  I am heir, and this my kingdom. Shall the royal voice be
  mute?
No, but if the rebel subject seek to drag me from the throne,
  Hold the sceptre, Human Soul, and rule thy Province of the
  brute.

This moral challenge casts back to *In Memoriam* (cxviii), but the
stanza is essentially about the restoration of man to spiritual dignity
and kingship. It contains an oblique attack on materialistic ethics,
and reads like a belated comment on the 'Man's place in Nature'-
controversy of the 1860's. The radical movement headed by Huxley
had 'degraded' man—dethroned him from his sovereign place in
Nature. It was imperative to reassert that man is indeed heir to
something more than 'the Province of the brute', that his soul has
royal command over the rebel subject of the flesh. The stanza seeks
to build up, in majestic size, a portrait of the ideal man as Tennyson
saw him; the man who 'bore without abuse/The grand old name
of gentleman'. Human dignity and nobility, the glory and greatness
of moral effort—it was necessary to insist on these threatened
values in the teeth of agnostic science and utilitarian ethics. The
wisdom of Old Age has something to say about the meaning and
rewards of the struggle:

I have climb'd to the snows of Age, and I gaze at a field in the
Past,
  Where I sank with the body at times in the sloughs of a low
  desire,

But I hear no yelp of the beast, and the Man is quiet at last,
  As he stands on the heights of his life with a glimpse of a
  height that is higher.

In two of Tennyson's last poems about Evolution, *The Dawn*
and *The Making of Man* emphasis is again on this moral and
spiritual progress. Though less direct in their exhortation to the
good life than *By An Evolutionist*, these too are built on an obvious
moral programme. Human evil is a predominant theme, and notably
in *The Dawn* the baroque verbal fury and strained imagery mark,
rather sadly, the change in Tennyson's treatment of the cosmic
theme since *The Two Voices* and *In Memoriam*. It seeks to drama-
tize the role of man in his evolutionary advance through a close
contemplation of evil, similar to the denunciations of *Vastness*,
but with this difference that here the misery of mankind is seen as
a phase that is slowly yielding to brighter prospects. The poet
surveys history as a nightmare panorama of infanticide, cannibalism,
holocausts, war and destruction. But, looking ahead, he finds that

the oppressive darkness is lifting, to reveal an upward movement: we are reminded of the struggle of Old Age (*By An Evolutionist*) climbing to the 'snows of age' from the 'sloughs of low desire'. In a universal perspective, here too is a movement from animal to man, death to life:

> Dawn not Day!
> Is it Shame, so few should have climb'd from the dens in the level below,
> Men, with a heart and a soul, no slaves of a four-footed will?
> But if twenty million of summers are stored in the sunlight still,
> We are far from the noon of man, there is time for the race to grow.
>
> Red of the Dawn!
> Is it turning a fainter red? so be it, but when shall we lay
> The Ghost of the Brute that is walking and haunting us yet, and be free?
> In a hundred, a thousand winters? Ah, what will *our* children be,
> The men of a hundred thousand, a million summers away?

The underlying impulse is still a craving for abundant life, and perfect happiness, for the race as for the individual. Yet the poet is going back on his old tracks and the pattern has become stereotype: there is no imaginative growth, no chiliastic concretion, no uprush of vision or theory. His question appears to beat in vain upon the future, as it did in *Locksley Hall Sixty Years After*:

> Far away beyond her myriad coming changes earth will be
> Something other than the wildest modern guess of you and me.

The same vagueness of anticipation persists in *The Making of Man*, which repeats the pattern of the final stanza of *The Dawn*:

> Where is one that, born of woman, altogether can escape
> From the lower world within him, moods of tiger, or of ape?
> Man as yet is being made, and ere the crowning Age of ages,
> Shall not æon after æon pass and touch him into shape?
>
> All about him shadow still, but, while the races flower and fade,
> Prophet-eyes may catch a glory slowly gaining on the shade,
> Till the peoples all are one, and all their voices blend in choric
> Hallelujah to the Maker 'It is finish'd. Man is made.'

The structure is lacking in inventiveness, for even the positive assertion of the second stanza is nothing but a reiteration of ideas similarly expressed in the two *Locksley Hall* poems: The goal of evolutionary progress on earth is peace and harmony—a 'federation of the world', and the 'crowning Age', more so than the 'crowning race' prophecy, foreshadows a moral attainment. This feature has not, however, gained in sharpness of definition, and it betrays a singular lack of imaginative challenge, which may be due to Tennyson's emotional conservatism. His ideal is all the time the 'perfect man'—a being of sweetness and light. Thus instead of preaching the superman, Tennyson rather tends to insist that man is not yet 'man', not yet 'made' or perfected into the 'shape and use' which he is meant to be, and which evolution seeks to realize.

The vast time-perspective which evolution always cuts into ages past and future, is a salient feature in Tennyson's later poems, as in those of earlier years. The process is infinitely slow, and takes *æons* to complete its successive tasks:

> Many an Æon moulded earth before her highest, man, was born . . .[2]

And yet, the past is as nothing to the future: in this certainty Tennyson finds a paradox:

> For we are Ancients of the earth,
> And in the morning of the times.[3]

The Princess advises patience with 'this fine old world', since it is still 'a child in the go-cart'. Man is heir to much imperfection, to pain and weakness and 'tiger spasms,' but, as the Ancient Sage assumes, 'this earth-narrow life' may be 'but yolk, and forming in the shell'. Similarly, the old man in *Locksley Hall Sixty Years After* anticipates future world harmony: 'for is not Earth as yet so young?' *The Dawn* explores infinite vistas of future ages, and trusts that, in the period calculated for this running down solar system to last, 'there is time for the race to grow'. Man has just begun his pilgrimage, and ahead of him there is almost unending adventure. In these prophecies Tennyson clearly, and it would seem deliberately, speaks as a representative of his age, for the idea of the perfectibility of man was one particularly dear to the Victorian, and could be shared by agnostics and Christians alike. Thus Stuart Mill made it the very basis for his religion of Humanity:

> Let it be remembered that if individual life is short, the life of the human species is not short; its indefinite duration is practically equivalent to endlessness; and being combined with indefinite capability of improvement, it offers to the imagination and sympathies a large enough object to satisfy any reasonable demand for grandeur of aspiration.[4]

2. *Locksley Hall Sixty Years After.*
3. *The Golden Year.*
4. 'The Utility of Religion', *Three Essays on Religion* (1874), p. 106.

In *The Making of Man* the poet returns to his favourite time-image—the 'æon'. In a sense he is, in this poem and in *The Dawn*, doing for the human race what he struggled to achieve for himself in *In Memoriam*; to expand life into eternity. Since the race shall have life and evolutionary growth in 'æon after æon', then the time-process, with its tragic inevitability of transience and death loses some of its frightening aspect. Without the belief in continued life for the individual after death, this thought would have been merely a philosophical consolation, but clutching at this assurance, Tennyson is able to identify his own life-zest with that of mankind and glory in its future greatness. Symbolized by the 'æon', temporal existence becomes, as it were, eternalized, and the evolution of man is felt as a process that somehow will bridge the two realities, heaven and earth, in its ultimate attainment. More life, not beatitude, is his answer to the 'black negation of the bier', which even the Ancient Sage hates. Hence the fusion of immanent and transcendent existence in *In Memoriam* through the spiritual ascent by which men rise 'on stepping-stones/Of their dead selves to higher things'. This theme recurs in the late poem, *The Ring*: There is

> No sudden heaven, nor sudden hell, for man,
> But thro' the Will of One who knows and rules—
> And utter knowledge is but utter love—
> Æonian Evolution, swift or slow,
> Thro' all the Spheres—an ever opening height,
> An ever lessening earth—

And thus, with temporal and spatial boundaries opened, there is free play for the expansion of life, from this 'earth-narrow' scene (*The Ancient Sage*) to unlimited growth and fulfilment in other forms and modes of existence. *The Ring* makes a condensed and precise statement of ideas more incoherently expressed in *In Memoriam*[5] of the continuous ascent of the individual soul in eternity. Here, once more, the underlying horror of death—less obvious but still corroding at the poet's Cosmos, is translated into a vision of life everlasting and triumphant. In this victorious mood, with its attendant certainty of the direction unfailingly pursued by life, Tennyson raises the promise of Evolution at the head of the movement. In no other passage or poem has he used the concept in the same explicit way—as a focal point to organize the poetic structure into a meaningful, coherent whole.

Perhaps, as T. S. Eliot claims, Tennyson never quite emerged from the torment and conflict of *In Memoriam*. It is undoubtedly true that there is no final reconciliation or resolution—no Cosmos once and for all replacing the Chaos, for Tennyson's belief is emo-

5. i. lxxxii, cf. also *A Memoir*, I, p. 321.

tional, not intellectual, and his vision of the world changes with the changing fortunes of his faith and doubt—hope and fear. Yet there is an increasing certainty and a prevalence of faith, and it seems gratuitous to explain this greater serenity by a failure or refusal to confront the implications of Chaos. As theology, as dogma and doctrine, his 'Cosmos' is a shaky structure, but as effort and aspiration, it is great and valid, and it informs some of his best and most vigorous poetry.

In his own day, both scientists and the educated public gave Tennyson credit for having pioneered the idea of evolution, and few of them realized that he was the heir of a tradition as well as a representative of his time and a prophet of the future. His position, in so far as his belief might be related to any body of doctrine, is somewhere between the neo-Platonism of the eighteenth century and the biological theory of Nature advanced in the nineteenth, and his intuitive achievement is to express a synthesis of the two at a time when science, in general, was striking out on a single-minded materialist track. From eighteenth century thought, as reflected in the Idealistic systems of *natura naturans*, he received, mainly through Coleridge, a vision of Nature as the manifestation of a world of spirit—'that true world within the world we see'; and in the poets of that century he found this cosmic belief persistently focused on the growing perfection of life and the unfolding of mind upwards in the 'scale of being'.[6] These poets often gave a very precise formulation to their faith in the rational, purposive order of the universe. To them, however, this order was a static, hierarchical whole, complete and sufficient unto itself. Tennyson, moving with the growing insight of his time, came to see the ideal, fixed system as development and a historical process. Even so, he retained the fundamental concept of philosophical Idealism, i.e. the world as an embodiment of spirit or mind. This implied both an insistence upon the non-material source of all being, and a teleological interpretation of the evolutionary process. For it seemed unthinkable that the increasing presence of mind in the cosmic scheme, so fully manifested in man, could be anything but the gradual attainment of a purpose—a taking possession of matter by mind to some definite end. It is true that, according to the principle of plenitude in the metaphysical speculations of the eighteenth century, man was not the crowning achievement in Creation: he was, according to Pope, placed in a 'middle state', and according to Young, 'Midway from nothing to the deity'. Yet, though other, more perfect beings were thought to exist in the universe, he was, on earth, the creature which above all others proved the excellence and purpose of the

---

6. Thus in Pope's *Essay*, Akenside's *Pleasures of the Imagination,* Young's *Night Thoughts.*

creative plan. 'If man were taken away from the world, the rest would seem to be all astray, without aim or purpose, . . . and leading to nothing'.[7] This statement by Bacon in the seventeenth century, but still as valid in the eighteenth, reads like a paraphrase of an important and recurrent theme in Tennyson's poetry. His spiritual plight, and the agony which doubt and death thrust upon him, made of the poet of *In Memoriam* a crusader for man's soul, against of the 'man machine', and against the evolutionary determinism the heritage of Renaissance materialism, with its late fruit, the idea which was to develop from Darwin's ideas of chance mutations and natural selection. Tennyson, in his search for Cosmos, sided with the neo-Lamarckians, who saw the process in nature as a penetration of matter by spirit and a growing command of mind over material aspects. This ancient idea had been given a suggestive Utopian formulation by Robinet in his *Vue philosophique de la gradation naturelle de l'être* (1768), in that he anticipated a time when the creative force—*la force active*—might possibly become wholly independent of matter: *Enfin elle se dématérialiserait entièrement, si j'ose ainsi m'exprimer, et pour dernière métamorphose elle se transformerait en pure intelligence.* Coleridge too forecasts a 'passing away of this Earth' and the emergence of a 'state of pure intellect'.[8] Tennyson's vision of the spiritual destiny of man is rooted in this Idealistic tradition.

The idea of evolution in Tennyson's poetry expresses an attitude and a belief which lend structural coherence—within the Chaos-Cosmos pattern—to poems set widely apart in subject-matter and time. Only to a superficial view does this poetry appear as a system or method to answer the questions of the age, in the form of a sermon or 'message' worked out in dialectic designs with antiactive forces tending towards balance and harmony, in the spirit of Hegel and Spencer. If Tennyson's poetry bears the impact of a collapse of dogmatic faith, and of the fretful search for certainty of his time, it is because he lived and struggled, often fiercely, with its questions and its fears. Tennyson's poetry about the universe and the destiny of man is important and sometimes great in the way it expresses the common lot of man within the emotional intensity and drama of the individual stance. One may regret Tennyson's lack of penetrating, consistent thought and vision, the often banal formulation of his themes of doubt and faith, and their monotonous repetition. Yet they seldom lose interest and persuasive force because they are alive with a sense of the inviolable holiness of the individual soul and the universal significance of its fate. Therefore, the lasting interest of Tennyson's poetry about the pilgrimage of life lies in his

7. Bacon, *De Sapientia Veterum, Works,*   8. *Religious Musings.*
vol. vi, p. 747.

tentative, incessant effort to integrate existence into a spiritual Cosmos—an effort that reaches its climax of force and expressiveness already in *The Two Voices* and *In Memoriam*. In these poems, as in later and minor ones, the idea of evolution is an integrative element: it helps Tennyson to escape the persecution of death by showing, in terms of historical fact, the way to a promised land of more and fuller life. This movement is the profoundest creative experience in Tennyson's poetry; and he stands therefore, not only as the 'master of melancholia', but as an ambassador of life.

Selected Bibliography

EDITIONS

The Complete Poetical Works of Tennyson, ed. W. J. Rolfe. Cambridge, Mass., 1898.
The Poems of Tennyson, ed. Christopher B. Ricks. London, 1969.
The Devil and the Lady, ed. Charles Tennyson. London, 1930.
Poems by Two Brothers, ed. Hallam Tennyson. London and New York, 1893.
Unpublished Early Poems, ed. Charles Tennyson. London, 1931.
The Works of Tennyson, ed. Hallam Tennyson. 9 vols. London, 1908. (The Eversley Edition.)

BIOGRAPHY, CONCORDANCE, BIBLIOGRAPHY

Baker, Arthur E. *A Concordance to the Poetical and Dramatic Works of Alfred, Lord Tennyson.* New York, 1914.
Baum, Paull F. "Alfred, Lord Tennyson," in *The Victorian Poets: A Guide to Research,* ed. Frederic E. Faverty. Cambridge, Mass., 1956.
Buckley, Jerome H. *Tennyson: The Growth of a Poet.* Cambridge, Mass., 1960.
Richardson, Joanna. *The Pre-Eminent Victorian.* London, 1962.
Ricks, Christopher B. *Tennyson.* New York, 1972.
Tennyson, Charles. *Alfred Tennyson.* New York, 1949.
Tennyson, Charles, and Christine Fall. *Alfred Tennyson: An Annotated Bibliography.* Athens, Ga., 1967.
Tennyson, Hallam. *Alfred Lord Tennyson: A Memoir.* 2 vols. New York, 1897.

BOOKS, CHAPTERS IN BOOKS, INTRODUCTIONS TO SELECTIONS

Auden, W. H. Introduction, *A Selection from the Poems of Alfred, Lord Tennyson.* New York, 1944.
Bagehot, Walter. "Wordsworth, Tennyson, and Browning; or, Pure, Ornate, and Grotesque Art in English Poetry," in *Literary Studies,* II. London, 1895.
Beach, Joseph Warren. *The Concept of Nature in Nineteenth-Century English Poetry.* New York, 1936.
Bradley, A. C. *A Commentary on Tennyson's In Memoriam.* Hamden, Conn., 1966. (First published 1901.)
Brashear, William R. *The Living Will: A Study of Tennyson and Nineteenth-Century Subjectivism.* The Hague, 1969.
Brooks, Cleanth. "The Motivation of Tennyson's Weeper," in *The Well Wrought Urn.* New York, 1947.
Buckley, Jerome H. *The Victorian Temper.* Cambridge, Mass., 1951.
Buckley, Jerome H. Introduction to *Poems of Tennyson.* Cambridge, Mass., 1958.
Bush, Douglas. *Science and English Poetry.* New York, 1950.
Bush, Douglas. Introduction to *Tennyson: Selected Poetry.* New York, 1951.
Johnson, E.D.H. *The Alien Vision of Victorian Poetry.* Princeton, 1952.
Langbaum, Robert. *The Poetry of Experience.* New York, 1957.
Lucas, F. L. *Ten Victorian Poets.* Cambridge, England, 1948.
Marshall, George O., Jr. *A Tennyson Handbook.* New York, 1963.
Mattes, Eleanor B. *In Memoriam: The Way of a Soul.* New York, 1951.
Paden, W. D. *Tennyson in Egypt: A Study of the Imagery in His Earlier Work.* Lawrence, Kan., 1942.
Pitt, Valerie. *Tennyson Laureate.* London, 1962.
Rader, Ralph W. *Tennyson's Maud: The Biographical Genesis.* Berkeley, 1963.
Ryals, Clyde de L. *Theme and Symbol in Tennyson's Poems to 1850.* Philadelphia, 1964.
Shannon, Edgar F. *Tennyson and the Reviewers.* Cambridge, Mass., 1952.
Stevenson, Lionel. *Darwin Among the Poets.* Chicago, 1932.
Swinburne, A. C. "Tennyson and Musset," in *Miscellanies.* London, 1911.
Tennyson, Charles. *Six Tennyson Essays.* London, 1954.
Young, G. M. "The Age of Tennyson," in *Critical Essays,* ed. John Killham. New York, 1960.

PERIODICALS

Burchell, S. C. "Tennyson's 'Allegory in the Distance,' " *PMLA,* LXVIII (1953), 418–424.

Cross, T. P. "Alfred Tennyson as a Celticist," *Modern Philology,* XVIII (1921), 485–492.

Dahl, Curtis. "A Double Frame for Tennyson's Demeter?" *Victorian Studies,* I (1958), 356–362.

Engelberg, Edward. "The Beast Image in Tennyson's *Idylls of the King,*" *ELH,* XXII (1955), 287–292.

Green, Joyce. "Tennyson's Development During the 'Ten Years' Silence' (1832–1842)," *PMLA,* LXVI (1951), 662–697.

Grob, Allen. "Tennyson's 'The Lotos-Eaters': Two Versions of Art," *Modern Philology,* LXII (1964), 118–129.

Johnson, E. D. H. " 'In Memoriam': The Way of the Poet," *Victorian Studies,* II (1958), 139–148.

Mitchell, Charles. "The Undying Will of Tennyson's 'Ulysses,' " *Victorian Poetry,* II (1964), 87–95.

McLuhan, H. M. "Tennyson and Picturesque Poetry," *Essays in Criticism,* I (1951), 262–282.

Potter, George R. "Tennyson and the Biological Theory of Mutability in Species," *P.Q.,* XVI (1937), 321–343.

Reed, John R. "The Design of Tennyson's 'The Two Voices,' " *University of Toronto Quarterly,* XXXVII (1968), 186–196.

Rutland, William R. "Tennyson and the Theory of Evolution," *Essays and Studies by Members of the English Association,* XXVI (1940), 7–29.

Ryals, Clyde de L. "The Moral Paradox of the Hero in the 'Idylls of the King,' " *ELH,* XXX (1963), 53–69.

Smalley, Donald. "A New Look at Tennyson—and Especially the *Idylls,*" *JEGP,* LXI (1962), 349–357.

Stange, G. Robert. "Tennyson's Garden of Art: A Study of *The Hesperides,*" *PMLA,* LXVII (1952), 732–743.

Stange, G. Robert. "Tennyson's Mythology: A Study of *Demeter and Persephone,*" *ELH,* XXI (1954), 67–80.

Stevenson, Lionel. "The Pertinacious Victorian Poets," *University of Toronto Quarterly,* XXI (1952), 232–245.

NORTON CRITICAL EDITIONS

HOMER   *The Odyssey*   translated and edited by Albert Cook
HOWELLS   *The Rise of Silas Lapham*   edited by Don L. Cook
IBSEN   *The Wild Duck*   translated and edited by Dounia B. Christiani
JAMES   *The Ambassadors*   edited by S. P. Rosenbaum
JAMES   *The American*   edited by James A. Tuttleton
JAMES   *The Portrait of a Lady*   edited by Robert D. Bamberg
JAMES   *The Turn of the Screw*   edited by Robert Kimbrough
JAMES   *The Wings of the Dove*   edited by J. Donald Crowley and
      Richard A. Hocks
Ben Jonson and the Cavalier Poets   selected and edited by Hugh Maclean
Ben Jonson's Plays and Masques   selected and edited by Robert M. Adams
MACHIAVELLI   *The Prince*   translated and edited by Robert M. Adams
MALTHUS   *An Essay on the Principle of Population*   edited by Philip Appleman
MELVILLE   *The Confidence-Man*   edited by Hershel Parker
MELVILLE   *Moby-Dick*   edited by Harrison Hayford and Hershel Parker
MEREDITH   *The Egoist*   edited by Robert M. Adams
MILL   *On Liberty*   edited by David Spitz
MILTON   *Paradise Lost*   edited by Scott Elledge
MORE   *Utopia*   translated and edited by Robert M. Adams
NEWMAN   *Apologia Pro Vita Sua*   edited by David J. DeLaura
NORRIS   *McTeague*   edited by Donald Pizer
Adrienne Rich's Poetry   selected and edited by Barbara Charlesworth Gelpi and
      Albert Gelpi
The Writings of St. Paul   edited by Wayne A. Meeks
SHAKESPEARE   *Hamlet*   edited by Cyrus Hoy
SHAKESPEARE   *Henry IV, Part I*   edited by James J. Sanderson   *Second Edition*
Bernard Shaw's Plays   selected and edited by Warren Sylvester Smith
Shelley's Poetry and Prose   edited by Donald H. Reiman and Sharon B. Powers
SOPHOCLES   *Oedipus Tyrannus*   translated and edited by Luci Berkowitz and
      Theodore F. Brunner
SPENSER   *Edmund Spenser's Poetry*   selected and edited by Hugh Maclean
      Second Edition
STENDHAL   *Red and Black*   translated and edited by Robert M. Adams
STERNE   *Tristram Shandy*   edited by Howard Anderson
SWIFT   *Gulliver's Travels*   edited by Robert A. Greenberg   *Revised Edition*
The Writings of Jonathan Swift   edited by Robert A. Greenberg and
      William B. Piper
TENNYSON   *In Memoriam*   edited by Robert Ross
Tennyson's Poetry   selected and edited by Robert W. Hill, Jr.
THOREAU   *Walden and Civil Disobedience*   edited by Owen Thomas
TOLSTOY   *Anna Karenina* (the Maude translation)   edited by George Gibian
TOLSTOY   *War and Peace* (the Maude translation)   edited by George Gibian
TURGENEV   *Fathers and Sons*   edited with a substantially new translation by
      Ralph E. Matlaw
VOLTAIRE   *Candide*   translated and edited by Robert M. Adams
WATSON   *The Double Helix*   edited by Gunther S. Stent
WHITMAN   *Leaves of Grass*   edited by Sculley Bradley and Harold W. Blodgett
WOLLSTONECRAFT   *A Vindication of the Rights of Woman*   edited by
      Carol H. Poston
WORDSWORTH   *The Prelude: 1799, 1805, 1850*   edited by Jonathan Wordsworth,
      M. H. Abrams, and Stephen Gill
Middle English Lyrics   selected and edited by Maxwell S. Luria and
      Richard L. Hoffman
Modern Drama   edited by Anthony Caputi
Restoration and Eighteenth-Century Comedy   edited by Scott McMillin